D0620816

THE UNIVERSITY PRESS

OF NEW ENGLAND

Sponsoring Institutions

BRANDEIS UNIVERSITY

CLARK UNIVERSITY

DARTMOUTH COLLEGE

UNIVERSITY OF NEW HAMPSHIRE

UNIVERSITY OF RHODE ISLAND

UNIVERSITY OF VERMONT

The Papers of
Daniel Webster

Correspondence, Volume 2

1825–1829

CHARLES M. WILTSE, EDITOR

HAROLD D. MOSER, ASSOCIATE EDITOR

PUBLISHED FOR

DARTMOUTH COLLEGE BY THE

UNIVERSITY PRESS OF NEW ENGLAND

HANOVER, NEW HAMPSHIRE 1976

CONCORDIA UNIVERSITY LIBRARY
PORTLAND, OR 97211

Copyright © 1976 by Trustees of Dartmouth College

All Rights Reserved

Library of Congress Catalog Card Number 73–92705

International Standard Book Number 0–87451–120–8

Printed in the United States of America

This edition of the Papers of Daniel Webster is published by Dartmouth College with assistance from the National Historical Publications and Records Commission and the National Endowment for the Humanities.

ADVISORY BOARD

Francis Brown, Chairman

Samuel Flagg Bemis (retired 1965,
    died 1973)

Dudley B. Bonsal

Harold H. Burton (died 1964)

Lyman H. Butterfield

Marcus Cunliffe

Paul Wm. Cutler

David Herbert Donald

Claude M. Fuess (died 1963)

Christian A. Herter (died 1966)

Herbert W. Hill

Oliver W. Holmes

Francis H. Horan

Mark DeW. Howe (died 1967)

Walter Johnson

Edward Connery Lathem

Roswell Magill (died 1963)

Richard W. Morin (retired 1968)

Elting E. Morison

Louis Morton

Allan Nevins (died 1973)

Stephen T. Riley

William G. Saltonstall

Arthur M. Schlesinger, Jr.

Charles Grier Sellers

Whitney North Seymour

EXECUTIVE COMMITTEE

Chairman Brown

Messrs. Lathem, Morison, Morton, and Riley

Acknowledgments

The libraries and librarians, archives and archivists, and individuals who have contributed materials for this volume are too numerous for individual mention, but those to which our debt is greatest are the National Archives, the Library of Congress, and especially to John McDonough, Manuscript Historian; the Massachusetts Historical Society and its Director, Stephen T. Riley; the New Hampshire Historical Society and its Director, John F. Page, and Bryant Tolles, formerly Assistant Director and now Director of the Essex Institute, Salem, Massachusetts. We owe a very special obligation to Baker Library of Dartmouth College, and especially to Edward Connery Lathem, Dean of Libraries; Virginia L. Close, Reference Librarian; and Kenneth C. Cramer, Archivist.

Equally great is our indebtedness to those who have made this project possible by their generous financial support: Dartmouth College, the National Endowment for the Humanities, and the National Historical Publications and Records Commission. Among individuals, our obligation is great to President John G. Kemeny of Dartmouth College, to Vice President and Dean of the Faculty Leonard M. Rieser, to Professors James M. Cox of the English Department, Louis Morton of the History Department, and Vincent Starzinger of the Department of Government; and to Mr. William B. Durant, Executive Officer to the Faculty of Arts and Sciences, who continues to be financial adviser to the project. At the National Endowment for the Humanities we are especially indebted to Dr. Simone Reagor, Director of the Division of Research Grants. Our obligations to staff members of the National Historical Publications and Records Commission extend in particular to the Commission Chairman, Dr. James B. Rhoads, Archivist of the United States, and to Dr. E. Berkeley Tompkins, formerly Executive Director, and Mr. Fred Shelley, his Deputy.

On the staff of the Webster Papers itself the editors of the volume could not have performed their duties as efficiently or as well if they had not been able at all times to call upon the special skills of Diplomatic Editor Kenneth E. Shewmaker, Legal Editor Alfred Konefsky, and Assistant Editor David Grayson Allen. Mrs. Mary Virginia Anstruther, who combines the roles of Secretary and Research Assistant, has consistently performed services above and beyond the call of duty.

Hanover, New Hampshire   C. M. W.
April 1, 1975

Contents

*For the page number on which each document of
the Papers begins, see the Calendar.*

A section of illustrations follows page 300.

Introduction

In the short half decade between the election of John Quincy Adams and the beginning of the age of Jackson the nation shed the remaining vestiges of its aristocratic past and moved decisively into the new democratic era that was the nineteenth century. So too did Daniel Webster pass through a transitional period, in his personal as in his public life.

The outward calm of the Adams administration was deceptive. The President, through no choice of his own, was both vehicle and foil for the political and economic transformation of the country. The elitism shared by Federalists and Republicans alike crumbled before the general extension of the franchise that marked the rise of the common man. The old leadership of talent backed by property gave way to managerial skill. The barely contained factionalism of the Era of Good Feelings exploded and the fragments recombined to form again two major parties. Jeffersonians and Hamiltonians, with the old issues long since resolved, freely crossed ideological lines to become by the election of 1828 Democrats or National Republicans. The latter group, soon to be known as Whigs, tended to represent the stable economic interests of the community, while the Democracy had greater appeal for the worker, the farmer, the small businessman who hoped with borrowed capital to grow large and powerful in his turn.

Yet as Webster and his National Republican colleagues realized all too well, in the United States of the 1820's policy was almost necessarily tinged with sectionalism, and measures, however carefully devised, could be interpreted as favoring one or the other protagonist.

The heritage of the Missouri controversy was manifest in the Southern reaction to the tariff and in the competition of North and South for the commerce and fealty of the West, where the balance of political power would clearly reside if it did not already. The Erie canal, promising to divert wealth from New Orleans to New York, was hardly in operation before Philadelphia sought a similar water route to Pittsburgh, and ground was broken for a canal to join the Ohio with the Potomac at Washington. More significant than either of these was the Baltimore and Ohio Railroad, chartered in 1827 and begun the following year, which by its very presence rendered all the canal systems obsolescent. Even in international relations, the politics of sectionalism was evident, for behind much of the opposition to United States participation in a Congress of American States was the unwillingness of the slaveholding South to recognize the legitimacy of a government like that of Haiti formed by revolted slaves. Indeed, the terms of the sectional rift were made explicit in the literature opposing the tariff and late in 1829 in the first defense of slavery as a positive good.*

Webster, like so many others of his generation, was forced to take a position before all the implications were clear. He contributed more toward the election of Adams by the House of Representatives than any other individual except Clay, but he became quickly disillusioned over the President's failure to use the patronage as a means of strengthening the party. He had transcended the particularism of his early years to become an outspoken nationalist, in full agreement both with the centralizing trend of the Adams administration and with the federal supremacy so clearly voiced by John Marshall. He now favored public investment in transportation, the protection of domestic industry, and a strong central bank—all the elements of the economic policy first sponsored by Henry Clay and characterized by Clay as the "American System." By 1826 or 1827 the two men, although still friends working together for the reelection of Adams, were in fact undeclared rivals for the party leadership and the presidential succession.

Even as the emphasis of his career shifted from the local to the national scene, Webster's personal ties with New Hampshire and New England generally were weakened by the death of his wife early in 1828, and of his brother Ezekiel in April 1829. These losses brought deeper personal suffering to Webster than anything he had before experienced, and left a permanent impress on his character. His remarriage, late in 1829, was motivated largely by the needs of his children and by his own requirement for a hostess to further his political career. The second Mrs. Webster, much younger than her husband, was the daughter of a prominent New York merchant, and that city became thereafter increasingly important in his social, political, and professional life.

When the first Congress of Jackson's administration gathered in Washington in December 1829, Clay was in retirement and Senator Daniel Webster of Massachusetts was by common consent and his own choice the active leader of the opposition. He was also the foremost spokesman, in Congress and before the Courts, for the large business interests of the nation.

* By South Carolina Governor Stephen D. Miller in his annual message to the legislature.

PLAN OF WORK

From its inception the Papers of Daniel Webster was planned as an integrated project, using both microfilm and letterpress publication. The persistent pressure of time and the steadily rising cost of book publication were important factors in the choice of the dual media, but the overriding consideration was the desire to bring all of Webster together, without abridgment or gloss, for those who were equipped to use it that way, while providing the less dedicated scholar and the general reader with the essential Webster in convenient annotated form. The microfilm edition, in four different groupings, is as complete as the surviving records permit. Webster's correspondence, including letters received as well as letters sent, together with miscellaneous notes, memoranda, briefs, drafts, formal writings, reports, petitions, and business papers have been issued with printed guide and index as *The Papers of Daniel Webster* by University Microfilms, Ann Arbor, Michigan. *The Legal Papers of Daniel Webster*, also issued with guide and alphabetical list of cases by University Microfilms, consists of records drawn primarily from the county courts of New Hampshire and Massachusetts and from the state and lower federal courts in New England. Records of the Department of State and of the Supreme Court are available on film from the National Archives and Records Service of the General Services Administration, but the user must select for himself the reels that may contain Webster material.

The value of this film, including as it does virtually all known Webster papers, cannot be overstated; but its very magnitude makes it unmanageable. It is relatively expensive, requires special equipment to use, is hard on the eyes, and effectively buries the grains of wheat by mixing them unevenly with an enormous amount of chaff. The user of the film, moreover, must decipher for himself often difficult or faded handwriting. He must search out the identity of persons and the nature of events alluded to, and finally he must rely upon his own judgment as to the significance of the given document. In the letterpress edition all this has been done for him, even to the selection of documents in terms of their significance, by editors totally immersed in the time and place and almost as familiar with the central characters as was Webster himself.

The letterpress edition in effect complements and renders more useful these various microfilm collections, whose very existence has made it possible to select more rigorously the documents important enough to be offered to the larger audience reached by the printed book. Each volume of correspondence, moreover, includes a calendar of letters written in the same time period but not selected for publication. For each of these the microfilm frame number is cited, as is volume and page citation for any document now available only in a printed version. Footnote references are also made to the film wherever appropriate. For the general reader and for the student of the period rather than of the man, the editors believe the selection of items printed will be ample. The biographer, and the scholar pursuing an in-depth study of some segment of the times, will need the film, to which he will find the printed volumes an indispensable annotated guide.

The letterpress edition is being published in four different series, overlapping in time but not in content, in order to make maximum use of subject matter specialists as technical editors. The edition has been planned in a total of fourteen volumes, of which seven are correspondence, three are legal papers, two are diplomatic papers, and two are speeches and formal writings. The present volume, including the period 1825–1829, is the second of the correspondence series.

EDITORIAL METHOD

Letters and other documents included in this volume are arranged in chronological sequence, irrespective of whether Webster was the writer or the recipient. The only exception is for letters that were sent as enclosures in later correspondence. These have been placed immediately after the document which they accompanied. Date and point of origin have been placed at the upper right of each letter. If all or part of this information has been supplied by the editors, it appears in square brackets, with a question mark if conjecture. The complimentary close, which in the original manuscripts often takes up three or four lines, has been run continuously with the last line of the text.

All letters are reproduced in full except in rare instances where the only surviving text is incomplete or is from a printed source which did not reproduce it in its entirety. Needless to say, texts from printed sources are used only when the original manuscript has not been found, but the letter is of sufficient importance to warrant its inclusion.

The letters themselves have been reproduced in type as nearly as possible the way they were written. Misspellings have been retained without the annoyingly obtrusive "(sic)"; and abbreviations and contractions have been allowed to stand unless the editor feels they will not be readily understood by a present-day reader. In such cases the abbreviation has been expanded, with square brackets enclosing the letters supplied. Punctuation, too, has been left as Webster and his correspondents used it, save only that dashes clearly intended as periods are so written. Superscript letters in abbreviations or contractions have been brought down, but a period is supplied only if the last letter of the abbreviation is not the last letter of the word abbreviated. In all other cases, periods, apostrophes, dashes, and other forms of punctuation have been left as Webster and his contemporaries used them. The ampersand, far more frequently used than the spelled out "and," has been retained, but diacritical marks over contractions have been omitted even where the contraction itself is retained.

Canceled words or passages that are obvious slips, immediately corrected, have been left out altogether; those which show some change of thought or attitude or have stylistic or psychological implications have been included between angled brackets. Interlineations by the author have been incorporated into the text, but marginal passages, again if by the author, have been treated as postscripts and placed below the signature.

In order to keep explanatory footnotes to a minimum, general notes have been interspersed from time to time with the letters that constitute the text of the volume. These serve to indicate what Webster was doing at a particular time or to explain a sequence of events that may help to clarify subsequent correspondence. Footnotes are used to identify persons, places, events, situations, problems, or other matters that help to understand the context of a particular reference.

Individuals are identified only once, generally the first time they are mentioned. For the convenience of the reader who may have missed this first reference, the appropriate index entry is printed in bold face type. Well-known individuals—those in the *Dictionary of American Biography* or the *Biographical Directory of the American Congress*—have not been identified at all unless the context seems to require it. For those in the DAB the index entry is marked with an asterisk and with a dagger for those in the BDAC. The extent of footnoting has been reduced by adding given names and initials in square brackets where text references are to surnames only.

Immediately following each document is an unnumbered note indicating the provenance of the document and if appropriate, giving some information about the writer or recipient. Symbols used in these provenance notes are the standard descriptive symbols and the location symbols developed by the Union Catalog Division of the Library of Congress. Those appearing in the present volume have been listed under Abbreviations and Symbols below.

Webster Chronology, 1825–1829

1825

January 18	Spoke in support of extending Cumberland Road from Wheeling, Virginia, to Zanesville, Ohio.
January 24	Kentucky and Ohio Congressional delegations, pledged to Clay, announced they would vote for Adams.
January 28	Clay publicly accused by Jackson partisans of entering into a "corrupt bargain" with Adams.
February 5	Urged choice of Adams in letter to Maryland Congressman Henry R. Warfield.
February 9	John Quincy Adams elected President by the House of Representatives, over Andrew Jackson and William H. Crawford.
February 20	Challenged for second time by John Randolph of Roanoke.
February 20	Clay accepted Adams' offer of the State Department.
March 4	Adams inaugurated; John C. Calhoun Vice President.
March 5	Clay confirmed as Secretary of State.
March 8	Ezekiel Webster, Daniel's brother, defeated in first bid for election to Congress from New Hampshire.
March 26	Clay published lengthy Address to the people of his old Congressional District, justifying his support of Adams and his acceptance of the State Department. Webster approved.
April 3	Defended election of Adams in speech at Faneuil Hall.
June 17	Delivered oration at laying of cornerstone of Bunker Hill monument.
June 24– August 2	Visited Niagara Falls with Joseph Story, their wives, and Eliza Buckminster.

October 26   Erie Canal opened.

1826

January 3   An Adams-Webster paper edited by David Lee Child, the *Massachusetts Journal*, began publication in Boston.

January 4   Spoke in support of his bill to reform judicial procedure and enlarge the Supreme Court.

January 18   The House Judiciary Committee, of which Webster was chairman, was instructed by indirection to investigate the conduct of Charles Jared Ingersoll, U.S. Attorney for Pennsylvania.

February 20, 21   Argued the case of the *Marianna Flora* before the Supreme Court.

April 8   Henry Clay and John Randolph of Roanoke fought a bloodless duel.

April 14   Delivered major speech favoring United States representation at Panama Congress of American Nations.

July 4   Deaths of John Adams and Thomas Jefferson.

August 2   Delivered commemorative discourse on Adams and Jefferson, Faneuil Hall, Boston.

September   William Morgan of Batavia, New York, disappeared after completing a book alleged to reveal secrets of Freemasonry, an incident that gave rise to the Antimasonic party.

November 6   Reelected to House of Representatives.

1827

January 2   Elected a director of the Bank of the United States at Philadelphia.

January 19   Argued before the Supreme Court for defendant in error (Saunders) in *Ogden* v. *Saunders*.

February 3, 5   Represented the bank in *Bank of the United States* v. *Dandridge* before the Supreme Court.

February 5	Spoke in support of the Creek Indians against Georgia.
February 10	Voted for the Woolens bill, which passed the House 106–95.
February 12	Attacked by the New York *Evening Post* for his vote on the Woolens bill, which reversed his free trade stand of 1824.
February 28	Woolens bill defeated in the Senate by casting vote of Vice President Calhoun.
April 20	Spoke in Faneuil Hall urging amalgamation of old Federalists and Adams Republicans.
May	Argued *Kelley* ads *Jackson ex. dem. Fowler et al.*, one of the Astor land cases, before the U.S. Circuit Court in New York.
June 8	Elected to the United States Senate from Massachusetts.
July 13	Death of Alexander Bliss, Webster's associate in his Boston law office.
July 30–August 3	Convention of "Agriculturists and Manufacturers" met in Harrisburg, Pennsylvania, drafting proposals that became the tariff of 1828.
August	Selected Henry Willis Kinsman as his law associate.

1828

January 21	Grace Fletcher Webster, Daniel's wife of twenty years, died after relatively brief illness.
April	Accused of having made a deal with Adams to bring old Federalists into office.
May 13	Voted for the "Tariff of Abominations," which passed the Senate 26–21.
June 5	Attended dinner in his honor and that of his congressional colleagues at Faneuil Hall.
August 4	Antimasonic convention met in Utica, New York, to nominate candidates for state offices.

October	Published, with Joseph E. Sprague and others, an "Address to the Citizens of Massachusetts" urging reelection of Adams.
November	Andrew Jackson elected President; Calhoun again Vice President.
November	Instituted proceedings against Theodore Lyman, Jr., for libel.
December 19	South Carolina legislature published an *Exposition and Protest* against the tariff, unsigned but written by Calhoun.

1829

February 14, 16	Represented defendant in error (Leland) before Supreme Court in *Wilkinson* v. *Leland*.
March 4	Andrew Jackson inaugurated and the "common people" swarmed over Washington.
April 2	New York Safety Fund, sponsored by Van Buren, became law, minimizing reliance of the New York business community on the National Bank.
April 10	Ezekiel Webster died suddenly of a heart attack in a Concord courtroom.
October 5	Virginia Constitutional Convention opened.
October 8	Argued for plaintiff in *Charles River Bridge* v. *Warren Bridge* before Massachusetts Supreme Court.
December 12	Married Caroline Bayard Le Roy of New York.

Abbreviations and Symbols

DESCRIPTIVE SYMBOLS

Abstract	Summary of contents, or a portion thereof, of a letter or document
AD	Autograph Document
AD draft	Autograph Document, draft
ADS	Autograph Document Signed
ADS copy	Autograph Document Signed, copied by writer
ADS draft	Autograph Document Signed, draft
AL	Autograph Letter
ALS	Autograph Letter Signed
ALS copy	Autograph Letter Signed, copied by writer
ALS draft	Autograph Letter Signed, draft
AN	Autograph Note
ANS	Autograph Note Signed
Copy	Copy, not by writer
DS	Document Signed
Extract	Copy of a portion of a letter or document
LC	Letterbook Copy
LS	Letter Signed

LOCATION SYMBOLS

CLCM	Los Angeles County Museum, Los Angeles, Calif.
COMC	Mills College, Oakland, Calif.
CSmH	Henry E. Huntington Library, San Marino, Calif.
CU	University of California, Berkeley
CtHT	Trinity College, Hartford, Conn.
CtHi	Connecticut Historical Society, Hartford, Conn.
CtY	Yale University
DCHi	Columbia Historical Society, Washington, D.C.
DLC	Library of Congress
DMaM	Marine Corps Museum, Washington, D.C.
DNA	National Archives
ICHi	Chicago Historical Society

ICU	University of Chicago
IGK	Knox College, Galesburg, Ill.
Ia-HA	Iowa State Department of History and Archives, Des Moines
MB	Boston Public Library
MBBA	Boston Bar Association
MBS	Social Law Library, Boston
MBevHi	Beverly Historical Society, Beverly, Mass.
MH	Harvard University
MHi	Massachusetts Historical Society, Boston
MNS	Smith College, Northampton, Mass.
MTaHi	Old Colony Historical Society, Taunton, Mass.
MWA	American Antiquarian Society, Worcester, Mass.
MWalB	Brandeis University
MdHi	Maryland Historical Society, Baltimore
MeB	Bowdoin College, Brunswick, Me.
MeHi	Maine Historical Society, Portland
MiD	Detroit Public Library
MiD–B	Burton Historical Collection, Detroit Public Library
NB	Brooklyn Public Library
NBuC	State University of New York, College at Buffalo
NBuHi	Buffalo Historical Society, Buffalo, N.Y.
NHi	New-York Historical Society, New York City
NIC	Cornell University
NN	New York Public Library
NNC	Columbia University
NNPM	Pierpont Morgan Library
NNS	New York Society Library, New York City
NPV	Vassar College, Poughkeepsie, N.Y.
NWM	United States Military Academy
NcU	University of North Carolina, Chapel Hill
NhD	Dartmouth College
NhExP	Phillips Exeter Academy, Exeter, N.H.
NhHi	New Hampshire Historical Society, Concord
NjMoHP	Morristown National Historical Park
NjP	Princeton University
OClWHi	Western Reserve Historical Society, Cleveland
PHC	Haverford College, Haverford, Pa.
PHi	Historical Society of Pennsylvania, Philadelphia
PPAmP	American Philosophical Society, Philadelphia
PPL	Library Company of Philadelphia

PU	University of Pennsylvania, Philadelphia
PWbH	Wyoming Historical and Geological Society, Wilkes-Barre, Pa.
RHi	Rhode Island Historical Society, Providence
ScU	University of South Carolina, Columbia
ViU	University of Virginia, Charlottesville
VtCasT	Castleton State College, Castleton, Vt.
VtNN	Norwich University, Northfield, Vt.
WHi	State Historical Society of Wisconsin, Madison
WaU	University of Washington, Seattle

SHORT TITLES

Adams, *Memoirs*	*Memoirs of John Quincy Adams, Comprising Portions of His Diary from 1795 to 1848,* ed. Charles Francis Adams. 12 vols. Philadelphia, 1874–1877.
Correspondence	*The Papers of Daniel Webster, Correspondence, 1798–1824,* ed. Charles M. Wiltse and Harold D. Moser. Hanover, 1974.
Curtis	George Ticknor Curtis, *Life of Daniel Webster.* 2 vols. New York, 1870.
DNB	*Dictionary of National Biography,* ed. Leslie Stephen and Sidney Lee. 64 vols. London, 1885–1903.
Fuess, *Webster*	Claude Moore Fuess, *Daniel Webster.* 2 vols. Boston, 1930.
Harvey, *Reminiscences*	Peter Harvey, *Reminiscences and Anecdotes of Daniel Webster.* Boston, 1877.
Hopkins and Hargreaves, *Papers of Henry Clay*	*The Papers of Henry Clay,* ed. James F. Hopkins and Mary W. M. Hargreaves. 5 vols., to date. Lexington, 1959–1973.
Mason, *Memoir and Correspondence*	*Memoir and Correspondence of Jeremiah Mason,* ed. Robert Means Mason and G. S. Hilliard. Cambridge, Mass., 1873.
MHi Proc.	*Proceedings of the Massachusetts Historical Society*
mDW	Microfilm Edition of the Papers of Daniel Webster. Ann Arbor, 1971. References followed by frame numbers.

mDWs	Microfilm Edition of the Papers of Daniel Webster, Supplementary Reel.
PC	*The Private Correspondence of Daniel Webster*, ed. Fletcher Webster. 2 vols. Boston, 1856.
Van Tyne	*The Letters of Daniel Webster*, ed. Claude H. Van Tyne. New York, 1902.
W & S	*The Writings and Speeches of Daniel Webster*, ed. James W. McIntyre. National Edition, 18 vols. New York, 1903.

SERIES ONE: CORRESPONDENCE

VOLUME TWO: 1825–1829

The Papers, 1825–1829

When Webster left Boston late in November of 1824 to attend the short session of the Eighteenth Congress, his family remained at home. His youngest son, Charles, then three years old, was in normal good health. No word to the contrary had been received by December 9, when Webster set out with the Ticknors on the pilgrimage to Monticello that had become a "must" for aspiring young politicians. It was only on his return to Washington shortly before Christmas that Webster learned of Charles' sudden death. In his grief he composed the following "lines," which he sent to Grace on January 5.

[LINES ON THE DEATH OF CHARLES WEBSTER, C. JANUARY I, 1825]

My son, thou wast my hearts delight
Thy morn of life was gay & cheery:
That morn has rushed to sudden night.
Thy fathers house is sad & dreary

I held thee on my knee, my son!
And kissed thee laughing, kissed thee weeping:
But ah! thy little day is done,—
Thou'rt with thy angel sister sleeping.[1]

The staff, on which my years should lean,
Is broken, 'ere those years come o'er me,
My funeral rites *thou* should'st have seen,
But thou art in the tomb before me.

Thou rear'st to me, no filial stone,
No parents grave, with tears, beholdest;
Thou art my ancestor, my son!
And stand'st in Heaven's account, the oldest.

On earth, my lot was soonest cast,
Thy generation after mine;
Thou hast thy predecessor past,
Earlier Eternity is thine

I should have set before thine eyes
The road to Heaven, & showed it clear;

But thou, untaught springest to the skies
               teacher
And leavest thy father lingering here.

Sweet Seraph, I would learn of thee,
And hasten to partake thy bliss!
And oh! to thy world welcome me,
As erst I welcomed thee to this.

Dear Angel, thou art safe in Heaven;
No prayers for thee need more be made
Oh! let thy prayer for those be given,
Who oft have blessed thine infant head

My Father, I beheld thee born,
And led thy tottering steps with care;
Before me risen to Heaven's bright morn,
My Son! My Father! Guide me there—

At Portsmouth N. H. April 29, 1810, at half past eleven o'clock, Sunday Evening, Grace Fletcher Webster was born.

Portsmouth N H. July 23d 1813, Friday Mng about half past eight o'clock Daniel Fletcher Webster was born.

Boston Mass: Jany 23. 1817 half past eleven o'clock on Thursday Evening Grace F. Webster died.

Boston Jany 16. 1818 on Thursday P M. 3 o clock—Julia Webster was born.

Boston July 20th. 1820. Thursday Mng 9 o clock Edward Webster was born.

Boston Dec. 31st. 1821. at half past twelve o'clock Monday Morning, Charles Webster was born.

Dec 19, 1824, Sunday <Evening> Morning, seven o'clock he died.

Copy. NhHi. Published in *PC*, 1: 376–377.

    1. The Websters' oldest daughter, Grace Fletcher, died on January 23, 1817, at seven years of age.

TO GEORGE TICKNOR

Wednesday Morning [January 5?, 1825]

My Dear Sir,

The weather is very fine & I hope cold enough for Mrs Ticknor's taste.[1] If you or she have a strolling disposition this morning, I should be glad to be of the party. Suppose we arrange to take a drive from the Capitol, at one oclock. That will give us a peep at the mail—before we go—two hours to drive—& an hour before dinner.

I hope you & the Ladies came safe from Mrs [John Quincy] Adams. Yrs always truly   D. Webster

if you come to the Capitol, send in for me.

ALS. NhD.

1. Mrs. Ticknor, nee Anna Eliot, was the daughter of Samuel Eliot of Boston. She had married George Ticknor on September 18, 1821.

FROM GRACE FLETCHER WEBSTER

Sat. morning Jany. 8th. [1825]

I cannot refrain my dear Husband, from sending you a line because you say you feel uneasy if you do not hear from us. It is a pleasure to believe I can do aught that can add to your happiness. I have nothing to communicate but the health of the family which blessed be God is pretty good, the children have slight colds. Julia complained of a sore throat last night which made me unhappy for a time and poor little Neddy coughs a little. I find I am very much alarmed if they are the least indisposed—but I know I ought not to indulge such fears but still with confidence to trust in that secure almighty love, which has always been my stay.

I had a very kind letter of condolence from Mr [George?] Hough.[1] You have had letters from your Brother—but I have not heard from him since you left us.

Adieu my dear Husband may heaven bless you and keep you! prays Your Ever affte   G.W.

ALS. NhHi.

1. Hough (1757–1830), the first printer in Concord, N.H., having set up a newspaper there in September 1789.

FROM GRACE FLETCHER WEBSTER

Jany 10th. [1825]

I have just received yours of the 5[1] my dear Husband, which I am very glad to see as I have had no letters from you for two days, and I feel uneasy if a longer time elapses lest something should be wrong with you. I hope your health is better than it was the last winter.

I thank you for the enclosed scrap of poetry which I found in your letter[2]—it is very beautiful. It makes me think of Edwards reflections on dear little Charles—tho' he saw him committed to the silent tomb he always speaks of him as alive, if any one mentions him as dead, Edward say[s] no, he is not dead he is alive in a beautiful place where he has everything he wants. The poor little fellow was at first inconsolable. I never saw a child so much affected at such an event. He wept till it seemed as tho' his little heart would break. Among other things which seemed to renew his grief was the little waggon—he said he had no one now to help him drag the waggon. Dr [John C.] W[arren] was here and saw Neddy's grief, and he tried to console him by describing the pleasures of the place to which the dear child had gone, and Edward smiled and said he would not cry any more—and the idea that Charles has every thing he wants has perfectly satisfied him. Is he not more rational than those who are older? *I* feel that he is.

I am glad you have been to see Mrs [Charles?] Vinson.[3] When you see her again remember me to her and hers. Julia saw a beautiful pair of socks which she wished to buy for Mrs. [Samuel] Jaudons baby[4] and I intended she should have had the pleasure but have been so much occupied in mind I forgot it or I could not attend to it—for I have been reminded.

We are almost frozen here. I hope it is more mild where you are.

Mrs [George] Blake[5] I think will go tho' she does not say much about it. Her only difficulty is to know what to do with George. I shall be too late for the mail. Adieu   Yours Ever

AL. NhHi. Published in Harvey, *Reminiscences*, p. 323.

1. Not found.

2. "Lines on the Death of Charles Webster," January 1, 1825, printed above.

3. Wife of a clerk in the third auditor's office.

4. Mrs. Jaudon, nee Margaret Peyton Alricks, had recently given birth to a daughter, Julia Webster Jaudon. Mrs. Jaudon was the step-daughter of Hugh Lawson White, Tennessee senator.

5. Nee Sarah Olcott Murdock (1789–1826).

TO JOHN CALDWELL CALHOUN

House of Reps. Jany 11th. 1825

Sir

I beg to call your attention to the Report of the Board of Engineers, and Naval Officers, made in May 1823, on the subject of the defence of Boston, "considered as a Commercial Sea Port, a Naval Depot, and a road of Rendezvous."[1]

By that Report you will perceive that certain Islands which are deemed essential to the military defence of the Port, and to its character as a safe Naval Depot, are in great danger of being carried away by the incessant encroachments of the Sea.

Since that Report was made, accurate observation has proved that the danger was not over stated, and that it is at this moment pressing and imminent.

I refer you on this point to the several documents, which you will receive herewith.[2]

Having recently, before the commencement of the present Session, felt it to be my duty to make a personal examination into the state of these Islands, I beg to express also, my own entire conviction of the great propriety of immediate attention to some of them.

I trust I may therefore ask your attention to the subject, and indulge the hope, that you will think it expedient to include a proper provision for this object, among the estimates for the present year.[3] I have the honor to be, with very true regard, Your most obt. Servt.   Danl Webster

Copy. DNA, RG 233.

1. In a petition to Congress of December 22, 1823 (mDW 41203), Josiah Quincy, mayor of Boston, refers to a survey "by several gentlemen of science and practical engineers, accompanied by Commodore Bainbridge, Commander of the Navy Yard at this place, and General Dearborn, Collector of the Port." Webster's reference was probably to this report, not found.

2. Webster had probably forwarded to Secretary of War Calhoun a copy of the Quincy memorial for Boston (mDW 41201), the memorial of the President and Trustees of the Boston Marine Society (mDW 41127), and letters from Bainbridge and Dearborn, not found but referred to in

John Calhoun to Louis McLane, January 14, 1825 (mDW 41114). On the question of islands in Boston harbor, see also Josiah Quincy to DW, January 4, 5, 1825 (mDW 4606, 4614).

3. In response to Webster's request, Calhoun forwarded documents on the question to Louis McLane, chairman of the House Ways and Means Committee, with the recommendation that an appropriation "may be made for the purpose of erecting the sea walls contemplated for the preservation of the above named sites [George's Island and Nantasket Head]." Calhoun requested an appropriation of $52,972.56; on March 2, 1825, an appropriation for that amount was approved (4 *U.S. Statutes at Large* 92).

The factionalism that sent the election of 1824 to the House of Representatives for decision was a step—perhaps a necessary step—on the way to a new party system. In the interval between the counting of the electoral vote on December 1, 1824, and the choice of John Quincy Adams by the House on February 9, 1825, congressmen and senators, state and local politicians, and aspirants to public office throughout the country bargained for support of their own favorite of the three whose names would be considered. Webster was one of those most energetic in Adams' behalf, working not only in Washington but by means of an active correspondence with political leaders in crucial states as well. In New Jersey, where most of the old Federalists had become Jacksonians,

oured to reconcile Daniel to the privation of doing without these things. There is the greatest folly at this day—*children* are *anticipating* all the *pleasures* and *amusements* of *Gentlemen* and *Ladies*. What there can be left for those, who shall arrive at that period I am unable to foresee. Boys even have supper parties and in some instances have drunk so much wine they could hardly be got home—and they could not be blamed how could anyone suppose they could have judgement sufficient to govern them.

I fear you will think this is pretty much like my *scolding* the *servants*. You have to hear it. I hope you will excuse it as it is a long time since I have exercised my *talent*. Mrs [George] B[lake] was here last evening she said she should not go to W. and that she doubted if Mr. B would. Ever Your   G.W.

I had a very kind letter from Brother Ezekiel.

ALS. NhHi. Published in Van Tyne, pp. 555–556.
   1. Not found.
   2. On January 6, Webster called up his "bill for the more effectual prevention of crimes against the United States."
   3. Not identified.

FROM GRACE FLETCHER WEBSTER

Friday morning Jany 14 [1825]

Yours of the 9th.[1] my dear Husband, tells me that you are solitary, and that you still have the rheumatism—both of which I regret without the power to cheer or alleviate. There is a striking, and painful contrast between the present season, and the last, with us my dear Love, but I hope we shall make this as profitable to ourselves as the las[t] was pleasant.

How is your family[—]agreeable? I have heard much of Mrs Wools[2] uncommon powers at conversation—extraordinary information &c. &c. And how do you find Mrs [Henry Williams] Dwight?[3] And Mrs [Christopher?] Rankin[4]—is she aught like your rib. You will excuse the vanity which leads me to remember that you was tho't by Mr. R. to be a model—you need not add he did not know her. I am well aware of that.

Are Mrs [Edward] Livingston and daughter at W[ashington] and is Mrs [Andrew] Stevenson there?[5] If they are when you see them I wish you would remember me kindly to them and all who you think would be gratified by the remembrance of Your   G. W.

P.S. You will probably soon see Mr E[benezer] Appleton Mr [William] Sturgis Mr. I[saac] McLellan,[6] who has been very kind in his attentions to me. He has called himself several times to offer his service and to take anything I might wish to send to you.

The children are at school tho it is a very rainy day. Our Man Abel[7] carries first one and then the other in his arms.

ALS. NhHi. Published in Van Tyne, p. 556.
1. Not found.
2. Probably Sarah Moulton Wool, wife of Colonel John Ellis Wool, Inspector-General of the Army.
3. Wife of a Massachusetts congressman. With Webster, the Dwights boarded at Mr. John Coyle's, Capitol Hill.
4. Nee Frances Fowler, wife of a Mississippi congressman.
5. Mrs. Livingston, Madame Louise Moreau de Lassey, the daughter of Jean D'Aveza de Castera, a Santo Domingo planter, was the widow of a French officer at the time of her marriage to Livingston in 1805. Mrs.

Stevenson, nee Sarah Coles, sister of Edward Coles, one-time secretary to President Madison and later Governor of Illinois, had married Stevenson in 1816.
6. Appleton (d. 1833?), Sturgis (1783–1864), and McLellan (1769–1849) were all Boston bankers and merchants.
7. Abel has not been further identified. He was probably a free black, one of a succession whom the Websters employed as house-servants. On occasion, Webster bought the freedom of a slave and employed him. Whether such was the case with Abel has not been determined.

The Websters' home on Somerset Street was sold in the spring of 1822. The next three summers the family spent in Dorchester, then a Boston suburb, in a house rented from Arnold [?] Welles (1762–1827; Harvard 1780), a prominent Bostonian and a general in the Massachusetts militia.

FROM GRACE FLETCHER WEBSTER

Sat. Jany 15th [1825]

My dear Husband,

I have intended to ask you several times, but have always forgotten it, about the key of the Dorchester house. And I now make a letter expressly for the purpose. Have you any recollection of the key? Gleason[1] says he gave it to you, I have looked every where I could think of, but cannot find it. I hardly suppose it possible you can recollect such a trifle at this time but still I did not know but you might, having a good memory. Mr [Arnold?] Welles wants to go into the house to take off the blinds. It seems as if we might find it, you could not carry it away—Dorchester 32! How many associations the name brings to my mind. Our residence there was one of the green spots in my life—that can never be renewed. The leaf is now sear, the roses have faded, and my beautiful blossom—the wind hath passed over and it is *gone*!!

We are all well. The children are at school. Julia shall have a message for Mrs [John] Coyle[2] before I write again. Please remember me to her and family. Yours Ever   GW.

I have no letter to day.

ALS. NhHi.
  1. Probably one of Webster's house servants.

2. Wife of a District of Columbia lawyer, with whom Webster boarded on Capitol Hill.

TO EZEKIEL WEBSTER

Jan. 16 1825

I have written to these boys,[1] that I will help them, a little, if you are satisfied it will do them good. I have told them that one of them would do well to come to Boscawen. I am willing to give them, outright, what I can afford; or to help them in any other way you may think best. If two hundred Dollars each, would, *certainly*, pay their debts, it is pity they should not have it. Please write them an encouraging word; & if they come down, let them have what you think proper, on my account, & on what terms you think proper—prefering, if it can be done, to make a small gift, rather than a large loan. I wd. be willing to *give* them 100 each. Yrs   D. W.

ALS. NhD. Published in *PC*, 1: 375.
  1. Sons of one of Webster's half-brothers, David (1769–?), who had

moved with his family to Stanstead, Canada, as a young man.

TO MRS. GEORGE TICKNOR

House of Representatives, January 17, 1825.

Mr. [Jules von] Wallenstein[1] has given me, my dear Mrs. Ticknor, your very kind note, and I cannot well tell you how much it has gratified my feelings. You have inferred nothing, my dear lady, and can infer nothing, of my regard and affection for yourself and your husband, more than the truth, nor equal to the truth. And I beg you to believe that there are none in the world whose regard and kind feelings I wish more to cultivate and secure.

Our six weeks' acquaintance has been to me a mixture of high enjoyment and severe suffering. The former I owe, mainly, to you and Mr. Ticknor; the last I take, and would wish to bear, as a common visitation of a kind Providence.[2] Yet I have felt it more than might have been expected, and my spirits recover slowly. I am sure that Mrs. Webster and yourself are congenial and assimilated spirits, and that she will cultivate your acquaintance with delight. Let us hope that circumstances may favor an habitual intercourse. At any rate, be assured that the *principle* of regard and affection will live in my heart.

I write this in the House, while Mr. [Henry] Clay is speaking on the Cumberland Road. The ladies are all present, inside the House. I have not reviewed them; for I am sure there is none of them that I have lately seen nor know, unless it may be Mrs. (A[lexander] H[ill]) Everett.[3] I see Wallenstein among them, as becomes a diplomatist. Mr. Clay speaks well. I wish you were here to hear him. The highest enjoyment, almost, which I have in life, is in hearing an able argument or speech. The development of *mind*, in those modes, is delightful. In books, we see the result of thought and of fancy. In the living speaker, we see the thought itself, as it rises in the speaker's own mind. And his countenance often indicates a *perception* before it gets upon his tongue. I have been charmed by observing this operation of minds which are truly great and vigorous; so that I sometimes am as much moved, as in reading a part of Milton and Shakespeare, by a striking and able argument, although on the dryest subject.

Mr. Wallenstein says you are to leave Baltimore on Thursday. There is, as yet, no Northern mail to-day. Should there be one, and in it letters for you, they shall be forwarded in due season. I shall flatter myself with the hope of hearing from you, not once only, but often, before you reach the little peninsula of Boston. Pray ask your husband if he has written to Dr. [John C.] Warren.   Yours most truly,   Danl. Webster.

Text from Curtis, 1: 230–231. Original not found.

1. Wallenstein, secretary to the Russian legation in Washington in the 1820's, and according to John Quincy Adams, "a person of extensive Literature, profound science, & elegant taste" (J. Q. Adams to John Adams, April 25, 1824, Letterbook, Adams Papers, MHi, Reel 147). Wall-enstein and Webster enjoyed a warm friendship even into the 1840's, when Wallenstein served as Russian diplomat in Brazil.

2. A reference to the recent death of Charles Webster.

3. Lucretia Orne Peabody and Everett had been married in September 1816.

TO EZEKIEL WEBSTER

Washington Jan. 18. [1825]

I am much obliged to you, for yours of the 10th.[1] It gave me much information that I wanted. I trust you have not forgotten to write me again, having seen Mr [Jeremiah] Mason at the Court.[2]

I hope you will pay all proper attention to your approaching election. The Patriot man,[3] I perceive, is very angry, & will be very active. If you save the House you will save all. I hope that public opinion, ever[y]where for Mr. Mason, will have some effect on the People of N. H.

As the 9th Feb. approaches we begin to hear a little more about the election. I think some important indications will be made soon. A main inquiry is, in what direction Mr Clay & his friends will move. There would seem at present to be some reason to think they will take a part finally for Mr *Adams*. This will not necessarily be decisive, but it will be very important. After all, I cannot predict results. I believe Mr Adams *might be* chosen, if he or his friends would act somewhat differently. But if he has good counsellors, I know not who they are. If Mr Clay's friends should join Mr Crawfords it would probably put him ahead of Mr Adams [on] the first ballot—& that being done, I know not what might follow.

I should like to know your opinion of what is proper to be done, in two or three contingencies—

1. If, on the first, or any subsequent ballot, Mr Adams falls behind Mr Crawford, & remains so a day or two, shall we hold out, to the End of the Chapter, or shall we vote for one of the highest?

2. If for one of the highest—say Jackson & Crawford *for which*?

3. Is it advisable, under any circumstances to hold out, & leave the Chair to Mr Calhoun?

4. Wd. <not> or would not, N. E. prefer a [man] of the power of Calhoun, to a choice of Genl. Jackson?

On these, & other similar points, I want your full opinions, by the first of next month.

I shall write you again in a day or two.   Yrs   D. W.

ALS. NhD. Published in *PC*, 1: 374.

1. Not found.

2. Webster was probably interested in Mason's plans for the senatorial contest, to be decided by the June 1825 New Hampshire legislature. Mason had already been a candidate for the U. S. Senate in the June and November 1824 sessions. Republicans dominated both houses of the New Hampshire legislature, but the Senate persistently refused to concur in the House's nomination of Mason, await-ing, so some argued, the outcome of the presidential election. On May 25, 1825, Webster had sent a note to Adams asking the President to use his influence to secure Mason's election in June. Adams declined, however, on grounds of propriety, and the legislature elected Levi Woodbury (Adams, *Memoirs*, 7: 14; Mason, *Memoir and Correspondence*, pp. 292–296).

3. Isaac Hill.

TO GEORGE TICKNOR

House of Representatives, January 20, 1825.

My Dear Sir:

I owe you for two very kind letters, and the only painful circumstance they mention is Mrs. Ticknor's health. I am truly sorry that any thing should interrupt her enjoyment of the society of Baltimore. You must certainly stay long enough for her to see Mr. [Charles] Carroll. The opportunity may not again occur.

We are to-day engaged on the [Chesapeake and Delaware] canal. Several speeches have been *filed in*. Mr. [Samuel] Breck is now speaking. It must have been the good Wallenstein[1] who wrote you about my little speech—for it was a very little one.[2] We think our Eastern candidate grows a little stronger in the prospect of the presidency. As the time draws near, we hear more conversation on the subject; but every thing is yet uncertain.

I go to-night to pass the evening with Wallenstein. My friend Dr. [Thomas] Sewall[3] has proposed him as a member of the "Columbian Institute"; so the doctor and I are going to pick a pheasant's wing on the occasion.

I have to-day no letters from Boston—and hear little news from that quarter, since the great explosion. Mr. [Ezra Stiles?] Gannet[t] has gone to-day to Mount Vernon. He left me a card without notation of place, and I know not where to seek for him.

Give my best and most true regards to Mrs. Ticknor. I should be glad to read Shakespeare—or Mr. [Josiah?] Tucker—or Mrs. [Lucy] Hutchinson[4]—or any thing else to her, that would make her forget the oppression of her cold. I hope to hear from her soon, and hear that she is better. Yours always truly, D. Webster

I sent you one letter, enclosed, yesterday—have none to-day.

Text from Curtis, 1: 232. Original not found.

1. George Ticknor had first met Wallenstein in Madrid, Spain, and Webster's acquaintance and friendship with him probably came through Ticknor.

2. Over the past few days, Webster had delivered speeches or remarks on several questions: the Cumberland Road, United States real estate purchases, and crimes against the United States. Ticknor had probably commented on Webster's remarks on the latter question.

3. Sewall (b. 1786), prominent figure in the Columbian Institute, Washington physician, and later, Webster's personal physician.

4. Tucker (1712–1799) was a British economist, minister, and author. Mrs. Hutchinson (b. 1620) was the author of the *Life of Colonel Hutchinson*, first published in 1806 (*DNB*).

FROM GRACE FLETCHER WEBSTER

Sat morning Jany 22d [1825]

My dear Husband,

I was sitting alone in my chamber reflecting on the brief life of our sainted little boy, when your letter came enclosing those lines of yours, which to a "mother's eye" are precious.[1] O my husband, have not some of our brightes[t] hopes perished! our fairest f[l]owers are indeed "blossoms gathered for the tomb." But do not my dear Husband, do not, let these afflictions weigh too heavily upon you. Those dear children, who had such strong holds on us while here, now allure us to Heaven.

> "On us with looks of love they bend,
> For us the Lord of life implore
> And oft from sainted bliss descend,
> Our wounded spirits to restore."

Farewell my beloved Husband! I have not time to write more—only to say I regret you have lost the pleasure of Mr and Mrs Ticknors society —which you so much need. I fear Mrs [Henry Williams] Dwight is not much benefitted by her voyage—so the last accounts appear—tho' at first they tho't her better. The children are tolerably well tho' not free from colds. Your ever affte   G.W.

ALS. NhHi. Published in *PC*, 1: 375– 376.

1. Webster had probably drafted and sent to Grace another poem, in addition to the "Lines on the Death of Charles Webster," printed above and mentioned in her letter of January 10. The second composition has not been found.

TO JEREMIAH MASON

Washington Jan. 25. 1825

Dear Sir

Ohio & Kentucky have agreed, I believe without doubt, to go for Mr Adams. This makes his election nearly or quite certain. I have thought this might, perhaps, be important enough to write a word to you, to mention it.

We have no other news. Yrs   D. Webster

ALS. MHi. Published in Van Tyne, p. 110.

TO GEORGE TICKNOR

Tuesday evening [January 25, 1825], 8 o'clock.

My Dear Sir:

This is all I have for you. I expect, indeed, something further, as Wallenstein said he should inquire at the P. O. about this time. If it comes, I shall enclose it to you.

I have been to dine with Mr. Calhoun. He talked to me, among other things, of your good fortune in picking up a *companion* on the road of life. I did not think that a subject on which I was bound to quarrel with a Secretary of War, whatever I might think of the matter. Mr. Calhoun is a true man.

Shall I learn, to-morrow, when you leave Baltimore?

God bless you and yours!   D. W.

Text from Curtis, 1: 233. Original not found.

FROM GRACE FLETCHER WEBSTER

Friday Jany 28th [1825]

My dear Husband,

I had just said mentally, I shall have no letters to day, and taken my paper, to write when I was very agreeably surprised by one—of the 22d. inst.[1]

Do you indeed, *believe* Mr Adams will be President? The important day is at hand, "big with the fate of Caesar and of Rome." Mr George [Washington] Adams[2] is going to be present. It will be a proud day. I have been expecting Judge [Joseph] Story yesterday and this morning. This was the day fixed for his departure. Mrs S. was here a short time last week and promised to spend a few days with [us] the next week. She looked almost as sad at the thoughts of parting with her husband as some other folks. Mr Bodowin[3] is going to W—he probably goes with the Judge. Mr [George] Sullivan will have a delightful time as we say with the addition of Julia's animated society.

Poor Mrs [George] Blake is quite sick, confined to her chamber, and almost to her bed. We are all better here but Daniel and Eddy not quite well enough to go to school.

Tomorrow I am to have the misery of a new face in the family in the all important character of COOK. Mary thought she must go home— Betsy has left me—she is at Phila's she has another little daughter—I mean Phila.[4] You must now & then have a little touch of domestic history. Your Ever affte   G. W.

ALS. NhHi. Excerpt published in Van Tyne, p. 558.

1. Not found.
2. Adams (1801–1829), son of John Quincy Adams.
3. Probably James Bowdoin Win-throp (1795–1833), Boston lawyer. He had dropped the name Winthrop.
4. All were probably at one time or another domestic servants in the Webster household.

TO JOSEPH HOPKINSON

Washington Jan. 29. 1825

My Dear Sir

I send you the document which you have expressed a wish to receive.[1]

I entertain no doubt of Mr Adams election. Probably he will be chosen the first ballot. New England, (6 states) Kentucky, Ohio, Missouri, Illinois, Louisiana, Maryland and N. York will, in my opinion be very likely to vote for him on the first trial. At any rate, his final election is as certain as such events well can be.

I hope you will come here, at some time during the *Court.* It is very possible you might do good by it. At any rate many will be glad to see you, none more so than Your true friend   Danl. Webster

ALS. PHi.
   1. Not identified.

FROM HENRY R. WARFIELD

Washington 3d. Feby. 1825

Confidential
My dear Sir
   I am induced from the good feelings which I trust have always existed between us to make to you this communication. The approaching Presidential Election gives me great anxiety. I am peculiarly situated, for altho. directly and indirectly I have been applied to at least, I am sure in a hundred instances, I have never expressed to a human being the Vote I intend to give. The representation as you know is composed of nine members from Maryland, every member except myself has expressed his opinion. The awful responsibility of the vote of that state may devolve on me—Nay more—Situated as the Votes of the different States are Maryland may make the President on the first ballot. Now Sir I am oppressed with this difficulty. Those with whom I am in the habit of associating in Maryland are for the most part called Federals and they constantly express to me their apprehensions that should Mr. Adams be the President, he will administer the government on party considerations— that the old Land marks of party distinction will be built up—that an exclusion of all participation in office will be enforced with regard to those who have hitherto been denominated Federals. I cannot for my own part believe that such a course wou'd be pursued. I shou'd trust that Mr. Adam's administration wou'd be on liberal and Independent grounds and that (regardless of names) he wou'd not deny to talents Integrity and competency a due participation. For in truth I consider all the old party distinctions to exist only in the name. I shall feel particularly obliged if you will give me your candid opinion on those points. I am with true esteem yrs &c.   Henry R. Warfield

ALS. NhHi. Published in *PC*, 1: 377–378. Warfield (1774–1839), representative from Maryland, had been elected as a Federalist to the Sixteenth, Seventeenth, and Eighteenth, Congresses.

TO MRS. GEORGE TICKNOR

House of Representatives, February 4, 1825.

My Dear Lady:
   I am right glad to find a little place left for me in Mr. Wallenstein's

letter, and to find it so flatteringly filled. I use the present moment to acknowledge this favor, while Mr. [George] McDuffie is making a very warm speech, I hardly know why or wherefore; but it relates to the rules of proceeding in electing a President next week, and he, being a pretty ardent Jackson man, seems inclined to make a kind of Jackson speech. I told Mr. Wallenstein to tell you that I should write you during the first long speech—and, depend upon it, the act of *writing* is, in such cases or most of them, less onerous than the act of *listening*. The Hall of Congress is an admirable situation to cultivate the powers of an organ which has been generally too much neglected in its *education*; I mean the *ear*. Now I have so disciplined this little member that, on being informed that I am not particularly concerned to know what is said, and requested to "bring me no more reports," it very faithfully performs its duty, and leaves me quite at ease to pursue any vocation I may choose. The "enclosed petty spirits" are left entirely undisturbed by what prevails without. This is an admirable improvement on the old maxim, "Hear with both ears." I hear with *neither*.

Times have a good deal changed with me, my dear lady, since your departure. The business of Congress has become more urgent—the event draws near—the session is wearing off—I begin to see *home* at the end of no long prospect, and all these things create a little activity and bustle, which serve, in some poor measure, to fill up such portions of time as I usually passed in your house, while you remained here.

I am glad to learn that you are entered so favorably into the society of Philadelphia. I think you will find it very intelligent and agreeable; but am not afraid, nevertheless, that it will lead you to be dissatisfied with a little peninsula running into Massachusetts Bay.

Give my love to your husband. There seem to have been proceedings about the college, which must interest him. I hope he is satisfied with the result.[1] Remember me also to Miss Gardiner.[2] Yours most truly,

D. Webster

Mr. [William] Sturgis says he had the pleasure of passing a very gratifying hour at your room in Philadelphia. Let me have a letter from you before you leave Philadelphia.

Text from Curtis, 1: 233–234. Original not found.

1. Webster was probably alluding to Professor James F. Dana's efforts to secure financial aid for Dartmouth College from the New Hampshire legislature. At the time, however, the legislature failed to appropriate any money from the literary fund of the state for the support of the College (John King Lord, *A History of Dartmouth College, 1815–1909*, Concord, N.H., 1913, pp. 208–209).

2. Not identified.

A good two weeks before the House of Representatives was to elect a President on February 9, it was known in Washington that the three states carried by Clay—Kentucky, Ohio, and Missouri—would switch to Adams. That would have been enough to arouse the enmity of the Jacksonians, without rumors that the Kentuckian was also behind a visible wavering in the Louisiana and Illinois delegations. Clay was promptly charged with selling out the West for the State Department and the succession. On January 28, George Kremer (1775–1854) an obscure and eccentric Jacksonian in the Pennsylvania delegation, published the charge of "corrupt bargain" in the Philadelphia Columbian Observer. *A few days later, Clay published a "card," calling the originator of the charge "a base and infamous calumniator, a dastard and a liar." Rumors of a duel arose and subsided, and Clay requested an investigation by a committee of the House of Representatives. Kremer declined to appear before the special committee, but responded in writing. The Kremer charges had little influence on the current election, but they were "the first skirmish in the great Clay-Jackson struggle" of 1828 (Glyndon G. Van Deusen,* The Life of Henry Clay, *Boston, 1937, p. 190).*

TO EZEKIEL WEBSTER

Feb. 4. [1825]

We have a little excitement, here, as you will see, but there is less than there seems. Mr. Clay's ill-judged card has produced an avowal—or sort of a[n] avowal, which makes the whole thing look ridiculous. Mr. Kremer is a man, with whom one would think of having a shot about as soon as with your neighbor Mr. Simeon Atkinson,[1] whom he somewhat resembles.

Mr Adams, I believe, & have no doubt, will be chosen, probably the first day.

Judge [Arthur] L[ivermore] means to go home so as to be at Haverhill C[ourt of] C[ommon] P[leas]. He has recd Mr [Israel Webster] Kelly's letter, & expresses, in general terms, friendly feelings towards him.[2]

How do you come on in your various matters? — Yrs   D. W.

ALS. NhD. Published in PC, 1: 380.

1. Atkinson (1754–1830), resident of Boscawen.

2. Kelly (1778–1857), sheriff in Salisbury, judge of the Hillsborough Court of Sessions, and Grace Fletcher Webster's brother-in-law. The subject matter of Kelly's letter to Livermore has not been determined.

The following letter to Henry Warfield, advising the Maryland Congressman that an Adams administraion would be "just and liberal toward Federalists as toward others," was probably written less to convince Warfield than to commit Adams, to whom the letter was shown before the concluding note was added. Commenting on Webster's visit and its object, Adams wrote: "I said I approved altogether of the general spirit of his answer, and should consider it as one of the objects nearest to my heart to bring the whole people of the Union to harmonize together. I must, however, candidly tell him that I believed either General Jackson or Mr. Crawford would pursue precisely the same principle, and that no Administration could possibly succeed upon any other" (Adams, Memoirs, 6: 493). With Webster's assurances thus ratified by Adams himself, Warfield gave his vote to the New Englander, carrying the Maryland delegation with him.

TO HENRY R. WARFIELD

H. R. Feb. 5. 1825

My Dear Sir

I have recd your note of yesterday, & reflected on its contents; and am very willing to answer it, as far as I can, without incurring the danger of misleading you, in the discharge of the delicate and important trust belonging to your present situation.

I must remark, in the first place, that my acquaintance with Mr Adams, although friendly & respectful, I hope on both sides, certainly so on mine, is not particular. I can say nothing, therefore, on the present occasion, by any authority derived from him. Being in a situation, however, not altogether unlike your own, I have naturally been anxious, like yourself, to form an opinion as to what would be his course of administration, in regard to the subject alluded to by you. For myself, I am satisfied; and shall give him my vote, cheerfully & steadily. And I am ready to say, that I should not do so, if I did not believe that he would administer the Government on liberal principles, not excluding Federalists, as such from his regard & confidence. I entertain this feeling, not because I wish to see any number of offices, or any particular office, given to those who have been called Federalists; nor because there is a number of such individuals, or any one, that I particularly desire to see employed in the public service. But because the time is come, in my opinion, when we have a right to know, whether a particular political name, in reference to former parties, is, of itself, to be regarded as cause of exclusion. I wish to see nothing like a proportioning, parcelling out, or distribution, of Offices of trust among men called by different denominations. Such a proceeding would be to acknowledge & to regard the existence of distinctions; whereas my wish is, that distinctions should be disregarded. What I think just, & reasonably to be expected, is, that by some one clear & distinct case, it may be shown, that the distinction above alluded to does not operate as cause of exclusion. Some such case will doubtless present itself, & in proper time & manner[1] may be embraced, probably, if thought expedient to embrace it, without prejudice to the pretensions or claims of individuals. The Government will then be left at liberty to call to the public service the best ability, & the finest character. It will then be understood, that the field is open, & that men are to stand according to their individual merits. So far as this, I think it just to expect the next administration to go. At any rate, it is natural to wish to know, what may probably be expected, in this regard.

While, with these sentiments, which, My Dear Sir, are as strong in my breast as they can be in yours, I am willing to support Mr Adams, & to give him my vote & influence, I must again remind you, that my judgment is made up, not from any understanding or communication with him, but from general considerations; from what I think I know of his liberal feelings, from his good sense & judgment, & from the force of circumstances. I assure you, very sincerely, that I have a full confidence, that Mr. Adams administration, will be just and liberal, towards Federalists as towards others; and I need not say there is no individual who would feel more pain than myself if you, & the rest of our friends should ever find reason to doubt the solidity of the foundation on which this confidence rests.

Note. I read this, precisely as it now stands here, to Mr. A. on the Eve' of Feb. 4. He said, when I had go[t] thro, that the letter expressed, in general sentiments, & such as he was willing to be understood, as his sentiments. There was one particular, however, on which he wished to make a remark. The letter seemed to require him—or expect him to place one Federalist in the Administration—here I interrupted him, & told him he had misapprehended the writer's meaning. That the letter did not speak of those appointments, called Cabinet appointments, particularly—but of appointments generally. With that understanding, he said the letter contained his opinions, & he should feel it his duty, by some appointment, to mark his desire of disregarding party distinctions. He said, also, that in his opinion it would be impossible for any other of the Candidates to do otherwise than to disregard party distinctions. He thought either of them if elected must necessarily act liberally in this respect.

In consequence of this conversation, I interlined, in this letter, the words, in proper time & manner—& made no other alteration in it.

AL draft and AN. NhHi. Published in *PC.* 1: 378–380.

1. As Webster explained in his note, he inserted "in proper time & manner" after he read the letter to Adams.

FROM GRACE FLETCHER WEBSTER

Friday morning Feby 11th. [1825]

I am very happy in receiving a short letter from you my beloved Husband.[1] I know your time must be all filled, and that you can have very little for me. The great question is undoubtedly decided, which has for a long time agitated the Public. Tho' we have very little doubt as to the success of the Northern Candidate, yet we are anxious to *know* how it is. And I am anxious also to know how Mr. Clay and [George] Kremer are coming out. I think you have a great many silly heads as well as wise ones in that honorable body. I can not tell you how happy I am that the fourth of March must put an end to those wise deliberations—otherwise I should fear that the whole winter would be taken up—in debating how the office should be settled. I fear you think it very foolish in me to meddle with these high matters, but I am so much interested in whatever you are engaged I must prate a little.

Poor Gov. [William] Eustis is to be buried to day with all possible pomp and parade. I am going to take the children to Mrs [Nathan] Hales to see the procession.[2] Yours Ever   G Webster

ALS. NhHi. Published in Van Tyne, pp. 560–561.

1. Not found.

2. Mrs. Hale, nee Sarah Preston Everett, was the sister of Edward and Alexander H. Everett.

TO [JEREMIAH MASON]

feb. 14. 1825

Dr Sir

You will have heard that Mr. [William H.] Crawford declines the Treasury. I have understood his reason to be, that he preferred to leave his friends in a situation to support, or oppose, the Govt. as they might here after think their duty required, without embarrassing them by his own connexion with the Administration.

The Department of State is offered to Mr Clay. He has it under advisement. It is thought to be doubtful whether he will accept it; but my opinion is that he will. Nothing further is known, & I have no secrets. Mr [Langdon] Cheves' name is mentioned, in conversation, for the Treasury. DeWitt Clinton, Mr [John] McLean, Post Master Genl., & one or two others have been suggested as Candidates for the War Department. But these are, I presume, all rumours, & nothing more is known, or decided at present. Mr. [William] Wirt, & Mr [Samuel L.] Southard, it is understood, will remain in their places.[1]

I took care to state my own views & feelings to Mr. Adams, before the election, in such manner as will enable me to satisfy my friends. I trust, that I did my duty. I was very distinct, & as distinctly answered; & have the means of showing, precisely, what was said.[2] My own hopes, at present, are strong, that Mr. Adams will pursue an honorable, liberal, magnanimous policy. If he does not, I shall be disappointed, as well as others; & *he will be ruined.* Opposition is likely to arise, in an unexpected quarter; & unless the Administration has friends, its enemies will overwhelm it.

It is not necessary, in writing to you, to deny the rumour, or rumors, which the press has circulated, of a place provided for *me.* There is not a particle of probability of any such offer.[3] My own sentiments about those things are very much as they were when I saw you. The Court is going on slowly. Judge Story has very much recovd. his health, & is in good spirits. The Chief Jus is uncommonly well.

I hear little from your State. If you have half an hour from Courts & Juries, I should be glad to hear from you. Yrs as always   D. Webster

ALS. NhD. Published in *W & S*, 16: 99.

1. Attorney general and secretary of the navy, respectively.

2. See above, DW to Henry R. Warfield, February 5, 1825.

3. The rumor was that Webster would be appointed minister to England, a position he very much desired but for which he was willing to wait (see Charles M. Wiltse, "Daniel Webster and the British Experience," *MHi Proc.*, 1973).

FROM JOHN WILLIAMS

Knoxville, Feb. 14th 1825

D Sir,

I seize a moment of leisure from the business of court to say a few words to you. I presume from the Washington news that Mr Adams is made Prest. & that your Judiciary bill[1] will pass. If this be so it will be in your power to render an important service to your country by having Jere[miah] Mason made a Judge of the Sup: Court. If worth had been consulted Mason or [James] Kent would have succeeded [Henry Brockholst] Livingston. With the example of Ky. & other states before us, every real friend to rational liberty should unite to make the Judiciary impregnable. This can alone be effected by selecting the best materials in the Country. All who know Mason will agree that he unites intelligence; & firmness to do his duty. The latter with me is not the least important qualification. I once had some agency in passing thro the Senate a Judiciary bill.[2] If it had become a law my eyes were fixed on Mason. Times have changed with me. At that period I had some influence at Court. Now I am *Hors de Combat.* Having fought and *fell* in the last ditch—I am content in future to attend to my own concerns But shall be gratified with the well doings of others. I am assured that your feelings in relation to the Judiciary are like my own. And that you will do what ought to be done. Make my respects to Judge [Joseph] Story & accept for yourself the best wishes of your friend   John Williams

ALS. NhD.

1. Williams was referring to the Committee on the Judiciary's bill extending and broadening the court system for the western states. See *Register of Debates*, 18th Cong., 2nd sess., 1824–25, 1: 370.

2. On March 7, 1820, Williams, then senator from Tennessee, introduced a bill to form an additional judicial circuit of Alabama, East and West Tennessee, and to appoint a circuit judge (*Annals of Congress*, 16th Cong., 1st sess., 1819–20, 1: 477).

TO EZEKIEL WEBSTER

Washington Feb. 16. 1825

D'r E.

You are acquainted with all the particulars of the Election. The appointments are now under consideration. Mr Clay will be Sec. of State. Mr [Samuel L.] Southard &c [?]¹ will remain. For the War, DeWitt Clinton, Jno. W. Taylor, & Mr [John] McLean, present P[ost] M[aster] G[eneral] are spoken of—for Treasury Mr [Langdon] Cheves. I know not, now, how these appointments, will go; but perhaps may know before Evening. If there is any faith in man, we shall have a liberal Administration. I think it not unlikely, that if it were pressed, there might be a *Federalist* in the Cabinet, but our friends are not all satisfied that such a measure would be discreet, at this moment. No doubt the true course at present is to maintain the Administration,—& give a fair chance. We may be deceived, but if we are, it will be *gross* deception.

I have strong hopes Mr. [Jeremiah] Mason will be elected [senator], unless your spring elections should go *very* bad. He will stand as a friend to the Govt. & the new elected President, & his principal opponent will be *e contra*. In this state of the question, causes will then act strongly, which last session only acted *feebly*. Mr [Samuel] Dinsmoor² will not be chosen, I predict. It will lie between Mr. Mason & Mr. [John F.] Parrott.

I see by the N. H. papers that the State is getting a little excited. I should like to hear how things look,—& to know whether every body acquiesces in the election quietly. Yrs   D. W.

Eve. I have more to say than a P. S. will suffice for. Go on—support Mr. A[dams]—get elected if you can.³ There is no great danger of Mr Mason—there is more *time* in his case. Every thing looks well.

ALS. NhD. Published in *PC*, 1: 380–381.

1. The reference is probably to Wil-

liam Wirt, Attorney General.

2. Dinsmoor (1766–1835; Dartmouth 1789), Keene lawyer, post-

master, congressman, and gubernatorial candidate in 1823. In 1825,
some New Hampshire politicians considered him a strong contender for
the U.S. Senate.

3. Ezekiel Webster was a candidate
for Congress. Labeling Ezekiel a Federalist, Joseph Healy of Washington,
New Hampshire, defeated him by
about 4000 votes.

FROM GRACE FLETCHER WEBSTER

Friday morning Feb. 18th. [1825]

Whenever I receive a letter, my dear Husband, I feel as if I must reply.
Yours of Sunday was an unexpected favour as I had one yesterday[1]—
but tho unexpected, not the less welcome.

The papers are full of speculations about the offices to be filled and
the characters who are to fill them. Even you do not escape. Mr. Adams
situation is not an enviable one. I have felt very much interested in the
great affairs at W[ashington] and should rather have been there on
many accounts than at another session, but I doubt if I ever go there
again. Our children, if they live, will require my constant care—more
than I could bestow in such a place—and if it must be so, if your duty
calls you there, I must submit. It is doubtless best it should be so.

Mr & Mrs [George] Ticknor returned yesterday. Eliza [Buckminster]
is to spend this day with me. She call[ed] here yesterday. I tho't her
health had improved. Adieu   Yours Ever—   Grace Webster

ALS. NhHi. Published in Van Tyne, p. 562.
1. Neither letter found.

FROM ISAAC PARKER

Boston 19 Feby. [1825]

My Dear Sir

You will have seen by the papers that a concurrent nomination by the
two political parties has been made for persons to fill the office of Govr
& Lieut Governour.[1] This course is approved by the most intelligent of
both parties, and is unsatisfactory as might be expected to a good many
of the rank & file in each army. I believe the subalterns of the democratic party are the most disturbed for they see it diminishes their chance
of promotion.

I feel satisfied from a years intimate & frank acquaintance with [Levi]
Lincoln that he is a better man than he has appeared at times when
chasing the meteor of popular favour. No man could have discovered better dispositions, and been more ready to maintain sound principles than
he since he has been upon the bench. Indeed there is no better remedy
for democratic itching than a high judicial steam pressure; and I think

if he is to be our Governour, the year that he has passed upon the bench is of infinite value to the Commonwealth.

The rumor now is that he declines the offer of the crown, but this I do not believe; for I think to be Governour of the Commonwealth is among the indispensables in his estimate of life. Without doubt he would prefer to postpone the fruition [?] to a later period of life, but the prospect is too certain now, and the future too uncertain to admit of hesitation. But if I am mistaken, I suppose the present Lieut Governour[2] will succeed to favour, and I think the federal party will be quite as ready to concur. This Gentleman is of a higher order as to talents and moral qualities than he is generally known to be. Though perhaps less quick than L[incoln] he is not less strong. I have watched him for five years past in full practice in Bristol and I do not know a more able, or a more fair Lawyer out of our City.

I have been long persuaded that the great causes of party division having ceased, party itself ought to die. It requires time for the waters to subside after a tremendous storm; but they will subside & it is the duty of all to hasten the period. There is nothing of the old party objects to contend about, and those only wish to prevent or delay the calm who expect some of these distinctions to vanish in it. Your great affair at Washington has been accomplished in a manner very satisfactory to us here, and highly creditable to our institutions, abroad.

Probably if a session of Congress was immediately to take place, we should perceive the effects of disappointment if not of revenge, but the interval between this & next December will tranquilize turbid feelings, and the hope of a change in 4 years will keep within moderate bounds vexation at the present state of things.

We have now to look for the filling up of the Cabinet & for the inaugural speech both of which will be looked to for indications of the character of the administration. I think the King elect cannot anticipate a very easy throne.

Our democrats in the Legislature have not done much if any thing which federalists in their place would not have done; why then is it not as well they should be there? Indeed I cannot but think that the ark is more secure with them, for the reason only that they are nearer allied to the people, (as the people suppose), and their doings will be more cheerfully approved.

I should lay by the old federal armour to be buckled on, when the times shall require a sturdy defence of principle.

These may appear strange sentiments, but I cannot but think they are just & necessary to the preservation of the things which as public men, we most value. Why should I write this letter? Merely to let you know that I approve what I see of your course, and that you may infer, as I am still among the highest toned of the federalists, that others of your friends think like men.

You may wish to know who will probably succeed L[incoln] upon the bench if he takes the chair. The western democrats say *Judge [Samuel] Howe*, than whom there is not a more fit man in the State. But I think it is too soon to expect that with the power in their hands they will be willing to lose the supposed advantage of one of their party in that place. I believe L will do his best, and that the Lieut Governour will be offered & will accept the seat. With this we shall be content. With great regard your friend & Serv   Isaac Parker

ALS. DLC.
　　1. Levi Lincoln and Marcus Morton had been nominated governor and lieutenant governor respectively, by both the Federalists and Republicans.

Both nominations were accepted (*Columbian Centinel*, February 23, 1825).
　　2. Marcus Morton.

FROM JEREMIAH MASON

Portsmouth Feby. 20. 1825

Dear Sir

I have your letter of the 14 Feby.[1] I am glad you got through [the] Presidential election so quick & quietly. I am glad not only on account of the advantage it affords Mr. Adams in being thus elected without creating further excitement, but also as it tends to allay public apprehension, on this most critical point of the constitution, the election of President.

I congratulate you on the success of your Bill agt. crimes, which I trust will pass the Senate.[2] It is certainly much needed. This, & the conspicuous part assigned you in the great election will sustain you, with the nation quite as well, & perhaps better than great speeches.

I expected the Department of State would be offered to Mr. Clay, but I doubted whether the fracas with [George] Kremer would not tend to prevent his accepting it. As K. is understood to be a vulgar fellow, & refused, when he had a fair opportunity, to establish his charges, I do not know that it ought to have any influence with Mr. Clay. Is the House to do nothing more in this matter? Having undertaken to enquire into it, & finding no evidence in support of the charges, it would seem, they ought to be declared to be false, slanderous & malicious. Would this bear harder on K than he deserves?

I think you did perfectly right in explaining yourself to Mr. Adams. If he expects the support of the Federalists, he must remove the bar that excludes them from office. Confidence must of necessity be mutual. One of the Departments ought to be offered to a Federalist. Considering their number & talents this would naturally be the case, unless they are excluded by design. They ought not, & I trust will not be satisfied with mere empty declarations of liberality in his inaugural speech.

I do not know how to understand your intimation of opposition to the new administration, from an unexpected quarter, unless it is to come from J. C. C[alhoun] & his friends, in union with the friends of Mr. Crawford. Such an union I had supposed would not take place. I conclude there will be no attempt to rally under the standard of Genl Jackson.

There is much more excitement in this State, relating to our spring elections than at any time since the war. The election of Senator of U. S. is made to bear on every thing. This is to be [the] turning point in the elections for the Senate & House of Reps. [Isaac] Hill is traversing the State, like a flying dragon, attending all the caucusses, & organizing his regulars. His activity increases as his influence declines. He has all the mail contracts in the State, which affords him great facility in disseminating his base slanders. The mails are said to be carried with great irregularity, & it is also said to be difficult to get news papers other than his own transported at all. Thus I, who have all my life studiously avoided being personally involved in electioneering turmoils, am unexpectedly & almost involuntarily drawn into the vortex. It was unavoidable, as it seemed to me, & I have made up my mind to meet it quietly, & bear the result as patiently as I can. It has so far given me less trouble than I expected.

The spirit of Jacobinism, which you know exists in this State in abundance, is pretty thoroughly roused. And although my friends seem to think my prospect, at present, good, my own opinion is that I shall fail in the end. A considerable portion of the moderate democrats are in my favour. If I were to be opposed by only one of the numerous candidates, & that one could now be designated I might succeed. But the friends of all of them unite in opposing me. [Levi] Woodbury is making great exertions. Govr. [William] Plumer has in his district set up [John] Broadhead a methodist preacher for the Senate. In this District [Clifton] Clag[g]et[3] has been nominated by a *regular caucus*. This augurs well. C is so contemptible I think he cannot succeed.

In this town there will be an attempt for electing to the House a set of true blue Jacobins, headed by Woodbury. It is quite uncertain what will be the result—perhaps a mixture by compromise. I have been told I could be elected, in this town. I have determined not to be. My situation in the House, the last session was painful & being there again by my own desire would not only be painful, but I think injurious.

I think the prospect of yr. brothers election is tolerably good, although doubtful. His opponent [Joseph] Healey is such a sad fellow that a considerable portion of the democrats will not vote for him—a part will go for yr. brother—others will give scattering votes, and in this case a plurality is sufficient. Truly yours   J. Mason

ALS. DLC.
1. See above.
2. Webster had introduced the "bill more effectually to provide for the punishment of certain crimes against the United States" on January 27, 1824; and on January 28, 1825, it passed the House. A few weeks later the bill cleared the Senate, and on March 3, the President signed the measure. See mDW 40808 for the

manuscript of the bill and for Webster's amendments; the act as passed appears in 4 *U.S. Statutes at Large* 115.
3. Brodhead (1770–1838), a native of New Market, was elected to Congress in 1828. Claggett (1762–1829) was a lawyer, congressman, and judge of probate for Hillsborough County.

FROM ISAAC PARKER

Boston 21 Feby. 1825

My Dear Sir

I have read your letter of the 16th.[1] with much pleasure, and shall communicate its contents only to such as you would have written to with equal confidence as to me. We should all have been gratified on many accounts at your appointment to one of the great offices, and yet none of us expected it. The charge of concealed Federalism on the part of Mr Adams though wholly untrue, would have been fixed upon him by such an appointment & would have retarded the fast approaching period when the merits of federalists will overpower the vulgar prejudices against them. I am very sure that in every personal view, your situation as an independent member of Congress with the opportunity it leaves for your professional concerns, is better than any situation in the Cabinet. The times are already such that you can support the measures of administration without any reproach from your political friends, and I have no doubt you will oppose them when they are hostile to the interests of our Country.

There is but one situation in which at present you can do more good, or feel more satisfied; and if the members of the next Congress are not mean in their feelings, that will be tendered to you.

Every body here is content with the election of President & some of course rejoiced. Our friend [George] Blake is about getting up a public dinner for the 4th. March.[2] There will be federalists enough to fill the table who sincerely rejoice, so that there will be no need of the aid of those who are merely acquiescent.

Judge [Levi] Lincoln, as I predicted, has consented to wear the crown of this little kingdom. Indeed, applied to by both parties I do not see how he could well refuse. I think better & hope better of him than during the convention I ever expected to. He has one great conservative [?] of rectitude in as great a degree as any man I know, *real pride of character*. The Worcester federalists, who are among the toughest among us, and who have been brought most in conflict with him, are among his warmest advocates. His being a Lawyer is something, his having been a judge is more; and my private intercourse with him for a year has raised him much in my opinion. You will receive a letter from me written two days before I received yours.[3] I am glad it so happened as it will contain decisive proof of the opinions of your friends here as to your course, without knowing any particular motive. A public man who is obliged to act upon emergencies at a distance from his friends will always be glad to find that they entirely confide in his doings. What you say of Mr. Calhoun has been hinted here before. It is unfortunate as it will lay the foundation of an opposition of which he will be the nucleus. And he certainly does not calculate well if he has a view to the Presidency hereafter. His popularity is high in N England; but when it is understood he has meddled in the election against Mr. Adams, all favour will be withdrawn, and he never can be Prest without N E votes.

We are apt to think all great men at the seat of Govt. have their present or future aggrandisement in view, in all their movements. Perhaps he is only influenced by personal dislike which I should not think very remarkable. We shall be glad to see you here at our law Term, and without doubt some of the cases will be left for you if you arrive by the 20th.

I am my dear Sir with true regard your friend & sert   Isaac Parker

ALS. DLC.
1. Not found.
2. Parker was probably referring to the public dinner scheduled at Faneuil Hall for March 4, to celebrate the inauguration of John Quincy Adams. Blake (1769–1841) was a Boston lawyer and close personal friend of Webster.
3. See above, February 19, 1825.

FROM GRACE FLETCHER WEBSTER

Monday morning Feb. 21st.[1825]

I am indebted to you, my dear Husband, for a letter of unusual length and spirits too.[1]

I have not written for several days for I fear if I write oftener my letters will be entirely without value. I, who never stir from my own fireside but to enter a Church, can have nothing to communicate but the health, or sickness of my family, as it please Providence—the shining of the glorious Sun, or the howling of the storms. My life is monotonous indeed, and somewhat dull—but it is doubtless best for me; it gives me time for reflections which the frequent intercourse with the world is too apt [to] banish—from a mind so trifling as I find mine;—and I have many, very many painfully mortifying reflections. It is mortifying to reflect how much I am behind you in every thing. I know no one respects, but rather despises those they consider very much their inferiors. You will perhaps say I am unusually humble, but these are not the feelings of an *hour* or a *day*. They are *habitual*.

Your friends are well—Mrs [George] Blake has been here twice. Eliza [Buckminster] spent a day with us last week and appeared in much better spirits as well as health. I wish you would write to her. As to writing to Mrs Blake I don't know—! that will occasion a demur. However, provided I may see the letter I should have no strong objections.

Mr and Mrs [George] Ticknor have returned. She made me a very friendly visit the day after her return. I have not yet seen Mr T. I would not forget that Mrs Ticknor desired me to mention her particularly to you. When you compare her letters with mine, my dear Husband, I am well aware that the difference in length would be the most trifling. You must have the mortification to reflect, that Mrs T is the daughter of a man of *Millions*, and has enjoyed [from] her infancy, every advantage, which wealth can bestow. While your wife is the daughter of a poor Country clergyman—all the early part of her life passed in obscurity, toiling with hands not "FAIR" for subsistance. These are humiliating truths, which I regret more on your account than any other. But, however poor or however obscure I am Always Affectionately—Yours   G W

ALS. NhHi. Published in Van Tyne, pp. 562–563.
1. Not found.

TO EDWARD EVERETT

H. R. Feb. 23 [1825]

My Dear Sir

If I were not the worst correspondent in the world, I should have written you long ago, to thank you for yr Plymouth Discourse,[1] & shew you that I keep alive the sense of a thousand other favors. Your kind & good long letter of the 14th[2] reminds me how culpable I am. I must say, however, that when conscience has stung me, in this matter, (as it often has done) I have soothed it, or attempted to, by saying that yr Brother was here—a *correspondent*, by profession;[3] & that through him you would be *officially* informed of all occurrences.

We have found a President. What next is to happen I know not. I might have said that we have also found a Secretary of State. People talk of Mr Senator [James] Barbour for the War—& conjecture that Mr. [DeWitt] Clinton will go to England,[4] & Mr. [Richard] Rush, perhaps, find employment at home;—in the Treasury or else where. These are rumours.

As to my leaving the House, I believe every body is willing I should remain as I am. At any rate, if there be any unwilling I am not one of them.

I am quite glad not to have the prospect of a contested election in Massachusetts—but I think Mr. Lincoln acts unwisely. He is too young, to be Govr. He should work 15 yrs first, on the Bench.

Prior's Life of Burke![5]—No I have not read it, but shall not fail to do so. With many imperfections, B. was still a prodigy. No other oration-maker, that I know of, whom England has produced, reminds one of Cicero.

But speaking of *Oration-makers*, makes me to recollect another part of your letter. I am sorry you have a speech to make at Concord. It would do better, if you were not so well known, all-over the Country, as well as at home.

If I were you, *I would not do it*. Tell the good people, that you have, within a few months, made two Orations,[6] (both very good ones) & that you think it inexpedient to make another so soon. This will satisfy all the reasonable. The truth is, the world will say, that in N. England we make too much of a good thing. I speak freely on this subject, because I am sure you will suppose I regard nothing but your permanent reputation. I would have you come out, *next*, in your[?] place in H. R.[7] To prove to you that I think of your case, as of my own, I will observe, that I have not made a Speech this session, although I have on hand pretty full preparation for *two* interesting subjects; & the sole reason is, that I may make an Address next June, at B[unker] H[ill] perhaps,[8] & I fear the reputation of being a *Speech-maker*. That hurt Burke. How can others, then, even if they were in his image, "hope to win by it"?

Nevertheless, if you are *engaged*, you must fulfill &c.

I saw A[lexander] H. E[verett] & wife at the Birth night Ball[9] last Eve. Yrs   D. W.

ALS. MHi.

1. Everett had delivered his Plymouth oration on December 22, 1824. Subsequent to its printing, he had forwarded a copy of the address to Webster.

2. Not found.

3. Probably a reference to Alexander H. Everett, whom Adams ap-

pointed as minister to Spain.

4. Clinton was nominated to the English post but declined. Adams subsequently appointed Rufus King.

5. Sir James Prior (1790?–1869), *Memoir of the Life and Character of the Right Hon. Edmund Burke*, published in Philadelphia in 1825.

6. Everett delivered the oration at

Concord on April 19, 1825. In addition to the Plymouth discourse, Everett had delivered the Phi Beta Kappa address at the Harvard commencement in August 1824.

7. Nominated for Congress in October 1824, Everett had been elected in November, his term commencing with the Nineteenth Congress in December 1825.

8. Webster delivered the address at the laying of the cornerstone of the Bunker Hill monument on June 17, 1825. For the speech, see *W & S*, 1: 235–254.

9. Celebrating Washington's birthday.

FROM JAMES MADISON

Montpellier Feby. 25. 1825

Dear Sir

I must not let the Session of Congress close without returning my thanks for the printed Documents for which I was indebted as appeared to your friendly politeness.[1] Tho' they find their way to me through the daily vehicles, there is an advantage in possessing them in a more compact, as well as less perishable form. Among the characteristic attributes of our Government is its frankness in giving publicity to proceedings, elsewhere locked up as arcana of State: And it will always be happy when they will so well bear the light; or rather, so much contribute to the reputation of our own Country, and the edification of others. Be pleased to accept, Sir, assurances of my high esteem & cordial respects

James Madison

ALS. NhHi. Published in *PC*, 1: 381–382.

1. The documents Webster franked to Madison have not been identified.

TO [JOHN QUINCY ADAMS]

H. R. Feb. 26. [1825]

Private

Dear Sir,

I recd. this letter this morning.[1] You know Mr. Mason's reputation & standing in N. E. In the events which have happened in *N. Hamp.* on the recent occasion, he took an active & prominent part.[2]

Although I did not expect to receive any letter from him, on these subjects, & have no reason to know, precisely, how far he would wish his sentiments to be known, yet I presume he did expect that I would make such use of his suggestions, as I might think discreet. And I have thought the best course would be to enclose the letter itself for your perusal. You will see, that, in general, his sentiments are like those which I have expressed to you myself.

This note does not require any answer. The letter you may return to me endorsed, at your convenience.[3]

My private letters correspond with the public accounts, as to the general satisfaction expressed, all over the north, at the result of the Election. There are letters, also, today, from Kentucky & Ohio, of a very favorable complexion. Yours truly   Danl. Webster

ALS. MHi. Published in Van Tyne, pp. 112–113.

1. Webster had probably forwarded Adams the Jeremiah Mason letter of February 20, 1825, printed above.

2. The New Hampshire legislature had under consideration the election of a United States senator. A dispute had arisen over the counting of votes, and as a result, no senator had been declared elected.

3. The address leaf, on which Adams' endorsement would likely have appeared, has not been found.

TO EZEKIEL WEBSTER

feb. 26. [1825]

Dr E.

I shall stay here probably till 15. or 16. March. Your election will be the 8—write me Wednesday Eve—the 9th & the letter will meet me here. Write me again on Monday the 14. & that letter will meet me in N. York —to which place let it be addressed.

Mr Clinton is offered the Mission to Engd. If he accepts, Mr. Rush is expected to [be] Sec. Treas: Gov. Barbour Sec. of War. There are some objections to these appointments. Mr Adams' situation is full of embarrassments, & I know not how he will get along. I retain however a confidence that he will act liberally, & in this hope I rest. Mr. Mason has written me a very sensible & judicious letter, on various topics, which I *have submitted*.[1] I think Mr Mason will yet be chosen. New influences will begin to bear on the case by June next.

I have a letter from Keene, (Mr [John] Prentiss)[2] saying there will be a scattering of the votes in that County for Mr. C[lagett]. I rather think you have some chance to be chosen—but shall not be disappointed if you should not. Judging from the Patriot, I suppose old *heats* must be much revived. If it be so, it is but a dying effort. Yrs   D. W.

ALS. NhD. Published in Van Tyne, pp. 113–114.

1. See above, Mason to DW, February 20, 1825.

2. Prentiss (1778–1873), printer and editor of the Keene *New Hampshire Sentinel*. Letter not found.

TO EZEKIEL WEBSTER

Washington Feb. 27. 1825

My Dear Brother

I am very glad that you have come to a result, which promises you so much happiness, in regard to the subject upon which you wrote me some days ago.[1] All that I know, and all that I have heard, of the Lady who is the object of your choice, leads me to believe that she is most deserving of your regard and affection.[2] I will thank you to give her my kindest respects & salutations; and assure her that I am anxious to become personally acquainted with one already well known to so many of my friends, & likely, soon, to form a link in a closer & dearer circle. I hope we may meet soon after my return.

We have nothing of particular interest in the political world since I wrote you last. Yours always affectionately   Danl. Webster

ALS. NhHi.
  1. Letter not found.
  2. Ezekiel's first wife, Alice Bridge, died in 1821; and on August 2, 1825, he married Achsah Pollard (1801–1896), a resident of Concord. She and Daniel became very close friends.

In 1825, for the second time in less than a decade, Webster found himself facing a challenge from the eccentric John Randolph of Roanoke. On February 20, after Webster had denied before Congress the truth of Randolph's attacks on the special committee investigating charges against William H. Crawford, Thomas H. Benton presented Randolph's challenge to Webster. Through Benton, Webster and Randolph managed to settle their disagreements without appeal to the code of honor, and both agreed that their dispute would be kept secret. Rumors of it quickly reached Boston, however, and, in the letter below, Grace Webster commented on it.

Until 1831, when a Washington correspondent of the New York Commercial Advertiser *recounted it, the dispute was kept out of the newspapers. Fuess (Webster, 1:326) attributed the leak to Randolph's talking "too much." That may have been the case, but there are other possibilities. Instead of the correspondence between Webster and Randolph being destroyed, it seems that most of it remained in Benton's hands; and Benton later provided Willie P. Mangum and Levi Woodbury with copies, either of whom could have resurrected the dispute in 1831. For additional correspondence between Webster, Randolph, and Benton on this issue, see the Calendar.*

FROM GRACE FLETCHER WEBSTER

Tuesday morning March 1st. [1825]
11 o'clock

My dear Husband, ·

Mr. [Alexander] Bliss[1] has just been here to enquire if I had any news from you knowing I had a letter this morning.[2] I told him your letter contained none. He then told me there was a report current in town last evening that Mr Randolph had challenged you for some remarks of yours last year which had just reached him. Mr B. did not for a moment be-lieve the report, but had manfully contradicted it, still he thought he should like to know what you had written, which happened to be merely a short notice of your dinner with the President, your engagement of our old rooms &c. &c.—not a word of duels or anything of the sort. I heard the same story at N. Jersey on my return last year. The duel excepted, as Mr R was then on the great and mighty deep, he could not have heard if you had made the threat. I told Mr [Richard] Stockton you were, I be-lieved very angry with Mr R. but you would not be very likely to threaten any man with a whipping. I have not the least disagreeable apprehen-sion of the truth of the report. My dear Husband, I neither believe Mr R would challenge nor if he did, that you would accept.

Mrs B[liss?] drank her tea with me last evening and staid till my hour for a potation.

We are all well—and happy in the trust that you are—and in the hope of seeing you ere long—I am as Ever Yours   G. W.

ALS. NhHi. Published in Van Tyne, pp. 563–564.
  1. Bliss (1792–1827; Yale 1812),

associate in Webster's law office.
  2. Not found.

TO EZEKIEL WEBSTER

Washington March 8. 1825.

My Dear Brother,

I have recd. yours,[1] communicating Mr [Enoch?] Gerrish's request;[2] to whom I will thank you to give my best respects. I did not see him, the last time I was in N. H. but remember him, as an old friend, much esteemed.

New York is full of Irish Laborers. There must be several thousands of them there. Some of them are likely, active young men, who get good wages. These, generally, find employment as house-servants, coachmen, &c. The great majority of outdoor laborers I do not suppose to be equal to our own Countrymen. Probably the best of the class of Laborers do not come over; & such as do come, prefer, I believe, to find employment in the Cities, rather than in the Country. There are, however, doubtless, many very excellent laborers. But our modes of farming & husbandry are not like what they have been accustomed to. They are said to be very good ditchers; and yet I was told at Nashua, last fall, that a gang of them, from Boston, offering to work on the Factory canal &c, were not found equal to the Yankees.

I will, however, inquire further into the matter, as I return through New York, & probably write you again from that place.

I hope now to be able to leave this place in a week or ten days. While

Congress remained in session, I could not pay any attention to my business in the Court. In that I am now engaged.

I have had a violent cold, which kept me in the House several days. But I have been in Court today. Yours very sincerely   Danl. Webster

ALS. VtCasT.
1. Not found.
2. Gerrish (1775–1856), Boscawen

merchant. The nature of "Gerrish's request" has not been determined.

FROM GRACE FLETCHER WEBSTER

Thursday morning March 10th.
[1825]

I must write this morning my dear Husband, if it be but [to] tell you how much I am disappointed in not having a letter. Your letters are indeed like Angel's visits, short and far between.

But I have done complaining—as I hope you perceive. I have even become quite stoical. This is the time you fixed on for your return but I have been silent. I am PATIENCE personified.

Mrs Story called the day before yesterday to tell me she could not come; that long anticipated visit is to be deferred till the good Judge comes home. I am truly sorry to relinquish the hope of that pleasure.

The Inaugural addresses have arrived. I have not finished the President's but as far as I have read I thot it sensible. I don't know what sort of an address is expected of a Vice President. Mr Calhoun is a sensible man and I suppose his is right.

I had a letter from your Excellent Brother this week. He intends to be here about the time of your return. It is before this decided whether he is to be one of the Representatives to Congress.[1] I very much fear he is not. If they do not elect him and Mr Mason—Newhampshire ought to be blot[t]ed out from the catalogue of States.

We are all well. Edward I think you will find grown considerably. Julia is about the same. I fear you will not find them much improved. I believe I have lost the art [of] managing children—and Julia requires a wiser head than mine, and a better heart I fear. She is very peculiar in her temper and feelings. I think it would be for her good to go from her Mother—but doubt if I could be happy without her.

Adieu, remember a little oftener—Your affectionate   Grace W

ALS. NhHi. Published in Van Tyne, pp. 565–566.
1. For the statistics of Ezekiel's defeat, see above, p. 26.

Although Webster had entered national politics as a sectional spokesman for New England, he had emerged by the 1820's as a leading nationalist.

It was in the framework of a strong and united nation that he supported in 1825 federal appropriations for the construction of the national road. In legislation, he had argued, Congress must "legislate for a whole, not for twenty-four parts." Internal improvements, whether in the construction of roads, canals, or railroads, should be decided on the question of where they were needed and not on the basis of which section they would benefit. As Joseph Vance, representative from Ohio, explained in his letter below, Webster had already earned the "gratitude" of the western people, in his role as spokesman of national interests. He was not yet the determined "Yankee suitor for the hand of the West," but her approval could not fail to encourage his emerging ambitions for the presidency.

FROM JOSEPH VANCE

Urbana March 29th. 1825

Dear Sir

From the interest you took during the last congress in favour of some of the important measures of the West,[1] you have not only a claim on the grattitude of this people, but are entitled to know the political feelings of this section of the union, both as it respects yourself personally, as well as those growing out of the late Presidential Election.

On my way home I passed through our State diagonally, and was every where met by our citizens with that cordiality and good feeling which spoke in a language not to be misunderstood that our stand in favour of Mr Adams was not only approved but received with a degree of enthusiasm unequalled in our state since its admission into the union. This enthusiasm and good feeling was no doubt as much the result of a well grounded confidence in our political institutions, owing to the manner in which the question was settled by the House of representatives, as it was to that of the elevation of the present incumbent to the chief magistracy of the nation.

As it respects yourself permit me to say that with our people no man in this nation stands on more elevated grounds and so far from a wish to proscribe any of the old Federal party their paramount wish is, that talent integrity and worth should be the only passport to office, regardless of party names or sectional distinctions.

In conclusion permit me to say that among the many valued friends I have made in congress none stands higher than yourself, and that nothing would afford me more pleasure than a conscious ability to serve you in attaining under this government a political standing equal to your merit.

Give my respects to friend [Francis] Baylies and accept for yourself the sincere regard of your friend,   Joseph Vance

Before me,

Justice of the

Timothy Williams

Peace.

Boston April 25, 1825, Received and entered with Suffolk Deeds, Lib. 299. fol. 158.

P[e]r Henry Alline Regr.

Printed document, with ms insertions. MWalB. Webster's endorsement of the deed reads: "Tappan's Deed[,] April 18, 1825[,] North part of Lot No. 19—where House in Milton Place stands—This land conveyed D. W."

1. See *Correspondence*, 3, and

mDW 39618 for plat map.

2. See mDW 39617, 39620 for that purchase. The cost of that land was $12,075.91.

3. See also Lewis Tappan to DW, February 14, 1826, below.

FROM JOHN EVELYN DENISON

New York, April 27, 1825.

My Dear Sir:

We got here last night from our tour in Virginia, which the long distances and bad roads made more of an undertaking than we had anticipated. I write to you, as I promised, without a moment's loss of time, but it is to tell you that all our hopes of another week with you at Boston are over. We have only eight days more on these shores, and intend to sail by the British packet on the 5th. It is not without great regret that I give up this last chance of seeing you in this country, and I certainly would have contrived it in some way if it were not for the good assurances I have that we shall meet at no very distant period in England, where I may pass much more time, and many hours of much more leisure in your company, than a hurried visit at Boston now would allow me. Mr. Rufus King's appointment[1] appears to have given very general satisfaction, in which I heartily join, and, out of many reasons, for none more than because I imagine it will fall in well with your views, and further the prospects you once mentioned in a conversation to me. I should be very glad to have this confirmed by you. I have written to our most excellent Judge [Joseph Story], as he desired me when we parted at Philadelphia, to tell him the day we sail, and how impossible it is for us to visit Salem again, but I have insisted that this is not to be a solemn leave-taking, and that the vision which now floats before my eyes, of our active and vigorous friend surveying his robed, and ermined, and gouty brothers of Westminster Hall, is to be realized. He is to see Lord Eldon on his woolsack, and we are to wander together through the aisles of Westminster Abbey.

I don't know what to expect about the continuance of the session of Parliament after our arrival in England. They have done a great deal of most important business; but I do not regret my absence from England, or think I could have spent one moment of my time better than in this country. You see we are verifying your predictions to Congress in April, '24,[2] as fast as we can reasonably be expected, by our policy at home and abroad. By the time you pay us a visit, Mr. [Frederick John] Robinson[3] will let us make you tipsy on good French wine almost for nothing. The first branch of [William] Huskisson's[4] new proposals for the regulation of colonial trade appears to me the most important measure produced for many years, as well as the most convincing proof of the real disposition of our Government. The way in which the people of England appear to be conducting themselves about the Catholics is still more important. I really believe that an effective cry of "No Popery" could hardly now be raised in the country. If it is so, the mighty change can be attributed only to the diffusion of light and knowledge among the people, and to the long and open discussion of the question. The triumph of discussion will be greater in this case, than even in the case of the emancipation of slaves. After this, Right and Truth need never despair.

I will not fail to write to you. You will direct me by your letters to the subjects about which you feel the greatest interest. [James Archibald Stuart]-Wortley and [Henry] Labouchere[5] desire their best remembrances to Mrs. Webster and you. Believe me, With great truth and friendship, Most sincerely yours,   J. Evelyn Denison.

I find an English road-book brought by accident among some others with us. As it is the best we have, and a late and correct edition, I thought you might like to have it. You may now travel from Liverpool to London with the same ease as you used to do from Hyde Park corner to the Bank, and learn the names of all the country-seats by the way.

Text from Curtis, 1: 243–244. Original not found. Denison (1800–1873), Viscount Ossington and member of Parliament, was on a tour of the United States with James A. Stuart-Wortley, Edward Stanley (1799–1869), and Henry Labouchere in 1824. Later, in 1857, Denison was elected speaker of the House of Commons. His friendship with DW was lifelong.

1. Adams appointed King minister to England, King's second term in that post. King remained in England for little more than a year, retiring in 1827, shortly before his death.

2. In his final comments on the tariff question in April 1824, Webster had made lengthy allusions to existing and proposed British trade policies. For Webster's comments (predictions), see *Annals of Congress*, 18th Cong., 1st sess., 1823–24, 2: 2026–2068.

3. Robinson (1782–1859), member of Parliament (*DNB*).

4. Huskisson (1770–1830), member of Parliament and on the Board of Trade. In 1825, Huskisson was the moving force behind the revision of Great Britain's revenue laws (*DNB*).

5. Stuart-Wortley (1776–1845), and Labouchere (1798–1869), both members of Parliament (*DNB*).

TO [JOHN EVELYN DENISON]

Boston May 2. 1825.

My Dear Sir,

I have recd yours of the 27th. April,[1] & most sincerely regret that we shall not see you again among us before you leave our Continent. The good Judge [Story] will be inconsolable. He is now in Maine, in the discharge of official duties, & will not, I fear, be home, in season to write you before your departure. You must try to keep our little Boston alive in your recollections. It will not be disagreeable to you, I hope, when you return to your own Country, & to the midst of your own associations there, to know that there are those, on this side the globe, wholly unknown to you a year ago, who entertain much regard for your character, & sincere good wishes for your welfare. For me, I shall take care to keep myself in remembrance. I shall contrive pretenses to write you often, & hope to hear from you sometimes.

Mr King's appointment gives very general satisfaction. I like it very much. He is a Gentleman of great worth & respectability, a little too much advanced in life, perhaps, to be expected to remain long in the situation. I think the President's selection fortunate, on all accounts.

I assure you, My Dear Sir, it is my fixed intention to see England, within two or three years. No disappointment, not connected with my own health, or that of my family, can be allowed to prevent the accomplishment of this purpose. Your acquaintance & friendship form not only an additional inducement, but an important reliance & resource, in relation to such a visit.

You will doubtless find Parliament still sitting, altho' many great questions will be disposed of before you will be able to show yourselves at Westminster. I have read the proceedings of the Session thus far with great interest, especially Mr Robinson's Speech, on bringing forward the Budget, & Mr Huskissons two speeches, on the subject of the proposed changes in the laws of trade. There appears to me to be, in each of these Gentlemen, so much clear-sightedness, so much enlightened liberality, united to so much general ability, as to fit them well to be leading ministers in your Government at this most interesting period of the world. I regard not only England but all the civilized States as greatly their debtors, for having set an example of a policy so wise, & so beneficial, in the intercourse of Commercial States. Their success, thus far, has been

greater, I think, than even they themselves anticipated; & I most sincerely partake in the gratification it produces.

I hope you will remember to send me any distinguished Parliamentary
speeches, that may happen to be separately published—although I believe I have not omitted this particular in the memorandum you were
good enough to take.[2] I believe I shall not receive, except through your
agency, the vol[umes] of Parliamentary Debates, of which you took a
note. On this subject, however, I will shortly write you, to your address
in London. I shall be very glad of the Road Book you mentioned. If the
present rage continues, one will need no *Road Books*. When I arrive at
Liverpool, I expect to embark on a *Rail way*, for London.

I beg you to make my best remembrances to Mr Wortley & Mr Labouchere. Mention me also to Col [Robert Kearsley] Dawson,[3] if he be
now with you. I saw less of him here than I wished. When you meet Mr
Stanley in England, be kind enough to remember my regards to him. I
expect to see a Speech from him, yet, before the close of the session.
Adieu, My Dear Sir, and I pray you to be assured of my faithful friendship & entire esteem,   Danl. Webster

Mrs. W. desires me to give her farewell to you and your friends Wortley & Labouchere. She wishes you fair winds, a prosperous voyage, & a
happy meeting with your friends.

If Mr Stratford Canning[4] should return to England, I beg you to make
acceptable to him my best regards.

ALS. DLC. Published in Curtis, 1:
244–245.

1. See above.

2. Not found.

3. Dawson (1798–1861), lieutenant
colonel in the royal engineers

(*DNB*), who had also toured the
United States with Denison, Stuart-
Wortley, Labouchere, and Stanley.

4. Canning (1786–1880), British
minister to the United States from
1820 to 1824.

TO JOSEPH HOPKINSON

Boston May 2. 1825

My Dear Sir

I have read Mr [Samuel D.] Ingham's address to his Constituents.[1] It
seems to me not likely to attract attention beyond the immediate sphere
of his friends. I have great repugnance to appear in the Newspapers on
such subjects. This habit of writing about what individual members
said, or did, seems to me to be a very undignified & improper proceeding.
Mr. Ingham is strangely misinformed, as to what he supposes to have
been said or done by me; but I would rather suffer some misrepresentation than to make public statements about such matters.[2] The disap-

pointed will complain. In some form, the grief must come out; & Mr I's pamphlet I think as harmless as almost any other mode.

I am glad to learn that you keep the good resolution of visiting us in June. I trust Mr [Robert] Walsh comes with you. You must let it be early in June. On or about the 20th, I think of going to the Springs—perhaps to the Falls, with Judge Story—& he begs me say to you that you must come along in season to find him as well as me here. It is long since you saw New England, & I hope you will put it off no longer. But, My Dear Sir, how do you expect to settle the matter with Mrs W. unless you bring Mrs Hopkinson with you? Or, I may say, even, how do you expect to settle the matter *with Mrs. W.'s husband?*—for I can hardly allow this long promised visit, which had a woman [in] it, at first, to go off with only a pair of Messrs. We should be truly glad that you would bring either Mrs H. or Elizabeth.[3] Either shall receive a most hearty welcome, & Mrs. W. would be particularly delighted. If Elizabeth will come, she shall not be requested to stir out of our House while she is in town, nor shall any body but yourself be allowed to set foot in it.

We have little news here. All things of a political nature go on well. An excellent spirit of harmony & concord is abroad. Yrs always

Danl. Webster

Let me hear from you, to know when you may be expected—& who will be with you.

ALS. PHi.

1. Ingham's letter "to the People of the Counties of Bucks, Northampton, Wayne, and Pike," in Pennsylvania, appeared in the *National Intelligencer*, April 30, 1825.

2. In his letter Ingham asked: "Why did Mr. Webster, a zealous, personal, and political friend of Mr. Clay, go to Mr. Kremer's lodgings that same night, seek and obtain a private interview with him—say to him that he had just written a letter to a friend, in which he had spoken of him (Mr. K) as an ardent, honest, and faithful Representative, expressing a *sincere regard* for him, and an anxious wish for the amicable adjustment of his difference with Mr. Clay—suggesting that some slight explanation would be satisfactory, and put an end to the investigation?" (*National Intelligencer*, April 30, 1825).

3. Joseph Hopkinson's daughter.

Although he publicly accepted Adams' assurances that Federalists would not be proscribed by the new administration, Webster wanted something more. Only by a general recognition of the key role Federalism had played in the early history of the Republic would members of that party be able to claim public office as a matter of right rather than on sufferance. Returning home in mid-March, he stopped in Philadelphia to visit with Joseph Hopkinson, and in New York, where he talked at length with Jonathan Goodhue (1783–1848), a prosperous merchant who was the son of a former Federalist senator from Massachusetts. According to Goodhue, Webster told him on March 23 that "in concert with Mr. Hopkinson of Philada. he had suggested to Mr. [Robert] Walsh the writing of a history of the Federal Government from its commencement to the end of Mr. Madison's Administration, and after some correspondence with Mr. Walsh he seemed disposed to undertake it. He told me the subject had been mentioned [as] yet only to two gentlemen in Boston, and one more, I think at Philada. and he proposed, if agreeable to me, that when he should get to Boston, he would write me on the subject to enable me to mention it to suitable persons here, with a view to raise by private subscription such a sum as would afford an adequate compensation to Mr. Walsh for the undertaking. He said that it had appeared to him extremely desirable, that while the materials were yet to be found, such a history should be written to preserve from misrepresentation the character of the Federalists who had so largely participated in the administration of the Government in the commencement of its existence, and the conduct and principles of the great Federal Party.

"He conversed with me at the same time very freely on the subject of the recent Presidential Election, in which he had taken a considerable share, and he gave me such a representation as convinces me that Mr. Adams starts at least with the intention of pursuing an honorable course as respects the former political parties. He had sent me a message requesting me to call upon him, as he spent but a few hours in town, and his conversation was quite a confidential one" (Goodhue Diary, Entry of April 1, 1825, NNS).

The confidence was broken, by accident or intent, before the end of the summer. According to Mordecai M. Noah, editor of Noah's New York National Advocate, the plan was "to pay Mr. Walsh for writing a history of the administration of Adams, Jefferson and Madison. . . . It seems that the project originated with Mr. Webster. . . . The sum of $4000 has been made up to give Mr. Walsh, with the privilege of making what he can from the sale of the work, for which he will receive at least $5000 more from the booksellers. . . . It seems that it is considered politic to praise the administrations of Jefferson and Madison, and unite in this commendation the cardinal features which distinguished the Adams administration . . ." (as quoted in the New Hampshire Patriot, August 1, 1825).

No doubt Webster saw himself as the ultimate beneficiary of any shift of political focus brought about by the contemplated work. If he was not yet overtly building an organization to further his presidential ambitions, he was certainly not discouraging others from such activity. More than a year earlier, for example, in February 1824, a New Hampshire cor-

respondent had suggested that Webster send a copy of the National Intelligencer *(presumably the issue of January 20 reporting his speech on
behalf of "the suffering Greeks") "accompanied with a 5 or 10 dollar
bank note" to a "very indigent, but honest and good hearted man" who
was an enthusiastic supporter (John J. Bryant to DW, February 10,
1824, mDW 3975).*

*Whether Walsh or anyone else ever completed the history has not been
determined. The scheme may have been superseded by the establishment
of a Boston newspaper to promote Webster's interests, which came to
fruition a few months later (see pp. 69–70, below).*

TO JONATHAN GOODHUE

Boston May 7 1825.

Private

My Dear Sir,

I now enclose you the letter which I spoke to you about,[1] when I had
the pleasure of seeing you. It explains fully its object. In my judgment,
it is a subject of great importance, and the present time is favorable and
seasonable for attending to it. I think it a duty of high obligation to
endeavor to present *truth*, to posterity. This undertaking seems to me to
be likely to contribute, in some good measure, to that end. I have undertaken to help it on, from a deep conviction of its utility and importance;
and as far as I have communicated it to friends here, it has met their
approbation. We expect that 20 Gentlemen here will give 50 Dlls each
to this object; & we should be glad to find as many, to give the same, in
your City. This is all we wish. From the nature of the case, the proposition can be communicated to very few persons, & those of the most confidential character. You were good enough to say, that the matter should
receive your attention, at the proper time, & I therefore now send you
the enclosed.

Whatsoever may be done about it, I hope may not be long delayed, as
it is understood that the arrangement is to be closed, if at all, the first of
next month. In the course of June, if the arrangement take effect, I expect our Philadelphia friends will visit your City, & ours, with some view
to the collection of necessary historical documents.

I can only repeat, My D[ea]r Sir, that I feel, for one, that some effort
of this kind is due, from us to our predecessors, of the last generation;
& that, all things considered, this mode of discharging that duty, promises, as much as any other which has occurred, or is likely to occur, to be
successful. I shall be most happy if yourself & your friends should concur
in this sentiment. I am, with the truest regard, Your Obt. Servt.

Danl. Webster

ALS. NNS.
    1. Not found.

TO JEREMIAH SMITH

Sunday Eve. [May 22, 1825]

My Dr. Sir

I send you a few letters &c.[1] It would be *queer* if you & I & Judge Story should happen to meet at Niagara. It is possible. The Judge & I intend to set off in that direction abt. June 20th. Yours always most truly

Danl. Webster

Copy. NhHi. Published in Van Tyne, p. 115.
    1. Webster sent Smith letters of

introduction to DeWitt Clinton, William Duer, and Chancellor Kent, mDW 4989, 4991, and below.

TO JAMES KENT

Boston, May 23, 1825.

My Dear Sir,

You know Judge Smith of New Hampshire, at least in his public and professional character. I wish to recommend him to you, on the score of private worth and social qualities. There are few men in the world I think more to your taste.

I entertain for him the highest regard, and true gratitude. When I came to the bar, he was chief justice of the State. It was a day of "the gladsome light" of Jurisprudence. His friends, and I was one of them, thought he must be made governor.

For this office we persuaded him to leave the bench, and that same "gladsome light" cheered us no longer. *Ponto nox incubat atra.* I need not continue Virgil, nor say how the east wind, and the north wind, and the stormy south wind, all rushed out together, and what a shipwreck they made both of law and parties.

Judge Smith has since occasionally practised the law, but for some years has lived entirely, I believe, with his books and his friends. He knows every thing about New England, having studied much its history and its institutions; and as to the law, he knows so much more of it than I do, or ever shall, that I forbear to speak on that point.

Indeed, I am ashamed to find myself commending to you one so well known to you and all other good men; but hearing he was about to visit your city, I could not resist the temptation afforded by the occasion of mentioning my regard for him, and of recommending him to the regard and friendship of yourself and friends. Yours, always truly,

Daniel Webster.

Text from *PC*, 1: 384. Original not found.

In the fall of 1824 and again the following spring Webster intervened unashamedly in the internal political affairs of New Hampshire in a valiant effort to get Jeremiah Mason elected to the United States Senate. The lower house of the state legislature nominated Mason but the state Senate refused to concur, proposing instead the names of William Plumer, Jr.; John F. Parrott, the incumbent; and Samuel Dinsmoor. Each of these was rejected by the House, leaving the election unresolved until a new legislature met in June 1825.

In the letter below, Webster details his efforts in behalf of his friend. He did not, however, mention his attempt to get Adams to intervene. Adams recorded in his diary (Memoirs, 7:14) that Dr. Watkins brought him an unsigned letter from Webster "urging the exercise of influence on my part to secure the election of Jeremiah Mason as Senator from New Hampshire; which I declined, from a conviction that such interference would not be correct in principle, and unavailing in result— there being not the remotest chance of Mason's election." Adams' analysis proved correct: Levi Woodbury, and not Jeremiah Mason, was elected senator.

TO JEREMIAH MASON

Boston May 23. [1825]

Dr Sir

I wrote you yesterday.[1] Last Evening I saw Mr [Salma] Hale, of Keene. In conversing with him on the subject, I found he entertained the same general impression as others, that the result of the elections was unfavorable. He said, however, that Cheshire would be 3 or 4 votes better. He had supposed that *Strafford* was much changed for the worst.

I perceive he is a good deal friendly to Mr. [William] Plumer[, Jr]. From what he says, as well as from some other things, I am fully persuaded that Mr. Plumer still thinks he has some tolerable chance. I have told Mr. H. (in hopes he might suggest it to Mr P) that I did not think your friends would vote for Mr. Plumer—that it was unreasonable to expect it—that your strength was greater than his, or any other candidate who was supposed to be favorable to this Administration, & that if they acted on principle, they ought to unite, in your favor. That Mr. Adams' friends could elect you, if they chose—that if they did not, I did not see why you & your friends should seek to uphold Mr. Adams' interest by electing Mr. Plumer or [John F.] Parrott. In my opinion, this is the right tone; & it ought to be held distinctly to Mr. P. & also to Mr. Parrott, & let the responsibility be *on them*.

Mr [Arthur] Livermore will doubtless be a candidate. It is said, & I incline to think it is true, that Mr. [Samuel] *Bell* would prefer Mr Livermore's situation to his own. Whether this chance of opening the other seat, to be filled this Session also, presents any new views, you can judge. I am at present a good deal inclined to think that [Samuel] Dinsmoor will be the leading candidate; & if you are not elected it seems probable he may be.

I shall leave town tomorrow for three days. On my return hope to find a letter from you. It is suspected an attempt will be made at Concord to repeal the Congressional District Law.

I think Mr. [Timothy] *Fuller* will be Speaker, here.[2] At least I hope so. The House, I believe, is *Federal.* Yet I think they will elect Mr. Fuller, & give Mr. [Levi] Lincoln just such a Council as he may wish. Yrs   D. W.

Let me know if any thing occurs to change the prospect.

ALS. MHi. Incorrectly dated 1824 by Van Tyne, pp. 105–106.

1. Webster was probably referring to his letter to Mason of May 21, 1825 (mDW 4983), dealing with the New Hampshire senatorial election.

No letter of May 22 from Webster to Mason has been found.

2. Fuller was elected Speaker of the Massachusetts House of Representatives on May 25.

A favorite sport of Webster was trout fishing, discussed in the letter below to Henry Cabot (1783–1864), a friend and colleague of the Boston bar. Often Webster combined fishing and work, as he did on this outing in June 1825. On this occasion, he composed his famous Bunker Hill address, drafted it over the course of the next few days, and delivered it on June 17. Webster himself commented in his Autobiography *on the composition of the Bunker Hill address during a fishing expedition. See* Correspondence, *1: 14.*

TO HENRY CABOT

Sandwich June 4 [1825]
Saturday Morning
6 o'clock

Dear Sir

I send you eight or nine trout, which I took yesterday, in that chief of all brooks, Mashpee. I made a long day of it, & with good success, for me. John [Denison][1] was with me, full of good advice, but did not fish—nor carry a rod.

I took 26 trouts, all weighing 17 lb. 12 oz.

The largest (you have him) weighed

at Crochars - - - - - - - - - - - - - - - -	2: 4 oz.
The 5 largest, - - - - - - - - - - - - - -	8: 5 oz.
The eight largest,	11: 8 oz.

I got these by following your advice; that is, by *careful & thorough* fishing of the difficult places, which others do not so fish. The brook is fished, nearly every day. I entered it, not so high up as we sometimes do, between 7 & 8 o'clock, & at 12 was hardly more than half way down to the Meeting House path. You see I did not hurry. The day did not hold out to fish the whole brook properly. The largest trout I took, at 3. P. M. (you see I am precise) below the meeting house, under a bush, on the right bank, two or three rods below the large *beeches*. It is singular, that in the whole day, I did not take two trouts out of the same hole. I found both ends, or parts of the Brook, about equally productive. Small fish not plenty, in either. So many hooks get every thing which is not hid away, in the manner large trouts take care of themselves. I hooked one, which I suppose to be larger than any which I took, as he broke my line, by fair pulling, after I had pulled him out of his den, & was playing him in fair open water.

Of what I send you, I pray you keep what you wish yourself, send three to Mr Ticknor, & three to Dr. [John C.] Warren; or two of the larger ones, to each, will perhaps be enough—& if there be any left, there is Mr [John] Callender,#2 Mr [George] Blake, & Mr [Isaac P.] Davis,3 either of them not "averse to fish." Pray let Mr Davis *see* them—especially the large one. As he promised to come, & fell back, I desire to excite his regrets. I hope you will have the large one on your own table.

The day was fine—not another hook in the Brook. John steady as a Judge—& every thing else exactly right. I never, on the whole, had so agreeable a days fishing tho the result, in pounds or numbers, is not great; nor ever expect such another.

Please preserve this letter; but rehearse not these particulars to the uninitiated.

I think the Limerick *not* the best hook. Whether it pricks too soon, or for what other reason, I found, or thought I found, the fish more likely to let go his hold, from this, than from the old fashioned hook. Yrs

D Webster

If they hold give Callender a *taste*.

ALS. MHi. Published in *W & S*, 16: 677–678.

1. John Denison, commonly called "John Trout," was a local angler who often accompanied Webster on his trout fishing expeditions.

2. Callender (d. 1833; Harvard 1790), a Boston attorney and former student under Christopher Gore.

3. Davis (1771–1855), Boston

manufacturer and businessman. In 1841, through Webster's influence as secretary of state, Davis received an appointment as naval officer of Boston, a post he held until 1845.

TO JOHN EVELYN DENISON

Boston June 6 1825.

My Dear Sir

You perceive that I do not intend to allow you time to forget your cis-atlantic friends, before you hear from some of us. I use this opportunity the more cheerfully as my friend Mr. [Warren] Dutton,[1] of this City, goes by the same conveyance, & although I believe he has a letter to you from your very good friend the Judge [Story], and although I believe also you saw him here, I must beg to solicit your attention & regard to him, if he should happen to come where you are in England. He is a very respectable and worthy man.

We all regretted here, very much, that you and your friends did not come here to give us a parting look. Nevertheless, we have prayed for prosperous gales, & an agreeable voyage for you all. For myself, I have been very quietly at home, since I returned from Washington, but the Judge & myself are thinking of making an excursion, to commence in the course of this month, to Niagara. Since the adjournment of Congress we have little political news. Mr Clay is gone to Kentucky, & expects, I believe, to be well received by his friends, notwithstanding some complaints, probably not general, for the support which he gave to the President. We look for Mr. Rush next month. Mr. King has already sailed to take his place. We have hopes of seeing Mr. [Henry Unwin] Addington[2] so far north as this place, during the summer. [Jules von] Wallenstein is already at New York. I believe Mr [Joseph] Hopkinson, & Mr [Robert] Walsh intend us a visit this month.

When you shall have composed yourself, My Dear Sir, & settled your brain, disturbed as it must be by such a whirl as you have made round so great a part of our Continent, I shall hope to hear from you. We have accounts from London to April 21. Mr. [George] Cannings[3] last Speech on the Catholic question is, I think, a most admirable performance. Some men, & he seems to be one of them, show great powers under the pressure of great responsibility. Certain it is, that his late Parliamentary efforts far exceed any thing which is to be found of his at an earlier date. I go far enough back, of course, to include among his great efforts, his Speech at Liverpool.

I am for the Catholic emancipation; but I should think, nevertheless, that its friends overrate its utility & importance by about as much as its enemies overrate its mischief, and danger. You must excuse this expression of opinion, on a matter, of the merits of which I know so little. If the leading Speeches on this (& other) subjects should be published in pamphlet form, I should be very glad to have them. I have made an arrangement with Mr. [James W.] Burditt, Bookseller, of this place, by which his correspond[ents] in London will receive, pay for, & transmit hither any *Books* which you may procure or order for me. The names & address of these correspondents are Messrs Peter, William & George Wynne Stationers, Pater Noster Row. When you took my memoranda it was left a little doubtful whether I should rely on you to be able to complete my set of Parliamentary Debates. My other hope has *failed*; & I now wish you to take the trouble to order what will complete my set, according to the minutes taken at Washington. I think of nothing in particular to be added to the list, with which I troubled you—but will thank you to exercise a pretty liberal discretion, in regard to such occasional publications, especially in the Department of politics, as you think may interest me. I would like well enough to see Sir [Samuel] Egerton Brydges' Book.[4] The Books, however, which I mean to trouble you to obtain, are only such as I should hardly be able to get otherwise—& therefore I shall not at present swell the list.

I pray you to remember me to your fellow travellers in America. We cherish the hope that you some times think of us. Mrs Webster joins me in remembrance and regard to you. I shall be likely to trouble you often, & trust you will let us know of your safe arrival. I shall expect, of course, that if any friend of yours shall be induced to visit America, you will allow me to be known to him. I am, Dr Sir, yrs very truly & sincerely

Danl. Webster

ALS. DLC. Published in Curtis, 1: 246–248.

1. Dutton (1774–1857; Yale 1797) was a newspaper editor, lawyer, and Massachusetts legislator.

2. Addington (1790–1870) was at the time secretary of the British legation in Washington (*DNB*).

3. Canning (1770–1827), British foreign minister (*DNB*).

4. Brydges (1762–1837), editor of early English literature (*DNB*). The specific work Webster wanted has not been established.

TO GEORGE TICKNOR

[June 15?, 1825]

"I did the deed" this morning—i.e. that is I finished my [Bunker Hill] Speech—& I am pretty well persuaded it is a speech that will *finish* me—as far as reputation is concerned. There is no more tone in it, than in the weather in which it has been written—it is "perpetual dissolution & thaw."

AL. NhD. Published in Curtis, 1: 251.

TO EZEKIEL WEBSTER

Monday June 20 [1825]

My Dear Brother,

I give this letter for you to Mr. G[eorge] W[ashington] La Fayette,[1] that you may be known to him, & that he may introduce you to the Genl. The Genl. will probably find you out. I have told him how good a *Greek* you are—a matter in which he feels great interest.

We leave here on friday morning for Niagara—have you any thing to say to us before we go. Yrs   D. Webster

ALS. NhD.
1. Lafayette (1779–1849) was the only son of the Marquis de Lafayette,

then on a tour through the United States.

On June 24, the Websters and the Storys left on a trip across New York state to Niagara Falls. A week earlier, Webster had delivered his now-famous Bunker Hill oration before patriots of the Revolution and La-fayette, the honored guest on the occasion. Soon after the celebration, Webster turned the address over to Ticknor, who sold it to a publisher for $300, the proceeds of which were to go to the Bunker Hill Monument Association. In the letter below, Webster directs Ticknor to make some last-minute corrections in the manuscript before publication.

TO GEORGE TICKNOR

Worcester, Saturday Morning
[June 25, 1825]

My D Sir

We are all safe here, with the prospect of a regular rain. I called at Cambridge yesterday morning & read to the 32nd. page of my address. It was then to be corrected & sent to you. I brought along the first 32 pages, & perhaps may look them over again, especially the latter part, & send them back. The passage about "propelling ships" &c, I altered again, so as that I think it may do.

Should not the word "monument," in the last sentence of the address be marked, by being in small capitals, or, more properly perhaps, by having a capital letter to begin with.

On page 24—10th. line—I find *so* for *to*—but I presume this has been corrected.

I understand the N[orth] A[merican Review] is coming out, today. Can you not send us a copy at Albany? Remember us to Mrs T. & believe us all to be Yrs   D Webster

ALS. MB.

TO JAMES WILLIAM PAIGE

Saratoga, Sunday morning
[July 3, 1825]

Dr Wm.

We came here yesterday, from Albany. As at present arranged, the rout[e] is pleasant. A coach brought us nine miles—we then entered a canal packet boat—ascended three or four locks, & came along through a country of very good scenery nine or ten miles, where we left the canal, & were brought here in a carriage. We had an opportunity of seeing the junction of the Western & Northern Canals, & the passage of the former over the Mohawk river, in what they call an aqueduct. The river here is about 400 yrds wide—stone piers are erected—& on them a plank canal is made, large enough for the canal boats &c. We saw also the falls called the Cohoes. At Ballston we stopped but a few minutes, our Ladies thinking that the Saratoga waters would suit their complaints better. This morning they have drank not a little from the Congress Spring. There is said to be more company here than is usual for the season. We shall probably stay till Tuesday. At Utica we expect letters from you. I hope to get a copy of my speech, somewhere along. I do not know what is the nearest Post office to Niagara Falls, on the American side. Some of the Gentlemen who have been there can tell you. I shall inquire for letters at Lewiston, & at Black rock, unless I hear from you at Canandaigua that you write to some other place. I shall also inquire at the nearest P. Office.

Mrs W. has told you, I suppose, all about Catskill Mountains. She professed to wish that you & Mr & Mrs Blake had been there with us. She says she has today no particular commission to charge you with.

I pray you remember me to Mr & Mrs Blake; I trust the Lady has recovered her voice, & wish they were setting out with us for Niagara. Love to the children. Yrs   D. W.

ALS. NhHi. Published in Van Tyne, pp. 691–692, under date of [July 10, 1825]. Paige (1792–1868), Grace Fletcher Webster's half-brother, was a prosperous merchant in Boston and one of Webster's most reliable financial backers.

TO JAMES WILLIAM PAIGE

Utica, July 8 [1825]

Dr W.

You perceive that our flight is not very rapid. We arrived here, evening before last, at the moment of the arrival of your letter, which, you may be assured, it gave us no small pleasure to receive. Yesterday we went to visit Trenton Falls, a famous *lion* 15 miles from this place. It is a succession of cascades, or water falls, in a stream called West Canada Creek, for a mile & a half or two miles. On either side, for the whole distance, is a wall of rock, nearly perpendicular, & varying, in height, from one hundred, to one hundred & fifty, feet. The passage, to view the falls, is at the bottom of this bank of rocks, & at the very edge of the torrent. It is difficult, & in some places, I think, *dangerous.* There are, however, chains fastened in the rock, in the most critical spots, to hold on by. Our Ladies accomplished the object of getting a full view, although it rained like a torrent, & to have fallen over would not have soaked them more thoroughly. We find all the inns, & all the roads, full of travellers, many of them from Boston. This Country is all alive. It is new, growing, & highly excited. An universal competition prevails, in every thing. Carriages—public houses—boats—all much more abundant than would seem strictly necessary—& all competitors. We leave this morning at 9—if our party should wake up by that time—& intend going 40 or 50 miles today.

I enclose Judge Story's draft for 200 Dlls. I have drawn a check on the B[an]k—for 400—& sold it here. You will please look in & see if there are funds. I believe they are abundant.

It will be Sunday before we reach Canandaigua, where we hope to find more of your letters. We often wish that more of our friends were with us when we see the great *sights.* I think Mr & Mrs Blake would like Trenton falls very much. We dined on very fine trout, caught in the falls, where some are found weighing five pounds. We have heard of nothing very good in Mr. Blake's particular line.

I do not know whether Mrs W. has any thing to send but love. I presume she is dreaming about you all.

Give my own to the children, & to Mr & Mrs Blake, & believe me truly yrs.   D. Webster

I threatened Mrs Blake with a letter, from [the] falls, which I shall remember.

ALS. NhHi. Published in *PC*, 1: 393–394.

TO MRS. GEORGE BLAKE

Niagara Falls, July 15. 1825

My Dear Mrs Blake,

It is one of my most agreeable duties, before leaving this place, to write to you, to tell you how much we have admired the great Spectacle here, & how sincerely we have lamented, every hour, that you were not with us to partake, & increase our pleasure. This is the third day of our being here. The weather has been uniformly fine, & we have seen the

Falls under all advantages. You have of course read many accounts of this Fall, to which no account can do justice; and altho' I am disposed to say something on the subject, I expect no better success than others, who have undertaken the description.

The Niagara River, at the moment of leaving Lake Erie, is one mile in width. It runs, nearly directly, north, with a rapidity of six miles & a half, an hour. We crossed it, from the East side to the West, at the village of Black Rock, two miles and a half below the end of the Lake. Here its current is less rapid, running probably about four miles an hour. This river, being fed from such vast reservoirs above, is subject to little variation in the height of its waters. Its annual rise does not exceed a foot; & it may give some idea of the immense distance through which its waters have flowed, to mention that the spring *fresh* is not felt here till July. It is now just about the time of high water. It is truly a noble River; rapid, but smooth & glassy; always full, but never over-flowing

"Tho' deep, yet clear; tho' gentle, yet not dull;
"Strong, without rage; without o'erflowing, full."

We passed down its western shore, along the bank, close to the water's edge, and over a level road. Lake Erie is 330 feet higher than Lake Ontario; but in descending the River, from Lake Erie, one perceives no very considerable, or great, descent, although the current is, all the way, rapid, till we get nearly down to the Falls. A little below the village of Black Rock, perhaps about five miles from Lake Erie, the River divides into two channels, forming a large Island in the centre, called Grand Isle, about 12 miles long, & in some places 6 or 7 broad. This Island terminates, and the two channels unite again, just at the head of what are called the Rapids, a mile, or a mile & a half, above the Great Falls. These Rapids are a succession of Cascades, spreading over the whole River, of different & various heights & appearances, rendering the whole breadth of the stream, which is here not less than two miles, white with foam. They would form a fine object, if there were nothing near which called the attention another way. Midway of these Rapids is Goat Island, which divides the river into two unequal parts, about one third, in breadth, being on the Eastern, or American side, and two thirds on the Western, or British. This Island runs down to the very brink of the Falls, & there terminates in a perpendicular precipice, or wall of Rock, which is part of the same great declivity over which the river pours. This Island thus divides the River, so that it falls over the precipice in two sheets. The length of the Fall on the American side is estimated at 380 yards,— then the distance across the end of Goat Island, 330 yards, and the length of the Falls on the British side, 700 yards. On the East side of Goat Island, is another small Island. I know not its name, but it is separated from Goat Island by 20 or 30 yards of water, which pours over here & makes a beautiful object, by itself, being wholly separate & distinct from the two great Falls. The Fall is rec[k]oned to be highest on the American side, being there 165 feet; & on the British side 150. Vastly the greatest portion of water, I should think three fourths, or even more, runs over on the British side.

I have seen no description which correctly represents the *line* of these Falls. I, also, shall fail in attempting to describe it to you; but, neverthe-less, I will make the attempt. But, in the first place, you must remember, that the land, or country, does not descend, or fall off, at the Falls. From the end of Lake Erie to Lewiston, which is seven miles below the Falls, the surface of the earth is uncommonly level; but here, at Lewiston, is a great descent, from the level of Lake Erie, to that of Lake Ontario. There-fore, as you come along down the river, from Lake Erie, when you get to the Falls, the river seems to fall away from your feet, & to pitch right down into the earth. Many miles before you reach the Falls, you see the *mist* or *spray*, rising up like a cloud. But this does not seem to be rising from the Earth into the air, so much as from the centre of the Earth to the surface. It appears to be coming out of the ground. From the bottom of the Falls to Lewiston, 7 miles, the whole channel of the river is one great *trough*, 100 or 150 feet deep, with sides of perpendicular rock. This has given currency to the opinion that the Falls were once 7 miles lower down than they now are; and that the force of the water, in time, has worn away the rocks, & forced the Falls back to their present position.

Now, as to the *line* of the Falls, as it appears to me, at the moment of writing this, from the upper rooms in Forsythes Hotel. The American Fall may be said to be *straight*. There are some little inequalities in the line, but on the whole it is very regular; next comes the little Island, near Goat Island, a little advanced, beyond the great American Fall; then the little separate cascade, a little more advanced; then the end of Goat Island, about on a line with the little Cascade; and then the great British Fall. The line of this Fall, leaving the point of Goat Island, advances, makes a bend forward, a sort of gentle sweep or graceful arch, perhaps two hundred yards in length, then retreats again, till it gets a little further back than the point of the Island where it set out, and making now an angle, or rather a curve, it goes downward, & across the River, & joins the western Bank, at Table Rock, which is a good deal below the end of Goat Island. This last mentioned bend, or curve, in the line of the Falls, is commonly called the horse shoe; for no reason, that I know of, except that a horseshoe is a ready figure to express any curving line. On the earth, at the bottom of the Falls, among the rocks, I succeeded, with a walking stick six feet long, in drawing, pretty accurately, the line of the Falls. I cannot do it on paper. The enclosed is as near as I can come.[1]

But I wish now to state something which I have seen mentioned in no printed account, but which is absolutely essential to any correct understanding of the subject. At the very foot of the Falls the whole River turns suddenly to the right; and runs off, in that direction. So that the water, which falls over on the British side, runs along at the foot of the American Fall. The American Fall faces, exactly & completely, the western Bank of the River. As you walk along down from the Table Rock, you have the American Fall precisely in front. Just at the bottom of the American Fall is the ferry. We land at the very edge of this Fall. But, on the other side, we set out near half a mile below the Table Rock. The whole, I think, may be understood, by bearing in mind that, at the very fall, the River makes a sudden turn to the right, so that all the Fall, out of the horse shoe, and especially the American Fall, fronts, not down the River, but directly across it.

I am afraid, after all, My Dear Lady, that you are little the wiser for this attempt at description. I can *draw* nothing; but if I find you in the dark on the subject, when I get home, I think, with a piece of shingle and a penknife, I may explain my ideas.

The Falls are seen from many different points, and the views are very various. I write this in an upper parlour, in Forsythes' Hotel, on the Canada side. The entire line of the Falls is in my view, but the whole is below me. The view, however, of the great curve, or horse shoe, is very good from this spot. I think as perfect, as from any point. I can see the water, as it pours over, nearly all round the semicircle. The sheet has all appearances of being very *thick*; probably, it is thought, 15 or 20 feet. It's surface, as it falls over, is streaked, with alternate white, caused by the foam, and the most brilliant emerald.

In descending, to get a nearer view, we go down a steep hill, or what may be called the upper part of the Bank, about 100 feet. This is about as much descent as the River makes, in the Rapids, above the Falls, so that having come down this distance we are on the level of the water at the head of the Falls. Here are several acres of flat land, between the foot of this hill, & the water's edge, thickly covered with trees and shrubbery. A planked walk leads along towards the River, at the head of the Falls, & I do not know that my attention has been more strongly arrested by any thing, than by the view which occurs, as we walk along this path. The water is seen, rather suddenly & unexpectedly, through a vista, or avenue of trees. It is, nearly, & seems to be, quite, on your own level. Great & unbroken ridges of billows come hastening & bounding along, & rush forward to the precipice, which, as yet, the spectator does not see. The magnitude, the strength, & the hurry of the mighty stream create deep & instant consternation. Proceeding onward, & turning a little down the stream, we come to the water's edge, at the top of the Fall. The water is even with the Bank, and we can wash our hands, in safety, in the River. Going along, now, on the Table Rock, we have what is generally thought the best view of the whole Falls.

Fronting us is the American Fall, & the little Cascade; further to the right Goat Island, & the commencement, by it, of the British Fall; & farther to our right is the great circular Fall, or horse-shoe, which will hardly allow the eyes to be withdrawn long enough to look at any thing else. You may stand by the water, just where it falls off, & if your head does not swim, you may proceed to the brink of Table Rock, & look down into the gulph beneath. This is all foam, & froth, & spray. As you stand here, it looks as if all the water of the globe was collected round this circle, & pouring down here into the centre of the earth. As we stood, today, at noon, on the projecting point of Table Rock, we looked over into this Abyss, and far beneath our feet, arched over this tremendous aggregate of water, foam, & vapour, we saw a perfect and radiant rainbow. This ornament of Heaven does not seem out of place, in being half way up the sheet of the glorious cataract. It looked as if the skies themselves paid homage to this stupendous work of nature. From Table Rock, or a little farther down, a winding stair case is constructed, down which we descend from the level of Table Rock 95 feet. This brings us to the bottom of the perpendicular rock, & from this place we descend, 50 or 60 feet further, over large fragments of rock, & other substances down to the edge of the River. We went this afternoon a little lower down the River than the upper stair case, almost indeed down to the ferry, & getting out on a Rock, in the edge of the River, we thought the view of the whole falls the best we had obtained. If, at the bottom of the stair case, instead of descending further, we chuse to turn to the right, & go up the stream, keeping close at the foot of the Table Rock, or the perpendicular Bank, we soon get to the foot of the fall, & approach the edge of the falling mass. It is easy to go in behind, for a little distance, between the falling water, & the rocks over which it is precipitated. This cannot be done, however, without being entirely wet. From within this cavern there issues a wind, occasionally very strong, & bringing with it such showers & torrents of spray that we are soon as wet as if we had come over the Falls, with the water. As near to the fall, in this place, as you can well come, is, perhaps, the spot on which the mind is most deeply impressed with the whole scene. Over our heads hangs a fearful rock, projecting out like an unsupported Piaza. Before us is a hurly burly of waters, too deep to be fathomed, too irregular to be described, shrouded in too much mist to be clearly seen. Water, vapor, foam, & the atmosphere, are all mixed up together, in sublime confusion. By our side, down comes this world of green & white waters, & pours into the invisible abyss. A steady, unvarying, low toned roar thunders incessantly upon our ears. As we look up, we think some sudden disaster has opened the seas, & that all their floods are coming down upon us at once. But we soon recollect, that what we see is not a sudden or violent exhibition, but the permanent & uniform character of the object, which we contemplate. There, the grand spectacle has stood, for centuries, from the creation even, as far as we know, without change. From the *beginning*, it has shaken, as it now does, the earth, & the air; & its unvarying thunder existed, before there were human ears to hear it. Reflections like these on the duration, & permanency of this grand object, naturally arise, & contribute much to the deep feeling which the whole scene produces. We cannot help being struck with a sense of the insignificance of man, & all his works, compared with what is before us.

"Lo! where it comes, like an eternity,
As if to sweep down all things in its track–"

I shall not, My Dear Mrs Blake, attempt any full description of this scene; & still less to represent its whole effect on the mind. It must be seen. It is something which speaks to the senses. No description can set it forth.

The ferry, as I believe I have already stated, leaves the British shore near half a mile below the Fall on that side, & passes over to the American shore just at the lower edge of the Fall there. The view of the whole fall, from the Boat, is very perfect; as much so, perhaps as from any spot. From the landing place on the American side, a new & well built stair case brings us up, close along by the falling water, to the top of the Bank. We then walk along up the River, & see that the American Branch is not only less wide but much less deep than the British. The Cascades, however, are beautiful, on this side. About half a mile above the Fall a good bridge is thrown over to Goat Island. This is a charming place, containing 60 or 70 acres of ground covered with large & handsome trees. We may walk all round it, & see the rapids, to great advantage, in both divisions of the stream. Its lower end, also, presents some good views of the Falls. We see here that the American Falls is not so straight, as it seems from the other side, but has various projections & indentations. The little stream, running at the east corner of Goat Island, & forming, as it falls, the little Cascade, is quite accessible, and might almost be waded over. In the morning the Bow is very fine, from this point. I saw one this morning, caused by the spray from the American Fall. It seemed to spring up from the little house, in which the Ferry man lives, on the British side, & swelling up along the Bank, it came down again near the Table Rock. The depth of the water in the River, below the Falls, is very great. It is said to have been lately sounded, by public authority, where the ferry is, & found to be more than 300 feet. It would *seem* to be dangerous, where the Boat passes, but I believe it is not so. The water is a good deal agitated, but it does not run with any current too strong to be encountered.

The Rock over which the waters of the Cataract fall is Limestone. No doubt the same sort of rock under lays this whole country, for a great extent. The Banks of the River, & the wall over which the Falls run, show great regularity of formation. In building the stairs, on the American side, lately, the workmen have blown-away the rock, in the side of the Bank, for some distance, to make room for the Stair case, & here the succesive *strata* are seen, generally from 6 inches to 3 feet thick, laid up with the precision of masonry.

We have been here now the whole or a part of three days; and although our eyes are not satisfied, with seeing, yet some of us complain of weary limbs, from walking about so much, & going down & climbing up the Banks so often.

We shall leave probably to-morrow. It will not be without pain that I part from the Falls.

And now, My Dear Mrs Blake, let me repeat how much we lament that you & your husband have not been with us, on this visit. Our whole party desire their best respects to you both. Mrs Webster, particularly, sends her love to you, & thinks you will deserve well, if your patience holds out through this long letter. However that may be, I assure you I have had much pleasure in writing it, & if I could think of any thing more to say, on the subject, should write still longer. But be not alarmed—I am through; and have only to add that I am, most affectionately Yours always   Danl. Webster

ALS. NBuC. Published in *PC*, 1 : 385–392.
1. Not found.

FROM JOHN EVELYN DENISON

London July 17. 1825.

My dear Sir

Your Parliamentary History, the continuation of the Debates, and five printed speeches will be sent by the Ship Crisis wh[ich] sails from the Port of London on the first of August. I have followed the directions of your last letter, wh[ich] says that Wynne, the correspondent of Mr Burditt, is to receive, pay for, and transmit all books thus ordered for you.[1] In the parcel you will find a little book directed to the Judge [Story], wh[ich] I will thank you to forward to him. I met with it by accident the

other day, it being sold out of the famous library of the Duke of Marl-
borough and is a scarce, and ought at Salem to be a curious book. I called
the other day on [William Scott,] Lord Stowell[2] but did not find him at
home, and as I am obliged to leave London the day after tomorrow, I am
afraid I must put off till a future opportunity the delivery of the Judges
message, and the complimentary reply that I know I shall be commissioned to transmit in return.

Mr Dutton has not called upon me, and I cannot find him out. Mr
Rufus King has not yet reached London, and I can obtain no news of
him either through official or other quarters. Mr [George] Canning has
been very alarmingly ill for the last three days, with an inflammatory
attack in the bowels—repeated bleedings, and leaches have overcome
the disease, and the medical attendants are now sanguine about his
recovery.

We have no political news, except very bad accounts from Greece. I
have seen Mr Stratford Canning two or three times since I last wrote.
He sets out very shortly for Constantinople. He desired his best remembrances to you, and that I would thank you for yours to him.

Is not [Nathaniel] Bowditch, or something very like it, the name of
your celebrated Mathematician, of whom Mr Jefferson spoke a great
deal. I understood that he had not only completely mastered LaPlace's
"Mechanique Celeste," but had detected some inaccuracies in the calculations, wh[ich] he had made known to LaPlace, & for it he had received
his acknowledgements. Is that so; & did he translate the work also?

The Prorogation of Parliament, and the unusual circumstance of an
almost insupportable heat of weather drives every body from London.
The Assizes and other country business summons them to their respective homes; and the Town will soon be comparatively deserted.

The House of Commons has decided on reprinting their Reports of
Committees, so as to complete the series from the Union downward. It
will hardly therefore be worth your while to have a few detatched copies
in the mean time, but I shall take upon myself to give directions to your
bookseller to watch a favorable opportunity of buying for you the 16 vols
already printed uniformly, to which you will hereafter add the new
Series.

You will not forget to let me have everything [in]teresting from your
side the world—especially every [thing which] claims to be your own
offspring. My best remembrances to Mrs Webster—to the Judge &c, and
tell him that I shall answer his letter from the country, that my delay, is
anything but neglect. Ever truly yours   J Evelyn Denison.

Col [Robert Kearsley] Dawson is to be married in three weeks to Miss
Seymour, a lady to whom he has been long attached.

ALS. DLC.
  1. See above, DW to Denison, June
6, 1825.

2. Lord Stowell (1745–1836), judge
and member of Parliament (*DNB*).

TO JONATHAN GOODHUE

Boston July 30. 1825.

My Dear Sir

On my return, two days ago, from a long journey into your State, I had the pleasure to find here yours of the 22. June. That of an earlier date had been recd, on the Eve of my departure.[1]

I regret that so unfounded a suspicion should exist in the mind of any of our friends, as to the intended object.[2] Certainly it never entered into my imagination that any thing should be written to disparage the well earned fame of Col Pickering or Genl Hamilton. Any expression of my regard for them would be wholly superfluous. It was to subserve no man's cause, nor to depress, on the other hand, any man's character, that I wished the history of the Administration of the Govt. to be written. I have been convinced that party & passion have very much discolored the truth, in many cases, & I wish to see historical justice established.

My view has been wholly & altogether *general*; & I repeat, that I would not aid any attempt to compose a political history so as to have a bearing on particular individuals, either for the purpose of praise or censure.

It is to be regretted, that this should have become a subject of Newspaper gossiping;[3] as it may lead to misrepresentation, & in that way hinder or embarrass the object itself. Still, I think it important, & that it ought to be pursued. You will probably have had opportunity of suggesting the subject as far as was contemplated before I shall be in your City in Novr. If any thing occurs, in the mean time, I will write to you. In the meantime conversation on the matter will doubtless subside; as it is desirable it should do. I am, Dr. Sir, most truly, Yrs   Danl. Webster

P.S. On recurring again to your letter, I perceive that you have *already*, suggested the object, to all the Gentlemen contemplated when I saw you.

ALS. NNS.
  1. Neither letter found.
  2. See above, DW to Goodhue, May
7, 1825.
  3. See above, pp. 46–48.

The response to Webster's Bunker Hill address was largely one of enthusiasm and praise; few raised objections to it. One anonymous writer, "Acacius" of Rhode Island, however, criticized the speech because it ignored the issue of slavery. Webster apparently did not respond—at least no response has been found. "Acacius" has not been positively identified, but may have been the Reverend Barnabas Bates.

Mount Hope, July. 1825.

Sir,

I have read with attention and interest your able and eloquent Bunker Hill Address. I was glad to find that you were more prudent than some others have been on similar occasions. I observed, however, one *omission*, which was to me an occasion of regret.

In your Address, you have appeared as an advocate for the rights of man. You have eulogized the prosperous state of our country, and the exertions of our fathers for liberty and independence. You have exulted in "the benefit which our example has produced, and is likely to produce, on human freedom and happiness,"—and you have sympathized with the oppressed Greeks. But I have not observed any expression of sympathy for the *two millions of slaves* in our own country, nor a word of regret that this land is emphatically a *land of slavery* as well as a *land of freedom*. Should such melancholy facts be forgotten or omitted in any of our celebrations?

You observe, "When Louis XIV said, 'I am the state,' " he expressed the essence of unlimited power. Our white people say, *We are the state*, and deprive the Negroes of the rights of man. Where despotism reigns, the greater the number of tyrants, the greater is the calamity. The subjects of Louis were *freemen* compared with the *slaves* of the United States.

While expressing your sympathy for the Greeks and suggesting a reason why some European Government had not interfered to their disadvantage, you say—"Let us thank God that we live in an age when something has influence besides the bayonet, and when the sternest authority does not venture to encounter the scorching power of public reproach. Any attempt of the kind I have mentioned should be met by one universal burst of indignation. The air of the civilized world ought to be made too warm to be comfortably breathed by any who would hazard it."

Prior to a resort to arms, the condition of the Greeks was far less deplorable and degraded than that of the slaves of our country; and the Negroes have far more cause of complaint against our government, than the Greeks had against the Turkish despotism. Why, then, should we feel more for the Greeks of Europe, than for the Negroes of America? Are we bound to feel *less* for the oppressed in proportion as they are *more* insulted and injured? Or should we feel more for them in proportion as their distance from us is greater? Who does not know that our Negroes have a thousand fold more reason to rise against their oppressors, than their Masters had to rise against the government of Britain? Shall we then celebrate the feats by which our liberty was obtained or secured, and still *do* nothing, *say* nothing, and *feel* nothing, for the millions we have deprived of their rights by the policy of our *free* institutions, or the power of our *republican* government? Why should we not try "the scorching power of public reproach" to reform or prevent abuses in our own land as well as to recommend its use in other countries? Why not make "the air" of the United States "too warm to be comfortably breathed" by any advocate for slavery, and especially by those who deride all philanthropic exertions in behalf of the slaves? If "we live in an age when something has influence besides the bayonet," why should we not try the efficacy of that "something" and do all we can to rouse public attention to the object of freeing our country from the infamy of the slave holding system, that it may be to all, except felons, a land of freedom?

In 1820, the number of our slaves nearly equalled the whole population of the six New England States. Suppose then that all the people of these six States were now slaves,—What should we be likely to think of those who could celebrate the liberty and glory of our country, without bestowing a thought on our wretched condition? In your Plymouth Address, you had an admirable paragraph on the slave trade; and for one, I regret, that in your Bunker Hill Address you had not introduced a paragraph of equal perspicuity and force, on the subject of slavery. Never perhaps had any person a better opportunity to make his countrymen feel their own inconsistency, than you had on that occasion. You were surrounded by many thousands of your fellow citizens, exulting in their freedom as purchased with blood. How affecting it must have been to them, had you described in glowing colors the condition of millions of slaves, held in bondage by men who can boast that their fathers fought for Liberty!

I doubt not that some will say, that you could not have touched the subject of slavery without offending our Southern brethren; and that it might also have encouraged an insurrection of the slaves. I very well know, Sir, that the subject of slavery is a delicate one; and I wish it may ever be managed with prudence. But if we are to forbear saying any thing about it through fear of offending the slave holders, how is the evil ever to be removed? And how are we to vindicate the conduct of our fathers in attempting to expose the injustice of those acts of Parliament which occasioned the Revolution? In respect to encouraging an insurrection of the slaves, I certainly have no wish to do this, or to have it done by others. But if any thing could *provoke* them to insurrection, I should think that our celebrations of liberty, regardless of their condition, would have that effect.

If the Bunker Hill Monument is intended to convey to future generations, correct views of the liberty, philanthropy, and glory of our country, at the time of its erection,—and should it be built during the present state of public feeling, it seems to me that there should be engraved on the Obelisk something like the following inscription.

In A D 1825,

Fifty years subsequent to the Battle for Liberty,

The Inhabitants of the United States were a

FREE PEOPLE,

Excepting TWO MILLIONS of *Slaves*,

Whose condition had excited but little sympathy,

and for whose emancipation no national

effort had ever been made!

Be assured, sir, that the foregoing remarks are not the fruit of any unfriendly or disrespectful feeling towards yourself or any other person. My object is, if possible, to occasion such reflections and such exertions as become a christian people, highly favored by God.

Too long have we been in the habit of regarding the Negroes as an inferior race of beings, who could not be profited by freedom. The success of the Haytians proves the falsity of such opinions. All things considered, their success is far more wonderful than that of any other people, who, in our day, have resorted to arms for the acquisition of liberty. What was the success of the French, the Spaniards, or the Neapolitans, compared with that of the Haytians! How much more consistent have the Haytians been than the people of our country! And what man of the United States has displayed more prudence and better talents for government than President [Jean Pierre] Boyer?[1] After the death of Henry [Christophe],[2] to unite the hostile districts of the island under one government, and so long to preserve the public tranquillity, must have required an assemblage of talents not very common in any country. May it not be doubted whether even a Governor [George Michael] Troup[3] would have done better than Boyer in the same situation? Compare the state papers of the two Chiefs, in respect to philanthropy, prudence, and magnanimity, and then judge.

I freely own, sir, that the people of our country have abundant reason to rejoice in the goodness of God to them. But when I hear them exult in our freedom—in our sanguinary achievements in a struggle for liberty—in our example as the light of the world—in anticipations of future unparalleled prosperity and glory—the black portentous cloud of NEGRO

SLAVERY presents its vast appalling surface to my view, and seems to say, FORBEAR BOASTING AND REJOICE WITH TREMBLING.

ACACIUS.

Text from the Boston *Columbian Centinel*, August 20, 1825. Original not found. In publishing the anonymous letter, the *Centinel* editors took an apologetic position. "We are aware," they wrote, "how restive some of our southern fellow citizens are whenever the subject of it [slavery] is discussed; but we cannot believe they can wish to suppress remarks on it, which flow from the pens of genius, sound argument, true Patriotism and Christian Philanthropy. We know the writer to be one of the most worthy and enlightened citizens, who has no other object in his address than the honor of his country, and the best good of his fellow men, and who would abhor to effect even a good end by disorderly or unjust means. We also know, that he has the highest respect for the Hon. Gentleman addressed; and would recommend no measure to him which in his opinion would lessen the sphere of his usefulness, or impair his deserved popularity."

1. Boyer (d. 1843), mulatto president of Haiti, had assisted in the expulsion of the French from the island and united it under his leadership in 1821.

2. Henry Christophe (d. 1820), Negro leader of the northern sector of the Haitian island, who had crowned himself King Henri I in 1811.

3. Troup, governor of Georgia, had been elected first by the General Assembly in 1823, and reelected in 1825 in the first popular canvass in the state. With Troup's election, the class conflict between the cotton planters and subsistence farmers had been resolved, whereupon the two united factions undertook to expel the Creeks and the Cherokees from the area.

FROM JAMES MADISON

Montpellier Aug. 12. 1825

Dear Sir

I have received the copy of your Oration delivered at Bunker's Hill on the occasion presented by the 17th of June last. It merits all the praise which has been bestowed on it. And I tender you many thanks for the pleasure it has afforded me, with assurances of my distinguished [esteem & cordial respects   J. M.][1]

AL (signature removed). NhHi. ALS draft. PHi. A note by Thomas Davis, dated October 13, 1828, states that Madison's signature was "cut out for Mr Sprague." Published in *PC*, 1: 396.

1. Bracketed insertion taken from ALS draft.

Concurrent with the negotiations to publish a "history" of the Federal party, Webster and some of his Boston friends—the Everetts, especially—moved to establish a new political sheet in Boston, the Massachusetts Journal, *with a strong Federalist, Webster, and Adams bias. The* Journal *commenced publication on January 3, 1826, and continued through 1831* (National Intelligencer, *July 26, August 9, 1825*).

FROM CALEB CUSHING

Newbury Port Aug. 17th 1825

Sir:

After having witnessed the interest which Mr [Edward] Everett & you condescended to take in the establishment of the Boston Journal, it has been with much regret that I have felt constrained to withhold myself from it. In making this decision, I have acted not more in compliance with my own judgment, than by the advice of two or three particular friends, whom I consulted, & whose opinions I was bound by every consideration to respect.

The risk of sacrificing my health by engaging in an enterprise, the faithful prosecution of which would require constant & daily attention through the year, but especially in the heat of summer, when I am very liable to febrile complaints, weighed much with me in this matter. In addition thereto, my connexion with the press as proprietor, which I found the plan to require, was a very prominent difficulty. This, besides the pecuniary responsibility, which might in some possible contingences prove very embarrassing to me, would, I feared, either entirely separate me from my profession; or else would so largely divide my time & attention between objects of a different nature, as to prevent my obtaining any share of the public confidence in a professional capacity.

I will not occupy your valuable time in stating more in detail these or other things conducing to my unwilling determination, which I have communicated to you in obedience to your commands. With sentiments of the highest respect, I am   Your most obliged humble servant,

C. Cushing

ALS. DLC. Published in part in Claude M. Fuess, *The Life of Caleb Cushing* (2 vols.; New York, 1923), 1: 63–64.

FROM ROBERT WALSH, JR.

Philadelphia August 22d. 1825

Dear Sir

Some weeks ago Mr. [Joseph] Hopkinson transmitted to me a letter from you to him,[1] in which you mention the subject of a communication from him & Dr. [Nathaniel] Chapman to you.[2] He requested me to write to him my views in relation to it, but as I knew that he purposed to visit Boston at the beginning of September & as I entertained the same design myself, I thought the reference of the whole matter to that period, the best course. At present, I consider it as doubtful whether either of us will be able to travel so far next month; it is uncertain how long he may be detained at Washington by the trial of Commodore [Charles] Stewart, & the state of my health & the demands of my gazette upon my time prevent me from being the master of my weeks or days.

Such being the case, I deem it due to your kindness, & advisable on my own account, to address you at once & directly touching the "aforesaid" matter. If you continue to think well of the plan, I could wish your arrangements to be completed in the course of the next month, as mine can be so very soon after, & have been begun already. There are some points upon which I would not have you misunderstand me. Whatever money may be advanced will be returned absolutely, in case the work should not be accomplished; and, if it should be, as I mean & trust that it shall—then likewise the advance will be refunded as far as there may be profits. My design is to be enabled to undertake it without considerable difficulty. I reserve an entire independence in the expression of my views of characters & events; but it is certainly my aim to do justice particularly to the Federal administration of the government, which, few, now a days, have the courage to defend.

Quid *verum* atque decens, *curo* et rogo, et omnis in hoc sum.

There has been some exaggerated awkward mention of the subject in the newspapers, not, however, in consequence of any indiscretion on my part. No harm has been done. There is nothing in the matter, as it really stands, of which any one needs be ashamed, though re[serve ought] to be practised in order to prevent [widespread?] malicious reports.

Your Bunker's Hill Discourse has *passed* without a dissenting voice. It was a *bonne bouche* for me, who relish in the highest degree, the *simplex munditiis*—sound, clear sense garnished with taste and *stint*.

You will be pleased to accept my best wishes & the assurance of the sincere respect with which I am Dear Sir, Your Obliged & faithl. Servt.

Robert Walsh Jr.

ALS. DLC.   2. Not found.
    1. Not found.

TO EDWARD EVERETT

Sandwich Aug. 25 [1825]

My Dear Sir,

I very much regret that Messrs. [Sewall] Phelps and [Samuel] Whitcombe should think the success of their proposed paper requires any announcement that particular individuals are expected to aid it.[1] For my part, I cannot consent that my name be used, for such purpose. I think there are great objections against any proceeding, which should amount to, a sort of promise to contribute to a public political Journal. In the first place, such a thing is wholly *new*, with us; & would, therefore, be regarded as *extraordinary*. In the next place, I am sure I should be very likely to disappoint the expectations of the Publishers, & of the Public also, if the public should think fit to form any expectation on the subject. And, lastly, it appears to me that I should find it very inconvenient, in many respects, while I remain in a public situation, to have any professed connexion with a political Journal.

In communicating this to Messrs. Phelps and Whitcombe I wish you to say that my opinion of the necessity of a political Paper, on the principles stated in the Prospectus, remains unchanged. That I wish to see such a paper established; that if a suitable person undertakes the Editorial Department, I shall take great pleasure in promoting subscriptions by recommending the Paper to my friends; and although I cannot consent to any use of my name, they can judge whether, by the communication of public papers, documents &c., of which I have collected many, I should be able to assist in the discussion of interesting questions.

We learn with pleasure the happy augmentation of the number of your Household.[2] Mrs W. desires her best remembrances to Mrs Everett on the occasion.

We are thinking of returning to Boston. At least *I* must go up, in a very few days. Yours always truly   Danl. Webster

ALS. MHi.

1. Sewall Phelps was a printer residing at 101 Salem Street. Whitcomb (1792–1879), born in Hanover, Massachusetts, had for several years been writing articles on his western travels and in support of internal improvements. In 1836, he settled in Spring-field, Vermont. The newspaper under consideration was probably the *Massachusetts Journal*, of which David L. Child became editor.

2. The Everetts' second child, Charlotte Brooks, had been born on August 13.

TO JEREMIAH MASON

Washington Dec. 11. 1825.

Dear Sir

I do not think there is the least probability that any arrangement will be made to supply, temporarily, Judge [John Samuel] Sherburne's place. When Judges become permanently incapable, they ought to resign. There is as much reason, at least, for proceeding vs Judge S. now as there was for the course which *he* pursued against his predecessor.[1] But at any rate, no *substitute* will be provided, I presume. If a vacancy should occur, in that Office, I will give my aid to support the Gentleman you refer to;[2] *unless* a new state of things should, in the mean time, arise. For example, if new Circuit Judges should be created, it might become an object, in our Circuit, to propose a candidate under such circumstances, that it might not be expedient, also, at the same time, to press for the appointment of the person you refer to as District Judge.[3]

We have done little here yet, & nothing more than you have seen. There will be opposition to Mr. [Rufus] King's appointment, in the Senate, but it is thought it will not be successful. The opposition, however, is strong, in that body. A very good temper prevails thro. the mass of our House. There is nothing of a spirit of *exclusion*, except among some of our N. England worthies, & perhaps a few others. It was not a bad thing that the friends of Mr *Crawford*, generally, supported a *Federalist* for the Chair.[4] Some of my friends thought that I might have obtained some votes for that place, but I wholly declined the attempt. If practicable to place me there, it would not have been prudent.

Virginia, as you will see, is in a great rage with the Message. We think it possible your old friend Mr [William Branch] Giles may come back again to the Senate;—unless the lot should fall on Mr [John] Randolph.[5] Yrs truly   D. Webster

ALS. MHi. Published in Van Tyne, pp. 115–116.

1. Sherburne was United States district judge for New Hampshire. He had been most influential in bringing on the impeachment of Judge John Pickering in 1804, to whose post he succeeded and in which he served until his death in 1830.

2. Mason was recommending Nathaniel A. Haven, Jr., for the post. He had recommended Haven to Webster in a conversation as early as 1823. Mason, *Memoir and Correspondence*, p. 285.

3. At the time, Congress had under advisement a bill, largely the work of Webster and Story, to amend the judicial system of the United States (mDW 41312).

4. John W. Taylor of New York, an Adams supporter, had been elected Speaker of the House of Representatives. Taylor had been opposed by John W. Campbell of Ohio, the Jacksonian candidate, and by Louis McLane, Delaware Federalist, who received the votes of many Crawford partisans.

5. Randolph was elected to fill the Senate post vacated by James Barbour's resignation.

TO ALEXANDER BLISS

Washington Decr. 21. 1825

Dr Sir

I have recd yours of the 15.[1] I had no notion of the scarcity of Cash, in Boston, until I recd. a letter yesterday on that subject from Mr. [James W.] Paige.[2] I shall write you & him, tomorrow, forwarding what little funds I have, & saying what must be done for the rest. Yrs   D. Webster

You will probably also hear from Mr [Samuel] Jaudon,[3] to whom I have written today.

ALS. DLC.
    1. Not found.
    2. Not found.
    3. Jaudon (1796–1874) served as second assistant cashier and then cashier of the Bank of the United States at Philadelphia. In 1828, he accepted the post of cashier of the branch bank at New Orleans, where he served until 1832.

TO ALEXANDER BLISS

Washington Dec. 22. 1825

Dear Sir,

I enclose a check on the Bank for 500—a sum which I believe you will find there—& I have written to Mr. [Samuel] Frothingham[1] to give you his advice about matters & things. In about 4 or 5 days I think I shall be able to send you 1000 Dlls more—from here—& can forward more, if indis[p]ensably necessary. I had no expectation, however, that such a pinch would arise, & had thought all things were snugly provided for.

I shall write you again shortly—   D. Webster

P.S. I also enclose a check for $100—not exactly knowing what there may be. You will use one or both according to the fund.

ALS. DLC.
    1. Frothingham (1787–1869), cashier of the Boston branch of the Bank of the United States. Letter not found.

TO JOSEPH HOPKINSON

Dec. 28. 1825

Dear Sir,

I hear very little said here about your Collector.[1] For the last ten days, no one's name has been mentioned to me. Nevertheless, I presume the candidates are respectively making interest, in the expectation that there will be a vacancy. I hope you have written to Mr. Adams, *yourself*, *directly*, on the subject. Considering your long acquaintance, I think you would be well authorized to do that, & it would be the frankest course. Since I recd. yours I have not seen Mr. Adams, tho' I have endeav[ore]d to do so. If I had an opportunity, I should have mentioned the subject. I doubt whether the present incumbent intends to *resign* and therefore it may be some time before a vacancy occurs. You will I trust suggest freely to me, any thing which you wish me to do or say. Yours truly always

Danl. Webster

ALS. PHi.
    1. John Steele (1758–1827), a Revolutionary war veteran, had been appointed collector of customs for Philadelphia in 1808, reappointed by Monroe, and continued by Adams. During his last two years in that post he was under heavy fire for having

allowed a consignment of tea, imported by Edward Thompson, out of the customs house before duties were exacted (Samuel Flagg Bemis, *John Quincy Adams and the Union*, New York, 1956, p. 136; see also *U.S. v. 350 Chests of Tea*, 12 Wheaton 486 (1827), in which Webster appeared for the claimants). Although urged by Webster, Hopkinson, and others to remove him, Adams was still delaying action a year later when Steele resigned voluntarily on December 31, 1826.

FROM WILLIAM KING

Boston December 30th. 1825.

Dear Sir,

As my business will detain me in this City ten or twelve days I feel desirous of knowing more of the political arrangements and prospects at Washington than is presented through the papers. My opinions in relation to the late Presidential controversy I believe you were acquainted with; I did believe that we had not a person at that time with us, that we could offer that would be generally acceptable, but presumed after eight years this might be done. My opinion was therefore made up early in favour of Mr. Crawford presuming as I did that I understood something of his opinions, and that of his friends in whom he had most confidence. His indisposition contributed no doubt to his defeat, and has probably left him in a situation not again to be named.

My principal object in troubling you with this letter is merely to know something of your opinions in regard to men and measures to be pursued, in which there is nothing personal in regard to myself, as I shall not ask as I do not desire any employment from the Government. Your reply will be perfectly confidential if you desire it, which with persons who will have to perform the part you will have to for some time to come, may be considered the most prudent course.

Those persons in Maine, as well as the people of this place, who did not aid Mr. Adams Election, as far as I have been advised, take no part and probably will not either aid or oppose Mr. A's Ad[ministratio]n unless influenced by persons whose experience and general information will enable them in this entire absence of political feeling to decide as to the course most proper to be pursued.

I am desirous of knowing how you get on with the Massachusetts Claims. Respectfully Your Obedient Servant,   William King

ALS. DLC.

TO JOSEPH HOPKINSON

Jan. 8. 26

My Dear Sir

On the receipt of your two last letters,[1] I took immediate steps to make the President well informed of what your friends wished, in regard to the Collectorship. Since then, I have had no opportunity of seeing him personally, myself, but hope to do it this Evening, if the rain should abate & allow me to go out.[2] As yet nothing is done, in relation to the Office. I suppose, unless Mr. [John] Steele resigns, there will be necessarily an investigation into his conduct. I hear very little said here, about the matter. If any thing occurs, I will let you know, if it come to my knowledge, & will write you also when I shall have seen Mr. Adams. The Panama mission is still before the Senate. It will probably be acted on this week. There will be opposition, to the measure itself, but I presume it will be ineffectual.[3] Yrs truly   Danl. Webster

ALS. PHi.
   1. Not found.
   2. Expecting the Philadelphia collectorship post to be momentarily vacated, numerous factions had petitioned Adams regarding the appointment. The "Family party," made up of Samuel D. Ingham, George M. Dallas, William Findlay, Richard Bache, and Thomas Sergeant, all Calhounites, favored the appointment of ex-governor John A. Schulze. John Binns, on the other hand, probably representing the desires of the Adams-Federalist faction, pressed Adams to appoint Jonathan Roberts.

If Hopkinson supported either of the above, it was probably the latter. Adams, however, does not record in his manuscript diary any conversation with Webster on the appointment.
   3. Following his message to Congress in December 1825, Adams had nominated ministers to the Panama Congress. Over the opposition of southerners, the Senate eventually confirmed the nominations and the House voted appropriations, but neither of the American delegates reached the Isthmus of Panama before the Congress adjourned.

FROM TIMOTHY FULLER

Boston 13. Jan. 1826.

Dear Sir,

Your favor of the 4th of Dec. was recd.[1] It presents a *coup d'oeil* of the forces & views of parties at Washington, corresponding with an exactness almost prophetick with the subsequent development of their hearings. The support of Mr. [John W.] Campbell, I conjecture to have been *a ruse de guerre* intended to divert from Mr. [John W.] Taylor the support of Ohio & the west in general.[2] The public opposition to Mr. King's appointment by Mr [Robert Y.] Hayne & some demonstrations of feeling on the part of the redoubtable [James] Hamilton, are the only symptoms of hostility to the administration afforded us by the newspapers.[3] The election of Speaker therefore agt. such combined opposition must I think have dismayed the *malcontents* or to use a more gentle word, the *noncontents*.

A letter from an intelligent correspondent in Virginia informs me that

Mr. [John] Randolph was supported for the Senate as *a friend to Mr. Adams' administration* in opposition to [William B.] Giles, the friend to *no* administration! Had Mr. [Henry St. George] Tucker who is in deed & in truth a friend to the administration, been adhered to, Giles would have been elected. Now in my opinion tho' Randolph is a malignant enemy of the President & as harmless as malignant, yet Giles would have been nearly as impotent as he & from the same cause—the invectives of the latter & the sarcasms of the former, tho' they may attract attention & gratify many a greedy devourer of calumny & hatred, would have failed, & *will* fail, to attract the publick confidence, & consequently to attract coadjutors in the Senate. In fact *such* opponents with such temper & feeling, manifested in debate, are always desirable—They are the beacons, which warn navigators from approaching them & the shoals & breakers which beset them on every side. In the same point of light I consider Gov. Troup, & think Mr. Adams ought to proclaim a fast or at least to fast & pray himself for his recovery. The fervor of his, (Troup's) *patriotism*, which is consuming him, has absorbed or consumed also the present humors in that quarter of the body politick which otherwise might have ended in a general gangrene. But I must not venture to talk in metaphor, as I may lose the grain of wheat in the bushel of chaff. A sheet of letter paper affords room only for a few simple propositions, unencumbered with the tinsel of verbiage.

Your remarks in support of the Judiciary bill have attracted much attention.[4] I assent readily to your reasoning in favor of keeping the Judges *sufficiently* employed to facilitate investigation & to keep their faculties on the alert; & as to exonerating them from circuit duty your arguments are quite satisfactory. Your bill has the merit too of providing for the numerous & extended population of the new states, without *surcharging* the system in such a manner as to excite jealousy.

It strengthens the Judiciary where it most wants strength—in the S. Court. And in short I could mention several points in which it has peculiar merits, but must omit further remarks for want of paper.

Our Legislature are fulfilling their *high destinies* without threatening to "shoot madly from their spheres." The example of S. Carolina & Kentucky has no influence on the sober sons of N England.[5] Yet I assure you we have grave subjects to determine—the regulation of alewives & the change of a score of cognomens are lost in obscurity when compared with the new bridges, new counties, new manufacturing principles, & new—almost every thing, which is "under consideration."

Excuse my long delay, which shall not be my fault in future, & present my best respects to Mrs. Webster, who I hope is in good health. I am sincerely & respectfully Yrs,   Timothy Fuller

ALS. NhD.
1. Not found.
2. Campbell of Ohio and Taylor of New York had been the two chief contenders for the speakership of the House. On the second ballot, Taylor, the candidate of the Adams faction, was elected. *Register of Debates*, 19th Cong., 1st sess., 1825–26, 2: 795.
3. Announced in April, King's appointment as minister to England had been confirmed on December 20,

1825, over the opposition of men like Hayne and Hamilton of South Carolina.
4. In late December 1825 and January 1826 Webster had spoken on several occasions in support of his judiciary bill.
5. The legislatures of South Carolina and Kentucky had passed resolutions critical of the President's program as set forth in his first annual message.

Charles Jared Ingersoll had been appointed United States district attorney in Philadelphia by President Madison in 1815. In the election of 1824, Ingersoll backed Crawford, but Adams had nonetheless reappointed him to the district attorneyship, even though his performance in that post had been under attack since 1822. Once the nomination was made to the Senate, Samuel D. Ingham, leader of the Calhoun forces in Pennsylvania, introduced a resolution in the House of Representatives calling for an inquiry as to "whether any, and, if any, what, provision by law is necessary to prevent attorneys of the United States from rendering services to defendants, or their representatives, in suits brought by such attorneys in behalf of the United States; and, also, from receiving compensation therefor." Recognizing that Ingham's resolution was directed at Ingersoll, Webster proposed to the House a substitute which would authorize the Judiciary Committee to investigate whether any such cases as described by Ingham's resolution had occurred. Webster's amendment was immediately adopted, and as chairman of the Judiciary Committee, he headed the investigation into the allegation of misconduct, inviting Ingham to inform him of the charges against Ingersoll. Ingham charged that Ingersoll, in his prosecution against the estate of Robert Waln to collect debts due to the United States in 1819, had, on appeal from the assignees of the estate, consulted with the secretary of the treasury and had received from that official a stay of execution. For his services in their behalf, the assignees had agreed to pay Ingersoll $250 plus expenses, which totaled $40. Once the committee received the notice of the charges, Webster sent Ingersoll the letter below inviting him to defend himself before the committee.

In his defense Ingersoll did not deny the allegations, but he did assert that his appeal on behalf of the assignees to his superiors was in the best interest of the United States—that by granting a stay until property values rose, the United States was more likely to realize a full payment of

Waln's indebtedness to the nation. Nor did Ingersoll deny having re-
ceived compensation from the assignees. The committee, after a rather
lengthy investigation, reported the facts of the case, stating that "Mr.
Ingersoll does not deny the above facts, and vindicates his conduct as
being neither inconsistent with his duty to the Government, or injurious
to its interest, but in accordance with a fair and admitted exercise of
professional right." On the question of whether Ingersoll's action had been
injurious to the interest of the United States, however, the committee
took no stand. As Webster explained to Clay a year later, "we had great
difficulty, as you know, last year, to prevent the District Atty from being
disgraced. He must have gone, & would have gone, but for the President's
kindness towards him" (see DW to Henry Clay, March 25, 1827, below).
Adams retained Ingersoll in the post, but Jackson removed him in 1829.
Whether there was any element of reciprocation in charges of miscon-
duct brought by Ingersoll against Webster in 1846 cannot now be de-
termined.

TO [CHARLES JARED INGERSOLL]

[January 24, 1826]

In behalf of the J[udiciary] C[ommittee] I have to inform you that the
attention of the Com[mitt]ee has been drawn, under a Resolution of the
House of the [18th] inst, to a transaction in which you bore a part, in the
years 1819, & 1820, respecting some arrangement entered into between
the U. States, or those legally representing them, and Mr Robt. Waln or
his assignees. The Com[mitt]ee take the earliest opportunity to give you
information, & will receive any communication which you may see fit
to make. The substance of the suggestion which has been made to <us>
[the] Com[mitt]ee, as far as <we> they at prese[nt] comprehend it, is,
that in a legal proceeding, under your care, as District Attorney, in which
U. S. was party, you rendered professional services to parties in an opposite interest, & for which you recd. compensation from such parties.

AL draft. DNA, RG 233.

It is impossible to say with any certainty just when the "presidential fe-
ver" began to heighten Webster's temperature. As early as 1824 he was
behaving like a future candidate, and by 1826 he seems to have been so
regarded by friends and foes alike. His aspirations and the expectations
of his supporters were by no means unwarranted if we may accept the
estimate of John Davis, freshman congressman from Worcester, Massa-
chusetts, and brother-in-law of George Bancroft, to whom the following
letter was written.

JOHN DAVIS TO GEORGE BANCROFT

Washington Jany 29th 1826

My Dr. George

Your kind letter has reached me and I hasten to acknowledge it altho. I have little of interest to say. The public papers inform you of all our doings and I can assure you that the body called Congress looses none of its dignity and importance and does not sink any in public estimation by being seen through that medium. Men ordinarily to appear great must be seen at a distance for they are seen with less distinctness, and only the more commanding traits of character reach us. We do not see their foibles, their weaknesses, their blunders and the thousand other weeds which grow up & shade them, and are rendered visible as you come near to them. When you come within the halls of legislation you see men as they are and you are most surprised to find them differing so little from the common & ordinary race. The greater proportion of them certainly possess few qualifications for the places they hold for they have neither knowledge or talents and on most subjects which are brought before them are as much in doubt and uncertainty as a navigator would be at sea without Chart or compass. To these remarks however there are many honourable exceptions & no one forms a more obvious proof of it than our Mr. Webster. He stands in the house upon disadvantageous ground because he was a leading federalist during the war and incurred a hatred which cannot be effaced from the minds of his adversaries. They are the more willing to remember him too because of his greatness, considering this as the only means by which they can prevent his supplanting them. Yet with all this prejudice and envy to encounter he holds a place head and shoulders at least above all others. No man is listened to in debate with such attention. No man is so certain to convince his hearers and no man is so sure to carry the house with him. He however conducts with great prudence in debate, puts out his strength only occasionally but when it is exerted it is almost as destructive to his adversaries as that of Sampson. I have no hesitation in declaring him to be by far the greatest man that I have seen here & I can assure you I am not extravagant when I say the boasted statesmen of the South are mere pigmies to him—those who dislike him dare not deny this. He makes no long set Speeches for he has no occasion for it. He never declaims nor does he appear to possess the art, but when he seizes a subject he appears to understand it most thoroughly so that nothing stated is new to him and treats it in a manner which none can fail to understand. He seems not to seek embellishment but expresses himself with great strength and power in the most simple unadorned language. He would I think in any age and in any country be denominated a great man.

There are many men most highly respectable for their talents and acquirements and who are even called great but their claim to greatness is of a more doubtful character. They have industry & mind and call their powers into action with great effect but beside of Mr W. they are literally as the murmuring of the breeze compared with the dissoluting fury of the hurricane. This I am aware may seem like hyperbole, but I have no particular partiality for Mr W. as a man, his manners are not conciliating, he is both proud and haughty and doubtless feels his intellectual superiority but he is so distinguished above all others that I cannot but feel gratified that our State has at the head of its representation a man of such remarkable powers. To show you that I am not far from the truth I heard a democrat of the old school who has a most thoroughgoing hatred for Mr. W. say a few days since that he was the greatest man in the nation and it was in vain to deny it. Now I have run over almost all my letter to tell you just what you knew before though when I commenced I did not intend to occupy these lines with Mr W. I have become considerably acquainted with Mr. Clay since I have been in this City and can assure you I am pleased with him as a man apparently open frank and undisguised, free and easy in his conversation and always sensible. You feel yourself at home at once with him and discuss topics with as much freedom as if he were an old acquaintance. The president altho he labors to be agreeable seems not quite so accessible and is rather unentertaining upon the common topics of conversation. I am not certain that he does not feel it necessary to be upon his guard generally upon all topics of public interest and as to minor affairs he seems in the language of the country to have no small change. He is not interesting in his deportment but stiff and I think I may say without doing him any injustice awkward. I have attended the drawing rooms twice and dined with him once. Mrs. A seems a genteel accomplished woman. I could go on describing the manners and accomplishments of our Governours and public agents of one kind and another but it would be an unprofitable labor as most of them appear to more advantage by their titles and stations than by any other accomplishments they possess.

I wish you could see some of the books lately imported for the library of Congress—they are the most superb editions I ever saw. I have wrote over much more paper than I intended but have gone on as I usually do when I write letters at a dog trot. Whoever has me for a correspondent must neither expect labor[ious] method or good penmanship in my letters for I ordinarily commence without knowing any thing what I am to say and consequently what comes first falls from the pen to the paper. I never was made for a letter writer and I am certain I cannot make myself one. At any rate I shall not try. I can talk to Eliza about our home affairs and she thinks it is all very good and so it is in its place but it is only entertaining to us who are concerned. I do not expect to amuse you so when you get tired of your proposal you must cease to write. I acknowledge the receipt of Mrs Ghirardi's letter and should have answered it but I wrote her only a day or two before. She may depend on my feeble aid in her undertaking and I fear it will be feeble for I cannot promise much especially from this quarter. Members of Congress are so pressed and harrassed with applications for patronage from all quarters that it is difficult to persuade them to read a communication. I cannot tell what a multitude of cards I receive from tailors, grocers, merchants, teachers of schools, dancing masters and in short every one who wants public aid seeks it in this way. I mention this only to show that there is not much hope of making an impression but as far as I am able individually to do any thing you can assure her no labor of mine shall be wanting for nothing would give me greater pleasure than her success.

Write me on receipt of this. Sincerely yours   J Davis

I perhaps ought to say a word as to the school as you desire it. I have no means of forming an opinion as to the chances of success and it would seem wholly unimportant if I had for the measure appears to be resolved on and a prospectus issued to the public. I have however no hesitation in saying I should not buy real estate at present—the hazard of suffering by loosing a good bargain is less than the hazard of success and real estate is miserably bad property to have on hand—it will not do to go upon the principle that you may not loose much. It is a down right gambling principle and most unsafe to act upon. I have seen more people made poor by it than in any other way. I am not to be sure possessed of all the reasons which might induce to the steps you mention but I mean to be understood that nothing short of necessity should compel me to it.

J. Davis

ALS. NIC.

FROM HENRY CLAY

[c. Jan. 31, 1826]

(Private and Confidential)
My dear Sir

The lapse of time now renders the adoption of Mr. [James] Hamiltons resolution about Panama necessary.[1] The Senate wants a spur. Respect for it has heretofore induced the President to hold up his message to the house until the Senate acted. The same consideration continues to operate; but that ought not to prevent the House moving in the matter, if it think proper to do so. *We* really desire that you should, and, if you see no objection to the course, suppose you take up Mr. H.s resolution and pass it for him to day? I made this suggestion to [Robert P.] Letcher, [Henry R.] Storrs & one or two others who were at my house last night. I am Yours faithfy   H. Clay

ALS. DLC. Published in Van Tyne, p. 118, under date of [April 1826]; and in Hopkins and Hargreaves, *Papers of Henry Clay*, 5: 81–82, under date of [c. February 2, 1826). Webster's action to spur the passage of Hamilton's amendment in the House seems to have begun as early as January 31, 1826, and probably came in response to Clay's undated note.

1. On December 16, 1825, Hamilton introduced a resolution requesting the President to forward to the House all documents and correspondence relating to the invitation to America to send representatives to the Panama Congress (*Register of Debates*, 19th Cong., 1st sess., 1825–26, 2: 817). Webster's amendment of Hamilton's resolution, asking for general information regarding the expected participation of American delegates in the congress, passed the House on February 2 (*ibid.*, pp. 1253–1254). Letcher and Storrs supported the Webster amendment.

TO JARED SPARKS

H of R. Feb. 4. 1826.

Dear Sir,

It will give me true pleasure to aid you, in your intended collection of Genl. George Washington works,[1] in any, & all, ways in my power. Judge [Joseph] Story has not yet arrived, but we expect him this eve'. I will have an early conversation with him on the subject. I think your proposed work one of great importance, & which you could so execute as to do yourself great credit. Yrs very truly   Danl. Webster

ALS. MH. Published in Van Tyne, p. 692.

1. Sparks was beginning the collection of documents for his *Life and Writings of George Washington*.

FROM NICHOLAS BIDDLE

Bank of the U. States
Feby 4. 1826

My dear Sir,

The delay in deciding on the Panama Mission induces me to request at the instance of Mr [John] Sergeant[1] that you will at once engage Mr [William] Wirt to act with you in the case of the Bank against Dandridge.[2] Mr Sergeant will forward to you the record, I hope by this mail.

You will oblige me also by looking at the Docket of the Court, and giving me a memorandum of any causes in which the Bank is concerned, stating the degree of forwardness in which they are & the names of Counsel who are engaged to attend to them, as it is possible that some cases may hence come up with regard to which some provision is necessary. With great respect & regard Yrs   N. Biddle Prest.

ALS. DLC.
    1. John Sergeant of Pennsylvania had been nominated by Adams as one of the ministers to the Panama Congress.
    2. In *Bank of the United States* v.

Dandridge, 12 Wheaton 64 (1827), Webster and Wirt, the attorney general of the United States, appeared for the plaintiff; and Littleton Waller Tazewell, for the defendant.

FROM ISAAC PARKER

Feby 12th [1826] Boston

My Dear Sir
    I thank you for your attention to my letter, and shall wait patiently till you are able to communicate finally, without wishing you to perplex yourself about such an affair.[1]

Your exposé about the Panama affair is very pleasant,[2] and I shall be very happy occasionally to convey your notions & observations of things fit to be communicated, to the club.

I have an idea that you have become, not so much by your own will, as by a "fortuitous concurrence of circumstances" the Premier in the House of Commons—The chairman of foreign relations is in opposition —of Ways & Means has no predilection for the President, though too upright to be a mere opposition man.[3] The west seems to have come in, but their great leader is in the bureau d'etat. Others fall behind & get condensed into a mass. You are left in the front and according to appearances will have a powerful support from the columns which though not carrying the standard of Administration like that side better than the opposition. It seems to me that the Judiciary bill has served to conciliate the men of the west.

Our affairs are small compared to yours. Our Court is still in session, being to-morrow the 75th day. The determination is to go to the last action of the docket, where we shall arrive by the last of the week.

You see the controversy between the Governor & the Agent for the claim.[4] There is indiscretion somewhere, perhaps on both sides—A steady helm is perhaps wanted in both ships. The impeachment ended properly; it was concocted in vile conspiracy: and the poor magistrate was guilty of nothing but want of head.[5]

Among the multitude of speeches on the Judiciary bill, there were some which will do no honour to us across the water—some full of fustian & froth[—]others of gross exaggerations—a very few very excellent —the best in opposition I think was the first speech of Mr [Alfred H.]

Powell. How much the speakers are indebted to the newspapers I know not.

My best wishes to Mrs W. Yours sincerely   Isaac Parker

ALS. DLC.

1. On January 21, 1826, Parker had requested Webster to assist his son, Charles, in getting an appointment to some office in Washington in which he might support himself (mDW 5232).

2. On several occasions between January 31 and February 3, Webster had addressed himself to the question of the Panama mission (*Register of Debates*, 19th Cong., 1st sess., 1825–26, 2: 1210, 1212–1213, 1215–1216, 1241, 1242, 1253, 1271, 1279–1282, 1304).

3. John Forsyth was chairman of the Committee on Foreign Affairs; Louis McLane, of Ways and Means.

4. George Sullivan was the Washington agent for the state of Massachusetts whose claims for reimbursement of expenses incurred in the War of 1812 were pending before Congress. Because he disagreed with Governor Levi Lincoln over the wisdom of pursuing certain of the claims, Sullivan had resigned in mid-January.

5. The Massachusetts House of Representatives had charged that Samuel Blagge, a justice of the peace, had "at divers times and in sundry circumstances . . . given certificates of Protection to individuals as Citizens of the United States, and that they personally appeared before him, and made oath to their citizenship, place of nativity, age, &c. when in truth and fact said individuals never did so appear before him, and on oath make said declaration." Blagge was acquitted of all charges on February 6 (*Columbian Centinel*, January 14, February 22, 1826).

FROM LEWIS TAPPAN

Boston, 14 Feb. 1826.

Dear Sir,

Having been absent on a journey I take the first opportunity to acknowledge receipt of your letter of 30 Jany.[1] I feel somewhat awkward offering my advice in a matter affecting so directly my own convenience & interest. Dr [Chandler?] Robbins,[2] who is thoroughly versed in these matters, thinks that at a public and free sale land will bring more than in any other mode. I proposed therefore giving a fortnight's notice, and selling the lots by auction, absolutely. Money is not plenty. The Banks discount cautiously. Private negotiations are made, of respectable paper, at the rate of 9 per ct ann[u]m. On pledges of Stocks money can be had at 6 per ct. The two lots stand you in 235, I think, per foot. To this should be added a year's interest. I fear the lots would not bring now more than 200 a foot. Still, Robbins refuses to take, for the lot on the corner of Federal & High Streets, which I sold at 187 per foot, less than 250 pr foot.

I have no objection to postpone the sale until the middle of March, but it should be advertised by the first. It will be more agreeable to me to have you appoint some one to act on your behalf than to be sole judge of the best time & terms of selling. I request therefore that you will request some friend here to confer with me, with joint authority to act on the premises according to our best judgement.[3] I am respectfully yours

Lewis Tappan

ALS. DLC.
1. Not found.
2. Robbins (d. 1836; Bowdoin 1815, Harvard 1818), Boston physician.
3. Webster was probably interested in buying some property adjacent to that purchased from Tappan in 1825. See above, Deed to Land: Transfer from Lewis Tappan to Daniel Webster, [April 18, 1825].

According to the charter of the Second Bank of the United States, the president and cashier were required to sign all circulating bank notes. From the beginning, the provision imposed severe hardships on the bank's chief officers. Numerous appeals to Congress for an alteration in that requirement had brought no action; and by 1826, the time Biddle requested Webster's attention to the problem in the letter below, bank notes, particularly of small denominations, were exceedingly scarce. As Biddle explained, it was an impossibility for the bank's chief officers at the parent bank in Philadelphia to sign all the notes; he wanted congressional assent for the appointment of additional signers. Again, in 1826, however, Congress took no action, with the result that in the following year, 1827, the bank began to issue branch drafts, signed by the presidents and cashiers of the branches. In authorizing the issuance of branch drafts, Biddle based his action on the opinions of Webster, by that date a director of the bank as well as one of its lawyers; Horace Binney, also both director and counsel; and William Wirt, attorney general of the United States, that such drafts were not in violation of the bank's charter (Ralph Catterall, The Second Bank of the United States, Chicago, 1903, pp. 114–119). Webster's response to Biddle appears in the letter of March 1, 1826, below.

FROM NICHOLAS BIDDLE

Philadelphia Feby 16. 1826.

My dear Sir,

The increased demand through every part of the union for notes of the Bank of the U. States renders it essential to give every possible facility for the multiplication of them. While the charter appears to require that the notes should be signed by the President & Cashier, two officers whose duties in the general administration of the Bank necessarily occupy so large a portion of their time, it is physically impossible to supply the wants of the Country. I am desirous therefore of consulting you as to the propriety of procuring an alteration of the charter from Congress, so as to enable the Bank to issue notes signed by other officers than those mentioned. I have said that the Charter *appears* to require the signature of the two chief Officers, because I have never been entirely satisfied, that the phraseology of the 12th Article of the 11th Section, and of the 14th Section of the Charter are of so exclusive a nature as to prevent the issue of notes otherwise signed. Nevertheless I would not lightly disturb even a reasonable construction & should prefer that the change should be made by an Act of Congress. As to the general propriety of the change it is useless to say any thing. It was obviously an inadvertence to impose on the two Chief Officers of the Bank a duty purely mechanical, & the satisfactory execution of which is now utterly impossible. To the community the names of those officers give no security beyond the names of any two other officers of the Bank, and in truth, such is the perfection of the art of falsification at present, that the mere signatures are by no means so valuable safeguards as the mechanical execution of the engraving. During the issue of the Treasury notes by the United States they were obliged to employ a multitude of signers. The Bank of England has now ten officers occupied in that way. You may form some idea of the progress of circulation from the facts, that in January 1823 I found it at $4,361,000 & that it is now $9,579,000 and it would be more considerable, but for the impossibility of multiplying the signatures for the small notes. I have no doubt that we could at once give to the Southern & Western sections of the country two or three millions of sound & useful circulating medium if we could sign that amount of 5 & 10 dollars. But to make two millions of five dollar notes, it would be necessary to sign my name 400,000 times, which, to a person whose time is & must be absorbed during the day by the duties of his station, is wholly impracticable. The application for this purpose was made to Congress some years ago, but it was accompanied by a request that Congress would alter the Charter so as to prevent the universal receivability of the notes. This I am satisfied from experience, as I was at the time from theory, is not desirable, & all 'that the Bank now wants is, that it may carry into execution a purpose useful alike to itself & to the community, by assisting in the diffusion of a wholesome currency. I wish therefore to consult you as to the best mode of presenting that subject to Congress. I have been for three years past so anxious to keep the Bank out of view in the political world & to bring it down to its true business character as a Counting House, that I have been very reluctant to apply to Congress for any thing. It occurs to me therefore that the matter might probably be brought up by taking from the files of the House the Memorial of the

Bank, & the proceedings of the Stockholders with the report of a Committee of the House of which Mr [Joseph] Hemphill was Chairman, made in the Session of 1823.[1] There was then a report favorable to the Memorialists, but it was never acted upon. If that report could now be made the basis of an act, confined merely to the alteration as to the signing of the notes I should much prefer it to a new & original memorial. The Bank has been the object of so much disputation & odium, that it is now desirable that its proceedings should be as little the cause of excitement as possible. I believe it to stand better with Congress than it did some time ago, but the political odour of sanctity is very evanescent & if our purpose can be obtained without bringing on two weeks debate upon the constitutionality of the Bank, the usurpations of the Supreme Court, & omni scibile & quibusdem aliis, it would be a great satisfaction. It was my purpose in case I could go to Washington to ask the concurrence of half a dozen gentlemen of the House to get the Bill through if possible by general consent as a measure useful in the collection of the revenue. But I cannot at present leave the Bank, & must therefore give you the trouble of advising me as to the course which should be adopted. Mr [Horace] Binney who is a member of our Board has sketched the enclosed short bill as being adapted to the purpose & it is submitted to your consideration. The alternative would be, to authorize the signing by any officers named in the Bye Laws, though I think the designation of the officers in the Bill itself would be more acceptable to Congress & as useful to the Bank. I shall be happy to hear from you on this subject as soon as you have leisure & in the mean time remain with great respect & regard,
Yrs   N Biddle

LC. DLC. Excerpt printed in Reginald C. McGrane, *Correspondence of Nicholas Biddle . . .* (Boston, 1919), pp. 38–39.
    1. Hemphill was chairman of a select committee handling memorials from South Carolina banks, insurance companies, and the Bank of the United States.

TO ALEXANDER BLISS

Washington Feb. 18. '26

My Dear Sir

An acceptance of mine, due Feb. 27th, or thereabouts, for 1,000—must be provided for. I have written to Mr. [James William] Paige, on the subject, & when it appears you must get his aid, to take it up. Several persons have written me to be concerned in their causes, whom I have referred to you, telling them that *I am retained when I am* RETAINED. I do not learn whether any of them have deposited the needful.

I should be glad to hear from you, to know how the Court gets on;

what the news is, & so forth. For the ensuing month, I shall be a good deal busy with the Court. Mr. [Robert F.] Stocktons case[1] is now on trial. Yrs   D Webster

ALS. DLC.
1. *The Marianna Flora*, 11 Wheaton 1 (1826). Webster and Blake appeared for the respondents in the case before the Supreme Court.

FROM DANIEL FLETCHER WEBSTER

Boston Feby 18th 1826

My Dear Father

Julia, received a very kind letter from you, to day, and Mother, a very long one, from Mr. W.[1] We have had very pleasant weather here for the last three days, and to day "il fait à la printemps."

I held my place near the head of my class, till the day before yesterday, when by an unlucky mistake, I got down to the foot. Mr Wells[2] says I get my Greek lessons better than any other boy in the class. I shall go to Mr Emerson's[3] tomorrow evening as usual; I hope. I shall have learnt a good deal of French when you come home. I have got FE for my Exercise which is the highest of all marks. Uncle [James William Paige] has been down to Taunton and Troy to see the "Kellico" factory.

Hannah[4] has not got home from Portsmouth as yet but we hope she will soon.

We are all quit[e] well and send much love Julia in particular. Your very affectionate son   Daniel F. Webster.

ALS. NhHi.
1. Neither letter found.
2. Not identified.
3. Daniel Fletcher may have been referring to Daniel Barrell Emerson, Frederick Emerson, or Benjamin D. Emerson, all prominent educators in Boston. Most likely he was studying under Daniel B., but without additional corroborative evidence it is impossible to be certain.
4. One of the Webster's household servants.

FROM JOHN EVELYN DENISON

London, February 23, 1826.

My dear Sir:

In writing to you at this moment, I might with justice say, as one of our friends of Rome said of old: *"Cum tot sustineas, et tanta negotia*—I should err against the public weal, if I should occupy your time with too long a discourse." But, in truth, I am too much engaged just now myself to commit this fault. What prompts me to write at this moment is, that I was fortunate enough to hear yesterday from Mr. Rufus King that Captain [Charles] Morris was now in London. With Mr. King's assistance I found him out this morning; and as he tells me he is about to return to Washington, where he expects to meet you, I cannot let him pass between us without a few lines of friendly remembrance.

I received ten days ago the *National Intelligencer* containing your speech on the introduction of your proposition for the alteration of the judiciary, and about that time the first volume of the "Debates of Congress." I am much obliged to you for these two proofs of your kind remembrance. It does not fall within the compass of a hurried letter to enter upon the vast subject of your Supreme Court, the corner-stone of your whole edifice. I congratulate America that so solemn and weighty a subject has fallen into such hands as yours. Your speech commands my admiration, as your view of the question carries with it my concurrence. I am afraid you have fixed the last rivet in the chains of our friend the Judge [Story]. I shall be extremely sorry, indeed, to find that the hope of seeing him amongst his brethren here is utterly gone. Westminster Hall is swept and garnished for his reception, and there are many persons here who would be very happy to make the Judge's acquaintance, and in whose society mutual pleasure would be given and received.

I hope you received safely your package of books, and one or two letters that I wrote to you last summer, and that the Judge received a book I sent to him and a letter written early in September, which I believe is the latest communication I can profess to have made.

You will have been contemplating, not without astonishment, the extraordinary depression under which our affairs have been, and are laboring. Much of what has occurred was clearly foreseen, and plainly predicted by Mr. [William] Huskisson and some others; the extent to which it has gone (and it has not yet reached its ultimate point) was hardly within the power of human calculation. It happens, very unfortunately for the interests of truth and sound policy, that these embarrassments, concurring in point of time with the alteration in our commercial laws, are by a large and powerful body in this country attributed mainly (though very falsely) to their enactment.

February 28.—I wrote so far on the morning of the 23d—that afternoon I took Captain [Charles] Morris with me to the House of Commons, where, though no very particular business was expected, fortunately a debate of great interest occurred. I shall leave Captain Morris to describe it to you. The first debate arose on a petition from the city, that a select committee might be appointed to inquire into the causes of the present commercial distress, and to devise, if possible, some remedy for it. This was the ostensible object; the real one was to induce the government to issue exchequer bills as a temporary relief. On this subject, Captain Morris heard Mr. [George] Canning and Mr. [Frederick John] Robinson speak shortly; he heard one disagreeable, foolish man coughed down; he heard a Scotchman, and some country gentlemen, and an alderman or two deliver themselves, each in his particular line.

Then followed the question of retracing our steps on the silk laws. The subject itself was one of sufficient importance, and one of great immediate interest, from the pressing distress to which all branches of that trade are exposed through their own miscalculations. But much more was meant than met the eye, and through the sides of silk a deadly blow was aimed at the whole system of our new commercial regulations, and at Mr. Huskisson's character and fame. He rose under many disadvantages, at the close of a long debate, with a large party in the House hostile to his views, and with many of his friends faltering in their allegiance. He entered into a general review of the commercial policy of this country, past and present, and made the most masterly statement on the subject of trade that ever was exhibited before Parliament. By this he has accumulated a new load of reputation to his former great character. He has proved himself true, under the best of all proofs, a pressure of difficulties, and has raised himself to the second place, second only to Mr. Canning, in the House, and in the country. Captain Morris will tell you how his speech was received. If he thinks we were very tumultuous, we were so beyond our ordinary expression. I never recollect a speech with such loud and unanimous cheering since I have been in Parliament. Certainly upon none have greater consequences depended. If he had failed in his defence—for upon his trial he stood before a House of Commons which had already sanctioned his measures—I verily believe we might have been driven back step by step to the old fastnesses of selfish prohibition. His speech turned the tide, raised his character higher than it has ever yet stood, and has confirmed his policy even beyond the power of prejudice to overthrow it. I hope this speech will be published. I will take care you have it immediately.

I have been greatly delighted by receiving a very long and kind letter from Judge Story this afternoon. He gives me an account of your trip to Niagara, through the State of New York. I think the Trenton falls exceed any scenery of the same dimensions that I am acquainted with, in exquisite finished beauty, and the Falls of Niagara in their way surpass every thing in splendor and awful grandeur. He tells me, too, something of your political existence, of which I had partially informed myself through your papers, and from some private hands. I may well congratulate you on its general features. It is not right to meddle with the affairs of individuals, but I think some politicians have played safer games than a certain young—South Carolinian, is he not?—late of the War Department, is now playing at Washington.[1] I must trust to you and the Judge to keep me in a certain degree on a pace with the changes and the progress of your striding country. If I remain stationary for a few years, you will be out of my sight, and it will be then too late to resume the chase. It seems not improbable that affairs may keep you at home for the present, and that you cannot be spared for your visit here. If so, I shall only look upon it as a pleasure delayed, and not taken away. For I feel sure that you will some day come and afford me the very sincere pleasure of conducting you around this little sea-girt land.

Pray, say for me every thing most kind to the Judge, and give him my best thanks for his long and interesting letter. I wish we had him here to let us into the true secret of safe banking; we have all been racking our brains, and writing pamphlets, and making speeches on this subject, which practically we have certainly not administered well. We hope to go on sounder principles, and pursue them with a steadier course. I shall not answer the Judge's letter immediately, because you will give him my present thanks, and a short interval perhaps may produce something of greater interest. The commission which has been examining into the practice of our Court of Chancery has closed its inquiry, and framed its report. This will be published shortly, and shall immediately be sent for your and the Judge's examination. We shall do nothing this year about the Catholic question, or the Corn Laws. Both will be submitted to the new Parliament next year; the Corn Laws will probably be taken up by the government, the other has, I fear, made little progress in public opinion. I dare make no prophecy as to when it may pass, and receive the triple sanction of Parliament. The condition of Ireland in the mean time is decidedly improving, and has already made most essential advances, but it is still such as no Englishman can contemplate without regret and shame, and no Irishman without still more bitter feelings.

I am sorry to hear from the Judge's letter that a package of books I sent you, with one included to him, has never reached you. I shall send into the city immediately to make inquiries on the subject. I shall look out for a few pamphlets and books to send you by Captain Morris, who has been good enough to undertake to deliver them to you.

I beg you will make my respects to the President, and assure all those, who may be good enough to have kept me in mind, of the grateful remembrance I entertain of their individual civilities, and of my general reception in the United States. You will know several to whom I would be specially remembered.

I have seen Lord Stowell once or twice lately; he was much flattered by the assurances I felt authorized to give him of the great reputation he enjoys amongst you; he desired his best compliments to the Judge. The chancellor has lately rallied, which, if it was not treason to say so, I am almost sorry for.—Believe me, My dear Sir, Your sincere friend,

J. E. Denison

Stanley is yet in the country with his wife, Wortley with his wife in town. He moved the address in a good and sensible speech this year. Labouchere is in town, and very well. I met Mr. Addington, too, the other day here, very well.

I hear from the office through which the package to you was sent, that it was shipped, and the ship arrived safe at New York, probably in August last. It was sent to the care of Le Roy, Bayard & Co., and is now most likely lying in the custom-house, or some warehouse.

Text from Curtis, 1: 267–270. Original not found.

1. John C. Calhoun, who, although Vice President, had joined the opposition to the Adams administration.

TO NICHOLAS BIDDLE

Washington Mar. 1. '26

Private

My Dear Sir,

My engagements in the Courts, and elsewhere, have been such as to prevent an earlier answer to your letter of the 16. Feb. on the subject of a proposed alteration in the Charter of the Bank, as to the officers who sign Bills & Notes.[1]

The reasonableness of what you wish, is too plain to be doubted, & I think the public, as well as the Bank, are interested in accomplishing the object. It is, indeed, impossible to be *sure*, before hand, that the subject might not bring on *debate*; as almost every subject does, or may. Still, the matter is of so much importance, I think it advisable to bring it forward. Your suggestion, as to the mode of proceeding, meets my approbation. Let the old Memorial be called up, & referred to a Com-[mitt]ee. This should be done by Mr. [Joseph] Hemphill, as the City member. It may be referred, either to the Ways & Means, or Judiciary. Either of these Com[mitt]ees will doubtless report a Bill.[2] It may, possibly, be thought expedient *to originate the measure in the Senate*; although I think, at present, it may as well begin with us.

Probably you will think it most prudent to write to Mr. Hemphill, on the subject, des[ir]ing his attention to it, & saying that you have, or shall, ask *my* cooperation with him. Let *him* bring forward the matter. I, in the mean time, will consult with some other members. I feel confident the thing *can be done*; & altho. we may be disappointed, I think it proper the attempt should be made, & shall feel disposed to give it an earnest support. We can but relinquish it, at last, if we should find it likely to bring on a war of words of great duration. Yours, very truly,

Danl. Webster

ALS. PU. Published in *W & S*, 16: 122.
  1. For Biddle's letter, see above.
  2. The bill was referred to the Committee of Ways and Means, headed by Louis McLane, who informed Biddle that the committee would not make a favorable report. (Ralph C. H. Catterall, *The Second Bank of the United States*, Chicago, 1903, p. 117).

TO ALEXANDER BLISS

Washington Mar. 3. 1826

Dear Sir

The 730 Dll note was on my Book, but I had *forgotten it*, & forgot to look at it. I hope you got along with it. I am resolved I never will come here again leaving *any thing* to be remembered at home; for I have no time here to remember or think of any thing except the daily business before me.

Sundry things must now be attended to.

1. As to the two notes, 3000 each, about which you had so much trouble after I came away—*when do they fall due?*

2. Two notes, 1500 each, signed by me & endorsed by Mr [George] Blake, fall due March 17. I know not exactly where they are, but you will hear from them. I enclose 2 notes, with Mr. B's endorsement, one for 1500—& one for 1000. I send these in season, so that they may be discounted; & for the balance shall request Mr Paige to furnish you cash. If you anticipate any trouble, in getting these discounted please let me know immediately.

There is one other matter, but about that I am not quite prepared to write now, & a day or two hence will be in season.

I enclose a small draft on Mr [Nathaniel] Adams of Portsmouth,[1] which I will thank you to send down. He is a very good man, but rather poor; & therefore I would not have the dr[a]ft negotiated, lest he should not find himself able to pay it.

I am suffering a little from influenza and cold; & a little from the pressure of affairs. My concerns in Court are more than usual; & I have not used usual diligence in previous preparation. [Robert F.] Stockton is yet undisposed of—Mr Blake thinks he will succeed.[2] The Court will sit three weeks longer. Yrs   D. Webster

ALS. DLC.

1. Adams (1756–1829; Dartmouth 1775), clerk of the New Hampshire Superior Court and longtime friend of Webster's.

2. *The Marianna Flora*, 11 Wheaton 1 (1826).

FROM JARED SPARKS

Boston, March 14, 1826

Dear Sir,

A new work has reached me from London, & is in press I understand in this country, entitled, "Principles of Political Economy, with a sketch of the Progess of the Science; By J[ohn] R[amsey] McCulloch, Esq."[1] It is the article in the Supplement to the Encyc[lopaedia] Brit[annica] enlarged, & made into a book. You know McCulloch is now considered a leading writer on this subject, & is Ricardo Lecturer.

It will be an important thing, if we can have a good review of this book in the N[orth] A[merican] R[eview]; & still more important, if you can find leisure and inclination to do it.[2] Political economy, altho' a science of great intrinsic value, is gaining very slowly in this country, & it seems to me a duty, for those who are skilled in the matter, to take some pains to bring it often & forcibly before the public. It has many points, too, peculiar to this country, which have not been sufficiently elucidated. If you will favor the readers of the N. A. Review with an article on this work, you can take your own time, and I do believe your labor would be well bestowed. I am, Sir, with great respect & sincere regard, Your friend & obt. sert.   Jared Sparks

ALS. NhD. Published in Herbert B. Adams, *Life and Writings of Jared Sparks* (2 vols.; Boston, 1893), 1: 270.

1. McCulloch (1789–1864), British statesman and political economist.

His work was published in England in 1825 (*DNB*).

2. See DW to Sparks, March 20 and October 12, 1826, below, for Webster's response.

TO JARED SPARKS

Washington March 20. 1826.

My Dear Sir

I should not be unwilling to write an Article on Mr McCulloch's Book, if my leisure should be such as to allow it. I can do nothing, however, till Summer. If, in the mean time, no abler hand takes hold of it, I will see what I can do with it. Are you not coming South, in the course of the Spring? I have understood you were expected. Yrs with much regard

Danl. Webster

ALS. MH. Published in *W & S*, 16: 124.

TO NICHOLAS BIDDLE

Washington Mar: 21. 1826.[1]

Dear Sir,

I believe I have already advised you that four causes, in which the Bank was interested, & to which you asked my attention, have been argued and determined. They were, *Findlay* vs the Bank,[2] *Coleman* vs the Bank,[3] *Williams* vs the Bank,[4] & *Mills* vs the Bank.[5] They were all decided favorably to the Bank, except that in Findlay's case, the Court below had made an error in computing interest, which is to be corrected. I now send you, under other covers, the proper Mandates & Certificates for carrying the judgments rendered here, in these causes, into effect.[6] You will transmit them, of course, to your local agents.

The case of Magill & others vs the Bank, No 102,[7] was not reached. It will doubtless come on next Term. I have not seen the Record, in that case, & am uninstructed as to its merits.

Dandridge's case[8] was not reached until almost the last day of the Court, & until the Court had intimated that they should not take up another long or important cause. It was ready for argument, & printed cases are prepared, for the use of the Court. In this case, according to your request, I engaged Mr. [William] Wirt, on the part of the Bank, as I have already advised you. I wish it to be understood, in regard to this cause, that I consider myself as only filling Mr. [John] Sergeant's place temporarily. If he should be here at the next Term, he will conduct the case, with Mr Wirt. I make no charge in it. A Bill of Fees, in the other causes, with Clerks fees &c, I forward to Mr [Samuel] Jaudon,[9] of the Bank, with an order at foot to pay amount to him. I have the honor to be, with regard, Your obt. Sevt.   Danl. Webster

ALS. PU. Published in *W & S*, 16: 123–124.

1. A note—"Recd March 24th."— appears under the heading; it is not in Biddle's handwriting, however.

2. *Finley* v. *the Bank of the United States*, 11 Wheaton 304 (1826).

3. Dismissed by the Court in 1826, *Coleman* v. *the Bank of the United States* was a companion case to *Finley* v. *the Bank of the United States*. See 11 Wheaton 304 (1826).

4. *Williams* v. *the Bank of the United States*, 11 Wheaton 414 (1826).

5. *Mills* v. *the Bank of the United States*, 11 Wheaton 431 (1826).

6. Not found.

7. *M'Gill et al.* v. *the Bank of the United States*, 12 Wheaton 511 (1827).

8. *Bank of the United States* v. *Dandridge*, 12 Wheaton 64 (1827).

9. Not found.

In the contingency that Charles Jared Ingersoll should be removed from office as a result of the charges preferred against him by Pennsylvania Congressman Samuel D. Ingham, old Federalists such as Supreme Court

Justice Bushrod Washington and Webster himself were prepared to seek the appointment of one of their own persuasion to the vacancy that would thus be created in the office of United States district attorney for Pennsylvania. Few appointments would have been more gratifying than that of Joseph Hopkinson, a close friend of Webster's for more than a decade.

FROM BUSHROD WASHINGTON

March 24th. 1826

Dear Sir

The day before I left Washington I received a letter from a gentleman of the bar in Philadelphia who, after alluding to a rumour then in circulation,—that a change in the office of District Attorney for that district, might possibly take place,—recommends, in that event, Mr. Joseph Hopkinson as the successor to the present incumbent, & adds, that his appointment would not only be highly acceptable to the members of that bar, but would be generally popular in that place.

I had a conversation that evening with Mr. I[ngersoll] who appeared to entertain no apprehensions as to the result of the pending investigation, and he consequently induced me to indulge the hope that it would be altogether favourable to him.

Should his anticipations be realized, which I most sincerely hope will be the case, you will oblige me by putting this letter into the fire. But should the event, unfortunately, be otherwise, you will please make such use of it as may best promote the wishes of Mr Hopkinson's friends, in case you suppose it can at all contribute to that end.

I have been the presiding Judge of the third Circuit for 23 years, and profess to be well acquainted with Mr H. Until his temporary retreat from the bar at Philad[elphi]a, a few years ago, he ranked with those who stood at the head of it, and enjoyed a liberal share of the business. Need I, to you, speak of his distinguished legal talents, or of his general literary acquirements? I should think not. From my opportunities [illegible] of witnessing his professional conduct, & his social qualities, for so long a course of years, I may be permitted to add my testimony to that of others of his attention to business, of his candour & abilities as an advocate, & of his integrity as a man. Such were the results of my own observations, and such, I believe, was & is his general character in Phil[adelphi]a. Should he receive the appointment, I feel satisfied that the duties of the office will [be] ably & faithfully discharged, & that the publick interest will be thereby promoted. I am dear Sir very respectfully & sincerely Yr. Mo. ob. Servt. Bush. Washington

ALS. NhHi.

The first measure of the Adams administration to arouse an organized opposition was the nomination of John Sergeant and Richard C. Anderson as ministers to the Congress of Panama. Fearful that the delegates might discuss slavery, abolition of the African slave trade, or the Cuban and Haitian questions, southerners united to oppose the mission. This southern opposition forms the chief topic of Webster's letter to Mason below.

TO JEREMIAH MASON

Washington Mar: 27. 1826

My Dear Sir

During the session of the Court, I had not much leisure to attend to general correspondence. You must receive this, as an excuse for leaving your letter so long unanswered.[1] It happened, luckily enough, that the H. of R. were occupied on no very interesting subjects, during my engagements else where. You see *Panama*, in so many shapes, that you probably expect to receive no news, in regard to it. The importance of the matter arises mainly from the *dead set* made against it, in the Senate. I am afraid my friend [John C.] Calhoun organized & arranged the opposition. *He expected to defeat the measure.* That would have placed the President in his power, more or less, &, if the thing could be repeated, on one or two other occasions, *completely so.* Mr. Adams, then, would have been obliged to make terms, or he could not get on with the Govt.—& those terms would have been *the dismissal of Mr Clay.* As far as to this point, all parties & parts of the opposition adhere, & cohere. Beyond this, probably, they could not move together harmoniously. Vast pains were taken, especially with new members, to bring them to a right way of thinking. Your neighbor [Ichabod Bartlett] was soon gained.

At the present moment, some who acted a violent part in the Senate, wish to have it understood that they are not, therefore, to be counted as members of a regular opposition. I have been informed, that Mr [Levi] Woodbury, & Mr [John] Holmes, disclaim opposition. Others, again, say, they had not full information, & complain of that.

Others make quotations, of sentences, words or syllables, from the documents; & carp at them. But you see all. In H. R. it is likely the necessary money will be voted by 30 or 40 majority.[2] We may have a week's debate.

Our Massachusetts claim came up on *Saturday*[3]—one of the Jackson men attacked it with great bitterness. Generally speaking, they are exasperated with all men, & every thing, that ever did, or is ever likely to, oppose Genl. Jackson.

The Bankrupt Bill will be taken up, shortly, I hope in the Senate. If it shall come down to us, I shall press it hard. If the Senate reject it, I shall not think it worth while to introduce the discussion into our House.

I observe the state of your recent elections. As between Gov. [David L.] Morrill and Genl. [Benjamin] Pierce, I suppose you found it difficult to make a choice.[4] It appears to me your leading men are likely to classify themselves as opponents of Mr. Adams. Is it, or is it not, desirable to bring things as fast as possible to that issue? The Congress election takes place next fall. Would it not be well to set up a good strong ticket, & vote for it? Of the Gentlemen now in the H.R. I do not recon more than one, or two at most, who are really & truly in favor of the present administration. It is possible, however, that they may keep themselves from any overt & palpable acts of opposition. If it would do any good, I suppose means might be found to have letters addressed to Gov. Morrill, on this matter.

Mr. [Samuel] Bell seems uncommonly zealous, & determined, in favor of the President—& acts a liberal & manly part, in recent & present occurrences.

The real truth is, that Mr. Adams will be opposed, by all the Atlantic States, south of Maryland. *So would any other northern man.* They will never acquiesce in the administration of any President on our side [of] the Potomac. This may be relied on, & we ought to be aware of it. The perpetual alarm, which is kept up on the subject of negro slavery has its object. It is to keep the South all united, & all jealous of the North. The northwestern States, & Kentucky, are at present very well disposed. So is Louisiana. Tenessee and Alabama will agree to any thing—or oppose any thing—as Genl. Jackson's interest may require. The Crawford men in Georgia will doubtless go in the same direction. In North Carolina, there are some who prefer Mr. Adams to Genl. J.—& in Va. it may be doubted whether the Genl. can be effectually supported. Va. says little about the men whom she would trust, but opposes those actually in power. In our House, however, the Va. phalanx of opposition is not formidable. More than a third, in number, may be reconed favorable. There is some reason to think the Jackson fever begins to abate in Penna; & doubtless it is over, in New Jersey. Under these circumstances, if New York & N. England go steady, it is not likely that the South will immediately regain the ascendancy.

The news from England does not represent Mr [Rufus] Kings health as entirely restored. He is able, however, to attend to business. Yrs very truly D. Webster

ALS. MHi. Published in *W & S*, 16: 125–127.

1. Webster was probably answering

Mason's letter of February 4, 1826, mDW 5291.

2. The House of Representatives

voted appropriations for the mission on April 22, 1826; and the Senate concurred on May 3.

3. No appropriations were made for settling the claims of Massachusetts growing out of the War of 1812 during the first session of the Nine-

teenth Congress.

4. Both Morrill and Pierce ran for the governorship of New Hampshire on the Republican ticket; the former, however, supported by Isaac Hill, was elected.

FROM JAMES MADISON

Mar. 27. 1826

Having to thank you for a copy, just come to hand, of the Ex[ecuti]ve Communications to the H. of Reps. relating to the Congress at Panama, I take occasion to supply the omission to do so for a former favor of a like sort. I hope you will not doubt the value I set, as well on the motive, as the matter for which I am indebted: But as such documents generally reach me thro' other channels, I feel some scruple in permitting you to be at the trouble of forwarding them; possibly too at the loss of some other friend. Be so good therefore as to accept a release from your obliging promise, with an assurance of my continued and cordial esteem & regard.

AL draft. DLC.

FROM JOHN MARSHALL

Richmond Apr. 3d. 1826

Dear Sir

I had the pleasure of receiving a few days past under cover from you the documents accompanying the late message of the President to the House of Representatives on the Panama mission. We anticipate a tolerably animated discussion of this subject.

I thank you very sincerely for this mark of polite recollection, & beg you to believe that I remain with [sincere regard, Yours,

John Marshall.][1]

AL (signature removed). NhHi. Published in *PC*, 1: 405.

1. According to an endorsement on the letter, Thomas Davis "cut out for Mr. Sprague. Oct 13. 1828," Marshall's complimentary close and sig-

nature. A different Marshall signature was pasted in its place. The bracketed close was supplied in *PC*, 1: 405, where Fletcher Webster probably conjectured it.

TO ALEXANDER BLISS

Washington April 7. 1826

Dear Bliss,

There will fall due 15/18 of this month a note of $3000 by D. W. to N[athan] Hale. I send you one for renewal.

On the 18th. there will come due a note to Mr [Stephen?] Hartwell,[1] if I err not, for $1510. Dollars. He knows about it. I send a note, sum blank—wish you to send for him, & tell him to renew the note for such sum as he finds convenient—say 1000 or 1200 Dollars—& pay the balance. I believe Mr [James W.] Paige has some small funds of mine, which he will let you draw upon. These things being done, there will not be much more to vex your good nature with till my return. Please keep a minute of these notes.

The Massachusetts claim looks pretty well. The discussion, (which has been able, on the part of some of the Speakers) has certainly dissipated much delusion. The real difficulty in the case is, *that no new law seems needed.* That, I believe, is the truth.

Mr. [Peleg] Sprague made a very handsome speech yesterday. I think him quite an acquisition to the House. Yours very sin[cer]ely   D. Webster

ALS. DLC.

1. On December 22, 1825, Webster had purchased property from Stephen Hartwell for $1000; Webster's note to him probably derived in part from this purchase (mDW 39835-278). Hartwell, a resident of Boston, has not otherwise been identified.

Webster's success in representing clients before the Spanish Claims Commission made it inevitable that men with outstanding claims against France and other European countries should seek his services. In the letter below, five prominent New Yorkers solicit his assistance. Frederick de Peyster (1796–1882) was a New York lawyer and prominent benefactor of the city; Charles King (1789–1867) was the son of Rufus King and editor of the New York American; *George Griswold (c. 1778–1859) was a director of the Columbia Insurance Company and the Bank of America, as well as an election inspector; Philip Kearney (1770–?) was a founder of the New York "Exchange Board"; and Elisha Tibbits, like Griswold, was an election inspector, a tax assessor, and president of the Franklin Fire Insurance Company. Their Memorial, not found but further identified by the memorialists in a letter to Clay on the following day, concerned " 'claims on the French & other European governments' " (Hopkins and Hargreaves, Papers of Henry Clay, 5: 243). While most of the claims questions were not settled until the 1830's—the Danish, in 1831; the French, in 1832; and the Neapolitan, in 1833—Webster, as in the Spanish claims, took a long and active interest in the representation of numerous claimants before the commissions as they were established.*

FROM FREDERICK DE PEYSTER, CHARLES KING, GEORGE GRISWOLD,
PHILIP KEARNEY, ELISHA TIBBITS

New York April 12th. 1826

Sir,

As a Committee appointed to act in behalf of Merchants and others of this City that have suffered by the injustice of foreign powers, we have addressed to the President of the U. States the Resolutions and memorial of which a printed Copy is enclosed, and being desirous of your counsel in regard to what further measures it might be expedient to pursue (in conjunction with other claimants and their Committees in other Cities and particularly in those of Massachusetts) we beg leave to introduce to you the Revd. Mr. [Thomas] Warner,[1] who having our own confidence on this subject we use the freedom of recommending him to yours.

We have the honor to be With much Respect Sir Your most obt servants

> Fred. de Peyster
> Chas. King
> Geo. Griswold
> Philip Kearney
> Elisha Tibbits

LS. DLC.
  1. Otherwise unidentified.

Having campaigned vigorously against the election of Crawford in 1824, Henry Wheaton, Supreme Court reporter and longtime close friend of Webster, expected an appointment to some key post from President Adams. In the letter below, he discusses his desire to be appointed federal judge for the Southern District of New York, a post then held by the ailing William P. Van Ness, whose negligence had permitted a clerk of the court to embezzle more than $100,000. (For an earlier charge of impropriety against Van Ness, see Correspondence, *1: 309–310.) When Van Ness died in September, the appointment went to Samuel R. Betts. Wheaton had to wait until 1827, when Adams appointed him chargé d'affaires to Denmark.*

FROM HENRY WHEATON

N. Y. April 12, 1826

My Dear Sir,

I am sorry to trouble you so often on the subject of my own affairs. But as I wrote you some days since[1] about the *procureur du roi* here, I think it proper to add that in consequence of his uncandid behaviour to me I hold myself exempt from all obligations of delicacy towards him. The exhibition of his utter incapacity to manage the law concerns of the Govt, which he has made at the Circuit Court now sitting ought to be known to the P[resident]. A *hint* from the quarter would be enough to make him *retire*; & the P. owes it to the public to *give it to him*. When I speak of *incapacity*, I do not mean in comparison of other men of more experience & learning, but of absolute *incompetency*. It is truly disgraceful that in a City where more than half the revenue is collected, its security (so far as depends on law proceedings,) should be left in such hands. You may rely upon it that the unanimous voice of the Bar will confirm what I state—I have reason to believe that the place is becoming more valuable, & indeed that it might be rendered very much so in competent hands.

It is stated to me (how truly I don't know) that he relies on the protection of Mr Clay, & that is the reason why he has not resigned as he pledged himself to do.[2] But Clay is entirely mistaken if he supposes him of any sort of consequence.

I cannot *write* these things to [*John W.*] *Taylor*. But I think if you apply yourself earnestly to the thing, you may, through him, move the P. to do what I will venture to say he will never repent of. Be this as it may, I am sure there is no man, who has a stronger claim upon him than your faithful friend,   H.W.

P.S. Excuse my importunity. If it were not *absolutely necessary* to me, you would not find my name on the list of *office Seekers*. If I could live over again the years that are past, those who are in power should not know me in that character.

ALS. DLC.
1. Letter not found.
2. Correspondence with Clay on the question of the appointment was in-

deed heavy. See, for example, Hopkins and Hargreaves, *Papers of Henry Clay*, 5: 762–765, 876–877.

TO MRS. GEORGE BLAKE

H. of R. April 29. 1826

My Dear Mrs Blake,

We have heard thro Mrs Johnson,[1] of your rapid progress to New York; & if you have proceeded, with equal speed, thro the remainder of your journey, you are now in Summer Street. I wrote Mr Blake in New York, & hope the letter arrived in season to be recd before you left; but I did not expect, I confess, to hear of your being so far along so soon.[2]

We have gone, My Dear Lady, as well as we could, since you left us; but I need [not] say how great a change your absence has wrought in our establishment. The "mess" were in bad spirits, for a week.[3] Indeed they have not recovered yet. Mrs W. has diverted her melancholy, by an uncommon attendance on parties. I believe she bade me attend her, in such service, five nights successively. However little this looks like grief, I assure you we have had rather a dull—I will say, a very dull—time of it, since you left us. We now begin to occupy ourselves with the thoughts of our own departure, which at present is fixed for the 15th. We hope to emulate your speed, in some good measure, & to be home by the 22. or 23rd.

As to politics, for Mr Blake (I know you do not trouble yourself with such nonsense) I have only to say, that we have done with Panama, at least in our House, & we are now getting on with the ordinary business of the Session. Mr. Blake's friend Mr Johnson,[4] has a little claim, which we are in hopes of getting up today. I believe Mr. Amory's[5] hopes are now faint, as to his business. He came to see me last Evening, and argued the cause, fully, & elaborately. I thought he went thro the matter as if he did not expect to enjoy another opportunity very shortly, of delivering his sentiments on that subject.

I assure you, My Dear Mrs Blake, I am most tired of being here. I wish to be home. Mr. Blake must take care not to get too much engrossed in affairs, to prevent his being able to take seasonable recreation. For my part, I intend to see the *South Shore*, at the usual period; I hope you will join us.

I write this in the House, & therefore have not an opportunity of taking Mrs. Webster's commands to send her love; nor have Julia & Edward an opportunity of sending theirs. You must therefore content yourself with the affectionate remembrance, My Dear Mrs B, of yours always truly

Danl. Webster

ALS. NhD.

1. Not identified.
2. The Blakes had been in Washington for the February Term of the Supreme Court. Blake and Webster were co-counsel in *The Marianna Flora*, and opposing attorneys in

United States v. *Tappan.*

3. The Websters, and most likely the Blakes also, were residing at John Coyle's on Capitol Hill.
4. Not identified.
5. Not identified.

Although the population of the United States had tripled and its area doubled since 1789, the system of federal courts remained virtually unchanged when Adams, following the lead of Monroe and Madison, urged reform. The Supreme Court's dockets were jammed, and a huge backlog of cases carried over from term to term. Bills had often been introduced, but no legislation had been enacted.

In 1825–1826 Congress again undertook to reorganize the Supreme Court, with Webster taking the lead in the House and Van Buren in the Senate. (See mDW 41313 for Webster's bill.) Both called for increasing the number of judges on the Court to ten and for the creation of additional circuits in the West. Webster's bill passed the House on January 26. A few weeks later the Senate concurred, with an amendment, how-

ever, separating Ohio from the proposed Indiana and Illinois circuit—
Webster's proposal—and uniting it with Kentucky. On the placement of
Ohio the two houses disagreed, with the result that the bill failed to pass
Congress. In analyzing the reasons, Van Buren wrote that "there has
been a great deal of shuffling on the part of Webster & Co. to let the Bill
die in conference. This plan we have defeated by a pretty strong course.
With characteristic Yankee craft he has, though defeated in his main
object, seized upon some clumsy expression of Holmes (who reported the
bill or rather amendment during my sickness) to hide the true ground of
collision, the union of Kentucky and Ohio, by raising another question
upon the form of the amendment. But the matter is perfectly under-
stood here. Unless they can have a Judge in Kentucky (who is already
appointed) and one in Ohio also, they wish to defeat the bill, in hopes
of getting a better one next year. The great object is to get McLean out
of the Post Office which can only be effected by his promotion, as they
dare not displace him. It is also said that Ingham is to be P. M. G. and
Webster, Speaker. There may be some mistake about this latter part al-
though I am not certain that there is" (Van Buren to B. F. Butler, May
15, 1826, Van Buren Papers, DLC).

TO JEREMIAH MASON

Washington May 2. 1826

PRIVATE

My Dear Sir,

Letters came yesterday from Mr. [Rufus] King desiring his recall, &
proposing, that he may be permitted to return, as soon as possible, to the
U. States:[1] This is unlucky. It is a very unseasonable termination of that
mission, & perhaps will settle some things not exactly as might be
wished. The truth is, that Mr. King's health has been such that he has
been able to do nothing, since he arrived in England. In the mean time,
two or three things entrusted to him are of pressing & urgent importance; so much so, that I think it probable the President had determined
to send out somebody to aid Mr. King in the negotiation, & then, perhaps,
to proceed to France to act in conjunction with Mr. [James] Brown, in a
renewed effort to obtain indemnity from the French Govt. for spoliations
&c. I imagine it would have been thought adviseable, under all circumstances, to have entrusted this special service to Mr. [Albert] Gallatin.
Mr K's resignation has changed the state of things. I have not seen the
President, since the news came, but have seen Mr. Clay, who gave the
information. I incline to think the course will now be to send Mr. Gallatin immediately to England, to take Mr. K's place. Mr. G, I was told,
was willing to go on a special, but not on a permanent mission. He does

not wish, it is said, to be obliged to take a House, or any establishment abroad; being rather desirous of husbanding his outfit, &c. What may come of this, I cannot tell; but see no way but to leave things to take their course. My impression, at present, is, that it would be unreasonable, to make any movement to give another direction to the affair.

The Judiciary Bill is yet between the two Houses. It may possibly be lost, but I think it will not be. If the Senate do not yield their amendment, probably we shall agree to it. A pretty satisfactory arrangement will be made as to the Judges. The present Post. Mast. Genl. will be named, in case Ohio be separated from Kentucky; otherwise I conjecture the Judge in that quarter will be N[athaniel] F. Pope, at present Dis[trict] Judge of Illinois. In Louisiana, I presume, a Judge [Alexander] Porter will be appointed; in Tennessee, either a Mr. [Thomas] Emerson,[2] or a Mr. [Henry] Crabb.[3] I hope the former. In looking out for men for these places a very honest & anxious desire is felt, I believe, to find men who *concur* in the leading decisions of the Supreme Court. If any error be committed, on that point, it will be thro misinformation.

I intend to be home by the 22 or 23rd. of May. There remain no public subjects of great interest except the Bankruptcy, which has breezed up, somewhat too late, in the Senate.

Be kind enough to give our love to Mrs. Mason & the children. As the Judge [Story] will be with you about this time, you may shew him this. Yrs always truly   Danl. Webster

Copy. NhHi. Published in *W & S*, 16: 127–128.

1. On March 20, 1826, King resigned his post.

2. Emerson, a native of Virginia, had moved to Tennessee in 1800, where he served as the first mayor of Knoxville; on the Superior Court bench, 1807–1809; as judge of the First Circuit Court, 1816–1819; and as a judge of the Tennessee Supreme Court, 1819–1822.

3. Crabb, a Nashville lawyer and partner of John Bell, was United States attorney for the Western District of Tennessee. In 1826 he was named to the Tennessee Supreme Court.

FROM JOHN SERGEANT

Philada.
May 2. 1826.

Dear Sir,

I am much obliged to you for the enclosure in your letter of the 26th ulto.,[1] but much more for your speech on the Panama matter. It is a speech that will tell, because it is direct and clear, and in my humble judgment settles every point it touches. Mr. Clay owes you a great deal for bringing out the true colours of his conduct from under the dust and cobweb they have been covered with by his opponents. The view is a striking one, and its exact truth, as well as its appropriateness to the occasion, relieve it from all imputation of springing from mere feelings of personal regard. It will do him permanent good.

I have seen an English publication which states objections to all Baron [Alexander von] Humboldt's routes.[2] Yrs. very truly

John Sergeant

ALS. DLC.
1. Neither the letter nor the enclosure has been found.

2. Baron Humboldt (1769–1859), German scientist and traveler.

TO [JOHN EVELYN DENISON]

Washington May 3. 1826

My Dear Sir,

I recd yesterday your letter of the 28 Feb,[1] & am greatly obliged to you, as well for the letter itself, as for the valuable pamphlets with which you accompanied it. We are now within fifteen or twenty days of the end of our session, and according to our custom, (& I suppose according to your's also) these last days are excessively crowded with business. Upon the whole, it has not been a session in which we have dispatched many concerns of great moment. It has been a *talking* winter. The President's proposition to send Ministers to the Congress at Panama has led to endless debates, especially in the Senate. The measure has met with much opposition, by which more was intended than the defeat of the measure itself. Various parties, not likely to act together often, united, on this occasion, in a close phalanx of *opposition*. The measure, however, has succeeded by a small majority in the Senate, & a large one in our House.

Another long topic, has been a plan for amending the Constitution, in the manner of electing [the] President. This grew out of the events of the late Election. After much tedious discussion, we leave the matter as we found it.[2] Our other subjects have not been of particular interest.

Mr [John] Randolph was elected last fall a Senator, from Va. It was unexpected; but his great devotion to certain political opinions cherished in that State gave him the Election. He is a violent opposer of the present Gov't.; & has conducted his part of the discussions in the Senate in a way hitherto altogether unknown. The Vice President has found out that he has no authority to call him to order, or restrain his wanderings: so he talks on, for two, four, & sometimes *six* hours at a time; saying whatever occurs to him, on all subjects. This course, & its indulgence by the Presiding Officer of the Senate, has produced a very strong sensation throughout the Country. It is now said he will sail for England in a few days, to pass the Summer.

We hear that Mr. [Rufus] King is coming immediately home, on account of ill health. I regret, very much, his sudden return. It is quite *unseasonable.* I hardly know what will be done, not having seen the President since the information arrived. I *hope,* however, that somebody will be sent out to bring pending negotiations to a close, & should not be surprised, if, with that view, Mr. [Albert] *Gallatin* should be selected.

I have read your Debates, thus far, with great & peculiar interest. The questions in your House have been such as are connected with general principles of great importance. In my poor judgment, your friends are clearly right, on the currency question, the Silk trade question, &c. On the silk question Mr Huskisson's speech is most admirable. I read it in the [Boston] Courier, but am happy to have it, thro. your kindness, in a more correct form. I have read it, a second time, here in my study, with real delight, & enjoyed his triumph, when he resumed his seat, almost as much [as] he himself could have done. Pray tell him, what I hope he would not be displeased to know, that there are men on this side the globe, who admire his liberal principles, & the singular ability & excellent sense, with which he recommends those principles to the adoption of his Countrymen. His speech on the Silk trade question appears to me, on the whole, his greatest effort; & next to this I place that which he made several years ago, on, what I thought a very mild proposition in your House, for the equitable adjustment of contracts.

I entertain no doubt that the prohibition of the circulation of small notes is a good measure, & will produce all the benefit intended by it, altho' it may have some effect to continue the immediate pressure; or, rather, it may retard, in some degree, the natural progress of relief & restoration. As it is prospective, however, in its operation, & for the present deferred, perhaps this effect may hardly be perceptible. It is quite true that gold & paper will not circulate together. It is quite true, also, that two kinds of paper, of different values, cannot circulate together, however small the difference. We have much experience of this last truth. For example, we have in Massachusetts, many Country Banks, all being incorporated institutions, well [re]gulated, & in good credit. *Their notes are payable only where issued.* These notes get to Boston; they pass, in the common exchanges, & for all ordinary persons; yet, as they are payable fifty, or a hundred miles from Town, they are not quite so good, as notes of the Boston Banks. Now the consequence is, that these country notes fill up the whole circulation. Hardly is there a Boston note to be seen; and in order to correct this, it has been found necessary, that these Country Banks should make provision for the redemption of their notes in Boston, as well as on their own counters at home. You will experience as I should think the same thing in England, if you establish

Country Banks, making their notes payable only where issued. These notes will be so good, that they will be taken; & yet not so good, quite, as Bank of England notes, or the notes of London Bankers,# because the Bank & London Bankers will not receive them, in deposite, as cash. They will still pass, in all small payments, at all the shops in London; & the consequence will be that Brokers, will take them up, at small but different rates of discount, for gold or Bank of England notes. York notes will be at one rate. Welsh notes a little higher, Worcestershire a little lower &c, according to distance from London.* Let me tell you a short story. A year or two ago, a client of mine, a trader, came to my Rooms to pay me for a legal opinion. The sum was 50 Dlls. He handed me ten five Dollar notes on a country Bank, in good credit, not a hundred miles from Boston. He was a good natured man, & I address'd him thus. "You give me this fee in country notes. Now I wish to tell you what I suspect. I suspect, that when you left your Counting House, you filled up a check, on a Boston Bank, for fifty Dollars;—you put it in your pocket, and on your way hither, you have called at a Brokers, sold your check, for these country notes, & have recd a premium of 1 or 1½ pr ct—say 50 or 75 cts, with which it is your intention to buy a leg of mutton for your dinner. Now, sir, that mutton is mine. You shall not dine, at my expense, in your own House. The legal opinion which I gave you was not *below* par; I will not be paid for it, in any thing which is. Sit down, & draw me a cheque for $50."—He at once admitted that the process had been as I stated, very nearly.

I have, indeed, understood, that heretofore, the notes of Country Bankers would not pass in London. Possibly that may continue to be the case, but I should expect that they would make their way, & if so I have no doubt the same evil will be felt, in time, which we have experienced here. But, My Dear Sir, I am talking upon what you must understand much better than I do, & I will tax you no farther.

We have a Countryman of yours here, a Captain Wylde,[3] of the Artillery, who, I had the pleasure to find, is a Nottingham man, & an acquaintance of yours.

I have forgotten to tell you that my Books all arrived safe, soon after I wrote you last. I hardly yet know what accident detained them, but they arrived in good time, nevertheless.

You have a busy summer before you. I suppose you will be *dissolved* next month, & have a warm July of it. I should admire to be in England, during a general election. It must be an occasion, I think, in which one could see a good deal of the true Mr. Bull. I trust your Catholic vote will not endanger your seat, as you thought it might, if the Election had come on earlier. It would be unkind in your Constituents to let their resentment, on account of that vote, be *felt*. I shall continue to rely on your friendship to send me occasionally such speeches, pamphlets, &c. as you may happen to notice, & as you may think interesting.

Mrs Webster is with me here. She commands me to make her remembrances to you. I had occasion lately to write Mr [Edward] Stanley,[4] but must beg you to renew as well to him, as Mr [James A. Stuart-]Wortley & Mr [Henry] Labouchere my assurances of regard & attachment. Pray what [has] become of Colo. [Robert Kearsley] Dawson? I am, My D Sir, most truly Yours   Danl. Webster

I shall see the good Judge [Story] by 25th inst in the Court, in Boston. He will be most glad to hear from you.

I believe your London Bankers do not issue notes.
* This is of course conjectural; but such has been our experience.

ALS. DLC. Published in Curtis, 1: 270–273.

1. Not found.
2. The proposed amendment was one which would remove the election of President and Vice President from Congress in the event that no candidate received a majority.
3. Not identified.
4. Letter not found.

FROM SUSAN DECATUR

Baltimore May 7th 1826

My dear Mr Webster,

I am most dreadfully mortified to learn that my claim has been defeated through your opposition to it[1]—for altho you had not manifested so warm an interest in my cause as some others of my belov'd husband's friends had done, yet I must confess I had not the least apprehension that you wou'd ever do any thing to injure me; and I still hope that you will have the goodness to tell me frankly, the grounds of your objection, as I may possibly have in my possession some information that might tend to obviate them—for it is utterly impossible that you can really think that the achievement had less merit than many others that have been more liberally rewarded. I can assure you that your opposition has astonish'd every person who knows you, here, even by reputation; and they will scarcely believe that I have not been misinform'd!

I came here about a week since for the benefit of my health and to obtain some further medical advice. I shall return home tomorrow, and I hope you will have the goodness to let me find a line from you informing me what has caus'd you to take such a cruel part against me. In the mean time I will believe that it has proceeded from some misapprehension of the subject; and not from any unkind feelings towards me, or from any desire to disparage the memory of my belov'd and lamented husband who consider'd you as one of his warmest friends and admirers. I beg you to believe me very sincerely Yours   S. Decatur

ALS. NhD. Susan Decatur, nee Wheeler, was the widow of Stephen Decatur.

1. Susan Decatur's claim was for compensation, in behalf of Stephen Decatur and others of the crew of the *Intrepid*, for the capture and destruction of the frigate *Philadel-* *phia* in the harbor at Tripoli. Webster and others opposed the claim on the ground that since no condemnation had taken place in compliance with the prize law, no lawful right to the prize had vested in the crew. *Register of Debates*, 19th Cong., 1st sess., 1825–26, 2: 2593–2600.

FROM JEREMIAH MASON

Portsmouth May 7, 1826.

Dear Sir:

I have just received your letter.[1] I regret exceedingly that Mr. King is to return so speedily for many reasons. It is unfortunately timed for him. His bad health, of which I was before aware, is doubtless the chief cause. If however he knew it was determined at Washington to send Mr. [Albert] Gallatin out to aid him in his negotiations, it is possible that might influence him, in requesting leave to return sooner than he otherwise would have done. Unless his feelings toward Mr. Gallatin are now different from what they were ten years ago it would not be entirely pleasant to be associated with him.

It seems to me that you cannot under existing circumstances assert your claim at the present time. Should the Government offer you the appointment,[2] I think you ought to refuse it. But if I mistake not it will be thought you cannot at this time be spared from the House of Reps. And as far as I understand the state of that body, I am inclined to think your presence there at the ensuing session very important.

In my opinion you have a right to insist that such arrangements be made, if they can be without injury to the public interests, that you shall not be defeated of that appointment eventually, & *at a period not more than two years distant.* How this arrangement is to be made I do not know. If Mr. G. should be appointed for a special mission, & go out before Mr. King's return, I suppose all the duties of a minister resident would of course be devolved on him. I see no inconvenience in such a mission continuing for two or three years, unless there be something in Court etiquette forbidding it. A continuance of two years probably would not be unpleasant to Mr. G. Should he be appointed as a regular minister resident, it may be doubtful whether he would be desirous of returning as soon as may be wished. He remained in France several years after he first began to talk of returning.

Our Circuit Court sits tomorrow, when I expect from Judge Story a stock of Washington news.

With Mrs. Mason's and my best regards to Mrs. Webster & wishing you a safe return home I am Truly yours   J. Mason.

I have received your Panama speech which has reached here. It is all that it should be. It is read with eagerness & abundantly praised. The opposition can gain nothing on this subject. They misjudged in attempting to attach such vast importance to it. What I chiefly regret in that matter is the course adopted by [Louis] McLane. I fear it is an indication of his inclination favourable to the opposition.[3]

Typed copy. NhHi. Published in Curtis, 1: 273–274.

1. See above, DW to Jeremiah Mason, May 2, 1826.

2. As revealed in his letter of May 2, Webster was thinking again of the possibility of being sent as minister to England.

3. Although McLane, as chairman of the House Ways and Means committee, had reported an appropriation bill for the Panama mission, he had followed it a few weeks later with a proposal and speech to "forbid American ministers at Panama from discussing a foreign alliance or any bilateral declaration binding the United States to resist European interference or committing the neutrality of the United States." It was this "policy of impediment" to which Mason referred. John A. Munroe, *Louis McLane: Federalist and Jacksonian* (New Brunswick, 1973), p. 201.

TO ALEXANDER BLISS

Washington May 8. 1826

My D Sir

I have already mentioned to you my intention to leave here this day week. We propose to send the horses ahead, by some days, & to take, ourselves, the quickest conveyance to Philadelphia. We do not intend stopping, any where; & I hope to be home in 7 or 8 days from the time of setting out. This will enable me to be at the Circuit Court, the second week. I suppose there will be no difficulty in deferring, to that time, any thing in which I am concerned. But I have a *strong wish* to continue every thing, as far as possible, to next term. I hardly recollect what causes I am engaged in, but none occur to me as likely to be pressing, in their nature. After the second week of the Court comes Election; a time not suited to Judge Story's Court, tho' well adapted to a court holden occasionally by me & Judge Isaac [P.] Davis! Soon after the first of June, I must go to N. Hampshire, to be gone a fortnight. I am unluckily the proprietor of some lands in the North part of that State, which I must give some attention to. It will be my purpose to get thro this, so as to be home to attend the Sup. Court in July, if any one should need me there. August is not a working month.

This is my present plan for the Summer, which I mention that you may answer inquiries. For the present, the object is, as far as practicable, to continue the Circuit Court business to the next term. If any thing occurs to keep me here longer than I now expect, I shall give you due notice. Yrs always   D Webster

ALS. DLC.

TO JOSEPH STORY

Washington, May 8, 1826.

My dear Sir,

I have received your letter written at Portland,[1] and will not fail to attend to the subject of it. I had already found my attention turned towards the proposed law, which I very much dislike, and shall take care to oppose.[2]

The fate of the judiciary bill is quite uncertain. The Senate show much pertinacity in regard to their amendment; and it is doubtful whether the House will ever consent to it. You will have noticed the proceedings thus far. If the Senate decline a conference, the bill is certainly lost. If they agree to a conference, and in that conference consent to abandon that part of their amendment which does not relate to the districts, it is possible, and only possible, the bill may finally pass. The real truth is, the gentlemen in the Senate who are called the Opposition, do not wish the bill to pass; even those of them who are from the West have but a cool desire for it. I suppose the reason is, they do not wish to give so many important appointments to the President. I think we stand pretty well, either way. If the bill passes, well; if not, we have made a fair offer, and the court will remain at seven some years longer. Judge [Robert] Trimble's nomination is not yet acted on.[3]

There remain no very important measures now before congress, although there is a mass of subordinate business, and of private bills.

My plan is to leave here on the 15th; to send the horses along three or four days earlier, so as to proceed rapidly ourselves to New York. I shall hardly be more than seven or eight days going home; so that I intend to be in your court, the second week of its sitting. I believe I have very little to do there, and I shall write to Mr. [Alexander] Bliss to postpone to next term, at once, all that can be so disposed of. After the second week of the court comes election week, a week not convenient for courts; so that I think the business of the term had better be wound up, if practicable, the second week. I shall write to Mr. [George] Blake to that effect, as well as Mr. Bliss. My health is good; but still I am not anxious to go immediately to much hard work when I get home. From the first day of December, I have not been an inch from my place till Saturday, when I rode a few miles on horseback. I need motion and air, more than a court. If any thing occurs to change my present purposes, respecting the time of my departure, &c. I shall give you timely notice; this letter I direct to Salem. Very probably I may write you again in a day or two, under cover to Mr. Bliss.

Mrs. Webster joins me in love to you, and we both join in one other thing, that is the most affectionate remembrance to Mrs. Story. Yours truly, Dan'l Webster.

Text from *PC*, 1: 405–406. Original not found.

1. Not found.

2. Story had probably called Webster's attention to the Senate bill for "regulating process in the courts of the United States," which had specific reference to the resolution regarding "execution and sale, on final process, property and estate of the defendant which has not been made subject to execution by the laws of the United States, or the laws of the State in which the judgment was pronounced," a concern growing out of the decisions rendered by the Supreme Court in *Bank of the United States* v. *Hollstead* (10 Wheaton 51) and *Wayman* v. *Southard* (10 Wheaton 1). At the same time, a resolution had been introduced in the House calling for the repeal of Section 25 of the Judiciary Act of 1789, which the House Judiciary Committee rejected. Story and Webster's concern over the "proposed law" arose over Senate amendments to the House bill. *House Journal*, 19th Cong., 1st sess., 1825–26 (Serial 130), p. 41.

3. Trimble was confirmed as an associate justice of the Supreme Court on May 9.

FROM JOHN MARSHALL

Richmond, May 20th, 1826

Dear Sir

I returned yesterday from North Carolina & had the pleasure of finding your speech on the mission to Panama under cover from yourself. I had previously read it with deep interest but was not on that account the less gratified at this polite mark of your attenion. I can preserve it more certainly in a pamphlet form that in that of a newspaper.

Whatever doubts may very fairly be entertained respecting the policy of the mission as an original measure, I think it was not involved in much difficulty when considered as it came before the House of Representatives.

I congratulate you on closing a most laborious session and am with great & respectful esteem Your obedt   J Marshall

ALS. ICU. Published in *PC*, 1: 406–407.

FROM GULIAN CROMMELIN VERPLANCK

Washington May 22nd. 1826

Dear Sir

I enclose you Judge Story's letter.[1] Mr [Aaron?] Hackley remained on the watch untill the last of our night session on Saturday—or rather Sunday morning. One of my colleagues made some faint demonstration to get up the bill—but the slightest show of opposition was of course sufficient to defeat it.

From what I have reason to believe concerning H. & his connection with our Lobby at Albany, together with the Judge's letter, I am led to suspect an extreme project concealed under this specious bill.

Col [John] McKee & Mr [Thomas H.] Williams with me,[2] are only left to keep the field & finding ourselves in possession of sundry remains of military stores we have commissioned the Col. to pick up an old soldier or two to help us finish them today to prevent their falling into the enemies' hands.

We all join in begging to be kindly remembered to Mrs Webster. I am yours truly   G. C. Verplanck

ALS. NhHi.
    1. Not found. This is most likely the same letter referred to in DW to Story, May 8, above. As a fellow member of the "mess" at Captain John Coyle's in Washington, Webster probably asked Verplanck to pay particular attention to the "proposed alteration in the Revenue Law." See DW to Verplanck, [May 20, 1826], mDW 5459.
    2. McKee and Williams also boarded with John Coyle.

FROM WILLIAM PLUMER, SR.

Epping May 29. 1826.

Sir,

By the last mail I received under your frank your able speech upon the Panama mission; for which you will please to accept my grateful acknowledgement. Your argument upon that subject, appears to me, conclusive. I have for several months thot. if the president had not recommended that mission, the leaders of opposition, both in the Senate & house, would have moved resolutions declaring such a mission necessary, & censured him for his neglect. Men predisposed to find fault with an administration, are never at a loss for occasions to express their dissatisfaction, any more than nations to assign reasons in their manifestos for war. Propriety & consistency are seldom traits in the character of party opposition, except they are, in general, consistent in condemning whatever their opponents recommend. I am respectfully, Sir, your obedient   William Plumer

LC. DLC.

On May 20, 1826 (mDW 5461), William Gaston asked Webster to pro-
vide him with character references of numerous witnesses in a case to
come before the North Carolina Circuit Court in 1827. The Whitaker
case involved a charge of libel, the origins of which lay in theological
disagreements between two Unitarian ministers, the Whitakers, and a
Presbyterian, Frederick Freeman. Neither the case nor Webster's com-
ments on several of those men who had submitted written depositions
on the character of the litigants is the most important aspect of Web-
ster's answer to Gaston: the letter's significance lies in Webster's candid
statement of his attitude toward the Adams administration at the time.
It is one of the few instances in which he forthrightly reveals his posi-
tion, in this instance to an old Federalist friend and congressional col-
league from the War of 1812 years.

TO WILLIAM GASTON

Boston May 31. 1826

My Dear Sir

I lose no time in answering yours of the 20th, which was recd. yesterday. Most of the Gentlemen whom you mention I have the pleasure to
know, & know them to be most worthy & respectable persons. Dr. [Abiel]
Holmes, a distinguished Clergyman, author of the two vols of "American
Annals"; Dr. [Thaddeus William] Harris, author of several respectable
publications, & among others a "natural history of the Bible," which has
attracted much praise, abroad, as well as in U. S.; Dr. [Andrew] Foster,[1]
& Dr. [Edward] Richmond,[2] are all well known to me. Genl. [Elijah]
Crane, Sheriff of Norfolk,[3] I know quite well. Mr [George] Morey[4] is a
particular acquaintance. Mr [Samuel] Rodman I know, & Mr Lemuel
Williams jr, both of New Bedford.[5] I do not know any thing of the Messrs
Whitakers,[6] either personally, or by reputation; nor am I acquainted
with the characters or persons of Mr. [Daniel] Kimball,[7] Mr [William]
Ritchie,[8] or Dr. [Daniel] Stone.[9] Mr [John] Bailey I have known only
from our intercourse in Congress; & of Lemuel Williams Senr. I can say
only that I take him to be a respectable Gentleman, who was member
of Congress many years ago from Bristol County.

It will give me pleasure to oblige you; or to serve the cause of truth &
justice by stating, in any form, the general character & reputation of
those Gentlemen whom I have mentioned as being known to me. They
are all equally well known to the following persons, who, I presume,
would cheerfully join me in bearing testimony to their good character;
viz, Isaac Parker, Chf Justice of Mass: Levi Lincoln, Govr; Mr Justice
[Joseph] Story; John Davis Esqr. District Judge;[10]—I think it likely some
of these Gentlemen may know those persons, mentioned in your letter,

with whom I have said that I am not myself acquainted. Any wish of yours, in regard to this matter, will be complied with, with great readiness & pleasure.

I thank you, My Dear Sir, for your kind sentiments towards my poor [Panama] speech; but much more, I assure you, for the friendly dispositions which you express towards the Administration, & your disapprobation of this strange opposition. I believe Mr. Adams' feelings & purposes are extremely good. Be assured, there is nothing in him of narrowness, or illiberality, or local prejudice. The South, I very much fear, means to quarrel with him, right or wrong; or perhaps, it may be more charitable to say that it means to act on the presumption that he must and will be wrong, & act wrong, in all things. I trust it will turn out otherwise, however, & that his measures will be found not unmixed evil. I have long wished to write you, on these subjects, but have been restrained from various considerations. I know the posture of your State; & how difficult & dangerous it is, or may be thought to be, to support the measures or approve the conduct of one, with a Community that is disappointed at his elevation, & hopes soon to see his place occupied by another. Nevertheless, if you could spare a half hour to give me your views & feelings fully, I should be very much gratified. You see on what grounds the opposition places itself. The Leading Jackson Journal makes this great charge to be, *a tendency, in Mr Adams, to stand well with Federalists.* All this, notwithstanding the Genl's letter about Col [William] Drayton![11] [Samuel D.] Ingham, [Samuel] Houston, & twenty others have repeated these ideas, in their speeches in Congress. Yet you know whose follower Mr Ingham was, as late as 1823, & what was the *professed* principle on which he who then was (& now is) his leader, acted.

But, My Dear Sir, I will not avail myself of the little opening, which your letter affords, to inflict upon you a political epistle. I am, however, I confess, desirous of knowing more than I do know at present, of your sentiments, in regard to public affairs; & perhaps you will find leisure to tell me frankly what you think, & something of what you see & hear around you.

It caused me much grief not to be here last summer, when you did our town the honor of a visit. Your various friends will be gratified by your remembrance of them.

I am, My Dear [Sir], with unabated esteem & regard, Yours

Danl. Webster

ALS. NcU. Published in Van Tyne, pp. 119–120.

1. Foster (d. 1831; Harvard 1800), a physician in Dedham.

2. Richmond (1767–1842; Brown 1789), minister at Dorchester.

3. Crane (1754–1834).

4. Morey (1789–1866), Massachu-

setts legislator and member of the executive council.

5. Rodman (1792–1876); Williams was the son of the Massachusetts congressman and state legislator.

6. One of the Whitakers, the plaintiffs in the case, was Jonathan (1771–1835; Harvard 1797), minister in New Bedford who later moved to Virginia and North Carolina. Following his court action in North Carolina, he settled in Rochester, New York.

7. Kimball (1779–1862; Harvard 1800), principal of Derby Academy, Hingham, and brother-in-law of Jonathan Whitaker.

8. Ritchie (d. 1842), a Unitarian minister in Needham.

9. Stone (d. 1842; Harvard 1797), physician in Sharon, Massachusetts.

10. Davis (1761–1847).

11. Letter not identified.

TO HENRY CLAY

Boston June 8. 1826.

My Dear Sir,

We are glad to learn through the papers that you have been able to leave the City for a little visit into Maryland; as it gives us reason to hope that you have recovered from your recent indisposition.

You will have noticed Mr [James] Lloyd's resignation.[1] I did not expect it, at this moment, although I was apprised of his wish to leave the Senate, as soon as he could. It was with difficulty he was persuaded to attend the last session. The Legislature being now in session, his place will be immediately filled. I incline to think that the appointment will fall on Mr [Nathaniel] *Silsby*.[2] It has been intimated to me, indeed, that a different arrangement *might*, perhaps, be made, if I should approve it; but my impression at present is against it, & I believe for very good reasons.

Mr Silsby you know. He is entirely well disposed, & is a well informed Merchant, and a respectable man. It is not likely he would take much part in the discussions of the Senate; but would bring a good deal of useful knowledge into the body, & might be entirely relied on to support all just & proper measures. According to general usage here, a Senator would now be appointed for 6 yrs, commencing next March, at the end of Mr. [Elijah Hunt] Mills' present term of office; but I think it probable enough, that having to fill the vacancy, occasioned by the resignation of Mr Lloyd, now, the Legislature may choose to postpone the other election to the winter. If the choice should come on now, I understand Mr Mills will be reelected.[3] If postponed, it may be a little uncertain, it is said; as some suppose our Govr. has an inclination for the place. There are here, in the Legislature & out, a few very busy persons, who are hostile to the Administration. They have no system, but act, in every case, *pro re nata*, & content themselves with the general principle, applied in all cases, & indiscriminately, of *opposing*. They will probably support Mr. [Levi]

Lincoln, agt. Mr *Mills*, from an idea that Mr Mills' appointment would gratify the friends of the President, or is a thing arranged, by his friends; although Mr Lincoln is known to be equally friendly. Some embarrassment may happen from this source, very possibly; but I trust it can be overcome.

I have great pleasure in assuring you that nothing can be more correct, or more decisive than public opinion, in this part of the Country, in regard to the various transactions of the last Session.

The sentiment of the People is exactly what you would expect & wish it to be.

In N. Hamp. the Legislature meets next week. The two Senators will doubtless be present, on that occasion, & we are looking with some interest to see whether Mr [Levi] Woodbury, & the Editor of the Patriot,[4] (publisher of the Laws!) will be able to bring the Legislature & people of that State to their way of thinking. I am, My Dear Sir, very truly yrs

D. Webster

ALS. DLC. Published in *W & S*, 16: 136–137; and in Hopkins and Hargreaves, *Papers of Henry Clay*, 5: 420–421.

1. Lloyd had resigned his Senate seat on May 23.

2. Silsbee took over Lloyd's seat on

December 6, 1826.

3. Mills was not a candidate for reelection. In the spring of 1827, the Massachusetts legislature elected Webster to Mills' vacated seat.

4. Isaac Hill.

FROM HENRY CLAY

Washington 14th. June 1826

My dear Sir

Your obliging favor of the 8th. inst.[1] came duly to hand. My health, about which you kindly express an interest, has improved since the adjournment of Congress, but is susceptible of further improvement, which I hope to realize on a journey, which I purpose commencing in 8 or 10 days to Kentucky.

We have heard of Mr [Nathaniel] Silsbee's appointment. He is a worthy, useful and (what, in these times, is no small recommendation) a perfectly faithful man. There would have been some advantages in your entering the Senate. Some too would have been lost by your leaving the House. You could not have taken, during the whole of the first Session of your Service in the Senate, the strong and commanding ground which you now occupy in the house. My opinion is that you acted wisely, for yourself and the Country, in deciding to remain where you are.

I have received, with much satisfaction, your favorable account of the state of public feeling and opinion, towards the Administration, in your quarter. We have similar accounts from every other quarter, less favorable it is true from the South, but far more encouraging in that direction than could have been inferred from the vote of the Southern representation, during the last Session. I have perfect confidence of the entire success of Mr. Adams. He will be re-elected by a vote of more than two-thirds of the Union. I am cordially & faithfy Yr. ob. Servt.   H. Clay

ALS. DLC. Published in Hopkins and Hargreaves, *Papers of Henry Clay,* 5: 434.
    1. See above.

FROM FRANCIS JOHNSON

Bowling Green
7th July 1826

Dear Sir
    Since my return I have seen many of my constituents and I have been to most of the Counties in the district—the Admn is popular—the opposition execrated. [John] Randolph, with the exception of a few Virginians never had any friends in this country. Calhoun had some friends chiefly in the Jackson ranks—now he has none or very few, desperate Jackson men excepted and perhaps not more than half a dozen in the district—no one who ever had any pretensions to greatness or popularity, has fallen so low and so irretrievably as Mr Calhoun, save it be Aaron Burr. There was a time, when the Hero *the mighty Hero* had some friends in this part of the state. They are now few indeed, he is following in the Vice Presidents wake. Mr Clay never was so strong in Kentucky as at the present time—he has no friend, but [who] is also the friend of the President so far as my knowledge extends and so in regard to Mr. Adams friends—the opposition have completely identified them —this is the feeling in my district so far as I have been informed. I entered Kentucky at Maysville on the Bank of the Ohio, which is 200 miles from here—the same feelings and sentiments appeared to me to prevail every where on my route. Louisville I am told, holds out yet—[Thomas] Metcalfe, [David] Trimble, & [James] Clark, will without doubt I think be re elected without opposition—so I think will [Richard A.] Buckner, and in all probability [Robert P.] Letcher—how I am to come off—I can't say. I am almost as it were in the Generals Neighbourhood—4 of the 6 counties of my district lead[?] on Tennessee and he lives near opposite the centre. A Jackson Candidate[1] has been in training for some months, tho' the Election does not come on for 13 months yet. It is said [Robert P.] Henry's Jackson speech & [George] McDuffies & others of that cast sent by him to his district will aid in defeating his Election if he should be a candidate. [Joseph] Lecompte cannot be re Elected. As to the other Jackson & opposition members I am not sufficiently in-

formed to speak. They will doubtless however be opposed—any man who would say here that Genl Jackson or any one else but Mr Adams, will get Kentucky at the next Election would be laughed at. It is the height of folly for the Hero or his friends to count on Kentucky.

The appointment of the Postmaster in Nashville[2] which made some bustle among the Hero's friends, is all right. I am told one may speak in terms of approbation now of the Admn. in Nashville without being insulted—in one of the Tennessee districts adjoining this, I am told they are going to run an Admn. candidate and they fancy with good prospect of success.

I have recently seen persons from Missouri & Illinois[.] [Daniel P.] Cook it is believed will be re Elected, his father in Law, Hon N[inian] Edwards being candidate for Governor it is thought will injure Cook some. Govr. Edwards & his opponents are riding post through the State & *stumping* it, as he calls it—and making speeches to every gathering of the people they meet with and so are the candidates for Congress. The Governor it is said, is silent in regard to the Admn—he is therefore no doubt a Calhoun man or a Jackson man, as well as his brother in law *Gen Duff Green* of the Telegraph—but he will be with the strongest presently.

The information from Missouri, renders Colo. [T. H.] Bentons re-Election to the Senate at best extremely doubtfull. [John] Scott is opposed by a Mr [Edward] Bates, (who I knew when we were boys) and who is represented to be an Adams man, and was so in the presidential Election. The Jackson party it seems cannot raise a candidate there. The election in both those states comes on next month. I met with Genl. [Marston G.] Clark[3] from Indiana a few days ago. He is a member of the Legislature of that state. He thinks the Hero will never get Indiana again. I passed 225 miles through Ohio on my way home. I found the people much more unanimous for the administration than I had supposed, tho I had calculated largely on Ohio. Mr [John W.] Campbell of that state, by whose place of residence I passed, declined a re Election in three or 4 days after he got home. I was told in Mr [John] Thompson's [Thomson's] district that he could not be re Elected—he had sent [Joseph] Lecomptes speeches & Bentons speeches in great quantities to his Constituents. I have just heard from Mr [William L.] Brents district in Louisiana by a Lawyer who resides there. He says the opposing candidate has made & is making great exertions, that Brent had not returned from the City—but he would be Elected even if he did not get back. Some accounts say [Henry H.] Gurley will be hard run—his old opponent is said to be out again. I have not learned the politics of the Candidates in Mississippi, but I presume an admn man will be Elected.

As I passed through Lexington in this state, a gentleman from Natchez had just before arrived, and gave it as his opinion that [Thomas B.] Reed could not easily be re Elected, on account of not voting for the Panama Mission and for voting against [John] Sergeant's appointment. The latter, he said, formed the greatest objection, not that they liked Mr Sergeant, but it was making a difference between men from slave & non slavery holding States. It was understood some how there, perhaps from his own letters—that he voted agt Sergeant's appointment because he was from a non slave holding State and because he had been some what the champion in the opposition to Missouri—opposition which upon that ground was not approved. They were opposed to raising any question about slave and non slave states, or making it a test in any way.

I assure you, that you are enquired after by the people, with interest —your rising, and conspicuously rising popularity in this country, has caused the Jackson & Calhoun papers in Tennessee to *belabor* you very much—and so much the better. They lie on you, excuse the word; as they do very many others—they go so far as to say you were of the Hartford Convention. This I knew to be false and have *as in duty bound* contradicted it; all they can say will avail nothing against you. Your course in Congress and your doctrine are admired and approved, and should you make the contemplated visit to this Country next summer, you will meet with many friends, whom you never saw. Your speech has silenced all opposition to the Panama Mission. I wish it were in every mans hand, in the opposition districts. [David] Trimbles speech is also very popular—*appropos*—I would write to some Bookseller or printer in Boston, who has the copyright of your Bunker Hill address, to contrive [?] a parcel of them to this state if I knew who to write to and they would find ready sale. I am often enquired of for it—the one which was sent to me has gone through many readings. The feelings of the people in this country is turning pretty fast from the south to your section of the Union—they begin to see the policy of the North assimilate nearer their own, than the South states. We sell much to the south—but they are against our manufacturies, roads & canals. I confidently say if Kentucky had to elect two Senators now, neither of the present incumbents could succeed. The vote of the Vice President agst. the Illinois Canal has helped him along down pretty smartly—or rather after being down, it has nailed him there—and there he will as he ought remain—Accept assurance of my respect & Esteem Yr friend &c.   Fr. Johnson

ALS. NhD.
1. Probably Henry Daniel, a Jacksonian elected to the Twentieth Congress; Johnson was not reelected.

2. For postmaster at Nashville, Adams and McLean had appointed John P. Erwin, who was opposed by most of the Tennessee delegation and

by Jackson himself. The appointment was attacked in the *United States Telegraph*, March 29, 31, April 5, July 5, 1826.

3. Clark (1769–1846), a Virginian by birth, had moved to Indiana via Kentucky; he had served with William Henry Harrison at Tippecanoe.

FROM JOHN EVELYN DENISON

London July 11. 1826.

My dear Sir

I received the other day your agreeable and instructive letter,[1] through the hands of Mr J[ohn Alsop] King. I was very sorry to miss Mr [Warren] Dutton. He came to London while I was engaged in Election matters in Staffordshire, & before my return he had left it. Col [Robert Kearsley] Dawson was fortunate enough to fall in with him, and I believe explained to Mr Dutton the cause of my absence, and [James Archibald Stuart-]Wortleys & [Edward George Geoffrey Smith] Stanleys. You follow the course of our public business so closely, and remark upon it so justly, that it is really superfluous in me to attempt to give you any information. I predicted truly the effect my Catholic vote would produce at Newcastle. I could not have carried my seat without a severe contest, and a great expenditure. I declined it under such circumstances; secured the return of my friend & colleague, Mr [Robert John] Wilmot Horton[2]—and myself shall be elected for Hastings at the opening of the Session—when the Gentleman now returned means to retire. I am happy to say the result of the Elections is upon the whole not unfavorable to the Catholic concessions. They have gained in Ireland, & lost something in England, and as far as prospective calculations can be relied upon there will be a majority of abt. 20 or 25. for sending the bill to the Lords. How will they conduct themselves? If the Parliament sits four sessions, and the H[ouse] of C[ommons] sends the bill up every session, I am inclined to think the Lords must make a great gulp and swallow it. I was very much obliged to you for the information contained in your letter abt. the system of Banking with you. I am collecting all the information I can on the very important question of the Currency. Should I be asking you a very troublesome favor, if I was to beg that you would send me over, a detailed acct. of the Banking System in Massachusetts. I do not mean to put so heavy a tax on your time, as to ask for a description of it under your own hand. But you wd. perhaps send me the general laws that regulate the Banks, and the principles on which they are conducted. How is the paper kept at par. We find here convertibility not to be a sufficient check. How are over issues controlled or rectified. Is there any general understanding among the Banks, and a mutual interchange & exchange of each others notes, as is the case in Scotland. I must regret that I did not look more closely into all this while I was at Boston. Pray furnish me with such facts, as may enable me to comprehend the merits of your system, wh[ich] I know to be so very good. I dined with Mr [William] Huskisson the other day, and took the liberty of showing him your letter; he desired me when I wrote to you, to make you his best compliments, to thank you for your obliging message, and to say, how greatly struck he had been with your speech on the Tariff, wh[ich] he had read with the greatest pleasure. I went yesterday to Sadbrook near Richmond a Villa of Mr W. Hortons, where Mr Huskisson dined—& Mr [John] Randolph, your notorious Virginian. I had not the pleasure of his acquaintance in America, but we had a good deal of conversation in the course of the evening, & I brought him back to London in my carriage. He is certainly an extraordinary man; with a very accurate memory stored with minute facts. As you & I agree in politics, naturally he and I did not. He astonished me by some of his doctrines abt. slavery, and by recommending the policy, & maintaining the practicability, of cutting the throats of every inhabitant of the Island of Hayti. After what I saw in the papers, I expected to see him put on his hunting shirt, but was disappointed.

I leave England the day after tomorrow, cross to Calais or Ostend, and shall pass up the Rhine into Switzerland. There I shall spend two months in the neighborhood of Lausanne with my friend Lord Sandon[3] who has taken a country house for the summer. October & November I shall pass at Paris, and return to look about me in England for two months before the meeting of Parliament. I fear it will be a winter of great distress. Indeed it must be one of extreme pressure and difficulty. The unprecedented drought has heightened and aggravated every cause of preexisting distress. The hay harvest wh[ich] generally affords employment for so many laborers, has passed over in a few days. Cattle are perishing for want of water, and pasture. The spring crops—oats, barley and beans, have failed almost universally. Wheat still looks well, but after so long a drought we fear a rainy harvest. Prices are continually falling, and the manufacturing interest does not yet begin to revive—& add to all this, the potato crop must fail in Ireland. I have drawn you a gloomy but a faithful picture of the present state of this country. We cannot quite agree among ourselves as to the cause of all this. Some maintain it arises purely from over trading—Some purely from the fluctuations of the currency—one proposes a metallic circulation, one a paper circulation, and the more depreciated, the better. I must question myself whether gr[ea]t attempts will not be made in Parliament to reconsider the amount of depreciation during the War, and to try to accommodate the present standard of money to that rate. It will be a most important session. The Corn Laws, the Catholic vote, the currency—the new commercial system will be violently attacked—and almost every weighty matter will come under discussion—West Indies again, & what is to be done with the Colonial Legislatures. I most earnestly hope the negotiations pending between our countries will be speedily and satisfactorily concluded. Your Government has a character in Europe for an encroaching and aggrandizing spirit, wh[ich] makes it difficult to treat with it on even terms. I wish all men in your country, or at least the prevailing party, held the language that you do. As an American I think I should be quite satisfied with the tone of dignified importance that you properly think becoming the situation of the U.S. As a neutral, I should think stronger language hardly consistent with friendly intercourse. I write freely to you, as I should do to an intimate friend in England. Certainly my earnest wish, is for the establishment of a perfect understanding between the two countries. That wd be as much for the honor and interest of both, as a bad understanding wd be injurious to both; and to many of the greatest and most important interests of the world.

I was much obliged to you for the speeches you were good enough to send me. Mr Huskissons speech on the shipping interests of the United Kingdom is not yet published in a separate pamphlet, nor is there anything new or worth your attention.

I shall be really obliged to you for the information abt. the Massachusetts banks—particularly since some conversation that I have had with Mr Huskisson abt. them. If you read the Report of the Chancery Commission, I should very much value your opinion. I must insist on having the Judges opinion at length. You may vote upon it in the H. of C. if you please. If you agree in a common judgment, I will confirm it by my vote—for I am sure I shall not have time to read it myself, or knowledge of the subject, or patience of investigation to form an opinion.

Thank Mrs Webster for her kind remembrances, and give all assurances of my esteem. I am writing in a great hurry. It is now midnight, and at 4 in the m[ornin]g, I am to be on board the steam boat that is to convey me to Calais. You say nothing of your visit to England. If you will come I don't know but I will enter into a compact to visit you at Boston again some summer agreed upon between us.

Best remem[brance]s to the good Judge, & believe me your sincere friend   J E Denison

ALS. DLC. Published in Curtis, 1: 276–279.

1. See above, DW to Denison, May 3, 1826.

2. Horton (1784–1841), political pamphleteer (*DNB*).

3. Dudley Ryder, Viscount Sandon (1798–1882) at this time represented Tiverton in the House of Commons.

Boisterous celebrations of the nation's fiftieth anniversary on July 4, 1826, gave way to reverent awe at the inscrutable ways of Providence as news of the almost simultaneous deaths of John Adams and Thomas Jefferson on that day moved slowly across the land. Newspaper columns were edged in black and memorial services were held in city, town, and hamlet from Maine to Florida and westward beyond the Mississippi. Differing hardly at all from hundreds of similar responses, the Boston City Council resolved "That these venerable Champions of Liberty should have commenced their political career at the same time—should have sustained the same important trusts and high offices—should have each contributed so essentially to the achieving of our Independence—should have lived to see their children's children realize the blessings of that Independence, which fifty years before they jointly risked their lives to secure to them—and should be summoned on the same day and almost at the same hour, to receive the reward of their virtue and patriotism—constitute a coincidence without parallel in the history of the world." Columbian Centinel, *July 19, 1826.*

Established statesmen, ministers of the Gospel, and ambitious local politicians vied with each other for the honor of commemorating the occasion by the spoken word. In Boston, by common consent, it was Daniel Webster who was invited to deliver the eulogy. According to Story's letter below, the orator-designate had some reservations. Since the speech was scheduled for August 2 in Faneuil Hall, the time was short for preparation of what would surely be his greatest public effort up to that time; but he agreed with Story that he could not refuse.

In search of fresh material, Webster turned to Timothy Pickering, himself a veteran of the Revolution. He requested and received copies of Pickering's correspondence with John Adams in 1822 about the Declaration of Independence and a copy of the address Pickering had delivered at Salem on July 4, 1823, in which the Adams correspondence and the Declaration had been discussed. It is probable that the section of Webster's eulogy which developed the imaginary conversation between Adams and an opponent of independence was based on Pickering's 1823 comments and on Adams' letter of August 6, 1822, to Pickering. Charles W. Upham, The Life of Timothy Pickering *(4 vols.; Boston, 1867–1873), 4: 335, 463–469.*

FROM JOSEPH STORY

Salem July. 11. 1826.

My dear Sir

I saw Mr [Jeremiah] Mason this morning & he wished much that I should go to Boston tomorrow to talk over the pending negotiations about an Eulogy. My own judgt is that you must & ought to deliver it. But I think that it ought not to be a mere city council affair, but a *State* affair, in *form at least*, so as to prevent any like attempt in other quarters; & to give a dignity to the occasion, which would make it felt in other states as well as abroad. I would go to Boston tomorrow if I could be sure I could lead in any direction so as to induce the Govr. & Council to act. But I am uncertain whether it would now be practicable, or whether your city authorities have not gone so far as to settle the course. If however I can be useful send me word & I will be up at a moments warning. Yours very truly & affectionately　Joseph Story

ALS. CtY.

FROM TIMOTHY PICKERING

Boston July 19. 1826.

Dear Sir,

Yesterday I received from my son Octavius[1] a letter informing me that you wished to see the original letter from Mr. John Adams, referred to in my prefatory remarks to reading the Declaration of Independence three years ago, and the remarks also: both are inclosed. And for the more precise understanding of Mr. Adams's letter, I also inclose the copy of mine, to which it is an answer, and of my reply, making my acknowledgements for that answer.[2] Of all these papers I pray you to take particular care, and to return them to me by my son, or other safe hand, when you shall have done with them.

All unpleasant feelings towards Mr. Adams, had ceased long before the occurrence of the above mentioned correspondence. A subsequent event obliged me, in my own vindication, to expose publicly his faults. Still I view, as I have always viewed him, as a man of eminent talents, zealously, courageously & faithfully exerted in effecting the Independence of the Thirteen United Colonies: and I believe that he, more than any other individual, roused and prepared the minds of his fellow citizens to decide positively and timely that greatest revolutionary question. Very respectfully, I am, dear Sir, your obedt. servt.　T. Pickering

ALS. NhHi. Published in Van Tyne, p. 695.

1. Octavius Pickering (1792–1868; Harvard 1810) was a Boston lawyer and reporter for the Supreme Judicial Court of Massachusetts. William T. Davis, *History of the Bench and Bar.* Vol. 1 of *Professional and Industrial History of Suffolk County, Massachusetts* (Boston, 1894), p. 280.

2. Webster had requested John Adams to Timothy Pickering, August 6, 1822, a copy of which may be found in the Adams Family Papers, Microfilm Reel 124; Pickering's letter to Adams, August 2, 1822, may also be found in the Adams Papers, Reel 456. A copy of Pickering's response to Adams, August 15, 1822, can be found in the Pickering Papers, MHi.

About the middle of May 1826 the ship Constitution, *homeward bound to Boston from the Pacific, docked at Nantucket with seventeen slaves aboard. They had been a part of the cargo of the schooner* Decatur, *bound from Baltimore to New Orleans. Some of the slaves, joined by some members of the crew, had mutinied at sea. The captain and mate were thrown overboard and a course was set for Haiti, but no navigator was left aboard, and the vessel was hopelessly lost when overtaken by the* Constitution. *Two men, eight women, and seven children were taken off at their own request and brought to Boston, where their owners, Austin Woolfolk of Baltimore and his brother John of Augusta, both notorious slave traders, sought to reclaim them, soliciting Webster's aid through Representative Forsyth of Georgia. The mutineers were tried in New York, where the* Decatur *was brought by a prize crew from the brig* Rooke. *No Massachusetts case is recorded, nor is there any evidence that Webster responded in any way to Forsyth's letter below.* Columbian Centinel, *May 20, 1826;* Niles' Weekly Register, *May 20, 1826; Frederic Bancroft,* Slave-Trading in the Old South *(Baltimore, 1931), pp. 39–42.*

FROM JOHN FORSYTH

Augusta 12. Aug. 1826

Dear Sir

Mr John Woolfolk a respectable citizen of this place will deliver you this letter written to introduce him to you. He is part owner of some slaves who were carried into Boston from on board the Schooner Decatur bound from Baltimore to New Orleans, & goes to your City to recover his property. As he apprehends that publick prejudice may create difficulties in his way he wishes the benefit of your professional services, which I have assured him no publick prejudice will prevent you from rendering.

I recommend Mr W to you as a man of property & probity. I am quite sure he will find much less prejudice in Boston than he has been led to believe exists there, on the subject of the species of property in which he has been unfortunately trading. I am Dr. Sir very sincerely Your obt. servant   John Forsyth

ALS. NhD.

FROM RICHARD RUSH

Washington August 30. 1826

Dear Sir,

Yesterdays mail brought me your discourse in commemoration of the lives and services of Adams and Jefferson pronounced at Boston on the 2nd of this month, and I have just finished reading it. If I were to say that it is able and eloquent, I should give it only the common praise of common productions. It takes much higher rank. It is full of commanding thoughts, full of elevated patriotism, full of profound criticism applied to the great subjects, individual and moral, that you had in hand. It is disencumbered of all that is little in its facts, of all that is of every day's hearing, in its reflections. The former are well chosen, and we have not too many of them; the latter are rich, condensed, elementary. There were parts that thrilled me. I read them to my family and they thrilled them too. The speech beginning at page 38 made my hair rise. It wears the character of a startling, historical, discovery, that bursts upon us at this extraordinary moment after sleeping half a century. Curiosity, admiration, the very blood, all are set on fire by it. Nothing of Livys ever moved me so much. Certainly your attempt to pass the doors of that most august sanctuary, the congress of 76, and become a listener and reporter of its immortal debates, was extremely bold, extremely hazardous. Nothing but success could have justified it, and you have succeeded.

I pray you, Sir, not to regard this letter as idle compliment. I intend it not in that spirit, but only as a momentary record of the true feelings with which I have risen from the perusal of so admirable a specimen of discriminating and philosophical eulogy; of a composition which I have found all over as animating as it is intellectual. With my thanks for the copy you have had the goodness to send me, I ask permission to tender you the assurances of my high respect & esteem.   Richard Rush.

ALS. NhD. Published in Curtis, 1 : 279–280.

TO CHARLES FOLSOM

Boston Septr. 22. 1826
Sir

I have to acknowledge the honor of your letter,[1] informing me that the Committee of the P[hi] B[eta] K[appa] had appointed me the Orator of the Society for the next year.

Although I feel bound to contribute my part, in any way, to the usefulness & reputation of the Society, yet I have recently had occasion to appear so often before the Public, that I feel entirely unwilling soon, again, to undertake a public performance. I hope the Committee will feel the weight of this reason; & be assured, that if it did not appear to me wholly insurmountable, I should not, as I now most respectfully must, decline the honor which they have proposed to confer on me. I am, Sir, with entire regard, Your ob. servt.   Danl. Webster

ALS. MB. Folsom (d. 1872; Harvard   in Italian.
1813), formerly tutor and librarian at   1. Not found.
Harvard, was, at this time, instructor

FROM NOAH WEBSTER

New Haven Septr. 30th 1826

Sir,

Having, since my return from Europe, had no opportunity of seeing you, I take this occasion to express to you my acknowledgements, for complying with my request, & procuring an act of Congress, enabling me to import copies of my Dictionary & Synopsis into the United States, free of the duties imposed by the tariff.[1] When I wrote to you from Cambridge (Eng.)[2] I had not offered my manuscripts to the booksellers, & supposed that I should find no difficulty in procuring them to be published. But after I went to London, I soon found that the principal publishers were engaged in a new edition of [Samuel] Johnson, & in a new work of a like kind; & they would not bring into market a work that might come into competition with those in which they were engaged. The smaller booksellers & publishers could not undertake so heavy a publication. One of the principal booksellers who examined my manuscript, said the work would maintain its ground in England, but his engagements would not permit him to undertake the publication. I am therefore obliged to wait for types to execute the work in this country; & this has caused a great delay. But this delay, I find, will be very useful to the work; & on the whole, I have reason to be well satisfied with the result, both of my voyage & of my application to the English Booksellers.

There is another subject, Sir, to which I take the liberty to invite your attention.

Since the celebrated decision, respecting copy-right, by the highest British tribunal,[3] it seems to have been generally admitted that an author has not a permanent & exclusive right to the publication of his original works, at common law; & that he must depend wholly on statutes for his enjoyment of that right. As I firmly believe this decision to be contrary to all our best established principles of *right* & *property*, & as I have reason to think such a decision would not now be sanctioned by the authorities of this country, I sincerely desire that while you are a member of the House of Representatives in Congress, your talents may be exerted in placing this species of property, on the same footing, as all other property, as to exclusive right & permanence of possession.

Among all the modes of acquiring property, or exclusive ownership, the act or operation of *creating* or *making* seems to have the first claim. If any thing can justly give a man an exclusive right to the occupancy

& enjoyment of a thing, it must be the fact that he has *made* it. The right of the farmer & mechanic to the exclusive enjoyment & right of disposal of what they make or produce, is never questioned. What then can make a difference between the produce of *muscular strength*, and the produce of the *intellect*? If it should be said, that as the purchaser of a bushel of wheat has obtained not only the exclusive right to the use of it for food, but the right to sow it, & make increase & profit by it, let it be replied, this is true; but if he sows the wheat, he must sow it on his own ground or soil. The case is different with respect to the copy of a book which a purchaser has obtained, for the *copy-right* is the author's soil, which the purchaser cannot legally occupy.

Upon what principle, let me ask, can my fellow-citizens declare that the productions of the farmer & the artisan shall be protected by common law, or the principles of natural or social right; without a special statute, & without paying a premium for the enjoyment of their property; while they declare that I have only a temporary right to the fruits of my labor, & even this cannot be enjoyed without a premium? Are such principles as these consistent with the established doctrines of property & of moral right & wrong among an enlightened people? Are such principles consistent with the high & honorable notions of justice & equal privileges which our citizens claim to entertain & to cherish, as characteristic of modern improvements in civil society? How can the *recent origin* of a particular species of property vary the principles of *ownership*? I say nothing of the inexpedience of such a policy, as it regards the discouragement of literary exertions. Indeed I can probably say nothing on this subject, that you have not said or thought—at least I presume you have often contemplated the subject in all its bearings.

The British Parliament, about ten or twelve years ago, passed a new act on this subject, giving to authors & proprietors of new works an absolute right to the exclusive use of the copy-right for 28 years, with some other provisions which I do not recollect. But the act makes or continues the condition that the author or proprietor shall deposit *eleven copies* of the work in Stationers' Hall, for the benefit of certain public libraries. This premium will often amount to fifty pounds sterling or more. An effort was made by the publishers to obtain a repeal of this provision; but it was opposed by the institutions which were to receive the benefit, & the attempt failed.

I have a great interest in this question; & I think the interests of science & literature, in the question, are by no means inconsiderable.

I sincerely wish our legislature would come at once to the line of right & justice on this subject, & pass a new act, the preamble to which shall admit the principle that an author has by common law, or natural justice, the sole & *permanent* right to make profit by his own labors, & that his heirs & assigns, shall enjoy the right, unclogged with conditions. The act thus admitting the right, would prescribe the mode by which it should be ascertained, secured & enjoyed, & violations of the right be punished—& further perhaps make some provisions for the case of attempts to elude the statute by slight alterations of books, by mutilations & transpositions.[4]

Excuse me Sir, for the trouble I give you—& believe me, with much respect, Your Obedt. Servt.   Noah Webster

ALS. NjMoHP. Published in *Letters of Noah Webster*, ed. Harry R. Warfel (New York, 1953), pp. 417–420.

1. On March 3, 1825, the act passed authorizing Noah Webster to import his work into the United States for five years at the rate that was then imposed on books in foreign languages. 6 *U.S. Statutes at Large* (*Private Laws*), 330.

2. See *Correspondence*, 1: 365–366.

3. Noah Webster was alluding to *Donaldson* v. *Beckett*, 1 *English Reports* 837.

4. For Daniel Webster's reply to this letter, see DW to Noah Webster, October 14, 1826, below.

TO JARED SPARKS

Oct. 12. 1826

My Dear Sir

I have read Mr [Jacob Newton] Cardozo's Book,[1] & looked into [John Ramsey] McCulloch; but the field spread out so wide before me, that I gave up the idea of entering upon it, with any view of writing.[2] A great part of Mr Cardozos Notes are taken up in commenting on [Adam] Smith & [David] Ricardo. The very statement of the questions in difference, between him & them, so as to be intelligible to general readers, would occupy the space of a short Article. I must confess, moreover, that there is a great deal of solemn common place, and a great deal also of a kind of metaphysics, in all or most of the writers on these subjects. There is no science that needs more to be cleared from mists than that of political economy: If we turn our eyes from Books to things, from speculation to fact, we often, I think, perceive that the definitions, & the rules of these writers, fail in their application. If I live long enough, I intend to print my own thoughts, (not however, in any more bulky form, than a Speech, or an Article in the N[orth] A[merican Review]) on one or two of the topics, discussed by Mr Cardozo. But when that leisure day, necessary even to so small an effort, may come, is more than I can say. Yours very truly   Danl. Webster

ALS. MH. Published in Van Tyne, pp. 695–696.

1. *Notes on Political Economy* (Charleston, 1826).

2. Earlier in the year Sparks had asked Webster to review McCulloch's

Principles of Political Economy. See Sparks to Webster, March 14, 1826, and Webster to Sparks, March 20, 1826, above. A review of McCulloch's *Political Economy,* written by Caleb Cushing, appeared in the *North American Review,* 25 (July 1827): 112–153; J. Porter's review of Cardozo's work appeared in 24 (January 1827): 169–187.

Webster approached the second session of the Nineteenth Congress very much in the attitude of party leader. He had a definite legislative program for which he sought to organize support before Congress met. Carryovers from earlier sessions were bankruptcy legislation and reorganization of the judiciary. To these was now added a tariff on woolens, marking both the changing economic pattern of his constituency and the first partial reversal of his own antitariff stand of 1824.

TO JOHN C. WRIGHT

Boston Oct. 12. '26

My Dear Sir

Our woolen manufacturers are meeting with great difficulties, from the low prices of the imported article, & the high price of wool. It is supposed that several of the establishments, this way, will stop unless relieved by a further interposition of the Govt., either to reduce the tax on wool, or enhance that on cloth. I suppose your neighbours, engaged in that line of business, have heard, or will hear from their friends in this quarter; and I mention the subject to you now, by request, in order that you may confer with them on the subject, preparatory to the meeting of Congress. It always seemed to me that the tax on foreign wool was injudicious; and although I remain fully of opinion that the Tariff is, in general, high enough, &, in relation to some articles, decidedly *too high*, I yet feel that Congress, by the late act, did undertake to give a certain degree of *"Protection,"* to the woolen manufactures, which they have not realized, in consequence of the high duty on the raw material. And on this account, I think a state of things may occur, in which some alteration may be expedient.

On one other subject I hope you will come prepared with an opinion; that is the *Judiciary.* Our very good friends in the Senate may, perhaps, think to anticipate us, & to send us, immediately after the commencement of the session, *their bill,*—leaving the responsibility on us. Shall we be before hand with them?—or what course shall we take?

I shall feel it my duty to bring forward the Bankrupt Bill, as soon as possible; & I hope you will aid therein, & find leisure to look over the bill.

We hear nothing yet of yr elections. I suppose indeed that you are at this moment engaged in them. Mr [Elisha] Whittlesey wrote me a letter of pretty good *anticipations*, some months ago.[1] I trust your constituents will send you back, notwithstanding all your sins. Your Speech, at the dinner given you, was in the right spirit, & [I] think must have produced an effect. Our elections are the first of next month. They do not excite much attention. There will probably be few changes. [Aaron] Hobart declines; [John] Varnum has an antagonist, & probably [Samuel] Lathrop, [Henry W.] Dwight & [Samuel C.] Allen will also find that others are willing to take their places. These differences, however, will not respect support or opposition to the Govt. I suppose Mr. [Francis] Baylies will not be a candidate. To [John] Davis, [John] Locke, [John] Reed, [John] Bailey & [Benjamin W.] Crowningshield, I imagine there will be no opposition. Nothing is yet said or done in this District. We have here a Jackson *paper* & a Jackson *party*.[2] Whether they will think it expedient to nominate a *Candidate*, in the Genl's interest, is more than I know. The Maine elections are very well. In N. Hamp the choice takes place in March. The Legislative Caucus has nominated all the present members except [*Nehemiah*] *Eastman.*

I should be very happy to hear from you, if you find time & leisure to favor me with a line before our respective times of departure for Washington. I shall not leave home earlier than the 25th Novr. Yours with entire regard,   Danl Webster

I omitted to mention Mr. E[verett]. He is likely to come in again, notwithstanding his one *heresy*.[3] Probably no body will be proposed against him.

ALS. NjMoHP.

1. Letter not found.

2. The Jackson paper to which Webster referred was probably David Henshaw's *Boston Statesman.*

3. Everett's "heresy" was a defense of slavery introduced into a speech opposing a proposal to amend the Constitution as to the manner of presidential elections. "Domestic slavery, though I confess not that form of servitude which seems to be most beneficial to the master—certainly not that which is most beneficial to the servant—is not, in my judgment, to be set down as an immoral and irreligious relation." Everett began, and ended, his brief passage on slavery with a protest against the three-fifths ratio, arguing that Adams ap-

peared to be a minority president only because of the inflated electoral vote thus given to the southern states. The blow was softened by kind words for the peculiar institution, including the Biblical proslavery argument and a favorable comparison of southern *of Debates*, 19th Cong., 1st sess., pp. labor with that of Europe. (*Register* 1578–1580). According to Representative Charles Miner of Pennsylvania, Everett had submitted his "first position" to Webster, who had approved it. (Miner to his wife, March 15, 1826, quoted in Charles Francis Richardson and Elizabeth Miner Richardson, *Charles Miner, a Pennsylvania Pioneer*, Wilkes-Barre, Pa., 1916, pp. 114–115). Since Webster regarded Everett's defense of slavery as heresy, we may presume that the position he approved was the criticism of the three-fifths ratio. With respect to slavery itself, Webster shared the attitude of many conservative New Englanders in opposing any extension of the system but accepting it where it existed. It was on this ground that he had opposed the Missouri Compromise. Although mili-

tant abolitionism was not yet a force to be reckoned with, Everett was sharply taken to task both by House colleagues and by private citizens. Indeed he never quite lived down the indiscretion of his maiden speech in the House. Paul Revere Frothingham, *Edward Everett* (Boston, 1925), pp. 104–108.

TO HENRY CLAY

Boston Oct. 13. 1826

My Dear Sir

The subject of the recent British *Order*[1] is exciting some little attention, as you will have observed, in the Commercial Cities, & there are those, doubtless, [who] would embrace this, as they would any opportunity, to find fault.

Mr [James] Lloyd has probably written you, in regard to it.[2] He feels more than a common share of interest, on the occasion, as he recommended negotiation, in preference to meeting the English proposition by an Act of Congress. It may be well, perhaps, that some little statement, *made at Washington*, should appear, for the satisfaction of the public. I would not intimate that there is, in this part of the Country at least, any *dissatisfaction*; but I see attempts are making, in N. York & other places, to produce an impression that the National interests have, in this instance, been overlooked.

As to the general course of political affairs, we have nothing of much interest in this quarter. Our elections take place next month. In some Districts there may be personal changes, but nobody will be proposed on the ground of opposition, nor any body chosen who is suspected, on good grounds, of being *inclined to join the opposition*. Some few, perhaps, may be chosen, who profess friendship, & who will yet fly off, on the first, & on every, close question, according to the example of last winter. But on the whole, the great majority, from this quarter, will be well inclined, & steady in their course. The Jackson paper in this City[3] (for *we* have also a Jackson paper) seems to occupy itself at present very much with Mr. [Edward] Everett. Mr Everett, however, is likely to be reelected with great unanimity. I think, My Dear Sir, without intending a compliment, that your Speech at Lewisburgh has done real service.[4] It was happy & excellent, even for *you*, both in matter & manner. We all rejoice here—I mean all who do not fear that you were born to prevent Genl. J. from being President, in the improvement of your health; & you must allow me to express my most anxious & earnest hope that you will not *over-work* yourself, the ensuing session & winter. What cannot be done without the sacrifice of your health, must be left undone, at whatever expense or hazard. I have often thought of suggesting to you one practice, if you have not already adopted it, which I have found very useful myself, when my own little affairs have occasionally pressed me; that is, the constant employment of an *amanuensis*. The difference between writing at the table, & dictating to another, is very great. The first is tedious, exhausting, debilitating labor; the last may be done while you are pacing a large room, & enjoying in that way, the benefit of an erect posture, & a healthy exercise. If I were you I would not touch a pen, except to write my frank. Make the Clerks do all that Clerks can do, & for the rest, dictate to an Amanuensis. I venture to say, that if you once get accustomed to this, you will find your labour greatly lightened.

I have had the pleasure of hearing from several Kentucky & Ohio friends, during the summer; & have had much gratification in learning the favorable state of opinion in those important States. The only incident to be regretted much, in the West, is the loss of [Daniel Pope] Cook's election. His friends must remember him, & sustain him, in some public service, according to his merits. I am, Dr. Sir, with unvarying regard & esteem Yrs   Danl. Webster

ALS. DLC. Published in *W & S*, 16: 138–139; and in Hopkins and Hargreaves, *Papers of Henry Clay*, 5: 790–792.

1. The Order in Council of July 27, 1826, to which Webster referred, excluded American vessels from the British ports in the West Indies, South America, and Newfoundland. See Albert Gallatin to Henry Clay, August 19, 1826, in Hopkins and Hargreaves, 5: 629–632.

2. See Lloyd to Clay, October 16, 1826, in Hopkins and Hargreaves, 5:801.

3. *Boston Statesman.*

4. On August 30, 1826, at a public dinner in his honor, Clay had delivered a speech at Lewisburg, Virginia, in which, among other things, he defended his acceptance of the State Department post. The text of Clay's remarks appears in Hopkins and Hargreaves, 5: 654–661.

TO WILLIAM BUELL SPRAGUE

Boston Oct. 14. 1826

Dear Sir

I believe you have collected nearly every thing, in the shape of a pamphlet, that has been published as a production of mine. I think of but one, which you have not on your list: a fourth of July Address, at Concord N. H. 1806.[1] Of that Address, I have but one copy, & would send you that, but that it is bound up with other pamphlets. Probably I may obtain a copy when I next visit N. Hamp.

I fear, My Dear Sir, that you do *me* no great service by preserving even single copies of some of these things. I am aware that many of them are puerile, others indifferent, & none of much merit. If your collection were confined to pamphlets of *value*, I should not look up any unfound production of mine. As in your collection, however, the rich & the poor, the high & the low, are to lie down together, I will remember to get for you, if I can, the Address at Concord, that it may be joined in the great congregation, & forgotten, in company wih many others better than itself.

I have sometimes heard of you, My Dear Sir, in Boston as I often hear of you elsewhere; & if you will, when next here, give me the opportunity of making your personal acquaintance, you will confer a favor on Your very Ob. friend & sert   Danl Webster.

Be kind eno. to give my regards to Mr [Samuel] Lathrop.

ALS. NhHi.

1. See mDWs for Webster's July 4, 1806, address "delivered before the Federal Gentlemen of Concord and its vicinity." No copy of the address has been found in the Sprague Collection, CtY.

TO NOAH WEBSTER

Boston Oct. 14 1826

Dear Sir,

I have received yours of the 30th of September,[1] and shall, with your permission, lay it before the Committee of the Judiciary, next session, as that committee has in contemplation some important changes in the law respecting copy-right. Your opinion in the abstract, is certainly right & incontrovertible. Authorship, is, in its nature, ground of property. Most people, I think, are as well satisfied, (or better) with the reasoning of Mr Justice [Joseph] Yates, as with that of Lord Mansfield,[2] in the great case of Miller & Taylor.[3] But after all, property, in the social state, must be the creature of law; & it is a question of expediency, high & general, not particular expediency, how & how far, the rights of authorship should be protected. I confess frankly that I see, or think I see objections to making it perpetual. At the same time I am willing to extend it further than at present, & am fully persuaded that it ought to be relieved from all charges, such as depositing copies, &c. Yours
D Webster.

LC. NN. Published in Horace E. Scudder, *Noah Webster* (Boston, 1882), pp. 61–62.

1. See above.
2. Yates (1722–1770); William Murray, first Earl of Mansfield (1705–1793) (*DNB*).
3. *Millar* v. *Taylor*, 98 *English Reports* 201. In the case *Wheaton* v. *Peters*, 8 Peters 591–595 (1834), the

first copyright case before the Supreme Court, Webster appealed to the Millar decision as precedent on behalf of the plaintiff. Maurice G. Baxter, *Daniel Webster & the Supreme Court* (Amherst, 1966), pp. 147–152.

FROM STEPHEN VAN RENSSELAER

Albany Octo 26. 1826.

Dear Sir

I received your letter last Evening[1] on my return from attending the wedding of Mr C[harles] King.[2] Your proposal is very flattering to me to be associated with you next session of Congress.

I had last summer when [Louis] McLane was at my house agreed that he should provide for us comfortable accommodations. I have not heard from him since the Election. I regret that it will probably be out of my power to accept your invitation. We are all in a tumble here. Our politicians wax warm—the Bucktails having nominat[ed] Administration men provokes the Clintonians & I suspect alarms them. [William Beatty] Rochester will receive a considerable vote if not a majority—as many of Mr. Adams friends will support him who were friendly to [DeWitt] Clinton at the last Election. My most respectful regards to Madam. Yours truly   V Rensselaer

ALS. DLC.
1. Not found.
2. On October 20, 1826, Charles

King, editor of the *New York American*, had married Henrietta Liston Low.

The fall of 1826 was the critical period in the dissolution and recombination of factions from which the second American party system was to emerge. Campaigning for the Twentieth Congress and for state and local offices was influenced to greater or lesser degree by the efforts of those who opposed the Adams administration to revive the alliance of New York and Virginia that had put the Jeffersonians in power in 1800. Prime movers were Martin Van Buren, whose Albany Regency had absorbed the northern following of William H. Crawford; Thomas Ritchie of the Richmond Enquirer; *and Vice President John C. Calhoun, who would bring to the combination southern antitariff support. The ultimate beneficiary would be Andrew Jackson.*

The "Old Republicans" of Massachusetts were divided in their allegiance, some making common cause with Adams while others were already dedicated to the election of Jackson in 1828. It was the latter group that kept Webster from a unanimous caucus nomination to represent the Suffolk District for a third term. Calling themselves "Democrats," they put up another Boston lawyer, Henry Barney Smith (1789– 1861; Harvard 1809) in opposition. Webster won the election by a landslide, but a base was thus laid for the future substantial growth of the Jacksonian coalition in Massachusetts.

TO HENRY CLAY

Nov. 6. [1826]

Private

Dear Sir

The [Boston] Patriot of today which I send you, will shew you how we go here. There is a busy, but very small, party, ready in "the General's" interest. They do not incline to make a nomination for Congress; but they have been very industrious *to prevent the re-election of the present incumbent from appearing to be the Act of the Republican Party.* The meeting last evening has settled that matter. There will probably be but few votes given, but they will, I presume, indicate no great division of sentiment.[1]

Mr. [Edward] Everett is unopposed; so is [Benjamin] Crowningshield & [John] Davis. A counter nomination has been made agt. [John] Bailey, but it will come to nothing. [John] Reed will be re-elected & so will [John] Locke, probably. In the Districts now represented by [Samuel] Lathrop & [Samuel] Allen, there may be some diversity of opinion, & our law requiring a *majority*, more than one trial may perhaps be found necessary, in these & possibly in other Districts. These differences & preferences, however, are all personal or local; the only *political* change likely to occur being in Bristol District, where a *friend* to the present Administration will succeed Mr. [Francis] Baylies.[2]

The results in N. Jersey & Ohio are highly important.[3] I hope they will produce a proper influence on *New York.* Mr. [Robert S.] Rose was here a few days since. He says nobody is proposed on the ground of opposition to the present general Administration; but he knows not what may happen, from other views & motives. The political men in New York revolve round a centre of their own. Their bearing on the general government is uncertain. I think the course which Mr [DeWitt] Clinton is pursuing is plain enough. My opinion is, that born to fluctuate between extremes of fortune, he is not now *rising*; & that his decline is near. Yours very truly   D. Webster

Col [Henry W.] Dwight, it would seem, has *declined*, on the very eve of the election. I know not the reason.

ALS. DLC. Published in Hopkins and Hargreaves, *Papers of Henry Clay*, 5: 872–873.

1. In the canvass, Webster received 1545 votes; Smith and others of his opponents received 123. *Columbian Centinel*, November 8, 1826.

2. With the exceptions of Samuel Lathrop and Francis Baylies, all of the other incumbents mentioned by

Webster were reelected. James L. Hodges succeeded Baylies; and Isaac C. Bates of Northampton succeeded Lathrop.

3. In New Jersey and Ohio the administration forces had won decisive victories over their opponents.

FROM HENRY CLAY

Washn. 10th. Nov. 1826

(Private)

My dear Sir

I congratulate you on your nomination by the Republican party, although we really have in this Country no other than a Republican party. Names may be gotten up or kept up in particular States for local or personal purposes, but at this time there are but two parties in the Union, that of the Administration and the Opposition. You will share with me in the gratification which is derievable from the success which has attended the former in N. Jersey, Ohio &c. I consider it as altogether decisive.

I thank you for the view which your obliging letter of the 6th. inst. presents of public affairs in your quarter.[1] I am sorry that [Henry W.] Dwight declines, as he is both a very good and highly honorable fellow. If [Henry] Shaw can come in his place, I should find some consolation in the change.

I have just completed a paper on the colonial question.[2] I am greatly deceived if we do not furnish in it to our friends strong and impregnable ground to stand on. I think the Opposition will be as much taken in as they were on the Panama question. Yours' ever & faithfully   H Clay

ALS. DLC. Published in Hopkins and Hargreaves, *Papers of Henry Clay*, 5: 889.

1. See above.

2. See Henry Clay to Albert Gallatin, November 11, 1826, in Hopkins and Hargreaves, *Papers of Henry Clay*, 5: 895–916.

FROM GRACE FLETCHER WEBSTER

Boston Dec. 2d 1826

My dear Husband,

The last accounts I had from you was a letter from Princeton.[1] I am sorry there was no prospect of sport for you. To day I hope you are safe at Baltimore. I could not sleep quietly last night thinking of the discomfiture you probably were enduring between Steam Boats and Stage Coaches and perhaps worse. But still trusting in that Power, which has hitherto preserved I would not indulge in unreasonable fears and anxieties. You & [James] William [Paige] have doubtless sepperated and if he is prospered will soon be with us. Poor Mr [Elijah Hunt] Mills left here on Monday last. His wife has gone with him. I saw a letter from him to Mr [George] Blake. I fear there is but little ground to hope that he will see again his home and his family. Mr. B. tho't he wrote in pretty good spirits but I am quite sure he thinks there is not much hope in his case.

We are all well and happy as the state of things will admit. We had a very pleasant dinner at Mrs [Israel] Thorndikes. The children were quite delighted. It is quite an epoch in their lives. They never dined at such a table before—it was truly elegant. There seemed, however, a small diminution to Julias pleasure to perceive that things were so much more elegant than mine.

A carriage Mrs Bien [?][2]—and then a number of other ladies—Mrs B. desires to be remembered to you—and is gone with all the others excepting Mrs [George] Ticknor[.] She waits till I finish so I will only add her affectionate remembrance to that [of] your aff[ectiona]te   G W.

ALS. NhHi.   2. Not identified.
    1. Not found.

TO GRACE FLETCHER WEBSTER
                                Decr. 4. [1826] Monday Eve'
My Dear Love,

I have made an engagement to take lodgings at a Mr. McIntire's,[1] P[ennsylvania] avenue, between Mrs [Ann Eliza] Peyton's, & [Jesse] Brown's, on the opposite side. It is a new house, & the *people* seem to be good people. I have a large room, in front, to myself, & a very comfortable lodging room. There are some other persons living in the house, but my establishment is all to myself. *Charles [Brown]* is to be my servant[2] —I am to take possession tomorrow, & present prospects are favorable.

I dined today at Mrs [John] Coyles. Her house is not yet full. She says she has never had so much difficulty in making up a mess. Mr [Thomas H.] Williams, Mr [Francis] Baylies, Mr [John] McKeé, & Mr [Henry R.] Storrs are there; & nobody else at present. You will hardly be sorry to hear that poor old Mary is dead. She was sick all summer, & Mrs Coyle says she was a perfect slave to her many months—not an unjust retribution. She died a month ago.

Mrs Everett is well, & things look there much as formerly. I am going up this Eve' to see the Presidt. Ys always   D. Webster

I have your letter, of Thanksgiving day;[3] & [James] Williams from New York.[4]

ALS. NhHi.

1. Webster was the only representative lodging at McIntire's.

2. Brown, formerly a slave, had recently had his freedom purchased by Webster, with whom he remained as servant for many years. Curtis, 2: 20.

3. See mDW 5716.

4. Not found.

TO GRACE FLETCHER WEBSTER

Washington, Dec. 6. [1826]

My Dear Love,

I am so happy as to have rec[eive]d yours of the 2nd instant,[1] & to hear of the health & happiness of you all. For two days I have been busy in getting into my new lodgings; & by tomorrow Eve' hope to have all things in order. I am a good deal like Robinson Crusoe. I have an outer room, & an inner one for retreat, & a man Friday; & beside Friday, am quite alone. Thus far every thing looks well. The keepers of the house seem to be very obliging, neat, good people; & for convenience of work & business I have never been better off here. I am sorry to find that my *Books* have suffered much. They look as if they had all been tumbled into the cellar together. However, I hope in a day or two to get the mould off, tho' the scratches & bruises are likely to remain.

Mrs Brown[2] gave her *first* party last night. Having occasion to go to the Presidents, I called on my return. It was the assemblage, pretty much, of a Washington party of last year. Mrs [Francis] Johnson[3] was there, & spoke of you with great kindness, & inquired for you very particularly. Her youngest boy is six weeks old. Many other Ladies, (& Gentlemen also,!) asked after your welfare with much apparent interest, & one of them pronounced you a favorite of the whole city. Mr. [Charles] Vaughan is unbounded in his thanks for what he calls our kindness at Boston; &, by way of proof, has invited me to a small dinner on Monday. Mrs [Joseph] Lovell[4] has a party on Friday. And this, I believe, is all the Washington news I have.

I thank Julia for her very good & kind letter,[5] & Master D[aniel] for his imitation of an obedient medal. Whatever is properly *obedient* I hope he will continue successfully *to imitate*. I shall write Julia soon. I hope Edward will not suffer me much longer to languish for [a let]ter from his pen. A single one of his [deli]cate & delightful scrolls, would give me pleasure.

Adieu, My Dear G—give my love "to all the House."   D. W.

ALS. NhHi.

1. See above.

2. Not identified.

3. Wife of the Kentucky congressman.

4. Wife of the Surgeon General.

5. Not found.

TO GRACE FLETCHER WEBSTER

Washington Decr 8. [1826]
friday Eve'

My Dear Love

I am happy to have a letter today from Uncle [James] William [Paige],[1] under a Boston date. He seems to have had a rapid passage home, & informs me you were all well, Monday Morning. I am at length pretty well settled, in my new abode, & well pleased with it.

Together with this, I send a little box, in which when you have taken all the paper off, & opened it, you will find two little bits of articles, designed as presents. One of them, if you like it, you will place in your own cap; & the other in Col Paige's ruffle. Give him a box on the ear, & tell him to be a good boy. The one intended for him, is that with a single stone, & *pillar*. If you do not fancy yours, you can return it to me, in the same little box, & the proprietor will take it back again. If he does not fancy his, tell him he is no true man. Intending to put a thing of this kind in the Col's shirt, I sent for one, & the jeweller sent me two, to make a choice from. They both seemed pretty; & Mr [Jules von] Wallenstein thought the one with three stones would be very proper for a Lady. So I send both.

Mrs [Joseph] Lovell has a party tonight; & if I am not too sleepy at 8 oclock, I intend to go.

I hope to hear from you tomorrow, as I have no letter today.

Adieu—with love to all. Yrs always   D. W.

ALS. NhHi.
1. Not found.

TO NATHAN HALE

Washington Decr. 14. [1826]

My Dear Sir

I sent you yesterday the correspondence on the Colonial subject. Mr Clay's dispatch of the eleventh of November recapitulates the whole case, & states it, as you probably will think, ably & clearly. I very much doubt whether Mr. [George] Canning fully understood the effect & operation of all the Acts of Parliament, at the time he wrote his letter to Mr. [Albert] Gallatin.

You will see the Annual Report of the Secretary in the papers; & I shall send it to you in pamphlet form, when so printed. With the exception of a few paragraphs of speculative opinion, the Report is clear, able, & satisfactory. Mr [Richard] Rush has shown, I think, that he judged better than our Committee of W[ay]'s & M[ean]'s last year.

The Senate's Committee seem in earnest on the Bankrupt Bill. It is now thought best not to bring forward the subject in H. R. till we see what progress is made, in the course of this month, in the Senate, on the same matter.

I hope you are enjoying the same fine clear & moderate weather which we have here.

P.S. *Dec. 15.* Mr [Ichabod] Bartlett's resolution,[1] which, as you see, passed today, will probably do us good. We shall now write the Govr., I think, & recommend the appt. of some *agent*, to look into the matter, & see on what principles the claims of other States have been paid. If there be no impropriety, in appointing a M[ember of] C[ongress] *Davis* wd. be the best man to be found.

Mr E[verett] was not in the House today. He was kept at home by a headache.

I do not get yr *paper*.[2] Please order it sent. Tomorrow we shall know who is Mayor. What shall I do, if you rob me of my *shooting* companion? Yrs   D. W.

The *bitterness* of most [of] the Jackson men to our claim is excessive. [William] Drayton is an exception. He seems to have conscience, even in politics.

N.B. Mr J[ohn] Randolph is here, to get a Congress confirmation of the Lottery, &c. The effort will be in vain. I told him, today, that we should naturally wait to see what lead the Va. members would give. He said, "they wd. do nothing."—If so, why should *we* do anything?

ALS. MHi. Published in *W & S*, 16: 139–140.

1. Bartlett's resolution was to transfer the question of Massachusetts claims from the House of Representatives to the Secretary of War. *Register of Debates*, 19th Cong., 2d sess., 1826–27, pp. 531–537.

2. Boston *Daily Advertiser*.

TO [NICHOLAS BIDDLE]

Washington Dec. 28. 1826

Dear Sir

Mr [Louis] McLane has been home, for a fortnight, & returned only the day before yesterday. I have spoken to him on the Bank-note-signature Bill, and he says he will now immediately bring it forward.[1]

I learn from Baltimore that the Bank has very considerable sums depending in that City also, on the *Richmond* question. I have been busy a little with preparation for that case,[2] & hope to be able to bring the opinion of the Chief Justice into some doubt. Yours   D. Webster

ALS. PU.
    1. No action was taken on the measure during the second session of the Nineteenth Congress.
    2. *Bank of the United States* v. *Dandridge*, 12 Wheaton 64 (1827).

FROM NICHOLAS BIDDLE

Philada. Jany 2 1827

My Dear Sir

Our friend Mr [David] Sears[1] who has been attending the Board for the last week informs us that he will not be able to return to our meetings at this season of the year, and desires us to fill his place. This has given us an opportunity of which we gladly avail ourselves to ask you to come into the general Board of Directors at the election which takes place to day. You will accordingly be elected. I hope this will be acceptable to you, as it is very gratifying to me personally. With great respect & regard Yrs   N. Biddle

LC. DLC.
    1. Sears (1787–1871; Harvard 1807), a wealthy Boston merchant and sometime legislator, was at the time a director of the Bank of the United States. *MHi Proc.*, Series 2, 2(1885–86): 405–429.

FROM JOHN TEMPLE WINTHROP

Jan. 4. 1826 [1827]

My dear Sir,

It was my purpose to have written you before the commencement of the Session of our Legislature, but have been prevented. Among the most important of the duties which devolve upon us is the choice of a Senator. From such information as I can gather, I have reason to think that there will be a strong effort made by a certain class of politicians to prevent the re-election of Mr. [Elijah Hunt] Mills, under any circumstances. Much use will be made of his reported incapacity, from ill health, for discharging the arduous labours of his situation. There is a variety of opinions on this subject, and altho. I have some and heard of many letters from Washingon touching the actual state of Mr M's health, yet I have no certainty of information. Nor have my friends. May I therefore ask the favour of your writing me a few lines for the purpose of ascertaining my mind, and enabling me to speak with somewhat of certainty in answer to questions put. Mr J[ames] T[recothick] Austin has said I understand that Mr. G[eorge] Blake would be a proper successor; but this is as you know a departure from the immemorial custom of Comm[onweal]th, in taking one Senator from each of the great sections and interests. It is said that the present Gov. altho' not desirous of the situation, would if chosen, probably accept. In addition to these, Mr. Speaker [William C.] Jarvis[1] and Mr. [John] Mills,[2] Prest. of Senate, have been talked of. I hope you are Sir in the enjoyment of health. The choice of Senator will probably come on at an early period of the Session. I have no means of accounting for the very remarkable result of the proposition for nominating Gen. Jackson in So. Carolina. Can [it] be correct, as stated, that the vote was unanimous?[3] With great respect, Your ob. St.   J. Temple Winthrop

ALS. DLC. Winthrop (d. 1843; Harvard 1815), was a Boston lawyer, having studied with William Prescott.

1. Jarvis represented Charlestown in the state legislature, serving as speaker of the lower house in 1826 and 1827; in 1828 he was elected state senator.

2. Mills, a Springfield lawyer, had served in the state legislature for many years. In 1826, he also served on the Massachusetts-Connecticut boundary commission and in 1842 on the northeastern boundary commission.

3. The South Carolina legislature had nominated Jackson for the presidency on December 19, 1826. The *Columbian Centinel*, January 3, 1827, reported mistakenly that the vote had been unanimous. The actual vote stood 135 to 2, in favor of Jackson. *Niles' Register*, 31 (January 6, 1827): 290.

TO NICHOLAS BIDDLE

Washington Jan. 6. [1827]

My Dear Sir,

I thank you for your kind note, on the subject of my election as a Director of the Bank.[1] I fear it will not [be] in my power to render you much service. Whenever, however, my attendance at the Board may be agreeable to you, it will give me pleasure to attend. I suppose that once or twice a year is as often as you desire the presence of the distant Directors. Yours very truly & sincerely   Danl. Webster

ALS. DLC.

1. See above, January 2, 1827.

TO EMELINE COLBY WEBSTER

Washington Jan. 16, 1827

My Dear Cousin,

I forward you a communication which the Doctor[1] put into my hands for that purpose. I have recd, My Dear Cousin, your two letters,[2] for which I am much obliged to you. I hope you are aware of the interest I feel, for your welfare & happiness, & of the pleasure it will give me to continue & cultivate your acquaintance. You decided right, I believe, as to the proposed journey to this place; although you know there are those who would be most glad to see you. The Doctor's affairs appear to go on pretty well, & he seems happier than heretofore, in some respects; but I believe his intelligence from Mrs [Mary Choate] Sewall[3] is not favorable.

The gay world here is given to balls & parties, much as usual. Having, this winter, no duties to perform, in the character of an attendant on Ladies, I see these social assemblages seldom. The Baron [Durand de] Mareuil (French Minister) leaves us in the Spring; an event which I believe all Washington contemplates with regret.

Congress & the Court now begin to be somewhat attractive. I saw a crowd of Ladies, in each place, yesterday, but knew none of them. As yet there has been no interesting debate. Mr. [John] Randolph has scarcely opened his mouth, for the session; so that people do not go to the Senate *to see the show.* As Va. has refused to reelect him, for the next Congress, it cannot be foreseen whether he will remain silent, or break out with new vehemence.

The session is passing off; & in two months I hope to be home. You must consider it as a settled thing that you come to Boston in April, & pass some time with us. Doctor Sewall will probably visit N. E. in May or June. In the mean time, My Dear Cousin, I hope you will allow me to hear from you, & continue to make [me] the channel of communication to your friends here. Yours very affectionately   Danl. Webster

The Doctor has been long looking for Doctor [Reuben D.] Muzzy,[4] but he has not yet arrived. Let me hear from you *soon.*

ALS. DMaM. Emeline Colby Webster (1808–1892) was the daughter of Rebecca Guild Sewall and John Ordway Webster of Maine. On October 28, 1828, she married Harvey Lindsly (1804–1889), a prominent Washington physician. Both of the Lindslys were longtime friends of Webster, and on several occasions, he boarded with them in Washington. Although Webster refers to Emeline as "My Dear Cousin," there is no evidence that the two were related.

1. Probably Thomas Sewall.
2. Not found.
3. Mrs. Sewall, nee Choate (1792–1855), sister of Rufus Choate and aunt of Emeline through marriage to Dr. Thomas Sewall of Washington, D.C. She was probably visiting in New England at the time.
4. Mussey (1780–1866; Dartmouth 1803), Hanover physician, was Emeline's uncle.

FROM GRACE FLETCHER WEBSTER

Boston Jany. 18TH. 1827

I have been reading this morning a speech of yours[1] my beloved Husband, which makes me hail this anniversary of your birth with increased delight. May heaven add blessings with years! and many, many may it add to a life so valued and so valuable! I pity the man so dead to every sentiment not only of honor, but honesty that could need an argument to convince him of the justice of the claim you urged, and I blush for the honor of our Country that there should be a majority of such sordid souls in her Congress. I hope you will pardon me for meddling with such high matters. I hope you will find some relief from your labours now you have Mr [Alexander] Bliss. I am sorry he should be made unhappy by the illness of their little boy—but he will be doubly happy to know that it is *quite* well again—O that is happiness beyond expression! We are all well—tho' very cold. Some windows have not been free from frost since the night before last.

Julia wrote you a letter yesterday[2] which I shall send with this. She is mortified to send it but it costs her a good deal of labour to write—and I was unwilling she should go over it again—it is her first attempt at writing.

Aunt Nancy[3] & Daniel and Julia join me in love. Daniel says tell Papa I have read his speech—and he as well as Julia are very decided in favour of the Bill. Adieu! Yours Ever—

PP—I have said nothing of poor little Neddy—he has not yet returned from school; here he comes almost frozen—he says his feet were freezing at school—and Miss Bleney[4] would not let him warm them!—he wishes me to give a great deal of love to Papa.

We have had quite a discussion about the seal. "Forgive the wish that would have kept thee here" is the one Julia has chosen for hers. Neddy says he thinks that a good one for ["]we did not want Papa to go away."

AL. NhHi. Published in Harvey, *Reminiscences*, pp. 325–326.

1. The speech most likely was Webster's on the claims of the officers of the Revolution, delivered on January 5 and reported in part in the *Columbian Centinel*, January 13, 1827.

2. Not found.

3. Not identified.

4. Not identified.

FROM GRACE FLETCHER WEBSTER

Boston Jany 21st. 1827

I have not written to you my dearest Love, for three days. I hardly know how I can have been so negligent. I have nothing worth writing about nothing to communicate but the health of the family and the intense cold, which still continues and increases in the house. The water froze in our chamber last night for the first time I believe since we have lived here, tho' we kept a fire till twelve o'clock. The frost has not been off our parlour windows since Tuesday Evening—notwithstanding the awful inroad we make in our woodpile. Today is sunday and we all "with one consent," excepting [James] William [Paige] and Daniel, stay from Church. I intend, however, to venture out in the afternoon unless those who have gone out this morning give a very discouraging account on their return.

I am hoping for a letter from you this good day—it is rather long since I have had that pleasure at least I fear the space of five days— but I think nothing worse than business prevents you from writing— therefore I am not uneasy—tho' I cannot deny that a letter from you is one of my greatest pleasures. How are all my good friends? I should like much to see them. I have not been in general society so long in Boston—I feel reluctant to going into it again. I have been but once since you left and that was to Mrs. [Nathan?] Appleton's Gala. I have engaged to go to the Solicitors on Tuesday evening to a small party. The hope of hearing Hellen[1] sing was my inducement, and tomorrow evening I am to go to Miss Inches[.][2] Cousin Eliza [Buckminster] is staying there—it is only a social party.

Have you seen Mr. [William Ellery] Channings discourse at the dedication of a Church in N. York.[3] I wish you would read it & tell me what you think of it; for myself I am sorry he preached such doctrine. I should be unwilling to believe him right and I cannot but fear we are wrong to appear to be of that sect. I am anxious that our children should be taught the right way if it be possible to ascertain what that is. I fear my dear Husband that you have not sufficiently considered the subject and I have been myself too easy. If you have time to give some consideration to the subject I wish you would and write to me. With much love Ever Yours   G Webster

ALS. NhHi. Excerpt published in Van Tyne, pp. 566–567.
  1. Not identified.
  2. Not identified.
  3. On December 7, 1826, Channing had delivered the dedicatory address of the Second Congregational Unitarian Church in New York, one of his "happiest and most powerful efforts" in behalf of Unitarianism, one of his contemporaries observed.

Typical of the many appeals which influenced Webster's change of position on the tariff was the one below from Samuel Torrey, a Boston merchant and banker and one of the officers of the Wolcott Woolen Manufacturing Company at Southbridge, incorporated in 1820 with a capitalization of $50,000. Like Torrey, William Payne and Ebenezer T. Andrews were Boston bankers; John Williams (d. 1845; Harvard 1792) was a Boston attorney. See DW to William Coleman, February 23, 1827, and preceding headnote, pages 159–163, below.

FROM SAMUEL TORREY

Boston, January 26, 1827.

Dear Sir:

As it is possible that the fate of the new tariff on woollens may not have been decided on the receipt of this letter, and conceiving that a few statements of facts may be of some service to us, I take the liberty of forwarding to you, two votes passed yesterday by the Wolcott Woollen Manufacturing Company, in consequence of the great losses they have met with during the past year; their accounts having been made up to the 31st December, 1826; and show a loss of more than ten per cent. upon their capital stock, not by bad debts, as they do not exceed one hundred dollars, but in consequence of the large quantity of woollens sent to this country from England and Germany, and sold at auction to a very great loss, if the fair duties had been paid upon them.

The Wolcott Woollen Manufacturing Cmpany, have been incorporated several years; they have the most approved machinery, and the cloths made at the Factory, have been sold from 1^{75}/_{100}$ at 10$\frac{3}{8}$ per yard, they obtained the medal of the New England Society, for the best cloth exhibited in October last; there has been manufactured at the Factory, during the past year, forty-four thousand five hundred and seventy-five yards broad cloth, valued at from 1^{50}/_{100}$ to 8 per yard; the losses by other Woollen Manufactories must be about equal to ours, and we must suspend the business entirely, unless the Government grant us some protection by an increase of duties.

In the Factory at Woodstock, to which the second vote refers, we have had in full operation the last year, fifteen broad hand-looms, and other necessary machinery, for making superfine cloths; you will observe that mill is to be closed as soon as possible; and at Southbridge, we have had sixteen power looms and five hand looms, in operation, together with the necessary machinery for finishing. &c &c. One fourth part of the hands employed there, are to be dismissed immediately, and the wages of those retained are to be reduced, and it is our intention to continue to lessen the number employed, until the work is entirely suspended, unless we get some relief from Congress during the present session.

With the hope that you will afford us all the assistance in your power, I remain, with great respect, Your obedient servant,   Samuel Torrey

At a meeting of the Directors of the Wolcott Woollen Manufacturing Company, holden on Thursday, January 25, 1827.

Present, Wm. Payne, President, Ebenezer T. Andrews, John Williams, and S. Torrey.

Voted, That the Agent be required to dismiss, as soon as possible, one-fourth part of the hands now employed in the Factory at Southbridge, and that the wages of those retained in the employ of the Company, be reduced, so as to average about twenty per cent. from the prices now paid.

Voted, That the Agent be required to have finished all the cloth now in preparation at Woodstock, and to suspend all business there, by the 1st of April next, if possible.

A true copy of the record.

Attest, Samuel Torrey, Clerk.

Text from *State Papers*, 19th Cong., 2d sess., 1826–27 (Serial 151), Doc. No. 70, pp. 4–5. Original not found.

FROM EZEKIEL WEBSTER

Jany 27. 1827

Dear Daniel

I cannot give you any very favorable account of our condition in New-Hampshire. You will recollect, that when I last saw you—I remarked that the opposition in this state was much stronger—than the friends of the administration here,—seemed to believe. Every day's observation since has confirmed my belief in the correctness of the opinion then expressed. Mr. [William H.] Crawford had a strong party in this state; not very numerous, but powerful from their connections, their standing, & the influence they possessed. Mr. Crawford's friends have generally gone with the opposition. The heart of the opposition—its most active and efficient leader is the Editor of the Patriot.[1] From the moment of Mr. [John Quincy] Adams' election—the efforts of the opposition have been united—vigorous & unceasing. Their object has been to gain friends in every town in the state, & secure those men—who have heretofore directed & controuled public interest. And I do not believe there is scarcely a town in the state, in which the opposition has not men, on whom they can rely,—well instructed,—& well qualified to scatter the seeds of opposition—& to serve as channels of communication with the Head quarters at Concord. The party is perfectly organized. It acts by one impulse by one effort—& to one object. Having secured their partisans—their object now is, by means of pamphlets—speeches—& Newspapers to address the passions—feelings, & prejudices of the voters. They certainly have the means of carrying on their operations with great efficiency. In the first place the Patriot has more readers than all the papers—that support the administration. The new paper at Dover[2] & the Haverhill paper[3]—go strongly against the administration. The [Portsmouth] *New Hampshire Gazette* & the *Newport Specta-*

tor will both go the same way. Of the papers that support the administration—the [Concord] New Hampshire Statesman has the most extensive circulation. The circulation of the Portsmouth Journal is very limited, & that of the Keene Sentinel is confined to the county of Cheshire.
In point of diffusing information, by Newspapers, the opposition has very
great advantages. I have not named the [Concord] *New Hampshire Journal* because—it is not yet certain, whether it *supports* the administration or not. I know what its *professions* are. Up to this time I am certain
that it has done the opposition no harm—& the administration no good.
It is nothing but *dish-water*. It takes no ground. It makes no stand. It
has gained but little public confidence, & but little circulation. Its course
is very equivocal—& in my opinion very ill judged. Whoever established
that paper & selected Mr. [Jacob B.] Moore as the Editor, was most sadly
deceived in his qualifications. It is certain that he has not the talents
necessary to edit the paper as it ought to be, and as it must be, to produce any good effect. And it is more certain that he has no *integrity*
either *moral* or *political*. He is not to be trusted in any thing, so far as a
man could throw a mill stone. I do not speak too strongly in this particular. There is no soundness—no fidelity in him. He will betray his
friends & sell his establishment to [Isaac] Hill, whenever he can make a
dollar more by that—than by keeping it. If the paper itself & the *declarations* of the Editor are to be believed—the gentlemen committed an
other error in the establishment of the paper. Mr. Moore says the paper
is to be conducted on the old party lines, & that no aid or assistance was
expected or desired from the Federalists. Indeed they were rather afraid
that the Federalists would show them a little countenance. I am sorry
to say it—very sorry to say it—that Mr. Adams' friends in this state are
as exclusive, and proscribing as Mr. Hill himself. I regret this because, I
do not believe it to be principles on which the administration are disposed to administer the government. And I except from this remark—
Mr. [Samuel] Bell. I have never had any conversation with Mr Bell, nor
any communication with him on the subject. Yet from what I can learn,
he is desirous to take a liberal course of policy. This is certainly the true
course—for the friends of the administration in this state—and it is the
only course, that will not leave them in a minority. Certain I am that at
this moment—Mr. Hill commands a majority of the republican voters
in this state. This will be evident whenever the question is put to the
voters. The friends of the administration, I am well aware—do not believe this, but if they are not mistaken, I know nothing of the public
sentiment. Hill has many advantages over them. He has the controul of
all the Caucus Machinery, & by that he will secure the state Government. He will have the Governor, & in my opinion he [is] very likely to

get a majority in both branches of the Legislature at the March election. He nominates & supports Gen. [Benjamin] Pierce as the opposition candidate, & proudly defies the friends of the administration to prevent his election if they can. The enclosed paragraph from his paper[4] shows the ground on which he rests the election of Gen. Pierce. I have no doubt but the Gen. is as heartily opposed to the administration as Mr. Hill himself. In regard to the feelings of the Federalists—they are generally, not by any means universally,—inclined to support the administration; if they can do it consistently with a proper self respect. They would support the administration from a sense of duty—but at the same time there is a duty they ow[e] themselves. Mr. Adams' friends cannot expect, that when they have been proscribed through the whole year— that they will, on election day sneak up to the ballot-boxes & vote for those, who denounce and proscribe them. Can they expect us to put our shoulders to the wheel with a halter about our necks, that we shall toil & sweat in the furrow—*marked* & *badged* by *them*, as outcasts, & aliens of the commonwealth? Do they expect that we are to be treated like the Helots of Sparta—ready to fight for our masters when our masters are in danger & when that danger is repelled, to be remanded to our chains and servitude? When we consent to do this we shall be worthy of chains & fetters & servitude & contempt & degradation & ought to wear & bear them all, to the last hour of our lives. In a country free as ours, an independence of opinion, and an independent expression of opinion is not only to be tolerated—but encouraged. We formed our opinions honestly & we expressed them fearlessly. We differed no more from others— than others differed from us, & I do not see why we may not have the common rights of citizens accorded to us, especially by those, who may need our assistance. The friends of the administration may think—& I am aware they do—that they are strong enough of themselves to put down the opposition. In this their confident security lies their danger. They would take no advice from me. I now tell you what may save them & what alone will save them in this state. They must hoist the *administration* standard—& invite every man, friendly to the Adminis[tration] to join them. The only question to be asked is this—will you support the present administration—as long as they administer the government, on the principles professed by them. Former distinctions are to be done away—former animosities to be forgotten. This advance is to come from them—and it will be met in my belief—frankly & sincerely. A union of administration men—would now be a majority in this state. Unless this union be formed without delay and act vigorously—the opposition will have the majority & will keep it. But I see nothing doing by Mr. Adams' friends with any effect. Their adversaries are active & vigilant. They are making every effort. They have powerful means within their controul, and their means are used to the best possible advantage to accomplish their purposes. At present we can do nothing. We must wait till a better spirit prevails—& till an opportunity of doing some good is offered. I am sorry that I have written so long a letter on this subject—I can write of it—& dismiss it. Yours truly   E. Webster

ALS. NhD.

1. Isaac Hill.
2. In Dover there were two newspapers, the *New Hampshire Republican* and the *Dover Gazette*, both of

which were anti-administration.
3. *New-Hampshire Intelligencer*, edited by Sylvester T. Goss.
4. Not found.

FROM GRACE FLETCHER WEBSTER

Boston Jany. 29 1827

Full many a Mail has arrived without bringing a line from you my dear Husband, but I know how you are occupied and that your whole mind must be engaged in arduous duties and labours. I hear proud accounts of you by way of Mr [Alexander] Bliss—which reconciles me to the deprivation I mentioned. My Husband is the centre and the height of my ambition. I fear you will think it would be better if I were more so for myself. No one could more ardently wish to be all a woman ought to be than I do, but I have not the courage to pursue a course that would make me what I would be. The weakness of my sight is too discouraging. I cannot write a short letter without feeling uncomfortable. But no more of my infirmities. We are happily all well and we have a beautiful spring like day—& if it were not for the snow would be delightful. Yesterday it rained and melted it a good deal but the streets are piled up still and the walking is very wet. Julia has been to school to get her lessons marked and intends to go tomorrow. I have bought her a pair of India rubber shoes—which will protect her feet— and I hope she will be able to go. This is the first time she has walked so far for a month.

George [Blake][1]—is cutting capers again. He is a sad, sad boy—his ruin, I fear, is inevitable if he stays here. [James] William [Paige] has talked to his Father—but he thinks nothing can elude, or exceed his vigilance and it all does no good, the fellow has not one right sentiment or feeling. I should not wonder if his Father believed in "total depravity." John[2] told Mr B[lake] some of his conduct which incensed him greatly and he reproved George so severely that he packed up his affairs and was going to set off for Danvers—but John found him and brought him back. But I trespas on your precious time while I detail these unpleasant things. Therefore I will only add the love of your daughter & wife

G. W.

PS. I forgot to say that I called last week to see Mr & Mrs [Christopher] Gore. They are quite as well as usual and both desired particular remembrance to you.

ALS. NhHi. Excerpt published in Van Tyne, p. 567.

1. Blake was the only child of George and Sarah Olcott Blake, who died in 1826.

2. Not identified.

FROM GRACE FLETCHER WEBSTER

Boston Feb. 5. 1827

I am very glad to receive a short letter from you to day,[1] my dear Husband, together with the childrens bon bons. They will be much pleased to see something or anything coming under your direction. Julia asked me this morning to write for her. She wished me to say she was studying grammar and that she had got to the head of her class again in geography and goes again to dancing school—a new quarter and in Common Street. I feared to let her go but she was very desirous of going, and before whenever she went it was with reluctance. I shall take all possible care to prevent her getting cold. We have another snow storm—this [is] really an old fashioned winter. You are doubtless better for escaping our cold and storms. I could some times almost wish myself there on more accounts than one, but I am very happy at home. I can never be absolutely unhappy while those I love are well and happy. I feel that I have much, very much to be thankful for that our dear children are so well in your absence and you also have recovered your own health again.

I am much flattered by the kind recollections of Madame Huygins[2]— I hope you had a pleasant dinner. With suitable remembrances to all my friends I am as Ever Yours   G. Webster

Mr. [Cornelius?] Coolidge[3] called here this morning to say he should set out for Washington Wednesday morning and to take any commands —Julia has been wishing very much to send you something this will be so good an opportunity I think I shall indulge her.

ALS. NhHi. Excerpt published in Van Tyne, p. 567.

1. Not found.

2. Madame C.P.E.J. Bangeman Huygens was the wife of the Dutch minister to the United States.

3. Probably Cornelius Coolidge, Boston merchant and original shareholder in the New England Bank, established in 1813.

TO WILLIAM PLUMER, JR.

Washington Feb. 11. 1827

My Dear Sir

I am much your debtor, for a letter long ago recd.[1] and till this late hour unanswered. I trust you will find an apology for this omission, in the pressure of my concerns here, with a *long* session of the Court, & the *short* session of Congress going on together.

You perceive that the times are not entirely pacific. In my little experience, I have never witnessed such extreme heat & violence of opposition, as now exists in Congress. Our *war* debates were cool & temperate, compared to the *manner* of our discussions now. This zeal *to oppose*, seems to exist, in an inverse ratio with any *just grounds of opposition*. Those, inclined to find fault, are angry, above all, that there is nothing to find fault with; hence the introduction of such small subjects as Mr. [Romulus M.] Saunder's Resolution about the Printers,[2] & on which a style of debate is indulged, quite unusual. The real truth is, that the opposition is nothing more nor less than opposition to a *Northern Administration*. No matter who the man may be, if he live north of "Mason & Dixon's line." The sooner our people understand & *feel* this truth, the better.

The condition of things in the Senate is bad; nor is there much hope of immediate amendment. There is a great array of talent agt. the Administration, & a deficiency, at least, of speaking ability, in its favor. The only man, on the side of this New England Administration, from N. England, herself, who is favorable to it, & who is in the habit of defending it, by taking a part in debate, is Mr [Elijah Hunt] Mills; & yet you see what pains are taken, at home, to turn him out! Your (& my old) State seems destined to witness a distinct & permanent division, in the courses, which her two Senators respectively pursue. In regard to Mr [Samuel] Bell, nothing is to be desired, but a more frequent practice of debate. Few men have clearer views, or better judgment; & none can be more true & steady. But he does not much love debate.

In the H. R. there is a majority, (but not a large one,) disposed to give Mr. Adams a fair chance. This majority is not decreasing; I think, on the contrary, it is rather strengthening & consolidating. We do not fear to meet our adversaries, (if we must consider them so) & to discuss with them, their reasons of dissatisfaction, & grounds of complaint.

I incline to think the debate on the Woolen Bill, (which passed the H. R. yesterday) connected with the measure itself, (whether it finally prevail or not) will be attended with important political results. The occasion has very much *distracted* the Pennsylvania Votes. The prominent leaders of the Delegation, [James] B[uchanan, Samuel D.] I[ngham] & others, went over to the *anti protection* party, & made an effort to take their friends with them, but it *did not succeed*.[3] It is supposed Pennsylvania will perceive, ere long, that she must give up, either her favorite *Candidate*, or her favorite *system of politics*.

From the west, information is various, & opinions, as to future events there, quite different. Ohio is settled, & fixed, in her course; but a great contest is expected in Kentucky; & no one can exactly tell what will happen in Ind[ian]a, Illinois, & Missouri.

I see you have some excitement in N. Hampshire, & I hope that Mr. Adams' friends will see the necessity of compelling *real* enemies to become *open* enemies. It is one of the strangest things things which ever happened, that so many *determined* foes should come into Congress, under the name of friends; or at least as *neutrals*. In the whole of N. York, for example, last Novr., there were not *three* candidates who presented themselves on the professed ground of opposition; & yet it is quite doubtful how the *majority* of her 34 members may be. I shall be glad, if *farther north*, some few similar instances may not be found. It is certainly time to put an end to this course of proceeding.

I will thank you, My Dear Sir, to make my respects to your father. I shall probably remain here till the 15th. or 20th. of March, & shall be very glad to hear from you, if you are not quite out of patience with so ungrateful a correspondent. Yours with much regard,   Danl. Webster

ALS. DLC.

1. Not found.

2. On January 1, 1827, Saunders of North Carolina had introduced a resolution requesting the secretary of state to communicate to the House a list of such newspapers in each of the States, "in which the Laws of Congress were directed to be published in the years 1825 and 1826; also, a list of such in which the Laws are directed to be published in 1827; designating the changes which have been made, and the reason for each change." *House Journal*, 19th Cong., 2nd sess., 1826–27 (Serial 147), p. 226.

3. Buchanan, Ingham, and three others of the Pennsylvania delegation had voted against the Woolens Bill.

TO NICHOLAS BIDDLE

Washington Feb. 12. 1826 [1827]

My Dear Sir,

We argued Dandridge's case last week, but as yet we have no decision. I apprehend there may be found to be some difference of opinion on the Bench, on the questions arising in the case; but it would be useless to hazard a conjecture as to the result.[1]

Mr [Daniel P.] Cook tells me, today, that his Committee has not been able to decide yet, either one way or the other, on your Bill.[2] There would now be little hope of acting on it, if it were reported. Yours truly

Danl. Webster

ALS. PU.

1. *Bank of the United States* v. *Dandridge*, 12 Wheaton 64 (1827). Webster and William Wirt, the attorney-general, appeared for the plaintiffs. As Webster predicted, there was a difference of opinion on the court: Chief Justice Marshall dissented from

Story's majority opinion.

2. The Committee of Ways and Means, of which Louis McLane was chairman and Cook a member, had under advisement a bill to permit officers of the Bank of the United States other than the president and cashier to sign notes issued by the bank. The proposed bill did not reach the floor of the House.

Webster did not hesitate to intervene on behalf of office seekers outside his own congressional district, or even his own state, if he believed the appointment would strengthen the Adams administration. The letter below concerns the appointment of a collector of customs at Castine, Maine. Jacob McGaw (1778–1867; Dartmouth 1797), to whom it was written, was a companion of Webster's Fryeburg Academy days. (See Correspondence, *1:43–45.) McGaw had recommended the appointment of a Mr. Carr to replace the incumbent, Joshua Carpenter, collector at Castine from 1825 to 1829, who had been charged with misconduct in office (*Adams, *Memoirs, 7: 474).*

Webster quickly agreed to use his influence in Carr's behalf, but later withdrew his approval when he learned that Carr was a nephew of Henry A. S. Dearborn, collector at Boston, who for himself and through his numerous family connections had already received more than his share of political favors. (See DW to Richard Rush, April 16, 1827, below.) There is no record that Webster ever informed McGaw of his change of heart, but no political ground was lost, since Adams did not in fact remove the incumbent and the expected vacancy did not therefore occur.

TO JACOB MCGAW

Washington Feb. 21. 1827.

My Dear Sir

I have recd your letter,[1] and shall lose no time communicating its contents to the President, & adding my wishes to yours, in favor of Mr Carr.[2] It is not my habit to interfere often, in local appointments, out of my own neighborhood; but I shall go out of my usual course, for once, in conformity to your wishes, & to render your friend a service. I have heard that Mr. Lee, the son in law of Mr. [Josiah?] Hook[e], was a candidate for the office; but know not on what interest, or whose recommendation.[3] Probably there may be others. As soon as I shall have learned what the probable result may be, I will give you information.

We felt, My Dear Sir, a very serious disappointment, when, on our return home in the Summer of 1825 from our journey to the Falls, we learned that you & Mrs McGaw had just left Boston. I recd the note, which you were kind enough to address to me,[4] the day after it was written. Indeed, we were actually arrived, *before* you left town, as it turned out; for, hoping that you might still be there, I went in search of you, & came on your track when you had been gone but an hour. I need hardly say that there are few of my old friends who keep so green & fresh in my recollection as yourself & wife; but it has so happened that with few have I had the misfortune of such unfrequent interviews and communications. I dare not recon up how many years it was, last June since I escorted *Phebe Poor*[5] to the Bank of Sandy River. *Mrs McGaw* I have never seen.

Once, when I lived in Portsmouth, you was in my house, for 5 minutes; & with that exception I believe I have not seen *you* since I was a pedagogue, at *Pigwacket*,[6] & we used to play *cribbage, at one oclock.*

I need not say, and cannot well say, how much interest I feel in the election, pending in your District. I earnestly hope for a result, which while it will give me great personal gratification will, I am sure, promote essentially the public interest.

Pray make my best remembrances to Mrs McGaw; & be assured of the sincere & hearty regard of Your old friend   D Webster

ALS. Mrs. Lester W. Parker, Brimfield, Mass. Published in Van Tyne,
pp. 612–613.

1. Not found.

2. Carr has not been otherwise
identified.

3. Hooke (1744–1829) had served
as collector of customs at Castine
from 1817 to 1825.

4. Not found.

5. Wife of Jacob McGaw.

6. Webster is here using Pigwacket
to refer to Fryeburg, Maine. The
name, or variations thereof, was commonly used to refer to the tribe of the
Abnaki nation, which had earlier
lived and cultivated the land in that
vicinity.

Webster's support of the Woolens Bill in 1827 was inconspicuous compared to his opposition to the whole idea of protection in 1824. On the earlier occasion, he had delivered a major speech against the tariff, but in 1827 he remained silent on the proposed legislation, merely passing Torrey's letter of January 26, 1827 (see above) to Gales and Seaton for publication in the National Intelligencer, *where it appeared on February 6, four days before he cast his vote for the tariff increase. Most observers ignored Webster's switch on the tariff question, which was overshadowed by the political maneuvering that forced Vice President Calhoun to commit himself by his casting vote against the bill. In Boston, Henry Lee and several of his merchant friends published a long, mildly critical pamphlet,* Report of A Committee of the Citizens of Boston and Vicinity, opposed to a further increase of Duties on Importations *(Boston, 1827). But from the pen of William Cullen Bryant in the* New York Evening Post *came the strongest charge of inconsistency. Two days after Webster's vote, Bryant wrote: "There he stands, boldly staring him-*

self, as he was in 1824, directly in the face" (February 12, 1827). For more than a month, from February 12 through March 19, the Post *continued the attack. Always sensitive to criticism, Webster defended himself in the letter below, probably addressed to William Coleman, still titular editor of the paper, although Bryant was already editor in fact. The* Post *did not withdraw its charges against Webster, but it did publish an anonymous letter, printed in the* National Intelligencer *and signed "A Member of Congress," March 30, 1824, which Gales and Seaton certified was a letter from Webster to them. "I cannot concur in the opinion intimated in your paper of yesterday," Webster had written in 1824, "that the fate of the present Tariff Bill will settle that question for ten years. I know no foundation on which that opinion can rest. On the contrary, I believe if the present bill should be rejected, it is the intention of some of those opposed to it, to propose and support a measure, calculated to bring about that 'judicious' revision of the tariff, which some sneer at, but which seems to others to be practicable, proper, and necessary. The public ought to understand that there are Members of Congress who will feel bound to oppose the present bill, who, nevertheless, are desirous of promoting a new regulation of duties, favourable to domestic manufactures, but more discriminating, more moderate, and less dangerous to the existing interests of the Government and of individuals, than that which is now under consideration" (New York Evening Post, March 19, 1827).*

TO [WILLIAM COLEMAN]

Washington Feb. 23. 1827

PRIVATE

My Dear Sir

I have been informed of the observations made by you <in your paper> relative to my vote on the Woolen Bill, although I happened not to see the paper containing them. Of these observations, I do not claim any right to complain, because you are entitled to your own opinions, & to your own mode of expressing them; <but from the friendly relation, which has generally subsisted between> but I have thought <that I would> you would pardon me, if, in this way, I <called> should call your attention to some considerations, connected with the subject, which may possibly not have presented themselves to you, with as much force, as you would be disposed to yield to them on more full reflection. This is intended as a private letter. I do not write for the purpose of vindicating my vote publicly, thro' the means of the Press; but merely to suggest one or two things to yourself <you only as possibly deserving some weight in your>.

I am charged with inconsistency. To make out this it must be shown that my vote in 1827 is in opposition to my vote of 1824; that both were given on the same subject, & under essentially the same circumstances.

You must allow me to say, that I do not admit, either that these two votes *are* in opposition, or, if they were, that the circumstances under which they were respectively given *are* essentially the same.

Before the Tariff of 1824, it was evident to all, that <the bus> manufactures <of the> for the productions of the articles of our own consumption were beginning to make their way in New England. Their progress was slow, & in respect to woolen fabrics indeed it had <indeed> hardly begun. New England is <populous> thickly peopled, has no great agricultural staples, possesses <great> habits of industry, unlimited water power, & some capital, the accumulation of two centuries of labour & frugality. The general peace <had> produced a state of things unfavorable to her further present progress, in commerce & navigation; & on the former, indeed, *your* vast, & vastly encreasing, City had already made great encroachments. What then was she to do? It was clear, that her industry, in time, must take a direction towards manufactures. But we were willing to wait for <this> that time. We wished to make haste slowly; to let the capital of the country find its own channels, to rear no hot bed growths, & to leave our condition to be bettered, if it might, by our own skill & enterprise rather [than] by Legislative interference. <Those> These were my opinions, & they were the opinions of a majority of the Members of Congress from N England. <A> One main ground, on which these opinions rested, not to mention others, was an apprehension of that very difficulty which we now encounter; that is to say, the difficulty of persuading the Government in case of accident or distress to maintain, with <vigor> proper steadiness, in its system of protection, if it should establish one <it.>. No remarks of mine are worth hunting for, so far back as a dozen years,— but the truth is, that as early as 1814, I expressed my fears on this <full> part of the subject fully & at large.

In 1824, however, notwithstanding our opposition, we were outvoted. The law passed. It laid new & heavy burdens on one of our main interests, I mean navigation, by its augmented duties on iron & hemp. From the time of passing that bill, ships could be built cheaper in England, & much cheaper in her Colonies, than in the U. S. As a compensation, or equivalent, for this onerous charge, the Act secured, (what was hardly needed) a farther protection <and for> to the manufacturers of cotton; & it proposed, & promised, (what it has not accomplished,) a farther protection also to the manufacturers of woolen. This promised protection, however, immediately operated to divert capital. The law was considered as fixing the policy of the Country. My constituents so considered it, & acted accordingly. I can <no> enumerate, among them, man by man, not single individuals only, but I may almost say, hundreds, who have withdrawn capital from other objects, & invested it [in] manufactories of woolen, since the passage of the law of 1824.

Now, that law, so far as it regards woolens, has not given that degree of protection, which it proposed to give. It was capable of evasion, & it has been evaded. At the same time, also, other events have happened, at home & abroad, <rendering its pro> tending to render its provisions incompetent to reach that degree of protection, bounty, benefit, or whatever you call it, which was intended & expected when the law passed. The consequence has been, a most severe loss, already felt, & entire ruin threatened, to the capital invested in this business. As to this last part of the case, the loss, <& the> actually felt, & the greater loss threatened, I know the facts to be true.

Now, My Dear Sir, what is to be done? How are we New England men to act? We cannot control, or alter the policy of the Country? The iron duties & the hemp duties still press on our navigation; it can hardly hold up its head, & there is no demand for its encrease. What then, I repeat, are we to do? The Tariff system goes on, & we cannot stop it; but that part of it which alone did us any good, has become disordered, & ineffectual to its purpose; it ceases to do us good. Are we then, to endeavor to remedy this defect in the system, &, since it must continue, to <endeavor> wish to obtain our portion of its benefits, as we bear our portion of its burdens, or are we not?

You & I are going into the Country. I propose the saddle, & the open air, but you insist on a carriage, & I submit to your pleasure. On our way, the wheel, at my corner of the coach flies off, & I am dragged along <in the mud> with the axle tree in the mud. Shall I refuse to stop,—& have the wheel put on, because I was originally against the confinement & the close air of the a coach, & in favor of a more free & unrestrained <exercise> manner of motion?

As to the *details* of the Bill, I confess I am not entirely satisfied with them; but the subject is difficult, opinion is various, & we cannot have every thing as we would. I wish for no more than shall effectually accomplish what the Act of 1824 proposed; but I do not think practicable to do that without some *specific*, or *square yard*, or *running yard*, duty. You know as well as I, that from 1789, our *ad valorem duties* have been founded on the basis of the *Invoice*. But you know also that this invoice, until lately, generally if not always, expressed the price of an actual *purchase*. It exhibited, therefore, the real cost of the Article, unless when it was fraudulent. Recently, & especially in the case of woolen goods, the Invoice *does not express the* <*pur*> *price of any purchase.* The importer is the manufacturer himself. He makes out his invoice upon his own notion of what the goods *cost him*; & in making that estimate, he may say, if he chooses, "I will throw in the expense of labour, for my workmen, if not thus employed, would have been doing nothing." Invoices, in these cases, are opinions, or estimates. Is it not true, that in your great & rich City, 4/5th of the woolen goods are imported on English Acct? The fact has been so stated—it is alledged that official returns show it & it is not denied. You see the reason of this, in what I have said above, & in twenty other modes of evading the real intent of the law. Is this tolerable? For my part, I have no hesitation to say, that I should agree even to a much stronger measure than the present, <before> sooner than I would acquiesce in a state of things <giving> which gives this manifest & plain preference to foreigners, in our own trade.—

I have <this> thus, my Dear [Sir], in the few short minutes which I have at command, suggested <my views reasons> these things for your consideration. I do not expect them to change your sentiments; but I hope they will lead you to think that I may possibly have some apology for mine.

AL draft. MHi. Published in *W & S*, 16: 145–148, with the name of the addressee undetermined. If mailed, the letter would have been addressed to the editor of the *New York Evening Post*, William Coleman; the essays discussing Webster's inconsistency had been written, however, by William Cullen Bryant. Charles H. Brown, *William Cullen Bryant* (New York, 1971), pp. 159–160.

FROM GRACE FLETCHER WEBSTER

Sat. Feb. 24 [1827]

I have just received yours of Sunday[1] my dear Husband and came down stairs with the intention of sending an answer by this days mail but to my regret I find it wants but five minutes of one o'clock. I the more regret it as I have not written for two days and I have not the same excuse that you have. I should have had time enough this morning but for a long visit from Mr [Thomas] Wo[r]cester[2] of Salisbury and after he went away I ran up stairs to make my toilette and then engaged in some other things till it was too late. We are all well—the children have no school, or at least Julia & Edward owing to sickness in the family where their school is kept the "throat distemper." I hope it will not prevail I have a great horror of it. I find it quite difficult to make Julia happy in the house now that the weather has been mild. It will long be very bad. We have two or three feet of snow still in many of our streets and the side walks are very wet. Riding and walking are equally bad. It is well for me that I can live without exercise in the open air.

One week more and your Congressional labors will be over—which you will not I think regret. How long do you think the Court will sit after Congress adjourns? I hope not long.

I know not how Mr [Edward?] Everett got such news as you mentioned I know nothing of it. It is sometimes reported that Eliza [Buckminster] is engaged to Mr [George] Blake & sometimes to Mr. Farrar[3] one probably as true as the other.[4] Mr B[lake] shew[ed] me a part of a letter last evening from Mr [Elijah Hunt] Mills—in which he is very urgent that he should meet him at Philadelphia and more especially to be introduced to a lady who was last winter at the Presidents. They think if he were to search the world over he could not find a more suitable person—is it possible it can be Miss Brease?[5] It was stated that you were of the same opinion—that she was the person of all others. If Mr. B. ever has a wife she must possess some personal beauty—which I think it very doubtful if he would allow to the lady in question. It seems impossible they can mean Miss B. and yet I know of no other. Pray set me right as I have a little curiosity on this subject. I did not read all Mr Mills letter but I fear from what Mr B. told me that is great reason to fear that his case is almost hopeless. Mr. B is to eat salt fish with us today. I am very stupid now but hope to be brighter before [he] comes. I forbear to say aught of the sickness of the he[art] that too often comes over me when I think [of] you at such a distance and the time that must still intervene ere we can see you—but in the hope that that blessed moment will come I am Ever Yours   G. W.

Sunday 12 o'clock
I have just returned from church my dear Husband, where I have heard a very good sermon from Mr [John Gorham] Palfrey. We have one and all been out. Julia chose to go with her Uncle. I had no other objection than the badness of walking. I am quite willing she should be an Episcopalian. Neddy has returned and is committing a hymn for tomorrow if he should go to school. He desires, however, that I will give a *great deal* of love to Papa—and then goes on repeating loud—"the winter is over and gone. The hedges are bordered with tufts of primroses" so it is not. Here we are still enveloped in snow we had a fresh flight last night. Daniel & Julia have returned and both send much love—as does their mother and Your   G W

ALS. NhHi.
　1. Not found.
　2. Worcester (1768–1831) was

minister at the Congregational church Webster had attended in Salisbury. In 1801 he had received the honorary

Master of Arts degree from Dartmouth College.

3. Not identified.

4. Later in the year, Eliza Buckminster married Thomas Lee of

5. "Miss Brease" was perhaps a
sister of Sidney Breese, whom Adams
had appointed as United States attorney in Illinois.

Brookline.

TO NICHOLAS BIDDLE

Washington Feb. 25, 1827

Private

Dear Sir,

I have written you by this mail,[1] about various matters, since which
I have yours of the 23rd.[2]

As to the Loan Bill,[3] I shall pay strict attention to it, & thank you for
your suggestions. It will be in my way to make some inquiries, tomorrow,
as to the existing state of opinion in the Senate, & I may probably give
you a line.

All the needful will be promptly done in McGill's case,[4] & the necessary documents forwarded.

In my letter, I have spoken of success in Dandridge's case only on
the ground of general confidence, arising from the consciousness of a
good cause &c.; but you may take it for granted that my expectation
will not be disappointed.

There is one other thing which I forgot to mention. A suit is pending
here, between one of the District Banks & an individual, in which the
Defense is *usury*; on the ground of making a discount of interest for 64
days instead of 63—I am asked, by other counsel to take part in the
argument, on the ground that the Branch Bank here has notes whose
fates depend on the decision of the same question.[5] I shall see Mr
[Richard] Smith[6] tomorrow morning, & if I learn that the Bank has a
considerable interest in the question, I shall presume it to be your wish
that I should see that the question is, by some body properly argued.

—Again tomorrow—Yrs   Danl. Webster

ALS. PU. Published in W & S, 16: 143.

1. Not found.

2. See mDWs.

3. The Loan Bill, one "authorizing
the Secretary of the Treasury, to exchange a Stock, bearing an interest
of five per cent., to the amount of
sixteen millions of dollars, for certain
stocks of six per cent.; and to borrow
a sum equal to any deficiency in the
said amount authorized to be exchanged," had passed the House on

February 14; it failed to pass the
Senate. *House Journal*, 19th Cong., 2d
sess., 1826–27 (Serial 147), p.
299.

4. *M'Gill* v. *Bank of the United
States*, 12 Wheaton 511 (1827). Webster represented the bank in the case.

5. The case, *Thornton* v. *Bank of
Washington*, 3 Peters 36, was finally
decided by the Supreme Court in
1830. Webster again represented the
bank in the case.

6. Smith was cashier of the Wash-   United States.
ington branch of the Bank of the

FROM PHILIP REED

Huntingfield Farm 25 Feby. 1827

Dear Sir

The doings of the Ho: Rep: published in the news papers some time past left no doubt that the claims of the surviving officers of the revolution had been laid up in the *dry dock*.[1] I fear that too few honorable members have read the Latin maxim "Let justice be done tho' the heavens shall fall" &c. Poor as too many of the officers are they have never *yet* approached the door of the Legislature to ask its charity. They have asked but for something in the shape of *justice*—not even *strict* justice have they asked from their Country. Defeated as they have been it cannot be expected that they will abandon their claim[—]justice to themselves forbid it. The honor of the nation forbid it for no man know better than you do that it belong to national honor that its debts be faithfully paid. One word & I have done with this part of the subject. Nations as well as individuals are accountable to God for their sins for their injustice, for their oppressions, and altho' the day of reckoning may be long deferred, yet come it will, all history is replete with proof on this point and we, altho' in our infancy are on the course with *whip & spur*.

The exertions which you have made in behalf of the rights of the officers entitles you to their highest regard. It was to offer an expression of this feeling that I as the organ of the survivors (16 only) of the M[arylan]d force[2] as well as to express my individual respect, have thus been enduced to trouble you. We know that your course is prescribed upon this as upon other occasions by a high sense of justice of public duty but while writing I could not refrain from the above remarks in reference to our case. A[n] apology is deemed unnecessary. Accept the assurance of my entire respect.   Philip Reed

ALS. DLC.
1. The bill for the relief of the surviving officers of the Revolution had been tied up in House debate for several weeks before it was recommitted to the committee.

2. Although Reed was then a brigadier general of the Maryland militia, he had been a captain in the infantry during the Revolutionary War.

TO NICHOLAS BIDDLE

Washington Feb: 26. 1827

My Dear Sir

On conversing with Mr [Richard] Smith today, I learn that the Bank *is* extensively interested in this question about the 4 days.[1] He promised to write today to you, & to ask you to send on the *opinions*, under which the Bank has acted. I shall of course look after the case, as far as may be necessary.

I send my little bill for fees to Mr [Samuel] Jaudon, requesting him, if paid, to forward the proceeds to Boston. Mr [William] Wirt tells me today he has himself forwarded his own account, so that I do not pay it here, as I had mentioned.

If you prefer not to *close* my little acct till I come along, you may direct such a sum as you see fit to be paid to Mr Jaudon for me, *on account*, generally; to be liquidated & balanced, when I am next at The Bank. This will answer my purpose just as well. Yours truly

D. Webster

The Senate has not taken up the Loan Bill.

I hope tomorrow for the judgt in Dandridges case.

ALS. PU. Published in *W & S*, 16. 144.

1. See above, DW to Biddle, February 25, 1827.

TO SAMUEL JAUDON

Washington Feb. 26. 1827

My Dear Sir,

I wrote to Mr. Biddle yesterday,[1] that I should send on my Bank account (for fees) today. I now enclose it to you.[2] The amount I could wish placed to my credit in the Branch Bank at Boston by the *6th* of March. Will thank you, therefore, to hand the acct. to Mr. [Biddle] &, if he shall order it paid, to remit the amount to Mr. [Samuel] Frothingham, with a request that he place it to my acct.

As however, Mr. Biddle may not be ready to order it paid, or may not see the board together, for a day or two, or, for other cause, there may be delay, and as I wish to send a little cash to Boston to meet a draft from here, I now enclose a draft to be signed by Messrs. A. G. & S. Jaudon (or whatever the precise name of the firm is) payable to *your* order, & accepted by me, for $1000—at 60 d[ay]s.[3]

This acceptance, I will thank you to turn into cash, (in case my acct should not be paid) & remit the proceeds, in like manner, to Mr. Frothingham.

I write this in H. R. in the amidst of a debate—but hope you will understand it. Yrs truly   Danl. Webster

ALS. NHi.

1. Webster was clearly referring to his letter to Biddle of February 26, above.

2. Enclosure not found.

3. Draft not found. The type of business in which the Jaudon firm engaged in the 1820's has not been

established; but in the 1830's, Samuel Jaudon and his brother worked with Biddle in the purchase of cotton in the South and Southwest for sale in England. Thomas Govan, *Nicholas Biddle: Nationalist and Public Banker, 1786–1844* (Chicago, 1959), pp. 319–322.

TO JOHN QUINCY ADAMS

H. R. Saturday 10 oclock
[March 3, 1827]

Sir

The two Houses have suspended their 18th joint rule, so far as to allow bills to be presented to you today *which shall have passed the Houses by 12 oclock.*[1] Not knowing whether you are informed of this, I now give you the information, supposing you might think it proper for you to be at the Capitol.

The H. R. will pass, probably, three or four private Bills. It has, as you see, *adhered* to its amendment in the Colonial Bill.[2] Yours as always

Danl. Webster

ALS. MHi. Published in Van Tyne, p. 122.

1. The eighteenth joint rule stipulated that "no bill or resolution that shall have passed the House of Representatives and the Senate, shall be presented to the President of the United States, for his approbation, on the last day of the session." *House*

Journal, 19th Cong., 2d sess., 1826–27 (Serial 147), p. 492.

2. The House and Senate had been unable to reach an agreement on the House amendment to the colonial bill "to regulate the commercial intercourse between the United States and the colonies of Great Britain."

FROM GRACE FLETCHER WEBSTER

Boston March 5 [1827]

As Mr [Alexander] Bliss has doubtless left you my dear Husband, I think for a little time you may feel a sense of loneliness, and possibly, if you have time, think of your *own home* more than you otherwise might; and that a letter though short and poor as usual may have a little additional value.

You must feel quite relieved to have nothing but the court to attend to and rejoiced I should think that the turmoil of Congress is over. I suppose most of the members are gone or getting ready to depart. The travelling must be bad. We have a great deal of snow yet, it will be long ere the birds will greet us with a song. I cannot wonder if you dread to return to our chilly air and cloudy skies. We who have remained here are very well and none of the family mind the cold but myself. I go out so seldom I am very sensible of the cold.

We find by the papers that Mr [George] McDuffie lives to fight another day, tho' it was currently reported that he was dead.[1]

Mr I[saac] P[arker] & Mr [George] Blake ate "Popates" with us last evening and both well. Mr B talks of going [to] Philadelphia and taking George with him—he has been confined to the house for several [weeks? days?] with exception of one ride.[2]

Are Mr. and Mrs E[verett] going to travel South? Sometimes I hear they are, and then that they talk of waiting till you return.

I have only time to say Adieu! Yours   G W

ALS. NhHi.

1. Because of South Carolina representative George McDuffie's attempts to harass the administration during the fight for passage of a constitutional amendment on presidential elections, Thomas Metcalfe of Kentucky had challenged McDuffie. The duel aborted, however, when the two failed to agree on the weapon to be used. Charles M. Wiltse, *John C. Calhoun, Nationalist, 1782–1828* (Indianapolis, 1944), pp. 330–331.

2. See above, Grace Fletcher Webster to DW, January 29, 1827, for an earlier discussion of George Blake.

FROM GRACE FLETCHER WEBSTER

Thursday March 8th, [1827]

I have yet another unexpected pleasure my dear Husband, yours of Saturday.[1] You must indeed feel relieved from a load of care. I rejoice with all my heart that you have got over it so well and so soon too for I expected you would have to sit up all night but you anticipated and sat up on Friday night. I hope your good long nap of 24 hours has softened you and that we shall find there is something "left of you yet."

You do not tell me the news. It is said to be a fact that Miss [Abigail] Brooks is engaged to Charles Adams.[2] I did not believe it at all—but last evening at Mrs P. I.s[3] I was told it was true.

Poor Mrs [Alexander] Bliss expected fully to see her good husband last evening but he has not yet [arrived.] Whether the storm delayed the boat, or whether he waits for the next is uncertain. O! if a husband could *know* the disappoint[ment] a woman feels; if he could but *know* the meaning of this most true saying of the wise man hope defered makes the heart sick it would not be so often felt, but as they do not know—they cannot be so *greatly* to blame so here my re[a]soning ends.

Eight days of March have come and almost gone. When as many more have passed I hope you will be making preparations for home. We are all impatience to see you.

You have doubtless seen the death of Mr A[rnold] Welles. His indisposition was short. I believe he had a fever. Yours Ever—   G. W.

Julia wishes she had a speaking trumpet that would reach your ear she says she wants to talk with you.

ALS. NhHi. Excerpt published in Van Tyne, p. 569.

1. Not found.
2. Abigail Brooks, daughter of Peter Chardon Brooks, and Charles Francis Adams were married on September 3, 1829.
3. Not identified.

TO NICHOLAS BIDDLE

Washington Mar: 10 '27

My Dear Sir,

I have recd yours of the 7th,[1] & beg to express the gratification I feel at the satisfaction, manifested by the Directors, with the results of the cases here,[2] and at the arrangements proposed for our future relations. You will please therefore to signify to others the readiness with which I accede to what you in their behalf propose.

I hope to see you by the 20th. Yours very truly   Danl. Webster

ALS. Nicholas B. Wainwright, Philadelphia, Pa.

1. Not found.
2. *Bank of the United States* v. *Dandridge*, 12 Wheaton 64 (1827), and *M'Gill* v. *Bank of the United States*, 12 Wheaton 511 (1827). In both cases Webster had represented the bank.

FROM CHARLES RICHARD VAUGHAN

Washington Monday 12 March
[1827]

My dear Sir,

Pray let me know on what day, excepting Friday the 16th March, you will give me the pleasure of your company at a quiet dinner. When I am aware of the most convenient day for you, I shall be anxious to engage Chief Justice Marshall, & Mr Justice Story & Mr Everett to meet you— no one else.

Perhaps you will undertake to arrange with those Gentlemen a convenient day for our dining together. I except Friday the 16th as I am engaged on that day to dine with Mr [Richard] Rush.

I am not at all disposed to let you off from the snug dinner we talked about soon after your arrival at Washington. I have twice called upon you to make an arrangement but your engagements in the Supreme Court prevented my finding you at home. Most truly yrs

Chas R. Vaughan

ALS. George C. Whipple, Jr., Carmel, N.Y. Vaughan (1774–1849) was the British minister to the United States, 1825–1835 (*DNB*).

Washington Mar: 17. '27

My dear Emeline

I duly recd yours of Feb. 27.[1] You may be quite assured, that none of your friends feel a greater interest than I do for your welfare, & therefore none are more anxious that you should act wisely, in the greatest concern of life. I do not doubt your discretion, My Dear Cousin, & the readiness with which the excellent admonitions of Dr. Young[2] occur to you prove that you have a just view of what belongs to the important occasion. You must keep your heart a little under the control of your judgment; but do not, in such a case, follow either, where the other will not go also. One other thing I will add—most men marry *above* their pretensions,—most women *below* them. Most men marry, for love—too many women marry, to be married. But these are cold & poor maxims, My Dr Cousin; & I dare say you have probably settled the whole matter before you read this homily. I have no acquaintance whatever with the person who, as I conjecture, is the object that has raised these questions. My own sincere & ardent admonition & advice to you is, first, to be sure he is worthy of your love, & next that you do love him. It is a bargain to be made but once.

I forward you a letter from the Dr [Thomas Sewall]. He promises to go by way of Albany & Hanover & bring you to Boston. I hope he will keep his word. If he should not, you will certainly be expected to visit us this spring, & to pass some time with us. At the latter part of April I shall be at Ipswich & Salem; & if you should then be in any part of Essex Co. I shall have great pleasure in taking you home with me. At any rate, I wish you to consider that we have a claim for a visit, & that it must be paid. We will then talk over your interesting subject, if it should not be already settled; & you know that you may rely fully on my friendship & regard. Few things would give me greater pleasure than to see you well established in life.

The Court & Congress being now both over, I am preparing to depart for home. My expectation is to be in Boston by the first of April, or before the 5th. I wish you would write me, as early as the latest of those periods, to let me know <merely> that you have recd. this, & to say what you think of the time of coming to Mass.

With the most affectionate wishes for your happiness, I am, My Dear Emeline, truly, Yours   Danl. Webster

ALS. DMaM.   2. Not identified.
1. Not found.

*In the two years following Adams' inauguration the elements of the op-
position were consolidated into a powerful, smoothly functioning political machine, now calling itself the Democratic party and based upon the
old alliance of New York and Virginia that had elected Jefferson, Madison, and Monroe. Largely the work of Martin Van Buren, the Jacksonian organization was so effective that it forced the disparate Adams following to look to its own power base. Webster was one of those who
participated in the reconsideration of party strategy, shortly before Congress adjourned in March 1827.*

*The new emphasis included subsidizing friendly newspapers, and
getting state legislatures still controlled by National Republicans to pass
resolutions in support of the administration. More important, the North-
South alliance of the Democrats which was necessarily equivocal on the
tariff was to be offset by a pro-tariff union of New England, the Middle
Atlantic states, and the West. The visible evidence of this union was to
be a "General Convention of Agriculturists and Manufacturers," called
to meet in Harrisburg, Pennsylvania, in the summer of 1827. Although
the protection of domestic industry was its central theme, the Harrisburg Convention did not lose sight of its political aims, nor did those
who supported or opposed the movement. Much of Webster's correspondence for the remainder of 1827 deals directly or indirectly with the political and economic tactics of the National Republican party to which
he now belonged.*

TO JOHN QUINCY ADAMS

Philadelphia Mar: 23. 1827
Private & confidential
Sir,

Will you allow me to express the wish to you, for reasons which you
will readily understand, that you would order the *Baltimore Patriot* to be
sent to you? If you have any general rule, in regard to Newspapers,
which compliance with this suggestion would infringe, the suggestion,
of course, may be disregarded; but if not, the giving of such a direction,
would, I think, be a useful thing and have a healing tendency.

I give the intimation, without the knowledge of the Proprietor of the
Paper, & only in consequence of what came to my own knowledge ac-
cidentally.[1]

I trust it is your practice to read & *burn* communications of this nature; unless, indeed, you find it more convenient to burn them *without
reading.* Yours with most true regard   Danl. Webster

ALS. MHi. Published in *W & S*, 16:
149.

1. Isaac Munroe (1784–1859) was
the proprietor of the *Baltimore Pa-*

triot & *Commercial Advertiser*. A native of Massachusetts, Munroe had published the *Boston Patriot* previous to his settlement in Baltimore (*Maryland Historical Magazine*, 20 [September 1925]: 249). Webster's information regarding the *Patriot* probably came from Nathaniel F. Williams (1780–1864), a Baltimore merchant and lifelong supporter of Webster, who may have been part owner of the newspaper. In 1841, probably through Webster's influence, President Tyler appointed Williams collector of customs for the port of Bal-

timore, and in 1851 President Fillmore appointed him appraiser for the port. Nathaniel F. Williams should not be confused with Nathaniel Williams (1782–1864; Harvard 1801), also a resident of Baltimore, and United States district attorney for Maryland. As early as 1824–25, Nathaniel Williams was reportedly supporting Jackson (Nicholas G. Ridgley to Duff Green, June 17, 1829, Letters of Application and Recommendation during the Administration of Andrew Jackson, DNA).

TO PETER FORCE

Philadelphia Mar. 24 [1827]

Sir

Your bill, amt. to 17 Dollars, was sent me at so late a period, I had no opportunity of paying it, before I left Washington.

I now enclose a twenty dollar Bank note, & you will please pass the balance, three Dollars, to my credit for this years sub[scription] for the Journal.[1] The Bill is receipted. I give the items of it below—Yr ob sevt

Danl. Webster[2]

Daily, d[ur]ing 1. Sess. 19 Congress	5.--
1826 Nov. 12. Two yrs subscription &c	10--
Dec 100 Presidents messages	2--
	——
	17--

ALS. DLC.

1. At this time, Force was publishing the Washington *National Journal*, the major newspaper supporting the

Adams administration.

2. Force endorsed the letter: "$20.00 March 26, 1827."

TO CHARLES MINER

Philadelphia March 24 '27

My Dear Sir

I had the pleasure to receive a very kind parting salutation from you,[1] on the 5th, & have embraced this opportunity to reciprocate, most cordially, your good wishes. Your acquaintance & regard are valued by me most highly; & I trust we may yet be mutually useful to each other. I hope you found all well, in your domestic circle.

I left Washington soon after the rising of the Court, & staid a day or two in Baltimore to see *our* friends. The general sentiment there seems favorable; but friends need to be waked up and excited. The same may be said of the State of things here. This State is all important. No pains should be spared to obtain its vote. I do think, verily, the chance of success is such as to justify a great effort. Our friends, however, need organization, system, & action. You know how these things can be, or must be, accomplished. Can you not set them in motion? You are near to the [scene?] & could communicate with Gentlemen here with facility.

At any rate, My Dear Sir, let us act as if we knew our danger, & were willing to face it.

I shall be very glad to hear from you, & shall now be home in a very few days. Yrs mo. truly   Danl. Webster

(over)

Do not fail to *expose* that abominable *job* the Missouri business. Let the public know all about it.[2]

ALS. PWbH.

1. Not found.

2. Webster was referring to the charges leveled in April 1826 by Luke Lawless, attorney in Missouri, against Judge James H. Peck of the United States District Court of the state. Lawless alleged that he had been oppressively convicted of contempt by Peck's court. The impeachment trial finally came before the Senate in 1830–1831, after an intensive investigation of the case by the House and a select committee of the Senate, one member of which was Webster. On January 31, 1831, Peck was acquitted by the Senate.

TO NATHANIEL F. WILLIAMS[1]

Philadelphia Mar. 24. 1827

Dear Sir,

I recd your letter safely,[2] from the hand of Mr. [George W.] *Slacum*,[3] & have duly considered its contents.

It is not convenient to write much, on the subject, & I will express, in few words, the result of my reflections.

Of the 24, which you think no more than right, I will be, distinctly, answerable for 15,—one half to *your* order, any time, after 1st day of April; & other Decr. 1. 1827. The remaining 9 must be looked up, in your quarter, if it may be.[4]

I go now to New York, where I shall remain long eno. to hear from you. I hope you will think the foregoing satisfactory; if not, tell me frankly, for we must accomplish the object, some how, if possible. You will please write me, on receipt of this, addressed to New York—care of Henry Wheaton Esquire.

You know what care to take of letters of this kind.

AL. NhD.

1. For the identification of Williams, see above, DW to Adams, March 23, 1827.

2. Not found.

3. Slacum, a native of Alexandria, was United States consul at Buenos Aires. According to Edward Everett (Diary, Entry of March 23, 1827),

Slacum was then in Philadelphia.

4. The figures indicate hundreds of dollars, which Webster was apparently helping to raise in Williams' behalf. The purpose is pure conjecture, but presumably was political, most likely some form of subsidy to the Baltimore *Patriot*. See below, DW to Williams, April 7, 1827.

TO HENRY CLAY

Philadelphia Mar: 25. '27

Private & confidential

My Dear Sir

I staid a day in Baltimore, mainly for the purpose of seeing some of our friends; & had the good fortune to fall in with many of them. Indeed some pains were taken to bring them together.

The general state of feeling, there, seems entirely satisfactory. Nobody complains of the measures of Government, & Genl [Samuel] Smith, even, has few or no followers in his crooked path. Still, the state of the *Press*, in that City, is not quite so favorable as might be wished. The Proprietors & Editors of the Public Journals are, generally, well disposed; but they are not willing to *take a side*, & to make their papers political papers. In the mean time, engines from another quarter begin to act vigorously on the public mind. This requires counteraction; for unremitted efforts, to produce whatever convictions, will, in time, prevail if totally unresisted. You know the grievance of the *Patriot*, about the public printing. That has *neutralized* its Editor,[1] & all the rest were *neutral* before. I have felt it to be necessary to change this *neutrality* of the Patriot into active support; & <with> by the aid of friends measures are in train, which, I hope, may have that result. It is not necessary now to trouble you farther, on that head. I think what has been done will be satisfactory & efficient.

I wish I felt as well satisfied with the state of things here. I have now been here three days, & have heard nothing but one continued din of complaint; not at the general measures of Government, but at the disposition of the *offices* which have been recently in the gift of the Executive. I suppose there must be some, of course, who are gratified at the late Customs House appointments here, but upon my honor I have not found one such. Enemies laugh, & friends hang down their heads, whenever the subject is mentioned. Our friend [Philip Swenk] Markley is, I dare say, entirely well qualified for his Office, & was probably recommended by a great country interest:[2] but I doubt whether those recommendations came from any deeper source than mere good nature & good wishes. I doubt whether the recommenders themselves are *gratified*, still more whether any of them are *attached*, by his appointment; while it is too evident that warm & zealous friends here are, some disappointed, & others disgusted. The truth is, that there seems to be a feeling prevalent here, that to be active & prominent, in support of the Administration, *is the way to throw one's self out of the chance of promotion, & the sphere of regard.* Those who wish for Office, think the policy for them is to hold back, in the ranks of opposition until they shall be offered their price. All gratuitous support of Government, they seem to think a foolish abandonment of their own interest.

Then, again, as to the state of the Press. I cannot learn that there is any *one* paper in the City, except the Democratic Press, which may fairly be called an Administration Paper.[3] There are many neutrals—many *candid* papers—many whose devotion to good government carries them so far, that they will, occasionally, admit pieces, which others have taken the pains to write; & many others, I suppose possibly, waiting, either for *terms*, or for tokens of what is to ensue, in political affairs.

At the same time, I am persuaded, that a distinct majority of the City is with the administration, and that if there could be a proper spirit infused, and a just degree of *confidence* excited, not only might the City return us a favorable member, but it might act also, *efficiently*, on the State.

In short things here seem to me to be precisely in that State, in which there is every thing to encourage effort, & nothing to be hoped for, without effort.

This I think the truth; tho' I should be glad to write a more cheering letter.

I said something to you about the West point visitors. Since I came here, I have heard, tho probably it is without foundation, that they have been already appointed; & that the persons, or many of them, are *opposition men*; so that it would seem our friends cannot even have *feathers*. Do inquire about this. In short, all protection, all proof of regard, all patronage, which can justly be afforded by the Executive Government, must be given to friends; or otherwise it is impossible to give any general or cordial support to the Administration before the people. I speak freely, because you know I speak disinterestedly. I have neither relation, friend, or connexion, for whom I ask anything. I go solely on the grounds of the common interest of us all.

I have conversed with Gentlemen here about *a public meeting*. They think it hardly practicable, just now. Time must mollify the feeling produced by recent events, before such a meeting would be attended. I have not, however, seen Mr [Robert?] Wharton, but shall meet him today, & learn what he thinks of it.

We <took> had great difficulty, as you know, last year, to prevent the District Atty from being disgraced.[4] He must have gone, & *would have gone*, but for the President's kindness towards him. Yet, I do not believe he would now walk round one square of the City to prevent Genl Jackson from turning the President out of Office. In the meantime his 700 *ridiculous* Indictments, not only bring great expense to the Government, but what is much worse, expose it to censure & reproach. Add to this, that the whole influence of the custom house *has been*, & that much the greater part of it *is likely still to be, opposed* to the friends of the Administration, & then we see what the prospect is. In my poor judgment, the general interest of the Country, & the interest of the Administration, alike required that that custom house should <have> be thoroughly reformed. And I think, moreover, that even now <places> room should be found or *made*, to place there three or four competent & faithful men. After what the Judges of the Supreme Court felt it their duty to say, on the conduct of the officers of that Customs house, in the late *Tea case*,[5] I think public opinion would justify, & indeed that it will peremptorily require, some efficient changes in the subordinate branches of the establishment.

But I will not weary you further. In hopes of being able to make a less dolourous epistle the next time I write, I remain, My Dear Sir, with true regard Your's   Danl. Webster

Mar. 26. P.S. The rumour about the West point appointments is not, I am told, well founded. Col [Andrew M.] Prevost[6] is said to be one of the Board, which is as it ought to be. I do not know that it would now be important to ask Mr [Robert] *Walsh* to be of the number. Mr. Walsh leaves here for Washington tomorrow. You will of course see him, & I hope will converse with him fully. Perhaps I may venture to write you again, on this point, before I leave the City.

ALS. DLC.

1. Clay's selection of the *Baltimore American*, upon the recommendation of many of the Maryland delegation, had alienated Isaac Munroe, publisher of the *Baltimore Patriot & Commercial Advertiser*.

2. Upon the resignation of John Steele from the post of customs collector, Adams had appointed William Jones, formerly naval officer for the port of Philadelphia; to succeed Jones, he had appointed Markley.

3. John Binns edited the Philadelphia *Democratic Press*.

4. Charles Jared Ingersoll.

5. *United States* v. *350 Chests of Tea*, 12 Wheaton 486 (1827).

6. Prevost, born in Geneva, Switzerland, had emigrated to the United States with his parents. In the War of 1812, he commanded the first regiment of the Pennsylvania artillery (*Appleton's Cyclopaedia of American Biography*, 5: 116).

TO JOHN QUINCY ADAMS

Philadelphia Mar: 26. '27

Private

Sir

Mr [Robert] Walsh is going to Washington tomorrow, of which I give you notice only to express the hope that you may see & converse with him. He seems to be laboring under the influence of feelings, which I think would be changed, by a free conversation & explanation. His position, at present, is one of some influence, & his future course a good deal important.

Pray place this note to the account of zeal & friendly anxiety, rather than to that of officiousness; & believe me to be, as I am, most truly, yours   Danl. Webster

ALS. MHi. Published in Van Tyne, p. 122.

TO MRS. GEORGE TICKNOR

Philadelphia Monday Mar: 26.
[1827]

My Dear Mrs Ticknor

I shall feel so guilty, when I see you, for not having written a single word to you, nor your husband neither, for this whole winter, that I would be very glad to begin the work of propitiation, confession, &c &c a little before hand. And as Mrs [William] Meredith has put this letter into my hands, instead of bringing it, I will send it forward; & this shall go with it. Pray receive it as a sort of peace maker. When you rebuke me, for my unpardonable negligence, remember at least that I have had the merit, however small, of confessing my faults, before you set them in order before me. I find that when the children break the China, if they run to mama, look sorry, & tell her all about it, mama's displeasure breaks as easily as the China itself. I must beg to learn from this juvenile policy, & to say it was an accident, I did not do it on purpose, am very sorry, wont do it again, &c &c &c—

We have had a busy winter at Washington, & put off writing to you & Mr T from today till tomorrow, in the hope that tomorrow would have [an] unoccupied corner in it. But they all came on successively, as full as the Stage Coaches here, with 13 inside passengers.

There will only be the more things to talk about, when I get home.

Mrs W[ebster] has given me account of your social little visits. I trust the Potatos are not all gone. Yrs truly   Danl. Webster

ALS. DLC.

TO JOHN QUINCY ADAMS

Philadelphia March 27. 1827.

Sir

I hope you will pardon me for troubling you, once more, on a political subject. However infirm my judgment may be, in the matters about which I write, you may yet be assured that every word proceeds from entire singleness of heart, & devotion to that, which is the great immediate object of my thoughts and efforts, the support and *continuance* of the Administration.

One of the *observables*, here, is Mr [Robert] Walsh's entire neutrality, (if it be *entire*,) as to the existing contest. This is a great draw back, on the means of affecting favorably the public sentiment. It is important, as I think, and as all here think, to bring him out, in a moderate but firm manner, in support of the Administration. He circulates 4000 papers; & his Review, also, which is getting an unexpected extent of patronage, opens another field, which might be prudently and usefully occupied, for the discussion of certain principles, now becoming interesting, and on which we must hope to stand, if we stand at all, in this State.[1]

You are aware, that there are 40. or 50 thousand Electors, in Penna. who formerly belonged to the Federal Party. With these, Mr Walsh's opinions have great weight; and a majority of their votes is necessary, in any calculation, which anticipates that this State may be found in favor of the continuance of the present state of things.

I have now been here near a week, have seen very many people, & conversed with all I have seen, who are favorably disposed, whether Greek or Jew. I have learned the grievances of the Democratic Press; & what I could do or suggest, in that quarter, tending to promote satisfaction, & to ensure active exertion, has not been omitted. The present state of feeling here is certainly not the best, so far as it has been produced by the recent appointments. This I have endeavored, by all the means in my power, to mollify & satisfy; & I hope with some success.

I have endeavored also to learn the causes of Mr Walsh's coldness & to find out what might propitiate his good feelings, & secure his efforts. He sees nothing, I believe, to disapprove, in the general measures of Government, but certainly is, at present, in rather an unsatisfied mood towards the Administration. I am happy that he is going to Washington,

& that you will have an opportunity to converse with him. He is an old & an attached friend of Mr [Joseph] *Hopkinson*, & he feels that Mr H. as an early & true friend to the President, has been *neglected*, & injured. Mr Hopkinson, himself, does not talk in that way; still, if something fit for him to receive, could be offered to him, I have no doubt it would gratify Mr Walsh more than any thing else whatever. The District Judge of this District will hardly last long. It is a small office, but I presume Mr H. would take it.[2] No doubt he is entirely well qualified for it, & would probably be recommended by nearly all the bar. I am persuaded a little effort would reconcile all our other friends here, or nearly all, to this measure. Some act of patronage or kindness, performed at the same time to them, would lead them easily to acquiesce in it.

The first fruits, of such an understanding, if it were found practicable to make it, would, I am persuaded, be seen in the appearance of quite a different tone & manner in the National Gazette. It would heal, too, much of the wound which is felt in N. Jersey; and would suffice, even in New England, to awaken the activity of many friends.

I know not what objections there may be, to this arrangement; but it strikes me that the good must greatly overbalance the evil. <Men> Friends here are in sections & parties; & unless *union* can be produced, great mischief will, or may, ensue. If things should remain in their present State, I think it more than probable, that Mr Hopkinson <would> will be run for Congress, with or against his consent, in October, *agt. Mr. [John] Sergeant*.

I see not why the Nat. Gazette, & the Press might not go on, well enough, without collision. There are measures of Govt. for Mr W. to defend; steps of opposition for him to expose, & reprobate; general good principles to be enforced, &c &c.—The Press, in the mean time, may very well pursue its own course, taking care not unnecessarily to annoy its neighbors. They might thus tend to the same point, altho' they should not walk in the same road. These ideas I have endeavored, by all means in my power, to enforce on all sides.

It is proper for me to add, what you already well know, that Mr Hopkinson is my particular friend. Make as much allowance for bias, & possible error of judgment, on this account, as seems proper to yourself. Be assured only that I speak as I really think.

Again begging you to pardon me for writing on such a subject, & so long a letter, I have only to renew the assurances of my sincere & constant regard   Danl. Webster

ALS. MHi. Published in Van Tyne, pp. 122–124.

1. Walsh edited the Philadelphia *National Gazette and Literary Register.*

2. Then eighty-three years old,

Richard Peters, Sr., had served as judge of the court of the Eastern District of Pennsylvania since 1792.

Upon his death in 1828, Adams appointed Hopkinson to the post.

FROM JOHN TEST

Brookville [Indiana] Mar 29th.
1827

Dear Sir

Since my arrival here I have been a considerable part of my time among the people and particularly those who were the supporters of Genl. Jackson. I find them all, or nearly so, disposed to desert him. They are disgusted with the course the opposition has taken. The leading men of that party are all unpopular here—and the general remark is, "we were in favour of Jackson, but we do not like his friends, and we are afraid he will be swayed by them." The opposition to the woollen-bill, and the course pursued by the *opposition* in relation to the collonial trade-bill has injured their Cause very much—Govr. [Jonathan] Jennings's course I suspect, has injured, if not intirely destroyed his popularity here. He is considered as having gone over to the *"enemy."* My successor [Oliver H. Smith[1] printed] Hand-bills over feigned signatures (last election) charging me with voting $25,000 to the president to furnish his house, and for purchasing Billiard tables, Balls, chess-men &c, while he was pretending, among the friends of the administration to be favourable to them. His whole scheme is blown, the people have been undeceived. He has ventured lately, it is said, to speak something in favour of the adminis[tratio]n openly, for which some of the Leaders of the Jackson party have threatened to scalp him—not that they seem to care so much about Jackson at present, but for the fraud practiced upon them. However these things aside, I think you may now venture to put Indiana down, as certain for the Administration. I saw a man yesterday who has just returned from <South> North Carolina. He came through Kentucky, Tennessee &c, he says there are very few Jackson-men in Kentucky, and not so many in Tennessee by a vast number as he expected and he tells me, what I did not expect, that in the last mentioned state, the poorer class of people are against Jackson. He (my author) is an intelligent, moderate man, and I place much reliance upon what he [tells me. Will De Witt] Clinton be out for president. If so, what effect will it have, he will do nothing here nor in Ohio. He is considered an apostate in politicts. If he does not, will Van Buren be a candidate for V. Prest. and if so what effect will that measure have. He will do nothing in the west. Please give me your views on those subjects when you have leisure—or on any other points you may think proper, and *that* confidentially, or otherwise—You see I have set the example. Old uncl Saml. Smith has blowd. himself *"sky high" "sky high sir."* The presidents proclamation is here, and the measure approved, while those who imposed the necessity of it, are condemned. Let me hear from you when convenient. I have embarkd. with you, and I intend to *sink* or *swim* with you. *But we shall swim.* respectfully, Your friend   John Test

Indiana feels that her interest has been promoted by the friends of the administration during the last session of Congress—she will not forget it. I have written a long letter to Mr. Clay.

ALS. NhHi.
    1. Smith, a Jacksonian, defeated Test in the latter's bid for reelection to the Twentieth Congress.

In accordance with the strategy agreed upon in March, Webster wrote Ezekiel urging him to introduce resolutions supporting Adams in the New Hampshire legislature. When the legislature convened, however, the self-styled "Republican friends of the administration" issued a call for a caucus to agree on appropriate resolves. Old Federalists, also friends of Adams, regarded the gathering as exclusive and boycotted it; and when the resolutions came before the lawmakers, Ezekiel and other Federalists voted to table them, with the result that no resolutions passed. See Ezekiel Webster to DW, June 17, 1827, below. Webster went to great lengths to explain to President Adams and Secretary of State Clay the historical basis for the disagreements in New Hampshire, but there was no concealing his disappointment with the situation. Later in the year he discussed the matter with Governor Samuel Bell, with whom he worked out an arrangement to bring the two factions together.

TO EZEKIEL WEBSTER

Boston April 4. 1827

Dear E.

I arrived here on friday, well; & found all well. The Supreme Court is sitting here, but will wind up this week. I shall then have a little leisure, & as Miss Paige[1] is about going to Salisbury, I think of accompanying her. I wish first, however, to learn, whether you will be at home, say the last of next week. I propose to go up, on friday the 14—& to stay till Tuesday following. Please let me know, as soon as you can, whether you will be at home.

I have seen no New Hampshire Papers, but hear from Mr [James W.] Paige that you are to be in the Legislature. I am very glad of it. This is a time for *action.* I wish to confer with you & Mr. [Jeremiah] Mason. I shall have no objection to return by way of Portsmouth, if you will accompany me.

I submit for your consideration this course. Early in the session, introduce a string of Resolutions, approving of the election of Mr. Adams—& of the general measures of the Administration—& characterizing the opposition as groundless. In support of these Resolutions, make your best *speech*—print it & circulate it thro' the State. So favorable an opportunity to do good & to distinguish yourself, will never occur to you again.[2] Let me hear from you by return of mail. Yrs   D. Webster

ALS. NhD. Published in *W & S*, 16: 152.

1. Not identified, but probably a half-sister of Grace Fletcher Webster and a sister of James W. Paige.

2. James Wilson (1797–1881) of Keene introduced resolutions to the effect that the legislature of New Hampshire "entertains the highest confidence in the talents, integrity, and the public service of John Quincy Adams." *Journal of the New Hampshire House of Representatives*, June Session, 1827, pp. 123–124, 139–140.

TO NATHANIEL F. WILLIAMS

Boston April 7. 1827.

My dear Sir,

I have your's of the 27.[1] & without multiplying words, agree to what is proposed. Consider it settled on the following basis.

$750 to be drawn for, by *you*, on me; payable May 15. I mention this time for reasons not necessary to trouble you with. $750. to be paid December 1. as I go South; & $500.—a year hence.

Acknowledge the receipt of this in general terms; and consider it *done*; & let me see the *fruits* of it; in due season &c.

Dictated letter, unsigned. NhD. The letter appears to be in the handwriting of James W. Paige.

1. Not found.

TO JACOB MCGAW

Boston April 10. 1827

Dear Sir,

I see that your District has again failed to make an election.[1] A friend of yours was here the other day, & regretted very much that you had *withdrawn*.

Would not the present be a favorable opportunity to offer your name again to be presented to the People?

Excuse this suggestion, from an old friend. Yours   D. Webster

ALS. Mrs. Lester W. Parker, Brimfield, Mass.

1. With seven candidates in the field, the voters of the Somerset and Penobscot district of Maine had failed for a third time to elect a representative to Congress. Boston *Columbian Centinel*, April 11, 1827.

TO JEREMIAH MASON

Boston, April 10, 1827.

My dear Sir,

You will have heard from Mary,[1] since her arrival here. We had a pleasant passage, and I was glad of her company. Since I have been at home, my attention has been occupied with various matters, private and professional. I have, nominally, some little business yet in the State courts; although my long absences have very much severed me from them. In the neighboring counties, where courts are held at seasons when I am at home, I have also an occasional engagement, and these affairs have required my attention since my return.

The business in the [Supreme] court at Washington was heavy, as you have seen; and my participation in it greater than usual. We got on with the Virginia cause famously;[2] you will see, when you see the report, that our friend Judge [Joseph] Story laid out his whole strength and made a great opinion. The attorney-general [William Wirt] argued the cause with me. It was not one of his happiest efforts. By the aid of your brief, I got on tolerably well, and took the credit, modestly, of having made a good argument; at any rate, I got a very good fee; and although I shall not send you your just part of it, I yet enclose a draft for the least sum which I can persuade myself you deserve to receive.

I was sorry not to be able to get good materials from you, in the lottery case,[3] also. But we got along with the cause, and hope sometime to get the money.

As to political matters, I wish to say something, but hardly know where to begin. A survey of the whole ground leads me to believe, confidently, in Mr. Adams's reëlection. I set down New England, New Jersey, the greater part of Maryland, and perhaps all Delaware, Ohio, Kentucky, Indiana, Missouri, and Louisiana for him.

We must then get votes enough in New York to choose him, and I think cannot fail of this. It is possible we may lose four votes in Kentucky, but I do not expect it. At the same time it is not impossible that Pennsylvania may go for Mr. Adams. Beyond doubt, public opinion is taking a very strong turn in that State, and it is not now easy to say how far the change may proceed. That there is a change, and a great change, is too clear to be questioned.

In New York, affairs wear the common complexion of New York politics. Mr. [DeWitt] Clinton and some few of his friends have the credulity to think that he has yet some chance of being President two years hence. They flatter themselves that General Jackson's friends will abandon the General, and take him up. You will think none can be so weak or so ill-informed as to entertain such a hope, but, in truth, there are such men, and Mr. Clinton is himself one of them. The choice is with the people in districts, and unless some change takes place, Mr. Adams will get a majority, perhaps a large one.

You perceive how local questions have split up our good people here. You see the worst of it. In truth, right feeling very generally prevails, and nothing but prudent conduct is necessary to manifest it. Measures are in train, in relation to the ensuing choice of representatives, which I think will show that Boston is yet Boston. Care will also be taken to induce other towns to send good, and a good many, members to the general court. We shall have a Senator to elect. Our difficulty will be to find a man fit for the place, and with popularity to carry the election.

I had a great deal of conversation with Mr. [Samuel] Bell, in the course of the session, respecting the state of affairs with you. I have confidence in his good dispositions, but I do not think his policy bold enough. He understands my opinion, and guesses at yours, on that point. Experience, one would think, must have taught him by this time that there is but one course; and that is to rally, as administration men, without reference to bygone distinctions.

I wish you could see and converse with him, about the 19th or 20th. I shall go up to Boscawen to see my brother. If I can persuade him to accompany me, I would return by way of Portsmouth, to pass a single day with you. It seems, that without his consent or knowledge, he is chosen to the State legislature. He is so much displeased and dissatisfied with the course adopted by Mr. Adams's republican friends, in New Hampshire, that I know not whether he can be persuaded to do any thing. I have, however, thought it would be worth considering whether he should not bring forward resolutions, approving the conduct of the administration, and disapproving that of the opposition, and supporting them by a good strong speech. This would, perhaps, have two good effects; it would, in the first place, compel Mr. Adams's friends to act with him, and, in the second place, it would oblige Mr. [Isaac] Hill's friends to take their side. All this, however, is for future consideration.[4]

When you have time, not better employed, I shall be glad to hear from you. If I should not return from Boscawen by your way, I shall take another early opportunity to go to Portsmouth.

To-morrow, Thursday, I am going down to dine with the judge [Joseph Story]. Yours, always truly,   Daniel Webster

Text from *PC*, 1: 417–419. Original not found.

1. Daughter of Jeremiah Mason.
2. *Bank of the United States* v. *Dandridge*, 12 Wheaton 64 (1827).

3. *Clark* v. *City of Washington*, 12 Wheaton 40 (1827).
4. See above, DW to Ezekiel Webster, April 4, 1827.

TO RICHARD PETERS, JR.

Boston April 10. 1827

My Dear Sir

I am obliged to you for your letters,[1] & gratified with the information which they communicate. The result of the attempt to get up an imposing Caucus at Harrisburg is very significant.[2] It shows, at least, much abatement in the zeal which has heretofore been felt for the opposition candidate. Two years ago, it would have been no objection that the meeting was a Legislative *Caucus*, & not a *Convention*.

In this part of the Country, the friends of Mr Adams begin to think it necessary or at least useful to *bestir* themselves. They constitute 9/10ths of the people, & have not heretofore felt it to be necessary to take any particular measures to rally friends, or to express opinions. But since there are *some* busy friends of the opposing Candidate, & since they make some *noise*, it is likely to be thought proper to adopt measures to show their *real* strength & number. I incline to think the question will be tried, in some of the State Legislatures this way, at their summer sessions; & have no doubts how the result will be.

You may learn, perhaps, thro. another channel, that I have not been inattentive to such things here, as might be useful with you. As yet, there has not been time for much; but I trust something useful will be done.

It will give me pleasure to hear from you often, although our state of things will not probably allow me to give you much that shall interest you in return. Remember the great importance of Pennsylvania. Yrs very truly   Danl. Webster

ALS. PHi. Peters (1779–1848) succeeded Henry Wheaton as reporter for the U.S. Supreme Court.

1. Not found.

2. A Jackson legislative caucus had met in Harrisburg on April 5. Because only thirty-five of the 132 state legislators attended, it was considered a victory for the Adams forces.

Since January the Massachusetts legislature had been trying intermittently to elect a senator for the term beginning March 4, 1827. The two houses could not agree on a candidate, and in mid-February the election was postponed until May. When the incumbent, Elijah Hunt Mills, an able administration man, gave the impression that his health would not permit his being a candidate for reelection, Webster's name began to be mentioned, along with that of Governor Levi Lincoln.

Throughout the discussion of the candidates in May it remained Webster's contention, seemingly sincere, that Lincoln was the man for the

*post. Indeed, Webster himself urged the governor to run. As the ac-
knowledged Adams spokesman in the House, with seniority and thorough
familiarity with its rules and procedures, Webster and other party leaders argued the importance of his staying where he was. The House, not
the Senate, was still the chief forum for legislative deliberations, and
there would be no one left in that body capable of the kind of leadership
Webster had given.*

*When the election came before the legislature, Webster was in New
York to argue the Astor case (Kelley ads. Jackson, 14 Federal Cases 244,
1827). He had left Boston still hoping that Lincoln would consent to run,
but he had given assurances that he would accept if there were no other
alternative. Governor Lincoln, as revealed in the correspondence below,
flatly refused to be a candidate, and on June 7, the Massachusetts legislature elected Webster to his first term in the Senate.*

TO JOHN BARNEY

Boston April 13. 1827

My Dear Sir

I am very much obliged to you for your kind & friendly letter from
Washington,[1] & highly gratified with the good news it communicated
from Virginia, & especially from Mr. [Alfred H.] Powell's District. If *all*
our Virginia friends should succeed, in their reelection, it would be a
signal triumph, after what we have heard of the want of popularity of
the Administration, in that State.[2]

I have today a letter from Mr [John] *Test*, written not long after his
return.[3] He says *Indiana* is certain; that the course pursued by opposition
has been very unpopular, & that the people are afraid of Genl. Jackson's
friends, &c. &c.

In our part of the Country we have little or no excitement. There is,
to be sure, a little knot of very busy men, who make some noise, & take
infinite pains; &, if altogether *unopposed*, might in time mislead many.
But the friends of the President are getting to be wide awake, & I think
we shall have, in N. England, very clear & strong expressions of opinion,
in the course of the summer.

The topic, connected with myself, which you say something on, in
your letter, is important; and a little difficult. Many of our friends here
I suppose, may be of *your* opinion; & will wish to see me transferred to
the Senate. My own feelings, I confess, are very much against it; & I
shall consent, if I consent at all, only from a sense of duty, & from
deference to my friends. The situation was offered to me five or six
years ago; & I declined it, intending, then, if I again went into Congress

at all, to go into the House. Last June I again absolutely declined to be voted for, to supply the vacancy occasioned by Mr. [James] Lloyd's resignation. My habits are formed for the House, & I doubt if I should feel so much at home elsewhere. However, I suppose I shall not be allowed to be judge myself, in this matter. If it be the general opinion of friends that I ought to go into the Senate, I shall submit, tho' with much reluctance.

What has become of our friend Genl. [Samuel] Smith? I hear nothing of him. You perceive that the Colonial question has gone off, very quietly.

Let me hear from you, My Dear Sir, as you have leisure. Yours very truly & sincerely   Danl. Webster

I have often recollected, with pleasure, the very respectable and intelligent Gentlemen, with whom you made me acquainted, at Baltimore. I was extremely pleased with their conversation. If any of them, or indeed any other friends of yours, should be coming this way, I hope you will give me an opportunity of seeing them, & of being useful to them.

ALS. NhD.
1. Not found.
2. Barney was overly optimistic.

Powell was defeated by Robert Allen, a declared Jacksonian.
3. See above, March 29, 1827.

FROM JOSEPH HOPKINSON

Philad. Apl 13. 1827
My dear Sir

Since Mr [Robert] W[alsh's] return from Washington I have daily intended to write to you; but have really been at a loss what to say to you, inasmuch as in his communications there with the President and Mr C[lay] nothing was obtained but general impressions, without any of that certainty or assurance that I think good policy as well as fair dealing required.[1] The reception given to Mr. W[alsh] by both was frank, kind & apparently confidential in a most flattering degree; and he spoke to them with the same freedom and strength that he did to you. Nothing could be more explicit both in manner and matter, as regards his own views & intentions, & his opinions of their entire ignorance of publick sentiment here. As to Mr. A[dams,] Mr. W[alsh] believes his wishes are as they ought to be, and if he were permitted to follow his own dispositions there would be little reason to complain of him. As to the other he is full of subtile explanations, and polite reasons, derived from persons here who entirely deceive him; and he the more readily falls into their errors as they favour his inveterate dislike to all federalists, & particularly to the one in question.[2] There is no faith to be put in this man; he is evidently playing his own game, without the least regard to the interests or character of Mr. A—except so far as he is connected with them. He said with one of his significant leers, "Nobody can say that I neglect *my* friends." *I beg* you *to consider this as confidential.* He admits you are indispensable to them; but thinks you are perfectly secured in the service. These are in general the impressions I have received; with one more that whatever you may choose to *demand*, they will not choose to refuse. On the whole I think Mr. W[alsh] believes he has made an impression, certainly on one of the gentlemen, & probably on both; but nothing passed which he could consider to give any assurance for the future.

I am glad my review is well received at your good City;[3] but I shall not be satisfied unless it meets your approbation, & that of our quick sighted friend Judge [Joseph] Story—Mo[st] affectly yrs   Jos. Hopkinson

ALS. NhHi.

1. According to Adams, Walsh had visited him for an hour on March 31, during which time he pressed for some appointment for Joseph Hopkinson. Rather than making a commit-

ment on Hopkinson, however, Adams referred Walsh to the many federal appointments which had been made (Adams, *Memoirs*, 7: 251–252).

2. The allusion is to Clay.

3. Not identified.

TO HENRY CLAY

Boston April 14. 1827.

Private & confidential

My Dear Sir

I wrote you last from Philadelphia.[1] Before leaving that City, I did what little I could towards allaying feelings of partial dissatisfaction, & inspiring confidence & zeal among friends. What I learned there, & what I have heard since, make me *almost* confident that Pennsylvania will go right, in the autumn of next year. New York presented a better state of things than I expected. I saw many people in the City, & some members of the Legislature direct from Albany. All concurred in saying that the Administration not only stood well, but was gaining ground daily. It is difficult to conceive of such credulity, yet the truth seems to be that Mr [DeWitt] Clinton believes, & his friends believe, that it is possible & *probable* that Genl. Jackson's friends may take *him* up, & abandon the Genl. A New Yorker naturally attaches great importance to New York; & supposes that whoever can secure that state in his favor must necessarily prescribe his own terms; & Mr C[linton] I believe, is as confident as Mr. V[an] Buren is, that *he*, too, can control the votes of the great state. Both will be disappointed. If we can continue to create a little more activity & exertion among our friends, a large majority of the New

York votes will be certain for Mr. Adams. The recent appointments, [Peter] Stagg,[2] [William Beatty] Rochester[3] & [Henry] Wheaton,[4] are thought to be very judicious & acceptable. I doubt whether any thing but a *good judge* was obtained by the appointment of Mr [Samuel Rossiter] Betts.[5]

In this quarter, there is nothing very interesting. Our Legislature meets the end of next month, & will have to make a Senator. There will be some difficulty in finding a suitable man for the exigency of the case.

I have persuaded myself to think that it would be well for the New England Legislatures, or some of them, in their summer sessions, to take occasion to express their opinions, respecting Mr. Adams' election, the merits of his Administration, and the conduct of the opposition. It seems to me high time to let our opinions be known. My wish would be to bring this matter forward in that State, in which, (of the N. E. States) there is most show of opposition; I mean New Hampshire. I could wish that some competent member of the popular branch should bring forward Resolutions, expressing distinct opinions, on the topics above mentioned, & support them by an able discussion. They would pass, by a large majority; & friends would then be known from foes. If you concur in these opinions, I wish you would take occasion to suggest them to Mr [Samuel] *Bell.* His opinion would have much weight with the good people in the New Hampshire Legislature.

I have some communications from beyond the mountains, which <all> are agreeable & encouraging; but your information from that quarter must be much more correct than mine, & I shall be glad to learn what you hear. At what time do you expect to leave W[ashington] for Kentucky?

The Newspapers, I observe, repeat the report that Mr [Albert] Gallatin is to return in the summer.[6] I trust it is not true. He ought to stay at least till the matters now pending are all disposed of;—I mean such as are subjects of pending negotiation. Yours, with most true regard,

Danl. Webster

ALS. DLC.

1. See above, DW to Henry Clay, March 25, 1827.

2. Stagg, of New York, was appointed surveyor and inspector of revenue for the port of New York.

3. Adams appointed Rochester of New York chargé d'affaires to Central America in 1827.

4. Wheaton, also a New Yorker, was appointed chargé d'affaires to

Denmark.

5. Betts had been appointed and was subsequently confirmed judge of the district court for the Southern District of New York.

6. At the time, Gallatin was minister to Great Britain, from which post he returned on October 4 to become president of the National Bank of New York.

FROM HENRY CLAY

Washn. 14th. Apl. 1827.

(Private and Confidential)

My Dear Sir

As I observe from the public prints, that you have reached Boston, I will no longer postpone the acknowledgement of your obliging favor of the 25th ulto under date at Philada.[1]

The state of things you found in that City were not very encouraging; but there was some misrepresentation to you. In the City, I fear, our friends are not all the most disinterested. On the contrary, there are some whose sole object is the aggrandizement of themselves or their immediate connexions. These it is extremely difficult to satisfy. From other parts of Penna. the information which reaches me (and it is not a little) is of the most satisfactory kind. The abortive movement at Harrisburg (in which only 35 members of the Legislature could be got to recommend Jackson) is very significant.

Henceforward, I think the principle ought to be steadily adhered to of appointing only friends to the Administration in public offices. Such I believe is the general conviction in the Cabinet. It appears to me to be important that we should on all occasions, inculcate the incontestable truth that *now* there are but two parties in the Union, the friends and the enemies of the administration, and that all reference to obsolete denominations is for the purpose of fraud and deception. In this way, the efforts in particular places to revive old names may be counteracted. It is curious to see [Louis] McLean [McLane] and Van Buren (the former endeavoring to keep alive the Federal party in Delaware, and the latter to crush it in New York) co-operating in the cause of Jackson.

I mentioned to Mr. [Edward] Everett that some of you who have leisure and talent ought to prepare a series of pieces, calculated for the region and to be first published in Penna., in which a solemn appeal should be made to her patriotism and intelligence to stand by the great principles of National policy, which she has hitherto so uniformly favored. The text ought to be Mr. [William Branch] Giles' late resolutions in the Legislature of Va.[2] Such a production, well executed, would have great effect in and out of Penna. We ought not too hastily to conclude that the state of any portion of the American population is such as to render it inaccessible to reason. Such a conclusion would strike at the foundation of all our institutions.

[Alfred H.] Powell has lost his election in Va. by a small majority. I regret that event very much.[3] In other respects, and so far as we have yet heard the elections in that State have resulted more favorably than could have been anticipated.

From the West, the information continues good.

[Robert] Walsh has been here; and left the city more favorably impressed than when he came. He says that some prominent appointment must be given to a Philada. federalist, and that that Federalist must be [Joseph] Hopkinson; and he also says that you concur with him in both particulars. Towards Mr. H. I have friendly feelings; but I really fear that any other Federalist in Penna. (not excepting James Ross) may be appointed with less injury to the Admin. than Mr. H.

You were misinformed about the West P[oint] visitors. I believe very good selections (and generally friends) have been made. I mentioned [Robert] Walsh and I think he is to be one. The Secy. of War is at present absent.

I have sent you a letter recd. this morning from Mr. [Thomas] Smith (Editor of the Lexington [Kentucky] Reporter) who has just passed from Philada. to Pittsburg through Harrisburg. His opportunities of collecting information were not bad. [H. Clay][4]

AL (signature removed). DLC.

1. See above.

2. In the session of the Virginia legislature just recessed, William B. Giles, shortly to be inaugurated governor, introduced resolutions requesting a committee to investigate and to report on the constitutional power held by the state and federal governments in Virginia. Specifically, Giles requested the committee to determine if the tariff and internal improvements were not in violation of those powers. *Niles' Register*, 32 (April 21, 1827): 135–139.

3. See above, DW to John Barney, April 13, 1827.

4. According to an endorsement by Thomas Davis, Clay's signature was "cut out for Mr. Sprague, Oct 13. 1828."

TO RICHARD RUSH

Boston April 16. 1826 [1827]

Private

My Dear Sir

I wrote you some days ago,[1] enclosing sundry letters in favor of Mr *Peabody*,[2] to be Collector at Castine [Maine]. At the same time, I expressed, I think, the opinion which I had intimated to you before, that it would be well to appoint Mr *Carr*.[3]

Soon after writing that letter, I learned one thing, which, if I had known it before, would have had some influence on my judgment, in that matter. I mention it now, confidentially, & wish you to suggest it to the President, that he may consider what weight ought to be given to it. Mr Carr is a relative, as it appears, I believe a nephew, of *Genl. [Henry Alexander Scammell] Dearborn*. There has been a feeling in that

State, for many years, that something too much of office & patronage has been bestowed on that Family. Its branches are numerous, and many places of importance have been & still are held by them. Of the existence of this feeling, I am certain, from my own knowledge & observation; & I am convinced also, that it is somewhat general. Other things being equal, I should think it the safest course to avoid giving fresh occasion for renewing or strengthening it; & therefore if another man, equally qualified & recommended by an equal weight of intelligence & influence presents himself, I should think it better to give him the preference.

I learn that Mr. [John] Davis,[4] of Augusta, is a candidate, with very high & general recommendations. Without doubt he is a highly respectable & very fit man; and the persons who have, as I am informed, interested themselves in his behalf, are the leading men in the State. Of all this, however, and of other applications, the President can judge. My main object, in this letter, having recommended Mr. Carr, is now to say, that if I had known, when I did recommend him, the fact which I know now, & which I have stated above, it would have produced great hesitation, in my own judgment, as to the expediency of appointing *him* to this office.

I have felt it be my duty to make this suggestion to you & the President, in entire confidence; & I do not doubt that that which is on the whole best will be done. Yours with entire regard,   Danl. Webster

ALS. NjP. DW's letter to Rush incorrectly appears on mDW as 1826. See Rush to DW, April 25, 1827 (mDW 6112) for Rush's response to Webster's letter.

1. See DW to Richard Rush, April 7, 1827, mDW 6073.

2. Not identified.

3. On Carr's appointment, see above, DW to Jacob McGaw, February 21, 1827.

4. Davis was then a member of the Maine House of Representatives.

FROM HENRY CLAY

Washn. 20th. Apl. 1827

(Private and Confidential)

My Dear Sir

I duly recd. your favor of the 14th inst.[1] Meetings are beginning to take place in Penna. of the friends of the Administration. One was held at Chambersburg a few days ago which is represented to have been the most numerous and respectable that ever assembled in that place.[2] You will see an account of the proceedings in the [Washington Daily National] Journal. I think with you that there is much reason to hope of a good result in that State. [Jabez Delano] Hammond gives me assurances, from Albany, that there is ascertained to be a majority in the Senate, and a large majority in the Assembly, favorable to the Administration. They have determined to establish a new and efficient paper there to expose both Clinton & V[an] B[uren]. The delusion of the former which leads him yet to suppose that Jackson will be abandoned and he be taken up is wonderful.

I have written to Mr. [Samuel] Bell of N. H. as you desired. I think the time has come when demonstrations should be made, and be made too in N. England, as well as elsewhere. You have no doubt heard that they had a preliminary meeting in Balt[imor]e of a most gratifying character as to the persons composing it, in which it was resolved to take the field in May, and organize the friends of Mr. Adams throughout the State.

My information from the West continues good. I feel perfectly confident that there will be no loss in that quarter.

Information has just reached the City that the re-election of [Thomas] Newton[, Jr.,] is placed beyond all doubt by the vote of Norfolk County at the beginning of this week in which he obtained about 390 to 90. [John] Taliaferro and [Charles Fenton] Mercer are run, so will be both re-elected. I think we shall make up for the loss of [Alfred H.] Powell by the election of a friend in place of W[illiam] Smith. So that the vote of Virginia will probably remain relative to the parties the same in the next that it was in the last Congress.

I have written to Mr. [Albert] Gallatin that it is not expected that he will return until he shall have brought the negotiations with which he is charged to a conclusion. And I have given him a rebuke for the reports, traced to himself, of his intention to return this Summer. Unless therefore he comes away in violation of all rule, I do not think he can get back this year, or at any rate, until the last of the year. [William] Huskissons illness prevented the renewal of the negotiations on the first of Feb. as was arranged; and, from the late accounts, it could not have recommenced as late as the 10th. March, if it indeed has by this time. If there should be a change of Ministry (and I think a total change not improbable—some must take place[)]—it may be the fall before they get to work again. Yours with sincere esteem   H Clay

P.S. Say, when you have occasion again to write, what you hear from or about [Thomas Jackson] Oakley.   H C

ALS. DLC.

1. See above, DW to Henry Clay, April 14, 1827.

2. On April 10, 1827, numerous citizens of Franklin County, Pennsylvania, assembled in the courthouse at Chambersburg and adopted resolutions defending Adams' administration.

TO JOSEPH E. SPRAGUE

Boston April 27, 1827

My dear Sir,

I was very happy to find here yours of the 21st.[1] on my return from N. Hampshire the day before yesterday; and rejoice to see today, how well you have begun in Salem.[2] *The thing will go.*

I have letters from Maryland, New York, Ohio, and Washington all giving very gratifying accounts. Indeed there seems to be a general awakening among our friends. I am going to Ipswich on Tuesday, and will endeavor to see you a moment as I go along, say about 10 oclock. Yours truly,   Danl. Webster

Copy. NhHi. Published in Van Tyne, p. 125. Sprague (1782–1852; Harvard 1804) was an attorney and postmaster in Salem, and at times a member of the Massachusetts General Court and Executive Council.

1. Not found.

2. On the evening of April 26, friends of the federal and state administrations had held a meeting in Salem, at which resolutions were adopted favoring the Adams administration and committees were appointed for nominating candidates and conducting the upcoming elections. The meeting, according to reports, "was more fully attended than any we recollect to have ever seen in Salem, and was conducted altogether without reference to the old party divisions." *Salem Gazette*, as quoted in the Boston *Columbian Centinel*, April 28, 1827.

TO JOHN C. WRIGHT

Boston April 30. 1827

My Dear Sir,

I thank you for your very interesting letter from Pittsburg;[1] & applaud your zeal & activity in the good cause. Your suggestions respecting the paper at that place will be *immediately* attended to, by friends here, & the price of fifteen or twenty subscriptions forwarded. I am aware that in your present situation you must be exposed to expense, as well as loss of time. I trust, however, that care will be taken that *individual* sacrifices, of this sort, be not heavy.

As this is the very moment for making right impressions, pains ought not & must not, be spared. It is essential, all important, *now* to put the proper means of forming right judgments into the hands of the People; the opportunity must not be lost. I recd the list of *names*.[2] Among the Newspapers in this City is the "Massachusetts Journal." It is a tri-weekly publication, well disposed, occasionally able, & well fitted for country circulation. It is for the Administration, & all its great measures. Would it do to send this paper regularly to the names on the List? I should be glad to do so, if you thought it would be well; but hardly dare have it done, without your advice.

I hear nothing definite from [Thomas Jackson] Oakley. If it were not for the *noise* made by a journey, I should see him, in next month. I feel very anxious, on the subject, for many reasons.

If I can learn any thing, I will let you know.

I returned from N. H. two or three days ago. There is a good deal of excitement in that State, but a great majority of the People are sound. Mr [Isaac] Hill & his party have thus far, owed all their success to the narrow notions of the Adams Republicans. These last undertook to put Hill down, by their own strength. With this view they established the Journal,[3] which was to reject all Federal support, & yet expected to overcome the opposition. In this, it has been found, that mere *news & circulation* do no wonders. Hill's party is too strong, not in numbers, but in management, & means of influence. I trust Mr. [Samuel] Bell will set these matters right. It is but [to] bring the friends of Mr Adams together, & they will show 4/5ths, both in numbers & talent, of the State. Their Legislature sits in June, & I hope a proposition approving the course of the Administration, & disapproving that of the opposition, will be brought forward. Such a measure is in contemplation.[4]

In this state the elections to the Legislature (except Senators) take place immediately. Sundry local objects will have their influence, but some reference will also be had to general politics. The important object, of this latter kind, is the choice of a Senator, in Mr [Elijah Hunt] Mills' place. This gives us trouble. I wish to ask your conscientious opinion whether the general good requires that *I* should go into the Senate. But at the same time that I ask your advice (& I have as yet, asked nobody's else) I ought to say that it may not be in my power to follow it, even if it should agree with my own opinion. In the first place, the Legislature may not be such an one as would chuse me; and in the second place, (& what I suppose more probable) the feeling among friends here may be so strong, that I shall not be able to oppose it. Nevertheless, as it *may* so happen that my own judgment may decide the matter, I should be glad of your impressions on it. Such a removal would be sorely agt. my inclination, & personal preferences. I think I am at home, where I now am, & should be transferred, with great reluctance. This, of course, all to ourselves, & let me know what you think of it.

You will have seen that all went well in the Connecticut Elections. [Orange] Merwin & [Noyes] Barber, whom the Caucus voted *out*, the People have voted *in*. Govr. [Cornelius Peter] Van Ness has made a sad business of the *interference* of the President &c.[5] Vermont is remarkably correct, & spirited; & agrees with Mr. [Jonas] Galusha, her former Govr.

that it would have been *unequal* to have sent Van Ness to the Senate, for N. York would have had *three* Senators, & Vermont but *one.*[6]

Our accounts from New York, are, in general, very favorable; but I have few particulars. [John W.] Taylor writes that in his District Mr. Adams is more popular than at any former period. I have learned nothing, or very little, from Maine; but believe all is well in that quarter.

I hope you have the good practice of *burning* such communications as this. It is the only *absolutely* safe course. Yrs truly   D Webster

N.B. You will *hear from me*, or from friends here, in a few days.

ALS. NhD.
1. Not found.
2. Not found.
3. The Concord *New Hampshire Journal*, published by Jacob B. Moore, was established at the insistence of Samuel Bell in 1826.
4. A resolution defending the Adams administration did come up in the New Hampshire legislature in the summer of 1827. However, it praised the administration as "strictly democratic" and hence offended the

Federalists, who combined with the Jacksonians to defeat it.
5. Van Ness (1782–1852) was governor of Vermont from 1823 to 1826. In October 1826, however, he lost his bid for a seat in the U.S. Senate to Horatio Seymour. Van Ness, in his bitterness, accused President Adams of using his influence to help Seymour in the election.
6. Galusha (1753–1834) was governor of Vermont from 1809 to 1813 and from 1815 to 1820.

TO HENRY CLAY

Boston May 7. 1827

Private & confidential
My Dear Sir,

I have to thank you for your's of the 14. & 20th of April.[1] The general information they contain, respecting the state of things in the South & West, is encouraging, & confirms what I learn from other quarters. The means agreed on, at the close of the session, & which have been partially applied, have, evidently, tended to awaken a good spirit. We cannot I think too strongly feel the conviction that public opinion is very likely to take a decisive direction between this time & the next meeting of Congress. We are all ready & willing, here, to do our part, that the direction shall be the right one.

A principal part of my present purpose is to ask your attention to a matter personal to myself. The state of Mr. [Elijah Hunt] Mills' health puts his re-election to the Senate out of the question. Of course, our friends here have to find a successor, & I see pretty significant signs of an intention to offer the place to me. A similar proposition was made to me last June, when Mr [James] Lloyd resigned; & repeated, with some urgency, afterwards, when an attempt was making to supply Mr Mills' place. On those occasions I was able *to get excused*, without great difficulty, & without giving offence. If the same thing should be proposed again, it will come under different circumstances, & it is necessary, therefore, to consider beforehand, what will be proper to be done. I need not trouble you with particular details of our politics: Suffice it to say, that the opposition, (for there is a little knot of Gentlemen, desiring that appellation) have seized on some local subjects,—especially a taking proposition for a *free-bridge*, by means of which they hope to strengthen their ranks. The leader of the *free-bridge* party is Mr [William C.] Jarvis, now speaker of the H. R. & who was one of the candidates for Senator last winter. He will probably be so again.[2] He *professes* friendship for Mr. Adams; but Mr. Adams' friends in the Legislature, when he is proposed for Senator, think of what happened in N. Hampshire, & *almost* happened in Vermont.[3] They do not incline to choose him. Mr. John Mills will, or may, also be thought of. I believe *he* is a very true man, but not one likely to take an active part in affairs. If Gov. [Levi] Lincoln would take the appointment, it would be highly satisfactory; but I believe he is not willing, at this time, to go to the Senate, & his friends are, also, a good deal averse to his leaving the place he now fills. Beyond all these reasons, a considerable degree of new feeling is springing up, in the State, in favor of the administration; & this feeling will require that *Something be done*. The Senate is looked upon as weak, & a strong desire is felt, to do all that can be done to give the Govt. aid *there*. From these & other considerations, added to what I hear & see, I fear a strong disposition, to the effect I have intimated, may prevail, unless it be prevented, or <directed> diverted by seasonable means. I have made some attempts to this end, myself, but with no great success. I have <told> stated my own *decided wish* to stay where I am; but am told, that I have no right to my own preference, but must be disposed of as others think best. I have hinted, that my appropriate place was in the House; that my habits were made up to it; that it was accustomed to the sound of my voice—& that I could do more good there than elsewhere, &c. &c. The answer is; the House will provide for itself; it is a numerous body, & somebody will appear to supply my place, &c. But the Senate is a small body—in which vacancies occur seldom, & which now, most woefully, requires amendment.

I need not say to you, My dear Sir, that both my *feelings* & my *judgement* are *against* the transfer. It would be to me a great sacrifice to make the exchange. And yet, on the other hand, as I am situated here, it would be extremely unpleasant & perhaps impossible, for me, to meet the offer if it should be made, *with a flat refusal*. I have therefore taken the liberty to write to you on the subject, for the purpose of asking you to consider of it, a little, & then to suggest what occurs to you for the use of confidential friends here. The Legislature meets the last Wednesday of the present month; & one of their first acts will probably be the choice of Senator.

You will perhaps find occasion to mention the matter to Mr Adams, & having done so, I will thank you to write a line to Mr [Nathaniel] Silsbee, such as may be shown to the Govr., & other confidential friends, expressing your opinion & feeling. If it be possible to persuade the Govr. to accept the place, all will be well; but if not, I greatly fear, I shall hardly escape. Upon the whole, having distinctly expressed my feeling, & my opinion, I must now leave the matter to the decision of others. A professional engagement will call me to New York, the 25. inst.; so that I shall not be at home, probably at the election.

I conclude by repeating that for the little time I may remain in Congress, I have a strong,—a very strong—personal wish to stay in the House; Nevertheless, *if it is clearly better* that *I go elsewhere*, I must be disposed of as the common good requires.

On one or two other subjects I had intended to say something; but shall spare your patience till another post.

Have you anything new as to Mr [Louis] McLane's intended course? I fear he is gone, but have thought it *possible* that the public sentiment in Del. might keep him right.[4] Yrs always with mo[st] true regard

Danl. Webster

ls. DLC.

1. See above, Henry Clay to DW, April 14 and 20, 1827.

2. Following several attempts and rebuffs by the legislature to secure approval for a free bridge across the Charles River, the Massachusetts legislature finally granted the Warren Bridge Corporation a charter in March 1827 over the opposition of the Charles River bridge investors. But Governor Lincoln vetoed the bill, with the result that the bridge question became an issue in local politics, dividing the forces which had earlier been united in their support of Adams. In the next gubernatorial contest, William C. Jarvis, representative from Charlestown, ran as the opponent to Lincoln, the incumbent governor. Lincoln won the election, but Webster's concern at this time was with the impact the bridge controversy might have on the base of Adams' support. Since the free-bridge faction had just forced their bill through the legislature, the legislature might also elect Jarvis senator, defeating the designs of the Adams forces. Over the next few years the bridge controversy, in which Webster continued to be involved as counsel for the Charles River Bridge, had far wider political and social ramifications. Stanley I. Kutler, *Privilege and Creative Destruction: The Charles River Bridge Case* (Philadelphia, 1971), pp. 18–34.

3. Although he continued for some time to deny any opposition to Adams, New Hampshire's Senator Levi Woodbury had shifted his support to Jackson in late 1826. Cornelius P. Van Ness, recent candidate for

the United States Senate from Vermont, had just come out against Adams by accusing him of tampering with the Vermont election.

4. McLane, an old Federalist from Delaware, was fast shifting his support to the opposition.

FROM NICHOLAS BIDDLE

Phila. May 8. 1827

My Dear Sir,

I have stolen from the quarter for accts the necessary time to perform the duty imposed on me by the Philo[sophical] Society—and cannot deny myself the pleasure of asking you to put the accompanying pamphlet among your books as a mark of my respect & esteem.[1] You will perceive in it still some thing of the character of my present pursuits—for being largely indebted for satisfaction "had & received" from many speeches of yours I am endeavoring to discharge my obligation at its nominal amount with a rate of exchange tremendously against me. I am however at least an honest insolvent, for if I do pay you as they phrase it, with a ticket, it is all I have. As such you will receive it from yrs very truly   N B

Mr. [Samuel] Jaudon will console you with a much better speech from Judge [Joseph] Story, in a day or two[.][2]

ALS draft. DLC.

1. Biddle forwarded a copy of his "Eulogium on Thomas Jefferson," which he had delivered before the American Philosophical Society on April 11, 1827.

2. The meaning of the allusions to Jaudon, Story, and a "speech" in Biddle's postscript has not been determined.

FROM HENRY CLAY

Washington 14th. May 1827

(Private & Confidential)

My dear Sir

I duly received your favor of the 7th. instant[1] and on the interesting subject of it, I have conversed with the President.

I had previously written to Mr E[verett] that the pro's and con's on the question of your translation from the House to the Senate were so nearly balanced that I thought you might safely pursue the bent of your own inclination.[2] The public interests require you in the House, and you are wanted in the Senate. So far as your personal interests are to be advanced, I incline to think you had better remain where you are. If your place could be supplied in the House, then I should say go to the Senate. [Thomas Jackson] Oakley or [John] Sergeant might enable the Administration to get along in the popular branch, but the course of the one and the election of the other is uncertain. If neither of them come to our aid, we *possibly* may do without them, should you be compelled to accept a place in the Senate. The Administration loses much directly as well as morally for the want of such abilities as you would carry into that body—directly by the array of talents on the one side (which it must be owned the opposition there exhibits) without an adequate counterpoise on the other; which has the effect of disheartening friendly Senators—morally by the extraneous effect on the Country of this unequal contest.

What the President would be glad to see is, that Mr [Levi] Lincoln should come in place of Mr Mills, as the state of this latter gentleman's health does not admit of his longer serving; and if, as is said to be probable, Mr [Nathaniel] Silsbee should resign, in consequence of his being elected Governor, or from any other cause, that you, after the ensuing Session, should take his place. But if Governor Lincoln cannot be prevailed upon to accept a seat in the Senate, then the President decidedly prefers your coming in at the next Session, as Mr Mills successor.

From [Louis] McLane I have heard directly nothing. I have hoped that, if Delaware should send to the House of R. next fall a friend of the Administration, and no very adverse twists should occur elsewhere, Mr. McL[ane] might see that it was his interest to adhere to his principles, and disentangle himself from his new associates; and I had thought that the probability of his adopting a correct course might be influenced by the consideration of his being the leader of one party, instead of being eclipsed in the ranks of the other. But all this is speculation; and, should you go into the Senate, he may still find that his future advancement lies rather on the side of working with you than against you. Unless I am much deceived Delaware will send to the H. of R. a friend to the administration.

The recent changes in the British Ministry are very great, and they must have been the result of a radical difference of opinion on some important subject. We have no explanation of them from Mr. [Albert] Gallatin, from whom I have received no letter subsequent to the resignations. The most obvious cause is that of the Irish Catholics. On the last day of March Mr. [William] Huskisson remained too unwell to resume the negotiation with Mr. Gallatin. He was trying to settle a preliminary point, respecting our North Eastern boundary with Mr. [Henry Unwin] Addington, but was able to make very little progress. I should think that the new ministerial arrangements would occasion some further delay. I see therefore but little prospect of Mr. Gallatin's speedily coming home.

I have very little late political news. The meeting in Balto. was all that we could have desired it to be. The progress of correct thinking in

Penna. continues to be encouraging. And in New York our friends are as confident of success as they need be. They are about to establish a newspaper to be edited by Mr. [Isaac Q.] Leake,[3] formerly senior editor of the Argus, and I hope they will not fail in that object. It is much wanted.

From K[entucky] my friends write me in good spirits. We shall have however warm work there growing out of our "Free bridge" question, alias the Relief system.

I have written a short letter to Silsbee[4] communicating the preceding views in regard to the Senate.

I am making efforts to get off to Kentucky in about a fortnight. Unless there should be some unexpected occurrences I think I shall go about that time. I am Cordially Your friend & ob. Servt.   H. Clay

P.S. Your late Speech at Faneuil Hall was all that it should have been.[5] It presented the true condition of the existing state of things, and pointed out clearly the only correct line of policy. In spite of all the carpers, it will have good effect.   H C.

ALS. DLC. Published in Curtis, 1: 296–298.

1. See above.

2. Clay repeated this sentence almost verbatim in his letter to Edward Everett, May 2, 1827 (Everett Papers, MHi, Microfilm Edition).

3. Leake, previously a clerk in the Mechanics and Farmers Bank in Albany and cashier of the Niagara Bank, had joined with Moses I. Cantine in 1821 to edit and publish the anti-Clintonian *Albany Argus*. It has not been determined that the paper Clay referred to was ever established.

4. Clay's letter of May 15, 1827, to Nathaniel Silsbee has not been found. Silsbee's response, of May 23, 1827, appears in Curtis, 1: 298–299.

5. See W & S, 13: 24–30, for Webster's speech of April 20, 1827, at Faneuil Hall. In that address, Webster stated that the ideological differences which formerly separated Federalists and Republicans were no longer revelant and urged partisans of both factions to unite behind Adams.

TO HENRY CLAY

Boston May 18. 1827.

Private & confidential
My dear Sir

Notwithstanding the *insanity* of some men, of all parties, & especially of some Federalists, by means of which this City will not be fully represented in the Legislature, yet the returns show that the House will be very strong, both in numbers & talents.[1] No opposition man will be in either Branch, from Boston; nor hardly one from any other part of the State. All the large towns have acted on the *Union* principle; & the House will therefore be mainly composed of friends of the Administration, of both parties. The folly of a part of the Federalists, here, is mortifying enough, but perhaps has done no great mischief, on the general scale.

Since I wrote you last, I am strengthened in the conviction that I ought not to be a candidate for the Senate. The more I think of it, the more fully I am persuaded of the propriety of remaining where I am. I hope an effort will be made, *from all quarters*, to persuade Govr. Lincoln to take the situation.

A *pamphlet*, for the especial benefit of Pennsylvania, will make its' appearance from Philadelphia, soon. It will be printed in English & German, and circulated as widely as may be. I think it will do good. Its' leading object is to present, by way of contrast, the politics of the Administration, & those of the opposition. As manifestations of the leading principles of the former, the Presidents first message, the doctrines of your speech, &c &c are fully exhibited; & as sure guides to a knowledge of the latter, Mr [William Branch] Giles Resolutions & other things equally authentic, are prominently put forth. I think the work will hit the sentiments of Pennsylvania, Ohio, & Western Va. Copies will of course be sent to you.[2]

I have seen a good deal of the New Hampshire People, in the course of the Spring. A warm battle is to be fought, in that State; & the sooner our friends understand it so, the better. For two years, the attempt has been to put down Mr [Isaac] Hill, by the *organization of the Republican party*. It has not been done, & cannot be done. Although four fifths of the people, in that party, are friends of Mr Adams, yet Hill, himself, & a few other cunning & indefatigable *Caucus* men, control the movements, & arrange the organization, of the *party*. Mr Hill himself would not, probably, have been elected Senator, if the [New Hampshire] Journal would have consented to nominate *any other* candidate, Federal or Republican; but it would not, as I have understood; because Mr Hill was the *regular caucus candidate*. The only way is to appeal directly to the *People*. The great popular current is with the Govt. there, as well as elsewhere; but half the benefit is not derived, which ought to be derived, from the favorable course of opinion. However, the Journal seems to be more in earnest, at last; & I think it likely the ensuing session of the Legislature may produce some new movements. The Federalists in the Legislature, a third in number, or more, & three thirds in talents & ability, are entirely willing to do any thing they can do, without personal dishonor; but they will not, & cannot, & ought not, to act with Mr Adams' Republican friends, until these last will cease to keep any terms with Mr Hill, & his party. I believe Mr [Samuel] Bell will see the state things are in, when he goes to Concord, & trust his fidelity & good sense to give them a proper direction.

I go to New York next week, where I shall see Mr [Thomas Jackson] Oakley. Before leaving the City, will write you, unless I shall previously learn that you have gone west.

I have today a very encouraging letter from Washington Co. Tenne. Yours always truly & faithfully   Danl. Webster

ALS. DLC.

1. After the votes were counted for the spring elections for state Senate, four of the seats from Suffolk County (Boston) were left vacant because no candidate polled the required number of votes. The same problem occurred on May 12, when Boston was able to choose only eight men for thirty places in the Massachusetts House of Representatives. All of the representatives elected, however, had been on the administration Union Ticket.

2. The title of the pamphlet referred to has not been determined; but apparently it was Webster's and Clay's intention to flood Pennsylvania with publications in support of the Adams administration. For example, according to Edward Everett,

Webster requested him, in pursuance of Clay's suggestion, to write an essay on "domestic industry and internal improvements for circulation in Pennsylvania" (Diary of Edward Everett, Entry of April 30, 1827, MHi). It is conceivable that the publication mentioned by Everett and the one referred to by Webster were one and the same. A publication with the unwieldy title, "Mr. Clay's Speech upon the Tariff: or the 'American Question,' so called; Mr. Giles' Speech upon the Resolutions of Inquiry in the House of Delegates of Virginia, in Reply to Mr Clay's Speech . . ." did appear under a Richmond, Virginia, imprint in 1827. Whether that publication, or other copies published in Pennsylvania, were circulated in that state has not been determined.

TO LEVI LINCOLN

Boston May 22. 1827

Private & Confidential
My Dear Sir,

It was my misfortune not to see you, on your late visit to this place, owing, partly, to engagements, in & out of town, & partly to a misapprehension, as to the time of your leaving the City. Disappointed, thus, in the expectation & hope of a personal interview, I now adopt this mode of making a few suggestions to you, on a subject of some interest; I mean the approaching election of a Senator in Congress. The present posture of things, in relation to that matter, is so fully known to both of us, that I need not trouble you with much preliminary observation. I take it for granted, that Mr E. H. Mills will be no longer a candidate. The question, then, will be, who shall succeed him? I need not say to you, that you, yourself, will doubtless be a prominent object of consideration, in relation to the vacant place; and the purpose of this communication requires me to acknowledge, that I deem it possible, also, that *my* name should be mentioned, more or less generally, as one who may be thought of, among others for the same situation. In anticipation of this state of things, & more especially since I have been awakened by its probably near approach, I have not only given it a proper share of my own reflection, but have also consulted with others, in relation to it, in whose judgment & friendship I have confidence. The result is, that there are many strong personal reasons, and as friends think, (and as I think too,) some *public* reasons, why I should decline the offer of a seat in the Senate, if it should be made to me. Without entering at present, into a detail of these reasons, I will say that the latter class of them grow out of the public station, which I at present fill, & out of the *necessity* of encreasing, rather than of diminishing, in both branches of the National Legislature, the strength which may be reconed on as friendly to the present Administration. I hope you will understand what I would now wish to communicate, without imputing to me the vanity of supposing that my *services*, to the Administration, or to the Country, in the H. of R. are of any particular importance; or, on the other hand, that it is [a] matter of option with me, to change that place for another. I think quite differently, in both respects. Nevertheless, however inconsiderable the first of these things may be, & however contingent, or improbable, the last, they are such as make it convenient, at the present crisis, to act upon the one, as if it were of some consideration, and to regard the other, as if it might probably, or possibly happen. To come, therefore, at once, to the main point, I beg to say, that I see no way in which the public good can be so well promoted, as by *your* consenting to go into the Senate. This is my own clear & decided opinion; it is the opinion, equally clear & decided, of intelligent & patriotic friends here; and I now [am] able to add, that *it is also the decided opinion of all those friends, elsewhere, whose judgment, in such matters, we should naturally regard. I believe I may say, without violating confidence, that it is the wish, entertained with some earnestness, of our friends at Washington, that you should consent to be Mr. Mills' successor.* You will probably, as soon as you arrive here next week, learn the same thing, thro another channel. I need hardly add, after what I have said, that such also is my own wish. We are in a *crisis*; & it requires all the aid which can be mustered. If I have not misunderstood you, on some former occasions, you do not desire a long continuance in your present situation. If so, this occasion is apt & convenient to resign it. If you should find your employment at Washington not agreeable, that also may be relinquished, without particular inconvenience, in a short time. The "crisis" will terminate, one way or the other, about the end of the next session, or by the beginning of that ensuing. You will then be able to regard your private wishes, probably, as to prolonging your official service there.

A professional engagement will take me to New York, at the end of this week.[1] I hope to return by the 5th. or 6th. of June, but possibly may be detained longer. If you wish to address me soon, please enclose your letter to Nathan Appleton Esq, of this City, & he will forward it to me, wherever I may be. Mr. Appleton is one of our (few) Representatives. He is intelligent, & perfectly well disposed; & I shall leave him possessed of my confidence, & with power to communicate my views on this subject to other friends, as convenience may require. He is well known to you, I suppose; if not, you may safely regard him as a man of high honor, & fit to be treated with confidence. I am, Dr. Sir, very truly, Yours

Danl. Webster

ALS. MHi. Published in Curtis, 1: 293–294.

1. Webster was to appear with Martin Van Buren and S. A. Talcott for the defendants in *Kelley* ads. *Jackson*, 14 Federal Cases 244 (1827), one of the Astor land cases.

TO JOSEPH E. SPRAGUE

Boston May 23. 1827.

My dear Sir,

I am obliged to you for your letter of yesterday.[1] The opinions you express are in general my own opinions precisely. I see but one way of escaping from our present difficulty, and that is to *prevail* with the governor to be a Candidate. To this end a united and vigourous application should as I think be made to him at the very earliest opportunity, after he arrives here. I have explained myself freely on this subject to Mr. [Nathaniel] Silsbee whom I saw yesterday. Yours with entire regard

Danl. Webster

Copy. NhHi. Published in Van Tyne, p. 126.
1. Not found.

FROM LEVI LINCOLN

Worcester May 24 1827

Confidential
My *Dear* Sir

I hasten, on the moment of the receipt of your letter[1] to a reply, in the hope that it may reach you before you leave the City, on your proposed Journey. Believe me, my Dear Sir, I am strongly impressed with a sense of the confidence and kindness of my Friends. Your opinions too, came to me with the added weight of suggestions of friendship. But I have to regret that, under existing circumstances, I cannot feel at liberty to yield a conformity to them. My course, in reference to the subject to which you allude, was originally directed by considerations, over some of which I had no power of control, and others had relation to the situation of Friends, and to what I believed was due to public sentiment. The expressions of *personal disinclination* to the office of U S Senator were sincere, and from the delicacy of my position the last year, were called for, and openly and repeatedly made. Indeed it became necessary for me to say that I should absolutely decline the place, if offered to me. I have since believed, and am now confirmed in the opinion (Mr Mills being out of the question) that the *transfer* to which *you object*, should be made. In this expression of this sentiment I have no disguise. If the strength and support of the Administration is regarded, it should most certainly be done. To your private interests, it seems to me, it could produce no additional prejudice. The sacrifice of business and of domestic duties and enjoyments are no greater in the one place than the other. To the Administration, this arrangement must be all important. I consider the deficiency of power in the Senate, as the weak point in the Citadel, the breach already made in the walls. The Force should there be strengthened. No individual should be placed there, who was not *now* in armour for the conflict; who understood the proper mode of resistance, who personally knew, and had measured strength with the opposition, who was familiar with the political interests & foreign relations of this country, with the course of policy of the Administration, and who would be prepared, at once, to meet and decide upon the character of measures, which should be proposed. This I undertook to say, no *novice* in the National Councils could do. At least, I would not promise to attempt it. I feel deeply, that I could not do it successfully. I should disappoint the expectations of my Friends, and do injustice to the little reputation I might otherwise hope to enjoy. There is no affectation of humility in this, and under such impressions, I *cannot suffer myself* to be thought of in a manner, which may make me responsible for great mischief in defeating the chance of a better selection.

As to the objection which I have heard urged from your present situation in the House, it has force, but is yet susceptible of a satisfactory answer. Even, *from* the Senate, that influence would continue to be *indirectly felt where* it has heretofore been *effectually exercised.* It cannot but be selfish, I had almost said *cowardly,* in the *Host* which will remain to the side of the Administration in the popular Branch, to avoid that responsibility, which their *numbers,* and I am well persuaded their *talents* will enable them triumphantly to meet.

But I have already written more and with greater haste than I should. I have to repeat that I beg not to be considered a candidate for the Station, to which, I feel, that the best and kindest motives in my Friends would assign me, but which I venture to assure them upon such explanations as I might more fully offer, they would excuse me at this time, for declining. In this act, it will be among the first of my wishes to retain that good opinion, with which you have so highly honored me.

I shall have pleasure in seeing Mr [Nathan] Appleton & hope that he may favor me with the opportunity on my arrival in the City. With sentiments of the most respectful & friendly consideration Your obedient Servt.   Levi Lincoln

ALS. DLC. Excerpt published in *W & S*, 16: 163.
    1. See above, DW to Levi Lincoln, May 22, 1827.

FROM JOHN C. WRIGHT

Steubenville, 24th May 1827

My Dear Sir,

Your favour of the 30th ult.[1] reached here some days since during my absence for a week attending Court, and to the giving certain men a proper political impetus in a neighbouring county. This absence has occasioned the delay in acknowledging your letter.

I had understood from another quarter that our friends in the "Bay State" had it in contemplation to send you and some other "strong man" to the U. S. Senate. I supposed [Nathaniel] Sillsbee would give place to some more efficient man, & that you were thought of to take [Elijah Hunt] Mills place. This information had occasioned me to reflect on the probable effect, of moving you to the Senate, & had really given me much trouble. It is useless to disguise the fact, your presence in the House has been thought essential, in sustaining our cause in that body —and although Providence, or exertion, might bring forth men, if you were absent, equal to any emergency, yet no one can say where they are to come from, or point out the men now in the House to supply your place. Your absence will be sensibly felt by our side & will inspire our adversaries with new hopes and courage. Should [Thomas Jackson] Oakley, be *against us*, and *Phil Barbour* be active & zealous on the same side—they with [George] McDuffie, [Samuel D.] Ingham & [James] Buchanan, aided by the sarcasms of the crazy [John] Randolph, even if [John] Forsythe, should be elected Governour & [Charles Anderson] Wickliffe fail,[2] will give us a hard trip. I fear Oakley more than any of them, and [am] exceedingly anxious to have him with us, though I am yet unable to learn how he is. It is equally useless to attempt to deceive our selves [of] the fact, that our opponents array more energetic operating talent on their side in the Senate than we do on ours. I do not intend to disparage our friends there, but the world says, and we have all *felt* the inferiority of our force in that body. We ought to have there, some of our most powerful minds. I have been astonished that New

England had not placed in that Station some men of more force. But we must look at the body as it is. We must recruit our force there, & where have we the men at command? *You we want in both places.* It is difficult to see how we can get along in either House without you. In the Senate there is little hope of renovating the present members, and imparting to them increased moral energy & exertions. In the House we have I think better ground to rest our hopes on—our men are younger[,] have more elastic[it]y of mind, and perhaps pressing necessity may bring out talents & exertions equal to any emergency we shall be called to encounter. If *Oakley & Phil Barbour* be warmly against us, they, with McDuffie & Buchanan & Randolph (with his dreaded sarcasm), even if Forsythe should be Governor & Wickeliffe have liberty to stay at home, will present a force we cannot despise, a force requiring strong power & efficient discipline to conquor. Yet I incline to the opinion the chance for us in the House, is better than in the Senate. And, though not without great distrust of the correctness of my opinion, I think you should go to the Senate. If it be true that Mr Sillsbee will retire who will succeed him? Give us a strong man—and when you are about "improving the condition" of the Senate suppose some of you put [Levi] Woodbury out of the humour of continuing any longer, that his place may be supplied by [Jeremiah] Mason, who will succeed you? Boston ought to be able to supply of the first order of intellect.

The N. Hampshire plan of sustaining the administration party without the aid of the federalists is certainly injudicious—the cry of old party names, at this day, is of no use except to demogogues; honest men ought to discountenance it. I regret your views in the Boston [speech] were opposed by any local & selfish views—these seem to have prevented an election of part of your Representatives.[3] Although your city is denominated "headquarters of correct principles" you can't boast much of union in this last election. I hope for the success of the remainder of your ticket on the next trial. I see [Francis] Baylies has *agreed* to try his luck again.[4] Cannot one of the administration opponents be induced to retire, & the other be elected.

I see no particular objection to sending the [Massachusetts] Journal to those names on the list.[5] It will do good in Ohio. You will observe, however, that Nashee & Co. Columbus,[6] Howard of St. Clairsville,[7] Beatty of Guernsey,[8] Wilson of Steubenville,[9] Patrick of N[ew] Philadelphia,[10] & Saxton of Canton[11] are printers of papers, & the Journal might be *exchanged* with them. In the Pennsylvania list, *John* Scott of Wilkesbarre should be *David Scott.*[12]

My news from Kentucky is very cheering. We should hold our own in the Reps. & probably leave [Joseph] Lecompte at home,[13] and also Wickeliffe if his own county where there are about 3/4th. admn. men, vote on the *question*, without regard to local feeling. [Thomas Patrick] Moore will be hard run.

Ohio & the western part of Penna. is doing well—but our opponents are *active* & *unprincipled*. They stop at nothing. We must be vigilant. [Cornelius Peter] Van Ness is laughed at for his folly. Jackson's adulterous intercourse is secretly doing us good.[14] The pamphlet is a good one & will soon be printed[15] We will get up an Ad[ministration] meeting here the last of the month. Truly your's,   J. C. Wright

ALS. NhD. Published, in part, in Curtis, 1: 300–302.

1. See above, DW to John C. Wright, April 30, 1827.

2. John Forsyth's election as governor of Georgia in 1827 took him away from Congress, but Wickliffe, also a Jacksonian, was reelected to the House of Representatives, despite Wright's prediction.

3. See above, Henry Clay to DW, May 14, 1827.

4. Baylies lost his 1827 bid for reelection to Congress.

5. See above, DW to John C. Wright, April 30, 1827.

6. George Nashee and John Bailhache owned the *Ohio State Journal and Columbus Gazette*.

7. Horton J. Howard published the *National Historian* of St. Clairsville, Ohio, and also the *National Enquirer* of Columbus.

8. Not identified.

9. James Wilson, formerly of Philadelphia, edited the *Western Herald and Steubenville Gazette*.

10. James Patrick published the *Tuscarawas Chronicle*, New Philadelphia, Ohio.

11. John Saxton published the *Ohio Repository*, Canton, Ohio.

12. David Scott, of Wilkes-Barre, Pa., had been admitted to the bar of Luzerne County in 1809. He was elected to Congress in 1817, but resigned the same year to receive appointment as President Judge of the courts of Luzerne County, a post which he held until 1838.

13. Lecompte (1797–1851) was not, as Wright predicted, "left at home" in the 1827 election. He served as a Kentucky Democrat in Congress from 1825 to 1833.

14. Wright was probably referring to a story in Charles Hammond's Cincinnati newspaper, the *Daily Cincinnati Gazette*, which asserted that Jackson's wife was an adultress and his mother a prostitute.

15. For a discussion of the pamphlet, see above, DW to Henry Clay, May 18, 1827.

FROM HENRY CLAY

Washington 28th. May 1827.

(Private and Confidential)
My dear Sir

I recd. your favor under date the 18th. inst. from Boston.[1] I regret the state of things there which defeated the election,[2] but it will have no bad effect, on the general scale.

Govr. [Levi] Lincoln, I fear, will not be prevailed upon to run as Senator. I transmit you a letter this day recd. from Mr [Nathaniel] Silsbee on that subject.³ The Govr. I believe is well apprized of the President's anxious desire that he should be in the Senate. I know not of any further exertions that can be made to induce him to alter his determination. Should he adhere to it, I have ventured to express the opinion that it would be expedient that you should be sent. Should Oakley be friendly, that will abate the objections to your transfer, although, as it regards yourself personally I do not think they will be entirely removed.

The conditions of affairs in N. Hampshire is to be regretted. But if you are right in supposing four fifths of the Republican party in that state to be favorable, Mr. [Isaac] Hill can not effect much. And sooner or later he must meet with the fate which he merits. I have always supposed that N. England, in all its parts, was so friendly as not to leave any doubt of its' final decision. I have not a single regular correspondent in N Hampshire. I think Govr. [Samuel] Bell (with whom I have occasionally exchanged a letter) may be entirely confided in.

From the West, and from Pennsa. and Maryland the current of news continues to run in a good channel. They are getting very warm in Kentucky, but unless I am entirely deceived there is no uncertainty in the final issue.

I *wish* to leave here about the middle or last of next week. I shall go by Pittsburg, where I anticipate a cordial reception.

I shall be glad to hear from you, while you are in New York.

The affair at Rio is much less serious in fact than it is represented to be in the papers. I think Mr. [Condy] Raguet acted rather precipitately. And I hope we shall be able to arrange it satisfactorily.⁴ I am always Cordially your friend   H Clay

ALS. NhD. Published in Curtis, 1: 299–300.

1. See above.

2. See above, DW to Clay, May 18, 1827.

3. See Silsbee to Clay, May 23, 1827, in Curtis, 1: 298–299.

4. In 1827, Raguet, chargé d'affaires in Rio de Janeiro, had abruptly returned to the United States, asserting that his efforts to settle disputes between the United States and Brazil were not supported by the State Department.

TO [NATHAN APPLETON]

New York May 30. 1827

My Dear Sir

I recd yours,¹ enclosing the Govr's letter,² which you did right to open & read. From the manner in which he expresses himself, I see little reason to hope that he will alter his resolution.

Nothing has occurred, since I left home, to change the view, which I communicated to you. If the Govr. *cannot be persuaded*, then a case will have arisen, in which I am content the Legislature shall act as its own sense of public interest may dictate. I repeat what I observed to you, on parting, that in my opinion the choice should be made, without loss of time. Enclosed is a letter for the Govr. which I will thank you to hand to him.[3] Yours, very truly,   D. Webster

The length of my stay here, is, as yet, a good deal uncertain.

ALS. MHi. Published in Van Tyne, pp. 125–126.
   1. Not found.
   2. See above, Levi Lincoln to DW,

May 24, 1827.
   3. See DW to Levi Lincoln, May 30, 1827, below.

TO LEVI LINCOLN

New York May 30. 1827

Private & Confidential
Dear Sir,

I have recd here your letter, communicated thro. Mr. [Nathan] Appleton.[1] I could very much have wished that you might have arrived at a different conclusion, on the question of going into the Senate. Nevertheless, I see that there is weight, in some of the reasons, which you mention, & I am aware also that there are other considerations, not stated by you, which, however little they may affect your own mind, very naturally, would create, in others, regret at y[ou]r leaving your present situation. Under existing circumstances, I feel it my duty to leave it to others to decide how the place shall be filled. If a satisfactory appointment can be made, without removing me from the place I am in, it will be highly agreeable to me; *if it cannot*, the matter must be disposed of as others may deem best. I am, My Dear Sir, with most true regard, Your ob. servt   Danl. Webster

ALS. MHi. Published in Curtis, 1: 296.
   1. See above, Levi Lincoln to DW, May 24, 1827.

TO JOSEPH E. SPRAGUE

New-York May 30 1827

Confidential
Dear Sir,

Your letter was forwarded to me here, and I now return its enclosure under another cover.[1] I left the subject on which your letter treats in this position; namely, that if the Governor could not be persuaded, my friends might dispose of me as they saw fit. Since I left home, I have seen or heard nothing which should have any material weight in determining the matter. What I have seen however as far as it goes rather tends to show that I may be spared, without great inconvenience from the place where I now am.[2] I shall probably be home early next week, but in the present attitude of the case I do not perceive that my presence is likely to be important. Yours truly,   D. Webster

Copy. NhHi. Published in Van Tyne, pp. 126–127.

1. Not found.

2. Upon meeting with Oakley and several of his friends in New York, Webster apparently felt that the New Yorkers' inclinations were to continue to support the administration.

TO HENRY CLAY

New York June 2. 1827

Private & confidential
My Dear Sir,

I thank you for yours of the 28 May,[1] which I recd. yesterday. My fears are as great as yours, as to Govr. Lincoln's consenting to go into the Senate. I enclose a copy of a letter which I have recd. from him since I left home.[2] My friends in Boston are instructed by me to say, that if the Governor persists in declining the place, I may be disposed of, as the general opinion of what is useful & expedient may decide; prefering, however, on my part, not to be placed in the Senate, if any other satisfactory appointment can be made. I know not exactly what will be done; & having now the advantage of being *away* from the scene, I intend to retain that advantage till the affair shall be settled.[3]

I have seen very many persons since I came here, & had much conversation about the politics of this State. The public attention seems to begin to be roused, at last; and as far as I can judge, the general feeling is good, very good. More union among friends is now manifested, & something like common understanding, & general system, prevails. The paper at Albany is likely to commence under very good omens,[4] & it is believed that the *Advocate*, which is supposed to have some weight & consequence in the *Country*, will, ere long, come out on the right side.[5] Mr Oakley is here, & I have had some conversation with him, & learned something also respecting him from other sources. I am satisfied of what his course will be, *so far as it may not be altered hereafter by events.* He will not be made a tool, in the hands of the Southern members of opposition. So far, I have no doubt. I have no doubt, also, that he will vote for Mr. [John W.] Taylor to be the Speaker; that he will support the woolen bill, and, generally speaking, go with that interest on which the strength of the Administration rests. But, then, there is another side of the account. He is *against* roads & canals, & internal improvements, except so far as the Tariff goes. This will be a considerable drawback from his usefulness. He is, too, an attached friend of Mr [DeWitt] Clinton, altho' I believe he now has very little intercourse or communication with him. This part of his character will cease to be hurtful, as events shall, as I suppose they probably will, more & more remove Mr Clinton from the theatre of political competition. I do not think that Mr. Oakley has any idea of a permanent connexion with the Government; at least, not in the Legislative Department. His objects lie in the line of his profession.[6] His standing, too, in his District, is rather precarious, having recd a majority of 40 only, where 6 or 7 thousand votes were taken. Upon the whole, I am rather inclined to think, that we have little to fear, & something to hope, from Mr Oakley's course in Congress; & that that course will, probably, be rendered more favorable, rather than less so, by events. What I have stated, I have gathered from such sources, that I would not wish to have much said of it, even to friends. I believe it may be relied on, as presenting a true view of the case, as it at present stands.

[Joseph] Vance has been here, & is now gone to W. Point. He says he left every thing well at home, & found every thing well in the Western Districts of this State. Gen [Solomon] Van Renns[e]laer I have met with also. He has become decided, & spirited, in his efforts to sustain the Govt. Depend on it, the "Universal Yankee Nation" will give a good account of themselves, from the bottom of Lake Erie to Penobscot River.

I am anxious to hear that you have departed for Kentucky. To that State, more than any other, at the present moment, I look with anxiety. If that be safe, all is safe. Pray when you get there make some of our lazy friends write to us, & inform us how things look.

I am yet to be here two or three days longer, & if I learn anything interesting will write you again. Yours always truly   Danl. Webster

ALS. DLC.

1. See above.

2. See above, Levi Lincoln to DW, May 24, 1827.

3. Webster's election to the Senate occurred on June 8. He had, contrary to his stated intentions, returned to Boston on the evening of June 6.

4. That newspaper was to be edited by Isaac Q. Leake. See above, Clay to DW, May 14, 1837.

5. *National Advocate*, formerly edited by Mordecai M. Noah but at this time edited by Thomas Snowden.

6. Elected as a Clintonian Democrat, Oakley resigned in 1828 to accept the judgeship of the newly created Superior Court in New York City.

TO [JOSEPH] GALES AND [W. W.] SEATON

Boston June 7 [1827]

Private

D Sirs

I arrived last Eve' from N. York. A great deal of embarrassment had been created by a letter from Mr [Elijah Hunt] Mills[1]—but a meeting of his friends had been held, & they did not feel *justified* in supporting him, under present circumstances. When I left home it was hoped Gov. L[incoln] would have been willing to succeed Mr. Mills; but he absolutely declined—& I was *forced* into it, very much against my inclination, you may be sure. I am quite certain I have gone from home;—but it could [not] be helped, without trouble, & perhaps disaffection. Yrs.

The truth is, this election was made, in the hope thereby of *strengthening* the Administration in the Senate. The argt. was, "the House is numerous—some one will take your place & the general disposition is more favorable. We must have *somebody, in Senate, from N. E.*—who can take part in debate &c &c &c—in order that our N. E. President may have fair play."[2]

I shall write you tomorrow.

AL. NN.

1. A few days before the senatorial election, Mills had written a Massachusetts legislator that his health "was so far restored, that his arrival at his home in Northampton" could be expected on June 6. If true, that disclosure destroyed the basic reason —Mills' poor health—for which the Massachusetts lawmakers were considering other candidates for Mills' post. *Columbian Centinel*, June 6, 1827.

2. The added paragraph, probably written shortly after the election on June 8, appeared in a revised form in the *National Intelligencer*, June 14, 1827.

FROM HENRY CLAY

Washington 7th. June 1827

(Private)

My dear Sir

I recd. yesterday your obliging letter of the 2d. inst.[1] with a Copy of one from Gov. Lincoln.[2] Since he so positively declines, I sincerely hope you may be elected. I have some fears however that Mr. Mills will create some trouble and difficulty.

The tone of confidence which the public prints of K[entucky] & the letters which I receive from my friends there assume, I think, is evidence of their conscious strength and certain success. I am fully aware of the very great importance of a favorable issue in the elections in that State; and I am much deceived if the Administration does not maintain its relative strength, that is two thirds of the members of the H. of R.

I take my departure for Lexington on the 10th via Pittsburg. I intend to return to the City by the first of August.

Oakley's opinion about Internal improvements will do no harm. What I am most anxious about, on that subject, is that they should be supported in New England, and that the West and Pennsa. should be made sensible of that support. After the next Caucus, we shall have a great increase of strength to the cause from the West. You have some difficulty to sustain it in New England, but I hope notwithstanding your limited territory and its improved condition you will be able to sustain it by prudence & discretion. You have your equivalents in other forms, if not in that of I[nternal] Improvements. We must keep the two interests of D[omestic] M[anufactures] & I[nternal] I[mprovements] allied, and both lead to the support of that other great & not less important interest of Navigation. Always Cordially Your friend   H Clay

ALS. DLC.   2. See above, Lincoln to DW, May
    1. See above.   24, 1827.

FROM ELIJAH HUNT MILLS

New York June 9. 1827

My dear Sir.

I have just learned the result of the choice of Senator on the part of the H. of R. and I assure you, with the utmost sincerity, that it is as gratifying to me, as it is creditable to the House, & will be beneficial to the Com[monweal]th and the Nation.[1]

I regret however that I had not known your views in season to prevent any votes being thrown away upon me. I should certainly have done so, had I not been assured, by an extract of a letter read to me as coming from you, that you *would not consent* to be a Candidate, and that the choice would probably fall on Mr. Jno. M[ills]. This I was willing to prevent, I confess, and in consequence of all this, I now appear before the public as an unsuccessful Candidate for an office which, Heaven knows, I sincerely wished not to hold—and as having incurred an implied vote of censure for my past services.

I have the vanity to believe however that this was not intended, and that I shall have credit for honest intentions & pure motives in the discharge of my public duties, and <that I have> of having served the State which has so long honored me with its confidence with fidelity & zeal, and a sincere <regard> desire to promote <their> its' honor & interests, however inadequate my capacity may have been to accomplish the object. The consciousness of this, will at any rate, be a source of no small gratification to me through life.

My health is gradually improving and I hope to reach home in the course of next week. I shall leave N. Y. on Monday, & probably stop a few days in N. Haven. With great regard & esteem, I am Dr Sir very respectfully Your obt servt,   E. H. Mills

ALS. NhHi. Published in PC, 1: 419–   1. The above paragraph of Mills'
420.   letter, with a summary of the remain-

der, was published a few days after
Webster received it in the *Boston
Daily Advertiser*, from which the

National Intelligencer, June 19, 1827,
copied it.

TO LEVI LINCOLN

[c. June 9, 1827]

Private

My Dear Sir,

I have addressed a letter to you signifying my acceptance of the place of Senator.[1] Supposing that nothing was to be done with this letter but to put it in the files of the Executive Department, I have confined it to the single purpose of expressing my intention to take the Office. If custom requires, as I suppose it does *not*, that this letter should be sent to the Legislature, I will be obliged to you to return it to me, that I may add a suitable expression of acknowledgements, &c.

This I could not do, I thought, with propriety, in a communication made to the Executive, & not intended to be communicated. I presume no communication to the Legislature is necessary. Yours, very truly,

Danl. Webster

ALS. MHi. Published in *MHi Proc.*, 49 (1915–1916): 207.
1. Not found.

FROM JOSEPH STORY

Salem June 10. 1827.

My dear Sir

I congratulate you with all my heart on the recent election of you as Senator. The vote is truly honorable to both Houses, & under all the circ[umstance]s a proud triumph of Massachusetts & national feeling, over the Discontents of all sorts. But I can truly say I congratulate the country more than I do yourself, for I am by no means sure that your personal ease or influence will or can be enhanced by this elevation, though it speaks as the voice of the State. So far however, as it speaks that voice, it is most important. Have you seen Oakley? How is he? How is New York? If the *national* men do not now lay in N Eng[lan]d a broad ground for a union among the best of all the old parties, it will be because there is a contagious madness. Never was there a more golden opportunity.

I am sorry to say that it is impossible for Mrs Story to leave home. Ever since Tuesday last our youngest child has been quite ill of a fever. She now seems a little convalescent; but we have been obliged to devote ourselves all night & all day to her, & to my poor sick sister, Mrs. [Stephen] White.[1] The latter is now in the last stage of life. I think she cannot live a week. She may not live for a day. Indeed for the last three days, she has been expected to quit us hourly. From our own sick house & hers we have been exceedingly distressed.

I intend to go to Rhode Is[lan]d if possible. Unless Mrs. W. dies in the intervening time, I shall be able to go. If otherwise, I shall write Judge [John] Pitman[2] to adjourn the Court for a week or two, when I can attend. He may try all the causes, if he pleases.

I shall write you again on Wednesday. My rest has been so much broken that I have not time to say more.

God bless you—Your affectionate friend   Joseph Story

ALS. MHi. Published in *MHi Proc.*, 2nd Series, 14 (1900, 1901): 412–413.

1. Harriet Story White was the mother of Harriette Story White, who was to become the wife of James

William Paige, Grace Fletcher's half-brother, in 1831.

2. Pitman (1784–1864) was judge of the United States district court of Rhode Island for forty years.

TO EZEKIEL WEBSTER

Monday Eve' [June 11, 1827]

Dear E.

On my return from N Y. I found Mrs W[ebster] a good deal sick. She has taken a very sudden cold, and was affected with *Erysipelas*. She is now much better, & I hope will soon be quite well. We look for D[aniel Fletcher Webster] tomorrow.

If any body should wish you to go to Penna, to attend a meeting, it might be well perhaps to go. You will have good company, & a good opportunity to see the middle States. Probably the meeting will be postponed till Sept[embe]r.[1] Yrs   D. W.

ALS. NhD.

1. The Harrisburg Convention, a gathering of delegates from the various states friendly to a protective tariff, had been proposed for late summer. Already, Boston citizens "interested in the protection of domestic industry" had named Bezaleel Taft, Jr., Joseph E. Sprague, James Shepard, Abbott Lawrence, Samuel D.

Colt, Edward Everett, and Jonas Brown as delegates. At a meeting of the "Wool Growers and Manufacturers" in Concord, New Hampshire, on June 14, Samuel Bell, Ichabod Bartlett, Ezekiel Webster, Samuel Smith, and Asa Freeman were also named as delegates. *National Intelligencer*, June 12, 28, 1827.

TO EZEKIEL WEBSTER

Boston June 13. 1827

Dear E.

Daniel arrived safe this morning. I have recd a summons, lawful in form and substance, to attend the Circuit Court, in Newport, & must set out tomorrow morning.[1] Mrs W[ebster] is getting well.

Your Resolution, as to the course to be pursued by yourself & friends seems reasonable, & just.[2] *Will your friends stick to it?* If they will remain firm, you will accomplish your purposes; but in such cases some are generally to go on separate account. If the Adams Republicans of N. H. do not, by this time, see the hopelessness of success, without a change of system, nothing but the utter ruin of their cause will ever open their eyes.

I shall be back on Sunday. Let me hear from you, by that time. Yours
D. W.

ALS. NhD. Published in Van Tyne, p. 127.

1. Webster was to appear in Newport to argue the case *Leland* v. *Wilkinson* (decided in June 1827), which was subsequently appealed to the Supreme Court. See *Wilkinson* v. *Leland*, 2 Peters 627 (1829).

2. The letter in which Ezekiel stated his "Resolution" has not been found, but it was most likely that he and other old Federalists in New Hampshire would introduce and pass resolutions supporting the Adams administration, as DW had recommended to him on April 4.

FROM CHARLES MINER

West Chester June 13, 1827

My dear Sir,

The mail, last night, brought the account of your election to the United S. Senate. How can we possibly spare you from our House? Who, when the storm is up and the billows roll, can we see at the helm, and each one feel that the vessel is safe? Well, they need a pilot in the Senate. I have felt that our friends there needed aid of a kind no one is so able to afford them; for the opposition happen to be strong in talent there. Believing the public good will also be promoted I congratulate you, sincerely, on this accession to your well deserved honours—on this gratifying testimonial of confidence from your noble State. The feeling of my heart is—*onward*—and may the highest honours be awarded to the greatest merit. With sentiments of perfect respect   Charles Miner

ALS. DLC. Published in Curtis, 1: 302.

FROM EZEKIEL WEBSTER

Londonderry June 17th 1827

Dear Daniel,

I came here yesterday. My wife has been here a fortnight with Alice [Bridge Webster].[1] Alice is gaining very slowly & it will be probably another fortnight before she will be able to go home. Gov. [Samuel] Bell &

his friends took the course, I expected. They called by a printed notice a meeting of the *"republican* friends" of the administration at the Court House. This adjective was inserted upon deliberation & consultation. I did not attend feeling myself excluded by the terms of the invitation. The Meeting was large & a good *many* speeches made by Gov. Bell, [Ichabod] Bartlett[,] Gov. [David L.] Morrill, Richard Bartlett[2] & Speaker [Henry] Hubbard. The object of *all the speakers*, except Gov Bell, was to prove Mr Adams to be a democrat & his administration to be strictly democratic & more purely & entirely so than Mr Munroe's or Madisons' or even Jeffersons'. They vindicated him from a charge of being a federalist or enclining to favor the federalists. *This was the substance of their story.*

After the meeting Gov Bell wished to see me & I called upon him. He said the manner of calling the Meeting might not be satisfactory to me. He hoped it would upon reflection. That he & his friends had determined to have resolutions introduced into the House, approving the measures of the administration & hoped the Federalists would support them. He restated very much his former conversation—renewed his declarations of good Feelings, &c &c &c &c &c.

In reply I calmly told him—that in our former conversation I had suggested to him the course, which I thought the republican friends of the administration ought to pursue. I was willing that he & his friends should adopt the principles on which they should support the administration in this State, & as far as I was concerned they might support it on their own principles as well as they could. That if those principles were *exclusive* & *proscriptive* of the federalists, they could not complain if they had not the aid or assistance of the federalists. I told him that he knew that the course of the federalists in N H. had been honorable, & marked with the greatest integrity. That in all divisions of the republican party, upon men or measures, the federalists had gone in favor of the best men & best measures. That when they were candidates for office they were very desirous to have no concert with federalists, but no objection to receive federal votes & federal support. At other times they were treated as outcasts and aliens. I referred him to the conduct of the federalists in this legislature—in the organization of the House & in the choice of the *Commissary General*. That the friends of the administration represented to us that the salvation of Portsmouth certainly & perhaps of the State depended upon this election, as insignificant as was the office. That it was made a party question, on this point the Jacksonians were to rally & if *Nelson*, their candidate, was to succeed, it would give such confidence to the Jacksonites in Portsmouth, that they would carry every election in town ever afterwards. That they courted the influence & solicited the votes of the federalists & that the federalists did give their votes to a man for their candidate & elected him.[3] Yet in two days these same men in express terms declared that they would not admit us into the meeting of the friends of the administration. I told him I considered this treatment of the Federalists from the friends of the administration, impolitic, ungenerous & unjust; & such as Federalists, who have any respect for themselves, would not submit to. I enquired of him why the friends of the ad[ministratio]n did not support the ad[ministratio]n, in N H., on its own principles; & if they expected the aid of the Federalists in other states when they proscribed them in this? He said in answer that his own feelings were liberal & said that the time would certainly come when there might be an union, with Federalists on the principles mentioned by me—but as yet the public sentiment was not ripe. I told him that on that point I differed from him; that I believed the sentiments of the people to be ripe for such a union at this moment; that it was not the sentiments of the people, that needed correcting, but the sentiments of those, who affected to be the leaders of the people; & that, in my opinion, the public sentiment would be right on this subject just when he & his friends wished to have it so. That this was a question altogether with him & his friends; that when they were willing to unite with the Federalists they might enlist the aid of the Federalists & not before—in favor of their resolutions or any other measure. We parted under a good deal of excitement.

The resolutions, I expect will be introduced on Monday; and if they are a motion will be made to postpone them indefinitely—for which I shall vote—if no other man in the house does. My present intention is to have the resolutions postponed, and if it becomes necessary in the debate on that question to give to the House the true reasons plainly & frankly for the motion. If that motion fails & we have to act upon them, amend them—give them pith & character & advocate their passing, giving my hearty support to the adm. on its own principles—& not on those of its *exclusive* friends in this state.

We are glad to hear of Mrs. Webster's recovery. Let me know the appearances of things at N York, &c. Yours truly   E. Webster

ALS. NhD.

1. Alice Bridge Webster (b. 1814) was Ezekiel's daughter.

2. Bartlett (1792–1837; Dartmouth 1815) was a Concord, New Hampshire, lawyer and at the time secretary of state.

3. As Ezekiel reported, Federalists had united with the "Republican friends of the administration" in the election of Robert Neal as commissary general.

TO NICHOLAS BIDDLE

Boston June 18. 27

Private

Dear Sir,

I enclose you an extract from a letter lately recd. by me from Col [Timothy] Upham, the Collector of the Customs, at Portsmouth N. H. relative to the appointment for Directors for the office there.[1] Mr Upham himself is a valuable officer & an excellent man, & much trust may be safely reposed in him. I know all the persons, whose names he mentions; most of them, very well; and I agree entirely with what he suggests, except as to leaving *him* out. Mr [John F.] Parrott, I think, *should be put in*;[2] & if this cannnot be done, without leaving Mr Upham where he now is (out), I think he should remain out. Mr. Parrott was the late Senator in Congress. I have known him a long time, & there can be no doubt, I think, of the propriety of Mr [Jacob] Wendell's[3] place being supplied by him.

I have marked this letter private; not wishing, however, that it should be withheld from communication to the Board. Mr Upham doubtless expected me to treat *his* letter, as in a proper degree, confidential; & I send the extract to you, therefore, in the same character. Yours, with great regard,   Danl. Webster

ALS. Nicholas B. Wainwright, Philadelphia, Pa.

1. Letter not found. Upham (1783–1855), a veteran of the War of 1812, served as collector of customs for Portsmouth, 1816–1829. He was renamed a director of the Portsmouth branch of the Bank of the United States.

2. Parrott was not appointed a director at this time.

3. Wendell (1788–1865), of Portsmouth, was a textile manufacturer, merchant, and importer in the Russian and West Indian trade. A previous director of the bank, he was not renominated in 1827.

TO JOHN W. TAYLOR

Boston June 19. 1827.

My dear Sir,

Some of our gentlemen, in this part of the country, who take an interest in the Agricultural & Manufacturers' National Meeting at Harrisburg, feel a good deal of solicitude that Delegates should appear there from the State of New York. They are fully aware, that there may be difficulty in assembling persons together from all parts of the State, to appoint the Delegates; but the great importance of having New York represented at the meeting, will, they hope, lead to the adoption of some measure calculated to bring about so desirable an end. It is not, perhaps, essential, that these Delegates should all be chosen at one general meeting. Local meetings, each appointing its own Delegate, might, it is thought, accomplish the purpose, if it should be found impracticable to convene a general one.

As the gentlemen concerned are desirous of corresponding with their friends in New York on the subject, I have taken the liberty to address this to you, & similar letters to three or four others,[1] to the end, mainly, that the gentlemen may themselves communicate with you, for the more full statement of their objects & wishes. I am, Sir, with very true regard, Your's   Danl. Webster

LS. NHi.
   1. Not found.

TO HENRY CLAY

Boston June 22. [1827]

Private

My Dear Sir,

We have heard of your departure from Washington, & are expecting daily, to see the account of your reception at Pittsburgh. This will find you, probably, at Lexington.

Since I wrote you nothing unexpected has occurred here. Mr Mills' letters, or those of his friends, caused some little difficulty, & gave *me* great pain, personally. He has been informed, however, of the considerations which led to the actual result, and is entirely satisfied, & indeed professes to be highly gratified.

The N. Hampshire Legislature is in session. That State is so absolutely *safe*, that one may as well laugh, as cry, at the strange management of our friends there, since no degree of imprudence can lose us its votes. The degree of imprudence, however, which has been manifested is surpassing. I took the liberty of suggesting to them, one & all, the expediency of bringing Resolutions in the Legislature at once, in which *all friends* could unite. Instead of taking this course, a meeting was called of the "Republican" friends of the Administration, at which Mr Bell presided, & where he & Mr [Ichabod] Bartlett & Mr [Thomas] Whipple made speeches.

I send you, herewith, a copy of a letter which I recd. from my brother,[1] two or three days ago, who is a member of the Legislature. Mr Bell's good sense appears to me to have strangely forsaken him. He cannot, I am sure, go one step, without the votes of the Federalists. If he were now a candidate for re-election, it would depend on *them* to say whether he should be chosen. Yet he still adheres to *exclusive caucuses*, & *party discipline*. This *party* confidence, & *party* blindness, which are so unworthy of so wise a man, will assuredly defeat all his objects. The *Reso-*

lutions cannot be carried, in the way & by the means Mr Bell & his friends propose. I have before told you of the condition of the Legislature, & of the State, in regard to ancient party divisions; & it will all prove true. This administration meeting *was not* attended by the men of weight & influence, either in the Legislature, or out of it. The *People* are wholly averse to the perpetuation of these old differences; but a *union* meeting would have brought out every body, of all sides, & carried every thing before it. Enough of this. In the end, all will be right, in that essentially *sound* State, tho' there will & must be some previous fermentation.

The New York Nat. Advocate has passed into other hands, & much good is hoped from its future operations.

The Baron Mareuil & family passed yesterday with us. They embark at New York on the first of July. Our latest English dates are still only to the 8th. of May. No vote, indicative of the strength of the new Ministry, had been taken, in either House of Parliament. I am not so positive, as most people seem to be, that the new Premier will achieve an easy triumph over his adversaries; and I cannot say that I feel quite so much interest in his success as I should do, if his feelings were more kind, or I may say, more just towards us. Yours very sincerely & truly

Danl. Webster

ALS. DLC.

1. Webster corrected the grammar and sentence structure of Ezekiel's letter of June 17, above, and forwarded a copy to Clay.

TO EZEKIEL WEBSTER

Boston Friday Eve' June 22. '27

Dear E.

I recd your letter of Thursday morning (yesterday) in the evening, giving an account of the fate of the Resolutions &c.[1] In the actual state of things it would seem desirable that you should not break up the session, without coming to some arrangement as to future political movements. Doubtless the only true course is to rally those, of whatever name or party, who are willing to unite to support the Administration, without reference to former divisions. If the Republican Gentlemen will not lead, in such a system of action, then of necessity, the Federalists must. Give them a fair option; if they decline taking a leading part, assume it yourselves. There would seem to be no other course.

In the present posture of things, *you* are bound, I should think, to do something. It would hazard too much to leave public opinion without a rallying point for another twelve months. For some purpose or another, there should be, I think, a union meeting, more or less public, before the legislature separates. I cannot see thro' the matter very clearly, but I suppose there must have been many Republican friends of the Administration, who voted with you, & who would not be adverse to *a union*. How this is to be brought about, those who are on the spot can best judge; but in some form it seems most desirable.

The main purpose of this is to suggest the importance of doing something, which shall produce these two effects; 1. To prevent any impression, from the postponement of the Resolutions, that a majority of the Legislature is agt. Mr. Adams; 2nd. to agree on some system, or mode of action, which shall unite as many as possible of the friends of the Administration, in future movements. It would now seem especially incumbent on *you* to do all you can, & to take the responsibility in regard to these two objects.

As soon as the weather is fair, I go off [on] a little journey with Mrs. W. Write me often, directed here, & your letters will be sent to me by Mr. [Alexander] Bliss. I shall be very anxious to learn your proceedings, & to hear of the effect produced by the facts. Yrs as always   D. W.

ALS. NhD. Published in Van Tyne, pp. 127–128.
    1. Not found.

TO JOHN QUINCY ADAMS
                                                    Boston June 30. 1827.
Private
Sir,

Having occasion to write you, today, on another subject, it occurred to me that it might not be amiss to use the same opportunity to say a few words in relation to the late ocurrences in *N. Hampshire*. The failure of the Resolutions, moved in the Legislature, may, I fear, have some little bad influence elsewhere, but ought not to be recd. as evidence of any unfavorable state of feeling & opinion in that State. It was produced by a difference among friends, which is greatly to be lamented, but which has been threatening, for some year or two, to break out. A short state-[ment] of the case is this. Ten or twelve years ago, the Republican party having attained a *very small* majority over the Federal party, all political contests, from that time forward, *on the former grounds of controversy*, ceased. It has never, since, been revived by the Federalists, on any occasion. Still, however, the Republican Party have kept up their organization, & had their caucuses for nomination, their County Conventions, &c &c. When the division took place, in that party, between the friends & enemies of the Administration, a division, which became manifest soon after the election of President, or indeed rather before that event, each *section* of the party wished to retain to itself the character

& denomination of the *Republican Party*; & to prove its title to this character, each kept up the same tone of hostility towards the Federalists, as in the days when there was a Federal party. This struggle, for what is called the "organization," & "machinery" of the Republican party, has been going on, now, for some time; a great majority of members being with the Administration, but much the greatest portion of management & activity, on the other side. Both have constantly disdained all Federal aid or cooperation. This was sensible enough, on the part of the opposition, because few or no Federalists could be expected, even if invited, to join those ranks. But it was obviously a good deal dangerous for the Republican friends of the Administration; because the Federalists constituted, whether in the Legislature, or in the State, almost one half, certainly a large third, of the whole, in point of numbers, & their proportion was still larger, in other respects. Yet this course has been steadily pursued, altho. with such results as might, one should think, have inspired a diffidence of its practical utility. Mr Hill's election to the State Senate, last spring, affords an apt illustration of these results. He was nominated by the Caucus, & being so nominated, the *Journal* would not support any body else, Federal or Republican. I suppose there is no doubt the Editor himself voted for Mr. Hill. At any rate, I have been assured, that if he would have opened his paper to the nomination & support of any other *Republican* Candidate (whose opinions were friendly) Mr Hill would not have been elected. Thus far, in almost every instance, the opposition, tho a small minority, has succeeded in obtaining the command of the "machinery & organization" of the party. I had last winter several conversations with Mr Bell, on this subject, & expressed to him my decided opinion, that the true course was to appeal directly to the people, on broad & popular grounds, with an abstinence from all reference to former party. He signified, uniformly, that his own feelings would lead to such a course, (& I have no doubt they would) but that he was afraid to risk it, as matter of policy. I believe that, in regard to the Federalists, their opinions & feelings were fully made known to Mr Bell, before the meeting of the Legislature; that they expressed their entire readiness, & their solicitude, to join in any measure calculated to strengthen the course of the Administration; but they stated, distinctly, also, that if this was expected of them, no *mark of opprobrium* must be set upon them. While they did not wish any thing to be done, to shew any *union* with them, they still expected that nothing would be done, designed to exclude & proscribe them, publicly, & offensively.

Notwithstanding this, as you will have seen, this meeting which was called, was limited, in the terms of the call, *ex industria*, to the "Republican" friends of the Administration. This call did not embrace, in its terms, one half, in numbers, or a fifth, in talent & character, of all the friends of the Administration, in the Legislature. What happened afterwards, & by consequence, you have noticed.

If I had been in my Brother's situation, I probably should have supported the Resolutions, notwithstanding the previous proceedings had been conducted in such a spirit. I have made so many sacrifices of feelings, in such cases, that they come easy to me. But, it seems, he did not chuse to brook it. There is not a faster friend to the Administration in the State, nor a more devoted supporter of the President, personally, than he is. I may say also, as you do not know much of him, that his weight & consideration, with the community, & in the Legislature, are second to what belongs to few.

No harm in regard to N. Hampshire politics will grow out of this business; altho', as I have before said, its effects, elsewhere, may be feared. It will probably impress one salutary truth, on the minds of our friends, in that state; to wit, that this Administration cannot be supported, but upon the merits of its acts, & by a direct appeal to the judgment of the People. I am thoroughly convinced that it cannot be upheld, any where, by combinations & arrangements among political leaders. It is the singular fortune, (for good or bad) of the Person now at the head of the nation, that if he has any *party* disposed to support him, it is the party of the People.

Craving your pardon, for the unexpected length of this letter, I beg to repeat the assurance of my sincere regard.   Danl. Webster

ALS. MHi. Published in Van Tyne, pp. 128–130.

TO JOSEPH GALES

[June ?, 1827]

Private and confidential

My Dear Sir,

My professional duties, to which such long absences in the winter make it necessary I should pay attention in the Spring, & early Summer, have so occupied me, since my return from New York, as not to allow me an earlier opportunity to write to you. My transfer to the Senate was, as I have said before,[1] & as you have rightly conjectured in the N[ational] Int[elligencer] quite against my personal wishes. Nevertheless, it is done; & the most, & the best, must be made of it.

I have thought, a great deal, on the interesting topic of your first letter.[2] I say *interesting*, because it is, with me, &, as I think, ought to be with all well wishers of the public, a *great object* that the situation of your press should be kept *independent*, & easy, in relation to pecuniary matters. I cannot help thinking, notwithstanding the difficulty usually attending such attempts, it might be practicable to make a useful arrangement here. To this end, however, one of you should *come here*; nothing can be done without somebody on the spot. The next thing would be, to find some agent, to take Mr. Rome's[3] place, to act as a correspondent, & to take care of yr money concerns. Probably your acquaintance here might lead to the knowledge of some such person. I can assure you of the zealous & friendly interest of Mr [James] Lloyd, Mr [Nathaniel] Silsby, Mr [Edward] Everett, &c &c, in the accomplishment of your wishes. Acceptances, in the usual way, by Mr. Clark,[4] with his certificate that he shall, probably, be in funds &c, would be a foundation, on which, I think, we could *now* raise some money, with the aid of your presence, or that of Mr. Seaton. One more *Court* I must *attend*; viz, among the whalemen of Nantucket. I shall return about the 10th July, & thence forward to the Middle of August shall be in or near Boston. I need not assure [you] what pleasure it would give me to be able to be useful to you.

You printed my hurried remarks very well, & every alteration was much for the better.[5] I hope to find an hour to make a short *argument*; but, in the mean time, there is a paragraph or two more of *preliminaries*, which I wish to send on.[6] Yours always truly   Danl. Webster

ALS. NhD.

1. See above, DW to Gales and Seaton, June 7, 1827.
2. Not found.
3. Not identified.

4. Not identified.
5. See the *National Intelligencer*, June 14, 1827.
6. Not found.

FROM JOHN QUINCY ADAMS

Washington 8 July 1827.

Dear Sir

I have received your recent and obliging letters.[1] Those of recommendation will receive the most friendly consideration, though possibly the wish of Dr [Nathaniel] Niles[, Jr.,] may be a little in advance of the age, and that of Mr Pine[2] in arrear of the time. They have my good wishes as and because they have yours. But the success of both is problematical.

Your explanation of the recent proceedings in New Hampshire confirms the opinion I had entertained of them upon perusal of the debate in the House. That they who have the same object in view should fail of the end by disagreeing upon the means, has excited in my mind rather regret than surprize. Mutual concession and conciliation between those who have been heretofore divided, but are now of accord in sentiment and principle, are so obviously necessary, that I have no doubt they will ultimately prevail. It has been gratifying to observe that this was the marked character of the proceedings in the Legislature of Massachusetts at their late Session.

I hope to have the pleasure of seeing you before the close of the summer at Boston, and remain Very cordially, Yours

LC. MHi.

1. See DW to Adams, June 4, 1827, mDW 6192; and above, DW to

Adams, June 30, 1827.

2. Not identified.

TO EZEKIEL WEBSTER

Boston July 12. 1827.

Dear E.

I arrived from Nantucket, the Evening before last. Your letter was sent as far as Sandwich, but did not follow me on to the Island,[1] and I was gone longer than I expected to be.

I am really desirous that you should go to Harrisburg.[2] I am sure you will be pleased with it, as it will give you an opportunity to see much of the Country, & a good many important men. Mr. A[bbott] Lawrence spoke to me on the subject yesterday. He said he, & many others, were anxious that you should attend the meeting, & I have no doubt he spoke truly. It is generally desired, by the Gentlemen here, I know, that you should be there. Mr. Lawrence says he shall leave this City on Saturday Morning the 23rd inst; & be back again by the 7th of August; this will give a day for N York, & another for Philadelphia.

For myself, I think it a matter about which you ought not to hesitate. Say at once, you will go, & the thing is done. Come down in season to spend a day or two here. As Mr. Lawrence will expect you, let us know, on receipt of this, your final determination. Yrs as always   D. Webster

ALS. NhD.

1. Not found.

2. See above, DW to Ezekiel Webster, [June 11, 1827].

TO [JOHN W. TAYLOR]

Boston July 15, 1827

My Dear Sir

I am obliged to you for your letter of the 3rd,[1] and gratified with the favorable accounts you present of political appearances around you. I believe the general current of intelligence from New York & Pennsylvania confirms your impressions. Mr. Van Buren, I perceive, has been too wise to place himself in opposition to the woolens bill.[2] How his Southern, & *City*, friends will like this, I know not, but think it will cause them some embarrassment. At any rate, the opposition, generally speaking, is so far identified with opposition to that measure, & the papers in favor of Genl. Jackson have so generally denounced it, not only in the South, but in the West & North also, that it cannot now be an easy task to change the tone, & to profess friendship for the "rogue's bill," as the Jackson papers in Kentucky have denominated it.

I thank you for your congratulations on my election to the Senate. If the greater good shall be produced by it, I shall be satisfied, altho' my personal wishes were very strong for remaining with you. It is now probable that Mr [Benjamin] *Gorham* will be my successor.[3] Mr. [George] Blake has been thought of, but he is disinclined to give up the office which he now holds.

While at New York, at the first of last month, I saw Mr. [Thomas Jackson] Oakley. I am tolerably well satisfied, as to his course, & as to his good disposition. My impressions, as to what he will do, are drawn from different sources, all, I believe, correct, & I will state the amount of them shortly to you, desiring you to consider the suggestions as *confidential.*

In the first place, I entertain no doubt of his voting for the Administration candidate for the *Chair.* In the next place, I think he will certainly go for the woolen Bill; and in the third and principal place, I am satisfied he will not enter into the opposition, nor do any thing from the motive of embarassing [the] Government, although he may not approve all measures, especially those connected with Roads & Canals. I believe he holds agt. us, on this power.

You will have noticed the death of Mr [William] Burleigh. I should not be surprised if this vacancy should be filled by the election of Mr. [John] *Holmes.*[4] There is no strong man, that I know, in the District, to run agt. him if he should incline to be a candidate. It is difficult to predict his course exactly, if he should be chosen, but my prevailing impression is that he would generally be with us. He & his old friend Mr. [John] Randolph might then settle their affairs, on a new theatre. I have heard nothing from the District; & this is but my own conjecture. Yet I think it highly probable that things will take the course I have stated. There is no strength in any part of N. England, for Genl Jackson, unless it be in N. Hampshire; & nothing then at all formidable, if our friends could persuade themselves to act together cordially. That State will certainly be right, & go with her neighbors.

Kentucky seems now the point of solicitude. I have a letter from F[rancis] Johnson,[5] who writes in good spirits, & seems confident of success, in his own District, & also of the success of [James] Clark, [Thomas] Metcalfe, [Richard Aylett] Buckner, [David] Trimble, [Robert Perkins] Letcher, &c. He even thinks Mr [Charles Anderson] Wickliffe will be hard run.[6] Nevertheless, I feel very anxious about Kentucky, & am of opinion that the elections in that State next month will form the *crisis* of our affairs. If they should go strongly agt. the Administration, the effect would be felt all over the Union. I am, D Sir, as always Yrs   D. Webster

ALS. NHi.

1. Not found.

2. Van Buren and several others were conspicuously absent when the Senate voted on the Woolens Bill. The vote ended in a tie, only to be broken by Vice President Calhoun's negative vote.

3. Gorham was elected to Webster's seat in the House of Representatives.

4. Instead of John Holmes, Rufus McIntire, from York County, Maine, a Jacksonian Democrat, succeeded to Burleigh's seat.

5. Not found. For an earlier letter from Johnson, similar to the one he must have written in 1827, see above, Johnson to DW, July 7, 1826.

6. All were reelected except Trimble.

When on July 13, 1827, Alexander Bliss died unexpectedly, Webster felt a deep loss. For eleven years, ever since he moved from Portsmouth, Webster had found Bliss an able assistant, one who proved dependable in supervising the law office when Webster was away and who proved equally trustworthy in his occasional errands to Washington on legal and claims matters. As Bliss's replacement, Webster selected Henry Willis Kinsman (1787–1858; Dartmouth 1822), a native of Portland, who had previously read law in his office. The Kinsman-Webster association in a law practice lasted ten years.

TO JOSEPH STORY

Boston Thursday Morning
[July 17, 1827]

My Dear Sir

You will be shocked to hear of the death of Mr. [Alexander] Bliss. He died at 10 oclock, on Sunday Evening, at Plymo. after one week's illness, of a fever. Mrs W. & myself go down today to attend his funeral, & shall return tomorrow at noon.

It is a dreadful calamity. I should feel that it fell heavily on me, if I did not see how it must crush others.

The bearer is Mr Hopkins, of Philadelphia,[1] whom you may remember to have seen last winter at W. He is a highly respectable Gent. of our profession, & as he goes today to look at Salem, I give him this introduction to you. Yrs always   D Webster

ALS. DLC.

1. Not identified.

TO HENRY CLAY

Boston July 24, 1827

My Dear Sir,

Your reply to Genl. Jackson's letter is admirable, & has been most favorably recd. every where, at least on this side the Alleghany.[1] It places the Genl. in a position where he cannot remain. He must move, in some direction; & whatever movement he makes will either embarrass his friends, or still more embarrass himself. I have a suspicion, that the respectable member of Congress is Mr [James] Buchanan. If this should turn out so, it will place *him* in an awkward situation, since, it seems, he *did recommend* a bargain with your friends, on the suspicion that such a bargain had been proposed to them, on the part of friends of Mr. Adams. I am curious to see how this matter will develope itself, &, in the meantime, am confident that Genl. Jackson is falling, in general estimation, daily & hourly. The present tide of things, if it should meet no counter currents of reaction, will & must overwhelm the opposition in another year. New York is growing stronger & stronger, daily, & at this moment I seriously doubt, whether, if the election were now to come on, Genl. Jackson could get *three* votes in the State. North of New York, from present appearances, there will be no such a thing as a Jackson ticket formed, except in New Hampshire. In that State our friends have, at last, opened their eyes; & seeing their danger, there is danger no longer. Govr. [Benjamin] Pierce turns out to be a *thorough Jackson man*, & completely under [Isaac] Hill's influence. This was predicted, to some of our friends, a year ago, but they would not credit the prophecy. However, since the Govr. so *turns out*, he himself will be *turned out*, at the next election, in March. Friends have agreed on this, & there is not the least doubt it will be done.

Mr [Benjamin] Gorham was elected yesterday, as my successor. The occasion created no great excitement, & tho' some of us did not like the premature movement of the Gentlemen who nominated him, there is no objection to him. He is very acceptable to every body, except the Jacksonians, who set up a candidate, & rallied three hundred votes.

It is probable Mr. [John] Holmes will succeed Mr [William] Burleigh in the Yorke District, in Maine. Yours always truly   Danl. Webster

ALS. DLC. Published in *W & S*, 16: 165–166.

1. In a letter to Carter Beverly of Wheeling, [West] Virginia, June 6, 1826, Jackson had renewed his charge of "corrupt bargain" between Clay and the Adams forces in the late presidential election. In the recently published letter, Jackson declared that his information came from "a member of Congress, of high respectability." From Lexington, Clay issued a public response (dated June 29), in which he denied the charges

and challenged Jackson or the respectable congressman to substantiate the charges. Both letters had been printed in the *National Intelligencer*, July 12, 17, 1827.

TO SAMUEL JAUDON

Boston July 25. 1827

My Dear Sir

I have not written you lately, I believe, on our little affairs of business. The draft, made by you & accepted by me, while in Philadelphia, becomes due tomorrow or next day, & will of course be paid. Your acceptance of my draft (300 d) falls due Aug. 20th; & I believe you must put yourself in funds to meet it by drawing on me. At least, it v.:ll be well to be prepared to do so; tho' I have some hopes of learning that a sum is at my disposition, at Washington, on which I can draw, instead of troubling you. Perhaps it will be convenient that you should send along the draft, pretty soon, & have it accepted & returned, as I may be occasionally from home, between this time & Aug. 20th.

The death of poor [Alexander] Bliss is a dreadful thing to us all. I ought hardly to speak of my own loss, when that of his wife and child are to be considered; but he was very dear to me. We have been together eleven years, in entire harmony, & to mutual benefit.

Mr Bliss' death will probably confine me more at home, for the summer, than I could wish. I have taken, in his stead, Mr. Henry W[illis] Kinsman, a young Gentleman who read law with me, has been in practice two years, & whom I can recommend for fidelity & capacity.

Be pleased to make our best respects to Mrs Jaudon. We wish to hear from you. Yours, truly, always   Danl. Webster

ALS. NHi.

In the following letter to his friend John Evelyn Denison, Webster's thoughts turned to British politics. George IV, in trying to replace Lord Liverpool, had a choice between pro-Catholic George Canning and anti-Catholics Arthur Wellesley, first Duke of Wellington (1769–1852), and Sir Robert Peel (1788–1850). On April 10, 1827, the ministry went to Canning; and on April 12 many of the Tories in what had formerly been Liverpool's cabinet resigned, forcing Canning into an alliance with the Whigs.

TO JOHN EVELYN DENISON

Boston July 28. 1827

My Dear Sir

It is a great while since you have heard from me; but this you must impute, not at all to forgetfulness, nor altogether to procrastination. I wrote you a long letter, at Washington, & when I supposed you had already recd it, it was brought back to me, having been dropped, in the Street, by my servant, on his way to the Dept. of State, & taken up by another servant who kept it, for a month or two, on the supposition, I imagine, (he being an ignorant Black,) that it might contain money.

The last letter which I had the pleasure to receive from you was dated in April,[1] & forwarded by your Brother[2] & Captain [Basil] Hall.[3] I have not yet had the good fortune to meet either of those Gentlemen, but on the strength of your letter I have written to Capt Hall,[4] now in Canada, solicited the honor of his acquaintance, & expressed the hope that we should see him here, & communicated, thro. him, my respects & salutations to your Brother. Capt Hall writes me that he will pay us a visit,[5] & I hope he may bring your Brother along with him.

I thank you for the Pamphlets &c which you were kind enough to send me. All such things I read with much interest, & shall be more & more obliged by every fresh instance of your recollection.

The recent political events in England have produced a good deal of sensation & speculation on our side the Atlantic. It is quite astonishing how extensively the debates & proceedings in your Parliament are read in U. S. Our interior papers, back to the shores of the Mississippi, contain more or less of them, & they everywhere excite some degree of attention. We are very generally on Mr [George] Cannings side of the question, although we have a suspicion that he does not love us Americans with quite all his heart. The general tenor of his political sentiments, especially so far as they regard the state of the world, & the cause of liberal opinions, & free Governments, is of course highly acceptable & gratifying to us Republicans. For one, however, I regret the secession *of some* of the Ministers who have retired, as I suppose you must also. Among these is Mr [Robert] Peel, who seems to have established a high character, as a man of useful & solid talents. I feel pain, also, that Lord Eldon[6] should not otherwise have terminated his long career. Perhaps something of the Professional feeling mingles in my regrets, in his case, for I confess I have the most profound admiration for his Judicial character. Nothing in your prints has disgusted me more than the fierceness of some, & the wantoness of others, of the innumerable attacks on the character of the Ex Chancellor. Of L[or]d Bathhurst[7] I know nothing, & of Lord Westmoreland[8] I suppose there is not much to be known, except that he is a Peer, a respectable person, & with powerful influence of property & connexion. These noble Lords, I suppose, could be spared, if such were their pleasure; but I should think it would have been desirable that the Duke of Wellington should have remained. Of course I am a very incompetent judge, but I must say I have seen no proof of that *incapacity*, which some of your Journals charge upon the Duke, in regard to the discharge of official duties. He does not appear to me to be a weak man, & I think his Speech in the H[ouse of] L[ords] made out a better case than was presented by any of his seceding Colleagues.[9] At any rate, considering his unequalled military achievements, in hours of peril & darkness, your Countrymen, many of them, will naturally regret an arrangement which *appears* to place him out of the favor of the Crown.

I congratulate you, most heartily, My Dear Sir, on your own accession to Office,[10] & the career that seems so auspiciously opening before you. May it equal its promise! I have looked after you, in the Debates, but have seen little of you this session. Our dates are now only to the 13th June. We do not know yet what the *Lords* have done with the Corn Law, & perhaps the *Lord* only knows what they may do.

Since you last heard from me we have become involved in a very warm canvass for the next Presidency. Genl. Jackson's friends have made, & are still making, very great efforts to place him in the Chair. He is a good soldier, & I believe a very honest man, but some of us think him wholly unfit for the place to which he aspires. Military achievement however, is very visible & palpable merit, & on this account the Genl. is exceedingly popular, in some of the States. The election will be close, tho' my present belief is that Mr. Adams will be again elected.

The good People here have seen fit to transfer me from the H. of Reps to the Senate. This was not according to my wishes; but a state of things had arisen, which, in the judgment of friends, rendered the measure expedient, & I yielded to their will. I do not expect to find my situation so agreeable as that which I left. Mr [Benjamin] Gorham, a highly respectable man, who was also my predecessor, succeeds to my place as Representative from this City. Our next session, we fear, will be stormy. There is nothing new, of an exciting character, either in our foreign relations, or our domestic condition; but the pendency of the President's election is likely enough to produce heat, as it has already created parties, in both Houses of Congress.

Your excellent friend, the Judge [Joseph Story], is very well. I believe he has recently written you. He always speaks of you with great regard & kindness.

We have heard, My Dear Sir, that you are soon to cease writing yourself Bachelor.[11] If this be true, it is another topic, on which we all send you our congratulations. Mrs Webster accepts the tender of your remembrance with pleasure, & bids me reciprocate respect & good wishes from her. Let us not be forgotten by your fellow travellers in America,[12] but give them our regards, as you may see them. I shall send you a little package, of such things as may be more likely to interest you; & in the hope of hearing from you, ere long, I am, Dear Sir, most truly yrs

Danl. Webster

Your new Chancellor, Ld. Lyndhurst, was born in this town, & christened in Trinity Church, July or Aug. 1772. His mother was a direct descendant, from one of the first *comers*, viz. one of the Company of the Mayflower, landed on Plymouth Rock, Dec. 22, 1620.[13] So you see there is a little of the blood of the Puritans in him. Being at Plymouth, the other day, their Village Antiquarian gave me this last part of the information.

ALS. DLC. Published in Curtis, 1: 302–304.

1. Not found.

2. Sir William Thomas Denison (1804–1871), an engineer and scientist, was in Canada in 1827 employed in the construction of the Rideau Canal (*DNB*).

3. Hall (1788–1844) had retired from service in the British navy and was a tourist in North America in 1827 and 1828. He authored many books on his experiences and travels (*DNB*).

4. Not found.

5. Not found.

6. John Scott, first earl of Eldon (1751–1838), had resigned as lord chancellor (*DNB*).

7. Henry Bathurst, third earl of Bathurst (1762–1834), had been secretary for war and the colonies in Liverpool's cabinet (*DNB*).

8. John Fane, tenth earl of Westmoreland (1759–1841), was lord privy seal for all but a few months from 1798 to 1827 (*DNB*).

9. For Wellington's speech, deliv-

ered May 2, 1827, see *Parliamentary Debates*, 17: 454–467.

10. In December 1826, Denison was returned to the House of Commons from Hastings without opposition, and on May 2, 1827, he was appointed to the council of the lord high admiral. Denison shortly resigned, however, when Canning was ousted. Reelected to Parliament in 1831 and intermittently thereafter until 1857, he served as speaker of the House of Commons from 1857 to 1872.

11. Denison married Lady Charlotte Cavendish Bentinck on July 14, 1827.

12. Denison had toured America in 1824–1825 with Henry Labouchere, James A. Stuart-Wortley, Edward Stanley, and Colonel Robert Kearsley Dawson.

13. John Singleton Copley, the younger, Lord Lyndhurst (1772–1863), replaced Lord Eldon as lord chancellor in Canning's ministry. Lord Lyndhurst was the son of the painter John Singleton Copley, the elder (*DNB*).

TO THE MARQUIS DE LAFAYETTE

Boston July 28. 1827.

My Dear Genl,

I am indebted to you for several kind letters,[1] & infinitely obliged by your remembrance and friendship. I would now gladly requite you, by such intelligence from your friends, in America, as it may be interesting to you to receive.

The last year, as you know, was distinguished by the simultaneous deaths of two of your old friends, Mr Adams, & Mr Jefferson. You have seen the proofs of regard paid them by their Countrymen. I now send you my own contribution to the great offering of national gratitude.[2] Mr Jefferson's daughter, Mrs [Martha Jefferson] Randolph, is now residing in this town, with her daughter, Mrs [Ellen Randolph] Coolidge, & is in good health. The States of South Carolina, & Louisiana have distinguished themselves by pecuniary grants to Mrs Randolph, so that, by the aid of some other means, her situation, altho' not affluent, is yet not necessitous.[3]

Mr. Madison, as the papers have lately informed us, has had a short illness, which, while it lasted, seemed to be dangerous; but he has now recovered, & was well at the last dates. We are looking for the President to pay us an Annual visit, to this his native state. He is said to be a good deal worn down by official duties, this summer, & exercise, & a brief relaxation from those duties, will, doubtless, be advantageous to him. His Lady has recently been here. Her health, tho' not good, is thought to be better than last year. Our Republic seems to be getting warm, on the Presidential election; but I hope we shall all be able to conduct ourselves with moderation & temperance, so as not, by our differences of opinion, & personal preferences, [to] carry things so far as to bring discredit on the general cause of Republican Liberty.

I congratulate you, most heartily, on the brightening prospects of Greece. The day, I trust, of her deliverance is now fast approaching, & none can pray for its hastening, more heartily than I do.[4]

Your friend Judge Story, of Salem, has just left my Chambers. He commands me to tender you his affectionate remembrances. My wife & children all desire to be brought to your recollection, with many assurances of attachment; & we all beg you to mention us kindly to your son & Mr [A.] Levasseur.[5]

I ought to tell you something of our [Bunker Hill] *Monument*. It begins to ascend. The foundations are all laid, & the monument itself is now showing itself many feet above the surface. It is to be 213 feet (English) in height. A fine quarry of Granite Stone has been opened, in Quincy, & a rail way constructed to transport the stone to the sea, whence it is brought in boats, towed by Steam Boats, to the foot of the Hill where the Monument stands.

We hope to be able to tell you of its progress, & of its completion.

I must beg you, My Dear Genl., to keep me in your kind remembrance, & allow me the pleasure of hearing from you, as occasion & your own leisure may permit. I shall venture to write you often, knowing the favor with which you will receive any thing which comes from your American friends. I am, most truly & devotedly, Yrs   Danl. Webster

ALS. NIC.

1. One of the letters referred to, that of May 20, 1827, was published in the *Portsmouth Journal*, October 6, 1827. The others have not been identified.

2. "A Discourse in Commemoration of the Lives and Services of John Adams and Thomas Jefferson," delivered in Faneuil Hall, Boston, August 2, 1826, and printed in *W & S*, 1: 289–324.

3. Martha Jefferson Randolph (1772–1836) was the daughter of Thomas Jefferson and the wife of Thomas Mann Randolph, governor of Virginia from 1819 to 1821. Thomas Mann Randolph had discontinued relations with his wife and family, so after Jefferson's death, Martha Randolph was left in need of support. The states of South Carolina and Louisiana, out of respect for her

father, each gave Mrs. Randolph $10,000. She went to live with her children, among them Ellen Randolph Coolidge (1796–1876), wife of Joseph Coolidge, Jr., a Boston merchant.

4. On July 6, 1827, Great Britain, France, and Russia signed a treaty pledging themselves to defend Greece against any Turkish claims to her territory, and to enforce an armistice between Greece and Turkey. Thus they gave Greece recognition as a country in her own right, not just a rebellious colony of Turkey. Later, in October 1827, the allies backed up their promises to Greece by almost completely annihilating the Turkish fleet in an attack led by Admiral Codrington in the bay of Navarino.

5. Levasseur was secretary to General Lafayette during his tour of the United States.

FROM HENRY CLAY

Washn. 19th. Aug. 1827.

My dear Sir

We have partial accounts from the K[entucky] Congressional districts nearest to us. [James] Clarke and [Thomas] Metcalfe are certainly and [David] Trimble probably re-elected.[1] The accounts do not furnish us with much information from the other districts, but our intelligence, such as it is, is not unfavorable. Judging from what I have seen, I think we shall be stronger than ever in the next Legislature of K. and that, if we do not gain (of which there is some hope) we shall not lose ground in Congress.

(Confidential)

C[harles] Hammond's paper at Cincinnati (published by Morgan, Lodge and Fisher) is I think, upon the whole, the most efficient and discreet gazette that espouses our cause. He is poor, disinterested, and proud. His paper is now published daily. I think he is every way worthy of encouragement and patronage. The only assistance he would receive would be in the extension of his subscription list. Perhaps he might receive a present of a new set of types. I write without his knowledge, and from a strong sense of his worth and morals. Can not there be something done for him in your quarter? I am truly your friend   H. Clay

ALS. DLC.
1. Trimble was not reelected.

TO SAMUEL JAUDON

Boston Aug. 20. 1827

My Dear Sir,

I lose no time in replying to yours of the 10th.[1] It would give me great concern, My Dear Sir, if you were to allow any thing to tempt you to go to New Orleans. No pecuniary compensation ought to be, to you, an adequate inducement. The unhealthiness of the climate is an insuperable objection, especially if one is required to take an Office which would necessarily confine him, the whole year, to the City. I suppose the chance would not be an even one, of your living *five* years; to say nothing of the exposure of others, parts of yourself.[2] Do not, therefore, my Dear Sir, think of it, even for a moment. Yours always truly
D. Webster

You needed no apology, for not answering my letter, respecting the little draft. In any little things of that sort, you may rely on receiving seasonable funds; give yourself no more letter writing trouble than is absolutely necessary.

ALS. NHi.
1. Not found.
2. In spite of Webster's plea, Jaudon moved with his family to New Orleans, where he served as cashier of the branch of the United States Bank from 1828 to 1832.

TO HENRY CLAY

Boston Aug 22. 1827

My Dear Sir

My letter to Col [Francis] Johnson[1] was not important, & the delay, in its transmission is of no moment.

You speak very modestly of recent events, in which you have borne so distinguished, & so *successful*, a part. I cannot think Genl. Jackson will ever recover from the blow which he has recd. Your speech at Lexington,[2] in point of merit, as a clear & well stated argument, is certainly at the head of all your efforts; & its effects on public opinion have not been exceeded by those of any political paper, I may almost say, within my recollection. [James] Buchanan is treated too gently. Many persons think his letter *candid*.[3] I deem otherwise. It seems to me he has labored very hard to protect the Genl, as far as he could without injury to himself. Although the Genl's friends this way, however, *affect* to consider Buchanan's letter as supporting the charge, it is *possible* the Genl. himself, & the Nashville Com[mitt]ee may think otherwise, & complain of Buchanan. I should expect this, with some confidence, if they recd. the letter a little earlier then they may have seen the turn which the Atlantic Editors have attempted to give it. As these last have pretty generally agreed to say that the letter does support the Genl, the Nashville Commentators, if they see the example in season, may be disposed to follow it. I do not yet learn what answer comes from that quarter to your Speech.

We must soon hear from Kentucky, & make up our minds to whatever comes. It would be bad, on many accounts, if we should lose any votes, in that State. In the first place, we have none to spare, & in the second place the general impression, produced by such a result, would be more or less injurious. Nevertheless, no extent of misfortune there, in these elections, would shake my faith in the final success of the Administration. With activity, zeal, & prudence, we shall succeed.

The President & Govr. [Joseph] Kent dined with me yesterday, both in good health, & excellent spirits. The President is fast recruiting.

I go to Barnstable County tomorrow, to pass a week or ten days, on the sea shore. Ever truly yours   Danl. Webster

ALS. DLC. Published in part in *W & S*, 16: 166.

1. Not found.

2. At a dinner in his honor on July 12, Clay had again denied the charge of a "bargain" with Adams.

3. In his public letter of August 8, 1827, to the editor of the *Lancaster Journal*, Buchanan, in explaining his reasons for the private conversation with Jackson on December 30, 1824, denied that he had conferred with Jackson on behalf of Clay. In essence, Buchanan denied the truth of Jackson's assertion to Carter Beverly. James Buchanan, *Works*, ed. John Bassett Moore (12 vols.; Philadelphia, 1908–1911), 1: 263–267; Philip Shriver Klein, *President James Buchanan: A Biography* (University Park, Pa., 1962), pp. 56–59.

TO SAMUEL JAUDON

Boston Sep. 11. 1827

D Sir,

I came up from Sandwich, yesterday, to see after some little affairs, & put my boy to school. Mrs. W. is still there, & I return tomorrow, to finish my *vacation*, & to bring home Mrs W. & Julia & Edward, at the end of this week, or first of next.

I have drawn a little bill of 1000 dlls on you today, which please accept, but do not trouble yourself to write about it. You will be placed in funds, seasonably to meet it.

The news from Kentucky looks *bad*. If the Electoral vote of that State should go for Genl. Jackson, he will be *elected*, if Penna. should not desert him. Yrs ever truly   D. Webster

I hope you do not think of N[ew] O[rleans].

ALS. NHi.

TO HENRY CLAY

Boston Sep. 28. 27

Confidential

My Dear Sir,

I hope you are recovered from such a *shock*, as the disappointment in Kentucky would naturally produce.[1] There is, doubtless, much cause for regret, but *none for despair*. We have a year yet, before us, & I trust time will aid our efforts.

For the last 3 or 4 weeks I have been with my wife & children down on our Southern shore, to get a little quiet. Professional duties have now called me home, & I expect to be a good deal engaged, till my departure for Washington. Not so much, however, as not to be able to attend to any thing which the *general good* may require. I am willing to make an effort to do something for [Charles] Hammond.[2] His paper is certainly ably & vigorously conducted. It is not a little difficult to excite an interest for objects so distant, yet there are a few Gentlemen here who would be willing to bear a part. A tolerable set of type, I learn, could be furnished at the foundry here for abt. 5 or 6 hundred Dollars. I will undertake to say that a fount, to that expense, shall be placed to his order, here, or transmitted elsewhere, if you think that such a mode would be the best way of serving him. I am not myself much acquainted with H. & do not know his feelings towards me. If you can correspond with him freely, & can learn whether he can be better served, to the same extent, in another way, it will be equally easy & agreeable to me. At your convenience, let me have your opinions & wishes, in regard to this matter, & they shall be promptly attended to.

The few elections which have recently taken place, in this quarter, have resulted well enough. I have no fears of [Rufus] McIntyre,[3] &, on the whole am reconciled to his election. [Samuel] Butman, elected in [David] Kidder's District, is a very true man. In the House there will be *three*, & only *three*, whose votes, in electing a Speaker I fear will be agt. Taylor; [John] Anderson & [James Wheelock] Ripley from Maine, & [Jonathan] Harvey from N. H. If [Kensey] Johns[, Jr.,] shall be chosen in Delaware, & [John] Sergeant in Philadelphia, they, with what has happened in N. Carolina, will make good the losses in Kentucky. Mr. Taylor thinks a *majority* of the N York members will be disposed to support him. If it should be but a *bare* majority, the Election will be very close. All our friends, I fear, do not rightly estimate the importance of this election; I hope we shall be able to impress it on them in season.

The President is yet with us. His health seems better, but he is not yet so well as I should wish to see him. I am, Dr Sir, mo[st] truly Yours

Danl. Webster

ALS. DLC.

1. According to reports, Kentuckians had elected seven Jacksonian congressmen and only five supporters of the administration. In addition, Jacksonians had made considerable gains in the state legislature. *Niles'*

Register, 9 (September 1, 1827): 1; 9 (September 22, 1827): 50.

2. See above, Henry Clay to DW, August 19, 1827.

3. See above, DW to [John W. Taylor], July 15, 1827.

TO JOHN QUINCY ADAMS

Boston Sep: 29. 1827

Private

Sir

I recd. the enclosed this morning,[1] & take the liberty of submitting it to your perusal. You need not give yourself the trouble to return it. If Mr. [Jeremiah] Mason, in case of vacancy, would accept the Office, I should suppose that Mr. [Samuel] Bell & other friends would be of opinion that he might be, with great propriety, appointed. But I cannot think he would take it. It is, by much, too *small* for him. I do not know, in the whole Country, another instance of so much talent, united to so high a character, so destitute of all fit employment.

As to Mr. [William] Claggett, I trust his appointment is not to be apprehended. He is a decided *enemy*, &, in the next place, those who know him, I presume, would not consider him competent to the situation.

It is not probable that an appointment will become necessary before the Meeting of Congress.[2]

The Delaware Papers recd. this morning hold out strong hopes of the Election of Mr. [Kensey] Johns[, Jr.]. The choice is to be made on Tuesday next.[3] Yours, with mo[st] entire regard,   Danl. Webster

ALS. MHi.

1. See Joseph Story to DW, September 28, 1827, below.

2. The appointment of a district attorney for New Hampshire was not made until April 1828, when Daniel

Miltimore Christie (1790–1876; Dartmouth 1815) of Dover became United States attorney for the District of New Hampshire.

3. Johns was elected.

ENCLOSURE: FROM JOSEPH STORY

Salem Sept. 28. 1827.

My dear Sir

Mr. [Daniel] Humphreys the Dist. Atty. of New Hampshire is very ill & will die soon, perhaps within a few days.[1] Pray take care, that some suitable person shall succeed him. I think Mr [Jeremiah] Mason, from a suggestion he some time since made to me, would like it. If so, nothing could be so good. There is Mr [William] Claggett in Portsm.,[2] who wants it, & he will move every way he can for it. You cannot be too soon in preparing the way for a *good* appointment. Verb: sat. Yours very truly   Joseph Story

ALS. MHi.

1. Humphreys (1739–1827; Yale 1757), a resident of Portsmouth, died on September 30.

2. Claggett (1790–1870; Dartmouth 1808), Portsmouth lawyer and occasionally representative and senator in the state legislature, had been appointed clerk of the United States Circuit Court in 1821. Jackson later appointed him naval officer for the port of Portsmouth.

TO PHILIP CARRIGAIN

Boston Octr. 3d. 1827

My Dear Sir

In compliance with the wishes of friends, I take the liberty of recommending to your notice and patronage the Massachusetts Journal, with the general reputation, of which you are doubtless well acquainted. It is published three times a Week, is not overloaded with advertisements; and its plan is stated to be to present important public documents at length, and to devote a proportionate share of its columns to matters of Scientific, literary and general interest. Its political character is probably well known to you. I am acquainted with the Editor, Mr [David L.] Child who is a gentleman of liberal and honourable feelings, and a Scholar of respectable attainments.[1] Your old & true friend,   Danl. Webster

LS. NhHi. Carrigain (1772–1842; Dartmouth 1794), a lawyer, first practiced in Concord and later at Epsom and Chichester. From 1805 to 1809 he served as secretary of state for New Hampshire. He also assisted in the survey of much of the state.

1. On the same day, Webster addressed a similar letter to Timothy Upham, recommending the *Massachusetts Journal* (mDW 6378).

TO SAMUEL BELL

Boston Oct 15. 1827.

Private & Confidential
Dear Sir,

I am obliged to you for yours of the 12th.[1] The preliminary steps, which you have adopted, appear to me to be very judicious, & I hope may result satisfactorily.[2] Undoubtedly there is a difficulty, in the case. Some Republican friends are unwilling to act with Federalists, & feel that they are strong enough to do without them. The Federalists, on the other hand, think that the number of this description of Republicans is very small; tho' that feeling does not pervade the mass, but is confined to the influential man, wholly or mainly; and they think, that the Federal friends of the Administration are at least as numerous as its Republican friends. It is natural that different views should be taken of these matters, by those who stand in different relations, & see things in different points of light. I have no confidence in my own judgment, in this case, because I know I have but a limited view, & I know also that it may be a partial one. Yet I frankly confess my opinion is, as it has been for some time, that meetings called of *all* friends is much the safest course. I will venture to suggest, in a few words, the reasons which lead me to give a preference to this, over the other proposed modes.

1—I do not think it practicable to secure majorities in the County & District meetings, under the present organization, & the reason is, that the zeal, the activity, & the management are, out of all proportion, greatest on the other side; and whenever a favorable majority *should* happen to be obtained, [Isaac] Hill would invent some *objection* to its proceedings, denounce it as illegitimate & get up another candidate. Wherever the existing organization should be found to thwart his purposes, he will contrive to get rid of it, or disregard it.

2d—Suppose county meetings are called of the Republican friends of the administration only.

    1—This mode would be more likely to increase the disaffection of the Federalists, than an adherence to the present system, because it would be a more marked separation from, & exclusion of them.

    2d—Would meetings called with this limitation, bring together, in most instances numbers enough & weight of character enough to make a suitable impression? I doubt it. Both Hills party and the Federalists would find their interest in detracting from the importance and the authority of such meetings.

There is another danger. If general meetings of *all* friends are not called by Republicans, they may, in all cases, & I think they will, in some, be called by Federalists, and such a measure would lead to great embarrassment.

Let us look to a particular case—take for example the 4th Senatorial District.

By the present organization, I presume the caucus in that District would nominate a Jackson man. Then he must be supported, if the present system is to be continued, by the Republican votes. This was the case last year & I am misinformed if the present Senator[3] could have been elected, if the [New Hampshire] Journal had insisted & supported another Republican Candidate. But I could not depart from the result of the caucus.

But suppose the present system is abandoned, by our Republican friends, & they call a meeting of Republican friends only, & nominate a candidate. The Federalists will undoubtedly set up *their* candidate, & there will then be, the *Regular* Republican candidate (as he will be called), the Administration Republican candidate, & the Federal candidate. There will be no choice; & nobody can foresee which two of the three candidates will be highest, except probably, that the Federal Candidate (being a friend of the Administration) might be one of them. If moreover, the Federalists in calling the nominating meeting should invite the attendance of *all* friends of the Administration, it would give greater effect to their proceedings & some Republicans, probably, from personal, local or other causes might attend.

From the complexion of some recent paragraphs & pieces in the Portsmo. & Concord papers & other indications, I think it evident that the Federalists, or some of them, are of a temper to make their weight felt, one way or the other. Now these men can be no more easily controlled, than those Republicans who are tho't likely to be disaffected by a union of action with the Federalists.

I believe it would be very easy, in case it should be thought best to call on *all* the friends of the Administration to form conventions, so as to arrange matters, as that the nominations should be entirely satisfactory to the Republican friends of the Admn., indeed that they should be *Republican nominations*, except perhaps, in an instance or two where every body would agree they ought to be otherwise.

On this point I should not apprehend any practicable difficulty. The only precise point, upon which I think a definite understanding would be necessary is, that the Electoral & Congress Tickets, to be agreed on in June should be framed on the principle of liberality & union.

There is one other consideration suggested by the concluding remark in your letter. It is this. If the meetings are to be called, & the elections carried on, only by the Republican friends of the Admn., I think they will be conducted probably, without much zeal, energy or perseverance. If on the other hand, these meetings should assume a different character, neither spirit nor ability would be wanting, to give them the utmost possible effect. The people would rouse themselves, with alacrity, as they have done in Maryland, Delaware & Phila. & with united strength carry the cause thro'.

In short my opinion is, that in this, as in other cases where the cause is good, the best way is to appeal at once to the People, upon the real question & disregarding personal & party combinations, to trust the result to them.

These my Dear Sir, are my notions. They may all be very wrong. I repeat that I place little trust in my own judgment, & that I see some difficulties, in what I recommend—which may very probably, appear to you greater than they do to me. I am perfectly aware of your own good feelings & dispositions, & thoroughly convinced that whatever course you may adopt, will be the result of your best judgment.

I have only to add, that if any thing could be done by me, to bring about a mutual understanding among those who, as I think ought to act together, I would spare no personal pains, labor or sacrifice to effect it. I must crave your pardon for one further remark. I would not recommend a *union*, if I believed the effect would be to impair in the slightest degree, your standing & importance in the State & in the Country; because I believe the weight of your character is most important & useful at the present crisis both to the Admn. & the country. But I really believe that the effect of union would be to give to you still stronger hold & still greater elevation in public regard.

I have no doubt of this, & it is one of the public benefits I should anticipate from the course which I think the true one.

I pray you excuse, both the length & the frankness of this & believe me with true & constant regard—Your friend—Danl. Webster

Copy. DLC. Published in *W & S*, 16: 157–160.

1. Not found.

2. Apparently the Republican friends of the administration and Federalists agreed, according to Webster's recommendations, to call "conventions of the people" without regard to old party labels. *Portsmouth Journal*, October 27, 1827.

3. Levi Woodbury.

FROM HENRY CLAY

Washn. 17th. Oct. 1827

My Dear Sir

Your favor of the 28th Ulto.[1] reached here whilst I was absent on a short excursion, undertaken to recover some strength which I had wasted during my devotion to business in the months of August and Sept.

I congratulate you on the present prosperous aspect of public affairs. The auspicious results of the elections in Maryland, Delaware, Philada. and of some other parts of Penna. have more than counterbalanced that of the K[entucky] elections which affected me personally more than its political importance merited. I hope the election of Speaker is safe; but this, in some measure, still depends on the course which a majority of the N. York delegation may take. Should that be adverse to Mr. Taylor, it is to be feared that an Opposition Speaker may be elected. A strong effort should be made on the three members from Maine and N. Hampshire to prevail on them to vote on that election, in conformity with the sentiments of their Section and Constituents. I have impressed some of our Western friends with the necessity of punctual attendance at the first of the Session.

As to the affair of Mr [Charles] Hammond and the types, be pleased to let it rest until you come here. Another & perhaps a better mode of accomplishing the object in view has presented itself. And that matter, therefore, had best remain over with the others on which we will converse when you come here.

The President is expected today. The incidents of the administration of the Government, during the current year, will enable him to exhibit a very satisfactory exposé to Congress.

In Virginia the indications are good, and such as to authorize at least strong hopes. I remain Cordially & faithf[ull]y yrs   H Clay

ALS. DLC.
1. See above.

FROM HENRY CLAY
Washington 25th. Oct. 1827

(Private and Confidential)
My dear Sir

The course adopted by the Opposition, in the dissemination of Newspapers and publications against the Administration, and supporting presses leaves to its friends no other alternative than that of following their example, so far at least as to circulate information among the people. At this moment, when at no former period was the prospect brighter in Virginia, there is danger, I understand, of losing the most efficient cause of the existing auspicious state of things, Mr [John Hampden] Pleasants and the [Richmond] Whig, from the want of pecuniary means. What ought to be done? It seems to me that our friends who have the ability should contribute a fund for the purpose of aiding the cause; and if that be deemed advisable, the appeal should be made in the large Cities where alone the capital is to be found. You stated, I think, last winter that such a fund would be raised, and that I was authorized to address you on the subject. I have not felt that I ought to avail myself of the authority, fearing that your own means might be encroached on too much. As for myself, if it were otherwise proper, I am too poor. I have not the pecuniary ability.

The best form of affording aid to the struggling papers is to supply it, and to require that a number of additional papers shall be circulated gratis, bearing some proportion to the contribution made. In this way the cause will be doubly served. I do not believe there is any part of the Union in which as much can be done, by the increase of the circulation of any paper, as can be effected, at this time, by extending that of the Whig in Virginia. Other papers (Mr Hammond's for example, and some others to the West) might be assisted with advantage in the same way.

If you coincide in these views, would it not be well for you to give an impulse to the creation of a fund for the above objects by conversation or other communication with some of our friends?

I think our cause stands well at present; but, we shall greatly deceive ourselves, if we think the time has arrived, or will for some months arrive, when exertions may be safely relaxed. Always and truly Yrs

H Clay

ALS. DLC.

TO HENRY CLAY

Boston Oct 29. 1827

Private & Confidential
My Dear Sir,

I recd the Enclosed this morning, & prefer directing a short answer, (which is all I have time for, as I am bound into Court) directly to yourself.[1] I do this for reasons of prudence, not knowing the writer.

Towards relieving the Gentleman mentioned, I have already done what I thought I could afford. The case, however, seems a pressing one, and I suppose friends here might be induced to lend a helping hand, if there were time & opportunity for consulting them. Indeed no difficulty would be felt about it, if there were not so many other similar cases. As it is, I will say to you, that $250 shall be forthcoming from this quarter, if eno[ugh] more should be obtained to ensure the accomplishment of the object. That you or others must judge of, & I shall be content with the result. A line from you, saying that you think there may be a fair chance of effecting good, by such a measure, on our part, shall be answered by an immediate transmission *to you* of the amt. above mentioned. Yrs   D. Webster

ALS. DLC.

1. The enclosure, not found, was probably a letter from Marcellus Smith to DW, requesting financial support for the *Richmond Whig*. Smith and Pleasants were co-owners of that paper.

TO HENRY CLAY

New York Nov. 5 [1827]
Monday Morning

Private & Confidential
My dear Sir

Professional business brought me to this City three days ago. Your first letter, on the subject of the [Richmond] Whig, came to hand the day before my departure; & your second, enclosing the letter to Mr Smith, has been forwarded to me here.[1] You will have recd. one from me, on the same subject, covering Mr [Marcellus] Smith's letter to myself.[2] I look upon it as of great importance to support the *Whig*, & am disposed to do all in my power to that end. To what I said in my last,[3] I will now add, that, under the pressing circumstances of this case, I will undertake for a remittance (to you) on my return, to *twice* the sum stated in that letter. I left some friends at work on the business, & have no doubt that as soon as I reach home they will be ready with, at least, the sum now mentioned. Indeed this matter is so material, & so urgent, that we must do what the case requires; & if it be absolutely necessary that even a thousand Dollars be forthcoming from our quarter, it will come forth. Nevertheless, there are so many other calls, & so few persons who feel the importance of aiding objects so distant, that we have hardly courage to be *generous* & *bountiful*, lest the burden should fall too heavily on the willing few. We should be glad therefore if some part of the thousand could be successfully looked for elsewhere. But, at any rate, the Establishment must not go down, nor its conductor be left in distress, for such a sum.

As to other more general arrangements, we are attempting to do what we can. I hope we may meet at W[ashington] with some settled System, and some ascertained means. Is there no danger in *writing* on these subjects? I hope your office is all confidential & trustworthy. All is safe at my end, because no one opens my letters.

Today is the beginning of the election here. I should be glad to tell you what the prospect is, if I knew, but I can form little opinion. There has either been a strong access of the Jackson fever in this State, since the Spring, or else the clamour is so loud as to frighten our friends needlessly. Mr. [DeWitt] Clinton, most unquestionably, is acting for Genl. Jackson, as far as he can. Mr. Van Buren, & his friends have the utmost confidence, in the result. They say, that all, or all but one, of the Senatorial Elections will terminate favorably to them; & that two thirds the H. of Assembly will be Jacksonian. The City, say they, will give a majority on that side, of 2 to 3 thousand votes. On the other hand, the friends of the Administration hope to divide the City, nearly equally; to elect sundry Senators, favorable to them; to elect such a House as shall not interfere with the Electoral Law.

My own impression is;

that the Jackson party will carry the City, but not by any great majority.

that in the Counties, where the question is fairly put to the people, on the administration question, such as Albany, Columbia, Rensselaer &c, the Administration Ticket will, in a majority of instances, prevail;

that in many Counties, *non committal* men will be chosen; all of whom Mr V. B. will of course claim, & most of whom he will ultimately control; & that in parts of the west, the Masonic & Anti Masonic dispute, will supersede all other questions; that the Anti Masonic side will be found generally the strongest; & that the collateral bearing of the results of this singular contest will not be unfavorable to the Administration.[4]

On the whole, I anticipate from this election some increase of hope, & much of exertion, among Genl. Jackson's friends; but nothing which need shake our expectation of carrying a majority of the District next Fall. You have doubtless, however, much fuller information than I have, although, for the moment, I am on the spot. Genl. [Peter Buell] Porter has been here. Unfortunately I did not know of it, in season to see him. He left yesterday morning. He will be himself in the Legislature, as is expected; which will be of some importance.

I hope to be able to get home at the end of this week, when I shall probably hear from you. By the 19th, it is my intention to set off, with my family, for Washington. Yours always truly   Danl. Webster

P.S. There is no part of the Country, in my jud[gmen]t, in which our cause has been so badly managed as here. If it survives, it will be because it has power to hold out against both the disease & the doctor. The prevailing error has been *timidity*.

ALS. DLC.

1. See above, Henry Clay to DW, October 25, 1827; and DW to Clay, October 29, 1827. The letter from Clay enclosing Smith's has not been found.

2. Not found.

3. See above, DW to Henry Clay, October 29, 1827.

4. Anti-Masonry stemmed from the unsolved disappearance in upstate New York in September 1826 of William Morgan, a Mason who had threatened to reveal the secret rituals of the order. Shrewd politicians like Thurlow Weed of the Rochester *Telegraph* were quick to capitalize on the wave of popular feeling against secret societies in general and Freemasonry in particular. Since Jackson was a Mason and Adams was not the lines in 1827 and 1828 were easily

drawn. The movement reached its peak in 1832, when the Anti-Masons nominated William Wirt for the Presidency. His crushing defeat ended the first third-party interlude.

FROM SAMUEL BELL

Chester Novr 8th 1827

Private

Dear Sir

Since the date of my last letter to you,[1] I have received answers to the letters which I had previously written to a number of the most influential republican friends of the Administration to elicit their opinions and wishes as to the system to be adopted to produce union, concert and exertion among the friends of the Administration in N. H. These answers, as I expected, exhibited considerable diversity of opinion, and in a few instances, timidity and want of decision. A majority expressed opinions which indicated the course which has been adopted. That is the appointment, from the most firm and decided republican friends of the administration, of a central Committee in Concord and its vicinity, as the organ of communication and interchange of opinion, and a committee of three persons in each of the Districts for the choice of Counsellors, requesting them to associate to themselves such other members as they should think proper, and prepare an address *to all the friends of the Administration* in their District requesting them to appoint Delegates from their respective towns to meet in Convention and select candidates for the County offices—suggesting that at those meetings the necessary arrangements and organization for senatorial District conventions should be adopted, and at them, arrangements should be made for a town organization calculated to bring all the friends of the Administration to the polls. I think the persons selected in the several Counties will exert themselves to carry the system proposed into effective operation. Considerable diversity of opinion exists as to the expediency of bringing forward a new candidate for Governor, but a majority are decidedly in favor of it. It has been thought best that the Convention for Hillsboro' should be first holden, and should first decide upon that question. The Committee for that County, (Gov. [David L.] Morril, Counsellor [John] Wallace[, Jr.,] & Col. David Steele[2]) are known to be in favor of bringing forward a new candidate, and it is believed that this opinion prevails more generally in that, than in any of the other Counties. There is supposed to be no doubt that the Convention in that County will decide in favor of bringing forward a new candidate, and this circumstance, taken in connexion with that of its being the residence of the incumbent, will secure its adoption in the other Counties.

A state convention for this object was considered, but most of those who were best acquainted with the present state of feeling, of existing circumstances and prejudices, thought the mode which has been proposed preferable. It is hoped that this arrangement will merit the approbation of the federal friends of the Administration, and when a union shall have taken place in the manner proposed all difficulties on that subject will necessarily cease. I will write by the next mail to Mr. [Jeremiah] Mason, to your Brother, and to Mr. [Boswell] Stevens of Pembroke[3] suggesting to them the system which has been proposed, and requesting, if it meet their approbation, that they would use their influence to induce their friends to cooperate in carrying it into effect. Union and a determination to make suitable exertions are all that is necessary to secure a decisive victory.

Permit me to suggest that letters from you to your most influential and active friends in N. H. would do much toward securing this desirable result. I am respectfully and truly your Friend and Obdt. Sevt.

Samuel Bell

P. The persons who have been named as Candidates for Governor are W[illia]m Badger, Ezra Bartlett,[4] Geo Sullivan, N[ahum] Parker, M[atthew] Harvey & D L Morrill. The County conventions are to be holden early in Decr.

Jacob B Moore of Concord is selected from the central Committee as the person to & thro whom the necessary interchange of opinion should pass. Genl. [Timothy] Upham, Col [Gilbert] Chadwick,[5] & W Plumer Jr. are the Com[mitt]e for Rockingham.   S. B.

ALS. NhD.

1. Not found.

2. Wallace (1756–1840) was a Milford farmer; Steele (1787–1866; Williams College, 1810), was a Hillsborough attorney.

3. Stevens (1782–1836; Dartmouth 1804) was a lawyer, state legislator, and, from 1828 to 1832, Judge of Probate for Merrimac County.

4. Badger (1779–1852), a native of Gilmanton, had served as state legislator and senator before his election as governor in 1834; Bartlett (1770–1848), son of Josiah Bartlett, was a prominent Haverhill physician and legislator.

5. Chadwick, a native of Deerfield, served in the New Hampshire legislature in the 1820's.

FROM HENRY CLAY

Washington 8th Nov 1827

My dear Sir

I recd. both your favor of 29th Ulto. from Boston, and Monday morning last from N. York.[1]

There is perfect security to your letters after they arrive at the office.

They are opened by no one but myself, especially when marked "private." Mr Daniel Brent,[2] who is worthy of all confidence, is some times charged by me with opening the Mail, but he never opens letters so marked.

I am glad that you are enabled to procure a contribution for the Whig to the amount mentioned in your last letter. It will afford at least present relief, and until some other arrangement can be made. I would prefer (if you have no objection) that the sum should be remitted to the Honble. J[osiah] S. Johnston, who is here, animated by the greatest zeal in the cause, doing more than any other person that I know, and who is in habits of correspondence with the Editors of the Whig. He knows the situation of the Editors, and has contributed himself handsomely to their relief. He will immediately pass the sum to its destination.

I regret very much the state of things in N. York. It was not expected until within a few weeks. It comes at a moment when almost every where else prospects were bright or brightening. In Virginia especially there is much reason to hope that the reaction, of which we have evidence in all quarters, will carry the vote to Mr Adams.

The elections in Ohio place about two thirds of our friends in each branch of the Legislature. The same want of organization which exists in N. York is wanted in Ohio, but the evil is about to be remedied.

I have a letter from [Henry R.] Warfield which I was glad to receive on your account. I have advised him to publish nothing for the present and until [John] McLean, who I take to be at the bottom of the business chooses to come out.[3] Expecting the pleasure of soon seeing you, I postpone for that occasion many things which I would otherwise now say, and remain Cordially your friend, H Clay

ALS. DLC.

1. See above, DW to Clay, October 29 and November 5, 1827.

2. Brent was the chief clerk in the State Department.

3. Postmaster General McLean, always harboring presidential ambitions of his own, had by this time cultivated the friendship of the Jackson forces and was using post office officials to boost the chances of anti-Adams candidates in state elections. Because of the alleged influence of post office officials in the New York elections, Clay had concluded, although he probably wanted nothing published on the matter yet, that a change in the department was necessary. Francis P. Weisenburger, *The Life of John McLean: A Politician on the United States Supreme Court* (Columbus, 1937), pp. 53–65.

FROM EDWARD EVERETT

[c. November 18, 1827]

My dear Sir,

I wrote Col. [Thomas Handasyd] Perkins a line yesterday, requesting him to pay over to you what he may get.[1] I think it will be $100 each for himself, his nephew, Mr [David] Sears, Mr [Peter Chardon] Brooks, Mr [Nathan] Appleton Mr [Israel] Thorndike $600. The Lawrences [Abbott and Amos] give $100. I have asked them to pay it to you & told them when you go. I have said the same to Mr [William] Sturgis (who said he would give something)[.] Isaac [Parker?] will get a trifle from Mr [Cornelius] Coolidge; & I have told J[oseph] E. S[prague] to send you in season whatever he can get from Salem. Yrs ever.

P.S. Since Writing the above, I hear from Col. P[erkins] that he is ready to pay 650$ to our order joint or single. So that you have but to receive it.

LC. MHi.
1. Most likely, the money was raised to support the *Richmond Whig*.

TO JOHN W. TAYLOR

New York Nov. 30. 1827

Private & Confidential
My Dear Sir,
Various unlucky occurrences have so retarded my journey as that I am yet only thus far toward Washington, & have now no hope of arriving before Tuesday. My presence earlier, I trust, will not be highly necessary. Mrs W. is with me, & her health is not entirely good, so as to enable her to encounter the risks of such bad weather as we have at present. If, in a day or two, circumstances should not change favorably, I must leave her, to follow me, & go myself by the speediest conveyance.

One reason for desiring to be early at W[ashington] was the hope of being, in some measure, useful, in the arrangements belonging to the commencement of the Session. Being unhappily prevented from attaining that object, I write now to make one suggestion, for the consideration of our friends. It is simply that *somebody* should take occasion to see Mr [John Heritage] *Bryan*. I intended to have had a conversation with him, if I had arrived in season. I would now write to him, but I fear it might not be quite prudent. I thought, at the end of the last session, his dispositions were favorable, & recent occurrences seem to strengthen that hope. He is desirous of making some figure, in the House, corresponding to the expectation of his friends & constituents. It would be well, therefore, that some friend should speak to him; & if the turn of the conversation should be such as to present an opportunity, I should be glad it might be said to him, that *I* was known, before I left the H. R. to have felt a wish for his support of our cause, in the House. This, perhaps, will satisfy him, that a conversation had between us last

Spring, is not forgotten by me. I repeat, I would write to him, but am not *certain* of the safety of such a course.

Will you mention to Mr [Nathaniel] Silsby that I cannot be in W[ashington] before Tuesday. Yrs always truly   D. Webster

ALS. NHi.

It was mid-November when the Websters, all except Daniel Fletcher, who was in school, set off for Washington. The weather was bitterly cold, storms battered the coast, and by the time they reached New York City both Daniel and Grace were overcome with fatigue and illness. The senator-elect suffered from a severe cold complicated by a crippling case of rheumatism; Grace's ailment, diagnosed as an abdominal tumor, was undoubtedly cancer. In New York, the Websters stopped at the home of Dr. Cyrus Perkins, an old college friend, to recover. Daniel slowly regained his strength, but Grace grew worse, and on December 3, the day Congress convened, Webster was still in New York, unwilling to leave his wife's bedside even to fulfill his obligation to his constituents. He even considered resigning his Senate seat to give Grace and the children his full attention, but friends urged against it. In mid-December after James William Paige, Grace's half brother, had joined them in New York, Webster hurried to Washington with the understanding that he would remain there if Grace improved enough for her to return to Boston. But she grew weaker, and in late December Webster rushed back to New York to stay constantly by her side for the next three weeks. During that time, he wrote to friends daily accounts of Grace's declining health and of his own grief at her pain and suffering. Webster's dependence on others at this trying time was so great that he occasionally closed his letters, whether addressed to man or woman, with "Yrs in love." On January 21, the sad scene ended: at the age of forty-seven, Grace Fletcher Webster died. Immediately, Webster arranged for her burial in Boston; and despite the harsh weather of late January, his illness, and his own emotional drain, he and the children made the trip to pay their last respects to wife, mother, and companion of twenty years.

TO NATHANIEL SILSBEE

New York Decr. 1. 1827

My Dear Sir

I am kept here by a concurrence of unfortunate circumstances. Mrs W's health was not entirely good, when we left home, but still such as to allow the hope that we should be able to travel with ordinary speed.

Our unfortunate passage from Providence encreased her debility, & since she has arrived here, an accidental cause has contributed to make her case worse. From this last, however, she is now fast recovering, & I trust will be able to travel on Monday. Today *I* have myself a very painful attack of *rheumatism*, occasioned, I suppose, by a violent cold I took on the way; & am not now able to leave my room. This will be better, however, I trust soon; so that my present hopes are to set forward on Monday. We shall not make a moments stop, for any purpose not connected with health. I hope I may not be needed before I can arrive, *with my family*. But if it were likely that I should be, I would leave them, at whatever inconvenience, & proceed by the most rapid conveyance, if my own health should be such as to allow of it. You will receive this on Monday, & I will thank you to write me, addressed to Philadelphia; saying whether any thing is expected to occur, in which my vote may be essential. I am fully aware of the general importance of every member's presence at this moment, in the Senate; & feel extreme anxiety, in consequence of my own unavoidable absence, even for a single day. Still, I am desirous of keeping my wife & children with me, if possible; as I should otherwise be obliged to return for them. Let me hear from you, as above requested. I write this, not without great inconvenience. I can neither walk, nor sit upright. Yours   Danl. Webster

ALS. NhHi. Published in *PC*, 1 : 422–423.

TO JAMES WILLIAM PAIGE

New York Dec. 3rd. 1827

Dear William,

Mrs Webster wrote you yesterday & I must now continue the melancholy narrative. I write by the hand of Henry Perkins[1]—I begin with myself. It seems to me that I am a little better to day than yesterday. I am free from pain, & while I lie still am easy & quiet—but I cannot get upon my feet, nor when on them walk across the room without help. But as I am convalescent & my complaint not dangerous I pay it little regard. The weighty matter is Mrs. Webster's illness, & this I fear has become alarming. Last night & to day she has suffered at intervals intense pain from her foot to her hip—to day she has been quite confined to her bed. I am fully convinced that it will not be proper to proceed farther with her until a favourable change shall take place—but how much of her present suffering arises from the disease itself, or from its natural progress, & how much from temporary causes I cannot tell. If Mrs Webster should again be as well as when we left home, I think I shall proceed to Washington, leaving her here for a while; & to come to

Washington, or return to Boston according to circumstances hereafter. But until she is much better than she now is, I should not leave her even if I am able to travel myself. As it is there is little prospect of my getting away before next week. I shall write you daily, & nothing remains but to hope & pray for the best.

We all send much love to you & Daniel. Yrs. always truly,

Daniel Webster

Dictated letter. NhHi. Published in Van Tyne, p. 570.

1. The son of Dr. Cyrus Perkins, at whose house the Websters had stopped.

TO JAMES WILLIAM PAIGE

New York 5 Dec 1827.

—7 P. M.

Dear William

I must now write you more fully upon the afflicting state of Mrs. Websters health. Dr. [Wright] Post a very eminent physician & surgeon has today been called into consultation with Dr. [Cyrus] Perkins.[1] Their opinion I am distressed to say is far from favourable. I believe they will recommend her return to Boston as soon as convenient. They seem to think that it is very uncertain how fast or how slow may be the progress of the complaint—but they hold out faint hopes of any cure. I hope I may be able to meet the greatest of all earthly afflictions with firmness; but I need not say that I am at present quite overcome. I have not yet communicated to Mrs. Webster what the physicians think. That dreadful task remains. She will receive the information I am sure as a Christian ought. Under present circumstances I should be very glad if you could come here; although I would not wish you to put yourself to too much inconvenience. I should be very glad myself to go to Washington though it were but for a single day; but I should not do that unless in the mean time Mrs. Webster could be on her return. I shall now make no move until I hear from you in answer to this letter. If you come on I think the best way will be to take the mail stage with the chance of finding an evening boat at New Haven. You must let Daniel know without alarming him too much that his mother's health is precarious & that she will probably return home. I am not yet able to write as you see though I think I am getting better. Yrs truly   Danl. Webster

P.S. 8 oClock—

I would fain hope that the foregoing is of too alarming a character. I have since seen Mrs. Webster & told her the doctors' opinions. She says she still has courage. If you can come so as to accompany Mrs. Webster home it will not be necessary that you should set out the very day you receive this. But I shall not myself go to Washington until I hear from you that you can come to take Mrs. Webster home, if need be.

Dictated letter. NhHi. Published in PC, 1: 424–425.

1. Perkins (1778–1849; Dartmouth

1800), a longtime friend of the Websters, was then a physician in New York City.

TO JOHN COLLINS WARREN

N. York Dec. 7 [1827]
friday noon

My dear Sir

You will have heard both of Mrs W's & my own illness, by which we have been, & still are, detained here. My own complaint, was a sudden attack of rheumatism. I say sudden, for so was the principal & main assault; tho' I have felt rheumatic affections & tendencies, occasionally, for a month. But I am convalescent, shall soon be well, & my case is not the great calamity.

I should have written you earlier, in relation to Mrs W. but this is the first day, or rather yesterday was the first, in which I could write, *propria manu*. I now perform the labor, not without some difficulty. You have probably heard from Mr [James William] Paige something of Mrs W's encreased illness. Our journey hither was one of great fatigue & exposure, & Mrs W. suffered much from it. The unlucky application, by accident, of a blister plaister, further irritated & inflamed her limb; & for several days she suffered great pain. She is now a good deal better; sleeps pretty well, & is, by day, nearly as free from pain, as when she left home. She was so unwell, however, that I deemed it expedient to have the best professional advice. Dr. Post & Dr. Perkins have examined the case together. Before Dr. Post was called in, Dr. Perkins had examined it, & thought it a dangerous & alarming case; & I understand Dr. Post agrees entirely with him, altho' I have not yet seen Dr. Post myself. They are both of opinion that it is not best for Mrs W. to proceed to W[ashington]. On the other hand, Mrs W. herself is very averse to going back. She thinks she shall soon be as well as when she left home; that she can more easily reach Washington, than Boston; that she can be well attended there; & so, on the whole, is *for going on*. But she has great confidence in you, & wishes for your opinion. She says, that the swelling is not materially encreased—that some days ago, there was an appearance, as if some *head* was forming; but that this appearance seems now diminishing. She has evidently, at this moment, less of flesh & strength, than when she left home; but how much of the loss of these has been owing to temporary causes, I cannot say. The blister plaster, undoubtedly, did a good deal of harm. Dr. P. had ordered a soothing anodyne plaster, & sent the prescription. By the blunder of the apothecary, a very strong blister plaster was sent, which Mrs W. put on, & went to bed. It woke her up, in the night, & on taking it off, it was found to have produced a very great blister, which could not be healed up, for some days.

Dr. P. & Dr. P. I suppose are afraid, that if Mrs W. goes on to Washington, the progress of the disease may be such, as that it will ulcerate, & that then it will be difficult or impossible for her to be carried home.

Laying all these things together, we wish for your advice. My own convenience, rather, is that she go to Washington—for I must be with her, wherever she is, & for the next six, or nine months, I can better be at W. than at home.

She will wait here, till she hears from you, in answer to this letter. I may be here also, but it is possible I may be gone. Let your letter, if you please, be addressed to *her*, & enclosed to Dr. Cyrus Perkins, 176 Fulton Street. If necessary, you can address another to *me*, enclosed in like manner, which the Dr. will forward, if I am gone.

I hope, My Dear Sir, you will give us an answer, at your earliest convenience. Your opinion will probably decide us, what to do. I only repeat that Mrs W.'s *desire* is very strong for going on; & that she would feel great *despondency*, if she must go back. Yrs   D. Webster

ALS. MHi.

TO JOHN COLLINS WARREN

New York Dec. 8 [1827]
Saturday Eve'

My Dear Sir

Since writing to you yesterday, it has seemed to me to be my duty to write again, & to put to you the important question, *whether you can* POSSIBLY *come here*, to see Mrs W. I am aware, what a call this is, on your friendship & kindness; & shall not feel hurt, if it cannot be complied with. At the same time, there is nothing I do or can more fervently desire. The truth is, Mrs W. thinks the Medical Gentlemen here are too *discouraging*; she feels, that if she could see you, you would, at least, try *something*. Next to the preservation of her life, the greatest object is to satisfy her that every thing is done, which *can be done*, for her recovery; & I fear she will not be entirely satisfied, without seeing you, & having the full benefit of your examination & advice.

I can say no more. I know how many concerns confine you at home; but if you could, *by possibility*, find 4 days to come here & return—or at most 5—it would confer an obligation, never to be forgotten. I cannot add all that Mrs W. says, & feels, on this point. Yours mo. truly always   Danl. Webster

ALS. MHi.

TO NATHANIEL SILSBEE

New York Decr. 9. [1827]
Sunday noon

My Dr Sir

I am sorry not to be able to give you a better account of myself, & especially that I am obliged to speak so unfavorably of Mrs. Webster's health. I have not yet been able to leave the House, nor indeed was I able to quit my own room till yesterday Evening. I am getting better, however, & if the weather were not so particularly unfavorable, I should have hopes of setting forward in a day or two.

My great affliction is the state of Mrs. W's health. Whether it is best for her to return to Boston, or to remain some time here, with a hope of being able hereafter to proceed to Washington, is a question difficult to decide. She is very unwilling to return; & the physicians do not encourage her further progress south. I am now in the hourly expectation of the arrival of her Brother, (Mr [James William] Paige), when we shall determine on something. It is most probable, I think, that she will return to Boston, with Mr Paige, & that I shall proceed South without her. It is possible, however, she may stay here, in the hope of being able to accompany Mr & Mrs [Joseph] Story, some three weeks hence, to Washington, as I have already said. Yours with mo[st] true regard
Danl. Webster

ALS. NhHi. Published in PC, 1: 425.

TO JOHN COLLINS WARREN

N York Dec. 9. [1827]
Sunday Eve'

My D Sir,

I wrote you last Evening.[1] Today, Dr. Perkins & Dr. Post have had another examination and consultation, & I am most happy to say that they think Mrs Webster's case apparently a *little* better. It seems to them that the tumour is not quite so hard, nor altogether so large, as when they examined it, together, last before. She passed a comfortable night, last night, & has been tolerably free from pain today.

Under these circumstances, My Dear Sir, if this letter should find you in Boston, Mrs W. thinks she will withdraw her request of a visit from you; or, at least, postpone it, for the present. She gets a good deal of courage, from these more favorable appearances; and as she knows how desirous you would be, of coming, if you could, & how difficult you must find it to leave home, she is very content to give up the expectation of seeing you here, for the present. We shall keep you, duly & daily, informed of the progress of affairs. The treatment is not materially altered; poultices, & other Emolients, occasional leeching, & rest & quiet are the main reliances.

We are looking hourly for Mr. Paige. Yrs always mo[st] truly
Danl. Webster

ALS. MHi.
1. See above, DW to John Collins Warren, December 8, [1827].

FROM JOSHUA PHILLIPS
Eldredge. County of Huron. Ohio
[December 10, 1827]
Dear Sir,

I hereby inform you that we had a County meeting at the Court House last Friday for the purpose of Appointing Delegates to meet with others from different parts of the State at Columbus the last of December to nominate Electors for President & Vice President & to take all laudable measures to secure the reelection of John Q. Adams.[1]

As there is little or nothing said publicly about Vice President I would suggest the propriety of nominating Daniel Webster of Boston as a Candidate for Vice President the ensueing election & you need feel no delicacy in answering me for I am your friend. Although I was not intimately acquainted with you in New Hampshire I was personly so. I have mentioned you as a Candidate for Vice President to some of my friends & have told them in addition to other things you would never fight a Duel.

Your Character as a Representative is well known here. If you think this worth answering let me hear from you as soon as possible. You can Counsel with your friends. Yours Respectfully   Joshua Phillips

N.B. Please to direct your Letter to be left at Florence Post Office. If this should find you at the City of Washington you will please direct your Letter to Pittsburgh, Pennsylvania as I expect to be there in January.   J. Phillips

ALS. NhHi. Published in part in Van Tyne, p. 131. Phillips has not been identified.

1. According to the *Ohio State* *Journal*, December 29, 1827, more than 200 citizens attended the pro-administration convention at Columbus on December 28.

FROM HENRY WILLIS KINSMAN

Boston 15th Dec. 1827

Dr. Sir

I recd. yrs. of the 13th. inst. this morning,[1] enclosing three checks for $1525, $250, $3000, & a blank note to be indorsed by Mr. [George] Blake. I find your a/c. at the Bank to be about $4373. Cr., which with Mr. [John] Dodge's[2] $100. makes $4473. If the one thousand dollars, which you mention in your letter, is deposited this morning, or Monday, I shall be able to get along without calling on Mr. Blake; but will keep the blank for any future contingency.

The first of Mr. [Henry] Wheaton's draft's has not become due yet, & the second is not payable until the 18th.

Your friends will be gratified to hear, that you are able to continue your journey, as well as, that Mrs. W. is better.

I wrote you at N. Y. the 12th[3] acknowledging the receipt of yr. blk. note for $1500.—& shall write you again in a few days respecting Mr. [Josiah] Marshall's case.[4] Respectfully Yrs.   Henry W. Kinsman

ALS. NhHi.

1. Letter not found.

2. Dodge had requested Webster to file a suit against Colonel Thomas Handasyd Perkins in the summer of 1827, one involving the settling of the estate of Unite Dodge, John's brother. On the Dodge-Perkins quarrel, see Carl Seaburg and Stanley Paterson, *Merchant Prince of Boston: Colonel T. H. Perkins, 1764–1854* (Cambridge, Mass., 1971), pp. 345–350; *Dodge* v. *Perkins*, 7 *Federal Cases* 798 (1827).

3. Letter not found.

4. *Gibson* v. *Marshall*, an unreported case in the Massachusetts Supreme Judicial Court, Suffolk County, filed November 1827 and decided in March 1829. Webster represented Marshall, a Boston merchant. The case involved the ambiguous financial situation of Susan Gibson. Her husband, Abraham, recently deceased, had been a Boston merchant with complicated financial dealings.

TO ELIJAH HUNT MILLS

Washington Decr. 19. 1827

My Dear Sir,

I arrived here only on Sunday Evening, the 16th. inst.[1] You are acquainted, probably, with the causes of my detention, for a fortnight, in N York. I left Mrs W. there, still quite unwell. My last letters represent her as much more comfortable & free from pain, than she had been; but I yet feel the greatest anxiety, as to the original cause of her illness.

I found here your letter of the third,[2] & dispatched its enclosure to Mr. [Samuel B.] Barrell.[3] It gave me great pleasure to hear from you, & to know that thus far you are getting along thro. the winter with less inconvenience than was expected. I hope we shall have little weather more severe than was experienced the latter part of last month.

As yet, I feel new & strange, in the Senate. My habits have become conformed to the course & manner of things elsewhere; & it will require time, to enable me to feel at home, where I now am. According to present appearances, there will be little for *me* to do. Our adversaries undoubtedly have a majority, & I think the true course is to let them exercise it, as seems to them good. Why should *we* be responsible for what we cannot control?

Today we have heard Col [Richard Mentor] Johnson's *Annual* on abolition of imprisonment [for debt];[4] sound, practical, systematic & coherent! I really think he is not half the man he was, ten years ago.

The good Deacon [Alden] Bradford is here,—a sort of agent for the Revo[lutionary]y officers. He has, as you will see, trusted their cause, in the Senate, to Mr [Levi] Woodbury.[5] Be it so. No considerable debate has arisen yet, in either House. P[hilip] P[endleton] Barbour's resolution, to sell out of the B[an]k, is expected to be called up tomorrow.[6]

The Senate room is *transmogrified*, since last session. The V. President sits opposite the main door, & faces his former seat. The seats are crowded, &, altogether, the arrangement is not good. My place (Hobson's choice) is nearest the Chair, on its left hand. It was left by 47 wiser heads than mine, & yet I believe it the best seat in the Chamber.

Mrs Adams' first drawing room was last night. I was not there, but believe she is not at all well. The President is tolerably well, & Mr Clay also, whose faith & courage still hold out. I hear he has thought it necessary to put forth another publication on the *combination* question, which is expected soon to appear.[7] I regret it; tho I am told it is very satisfactorily done. This, I believe, is not yet a *public* matter.

It will be one of my most agreeable duties, My D Sir, to write to you, & to forward you any thing to occupy your hours; or it will be still more gratifying to be useful to you, in any more important respect.

When you have leisure & strength, I shall be happy to hear from you. Yours always truly   Danl. Webster

ALS. MHi. Published in *PC*, 1: 427–429.

1. Webster traveled to Washington from New York with Congressman Thomas Jackson Oakley. He took his seat in the Senate on Monday, December 17, 1827, two weeks after the opening of the session.

2. See Elijah Hunt Mills to DW,

December 3, 1827, mDW 6460.

3. Barrell was an attorney in Washington.

4. For Johnson's speech in the Senate, see *Congressional Debates*, 20th Cong., 1st sess., 1827–28, pp. 11–15. Johnson was responsible for much agitation in support of the abolition of imprisonment for debt, and

his speeches on this subject in the Senate during this period actually occurred much more frequently than annually.

5. According to the *National Intelligencer*, December 20, 1827, Woodbury on December 18 "presented the petition of the surviving officers of the Continental Army," asking that they be granted the half pay promised them.

6. On December 13, 1827, Barbour presented to the House of Representatives a resolution "to inquire into the expediency of providing by law for the sale of that portion of the Stock of the Bank of the United States which is held by the Government of the United States, and the application of the proceeds thereof to the payment of the public debt." The bill was, as Webster predicted, called up again by Barbour on December 20, and defeated in the House, 173 to 9, on December 21.

7. A long essay by Clay, attempting to vindicate himself of Jackson's charges of political intrigue in the 1824 election, appeared in the *National Intelligencer* of January 3, 1828.

TO DAVID DAGGETT

Washington Decr. 22. 1827

My Dear Sir,

Fortunately, I am recovered from rheumatism, or I might be tempted to try your prescription, which seems to be a process *to burn it out*. If there be any thing, good or bad, in the human Constitution which can resist the joint flames of *whiskey & brimstone*, it must certainly be *fire-proof*.

I am nearly well; but my poor wife is still quite ill at New York. I learn, here, nothing—except that a hot *winter & summer* are before us. When I see & know more, I will write you. Yrs in love   D. Webster

ALS. CtY.

TO JAMES WILLIAM PAIGE

Decr. 25 [1827] Christmas noon—

Dear William,

Your letter of Sunday[1] has this moment reached me, in which you say Mrs W. would be glad, if it should be quite convenient for me, that I would come to New York, to meet Judge [Joseph] Story—and I certainly shall do so. I cannot go for a day or two, because my cold is too severe; but there is nothing to preventing my setting off, so soon as I am quite well. Judge Story wrote me that he should probably set out abt. the 29th—which is next Saturday.

Possibly I may not leave here before *Monday*, the 31st. but even, then, I shall be in N. York as quick as the Judge. On receipt of this, [I] will thank you to write me, saying whether Mrs W. wishes me to bring any of hers, or the childrens, things along with me. Your letter, if written on friday morning, will be here on Sunday, so that if I happen to stay till

Monday, I shall get it. *Probably*, I shall go off before Monday—this will depend a little, as well on the weather & the state of the public conveyances, as on my getting rid of my cold.

I hope, if it be not too inconvenient, you will stay till I come; & then we can talk about Grace's going to Boston, or Washington. The tone of your letters, for three or four days, has been so much more favorable than before, that I feel encouraged. It will be dull to her, I fear, to be left again, by me, after you are gone; but, then, I must come here, dispatch some few things, & return to her again. I shall let no business, public or private, prevent attention to her, as the first duty.

My cold is better today, but still I am not quite well. Indeed so much of rheumatism, & then so severe a cold, have rather reduced this corporeal system of mine, to some little degree of weakness. Two or three days of good weather, (which I know not when we shall see again) would do me a great deal of good.

What did you mean to say of Mr [George] Blake— Is he going to marry Mrs [Caroline Langdon] Eustis?[2]

You will of course send this to Grace, as I shall not write another today.

As I have begun, I shall continue to "Stone & Otis,"[3] for the present. Yrs always truly   D. Webster

—Again tomorrow—
My Christmas dinner is a *handful* of magnesia, a bowl of gruel.

ALS. NhHi. Published in *PC*, 1: 429–430.

1. Not found.

2. Blake had been an intimate personal friend as well as a political ally of William Eustis, governor of Massachusetts. Eustis had died in 1825; Sarah Olcott Blake, Blake's second wife, had died at the age of thirty-seven on May 13, 1826. Although it has not been established that either Blake or Eustis' widow, Caroline Langdon Eustis (1781–

1865), ever remarried, Paige had probably passed on to Webster a rumor of romance between the two. Mrs. Eustis was the "beautiful and accomplished" daughter of Hon. Woodbury Langdon (1739–1805) of Portsmouth, New Hampshire (*New England Historical and Genealogical Register*, 23: 206).

3. The meaning of the allusion to "Stone & Otis" has not been determined.

TO JAMES WILLIAM PAIGE

Friday 1 oclock
[December 28, 1827?]

Dear William,

I have yours of Wednesday,[1] in which you say something of going to Boston &c.

I really know not what is best to be done, but will suggest what occurs to me.

In the first place, I am not now well eno' to set off, on a journey, to N. Y. My cold, or what remains of it, (which is more than I could wish) is on my chest & lungs. I have a *cough*, though not hard & obstinate, yet so serious as to admonish me to be *careful*. Taking chances of health & weather, *Tuesday* or *Wednesday* would be the earliest day that I should expect to be able to go away. That would bring it near the end of the week, before I reached N York. Now, if Judge & Mrs [Joseph] Story left home at expected time, they will be *leaving* N York by the time I shall arrive. So that, after all, I must come back very soon, or come alone afterwards.

I have looked at all my causes in Court, & am satisfied that I can *very easily* make such arrangements, as that I may be gone a fortnight any time before the 1. of *Feby.*

Now the question is—whether I had not better wait till the Judge & his Lady come here, & get settled—& then go & see Grace?

I should prefer, it is true, going while the Boats yet run; but a land journey, in health, is less hazardous than water passages, while sick.

What occurs to me, as best, on the whole, is; that on receipt of this, you go to *Boston*; & give the necessary attention to your own affairs. If, after being there a few days, you could return, without *any* degree of inconvenience, I should be glad. But I would not have you derange your own affairs at all. In the meantime, I will be governed by my own health, & by what I hear from N. York, as to my going there before your return. I do most devoutly wish I was able to go tomorrow!

It is obvious to me, that if Mrs W's case should continue, without material alteration for some time, I must vacate my place here. Personally, I care very little about it, but wish only to fulfill the expectations of my friends, as far as circumstances will allow. But on this point, I shall do nothing hastily.#

You will receive this on Monday Morning. I shall get your answer on *Wednesday*—but, in the mean time, if I hear that Mrs. W. is worse, or I should get well myself sooner than I expect, I may probably set off.

The most I shall fear, after you go, & while you are gone, is, that I shall not get, daily, true accounts. The Dr. will naturally think that I could do no good, & therefore if Grace should be rather worse, might not think it worth while to give me notice. *I must depend on you to make some arrangement by which I shall know, from day to day, & every day, precisely how she is.*

P.S. Mr. [Edward V.] Sparhawk,[2] one of the reporters of the Senate, thinks of leaving this place for New York Tomorrow—if he should, I will try to send a small trunk of childrens clothes—if I can get them selected & packed. Yrs   D. Webster

A certain other situation, abt. which the Papers talk, is equally inconsistent with the present condition of things, even if I had the option.[3]

ALS. NhHi. Published in Van Tyne, pp. 571–572.

1. Not found.

2. Sparhawk was a reporter for the *National Intelligencer*.

3. Webster was probably referring to suggestions that he run for the vice presidency in 1828. He does not himself comment one way or the other, but to run with Adams would have presented a constitutional problem, since both were citizens of the same state.

TO NATHANIEL SILSBEE

New York Jan[uar]y 4. [1828]

My Dear Sir,

I arrived here yesterday, at 11 o'clock, after a very tolerable journey, & without having added any thing to my cold. Indeed I think it is better than when I left Washington.

I find Mrs Webster more comfortable, on the whole, than I expected. She has now enjoyed more rest & repose, & more freedom from pain, for three days together, than in any equal time since we came here, six weeks ago. She has lost flesh, since I left her, however, and is now feeble.

As to the original cause of her illness, I do not know exactly what to think of it. Some symptoms are certainly a little more favorable. The tumour, itself, has not enlarged, lately; & the parts adjacent are evidently less swelled & inflamed.

I cannot help getting a little new hope, on the whole; tho' I fear I build on a slight foundation.

I find here the Judge [Story] & his Lady. They are in very good health. He has not looked so well, [for] a long time. It is a great thing to get him out of his study. They set off this afternoon, being anxious to get over the Chesapeake, before the Boat stops. They will take possession of the rooms, at Mrs [Ruth] McIntyre's;[1] where I hope to join them soon. Mr [James William] Paige went to Boston yesterday. As soon as he shall be able to return, which I think will be in a few days, I shall return to Washington, if Mrs W. remains as comfortable as at present. I am, My Dear Sir, with mo[st] true regard, yours   Danl. Webster

Mr Clay's address[2] seems to meet with universal approbation.

ALS. NhHi. Published in *PC*, 1: 431.

1. Mrs. McIntyre, a widow, kept a boarding house on Pennsylvania Avenue in Washington.

2. In his address "To the Public,"

printed in the *National Intelligencer*, January 3, 1828, Clay defended himself against the "corrupt bargain" charges.

FROM NATHANIEL SILSBEE

Senate Chamber
Washington 4. Jan. 28

Dear Sir

Agreably to your request, I yesterday asked and obtained leave of absence for you, for one week from that time. I am induced to make this known to you from not seeing it noticed in the "Intelligencer" of today, which omission I mentioned to Mr. [Joseph] Gales a few minutes since, who said he would speak to their stenographer about it, & notice the omission in tomorrow's paper.[1]

I stated to the Senate, that the request was caused by the indisposition of Mrs. W. which had for sometime past detained her, on her way to this City, at New York, where she was now quite sick, so much so, that however your absence from the Board might be regretted by myself or others, I confidently hoped the request then made in your behalf, would be granted.

I am not without apprehensions that the unpleasant weather which we have had since the day after you left here may cause an increase of your own indisposition; I hope, however, this will not be the case and that you may have the satisfaction to find the state of Mrs. Webster's health better than you seemed to apprehend.

It is said to have been agreed in the Committee on Manufactures of the House, that for the purpose of obtaining the information contemplated by the late Resolution,[2] each member of the Committee should select two persons to be sent for, and not more—who these fourteen persons are to be is not yet publickly known.

No other news. Yours most respectfully   Nathl Silsbee

ALS. NhD.

1. A small item explaining Webster's absence from the Senate appeared in the *National Intelligencer* of January 5, 1828.

2. The resolution, as amended and passed by the House of Representatives, was: "Resolved: That the Committee on Manufactures be empowered to send for, and to examine persons on oath, concerning the present condition of our manufactures, and to report the minutes of such examination to the House." The data gathered presumably were meant to aid in designing the tariff of 1828. This resolution, however, was opposed by the friends of manufactur-

ing, who suspected that it would be used to stall protective legislation. The resolution was discussed and passed by the House on December 31, 1827; for the text of the arguments, see *Register of Debates*, 20th Cong., 1st sess., 1827–28, pp. 862–890.

TO JAMES WILLIAM PAIGE

Sunday Eve' 7 o'clock
[January 6, 1828]

Dear William,

Mrs W. has suffered today, rather more than for some days past. Her system, generally, has been a little deranged, & it was not till since three o'clock that some medicine, which she took for the purpose, has had its proper effect. She is now somewhat easier, & I trust will yet have a comfortable night. The tumour today seemed rather harder than yesterday; probably from the pain, occasioned, in great part perhaps, by the cause above mentioned.

Under cover to you, I send an unsealed letter to Dr. [John Collins] Warren.[1] I wish you would read it, & then see the Dr. You will see, that in one part of it, I say you will speak to him further. The object of that, is, that you should tell him that the *expense* of procuring some one or more to take the temporary charge of his affairs at home, is not at all to be regarded—nor indeed any other expense. Tell him at once, that if I knew the case was hopeless, absolutely so, still, I would regard a thousand dollars as well laid out, to give Grace the comfort of seeing him. No considerations of expense must weigh at all. Perhaps you may tell him, also, that you & other friends will, if he wishes it, go to some other, or any other Physician, and ask of them the favor to aid in the care of his concerns, in his absence. Mr [George] Ticknor & Mr [Nathan] Hale, I am sure, would gladly join you, in any thing of that kind which it might be necessary to do.

As to the *time* of the Dr's coming, a day or two, or two or three or four days, perhaps, will make no material difference. Other things being Equal, however, the sooner, the better. Perhaps he might prefer not to come till you come; & your affairs may necessarily detain you some days. Again; tho' he should not wait for you, it might require three or four days to put his affairs in train. If he should come by N London, he would do well to come to Fuller's, overnight; so as to shorten the next day's ride. On all these matters, I must leave much with you & him. *If the thing be possible, I wish him to come*; & I can say no more.

As to your own return, My Dear friend, I would not have you make too great a sacrifice. I can stay here now, for ten or twelve days, without *great* inconvenience. And, indeed, as I have before mentioned to you, nothing will be allowed to take me away from Mrs W. so long as my presence is in any degree essential to her comfort. Nevertheless, I should be very glad to be at Washington, about the commencement of the second week of the Court—say about the 21st. or 22nd. inst.

8 o'clock:

Mrs W. is now in a very quiet sleep. I trust she will have a good night. I shall of course write you every day, & shall now look out soon for a letter from you. I wish you would see Mr [George] Blake—give my love to him—& if convenient show him, or read him, my letter to Dr. Warren. He was very kind when I wrote on the same subject before.[2] Adieu!

D. Webster

Do not forget to give all our loves to Danl.

ALS. MHi.

1. See DW to Dr. Warren, January   6, [1828], below.

2. Letter not found.

TO JOHN COLLINS WARREN

New York Jan. 6. 1827 [1828]

My Dear Sir

Before the receipt of this, you will have seen Mr. [James William] Paige, & learned from him, not only the present condition of Mrs Webster, but also our anxious wish that you should see her, if such a thing be possible. As on the former occasion, so now, I would have you believe that I am fully sensible of the nature of this request, & of the inconvenience it must put you to, to comply with it. Nevertheless, I hope you will consider the circumstances to be such as to render it not altogether unreasonable. I have entire confidence in Dr. [Cyrus] Perkins, whom I have long known, & in Dr. [Wright] Post, whose reputation & standing are so high. Still, there are reasons which impel me strongly to desire your consultation with them.

In the first place, you have known the case longer, & are better acquainted with its early appearance, & history.

In the second place, cases of this nature are of such rare occurrence, that the opinion & advice of any experienced & distinguished practitioner, whose range of practice renders it probable that he may have met with a similar case, are highly to be prized, & much to be desired.

But, mainly, & without mentioning many other things, it will be, in the highest degree, gratifying to Mrs Webster, to see you, & have the benefit of your advice. Whatever your opinion may be, & whatever the result may be, it will afford her the greatest satisfaction, to see you again; she will then feel that all has been done, that can be done. I assure you, also, my Dear Sir, that of our numerous friends at the East-ward, many of them are particularly anxious that you should visit her. They seem to understand that there is some degree of difference, be-tween you & the Physicians here, as to the degree of danger in the case. I, indeed, can reconcile such a difference, if there be one, by consider-ing the different periods, at which you & they examined the case; but such a reason might not satisfy all.

It seems, My Dear Sir, as far as I can understand it, to be a case of uncommon occurrence—of somewhat anomalous character—& hardly to have been looked for, in so good a constitution. Under all these cir-cumstances, I feel that something will still remain to be done, until you have seen the case once more, & conferred with your brethren here re-specting it. I should not be at all surprized, if, on your examination of the case, you should find it to be more dangerous than you thought it at first. Nor, have I any great reason to suppose that you would advise to any mode of treatment, essentially different from that which has been followed here. Still, in a case of this kind, it is *possible* you might suggest something useful. This is the view which both Dr. Post & Dr. Perkins have of the matter, & they would therefore be very glad to have the benefit of your experience and advice, in consultation.

Enclosed you have a short account of the history & symptoms of the case, since Mrs W. has been here.[1]

Allow me now, My Dear Sir, to say a word or two, as to the practica-bility of getting here, & the necessary time for the journey. And in the first place, I may say, that Mr Paige, if desired, will come with you, & take the charge of your conveyance. When the weather is not stormy, nor excessively cold, you may reach here in a day & a half, by way of New London. The mail coach goes regularly in two days.

I do not expect you can leave home, without engaging some friend to take care of your patients in the City; & also procuring some suitable substitute to carry forward your lectures. The inconvenience & expense of these things, I have fully considered. On this point, Mr Paige will speak to you further.

And now, My Dear friend, I can only repeat the extreme solicitude which I feel, on this subject. It does not seem to me that if it were my own life, which was at hazard, I could experience so much. I know well, My Dear Sir, that if the kindest feelings, and truest friendship can overcome the obstacles, we shall see you—& there I must leave it. With the most sincere esteem, Yours   Danl. Webster

ALS. MHi.
    1. Not found.

TO NATHANIEL SILSBEE

New York Jan. 8. [1828]
Tuesday Morning

My Dear Sir,

I thank you for your letter of the 4th[1]—& for the friendly manner in which you applied for my leave of absence.

Mrs Webster remains essentially the same, as when I wrote you last, except that I think she had not quite so comfortable a night, last night. The tumour is evidently making progress towards breaking thro. the skin. What character it may then assume is uncertain; but my fears are great. Of the three Physicians who have attended her here, (Dr. [Cyrus] Perkins, Dr. [Wright] Post, & Dr. [David] Hosack,) the former only thinks he ever saw such a case before. A description of it, made out by Dr. Perkins, has been sent to Dr. [Philip Syng] Physic[k], & also to Dr. Nathan Smith, of N. Haven, for their opinion and advice. I have written an urgent letter to Dr. [John Collins] Warren, to come to N York, to consult with the Physicians here.

My own health is mending, & if we could have a little clear weather, I think I should soon be well.

We have no news here. The thick weather is supposed to have kept back the packets. That of Nov. 24. is not yet arrived. Yours very truly

D. Webster

I suppose Judge [Joseph] Story will be with you nearly as soon as you receive this, unless he stopped in Philadelphia.

ALS. NhHi. Published in part in PC, I: 432.

1. See above, DW to Nathaniel Silsbee, January 4, 1828.

TO EZEKIEL WEBSTER

N. York Jan. 8. 1828

Dear E.

I came here from W[ashington] on friday, the 4th. There are so many friends to write to, on the subject of Mrs. W's health, that I fear I may neglect some; and hardly know how long it is since I wrote you. [James] William [Paige], however, has written occasionally, to his friends in your vicinity.

I cannnot say any thing new, in regard to Mrs. W. Her case is most serious. It is one of rare occurrence, no Physician here but Dr. Perkins thinking he ever saw one like it. The tumour has not yet broke out, but threatens it, & will, doubtless, soon. Its character will then be better known; & I fear the worst. Dr Nathan Smith, Dr. Physic[k] &c have been written to, for opinions & advice; & I have written an urgent letter to Dr. Warren to come here. After all, the case is very much out of the reach of medical application, or surgical aid. The tumour is so large, so situated, embracing so many muscles, nerves & blood vessels, that an *operation* is not to be thought of. Internal remedies do not reach it, & external applications have little effect. The result must be left with Providence; but you must be prepared to learn the worst. For three or four days, she has been more free from pain, than for some time before —but yesterday she was a good deal distressed, again. William P. went home the day I came. He thinks he can return, in a week or ten days, & stay till I make a visit to the [Supreme] Court at Washington, if Mrs W. should be so as to allow of my leaving her. You will of course not alarm your wife & Mrs [Israel W.] Kelly & Nancy too much, in regard to Grace.[1] There is yet a *hope*; but I have thought it best to tell you my real opinion.

My own health has suffered from continued colds, & catarhs. Though not quite well, even yet, I have no dangerous, or bad symptoms. I feel no inflamation of the lungs, or soreness of the chest; nor any febrile symptoms. An epidemic cold is all about here, & I partake in it, but it appears to be getting better, & I have no doubt that two or three clear days would finish it. Julia & Edward are pretty well. They go to school. Grace & the children desire their best love to Mrs W. and the little girls —as well as to you. Yrs always truly   Danl. Webster

ALS. NhD. Published in *PC*, 1: 432–433.

1. Grace Fletcher Webster's sister, Rebecca Fletcher (1776–1853) had married Israel W. Kelly. Nancy has not been identified.

FROM JEREMIAH MASON

Portsmouth Jany. 9. 1828

My dear Sir

On coming home today from Salem, I received your letter of 26 Decr.,[1] which had been lying by several days. I had been desirous of writing to you from the time I first heard of your & Mrs. Websters sickness at N. York. But I was very soon told that it was your intention to go to Washington & return to N York, which made it uncertain where a letter would reach you, at any particular time. We have been greatly distressed by the various accounts of your & Mrs. Websters situation, which have not been so alarming as that in your letter. I was at Boston last Sunday, & saw Mr. Paige immediately on his return from N. York. His account of Mrs. Websters situation was greatly more favourable, as you know. He had not then seen Dr. Warren, but said that the N. York surgeons thought much better of the case than they had, believing (as I understood him) that present appearances were *greatly* more favourable. As to your own health he said he had never before seen you so much reduced, & so feeble, but that he supposed the cause of your sickness to be, in a good degree at least, removed, & that there was good ground to hope that rest & quiet would speedily restore you.

I am aware that your sufferings have been excessive & with all the alleviation of present favourable appearances, if they continue as when Mr. Paige left you, that your situation must still be full of distress. In case Mrs. Webster still continues in a condition actually critical, in the opinion of those most competent to judge of it, I do not think that your duty to the public requires you to leave her to resume your seat in the Senate. Indeed it seems to me that under such circumstances it must be quite impossible for you to attend to your duties in the Senate, and I think you ought not to attempt it. Nor do I think you ought to return to Washington till your own health is in a good degree restored, & confirmed. But I hope & trust my dear Sir that when you receive this, Mrs. Webster may be deemed to be out of danger. If however she should unfortunately be otherwise & that you should be obliged to remain with her (as I think in that case you would) I much doubt whether that would justify you in *immediately* or *soon* vacating your seat in the Senate. This I understand to be the intimation in your letter. Whether her continuing long in such situation would not render your resignation expedient can be determined hereafter. I most cordially wish under present circumstances that you was out of the Senate. But I do not see how you will justify resigning at *this time.* Your motives will be misunderstood by many of your political friends & misconstrued & misrepresented by all your political enemies. Your resignation would unquestionably be imputed to your supposed dispair of success of the Administration party. I am sure it would be so represented by all the opposition papers in the U. S., and I think it very probable that many not under their influence would believe it. Considering your standing, such a belief might at the present time do the administration & the Country vast injury. I think the injury arising from absence from the Senate would be immeasurably less than from your resignation. Having accepted the place so recently nothing but imperious necessity will be or ought to be considered a justification for resigning it under the present circumstances of the Country. At all events I hope you will not come to a determination to do this hastily. If you find it probable that you must be absent from the Senate the whole or chief part of the present session I think you ought to state your willingness to resign to some of your political friends at Washington & be in some measure guided by their opinion of its expediency. There can be no danger of thereby exposing yourself to the suspicion of wishing to obtain their advice to retain it altho, I doubt not such will be their earnest advice. You are too well known at W. to fear anything of that sort.

After giving you my opinion thus frankly on this point, I think I am bound to say with equal frankness that not only Mrs. Websters situation, if it continues to be dangerous & critical, but in my opinion a due regard for your own health, if it be as low & slender as I fear, makes it your duty to remain quietly where you are for the present. I know the calls for you in the Sup[rem]e Court will be urgent, but I really fear that any extraordinary exertions with your present feeble health & anxiety may destroy you. If you do return to Washington I most sincerely advise you to abstain as much as possible from occasions of high excitement & exertion. Such a course under circumstances cannot injure your reputation.

Since I saw you at Boston I have been twice to Salem to attend the trials of the Argonaut. We have had two tedious jury trials, & have obtained two successive verdicts much against the wishes of Judge [Samuel] P[utnam][2] He seemed to think it his duty to obstruct the Pl[aintif]fs course as much as he could, but I believe we have got our verdicts on such grounds as must end the litigation, though not on the ground we ought to have had them. I left Salem immediately after the last verdict was given. I have no doubt the judge has in some way reserved the cases for the whole Court.[3]

I have been so engaged that I have not had time to read Mr Clays letter.[4] But I have been told by several who have read it, that it is entirely conclusive, & that it cannot fail to produce extensive effects.

The prospect is now favourable for our spring elections. There will be greater exertions & excitement than we have experienced for many years.

We shall be very desirous of hearing occasionally how you & Mrs. Webster are. Mrs. Mason joins me in affectionate regards to her & yourself. I am my dear Sir most sincerely yours   J. Mason

ps. I have not time to transcribe this & make it more legible.

ALS. NhHi. Published in part in Van Tyne, pp. 131–133.

1. See DW to Mason, [December 26, 1827], in PC, 1: 430–431.

2. Putnam (1768–1853; Harvard 1797) had served as state senator and representative before his appointment to the Supreme Judicial Court in 1814.

3. The Argonaut, a ship owned by Willard Peele and others, had struck rocks on its way to Salem on March 24, 1821, and was abandoned off Portsmouth harbor. The insurance companies refused to declare it a total loss, and finally tried to return the Argonaut, patched and mended, to its former owners. When the owners took the matter to court, the juries consistently decided against the insurance companies, while Putnam, judge of the Supreme Judicial Court,

apparently was of a different opinion. In the case, *Peele et al.* v. *the Suffolk Insurance Co.*, decided in the November term, 1828, Leverett Saltonstall appeared for the defendants, and Mason and Nichols for the plaintiffs. The decision was in favor of the plaintiffs, with Chief Justice Isaac Parker stressing in his opinion that the insurance company had constructively accepted the offer of abandonment by the unreasonable delay in making the necessary repairs. See 7 *Pickering Reports* 254 (1828).

4. See H. Clay, "To the Public," *National Intelligencer*, January 3, 1828.

TO JOSEPH STORY

N. York. Jan. 10. '28

My Dear Sir

I imagine you are in Washington ere this time, altho' I have heard nothing of your progress since you left us. On your account, I have kept an anxious eye to the weather, & am happy in thinking that, in all probability, you skimmed over, & were not obliged to plough *round*, the Chesapeake. As you are now arrived at your resting place, before adverting to other topics, let me say a word or two about matters there—I mean matters *domestic*. *Impr[imis]*. The small parlour is the warmest, and has the pleasantest aspect—therefore, probably, Mrs S[tory] will like it best, as a sitting room. If she prefers the larger room, however, she can have her choice.

Item. Mrs [Ruth] MacIntyre will arrange her lodging room and your study, on the first floor—i. e. the same floor (only a little lower) as the parlours.

Item. In the closet, in the small parlour, is some *wine*, of various sorts— *look & see*. There are some bottles marked "Canton"—others "Gov. Jones." These are honest madeira—perhaps, also, some J[?]. A. G. Some sherry may be there, marked E. I. & something else.

In the two small Decanters, you will find brandy, & choice old rum. The old rum is in bottles, in the small box, in the garret. The box has been opened—is just tacked together again, & is under the other boxes. Sampson[1] can get a bottle of it, easily.

As to a Hackney Coach man, there is a man by name Dennis, a colored man.[2] He seems a careful fellow, & has a decent carriage—Sampson knows him.

And now, My Dear Sir, as to other matters.

Mrs W. is not quite comfortable, for her. About Monday & Tuesday, she had a good deal of pain, having become a little deranged, in her general system. This, of course, inflamed & irritated the local affection. She has now got over that, & for yesterday, & today, & the two last nights, has been, I think, more comfortable, than for some weeks—perhaps than ever since her arrival here. The tumour itself has not materially changed, except that it appeared yesterday less inflamed, & a little softer, with rather less swelling around it, than the day or two preceding. Its appearance, in these respects, naturally varies, from day to day, from the operation of divers causes. I hope Dr. Warren will come here next week—he gives some encouragement. The case has been laid before Dr. Physic[k], and we have his answer.[3] It sheds no new light.

My own health is much improved; & in a few days I hope to be quite free from the remnant of my cold. Mr Paige arrived, safe and in season, at Boston. He is dispatching his affairs, so as to return here, soon as possible. If Mrs W. should be no worse, I shall be looking south next week, on the moment of his arrival. Mrs W. sends a world of love to Mrs S. She hopes she may find herself not so badly off at W. as she feared. I shall write you a line, nearly every day.

I send you a Salem letter.[4] Tell Mr [Henry] Tims[5] to open all letters, having Salem P. marks. I believe Mr. Mason is now at Salem trying the Argonaut once more.[6]

Little or no news here. Yrs always   D. Webster

ALS. DLC.
1. Probably a servant at Mrs. McIntyre's.
2. Dennis is not otherwise identified.
3. Not found.

4. Not found.
5. Tims was assistant doorkeeper of the Senate.
6. See above, Jeremiah Mason to DW, January 9, 1828.

TO JOSEPH STORY

Saturday 1 oclock
[January 12, 1828]

My Dear Sir

By a letter from Mr Silsbee I learn that you arrived safe at Baltimore on Tuesday;[1] from which I infer that you did not put your water conveyance at hazard, by a day's stay at Philadelphia.

Mrs W. is much as yesterday, tho' I think not quite so well. She appears a little weary, this morning, & more flushed than I could wish. Tho' her constitution is so good, yet I have been constantly afraid that this dreadful tumour might eventually affect her lungs.

Mr Paige writes me that he shall leave Boston, the first of next week. The moment of his arrival, I shall set out, provided Mrs W. remains as at present. Mr [David Bayard] Ogden goes on Monday morning. I shall give him information, in regard to such causes of mine as may be early on the list and, in the meantime, have written to the Clerk in relation to one or two which may be mentioned possibly before Mr. Ogden arrives.[2] Yours always   Danl. Webster

ALS. DLC.
1. Not found.
2. See DW to William Thomas Car-

roll, clerk of the United States Supreme Court for over eighteen years, January 12, 1828, mDWs.

TO [JOSEPH STORY]

Monday 12 oclock
[January 14, 1828]

My Dear Sir,

Mrs W. is better, & brighter, this morning, than I had anticipated. She slept tolerably well, complaining little of pain in the limb, but a good deal of pressure about the chest, & difficulty of breathing. The tumour looks constantly more & more like coming thro the skin. She is quiet this forenoon, & inclined to sleep. The manifest cessation of acute pain, would give me some hope, if it were not for these other symptoms. And tho' there is less of pain, there is more of numbness, & stiffness, in the limb.

I still hope for the best—but must say I am filled with the greatest anxiety. I am satisfied, however, that every thing has been done, & the issue I leave to Heaven.

By this mail I write to Mr [David Bayard] Ogden, (I suppose he goes today) with a memorandum of my actions, & have asked him to make the proper suggestions to the Court.[1]

Mr Abbott Lawrence, & wife, are now here, on their way to Washington. He is a very sensible & worthy man, probably known to you; & his wife, Mr [Timothy] Bigelow's daughter, is an amiable & excellent woman.[2] She was our next door neighbor, in Somerset Street, for several years. They will stay at Washington, perhaps three or four weeks. Mrs Lawrence will not go into the beau monde a great deal—nor her husband either. He is neither a suitor in Court, nor an applicant for office—but goes on, partly for health, & partly, I suppose, to look after the manufacturing interests. It has occurred to me that perhaps it would be agreeable to Mrs Story to have such quiet people in the House with her, for company. You will see Mr Lawrence, on his arrival, & can suggest it, or not, as you see fit. I feel very anxious that Mrs Story should find herself agreeably situated.

I have little news from the East. Mr Paige & *Hannah* I suppose are now on their way. The travelling is very heavy. Tell Mr [John] Agg[3] to send the *Journal* to Mrs McIntyre's *for me*, every morning (that you may see it). Do you get my newspapers? Can I do any thing to make you & Mrs. S. more comfortable or better off? I am anxious to hear from you. Yrs mo. truly   D. Webster

ALS. DLC.
1. Not found.
2. Katherine Bigelow Lawrence (1793–1860). Her father, Timothy (1767–1829; Harvard 1786), was a Medford lawyer, who had served

eleven of his twenty years in the Massachusetts legislature as speaker of the House.
3. Agg was on the staff of Peter Force's *National Journal*, the chief administration paper in Washington.

TO JEREMIAH MASON

New York, January 15, 1828.
My dear Sir,

I thank you for your kind and friendly letter,¹ and wish I could feel justified in confirming those favorable hopes which your friendship leads you to form, in regard to my sick wife. Would to God I were able to encourage my own hopes, and yours also. But I fear, greatly fear, that Providence has not so ordered it. Although she is better one day than another, that is, more comfortable, more free from severe pain, yet I do not see any material change in that which has occasioned her illness. The tumor remains as hard and unmanageable as ever. It seems altogether beyond the reach of human art. Nothing removes, nothing softens it. In the mean time, so much pain and illness begin to affect the general health, and some indications appear of what I have all along feared, since I formed any notion of the disease, of an affection produced by it on the chest and lungs. For the last two days there has been less of acute pain in the limb, but more of stiffness and numbness; I mean in the whole limb below the tumor. She has complained also of weakness of the breast, and manifested considerable difficulty in breathing. Large glandular swellings appear also in other parts of the body, especially about the abdomen. On the whole, though there is less of suffering, I think the danger is plainly increased. The tumor itself has not yet broken through the skin, and does not look quite so much threatening to-day as it did yesterday.

After all, my dear Sir, we have a ray of hope. I try to keep up my courage, and to strengthen hers; but it is due to our friendship that I tell you the whole truth. I have endeavored to prepare myself for that event of all others the most calamitous to me and to my children.

I thank you for your advice as to myself, and shall certainly follow it. In all probability, I shall stay here for some time yet. I fear circumstances will not be such as that I can leave, even after Mr. Paige comes, nor am I very anxious to do so. There seems nothing important in Congress; and I must try to make some arrangement of my business in court.

My health, though not entirely confirmed, is daily improving. I have the remnant of an epidemical cold, a little loose cough and catarrh; no soreness of breast, nor inflammation of the lungs, nor any feverish tendency. Be assured, my dear Sir, I shall take all possible care of my own health.

Ten o'clock P. M. Mrs. Webster is now asleep, and is free from severe pain, but breathes not easily. She is a good deal inclined to sleep. I leave a space to tell you how she may be in the morning.

Wednesday morning, eight o'clock. Mrs. Webster passed rather a comfortable night. She had less cough than I apprehended, and seems calm and quiet this morning. She thinks she breathes a little easier than yesterday. Her voice is faint, but natural in its tones.

Text from *PC*, 1: 433–435, where no   1. See above, Mason to DW, January 9, 1828.
signature appears. Original not found.

TO EZEKIEL WEBSTER

N. York Jan. 17. 1828

My dear Brother,

I cannot give you any favorable news respecting my wife. She is no better; & I fear is daily growing weaker. She is now exceedingly feeble. Dr. P[erkins] thinks she has altered very much the last three or four days.

The prospect nearly confounds me; but I hope to meet the event with submission to the will of God.

I expect Mr Paige tomorrow morning. He or I will write you again, soon. Yrs affectionately   Danl. Webster

ALS. NhD. Published in *PC*, 1: 435.

TO JOSEPH STORY

N. York Jany. 19. [1828]
Saturday noon

My Dear Sir,

I thank you for your kind letter,[1] & for taking care of the record from Boston. The place I hold, at present, I feel to be of no great importance to me; but if it is desirable to my friends that I should remain in it, I shall do so. Consider that matter, therefore, as at rest.

We have no change here, today; at least none for the better. Mrs W. has altered, since yesterday, only as she appears somewhat weaker. How long she may survive, is uncertain; but her recovery, I fear, is no longer, My Dear Sir, the object of rational expectation. With this calamity, one of the greatest, it seems to me *the* greatest, which could befal me, in this life, I hope to struggle, as becomes me. My feelings, it is true, sometimes overwhelm me; but I trust I shall be able, still, to act suitably to my situation, and my character. You are disciplined, in these distresses; & know how difficult it is to reconcile ourselves to misfortunes, which we know, nevertheless are inevitable. My own opinion, as to the result of this dreadful case, was formed soon after arriving here, toward the end of Novr. All that is to be suffered from expecting the worst, I then underwent. To what is yet to come, I hope to have patience to submit, with resignation to the will of Heaven. I have possessed the treasure long; & if it be the will of God now to withdraw it, I will still thank him, morning & evening, for having bestowed it. Yours mo truly & sincerely

D. Webster

My own health is very much improved. William is here; & I have no cares or trouble except what is inseparable from my situation.

ALS. DLC.
  1. Not found.

TO JOSEPH STORY

N. York Sunday 12 oclock
[January 20, 1828]

My Dear Sir,

I am sorry to say that Mrs W. is not quite so well today. She seems faint, feeble, & inclined too much to sleep. It may be an unnecessary alarm, on my part, but I greatly fear her present symptoms are bad. They seem to me to indicate that her system is at length yielding to the powers of this local disease. Glandular swellings appear, in other parts of the body, I suppose from a sort of sympathy. God knows what may be the result, or how soon that result may come. If you do not think it a burden, I would rather write to you daily, than to divide my letters among many friends—tho' I shall occasionally write my excellent Colleague. You will, I am sure, inform the Court of my present, I must say, distressed condition. I beg of you to make to each member of the Bench my best & truest regards. If events should keep me here, as very likely they may, I shall of course make such a disposition of my affairs in Court as may least interfere with the dispatch of the business of the Term.

I enclose a long letter, rather confidential, which I have recd today from Mr. [Jeremiah] Mason.[1] Yrs very truly, Danl. Webster

ALS. DLC.
1. Not found.

FROM NATHAN HALE

Boston Jan 20, 1828

My Dear Mr Webster,

I ought to thank you for myself & Mrs Hale for your kind letter informing us of the situation of Mrs W.[1] It comforted us to be so particularly informed & to hear so much that was encouraging. I need not say how much we are grieved to hear so little that is favourable of her progress since. It would be a great relief & gratification to Mrs H if she could sometimes be with Mrs W. when she is able to see her friends. That being beyond her power, we can only assure you of our sympathy and our most anxious hopes of more favourable news.

I have just seen Daniel, who is prepared to set out in the stage today. The weather being favourable, there is a prospect that he will get on comfortably & will arrive as soon as this letter. Very truly & affectionately yrs &c   Nathan Hale

ALS. NhHi.
1. See DW to Mrs. Nathan Hale, December 13. 1827, mDW 6489.

TO EZEKIEL WEBSTER

Monday 1/4 past 2 o'clock
[January 21, 1828]

Dr Brother,

Poor Grace has gone to Heaven. She has just breathed her last breath.

I shall go with her, forthwith to Boston—& on receipt of this hope you will come there if you can.

I shall stay there some days. May God bless you & yours—

D. Webster

ALS. NhD. Published in PC, 1: 436.

TO ELIZA BUCKMINSTER LEE

Monday, 1/4 past 2 o'clock.
[January 21, 1828]

My dear Eliza,

The scene is ended, and Mrs. Webster has gone to God. She has just breathed her last breath. How she died, with what cheerfulness and submission, with what hopes and what happiness, how kindly she remembered her friends, and how often and how affectionately she spoke of you, I hope soon to be able to tell you; till then, adieu. Yours,   D. Webster

P.S. We shall all proceed immediately to Boston.

Text from *PC*, 1: 436. Original not found.

TO JOSEPH STORY

New York Jan 21. 1828.
Monday Eve

My Dear Sir,

Our anxieties terminated at 1/4 past two oclock, this afternoon. For the last four days Mrs Webster declined, even beyond my fears. Her whole constitution seemed to give way, at once; & from about the time you left here, or rather a few days after, her general appearance left little room for hope.

In regard to the manner in which she left the world, I shall have much gratifying conversation with you, & Mrs Story, hereafter. Nothing could be more hopeful, cheerful, & happy. A heavenly smile overspread her face when she embraced us, for the last time; & pressed our faces to her cold lips. Enough!—I cannot now trust myself farther, only to say that she constantly spoke of you & Mrs Story, with the utmost kindness & affection. You were both, indeed, very dear to her.

And now, My Dear Sir, I must pray your candor, towards the resolution which I have found, & which, I fear, at first thought, you may not approve. Nevertheless, I think reflection will bring you to the opinion that I am right.

I must go with my wife & children to Boston; & perform her funeral service. After deep reflection, my mind cannot be brought to any thing else. I know it is an undertaking, of some difficulty, at this season; but I believe it may be accomplished without great inconvenience. Mr Paige will proceed tomorrow Morning, with the remains of his sister, to New London, in the Boat, & thence to Boston. I shall take Julia & Edward, & go (by land or water) by way of N. Haven. The reason for this is, that poor Daniel is not yet arrived, & we must try to meet him at N. Haven, & turn him back. The roads are now getting to be very good, & the stages will carry us rapidly.

I could not, at any event, go immediately to Washington, where I should inevitably be drawn, suddenly & at once, from the scenes I have been thro', to the business & cares of life.

My mind startles back, from such a thing. And if I were now to leave her here, it would be only to remove her hereafter. Then, again, we have so many friends, who loved Mrs W. most tenderly, & whom it will gratify to have an opportunity to unite in paying the last tribute to her memory.

On the whole, it is agreeable to my own feelings, & appears to me to be suitable, to my own character, to my affection for her, to my duty of manifesting that affection, & to the production of the proper impressions, on the minds of my children, that I should not part from my wife, until I have deposited her, in the presence of our living children, by the side of those others, who have left the world before her.

All this will not prevent me from being in W. very *early* in Feby. My health is good, & the prospect of weather is now fair. I shall write you every opportunity. Adieu, My Dear Sir, & may God bless you. Yours always mo. truly   Danl. Webster

ALS. DLC.

TO JOHN GORHAM PALFREY

New York Jan. 21. 1828
Monday

My Dear Sir

In our afflictions, it is natural that we should think of those, who are our friends, & to whom we have expected to look for succour and consolation, when our trials should come. I am now, My Dear Sir, a widower, & my children are motherless. Mrs Webster breathed her last at a 1/4 past 2 this afternoon. For the last week she fell off very fast, indeed; so that even I, who had as little hope as any one, I believe, was surprised at her rapid decline. Poor Daniel is not yet arrived; he lost the happiness of beholding again a living mother.

You will be mainly concerned to know, in what temper & frame of mind & spirit, she departed this life. And in this, the most important particular, I have infinite satisfaction in saying that she died, just as you & all Christians would have wished her to die. She died, full of good hopes, submissively, & cheerfully. A smile of ineffable sweetness irradiated her emaciated features, when her husband, & her children recd her last embrace, a few minutes before her death.

During the whole period of her sickness here, she was apprised of the *danger* of her situation; for it was fully disclosed to her; yet, there is no doubt, she at times entertained strong hopes of recovery, & certainly wished to live, if such were the will of God. She loved the world, she said, as the workmanship of God, & as full of a thousand beauties of his creation. She had too, as she thought, much to live for; yet her last connected declaration on the subject, was that "tho' she wished to live, her prevailing feeling, & her prayer was, submission to the will of her Heavenly Father."

These, & more details of her conversation, I know you would receive with pleasure; but for the present I must forbear.

Our only clerical acquaintance here was Mr [Jonathan Mayhew] Wainwright. He called to see us, first as an acquaintance; & his visits, as a religious friend, were afterward cheerfully paid, & gratefully recd. His kindness, liberality, accomodation, & disinterestedness deserve all our thanks.

Allow me now, My Dear Sir, to perform that duty, for which I principally write you, at the present moment; a duty, most grateful to me, & I hope acceptable to you.

My Dear wife, on friday, among other things, which she left me in charge, desired me, especially, to write to you; to send you her last affectionate farewell; "& ask him," she added, with suffused eyes, "to remember me."—"And tell him," she continued, "how much I have thought of him, & how often I have wished to see him, during my sickness."

It is my purpose to proceed immediately to Boston, with my children— & there to perform the last duties to the best of wives & mothers. I suppose there may be some difficulty in this, but I shall undertake it. I cannot leave her, till she is deposited with those of her children, that have gone before her. With entire regard & esteem, Yrs   Danl Webster

ALS. MHi.

FROM GEORGE TICKNOR

Thursday Morning.
[January 24, 1828]

My dear Friend,

We have just received your letter of Monday afternoon.[1] It was not unexpected; but there is no preparation for such losses. You have all our sympathy & our constant prayers; but there are no words of consolation in the first access of such sorrow. God be with you, & sustain you and bless you, for all earthly means fail, when he touches us with affliction. I wrote to you on Sunday, Monday & Tuesday,[2] &, with Anna, begged you to bring your children to us. Your anxious tho'ts will be for them—suffer us to do something for you through them. Our house is large, our arrangements abundant & suitable for many children—we have many unoccupied rooms—and if you will come yourself, & bring Hannah & all your household, we will do all we can to make our house one that will console your sorrow. It will be a happiness to us to be able to *do* something for you, and your children shall be as ours so long as you will leave them with us. We have abundant room & excellent servants—& it would be no care but a happy one. I do not know, what your arrangement & thoughts may be. Perhaps, you bring with you what remains of your fondest hopes. They shall find sacred shelter under our roof, & it will not be the first time that death has been among our young household. Indeed, we would gladly do all things for you & offer you all that is ours. We feel, that we can do it without inconvenience & that you may dispose of us entirely without thinking you are giving us trouble.

Our best love & sympathy to Mr. Paige. He comes with you, of course. Tell him, it will be a great pleasure to us to see him again; there are few so true hearted & thorough in affection as he is.

Dr. Warren has just been in. He feels this loss very much. He had disposed all his affairs except his family patients to go to N. York, though he did not hope anything but to show his sympathy, & gratify his feelings. Mrs. [Theodore?] Lyman was so ill on Sunday, that a consultation was called; but yesterday she was decidedly better. [Jonathan?] Mason is very feeble, & gradually fails. Dr. [James] Jackson thinks very unfavorably of his case. So full is the world of sorrow. God bless you, my dear friend, & enable you to draw from this great sorrow, the greater benefits for which it was sent. Kiss the children for us & believe us always your friends.

AL. NhHi.   2. Letters not found.
1. Not found.

FROM JEREMIAH MASON

Portsmouth Jany. 27. 1828

My dear Friend

Your two letters from N. York[1] prepared us to expect what has happened. We most sincerely sympathize with you in this event, in all its bearings & aspects, so melancholy & distressing. I know of no occasion, on which I have seen Mrs. Mason more deeply affected. Without perhaps fully appreciating their extent, I know your sufferings have been, & still are excessive. You have all the consolation that the sympathy of friends, & universal condolence can give. But my knowledge of you, my dear Sir, forbids the hope of much relief or benefit from this source. Your consolation must come from a higher source. Your relief in this great calamity rests with yourself & your God. And there I confidently trust & hope you will find it. This is one of those events which strikingly illustrates the vanity of human expectations, & the imbecility of all human power.

Mr. [George] Ticknor, in a letter of yesterday, says he understands your intention to be to return to Washington in eight or ten days. This as it seems to me ought to depend entirely on our own feelings & the condition of your health. I learn from Mr. Ticknor that your business in the Supreme Court will not be permitted to be pressed on you at this term. This I had anticipated.

We know nothing of the arrangements you have made, or think of making for your children this winter. We understand they are now with you at Mr [George] Blake's. Mrs. Mason desires me to say to you, that in case you can form no plan for taking care of them more satisfactory, she will most willingly take charge of the two youngest, till your return from Washington next spring. She is aware of the nature of the trust she offers to assume, & will of course execute it with all possible care. If this arrangement appears to you preferable to any other you can make, I request you will assent to it without fear of any apprehended trouble to us. For be assured, my Dr Sir, Mrs. Mason will undertake it most cheerfully.

When I first heard of your being at Boston, I thought of going there to see you. But I fear I shall not be able. A violent snow storm is now raging, & it is impossible to foresee how it will leave the travelling. I am likewise at this time much pressed with engagements for the winter session of our Supr. Court, which commences at Dover the first of next week. Mrs. Mason desires her most affectionate regards to you. I am Dr. Sir most faithfully yours &c   J. Mason

ALS. NhHi. Printed in Mason, *Memoir and Correspondence*, pp. 312–313.

1. See above, DW to Mason, January 15, 1828; and DW to Mason, [January 21, 1828], in *PC*, 1: 435.

FROM JOSEPH STORY

Washington, January 27, 1828.

My dear Sir,

I received in the course of the mail your letter announcing the melancholy news of the death of Mrs. Webster.[1] It has sunk Mrs. Story and myself in deep affliction. And prepared as we were for the heavy intelligence, it yet came, at last, with a most distressing power over our minds. We do, indeed, most sincerely and entirely from our whole hearts sympathize with you, and partake largely of your sorrows. We have long considered Mrs. Webster one of our best and truest friends, and, indeed, as standing to us almost in the relation of a sister. We have known her excellent qualities, her kindness of heart, her generous feelings, her mild and conciliatory temper, her warm and elevated affections, her constancy, purity, and piety, and her noble disinterestedness, and excellent sense. Such a woman, and such a friend, must be at all times a most severe loss, and to us, at our age, is irreparable; we can scarcely hope to form many new friendships, and our hope, our dearest hope, was to retain what we had. We have so hoped in vain. I can say with [Edward] Young,[2] in deep humiliation of soul,

"Our dying friends come o'er us like a cloud,

To damp our brainless ardor, and abate

That glare of life, which sometimes blinds the wise."

Of the loss to you, I can and ought to say nothing. I know that if we suffer, your sorrows must be unspeakable. And I can only pray God to aid you by His consolations and to suggest to you, that, after your first agony is over, her virtues and your own admirable devotion to her cannot but be sources of the most soothing recollection to you. I know well that we may do mischief by intermeddling with a heart wounded by grief; and it must be left to itself to recover its powers, and to soften its anguish. What some of us think of the dead, you may read in the National Intelligencer of Saturday.[3]

In going to Boston, and attending the funeral obsequies, I entirely agree with your own judgment. I should have done the same under the like circumstances, as most appropriate to my own feelings and to public propriety. We have in spirit followed your wife to the grave with you.

I do not urge your immediate return here. But yet, having been a like sufferer,[4] I can say, that the great secret of comfort must be sought, so far as human aid can go, in employment. It requires effort and sacrifices, but it is the only specific remedy against unavailing and wasting sorrow; that canker which eats into the heart, and destroys its vitality. If you will therefore allow me to advise, it would be that you should return here as soon as you can gather up your strength, and try professional and public labors. Endeavor to wear off that spirit of despondency which you cannot but feel, and which you will scarcely feel any inclination to resist. Saying this, I have said all that I ought, and I know that you can understand what is best, better than I can prescribe.

Mrs. Story desires her most affectionate regards to you and the children, and I join in them, being always affectionately, Your friend

Joseph Story

Text from *PC*, 1: 445–446. Original not found.

1. See above, DW to Joseph Story, January 21, 1828.

2. Young (1683–1765) was an English poet and playwright. The lines are from his "The Complaint; or

Night Thoughts."

3. Story wrote the obituary of Mrs. Webster that appeared in the *National Intelligencer* of January 26, 1828.

4. Story had lost his first wife, the former Mary Lynde Oliver, in June 1805.

TO CYRUS PERKINS

Boston, Monday, January 28, 1828.

My dear Sir,

You have learned by Mr. Paige's letter, that we reached Boston on Friday evening, and on Saturday committed Mrs. Webster's remains to the tomb. We used the occasion to bring into our own tomb the coffin containing the remains of our daughter Grace, who died January 23, 1817. My dear wife now lies with her oldest and her youngest;[1] and I hope it may please God, when my own appointed hour comes, that I may rest by her side.

Mrs. Bryant[2] came immediately to see me and the children, and manifests the kindest sympathy in the calamity which has befallen us. She is an excellent woman, and one whom Mrs. Webster very much regarded and loved. All our friends have received us with a sincerity of condolence and sympathy which we can never forget. The children are well. Daniel will resume his usual residence and occupation in a day or two. Mrs. Lee, (Eliza Buckminster,) Mrs. [George] Ticknor, Mrs. [Nathan] Hale, Mrs. [Nathan] Appleton, and others, have offered, in the most friendly manner, to take care of Julia and Edward, for the winter. We have not yet decided how we shall dispose of them.

I pray you to give my most affectionate regards to Mrs. Perkins. I never can express how much I feel indebted to her kindness and friendship. If Mrs. Webster had been her sister, she could have done no more.

In a few days, I intend to set out for Washington. If there should come a flight of snow, so as to make sleighing, I shall immediately improve the occasion to get over the hills to New Haven. I am, dear Sir, most truly, Yours, always, Daniel Webster

Text from *PC*, 1: 446–447. Original not found.

1. As Webster reported, Grace Fletcher Webster, daughter, had died on January 23, 1817; and their youngest son, Charles, on December 19, 1824.

2. Not identified.

TO JOSEPH STORY

Boston Jan. 28. [1828]

My Dear Sir

We arrived here on Friday, &, on Saturday, performed the last sad duties to my wife. She rests, with Grace & Charles, her eldest & her youngest, in our own tomb, under St. Paul's Church.

This scene, my Dear Friend, is closed. I would not make you unhappy by dwelling on it. The sorrows, & the reflections, which belong to it, are, peculiarly, for me & mine—& God grant we may improve them as we ought. Our friends have recd me & my children, with the kindest condolence & sympathy, & offer us every aid & assistance which we can possibly need, or require. Daniel will remain as he is. Julia & Edward will go to the home of some one of our friends—Mrs Lee, Mrs Ticknor, or Mrs Hale. Uncle William will be here, to look after them all.

In two or three days, I shall set off for Washington.

I have no time to say more at present; but would not let the mail go without taking a short line to you.

Pray mention me most affectionately to Mrs Story. Yrs always

D. Webster

ALS. DLC.

TO JEREMIAH MASON

Boston, January 29, 1828.

My dear Sir,

I thank you for your kind letter of yesterday.[1] It would give me great pleasure to see you, but I do not expect you to make a journey hither, at this season. I know also that your engagements must be pressing. I am at present at Mr. [George] Blake's, with the children. My brother came down yesterday. It is my purpose to stay till towards the end of this week, or to the first of next, according to the weather, and then proceed South. My own health is pretty good, although I feel in some measure fatigued and exhausted. I shall travel slowly, and must necessarily stay two or three days in New York.

As to my children, I think I shall dispose of them in this town for the present, without inconvenience. Daniel is perfectly well disposed of where he is. Mrs. Lee (Eliza B.) lays claim to Julia, of right, and would be glad of Edward; also, Mrs. Ticknor, Mrs. Hale, Mrs. Appleton, and others, have kindly offered to take them. I feel a reluctance to separate these two little ones, but still incline to think the best thing will be to let Julia go to Mrs. Lee's, and turn Edward, for the winter into Mrs. Hale's little flock.

As far as I have thought at all on my future arrangements, my inclination is to make no more change in my course and mode of life than the event necessarily produces.

I think I shall leave orders to have the furniture put up, in the house, with a view of taking home the children when I return, and, with the aid of Mr. Paige, keeping the family together. Except, perhaps, that it may be best that Julia should stay principally with Eliza, or in some other family, where there is a lady. Very probably both the little children may pass the summer at their uncle's.

I pray you give my most affectionate remembrance to Mrs. Mason. Mrs. Webster spoke of her often, and always with the strongest sentiments of esteem and affection. Her last letter was received, I think, before Mrs. Webster's death;[2] but when she was not in a condition to read it, or hear it.

In regard to this calamity, my dear Sir, I feel that every thing has conspired to alleviate, as far as possible, the effects of the calamity itself. All was done that could be done; the kindness of friends had no bounds; and it is now continued, also, towards me and the children. The manner of the death too, was, in all respects, such as her dearest friends would have wished.

Adieu, my dear Sir, Yours, always truly,   Daniel Webster

Text from *PC*, 1: 447–448. Original not found.
  1. See above, Mason to DW, Janu-

ary 27, 1828.
  2. Not found.

TO JOSEPH STORY

Boston Feby. 5. [1828]

My Dear Sir

I set out [for Washington] today, & shall get along just as fast as I can. I feel a good deal depressed, & have a great aversion to motion & action. But I feel it to be my duty *to go*; & trust I shall feel more energy, after I have set off. The weather is very mild, like spring. Our children continue in health. Yrs always   D. Webster

ALS. DLC.

TO JAMES WILLIAM PAIGE

Hartford, Thursday Eve 6 o'clock
Feb. 7. [1828]

Dear William

I reached this place at 3 oclock, this P.M. without injury or serious inconvenience, but not without weariness, from the time consumed in the journey. Tuesday evening & yesterday forenoon the travelling, tho bad, was not *so* bad; for altho' there was water & mud on the top of the ground, there was frost beneath, to hold up horses & wheels. But when the rain began, yesterday afternoon, pouring like a summer shower, things went rapidly, as things sometimes will, from bad to worse. Both horses & wheels sunk deep, & the end of yesterday's journey and the beginning of today's, were brought very near together. I "did not feel like" going on to N. Haven this afternoon, as Edwd. would say; but proceed in the mail stage, in the morning. The mail stage from Boston, 1 oclock yesterday, due here at 6 this morning, is not here *yet*. My intention is to travel every day, in good weather; but as little in the night, as possible. I presume it will take two days & a half to get to N York; as I have no expectation of aid from the Boats.

I do not know that I said all I intended, in regard to the *picture*, tho I believe I did so. My wish is, that Mr [Chester] Harding should finish it, whatever may remain to be done, immediately; that it should then be put in frame, & placed in some safe situation, perhaps at Eliza's, or such other place as you think best. I cannot tell you how I value it. It was a most fortunate thing, that we had it done.[1]

I feel no more anxiety about the children, than what is unavoidable. I know they are all well provided for, and as well off, as they can be. But, still, a sense of their loss adds poignancy constantly to the sense of my own.

I hope they will behave well, & be happy. You must see that they are properly attentive to our friends who have been so kind to us.

. I am sure I shall hear from *all* of them, they are so great writers.

Give my love to Mr [George] Blake, & other friends. Yrs   D. Webster

ALS. MHi.
1. See the reproduction of Harding's painting of Grace Fletcher

Webster in the portrait section of the *Correspondence*, 1.

FROM JULIA WEBSTER

Boston Feb 9 1828

My Dear Father,

I am sorry that I have so long Neglected to Write to you. I began to go to Miss [Elizabeth Palmer] Peabodys Wednesday and I think I shall like it better than I did the first day. Uncle went to Lowell Wednesday and got home last night. I saw Hannah this morning for the first time since you have been gone; then she was very well, and sent her Love. I went to Mrs [Nathan] Hales yesterday, and had a very pleasant time. Will you please to tell me whether the City hall in New York is Marble or Wood, for Mr [Thomas] Lee[1] says, he thinks it is Marble, and I think you told me that it was wood; So I bet him one cent, and he bet Me two; I wish you would inform Me in your next Letter, witch I hope will come Soon; I have begun to Learn Latin. do you wish I should Learn french and Latin at the same time, I have not begun the first yet. Cousin Eliza bought me a pair of india waders, but the mud has so dried up that I do not need them. I have Not seen Daniel today, but I expect him every minute. I like staying here very Much indeed. We all send Love, and I send a kiss. Your affectionate daughter   Julia Webster

ALS. NhHi.
1. Husband of Eliza Buckminster, Lee (1779–1867) of Brookline was

a merchant in the firm of Cabot & Lee.

In the Twentieth Congress, the major issue was the tariff. In mid-February when Webster resumed his Senate seat, the discussion was already under way. The Jacksonians, with their support coming as it did from both protectionist and free trade states, played both sides with great adroitness. Their strategy was to make the tariff so unacceptable to New England that it would be defeated by New England votes. The administration forces, on the other hand, hoped to bring duties into line with the recommendations of the Harrisburg Convention. The House bill, passed on April 23, was indeed objectionable to protectionists in general and to producers of woolens in particular, but Senate amendments brought it close enough to the Harrisburg schedules to win New England support. On May 13, the amended bill passed the Senate, with even Thomas Hart Benton and Martin Van Buren voting for it. Though they had failed to defeat the measure, the Democrats had nonetheless succeeded, for the tariff was no longer a campaign issue and Jackson could still run as an advocate of protection or free trade, as the locality required. Much of Webster's correspondence between February and May deals with the reaction of certain of his constituents—mostly manufacturers and merchants—to the political scramble in Washington over the tariff bill.

FROM PATRICK TRACY JACKSON

Boston 11th. Feby. 1828

My dear Sir

On reading the Bill for altering the duties on sundry articles, as reported by the Comm[itt]ee on Manufactures,[1] my attention was attracted to two alterations from the present duties, which in my opinion go to ruin one branch of domestic manufacture, which tho' yet in its infancy, bids fair to become important unless it is checked by Act of the Government. I refer to the manufacture of Carpeting. I am well assured that the coarse Carpets are made in England & Scotland principally if not entirely of Foreign wools; & that we can & do import the descriptions of wools used in this manufacture, from the same places, & at as low a cost to us, as theirs costs them. I am also assured that wool of this coarse quality and low price, cannot be afforded in this country sufficiently cheap to permit the manufacturers to use it for carpets & other coarse cloths. The wool from Smyrna, South America & from the north of Europe, usually sells here for 10 to 13 cents a pound. The present duty on all Foreign wool, the value of which at the place whence imported shall not exceed 10 cts. a pound is 15 Pr Ct. ad Valorem. In the Bill reported, section 2d paragraph 1st "On all unmanufactured wool seven cents a pound & also in addition thereto 10 per cent ad valorem on the cost &c." This duty is on the coarse wools equal to 140 Per Cent and I suspect on the wool from Smyrna is over 200 Per Cent on the Cost. The present duty on coarse Carpets is specific, 20 to 25 Cents pr. square yard. In the

Bill reported, section 2d paragraph 2d "on manufactures of wool" (sundries excepted but not carpets) "the actual value of which at the place whence imported, shall not exceed fifty cents Pr. Square Yard the duty shall be sixteen cents Pr Square Yard"—Thus reducing the duty on coarse carpets from 20 or 25 to 16 cents, and increasing the duty on the raw material from 10 to 200 Pr Cent. I may be mistaken as to the operation of the proposed duty on manufactures of wool, and Carpets may be intended to be excepted, if so, the duty on them remains as it now is, and is sufficient for the protection of the manufacture, which will flourish and become an important item in domestic industry, if we are permitted to import the material from the only places whence it can be obtained.

There is another manufacture vz. Negro Cloths which I am told are now made and sold here as cheap as they can or ever could be imported, which will be ruined by this proposed duty, on coarse wool; still perhaps those who are in favour of the protecting system, should not complain and refuse to the Cultivator of wool his share of protection. And it may be said, that the system once commenced must be carried through, all classes must be protected. In this particular case the wool grower has no interest in the question. Prohibit the importation of the coarse wools before described and you destroy the manufacturers of it. They cannot obtain the raw material for the Farmers here can do better than to raise any wool that is worth less than 25 Cents a Pound. I am just engaging in a manufactory for Carpeting, which must be my excuse for troubling you on this subject, & have not yet gone so far but that I can stop with small loss—and I must stop, if the Bill now reported is passed in its present form. Should you think it proper to act on this subject you will make such use of this communication as you may think proper. With much esteem & regard I am dear Sir Very respectf[ull]y Yrs

P. T. Jackson

Since writing the above I learn that there has been a small quantity of wool imported to this Country from South America, which, being very dirty, costs there so low as to be chargeable with only the 15% duty; & that when cleansed it is of a quality to compare with domestic wool. The quantity is trifling and it cannot so materially affect the wool growers as to induce Government to prohibit all coarse wool & destroy the manufacturers dependent on a cheap supply of it.

ALS. NhD.

1. A bill "in alteration of the several acts imposing duties on imports" was presented on January 31, 1828, by Congressman Rollin C. Mallary, spokesman for the Committee on Manufactures. *Register of Debates in Congress*, 20 Cong., 1st sess., 1827–28, p. 1274.

The tariff agitation brought into sharp focus a long-smoldering ideological controversy between North and South—between those who believed, with Webster and Marshall, that the national government must be supreme, and those who held, with Jefferson and Calhoun, that only the states could protect the individual from the tyranny of the majority. The ever-volatile South had opposed the tariff of 1824 on the ground that any restriction on the importation of British goods would quickly be balanced by a corresponding decline in American goods sold in Britain. When the price of cotton, which made up the bulk of the export trade, tumbled from 18 cents a pound in 1825 to 9 cents in 1827, no argument on earth could convince the planters that the tariff was not necessarily the cause. The southern answer to the Harrisburg Convention was voiced most trenchantly by Thomas Cooper, president of South Carolina College, who warned that the time must soon come to "calculate the value" of a union so unequal in its benefits, and to choose between "submission or separation." Equally "treasonous" were the newspaper essays of Robert J. Turnbull, published in pamphlet form as The Crisis; *but Cooper, friend of Jefferson, victim of the Sedition Act, former professor at the University of Pennsylvania, was better known in the North, and so his words were more widely publicized. It was to this controversy that Abiel Holmes, Massachusetts clergyman and historian, refers in the letter below.*

FROM ABIEL HOLMES

Feby. 16. 1828

My Dear Sir

The language I am master of is incompetent to give a correct idea of my feelings when I read the declamations which are spouted out in a place which ought to be sacred to truth and patriotism. On what a precipice does the nation stand by the ill-judged exertions of those who were bound by every principle of morality to protect it!!!

What will the end of these things be? When it is *men* and not *measures* which breaks the union of the community; when it is party spirit and not Patriotism that is the *primum mobile*; when instead of moderation the most boiling passions predominate; when Misrepresentation and downright fabrication are put in requisition; when loyalty stands on Tiptoe; when ambition like Aaron's serpent swallows down all the nobler passions of the mind; when malice, envy discord and revenge are brought on the stage with the Ensigns of civil war or a division of the states close in the rear: What are we to expect next? May it not be reasonably feared that the Union may need stronger bonds than Paper or parchment to hold it together? May Heaven forbid that those things that I fear should ever be reduced to Event.

How must Washington (whose sleepless nights were spent in holy ejaculations to Heaven; and whose breast was so often bared to the shafts of death for the securing our Independence and national glory) frown indignant from the Battlements of Heaven at the noxious fumes which exhale from the American Divan! I have spent much time in calculating the increase of our population; how long it would be before the population of the U. States would exceed the population of all Europe; how long it would be before the uncultivated regions between the Atlantic and Pacific, and between the rocky mountains and the Mexican Gulph would be transformed into cultivated fields and gardens; when the shores of those inland Seas of fresh water would be decorated with populous cities of greater extent than any now on the Atlantic shores. Often did I reflect on the difference between what is now the U. S. at the early period of my recollection, when the population did not exceed 2 millions, and what it is now; and what it probably would be during the lives of those who are now children. My recollection extends back to the time when it was doubtful whether the English settlements in N. America would remain such, or be transformed into French Provinces, or that the English and French populations in America would both be swallowed up by the aboriginal natives. What an astonishing contrast! I sighed for immortallity that I might realize what in reverie I had anticipated.

None but those who have taken similar views of the subject can form an idea of the pleasing sensations that I experienced in those contemplations; but the sad reverse! If I could indulge the idea that the Union of the States is to be dissolved; that faction is to rend the nation into discordant sections; that this may terminate in volcanic eruptions; that the luxuriant soil should have its richness augmented by the blood of its citizens, and the whole history become literally an [illegible]; my very soul would revolt at the idea of existence!

Are my fears the production of a disordered imagination? Would to Heaven that I could be convinced that is the case. I will endeavor to believe that it is.

A republican Government is comitted as to duration to the continuance of public virtue. As well could Lazarus in the grave perform all the functions of life as a Republican Government continue after the extinction of public virtue. When a people are so politically blinded as to intrust the management of National affairs to men wholly devoted to partyism it requires no great professional political skill to determine the state of health of the Body Politic. When an eating defection takes place on the heel, the part turns black and intermediate pains run along the interior parts the patient has great reason to be alarmed for the consequences. Not less alarming is the state of a Nation when public virtue ceases to be the principle which governs those that conduct it's affairs. The following lines from De Foes *Jure Divino* are lamentably true.

"Ambition Knows no bound; the meanest hand
If once cut loose would Pow'r itself command;
Would storm the skies, the Thunderer then dethrone
Be universal Lord and call the world his own."

Unfortunately there is a strong propensity in a people to Jealousy of those who are intrusted with the management of National affairs. This jealousy when governed by reason is a safeguard to the public interest; but it is a most dangerous instrument under the controul of an aspiring Demagogue. A suggestion (much more a positive assertion) made by one of those Dangerous animals that the people's rights (especially in money matters) are invaded, it extends from one to another with the agility of the electric fluid and it does not require any thing more than moderate abilities to extend its influence thro' a nation. The naming Mofussillo of Naples confirms this position. Thousands of instances as strong as this is recorded in the Historic Pages. Human Nature *abstractly* is much the same at all times and in all places; and it would be folly to imagine that any thing merely in the soil or atmosphere of America should make any radical difference. The education, inteligence and the political knowledge of the People of these states make a difference (in that respect) between them and the people of the states in the Southern Continent; and I know of no other difference.

These detached observations are made in the intervals of pain in a state of confinement by a fever sore. You may think they stand in need of apology; but I have none to make. May God in his mercy take you and the National Legislature with the Administration into his holy protection is the fervent prayer of him who takes the liberty of subscribing himself Your's &c   Abiel Holmes

ALS. NhHi.

TO JAMES WILLIAM PAIGE

Washington Sunday Eve'
[February 17, 1828]

Dear Wm

I found divers letters of yours here yesterday, & have another today;[1] for all which I thank you. A line from you, as often as you can write one, will always give me pleasure & satisfaction. I sometimes feel as if

I were troubling you too much, with so much care of the children, & so much attention to my concerns. But I trust you will not suffer me to wear out your patience & kindness. Notwithstanding the blessed spirit that has so long been the common bond of union between us, is now on earth no more, you will ever be to me one of the nearest & dearest objects in life; nearer & dearer, indeed, from this very calamity. Enough!

I find Judge S[tory] & his lady very well. Mrs Story has had the company of Mrs [Abbott] Lawrence, & has not been, therefore, lonely. But, alas! it is not such a winter as she promised herself.

I have not been out of the House today. A great many people have been to see me. Tomorrow I shall probably go into Court. Yours, Dear William, most faithfully,   D. Webster

ALS. NhHi. Published in *PC*, 1: 450–451.
   1. Not found.

FROM ALDEN BRADFORD

Feby 17th [1828]

Dear Sir,

Allow me to offer you my sincere condolence for the very great affliction with which you have been recently visited. But as it [is] a bereavement which cannot be estimated, neither is it one, which any but a most intimate friend can with propriety dwell upon.

I am aware that your mind is occupied with various important subjects; but fidelity to my constituents induces me to request your attention to the Bill before the Senate & House in favour of the surviving officers of the revolution. The Bill before the House was reported only last week & has not been discussed. There has been a debate on the Bill in the Senate of several days; But about fourteen days ago, it was laid on the Table & has not since been called up—tho' it probably will be on Monday or Tuesday of this week.[1] Messrs. [Levi] Woodbury, [John M.] Berrien, [William Henry] Harrison, [Ezekiel Forman] Chambers, [Asher] Robbins & [Martin] V[an] Buren & [Samuel] Smith of Maryland have advocated—[William] Smith of S. C.[,] [John] Tyler, [Nathaniel] Macon & [John] Chandler have opposed, & Mr [Samuel] Bell & Mr [Albion Keith] Parris proposed to get on privates who served for one year. Those who served *during the war* & not on pension list, we are willing should be provided for. The Bill proposes a sum in gross as an indemnity for the failure of government to discharge its own promises, either of half pay or 5 year pay in good money as was proposed. The Bill in the House proposes half pay in future, & an allowance for the past; say since 1810.

But we are content with the sum in gross, as it is most simple, will be most likely to give a larger sum, & as the Com[mit]tee of Senate seem rather tenacious of it. If it passes the Senate, we have no doubt of its passage thro' the House. The Committee of the Senate we presume, were unwilling explicitly to recognize the *strict legality* of the claim; & therefore, probably, propose an indemnity, in equity & good faith, for the loss sustained by the officers, by the nonpayment of both half pay & 5 years full pay, as was implied by the resolve of Congress; which really promised the 5 years pay, (in lieu of half pay for life) down, & in good money, or securities at 6 per cent.[2] And it was not 'till attempting for a year or more to obtain funds from the several States to fulfill the promise, that Congress issued certificates for the amount of 5 years' wages, that such a sum was due & payable. But the certificates were not *securities*, and were not paid in any way, till 1790, & then only partially. The 2d. promise then not having been performed, according to its true meaning & intent, the first is really good. But as the time is long, & the certificates were in part paid to the holders, it seems to me, that the Com[mit]tee of the Senate would not recognize an absolute legal claim. Yet under all the circumstances of the case, they think something is equitably due, & therefore propose a sum in full indemnity, & leave out half pay in future. By this, they avoid committing the government to allow the *heirs* any thing, if they should apply hereafter.

How Mr [Dudley] Chase & [Horatio] Seymour are, I do not know; but believe Mr Chase is for the allowance.

I pray you excuse this— respectfully   Alden Bradford

ALS. NhHi.

March 11, 1828.

1. On January 3, 1828, a bill had been introduced from a Senate select committee, composed of Levi Woodbury, William Henry Harrison, John M. Berrien, Martin Van Buren, and Webster. *Senate Journal*, 20th Cong., 1st sess., 1827–28, pp. 47, 69. A few weeks later, on February 11, 1828, Tristam Burges reported a similar bill to the House of Representatives. Burges represented the special committee appointed to consider the memorial of Aaron Ogden and Alden Bradford. *House Journal*, 20th Cong., 1st sess., 1827–28, p. 10. The bill had been laid on the table on February 6, 1828; and debate on the subject was not taken up again until

2. In May 1778, Congress passed a resolution granting seven years' half-pay to officers in the army who continued in the service until the end of the Revolutionary War. In October 1780, they resolved that all officers who stayed in the army until the end of the war were entitled to half-pay for life. However, in March 1783, Congress decided to give the officers five years' full pay, some of which was issued in 1784. The officers felt that the government had cheated them of both the full five years' pay and the option of half-pay for life, which caused the controversy in 1828 over their relief.

FROM WILLIAM TILESTON AND JAMES M. ROBBINS
Boston, February 18th, 1828.

At a Meeting of the Growers and Manufacturers of Wool, from various parts of the Commonwealth, holden at the *Exchange Coffee-House*, in Boston, on the 16th instant, the following Resolutions were unanimously adopted: —

Resolved—That we disapprove of the Bill recently reported to the House of Representatives by the Committee on Manufactures,[1] inasmuch as the protection so greatly needed by the Growers and Manufacturers of Wool, is not provided for by said Bill.

Resolved—That if the said Bill should become a law, all the Manufactories of Coarse Woollens in our Country, such as Baizes, Bockings, Negro Cloths, Carpets, &c. would be completely ruined; as it is proposed to increase the duties upon low Wools, (which are not raised, and probably will not at present be raised in this country,) from the present duty of 15 per cent. to 120 and 150 per cent., while at the same time, by the operation of said Bill, the duty upon the Manufactured articles is essentially reduced; particularly upon the article of Carpets, which now pays 25-100 per square yard, but which, according to the proposed Bill, will pay only 16-100 per square yard.

Resolved—That while it is proposed to add only 3½ per cent. to the duty upon Broadcloths, which are sold in our markets for about $2.50 per yard; (being a description of Goods of which a larger amount is manufactured here than of any other,) the proposed increased duty of 27 per cent. upon the kinds of Wools of which such Cloths are made, will not benefit either the Wool Grower or Manufacturer, but specially injure both of those classes of our fellow citizens.

Resolved—That the Recommendation of the Convention at *Harrisburg*, on the subject of Wool and Woollens, meet the entire approbation of this meeting.

Resolved—That the doings of this meeting be signed by the Chairman and Secretary; and that a Copy be forwarded to each of the Senators and Representatives from this State, in the Congress of the United States.

WILLIAM TILESTON, *Chairman*
JAMES M. ROBBINS, *Secretary*

Printed document. NhHi. Published in *Niles' Register*, 34 (March 1, 1828): 3. Tileston (1779–1834) of Boston and Robbins (1796–1885) of Milton were both businessmen dealing in American-made cloth and

1. John Quincy Adams, by Gilbert Stuart and Thomas Sully, 1825–1830. Bequeathed unfinished to Harvard College by Ward Nicholas Boylston, 1828.

2. Henry Clay, by Chester Harding, early 1820s. Herbert L. Pratt Collection, Mead Art Gallery, Amherst College.

3. (top left) Robert Walsh, by Thomas Sully, 1814. Andrew Mellon Collection, National Gallery of Art, Washington, D.C.
4. (top right) Joseph Gales, by Thomas Wood, 1856. National Portrait Gallery, Smithsonian Institution, Washington, D.C.

5. (bottom left) Charles Miner, by B. Otis, 1821. Wyoming Historical and Geological Society, Wilkes-Barre, Pennsylvania.
6. (bottom right) Nathan Hale, engraver and artist unknown, from an unlocated painting. Justin Winsor, ed., *The Memorial History of Boston, including Suffolk County, Massachusetts, 1630–1880* (4 vols.; Boston, 1881), 4:124.

7. (top left) Jonathan Goodhue, artist and date unknown. Essex Institute, Salem, Massachusetts.
8. (top right) Joseph E. Sprague, by Charles Osgood, c. 1834. Essex Institute, Salem, Massachusetts.

9. (bottom left) Henry Alexander Scammell Dearborn, by Thomas Badger, date unknown. Maine Historical Society, Portland, Maine.
10. (bottom right) Samuel Bell, by L. Bell after H. C. Pratt, date unknown. New Hampshire State House, Concord, New Hampshire.

11. John W. Taylor, artist and date unknown. Office of the Speaker, U.S. Capitol, Washington, D.C.

12. Bushrod Washington, attributed to Washington Allston, date unknown. Bequest to Harvard College in 1845 by Joseph Story.

13. View of the U.S. Capitol, by Charles Burton, 1824. Metropolitan Museum of Art, Joseph Pulitzer Bequest, 1942.

14. Ezekiel Webster, posthumously
by Sarah Goodridge, c. 1830.
Cincinnati Art Museum.

15. Mrs. Ezekiel Webster, by
Sarah Goodridge, c. 1830.
Cincinnati Art Museum.

16. (top left) Levi Lincoln, by
Chester Harding, 1830. Worcester
Art Museum, Worcester,
Massachusetts. Mrs. Daniel W.
Lincoln, owner.

17. (top right) George Ticknor, by
Thomas Sully, c. 1828. Dartmouth
College.

18. (bottom left) Edward Everett,
by Bass Otis, c. 1824. Gift to
Harvard University by William
Brooks.

19. (bottom right) Jared Sparks,
by Rembrandt Peale, c. 1830.
Bequest to Harvard University by
Lizzie Sparks Pickering, 1919.

20. Caroline Le Roy Webster, ascribed to John Wesley Jarvis, c. 1830. Phillips Exeter Academy, Exeter, New Hampshire.

21. Daniel Webster, by Chester Harding, 1828. Dartmouth College.

22. Andrew Jackson, by Thomas Sully, 1829. Historical Society of Pennsylvania.

woolen goods.
1. See above, Patrick Tracy Jack-

son to DW, February 11, 1828.

TO GEORGE TICKNOR

Washington, February 22, 1828,
in Supreme Court.

My dear Sir:

I find myself again in the court, where I have been so many winters, and surrounded by such men and things as I have usually found here. But I feel very little zeal or spirit in regard to the passing affairs. My most strong propensity is to sit down, and sit still; and, if I could have my wish, I think the writing of a letter would be the greatest effort I should put forth for the residue of the winter. I suppose, however, that a sort of necessity will compel me to be here for ten days or a fortnight, and to appear to take an interest in the business of the court. My own health, I think, is a good deal better than when I left home. Indeed, it is very good, and I have nothing to complain of in that respect.

The Judge and Mrs. Story are getting along very well. She has complained a little of *dyspepsia*, but now seems to be well, and enjoys Washington society with reasonable relish. They dine to-day (birthday) at the President's.

I hear that my children are frequent visitors at your house, much to their gratification. I know, my dear sir, with how much kindness you and Mrs. Ticknor treat us all; and feel how greatly we must lean on our friends under our present circumstances. I feel a much greater inclination, or, to speak more properly, a much greater necessity, of being at home than ever before; not at all on account of the children at present, as I know they are well disposed of, but for my own comfort and solace. There is little here to administer that, which I find I most need. But I did not intend, my dear sir, to write you a gloomy letter. My object was mainly to notify my safe arrival, to keep myself in remembrance, and to thank you for all your kind deeds. Both you and Mrs. Ticknor are persons to whom the art of writing is known, and the exercise of it not afflicting. I flatter myself, therefore, that one or the other of you will sometimes favor me with a few lines. I pray you make her my most grateful and kind remembrance. Mention me also to Mr. and Mrs. [Nathan] Hale. Yours ever faithfully,   Danl. Webster

Text from Curtis, 1: 319–320. Original not found.

TO HENRY WILLIS KINSMAN

Washington Feb. 25 [1828]

Dear Sir

If you have an opportunity, please send me a copy of the Debates in

Mass. Convention, of 1820. I wish it for a friend in Va.[1] Perhaps Mr J[onas] B[ond] Brown[2] will be coming on, about this time; or some other person who can bring it. Yrs   D. Webster

ALS. Dr. Gurdon S. Pulford, Palo Alto, California.

1. The Massachusetts Constitutional Convention, in which Webster had played a conspicuous role, met from November 15, 1820, to January 9, 1821. Virginians at this time were once again discussing the matter of a convention for revising the Constitution of the Old Dominion. In the session of 1827–28, the legislature agreed to submit the question to a plebiscite, which returned a decisive vote in favor of a convention. It was not until October 1829, however, that the convention assembled.

2. Brown (1795–1835), son-in-law of William Tileston, ran a woolens mill at Millbury (near Boston). At this time, he was going to Washington to appeal for tariff revision on behalf of a committee of New England manufacturers.

In early 1828, shortly after Albert Gallatin had resigned the English mission and returned to the United States, rumors began to circulate again that Webster would be named the successor. Unlike those of 1825, the reports in 1828 seemed to have had more basis in fact. President Adams and Secretary of State Clay had discussed Webster as the possible nominee, and Adams had acknowledged that in his qualifications, "Mr. Webster stands preeminent." Webster, as revealed in the correspondence below, entertained the idea of serving as minister to the court of St. James, even asking several of his closest friends whether he should accept if the post were tendered. Most of those friends, however, advised against it, and along with the question of the care of his children, this became a serious consideration for him. Political expediency, as is so often the case, was decisive. Webster was then deeply entangled in controversy over the so-called "Adams pledge," a factor in the President's election which some opposition editors charged was now to be redeemed by Webster's appointment to the British mission (see also pp. 334–336, below). With the Jackson press urging rejection of the Massachusetts senator should the appointment be made, Adams decided that "the moment was unfavorable," and Webster was again bypassed. On May 23, the Senate confirmed James Barbour of Virginia, secretary of war in the Adams cabinet, to be Gallatin's successor. (Adams, Memoirs, 7: 468; United States Telegraph, March 12, April 1, 1828.)

FROM ROBERT WALSH, JR.

Philadelphia Feby. 25. 1828

Dear Sir

The report is strong here that you have been nominated to the station of Minister plen[ipotentiar]y at the Court of St. James. Your friends rejoice in the idea, knowing that the country would gain incalculably while you yourself might obtain signal gratification & distinction abroad. I venture to address you, in mere reference to this subject, not with any view to the discovery of secrets or wishes or any kind of enquiry; but simply to make a suggestion. The son of mine whom you saw with me in Boston is not yet seventeen years of age, but is remarkably advanced, for his time of life, in his frame & intellectual habits.[1] He is well acquainted with the Latin & Greek classics, & with the French, Spanish & Italian languages; and besides writes his own tongue with remarkable terseness & accuracy. His penmanship is excellent. He is of a most ingenuous, honorable and docile spirit. I think I describe him impartially, & not as an overfond father. Now, in case you should go to London, I would be glad to place him in your official family. I state this wish merely as an intimation. I know that there may be many youth whose friends would seek the same advantage for them, with much stronger claims; some whom you would originally select in preference to any other, from affinity, acquaintance, &c. I throw out my vague desire on the score of chance or possibility. In case I should be well enough to travel in eight or ten days, I will visit Washington in order to place a daughter at school. I shall then endeavor to find an opportunity of laying open to you my views of politics, so that you may understand entirely my dispositions & notions, & give such counsel as you may deem it worth while to bestow. I am, Dear Sir, with lively respect, Your truly faith[fu]l servt.   R. Walsh Jr.

ALS. NhHi.

1. Of his twelve children, Walsh was probably referring to Robert Moylan Walsh (1811–1872; William & Mary), who did in fact go to London as attaché of the United States legation in 1830. R. M. Walsh afterward held numerous diplomatic posts, among them secretary of the legation at Naples and United States consul at Leghorn.

TO JAMES WILLIAM PAIGE

Wednesday Eve
[February 27, 1828]

Dear Wm.

I have recd today your letter of Saturday,[1] which makes me feel a good deal better. I have seldom been 5 days, before, without hearing from home; & altho' I have lost what mainly made home dear to me, there is yet that in it which I love more than all things else, in the world. I could not get along without cherishing the feeling that I have a *home*, notwithstanding the shock I have recd. You must try to make the children write, when *you* cannot; so that I may hear from some of you, once every two or three days, at least.

This morning was devoted to [Major] Genl. [Jacob Jennings] Brown's funeral;[2] & I went into Court at one oclock. For some days to come, indeed as long as the Court continues, I expect no leisure. Time has been, when I should not have cared much about it; and as it is, I shall get thro', some how or another. Mr [Andrew E.] Belknap's case will not be tried, probably, till next week.[3]

The arrangement you suggested sometime ago, as to the children's all dining with you on Sunday, & occasionally with our other friends, pleases me very well. I hope they are happy. Edwd. I am sure is as well off as he can be, *and since you cannot spare him*, I am content he should remain where he is.

[William] Riley's trunk is here.[4] I shall send it the very first opportunity. He will receive it, I trust in a week or two.

I am sorry to hear Mary[5] is sick, & hope her illness will not be of long duration.

Remember me kindly to Mr [George] Blake. I would write him, if I had time tonight—but must put it off for a day or two.

Give my love to all the children. I wish I had one of them here. Good night   D Webster

ALS. NhHi. Published in Curtis, 1: 318–319.

1. Not found.

2. Brown, the commanding general of the United States Army, had died on February 24; and on February 27, the day of his funeral, Congress recessed.

3. Belknap was a merchant in Bos-

ton, a partner of Rabaud, Brothers, and Co., of Marseilles. Belknap was one of the defendants in error in the case, *D'Wolf* v. *Rabaud et al.*, 1 Peters 476 (1828).

4. Riley was a free black, a clothes dealer in Boston.

5. Not identified.

FROM THOMAS HANDASYD PERKINS

Boston March 1. 1828

Dear Sir

The state of things at Washington, is such, that doubt seems to hang over every thing of a Public Character. Yet, as a New England man, you can make a pretty good *guess*, as to the probability, of the course which matters & things will take—the *uncertainty* in relation to what will be done on the Tariff, is much worse than the reality, to which we are now subject.[1]

At this time of the year the busy season begins, unless retarded by some extraneous cause. The people who usually buy teas for the spring demand, hold back, under the idea that the duty on the article is to be reduced and that the article will be sold cheaper after such change takes place. I have come to the conclusion that nothing will be done in the Tariff; but this idea is suggested by the fact that so far little has been done, and that there is much to do which *must be done*[;] consequently that subject upon which Gentlemen are so much divided in opinion will be left untouched. I am waiting for the moving of the waters. If there is no probability of a change in the tariff my course would be different from what it would otherways be. Anything but *suspense*, for a merchant. To give fair play to the trade, the change should look forward two years—that every one might make his election as to new undertakings—indeed it would be most important to the trade, if there was a periodical remission of the Tariff from ten years to ten years. This, however desirable, is not practicable. Genl. [Samuel] Smith asked my opinion as to the reduction that ought to take place, if any—it was my opinion that if any change takes place, that a reduction of 33⅓ to 25 Per Ct. would be that, which I should recommend—except that I think all Black tea, should be put at the same rate. I doubt if there is a pound of Bokin tea imported into the U States. I am not so confident that there is not tea paying a Bokin duty—it is difficult to determine where the Bokin quality ends, and the other black teas begin. I have no doubt that the Bokin, Congo, Souchong and other black teas are from the same shrub—the Bokin being the longer and grosser leaf—the Congo & Campoi, the link between, & the Picco, the fine tea, at the ends of the branches or new wood—the difference in quality of Bokin to Bokin, souchong to souchong, governed by soil & situation, as is the case with the Black tobacco & the Kite soot. There is no fear that the importers of teas will grow too rich this year. With the present duty I would not take the imports at the cost in China, the importer losing the charges of importation. If you can make a guess as to the probability of a change, I should be glad to have it.

What teas I have on hand are in the public stores in bond. I presume that all teas thus situated will be considered as new importations & come under the new duty—if not so, there would be a dreadful gulph between him who arrives to day & he who arrives the day after the bill takes effect! This is the period of the year when voyages are undertaken, either direct or circuitous, and the latter not terminated in many instances under 18 mo[nths]—an alteration in the Tariff at this session, which should look forward to March 1830 would place every one on a footing[;] any other arrangement would have an unequal operation. I do not know any thing more practical than the following fact. [Patrick

Tracy] Jackson, [William] Sturges, and several others have got hold of a mode of weaving Carpets, which induced them to form a Co. and get an Act of Incorporation—since when, the heavy duty on wool, has been upon the tapis. All the Carpets made either in England or in this Country, are made of wool, which is the production of *neither*—because the most inferior wool produced here, is too valuable for this manufacture. The wools of Turkey & the Grecian Islands, of Iceland & So. America, which cost 8/ to 10/. on what is made in England & here. The manufacture of Carpets in this Country, is as effectually put a stop to, by this duty, as if a law was passed that the article should not be made. John Bull will have no cause to complain, because he likes to be our manufacturer. In England the duty on Raw Silk a few years since for home use, was 5/ R[a]w St[ate]—it is now one penny, & the silk trade has increased 10 fold. I have always considered the discrimination between the duty on silks from England or Europe generally, and from India & China as very unjust, and onerous upon the trade. There is no doubt that the heavy duty was imposed on India & China silks to prevent the *export of Specie* to India & China. There is at this period, more *Specie sent to Europe than beyond the Cape of Good Hope*, as I verily believe—from 1816 to 1822, I was in the habit of sending from 500 to 800,000 Ds. in a year to China in Specie—since 1823, altho' I have had a larger property in China since than before that time, yet *not a Spanish Dollar* have I sent there. Our ships going round Cape Horn, to the Spanish & No. W. Coasts and Sandwich Islands go to China with Dollars, Copper, Furs, Woods &c and the China ships which prosecute the trade from this Hemisphere, take the products of this Country, Europe & Turkey, and comparatively but few dollars—now altho' the ground *was never tenable*, it is now baseless. Why should we encourage the manufacturers of England, France Germany or Italy more than those of India or China? I know not. If disposed so to do, I can import China Goods, cheaper thro' England than direct, but there would be management in the case, and I have neither time or inclination to do this, tho' others may. I have the enemy in the Camp, and have kept home the past 10 days so that I hear nothing, and do not see much to gratify me in the periodicals. I am told the Jackson people are chuckling. I cannot bring myself to think that he will be successful—time will show—I confess I submitted with becoming fortitude to the death of Mr. [DeWitt] Clinton;[2] under the impression that his influence lost to Jackson, would be a gain to Adams. With much regard, I am Yr friend & Servt.   T H Perkins

ALS. NhD.
1. The fate of the tariff bill, which was introduced into the House on January 31 where it had since been under discussion, was yet uncertain. Not until May 5 did the Senate take

up the measure; and it was May 15 before the bill finally passed. *Register of Debates*, 20th Cong., 1st sess., 1827–28, pp. 725, 785, 786, 1274,

2714.

2. Clinton had died on February 11, 1828.

FROM EZEKIEL WEBSTER

March 1. 1828

Dear Daniel

I returned last evening from attending the Court of C[ommon] P[leas] at Haverhill. A pretty good spirit prevails among the Friends of the Ad-[ministratio]n in Grafton. As I may not write you again, till after the 2d Tuesday of March, I shall give you some guessing, upon the result of our Election. Mr [John] Bell will be elected by a majority from three to five thousand. Four of the [Executive] Council—nine of the Senate— & 140 out of 215 members of the House, will be the friends of the administration. This is but "guessing," as there has been no popular election to test the *popular* feeling upon the Presidential question. The result may essentially vary the estimate.[1]

[Isaac] Hill doubts of his going into the Senate of the U. S. His candidate at present is Gen. [Samuel] *Dinsmoor*. If he cannot carry his Favorite Candidate—he says—(I am told) that he will go for any body in opposition to Gov. Bell. ☞ Hill will not be elected in this district. Yours as ever— Ezekiel Webster

ALS. NhD.
1. For Ezekiel's later and more detailed account of the New Hampshire

election, see Ezekiel Webster to DW, March 17, 1828, below.

FROM ELIZA BUCKMINSTER LEE

Boston March 2nd [1828]

My dear friend,

I was grieved to find by a letter I saw to day addressed to Mr [James William] Paige, that you had suffered any anxiety from the silence and neglect of your friends here; especially as I felt myself guilty, in not having answered your very kind letter to me.[1] I assure you my dear friend, I was grateful for so early an assurance of your remembrance, and should have written to you immediately, but I thought Mr. Paige was in the habit of sending you a daily account of the children, and that you could not feel the *want* or the *loss* of any further communication with Boston.

With respect to Julia, she has been only a pleasure to me, and a pleasure, which hardly any thing else could have given me. She has been an extremely good girl. She has not suffered in the least from cold, or any other illness. Her spirits have improved every day, & I find her now as ready for a frolic, as any little girl I was ever acquainted with. Her time has been very much occupied with her school, & with her little friends in the afternoons; but she really wishes to write to you every day, and has resolved, that this employment shall take the place of other pleasures.

I do not know that I can tell you any thing of this great City that will interest you. The [James] Wadsworths who have been the occasion of a great many parties, have at last themselves departed, and Miss Wadsworth has gone without "let, or hindrance" although I understand more than one gentleman has resolved on a tour to Niagara next summer.

Mr. [George] Blake and William have just been in here to pass an hour. The former was rather dull. He wanted some body to make him tell his long & wonderful stories.

Daniel dined with us yesterday. I do not think he could be in a better situation. He appears very happy, & I believe studies very well.

I feel perfectly sure that Ned [Edward] can never be spoiled, under any circumstances. He seems to have all the gifts that are bestowed in natures most generous mood. Every body loves him—and I feel sure that he will make a great & noble character. If you can consent to leave Julia with me, it will make me happier than any other circumstance which I can now imagine to be within my view. If therefore my dear friend, you should under any possible arrangement wish to cross the atlantic, the disposal of your children need not prevent it. I should not have mentioned this, if your conversation with me had not suggested it.

I hope you will not have any cause to feel anxious in future about your children, & that you will hear every day from some one of them. For myself I should be glad to write to you every day or two, if it would afford you any pleasure, or relieve you from any anxiety. Let us hear from you very soon, & believe me affect[ionate]ly yrs   Eliza Lee.

ALS. NhHi.
  1. Not found.

FROM HENRY ALEXANDER SCAMMELL DEARBORN
Boston March 7. 1828.

My Dear Sir,

I am extremely obliged to you for, Mr. [John C.] Wrights speech, in a pamphlet form. I have read it with i[n]finite pleasure. He has clothed himself with glory, by the manly, firm, independent & eloquent manner in which he has defended the administration, & scattered the forces of the opposition. It is a good thing, done in good time, & the best manner. Well may Ohio be proud of such an able, honest, & zealous patriot. He is a man after my own heart. I have not the honor of his acquaintance, but will thank you [to] say to him, how much I am indebted to him, for the satisfaction I have derived in reading his speech.[1]

You see our legislature has had a grand caucus & nominated Mr. Adams as President & Mr. [Richard] Rush as Vice President. All looks excellently well. New Hampshire will come out triumphantly.

I am right glad to hear you are to go to London; & hope the report is true. With great respect your most obt. St.   H.A.S. Dearborn

ALS. NhHi.
1. Webster had sent Dearborn a copy of Wright's speech on retrenchment, delivered before the House of Representatives on February 6 and subsequently printed as a pamphlet by Gales and Seaton.

FROM THURLOW WEED

Le Roy, March 7, 1828

Dr. Sir.

We have just closed a Convention of Anti-Masons from twelve Counties—77 Delegates present. All but one for the Administration, and he will be. Gen. [James] Wadsworth, of Geneseo, President. As I have told you before, we shall carry the State triumphantly. We have called a State Convention on the 4th of August, and shall nominate a Governor ([Francis] Granger) and Lt. Governor.[1] I do not entertain a doubt of the most complete success.

The Convention embraced the talents, character and *influence* of "Lion of the West."

Will you do me the favor to mention the subject of this letter to the Hon. [Josiah Stoddard] Johnston of the Senate, and if convenient, to Mr. [Henry Clinton] Martindale, of the House.

In haste Very truly   Thurlow Weed

ALS. DLC.
1. As Weed suggested, the Utica convention of Antimasons confirmed Granger as their gubernatorial candidate; for lieutenant governor, they named John Crary.

TO MRS. EDWARD EVERETT

Washington March 10. 1828

My Dear Mrs Everett,

Julia writes me that you have given to your little daughter the name of her dear mother. I cannot well tell you how much I am affected by this proof of your regard, for her whom I & my children have lost. As far as the truest friendship and affection could merit such remembrance from you, it was well deserved.

Mrs Webster & yourself had not been intimately acquainted for many years; yet long enough to awaken feelings of strong attachment, in a heart, in which the flame of friendship, once kindled, did not expire. The longer she had lived, & the more you had known her, the more, I am sure, you would have loved her; & the more affectionately would your regard have been returned & reciprocated. I shall ever feel, My Dear Mrs Everett, most tenderly & deeply, your kindness & affection, in thus calling your little daughter by a name, dearer to me than any thing in this world can ever be. May Heaven bless this young object of your maternal affections! & may I live long enough to tell her of the goodness and excellence of one, the memory of whose friendship for her mother her own name is designed to preserve!

I sympathise with you, My Dear friend, in the sorrows arising from the situation of your Brother's health. In that part of the school of affliction I have, also, been disciplined. Complaints, like his, belong to my own family, & I have seen both brothers and sisters victims to their steady progress & fatal termination. It will be a great consolation to your mother to be with him; & he will feel that all is done for him that kindness & love can do.

Your excellent husband came to see me last evening. We are both so busy, in our respective places, that I see much less of him than I used to do, & than I wish. The Court will close its session this week. I hope then to have leisure to pass a little time occasionally with him, and some others of a few friends.

Be pleased to make my kindest respects to your father & sister—& believe me, My Dear friend, with truth & sincerity, Yours

Danl. Webster

ALS. MHi.

FROM GERRY FAIRBANKS

Boston March 12 1828.

Dr Sir,

Your esteemed favour of the 25th came duly to hand.[1] The article in the Patriot alluded to was intended as clearly & distinctly as possible to give the *feelings* & *views* of the *Republicans* of *Massachusetts*. I felt at the time & now feel that an apology was due to you for going into minute points of character where even *Suspicion* had never found a resting place. But when I considered that here the game playing by the opposition was to prostrate if possible every man of *talents* & *influence* who was known to be in favour of the administration & that the higher & more noble the mark the greater would be the effort to strike it with a deadly blow, I was satisfied that an *honest sincere & frank* exposition of the course of the Republican Party in regard not only of their support of you but their views of your political course & of your private character, was due to them as well as to you. Not having been generally known as the author I have been able to hear it freely commented upon & have been happy to find that the sentiments it contains have met the warm approbation of all my republican friends.[2] The course which the Statesman pursued in regard to this article was quite fair & temperate with the exceptions of republishing the article from the Telegraph, which by the by was not done untill nearly a week after they received it & then without comment. This vile effusion of [William] Jarvis was thought by your friends here unworthy of notice. Young [Joseph Tinker] Buckingham had made up his mind at one time to notice it, he had in possession facts which would have completely put him in the wrong, but on consideration he thought the fellow below contempt.[3]

Our political prospects for the ensuing year look well. At a very full meeting of Republicans on sunday evening last it was unanimously voted that it was expedient that the friends of the administration with out distinction of Party should be called to gether to make arrangements for the ensuing elections. This course entirely meets the views of the Gent[lemen] of the other party, & measures are now in progress for calling such a meeting. We have now the *Courier with us* & *for the administration* and apprehend no difficulty. *From your exertions last year we think we shall reap a full harvest this.*

My Brother left Portsmouth yesterday & brought the returns which you will see in the Daily Advertiser of this morning. It was there confidently believed that Mr Bell's[4] election was perfectly certain. Mr. Ward[5] has just shown me a letter from Genl [Stephen] Low of Concord[6] which gives results from that part of that state, still more favorable than those from Portsmouth, with the additional inteligence that Isaac Hill had lost his election. I am gratified that you have so strong hopes of Mr. Adams's reelection. God grant that he may succeed. Respectfully & truly your obet.   G Fairbanks

ALS. NhHi. Fairbanks (1782–1829), was a hatter, saddler, and harness maker in Boston.

1. Not found.

2. In response to an article in the *United States Telegraph*, January 3, 1828, attacking Webster professionally and morally, Fairbanks had written an essay in the *Boston Patriot* defending Webster and showing why

he should be supported by the Republican party. It was Fairbanks' belief that the *Telegraph* essay had been written by William Jarvis (1791–1853; Dartmouth 1810), of Boston, a graduate of the Litchfield Law School and recently named as Duff Green's partner in the *Telegraph* office.

3. At this time Buckingham was

publisher-editor of the *Boston Courier*.
4. See p. 315.
5. Not identified.

6. Low was postmaster at Concord, New Hampshire.

TO JAMES WILLIAM PAIGE

Washington March 13. [1828]

Dear William,

My large note to you falls due the 20th. inst. For some days, I have been hoping, daily, to get the balance of my Lottery fee, (3000) but as yet it does not come. Those concerned do not act to please me. I believe I am ultimate[ly] safe, as the parties are able, & I have a written acknowledgment of the agreement—but I ought not to be delayed about it.[1] I have written very decisively to the principal party, who lives at Richmond, & expect hourly to see him here.[2] In the mean time I send you my signature, over which you must write a renewal note, & get along some how. I am sorry money is so scarce, just now. I should be glad to give a thousand to Mr. Pratt,[3] so that the House bills may be kept up. Some other smaller sums I hope to receive immediately, & shall remit them direct to you. Probably I shall send you something before 20th./23rd.

The Court will cease to hear arguments, at the end of this week—& then I hope to have time to look round & see where I 'am. For the last three weeks I have been quite too much pressed. From day light to 11 o'clock, I sit here at my table; & from 11 to 5 am [pm] in the Court or the Senate. I shall be glad when their Honors take leave of us.

I believe I told you the other day all that I knew, & what I thought, about this rumoured mission. I say nothing publicly about it, nor scarcely to any of my friends. Nor can I say that my own judgment is entirely made up, as to the course I should pursue, *in case* &c. I will say to you, however, as entirely between ourselves, what is, indeed, but repeating that which I have already stated to you, that my present inclination, on the whole, is *against* going. That result seems to me to be rather the most prudent; tho' a different one would be, in many respects, more agreeable. I should like to know your thoughts, *freely*.

I do not intend to harass myself with the debates of the Senate. Nothing very interesting is likely to arise, at present; & I feel no disposition to do more, in regard to any subject, than my duty requires.

Mr [Andrew E.] Belknap will be off, in a day or two. Yrs as ever

D. Webster

ALS. MHi.
1. On the matter of his fees in the lottery case (*Clark* v. *City of Washington*, 12 Wheaton 40, 1827), see-

DW to Thomas Swann, May 6, 1827, mDW 6123; and December 21, 1827, mDW 6506.
2. Letter not found.

3. Pratt was probably one of the seven carpenters ("housewrights") in Boston with that surname.

FROM THE MARQUIS DE LAFAYETTE

Paris March 13th 1828

My dear Sir

While I have been for more than eight weeks confined by illness, a situation much aggravated by the loss of one of my beloved grand daughters, and an intimate old female friend and relation, I have had also to grieve for the dreadful blow you are doomed to bear. My most affectionate sympathies are with you, my dear friend. George and M. le Vasseur beg to be remembered on the melancholy occasion. Of that sort of affliction I have too cruel an experience not to feel the whole extent of the calamity that has befallen you. Receive the affectionate regards of

[Lafayette]

AL (signature removed). NhHi. Published in Van Tyne, p. 574. The following endorsement appears on the letter: "Autograph cut out by direction of Mr Webster for Mr Sprague. Oct 13th 1828. Thomas Davis."

TO ELIZA BUCKMINSTER LEE

Washington, March 15, 1828.

Dear Eliza,

I return you Mr. [Nathan?] Parker's letter, which I have read, as you may well suppose, with great pleasure.[1] Nothing is more soothing and balmy to my feelings, than to dwell on the recollection of my dear wife, and to hear others speak of her, who knew her and loved her. My heart holds on by this thread, as if it were by means of it to retain her yet here. Mr. and Mrs. Parker were always kind to us, and are among those Portsmouth friends whom time and distance never separated from our acquaintance and affection. Mrs. Webster had very high esteem for them both.

I hear from Mr. Paige, and from Julia, and from Edward, that you are well. Julia has told me all about your party, and how long she sat up. I hear from others, as well as herself, that she is happy as possible under the protection of your care and kindness. You will love her, I know, for her mother's sake, and I hope for her own also; and I trust she will make herself agreeable to your husband. You are kind enough to say, that concern for Julia need not lead me to forbear any purpose which I might otherwise have, of crossing the water. It would be unpleasant, certainly, to leave the children, and especially a little girl of Julia's age, but I should not feel uneasy about her at all, while under your guardianship. There are other considerations, however, which are well to be weighed before I am water-borne. Even if what you allude to were supposed to be at my own option, and however desirable it might be in itself, times and circumstances may nevertheless be such as "give me pause." This is all I can say about it at present; except that I am now too old to do any thing in a hurry. I believe this almost the only time that I have alluded to the subject, to any one; and would not wish to be quoted as having said one word respecting it.

Mrs. Story left us the day before yesterday. The Judge goes in a day or two. I shall be sorry to lose him, though quite willing to have the court break up.

I have a very kind letter indeed from Mrs. Everett, respecting the name of her youngest daughter;[2] I wish uncle would carry Julia out to see her.

Is your husband a document reader? I should be glad to send him some of our papers, speeches, &c., but have been afraid he would vote it a bore. Pray give my love to him, and believe me, as Ever yours,

Dan'l. Webster.

Text from *PC*, 1: 452–453. Original not found.

    1. Parker (d. 1833; Harvard 1803) was minister at the South Parish Church, Portsmouth. Parker's letter to Eliza Buckminster Lee has not been found.

    2. Not found.

FROM EZEKIEL WEBSTER

March 17. 1828

Dear Daniel

The result of the election on Tuesday does not vary much from my prediction. There is a probability that there will be a vacancy in district No 6. When the Government shall be organized—*Four Counsellors, Ten Senators*—& 135 or 140—out of 215 representatives will be administration. The administration cause will be stronger in the House—than it was last year, & the Senate will be entirely changed. Mr [John] Bell[1] will have a plurality over [Benjamin] Pierce—of 4,000. He contested this election for Gov. under every disadvantage. Pierce was in possession—had been in but one year, had not declared himself for Jackson, was supposed to have been a revolutionary officer, & had done nothing in his office to give general offence, & his age, his very incapacity—his ignorance—his unfitness seemed to recommend him to the popular commiseration. We have given a very great vote in this district, at least 500 votes more than was ever before cast. We felt the importance of every vote. In this part of Boscawen among a population of 250 voters—we had only two Administration voters absent—& they were detained by sickness. Sick as they were, they would have been carried—at the imminent hazard of their lives—if their friends would have permitted it. The Friends of the administration have acted together cordially & in good Faith. When our *disabilities* were removed, when we could act with the republican friends of the administration on *equal terms*, with a proper self respect—& with our proper influence—we gave them all the support in our power. I think they will not complain of us. We did not attempt to procure the nomination of a single Federalist—for the Council or Senate. The determination of the *republicans* to call meetings of the *Friends* of the administration, without regard to former party names—has saved the cause of the administration in this state. It was my opinion last June—that this *measure only* could save it. And if the course—I took upon [James] Wilson's resolutions—led to the adoption of this measure—I am perfectly satisfied, though I know I gave offense to very many gentlemen, which they never will forgive.[2] If it promoted the interest of the good cause, it is not of much matter what were its effects in regard to myself. Had there been during this election any thing like lukewarmness or indifference among any considerable portion of the friends of the administration—the result would have been very different. In district no 4, for instance, if one out of ten of those who voted for Judge [Hall] Burgin—had staid from the polls—or one out of twenty had voted for his opponent—Hill would have been elected.[3] Our success in choosing Judge Burgin, illustrates strongly the necessity & the advantages of a union of counsel of feeling & exertions, among the friends of the administration. It will be still necessary to enable them to maintain their ascendancy.

I intend to submit some considerations to Gov. Bell on this subject, as soon as I have leisure. Yours truly—E. Webster

ALS. NhD.

1. Bell (1765–1836), brother of Samuel and the Adams coalition candidate for governor, had defeated Pierce, the Hill nominee. Benjamin Pierce was the father of Franklin Pierce.

2. See pp. 151–227, *passim*, for a discussion of the problems of uniting the Republicans and old Federalists of New Hampshire behind the administration in 1827.

3. Burgin (1770–1844), justice of the Court of Sessions from 1823 to 1825, defeated Hill in the state Senate contest.

It was in hope of eliminating the last vestiges of friction between the old Federalists and the Republican friends of the Adams administration in New Hampshire that the President's supporters prevailed on Ezekiel Webster to become a candidate for Congress. As one of the Federalist

*leaders in New Hampshire, Ezekiel had been a strong campaigner in
1827 and 1828. His qualifications included eleven years in the lower
house of the state legislature and one in the state Senate. No man was
better informed of the nuances and political cross-currents in New
Hampshire. He nevertheless proved reluctant to accept a nomination, as
he informed his brother, below. At Daniel's insistence, he finally re-
lented and accepted the nomination of the opposition caucus in December 1828, but was badly beaten when the election was held in March
1829. Only weeks later, while delivering an argument before the court
at Concord on April 10, he collapsed and died within a few minutes.*

FROM EZEKIEL WEBSTER

[March 17, 1828]

Dear Daniel,

I suppose the Friends of the Ad[ministratio]n would be willing to agree
upon a Congress Ticket, without reference to old party distinctions.
Some of my friends have requested me that I should consent to have my
name proposed, among others, as a *candidate* to be put on the list of the
administration Ticket. This has occasioned me to consider, & reflect
upon the subject, deliberately and maturely. The result of the whole matter is that I cannot be thought of as a candidate. I am decidedly of the
opinion that a ticket should be formed in June—upon the most liberal
principle—& that the election should be made in Nov. when the Electors
are chosen. I mean to mention this subject in my letter to Gov Bell.
Yours &c   E. Webster

ALS. NhD.

TO EZEKIEL WEBSTER

Washington Mar 18 '28

My Dear Sir

We are exceedingly delighted with the N. Hampshire news. It has
caused many gratulations, & rejoicings, among *some* of us, & disappointment & chagrin are very visible on the faces of *others*. It was really expected here that Genl. Pierce wd. be reelected. Several of the N. H.
members had little hopes, till I showed them your letter, written after
your return from Haverhill. They esteemed that *authentic*, & took courage. They all, *I believe*—& some, *I know*—see & *feel* how much *you*
have aided to bring about this excellent, excellent, result. I mean to be
proud of the old *natale Solum*, after all—(Mary [Ann][1] must translate
my Latin). I only beg you, now, *not to lose the fruits of victory*. Follow

up the blow. You know *one thing*, which I have very much at heart. *Be in season, in preparing for that.* You will never regret it.

I see a good number of good men returned to the House, [Boswell] Stevens, [Benjamin M.] Farley, [Oliver W. B.] Peabody, [Levi] Chamberlain, [John] Kent, [Samuel] Abbott &c &c &c.[2] It looks, too, as if [John] Wallace, [Jr.] & [David] Steele were both chosen into the Senate.

I have the pleasure to say that from other quarters the news is most cheering. Kentucky is now the great point of attention. Her election for Govr. &c takes place the first monday in August, [Thomas] Metcalf, vs [William Taylor] Barry. This will call out the whole strength of parties, & settle the final vote of Kentucky. It will be a severe contest, but our friends are in good spirits, & high hopes. Recent intelligence is very favorable.

In N. York the *Anti masonic* feeling is bearing down every thing. Nothing can stand before it, not even Genl Jackson. For once, an *incident* is helping the right side. Mr Adams *is not* a Mason—Genl J. *is*. A delegation from nearly half the State assembled ten days ago, at Le Roy, as an Anti Masonic Convention. Genl Wadsworth presided. Out of 77 members, 76 were for *Administration*. They will have a Convention, in the Spring or Summer, to agree to a Govr. It will be Ch. Jus. [John] Savage, or Mr [Francis] Granger, of Canandaigua.

I now *believe* Mr Adams will be reelected.

I shall send you more of Mr [John C.] Wrights speeches, & the other Documents you write for. The Court has adjourned; & I hope to have time to *breathe*—& to think of my friends.

Pray give my best love to your wife & children. Yrs always

D. Webster

ALS. NhD. Published in Van Tyne, pp. 133–134.

1. Mary Ann Webster (1816–1864), daughter of Ezekiel.

2. Stevens (1782–1836; Dartmouth 1804), of Pembroke; Farley (1808–1892; Yale 1832), of Hollis; Peabody (1799–1848; Harvard 1816), of Exeter; Chamberlain (1788–1868), of Fitzwilliam; and Abbott (1777–1853, Harvard 1797), of Wilton were all lawyers. Kent was a merchant from Barnstead.

TO EZEKIEL WEBSTER

Washington Mar: 20 [19]. 1828

Dear Brother

I wrote you yesterday.[1] The object of this is more private & personal. I want you to tell me what you think best, for the Adm[inistrati]on, & for me, in relation to a subject, upon which the Newspapers continue to be loquacious.[2]

Give your advice without favor or affection, and as a man who is "looking before & after." Yrs as always   Danl. Webster

ALS. NhD. Published in *PC*, 1: 453.   2. Webster was alluding to the
1. See above.   matter of the English mission.

TO JEREMIAH MASON

Washington Mar. 20th. 1828

My Dear Sir

The practise of asking the advice of friends, in one's own affairs, is a little old-fashioned. I do not think very highly of the custom, myself. Still, I now write mainly with the purpose of taxing your good nature with the request, that you will say, in a strait-forward way, & few words, what you think upon the subject, with which the newspapers have been busy, for some time past. I do not mean to trouble you for a long statement of *pros* & *cons*; nor do I mean to anticipate your impressions, by a single suggestion of my own. You see what all the world sees, & know what all the world knows, of the state of things here, & of *my* present condition. Will it be best for the *Administration*, & best for *me*, that I stay where I am, or that I go elsewhere? I care not how *shortly* you speak, but I pray you to speak *freely*.[1]

We are in very good spirits, with the news from N. Hamp. I believe certain Gentlemen here are a good deal disappointed. It was confidently expected by them, that Genl. Pierce would succeed. We trust he has failed—& it seems our friend Hill is out also.

Affairs here are wearing rather a better appearance. The intelligence, from interesting points, is a little cheering. Perhaps the most important contest, or rather one of the *earliest* of the important contests, will be in Kentucky. The election of Govr. &c takes place, in that state, on the first monday in August. The whole will turn, mainly, on the Administration question. Metcalf is candidate, for the Admn. side, & Barry, whom you know, for the opposition. The result of this election is likely to decide the ultimate vote (the *whole* vote) of Kentucky, & must necessarily have a great operation elsewhere. If Barry should succeed, by a strong vote, I should give up Kentucky; &, with Kentucky, nearly all hope of Mr Adams' reelection. New York is unquestionably *mending*. If it goes on, as it is now going, a great majority of votes in that state will be for Mr. Adams.

The Louisiana members are to be elected again, in July. It is believed Mr [Edward] Livingston will be left out, & a friend of the Admn. elected in N. Orleans.

Judge Story left us two days ago. The Court has had an interesting session, & decided many causes. The Judge of our Circuit has drawn up an uncommon number of its opinions, &, I think, some of them, with uncommon ability. Yrs always truly   D. Webster

ALS. NhD. Published in Van Tyne, pp. 136–137.

1. See Mason to DW, March 27, 1828, below, for Mason's response.

TO CHARLES BRICKETT HADDOCK

Washington, March 21, 1828.

My dear Nephew,

I thank you for your kind and affectionate letter,[1] and assure you its suggestions are all in strict accordance with my own feelings. It does not appear to me unreasonable to believe that the friendships of this life are perpetuated in heaven. Flesh and blood, indeed, cannot inherit the kingdom of God; but I know not why that which constitutes a pure source of happiness on earth, individual affection and love, may not survive the tomb. Indeed, is not the principle of happiness to the sentient being essentially the same in heaven and on earth? The love of God and of the good beings whom he has created, and the admiration of the material universe which he has formed, can there be other sources of happiness than these to the human mind, unless it is to alter its whole structure and character? And again, it may be asked how can this world be rightly called a scene of probation and discipline, if these affections, which we are commanded to cherish and cultivate here, are to leave us on the threshold of the other world? These views and many others, would seem to lead to the belief that earthly affections, purified and exalted, are fit to carry with us to the abode of the blessed. Yet it must be confessed, that there are some things in the New Testament which may possibly countenance a different conclusion. The words of our Saviour, especially in regard to the woman who had seven husbands, deserve deep reflection. I am free to confess that some descriptions of heavenly happiness are so ethereal and sublimated as to fill me with a strange sort of terror. Even that which you quote, that our departed friends "are as the angels of God," penetrates my soul with a dreadful emotion. Like an angel of God, indeed, I hope she is, in purity, in happiness, and in immortality; but I would fain hope, that in kind remembrance of those she has left; in a lingering human sympathy and human love, she may yet be as God originally created her, a little lower than the angels.

My dear nephew, I cannot pursue these thoughts nor turn back to see what I have written. Adieu,   D. W.

Text from PC, 1: 453–454. Original not found.

1. Charles B. Haddock to DW, March 12, 1828, mDW 6851.

TO JOSEPH E. SPRAGUE

Washington Mar. 22 1828

Private and Confidential

My dear Sir,

I thank you for your very kind and gratifying letter of the 16th.[1] and reciprocate your congratulations on the result of the N. Hampshire Election.[2] Most undoubtedly that result is to be wholly ascribed to the judicious arrangements made in the fall for conducting the elections. If our fellow citizens of the Republican party had adhered to their old usages, and gone with the machinery of the *Caucus*, it is certain now that the friends of the Administration would have been outmanaged, overwhelmed, and defeated—all the success is fairly to be ascribed to the *course* adopted, and I am fully sensible that *no man* in the U. S. had done so much as yourself to bring men's minds to agree to that course. Whoever else forgets this *I* shall not. I am persuaded that your efforts have been felt, not only in Mass. but also very deeply in N. Hampshire and generally throughout the country. I know no one who has done so much. The present united force of New England is mainly owing to the course which you have steadily and zealously urged on your Republican friends. Depend upon it—that you have been *abused* because you have been *felt* and that the loud cry against *Amalgamation* has originated in the terror which our enemies felt at the idea of a union among their adversaries. You will see Judge Story as soon as he returns. He and I had some conversation, which I asked him to state to you, and to which I ask your particular attention.

As to the mission to England, it is a subject on which I know little and say nothing. I heard what your opinion is, and assure you that you may rest satisfied of one thing—and that is—that nothing will be done, as far as I am concerned, but on the maturest consideration and nothing on grounds merely personal. Our friends think that prospects are getting better and better both on this and the other side of the Alleghany. The first great contest is to be I think in Kentucky on the 1st. Monday in Augt. If General Metcalf shall succeed by a large majority, the effect will be not only to secure the whole vote of Kentucky, but also to give great courage and activity to our friends elsewhere. In this last point of view even the recent Election in N. Hampshire has done good. We do not enough estimate the effect which an expression of public opinion in one state has in another, however remote. For this reason it is of great importance that the tone in N. England should be united decisive and strong. Yours always truly   D. Webster.

Copy. NhHi. Published in Van Tyne, pp. 134–135.

1. Not found.

2. The Adams faction in New

Hampshire had captured the governorship and two thirds of the seats in the legislature. Reports circulated that administration candidates had won in nine of the state's twelve senatorial districts. *Niles' Register,* 34 (March 22, 1828): 52.

TO EZEKIEL WEBSTER

Washington Mar. 23. 1828

Dear E

I have recd. yours of the 17th,[1] and am glad you propose to write Govr. Bell. If you have not already done so, when you receive this, lose no time in accomplishing your purpose.

I cannot listen, for a moment, to what you say about not being a candidate. I never shall consent to your declining, if you have a fair opportunity. Be assured, it will do you much good, to be here a year or two— & you will lose nothing by it. I beg of you, by no means, to come to a different conclusion, at least till I come home.

The N. Hampshire election has produced vastly more impression here than I had expected from it. It seems quite certain, that a pretty strong confidence of success was entertained by Genl Jackson's friends. I was told today that Mr [Jonathan] Harvey, shortly since, expressed the strongest belief that N. Hampshire wd. go for the military candidate.

I send you, today, a Militia Document. The preface & notes, &c, are understood to have been drawn up by Mr *Storrs;* tho', I suppose, if this be so, it is intended to be kept private.[2] I think you will find [it] a thing to make the People think. I shall send you several copies.

We need much a list of names in Mr Harvey's District, of intelligent People to whom this & other documents can be sent. Who is there, in Warner, Sutton, Fishersfield, Hancock, Henniker &c &c, to whom the N. H. Members might send something, calculated to enlighten the People, & to give them the truth? I really feel it a duty, to give the People light, in regard to the present state of public affairs.

We have every reason to think the tide has turned, in N York, & is setting the other way, with prodigious force. Something of the same nature is visible in Kentucky. Depend upon it, with proper exertions, we may yet save the Country. Yrs always truly   D. Webster

I am anxious for your answer to my last.

ALS. NhD. Published in *PC,* 1: 454–455.

  1. See above.

  2. The document was, most likely, the "Report of the Committee on Military Affairs . . . in relation to the proceeding of a court martial, ordered for the trial of certain Tennessee Militiamen." *House Reports,* 20th Cong., 1st sess., 1827–28 (Serial 177), Doc. No. 140.

Portsmouth, March 27, 1828.

My dear Sir,

I have omitted to answer your letter a few days because I did not well know how to answer it.[1] You ask whether I think it best for the administration, and best for you that you remain where you are, or go elsewhere, that is, accept the appointment to England offered you. On the first question, I have no doubt; for obvious reasons, I think it is certainly best for the administration that you remain where you are. In your present situation you can render the most essential aid and support, the loss of which at this time would be severely felt. The administration at the present time need all their strength, and that exerted to the greatest possible advantage. Your services in the Senate may be greatly important at the next session, and if Mr. Adams succeeds in his election, as I trust he will, your services will probably be vastly more important at the next Congress. But what I deem of still greater importance is your influence in the approaching election, which by leaving the country will be lost or greatly lessened. Without entering at large into the reasons, I am decidedly of opinion that your remaining where you are is most advantageous for the administration.

On the other question I have had doubts, but after giving it the best consideration in my power, I have come to the conclusion that what is best for the administration is also best for you. The success of the present administration deeply involves the best hopes and the highest interests of the country. You are a public man, and, as I believe, are destined to continue a public man, and as such you are in a great degree identified with the administration. Under such circumstances, it seems to me that you cannot well sever your personal interests from the interests of the administration and of the country. If I am right on the first question, of which I entertain no doubt, your services in England at this time will be of minor importance when compared with your services at home. If so, there seems to be something of the nature of public duty in the case. And I trust it is and will continue to be the true interest of an elevated public man to follow the path of his duty. The administration, believing you to be entitled to it, may be willing to give you the contemplated appointment, if you wish for it, but I presume they cannot be desirous that you should accept it. I do not think that the ribaldry of the opposition newspapers ought to be permitted to have any influence whatever on your determination.

I have in compliance with your request given you my frank opinion without any detail of reasons. And I think I ought with equal frankness to tell you that I do not feel much confidence in the correctness of my opinion. I am too far removed from the great world, and too little conversant with political affairs, to be competent to form a judgment of any value on this matter. I am aware there may be considerations of a private nature, arising from your own feelings at the present time, which may be entitled to much weight. Of these you alone can judge. I am as ever faithfully yours,   J. Mason.

Text from Mason, *Memoir and Correspondence*, pp. 319–321. Original not found.

1. See above, DW to Mason, March 20, 1828.

FROM EZEKIEL WEBSTER

March 29th. 1828

Dear Daniel,

When I saw you I gave you a history of the *infamous pamphlet*.[1] It is in substance—this. One of the Editors of the Castine American—a Mr Otis[2]—was related or connected in some way with Mr or Mrs [Jonathan] Russell. When they established their paper—Mrs Russell was a correspondent & contributor of many articles in prose & verse. Her hand writing was perfectly known. This pamphlet was sent to that Press in *her hand writing* for publication. They set up a greater part of it & became alarmed for the consequences of publishing a pamphlet so libellous & infamous—& then distributed the types. It was returned & offered to the Editor of the Statesman (Boston). He refused to publish it—it was sent to Hill—& he directed it to be printed. A workman in the Castine Press at that time is now in N. H. Statesman Office—Mr [George] Kent[3] gave some hints about this some time ago—& it brought Green[4] up to Concord, where he was closeted with Hill one day & two nights. This workman was sent for—was solicited to deny the facts—but he was stubborn & Green returned—without accomplishing any thing. I have seen the certificate signed by him. It is fact to the point of the manuscript being in her hand writing &c. &c.

I think this extract had better go into the Intelligencer or Journal. Mr Kent will publish the certificate—at a proper time if it should be necessary. The Editor of the Castine paper will also tell something more about it. The Truth will be out, before long in regard to it. Yours as ever—

E. Webster

ALS. NhD.
1. *Brief Sketch of the Life, Character and Services of Major General Andrew Jackson.* By a Citizen of New-England. Concord, N.H.: Printed by Manahan, Hoag & Co., for Isaac Hill,

1828. The authorship of the pamphlet has long been attributed to Isaac Hill, but if Ezekiel's information is correct, the pamphlet was "compiled and published under the direction, if not by, the ☞ HON. JONATHAN RUS-

SELL. 〰 " *New-Hampshire States-*
man & Concord Register, March 29,
1828.

2. The *Eastern American* was published in Castine, Maine. Otis has not
been identified.

3. Kent (1796–1881), Concord
lawyer, banker, and trustee of Dartmouth College, 1837–1840, was at
this time a publisher of the *New-
Hampshire Statesman.*

4. Not identified.

FROM EZEKIEL WEBSTER

March 31. 1828

Dear Sir

I have written Gov. Bell to day. I have stated to him my opinion of our
present condition. It is the best opinion I can form. I suggested to him
both the importance & *necessity* that our representatives in Congress
should make an address to the people of this state—under their own
signatures.[1] They should speak out. Something of this kind is certainly
needed. It should be published in a pamphlet form of 30,000 copies at
least. The people want *information, light,* knowledge of the character &
measures of the Administration. I say to you what I say to no person
here—*We cannot carry the election next Nov. without the greatest exertions.* Bold and manly measures only can defeat the Jackson party in
this state. It is necessary that every man should put into the support of
the good cause—all his talents—all his *personal* character—*personal* influence & exertions. The contest must be made to resemble the ancient
battle—where every man grapples with his adversary. The crisis is extraordinary—The contest is extraordinary—& both the crisis & the contest call for extraordinary efforts. Let our representatives give us the
example. Let them make an appeal to the good sense of the people &
warn us of our dangers. Let them lead & there will be enough to follow.
The public sentiment enlightened & informed by the address itself—will
support them & carry them & the State triumphantly through the contest. The present delusion is astonishing. No man, who does not witness
it, can believe it. Mr Healey can do more in those towns you mention
than any other man.[2] He should have documents plentifully. He knows
to whom it would be best to send better than any other *person.*

I have received the militia *document.* I think an edition of it will be
printed in this State. Yours &c   E. Webster

ALS. NhD. Published in *PC,* 1: 455–
456.

1. The chief "address" in behalf of
the Adams administration in New
Hampshire was one by Ezekiel Webster, "A Defence of the National Administration, in an Address to the

People of New-Hampshire" (Concord,
1828), written under the pseudonym
"Cato."

2. See above, DW to Ezekiel Webster, March 23, 1828. Healey has not
been identified.

FROM ESTWICK EVANS

Portsmo
April 1, 1828

Sir,

Resignation to the will of Heaven is as incontestably a matter of interest as of duty; interest, not because duty, as is often the case, but interest in & of itself, for the reason that a contrary course renders life useless & miserable without one counterbalancing advantage. All, sir, have a right to sympathize with their fellow men; but few, however,—very few, could, in the present case, venture upon the high & delicate ground of condolence. I beseech you to believe that I have no such presumption. I was unwilling, however, to speak to you upon the little affairs of time without a pause indicative at least of a respectful solemnity.

You will remember, sir, that I wrote you upon a certain subject.[1] The election in this town has passed. I mentioned my object to two or three men of character, but not to one of the committee of nomination, many of whom were particularly friendly. I do not know that they knew of my wishes. That I was not in nomination was a subject of surprise & remark. It is also a subject of regret with many of the most respectable & influential friends of the Administration; & should a vacancy now occur I should, undoubtedly, be elected. Indeed, it was concluded at the polls, that in case there should be no choice, as was expected by some & feared by many, I should be the first person run for.

Had I said one word to the *Jacksonians* I could have had every vote; & it is asserted by them that had I remained with them, even in opinion, they should have succeeded. I knew that they possessed more means of success than the other side, & that they would rapidly increase. My not acting with them was by no means a matter of policy but of principle; still I doubt whether I should do justice to those who are dependent upon me to sacrifice all my political prospects. It could not be expected that I should act even by merely attending the Administration meetings, which I have done, without calculating upon the same support that I had, without a question, lost. As to the strength of the parties I am always willing to fall as well as rise with my friends.

My election as representative was of no consequence, only as it might affect my nomination for congress next June; but it has been observed that my absence from Concord might favour that. The way now seems entirely clear for me, if a few of the most influential friends of the Administration should favour it. I venture to say that, so readily would the people, in favour of the General Government, support the nomination, that some half dozen individuals in Portsmouth, whom I might name, might secure my nomination. I am strongly impressed with the idea that such a step would be the means of effecting much & permanently for the Administration.

I have become an object of suspicion with the Jacksonians, & I think it is not right, it is not liberal, it is not politic, for your friends to meet me with a cold & barren embrace.

Further, I would ask, would my nomination for Congress be inconsistent with the public good? Will it do injustice to the claims of others? I have no doubt that your *will*, like the wand of a magician, can accomplish the object, & I would inquire, would the exercise of this power, made for some purpose, be inconsistent with your principles & feelings as a man & christian? Is not eighteen years of disappointment & the most keenly felt wrongs sufficient for one individual—who never tarnished his reputation by a single act of dishonesty or meanness?

My nomination in 1822 was made upon grounds highly honourable to me, because made by men who were influenced, not by selfishness or even personal friendship, but by, as they have said, propriety & a regard to the public good. Some of them I have reason to believe were on your side of the house. Should your brother condescend to give you a history of that session & of that affair I am sure you would consider my case a hard one. [Isaac] Hill defeated me by the basest means. The Federal party in the house sanctioned my nomination, reported to the general convention, like men & gentlemen; they sanctioned it with a fullness & a spirit not to be forgotten; & the same individual to whom I *refer* above, with a liberality, good sense, & good nature (characteristics which ought to be peculiarly dear to the friends of virtue & which you will recognize in one you love) said (I omit the complimentary part of it) "he has as good a right to it as any one." I am sir, Most respectfully & truly your obed Serv   E Evans

ps It is not exactly proper for me to write *you* in haste; but having done so, I must request that you will make any necessary allowance for this circumstance as to the matter & manner of this letter.   E E

ALS. DLC. Evans (1797–1866), a Portsmouth and Exeter attorney, regarded by many of his associates as eccentric because he championed cases involving the poor and sailors, had been an unsuccessful candidate for Congress in 1819. From 1822 to 1827, he had represented Portsmouth in the state legislature. In 1829, shortly after he failed to be named a candidate for Congress by either party, he moved to Washington, D.C., where he continued his law practice, and, in later years, wrote numerous essays in behalf of the Union and a national banking system. According to Jeremiah Mason, Evans had, in Portsmouth, " 'about as much influence as any one, because he was a clever fellow, honest, poor, and not

well treated, and the people sympathized with him.' " Charles H. Bell,
Bench and Bar of New Hampshire

(Boston, 1894), pp. 343–344.
  1. Letter not found.

TO EZEKIEL WEBSTER

Washington April 4 1828

Dear E.

I send you Mr [John] Davis' Tariff Speech,[1] & shall send you others. Having some Nos of an English Newspaper published in Paris, for the benefit, I presume, of English Residents there, I enclose them to you as you will find in them full accounts of the late ministerial changes in England, Mr [Henry Peter] Brougham's Speech on the laws, &c.[2]

I believe what you advise, in relation to a certain question, is right, & I presume the matter will have that termination.[3]

I have had a good deal of conversation here about N. Hampshire matters, with certain friends. I think a good disposition prevails, & that a satisfactory arrangement, in regard to future proceedings may be made in June. But you will find it *indispensable*, to this arrangement, that you be a candidate for a seat here. To that, there will be no objection, I imagine; but, on the contrary, a hearty assent. Other propositions would or might create difficulty. For one, *I* shall never agree to let you off.

It is quite uncertain whether any Tariff bill will pass. Nothing new has developed itself for a week, in regard to the subject. Yrs always

D. Webster

ALS. NhD. Published in *PC*, 1: 456–457.

  1. Davis' speech had been delivered before the House of Representatives on March 12 and 13, 1828. See *Register of Debates*, 20th Cong., 1st sess., 1827–28, pp. 1878–1909.

  2. Brougham (1778–1868), to become lord chancellor in 1830, had delivered a speech explaining his scheme for reform of the British legal system (*DNB*).

  3. Ezekiel's letter containing his recommendations on Webster and the English mission has not been found.

FROM PETER PAUL FRANCIS DEGRAND

Philá. 7th April 1828 A. M.

Confidential

Dear Sir

Let the friends of the Admtn. not be startled one inch, from the Ground of obtaining *substantially* the Harrisburg Platform and have the yeas & nays.

If they can only have *substantially* the Bill as Reported originally by the Committee of Manftrs., let them vote, in solid column, agt. it. I have no doubt I can get the whole Caucussing Machinery of the manufg concern, to approve the course, thus pursued by the Members friendly to the admtn: & to sustain accordingly, an administration, which thus sustained their own views.

Let no unmanly fear induce any of our friends to vote for the Bill as originally Reported; nor for any thing substantially like it.

If any one of our friends advises to a different course, you may rest assured such a friend does not understand the moving strings of the manufg. concern as well as I do.

You see that the course I recommend is plain, comfortable, consistent & honorable.

Our march is still onward in Pennsylva.

I thank you, for the kindness you have had of sending me various interesting Documents. I shd. like much to have [Richard] Rush's Report on Silk Worms[1] & any Statistical accts & whatever you may deem interesting. Yours with esteem   Dd.

ALS. DLC. Degrand (1787–1855), a native of Marseilles, had settled in Boston in 1804, where he became a prominent merchant and broker, most likely with a branch also in Philadelphia. In connection with his financial interests, he began publishing in 1819 *Degrand's Boston Weekly Reporter of Public Sales and of Ar-* rivals; and in later life he took a keen interest in railroad promotion.

1. Rush's report "In Relation to the Growth and Manufacture of Silk," referred to the Committee on Agriculture on February 7, 1828, is printed in *State Papers*, 20th Cong., 1st sess., 1827–28 (Serial 172), Doc. No. 158.

FROM MOSES HAYDEN

York Livingston Co Apl. 8, 1828

Dear Sir,

I am much obliged by your favor of March 25 recd yesterday.[1] I am glad that your attention has been drawn to the subject of Anti Masonry & I look forward to the time when you will be willing to "confess that the Morgan business not only *seems* to prove that there is some danger in the institution" but will be able conscientiously to declare that the comparatively trivial & unimportant circumstance of the assassination of [William] Morgan has providentially led to the detection & exposure of a more iniquitous & high handed fraud upon the free & equal rights of a republican people than any which has been developed in reference to any subject within the last century. The animal feeling such as is witnessed when a herd of Bullocks bellow on the spot where the smoking blood of a victim is rising from the ground has long since subsided—it has settled down into determination—it has with collateral circumstances produced the gristle of principle—as fixed & strong as revolutionary principle & as thoroughly imbued with the sentiment of patriot-ism—Only shew that the evil complained of cannot be removed without recurrence to arms & that such resort would be just & proper & I do not hesitate to express my belief that in the 12 western Counties an army of 5000 would come into the field as volunteers—this Spirit is contagious —it is migratory & will be united in its march to no narrow range. It *will affect & control* the proposed succession to the Presidency if Mr A should be elected a 2d time.

To be considered for a while as zealots & enthusiasts will be the fate of all those who maintain such opinions & foretell such events as those alluded to. The excitement of the People here is supposed abroad to be a wonderful matter & of course governed by no fixed laws which will regu-late it—& in this incorrect opinion lies all the mistake. The wonder lies not in the excitement but that such causes exist to produce it—at this late period—in the 19th Century; the excitement as it is termed is noth-ing but the sober & vigorous action of mens minds upon a well proved state of facts calculated beyond any other to Stimulate & arouse—Ex gr. The Masonic institution is charged with giving countenance to its mem-bers in taking the life of a fellow citizen in defiance of the laws of the land—& in pursuance thereof a well known undoubted & now undenied Masonic murder has been committed. They stand charged with taking on themselves the most solemn obligations to screen their brethren from harm in all situations of danger & the proof is that uncounted & unde-nied masonic perjuries have grown out of the Morgan trials—& the as-sassins most of them have escaped beyond the reach of law. They are charged with political concert in favor of each other & an examination of their oaths as given to the public by men of character who have taken them shews that they are under obligation so to act, & as practical proof is, most desirable, it is an ascertained fact that in many of the western Counties that while the masons compose not more than 1/6th part of the voting population they have contrived to obtain & hold untill re-cently about 3/4ths of all the offices. No doubt they have played with false dice. No doubt the institution is a constantly operating moral trea-son against every distinguishing feature of the government.

I concur with you most sincerely in the heartfelt desire that the Ad-ministration, may sustain itself. I feel a sort of confidence that it will do so. I have felt a great interest in your situation both public & *private* which I heretof[ore o]mitted not *neglected* to express. The oppositi[on] have [been w]onderfully exercised it seems by the exp[ectation] of your [su]cceeding Mr. [Albert] Gallatin at the Court of St. James. For myself I had hoped to have heard of your nomination before this—there would be more of the bugbear than of rea[l] danger in the President's making it. The old prejudices are now in my judgment rather nominal than real. New Hampshire & Maine probably retain more than is to be found elsewhere. The death of Mr. [DeWitt] Clinton & other circumstances to which I have alluded present a new phase in political affairs—accelerating the progress of events heretofore considered contingent & remote. Jackson does not as I can discover since I last wrote you[2]—advance— but is rather on the wane. I am very sincerely & truly Yrs   M Hayden

ALS. NhD.   2. Letter not found.
   1. Not found.

TO JOSEPH E. SPRAGUE

Washington April 13 1828
Confidential
Dear Sir,

I saw Mr. [Nathaniel] Silsbee's letter received from you yesterday, your election comes on nobly. From what I see, I shall confidently expect that you yourself will be in the Senate.[1] You certainly deserve to be there from your able and indefatigable exertions in the good cause, as well as from your ability to be useful in that situation. I fear we are getting into trouble here about the *Tariff*. The House of Representatives *will pass the Bill*—it will be a poor and inefficient aid to wool and woolens, and <will> [with] the molasses and hemp in it, what shall *we* do with it? Pray turn your thoughts to this matter a little.

   1. Can we go the *hemp*, iron[,] spirits an[d] molasses for the sake of any woolen bill?
   2. Can we do it for a poor woolen Bill?
Yours always truly   D.W.

   P.S. I think the Bill will positively *injure* the manufacturer, the "passing" though possibly it may help the woolen grower.

Copy. NhHi. Published in Van Tyne, pp. 135–136.
   1. Sprague had recently been nominated on the administration ticket to represent Essex County in the Massachusetts Senate; his campaign was successful.

TO [JOSEPH STORY]

Washington April 13. 1828
Dear Sir

I have recd your letter,[1] & had pleasure in executing your commissions. The Books & the letter have gone to Mr [Charles Richard] Vaughan. The note for Mr [Chester?] Harding, & the letter for Mr [Tench?] Ring[g]old have been recd & delivd.[2]

I regret deeply to hear of the illness of Mrs S's sister, knowing how much she is attached to her, & how deeply she must be affected by her present condition. I would fain hope her case may not be as bad as you fear.

We see that there is a good deal of excitement abt. Dr. [John Thornton] K[irkland]'s resignation.[3] I trust it will be but temporary, since the whole world knows the regard entertained for him by all who have had any concern with the College Government. I can well understand there will be difficulties in finding a successor. I confess I think of no one so likely to do good as Mr [George] Ticknor. I presume you will take some time to deliberate, on so important a matter. *I am agt. a clergyman.* Nor should I look for a man, himself distinguished by his acquisitions in any one particular branch of science or letters, tho' I think Mr T. is so distinguished. The place requires a man with powers of administration, and government, & knowledge of character, & competent to a vigorous supervision of all subordinate functionaries. He is not to run up the shrouds, nor to go out in the Boat; but to stand at the helm, & look at the needle.

Our House passed the process bill, in pretty good form.[4] It reposes, for the present, in the H. of R. to be taken up probably when the Tariff is done with. I believe the Tariff Bill will come to the Senate, in a very bad shape; in a shape to be injurious even to the woolen manufacturers, & retaining, still, the duty on hemp, molasses, &c &c.

We shall consider it cooly, &, as far as I am concerned, endeavor *to judge of it as it is*, & act accordingly. I hope not to commit any great mistake.

You express a friendly wish that I should say something, before the session closes, by way of keeping myself in remembrance. If I do say anything, it will be on the Internal improvement question. The House sent us a bill containing among other things, an appropriation for *surveys*, for roads & canals. In Senate, we amended it, as you will have seen, by confining it to such as are already commenced. The House will disagree to this Amendt, & we shall have the bill back. I have some thoughts of using that occasion to say *a few words*.[5] I really wish you could sit down & give me as many *suggestions*, as it wd. take you half an hour to write—either on the *power*, or the policy. Pray do so, if you can.

A certain subject remains *precisely*, as when you left. No alteration has occurred, either by events, or in opinions.[6]

We rejoiced greatly yesterday at the news from Boston & Salem. Boston at last seems disposed to act a part becoming her character.

It looks very likely our friend [Joseph E.] Sprague is chosen. Depend upon it, the day of exclusion has gone by, in N. E. as well as elsewhere.

Pray make my most affectionate regards to Mrs. Story. Yrs always truly   D. Webster

What do you think of the Chief Justice's letter to the Whig?[7] Is it not an excellent thing?

ALS. DLC.

1. Not found.

2. Ringgold was marshal of the District of Columbia.

3. Kirkland resigned as president of Harvard College on April 2, 1828, after disagreements over college administration with Nathaniel Bowditch, a fellow of the Corporation.

4. The Senate had passed "an act further to regulate processes in the Courts of the United States" on April 4, 1828.

5. On April 8, Webster delivered a short speech on the subject of internal improvements. *Register of Debates*, 20th Cong., 1st sess., 1827–

28, pp. 604–605.

6. The allusion is most likely to the appointment of minister to England.

7. The letter from John Marshall to John Hampden Pleasants, editor of the *Richmond Whig*, dated March 29, 1828, was copied in the *National Intelligencer* of April 5, 1828. In it Marshall denied "Marylander's" report that he had said he would "consider the election of Jackson as a virtual dissolution of the Union." Marshall did declare, however, that he thought the charges of corrupt dealings between Adams and Clay were entirely "unjust."

FROM LEVI LINCOLN

Worcester Masstts April 19 1828

My Dear Sir

The receipt of your interesting communication of the 15th[1] has been somewhat delayed by my engagement from home, or it would have been acknowledged by an earlier mail. I have now to regret, that since the adjournment of the State Legislature, my time and thoughts have been so exclusively engrossed by events of the most pressing domestic concerns, or by those subjects of official duty, which were devolved upon me by some recent Enactments, that I have had no opportunity for more regard to Congressional measures, than to mark their extraordinary character and gather from the public journals, something of their progress. It would indeed afford me pleasure to offer any considerations worthy of your attention, on the subject of the proposed Tariff—but I should feel more than common distrust in doing it, at this time, from the circumstance, that many articles are contained in the Bill, about which I have most unsatisfactory means of arriving at a safe opinion. On the subject of the woollen manufactures, and as connected particularly with this interest, the encouragement of the *wool grower*, I cannot perceive that any advantage is promised by the Bill. Indeed certain departments of the business will be quite as much prejudiced, as other portions will be bene-fitted, & the encouragement, up on the whole (*if any thing*) is alto-gether too inconsiderable and inadequate, to render the law, *on this account only*, very desirable. I might repeat facts and representations on the subject, which have already presented the question as well before Congress, as in the Country, in the most striking light. I adopt fully the reasoning, the powerful and unanswerable, and was it not for the ob-stinacy of prejudice and the array of party, I should hope, the *controlling* arguments of the advocates of protection. The vital interests of the na-tion have not been mistaken by them, and they will at least have the honor of having manfully vindicated, if they are denied the satisfaction of being able to sustain them.

My remarks are thus general, from the reason before suggested, that I am not sufficiently well advised of the bearing of the *whole* Bill upon *all* the interests which it embraces, to decide how much *worse than doing nothing*, it may be, to pass it. I confidently believe that it will be re-garded as no *boon* to the manufacturer of woollens. The extravagant duties on several articles, & most especially on Molasses & Hemp so deeply and so fatally affects other important interests, that there can hardly be formed a counterbalance to these positive objections. On the whole, I cannot but consider the Friends of the American System in Congress, as placed in a most perplexing and responsible situation,— but of this, I can offer you the most entire assurance, that they will be ardently sustained in *any* course which necessity may compel them to elect. The alternative to which they may be brought by the majority, has been long since anticipated here, and the principle of expediency upon which they must ultimately decide, is regarded as so equivocal, that nothing of personal confidence towards them, will be hazarded by the issue.

The friends of the administration in this State, and particularly in Boston, have decidedly and nobly vindicated their true sentiments in the late election. Even *I* may be permitted thus to respond to a general re-mark—because the canvass was conducted altogether in reference to the great questions of national concern. It was indeed [ms. cut for removal of signature],[2] for they had already [one line missing] convenient por-tion. They drop, as mischievous Boys hide, the moment they are de-tected. I think there will be no more getting up.

The measures which have been adopted by the National Executive in reference to the North Eastern Boundary,[3] have had the best effect upon public sentiment in Maine. Fears were certainly to be entertained, at one time, that the difficulties and excitements which existed on that subject, might be made instrumental in detaching that State from the Administration, but I feel warranted in saying, that there is nothing more to be apprehended, on that account.

I have written hastily, that another mail might not pass without bearing the expression of my gratification in your attention, and the renewed assurances of my highest esteem and respect   [Levi Lincoln]

AL (signature removed). NhHi.

1. Not found.

2. An endorsement on the manuscript reads: "cut out for Mr. Sprague. October 13, 1828. Thomas Davis."

3. The United States and Great Britain had agreed in 1827 to submit the disputed northeastern boundary to the king of the Netherlands for arbitration. Lincoln's reference here is to the implementation of the convention by President Adams. The decision, rendered in 1831, was rejected by the United States. See the forthcoming Diplomatic Papers for Webster's role in the ultimate settlement of the boundary question.

A corollary to the "corrupt bargain" charge was that Adams committed himself to appoint Federalists to office to secure the needed votes for his election in the House of Representatives in 1825. With the presidential election fast approaching in the spring of 1828, Jacksonian presses throughout the country added the charge of "the basest duplicity and hypocrisy" to the broader one of an understanding between Adams and Clay, whereby the one would get the presidency and the other the State Department. Webster, Joseph Hopkinson, and Richard Stockton, in addition to Adams, were central figures in the new charge (New York Evening Post, *April 16, 1828).*

The accusation was first made in April 1828 in the Buffalo Republican, *a newspaper edited and published by William M. P. Wood, a former resident of Trenton, New Jersey. Wood was an acquaintance of Richard Stockton, whose death on March 7 probably suggested the article. Wood's account, based on a reputed letter of Stockton's, was that Webster showed Stockton in the presence of Joseph Hopkinson and others a letter from Adams pledging to appoint Federalists in Trenton. According to Wood's printed excerpt, Stockton wrote: "I know Mr. A's. hand writing well; and was perfectly satisfied of its being genuine, by its being interlined by him."*

Wood's report, quickly reprinted in the Jacksonian papers throughout the country, had just enough truth in it to provoke the following exchange of correspondence between Webster and Hopkinson and the letter from Robert F. Stockton, May 14, 1828, below. Clearly, Wood was referring to Webster's letter to Henry Warfield, February 5, 1825 (see above, pp. 21–22), which Webster had shown to Adams. An addendum to the letter reports Adams' pledge that no party would be proscribed should he be elected. The interlineations referred to were Webster's, not Adams'. There was, in fact, no Adams letter making pledges, or even hinting at them. Webster's letter to Warfield was sufficiently equivocal, and Wood's report sufficiently garbled, to permit the flat denial Hopkinson proposes.

FROM JOSEPH HOPKINSON

Philada. April 19. 1828

My dear Sir

An article has appeared, first in a Buffalo paper, and is now passing into the opposition Journals, purporting to be an Extract from a letter written by our respected and departed friend, Mr [Richard] Stockton, on the subject of the asserted pledge made by Mr Adams in favour of the federalists. It is remarkable that this letter was concealed until the death of the alleged writer; that now an Extract only is given; that it has no date, and the person to whom written is not named. From these circumstances and other internal evidence I should pronounce the whole an impudent fabrication. There is however another and a stronger fact to bring me to this conclusion. Mr Stockton is made to say that "the letter" (containing the pledge) "was shewn me at Bispham's, in Trenton, in presence of Mr Hopkinson and one or two others." Now, my dear Sir, I have not the least recollection or belief of any such occurrence; nor that I ever saw you & Mr S. together at Trenton at any time or on any occasion. What passed between you & myself on this subject was in my parlour in Philadelphia; and I believe was mere conversation, in which way you made all the communication you ever made; for I do not remember that you showed me any letter; but I am not certain of this tho' you spoke of one from a gentleman from Maryland to you & your reply.[1] I beg you to refresh me on these particulars.

1. Have you & I ever been in company with Mr Stockton at Trenton— nay, any where except once at Princeton several years ago, and before this presidential controversy arose.
2. Did you ever show me, or Mr S. in my presence any such letter.
3. Will it be advisable to have a paragraph in the Natl. Gazette, charging the letter to be a forgery on the ground of these falsehoods, which Mr S. never could have written. What you write to me will, of course, be confidential; and merely to correct the error of my memory; or confirm my confidence in it. Answer me quickly.

[Joseph Hopkinson][2]

The two or three gentlemen said to have been present, are not named.

AL (signature removed). NhHi.
1. The reference is to the exchange of letters between Warfield and Webster, February 3, 5, 1825; see above pp. 18–22, for the correspondence.

2. Again, an endorsement on the letter reads: "Autograph cut out for Mr Sprague. Oct 13, 1828. Thomas Davis."

TO JOSEPH HOPKINSON

Washington April 21. 1828

My Dear Sir

On Friday I saw the Evening Post, containing the supposed letter from Mr Stockton, reprinted from the Buffalo Journal. I have no doubt at all it is a mere sheer forgery.

Your two first questions I can readily answer.

1. I have not seen you and Mr. Stockton together since the year 1819.
2. I never showed to you, nor to any body else in your presence, any such letter, as is supposed, or any other letter respecting the election of President.

As to the third question, I am disposed to leave the matter to your discretion & judgment, & those of the friends about you. Probably a denial under your authority, might do good.[1] One thing is to be guarded against; & that is, not to do any thing which may make it necessary for *me* to publish any thing in my turn. I do not, indeed, see that a denial of this story by you will induce such necessity, but rather have the contrary effect. Still, I thought fit to express the caution.

It is quite impossible Mr Stockton could have written such a letter. I *think* I have not seen him at Trenton since 1819; tho' it is possible I may have seen him there, as his Court has been sometimes sitting in that Town as I have passed. But *I am quite positive I never said one word to him, at Trenton, about Mr Adams' election in my life.* Yrs truly

Danl. Webster

ALS. PHi.
1. Apparently Hopkinson did respond publicly to the charges, for the New York *Evening Post*, May 16,

1828, reprinted from Walsh's *National Gazette* a response to the questions Hopkinson asked of Webster in his letter of April 19, above.

FROM ISRAEL THORNDIKE (TO DANIEL WEBSTER AND NATHANIEL SILSBEE)

Boston, 28 April, 1828.

Dear Sirs,

I observe that the Tarif has passed in the House and of course will be before the Senate or decided there when this reaches you. I am however of opinion that this Bill bad as it is, had better be passed than that the whole should be lost; respecting the Duty upon low priced Sheeps Wool that may be countervail'd by increasing the Duty upon Carpets and such other *coarse* articles as this kind of Wool is used for. I think the increase of Duty on Molasses will be prejudicial to our West India trade, and to our distilling business, and that of not allowing drawback upon the exportation of N. England Rum will be prejudicial to the N England States in as much as it will entirely prevent the exportation of that article, and of course of the importation of the proceeds, which now gives employment to considerable Shipping and many Sailors.

The proposed increase of Duty on Hemp I think injudicious and prejudicial, because it will drive Ship owners to direct their masters to supply their ships abroad, not only upon the Voyage which they may be upon but so largely as to require little or none for their next outward bound passage after their return.

I observe that Ravens Duck stands chargable with the same Duty as the heaviest Sail Duck, the Cost of which, at the places from whence it is exported is from ¼ to ⅓ of that of Sail Cloth, and besides if the Tarif passes as it now is without reducing the duty on this article, no revenue will be raised on it, because Russia Sheetings (sometimes called Flims) on which there is no additional Duty, will be used as a substitute.

When Mr [Alexander James] Dallas was Secretary of the Treasury I did by *his desire* correspond with him upon the subject of a then proposed Tarif, my Letters to him are (I presume) now on file in the office. I then felt more interested upon this subject than I now do, and was more *particular* upon the subject than I am now capable of being. I then thought as I now do that it would be good policy in the Government to give a drawback upon Cordage manufactured in this Country because the Hemp from which it is made would be first imported, and then the Cordage exported, it being thus twice waterborne would give additional employment to tonage, and besides the proceeds of the Cordage which would be brought home would pay a duty and thereby enrich the Revenue.

I am also of opinion that a duty of, say, two to three cents pr pound on *sheet* Copper would be beneficial, it would encourage the importation of Pig Copper (which ought to be free) and would encourage the manufacture of it in this country where it is made as good as in any part of the World. If the Duty upon Hemp is touched I am decidedly of the opinion that it ought to be upon this principle, say Riga Rhine, St Petersburg clean, and Bologna Hemp shall pay an impost Duty of $ [1] per ton of 2240 l[b]s and that outshoot half clean and all other inferior Hemp shall pay double the $ as before mentioned. The foregoing is bottomed upon this principle Viz—that inferior Hemp which cost perhaps half that of best kind is weak and actually unfit to be made into Cordage is often purchased in Russia and brought into this country and made into cordage, which looks as fair and as well as that made from the best Hemp, and no man can tell from the appearance of it, that it is not made from the best Hemp, the same reasons why this guard ought to [be] placed on Hemp apply to the government as to individuals to prevent the imposition being practised as upon individuals. If I am answered that as to the Government Ships there is no danger because the Agents will take care to fix a standard by which it shall be proved—to this I should answer that it is by no means certain that you will always have Navy Agents that are capable, diligent & honest [in] proving every coil, and besides a possible case may, in time [arise wherein a] subordinate officer may be bribed, all of which [must be] guarded against by making bad Hemp come higher to the manu[facturers] than good.

I mentioned to both of you Gentlemen that I had a case which I thought a very hard one with the Directors of the Bank of the United States, and asked the favour of you Gentlemen to call up the same for revision as you passed through Philadelphia. It is probable that the Directors may say that it has been settled a long time since, to which I should reply that I did receive such a sum on delivering up the Bills as they chose to give me, rather than lay out of the *whole* sum, and now ask the favour of having the transaction reviewed at a full board, and do by me in this business exactly what would be expected in a reverse of circumstances. I am with much respect your obt humble servant

Israel Thorndike

P.S. I think I gave to Mr. Webster the papers detailing the particulars of this concern.[2]

LS. NhHi.

1. Thorndike left a blank here, suggesting that Webster and Silsbee supply a specific rate.

2. Not found.

FROM THOMAS LORD & COMPANY

Boston April 29. 1829 [1828]

Sir

We have with the deepest solicitude watched the progress of the "Tariff bill" through all its discussions in the House of Representatives. [We,] having long been agents for a large number of "Woolen Manufacturers" and deeply engaged in the "Wool trade" are satisfied both these interests need further and immediate protection.

Therefore although the "bill" is not what we should have chosen, still we consider it will be of great benefit to a large proportion of your Manufacturing Friends in New England, who, we doubt not, will feel

themselves under additional obligations by your favourable consideration of the Bill, which we hope even in its present shape, will receive
the sanction of your vote. We are Sir with gratitude and respect, your
Mo H[umbl]e Servts   Thomas Lord & Co.

ALS. NhHi. Thomas Lord was a   American goods.
banker and merchant, specializing in

FROM WILLIAM GIBBES HUNT

Nashville May 1. 1828

Dear Sir,

Your polite note of the 8th ult. was duly received, acknowledging the
receipt of the little pamphlet I took the liberty to send you;[1] and I now
hope, it will not be deemed obtrusive or impertinent, as you have expressed your concurrence in the views it contains of the character of
the departed Clinton, to say to you that it was prepared, at very short
notice, amidst the pressure of many duties and the constant interruption
of my ordinary professional and editorial avocations. Had more time
and leisure been allowed me, I should have gone, at some length, into a
minute analysis of the character of the deceased, as it appears to me to
have been developed by his labors and services. I was compelled however me[rely] to skim over the surface of the subject, without attempting
to penetrate its most interesting details. I am looking with much anxiety
for the Address of my friend Mr [Samuel Lorenzo] Knapp on the same
occasion,[2] believing from his well known capacity and from the accounts
I have seen of it in the papers, that he has done ample justice to the
subject.

Suffer me, Sir, while availing myself of the opportunity, which seemed
to present, for opening a correspondence with you, to express to you,
at once, my high respect for you personally and my cordial sympathy
with you in your late domestic bereavement. I had once the pleasure of
an acquaintance with Mrs Webster, and have ever retained a recollection of it with much satisfaction. While a student a[t] Harvard University, in my boyish days, I boarded in the family of President [Samuel]
Webber,[3] where your lady, then unmarried, spent some time on a visit,
and where I recollect, once or twice, seeing you. Since that time I have
been, yankee like, a rover. After residing, for some years, at Lexington
Ky. I removed to this place, where I am engaged in the double pursuit
of attorney and editor.[4]

I have studiously endeavored, however, of late, in my editorial course,
strictly to avoid an offensive devotion to either of the presidential candidates or their respective partisans. Entertaining sincerely, from personal

intercourse, a respect for the character of Gen. Jackson, and finding some of my best friends among his zealous devotees, I have felt no inclination to oppose him; while, on the other hand, knowing the almost unrivalled qualifications of Mr Adams and the eminent talents and high moral worth of the members of his cabinet, I could not join in the denunciations, so general and so popular here, against the present administration. I have, consequently, subjected myself to the somewhat unpleasant, though not in my estimation dishonorable, imputation of being a nondescript—and occupying a station, as it is familiarly said, *upon the fence.* I must say however, that I could not, under any circumstances, join in the strain of unnecessary personal calumny, so disgraceful to the warmest partisans on both sides of the present controversy. I cannot but regard the struggle as a mere contest for the promotion of individuals, without involving, in its results, any important abstract principles. I am willing therefore, situated as I am, to stand by for the present, a calm and dispassionate spectator, to smile, as I frequently do, at the contortions and inconsistencies of exclusive partisans, who are apt to forget, in their present zeal, the sentiments they have heretofore expressed—and to indulge the hope, that whichever party may be triumphant, the good sense and moderation of the American people will prevent any of those evils, which the intemperance of heated politicians might lead us to apprehend.

I am pleased to find, that Mr [John] Bell, the representative from this district, who is a gentleman as well as a man of undoubted talents, has been, thus far, as I think he always will be, moderate, discreet and respectful, though he will be found not wanting in decision, firmness and zeal in the support of his own views, whatever they may be. He is a native of Tennessee, has travelled little, and has of course strong sympathies for the west, with little personal acquaintance with the other sections of our great republic. He is, however, too liberal in his feelings and too expanded in his views, to pursue a course, exclusively sectional, or to disregard the obvious claims of other portions of the Union. Although, from his modest, unobtrusive character, he may not, immediately, attain a high rank in the councils of the nation, he will be sure, if he remains in Congress, to gain the respect of his co-legislators and to become eminent for his clear, accurate, and vigorous mental powers. I am confident he will always endeavor to be governed by a sincere and conscientious regard to duty, & the honest convictions of his mind.

I have long felt much anxiety for the adoption of an amendment in our judiciary system, which you have heretofore been efficient, but unfortunately not yet successful, in endeavoring to effect. It is much needed by us in the west, and it is much to be regretted that party jealousy should have defeated an object so important to the interests of the people. I fear there is little prospect of its attainment for some time to come. The golden opportunity has been unfortunately lost.

On the subject of the Tariff and the construction, by the national government, of roads, canals, &c. our representatives in Congress seem to differ, radically and essentially, from the candidate they support for the presidency, as well as from the present administration. Nothing, probably, will be done at the present session, in relation to these subjects, at least nothing of much consequence to the nation.

Whenever you can command a moment not required for the discharge of public or private duty, nor occupied by more agreeable employment or recreation, permit me to assure you, that it would be highly gratifying to me, if you would devote it to the suggestion of your ideas of the present situation of our national affairs, the prospects of the country, and the duty of its politicians and citizens. A free interchange of sentiments between the remote sections of our Union cannot but be useful, and a communication from leading statesmen in the east to those of us in the west, who endeavor to give a tone in some degree to public sentiment, may be mutually beneficial. No improper use shall ever be made of any thing communicated to me. Respectfully Yr hum[bl]e ser[van]t

W. G. Hunt

ALS. NhHi.

1. Hunt, *An address on the character and services of De Witt Clinton* . . . (Nashville, 1828). Letter not found.

2. Knapp, *A discourse on the life and character of DeWitt Clinton* . . . (Washington, 1828).

3. Webber was president of Harvard, 1806–1810.

4. Hunt edited the *Nashville Banner and Nashville Whig*.

FROM SAMUEL H. BABCOCK

Boston May 7. 1828

Dear Sir,

You will pardon me in again writing you on the subject of the Tariff. The Bill as amended by your Hon. Body will give ample protection to the woollen manufacturers so far as can probably be expected in the present situation of our business—and will give entire Satisfaction to them. We consider this attempt as our last struggle & if we fail—our business is ruin'd. I feel confident you will advocate this Branch of our National Wealth & hope you will feel so far interested in the subject as to give us your assistance. Respectfully yrs &c   Saml. H. Babcock

ALS. DLC. Babcock was a mechant in Boston, dealing mainly in English goods.

FROM JOSEPH TINKER BUCKINGHAM

Boston, May 7, [1828]

Dear Sir,

Our friends here, the Manufacturers, after deliberation and consultation among themselves, have come to the conclusion that the Tariff Bill, as reported by the Committee on Manufactures in the Senate, will answer their purpose. It comes so near to the Harrisburgh Platform, that the operation[,] they think[,] will be satisfactory and advantageous. I have taken the liberty of stating this to you, although you have probably been apprised of their views from sources more direct and positive. Should the bill as amended pass the Senate, we hope that our representatives who voted against it, will see no good reason for continuing to oppose it, when it goes back to the House. I should make some remarks of this nature, in the Courier, but for a political reason. It is, perhaps, better that the Jacksonians of the south and middle States should not know that the bill has been made acceptable to the people of New-England.

There is nothing in the way of news here that you do not get in the papers. Our representative election is to take place to-morrow. There appears to be no opposition to the Administration ticket, except what is got up at the Statesman office; but I have some doubts whether *our party* will be elected. Yours respectfully   Jos. T. Buckingham

ALS. DLC.

FROM ABBOTT LAWRENCE

Boston May 7th. 1828

Dear Sir,

The amendments offered by the Committee on Manufactures to the Tariff bill in the Senate I have examined carefully and so far as Woollens are concerned the bill is very much improved and is thought by many to be now good enough. I must say I think it would do much good, and that New England would reap a great harvest by having the bill adopted as it now is. If the dollar minimum was stricken out and low wools admitted at a fair rate of duty there would be no sort of objection to it. As it is the amendments propose a heavy duty on the manufacture of this coarse wool, which makes it less objectionable, and it also increases the rate of advalorem duty on all the minimums; which materially alters the effects which would be produced by the bill as it came from the House. Molasses too is reduced—and I wish hemp was at $45 or $50—however the bill as it is or I should say with the amendments meets with great favor in this state, and if nothing better can be had I

am fully of opinion both as regards the *true* interests of the country—
and the political effect of accepting or rejecting it, that it will be wise
to take it. This bill if adopted as amended will keep the South and West
in debt to New England the next hundred years. I wrote you several days
since and have had no reply to the question whether a bill would be
obtained this session.[1] I hope Kentucky is secure for the Administration—you see we are upon the *real* amalgamation platform here. Your
plans of last year are in full operation this present political year. All is
going on well. What can be done for the Massachusetts Journal. Will
you write [David L.] Child a word of encouragement. He is doing great
good in this State and can do more in Maine and New Hampshire. If
this Tariff bill does pass I hope the time may be at least 60 days from
its passage before it takes effect. Orders have been sent abroad for
goods, which cannot be here till July or August. It would not of course
be proper to give time sufficient to obtain goods from England after its
passage—this cannot be done in 60 days. We are now surfeited with
foreign goods, and money is very scarce. I am Dear Sir truly your obt
Svt   Abbott Lawrence

ALS. NhHi.
1. Not found.

TO JAMES WILLIAM PAIGE

Saturday Eve' [May 10, 1828]

Pretty Private
Dr. William
The Senate has taken no important vote to day, except a foolish one
on the subject of *Indigo*—in which I was found, by mistake, on the
wrong side. It is a bad vote.[1]

We have fixed the adjournment for the 26.—in both Houses.

As to the Tariff—I have nothing to say different from my last. I think
it will pass the Senate—whether it may not be lost, in the subsequent
disagreements of the two houses, is more than can be exactly foreseen.
The *safe* course is, I think, to consider that the Bill will pass.

11 oclock—tired & sleepy.   D. W.

I mean to make one more effort to extend the time of this Tariff's taking
effect—but I doubt my success.[2]

ALS. NB.
1. Webster had voted in favor of
the amendment to increase the duty
on indigo. *Senate Journal*, 20th
Cong., 1st sess., 1827–28, p. 393.
2. See above, Abbott Lawrence to

DW, May 7, 1828. On May 12, the
Senate agreed to an extension of the
time before the tariff would take effect. *Senate Journal*, 20th Cong., 1st
sess., 1827–28, pp. 403–404.

Washington May 11. 1828
Sunday morning

My Dear Son,

Accustomed, in our happy days, to have my children round me, on Sunday morning, & being now deprived of that pleasure, & indeed never expecting to enjoy it again, in so great a degree as it has been enjoyed, I devote this morning to the only practicable way of holding intercourse with them. The rest & quiet of the Sabbath brings you all very freshly to my recollection, & now that the cares & labors of the week have ceased, I have pleasure in devoting my thoughts to my children, altho' accompanied with much melancholy & painful recollections. My first wish, on this occasion, My Dear Son, is to express my satisfaction with your conduct & character, & the good behaviour & amiable deportment of Julia & Edward. I am sorry to be absent from you, feeling how especially it has become my duty to redouble my care of you, by the death of your blessed mother. The prospect is, that I shall now soon be with you, & I anticipate the happiness of finding you all in good health, and of hearing good accounts of you from the friends among whom you have passed the winter.

Congress will adjourn the 26. inst. That will bring it to the first of June before I get home, which will be about the close of the vacation in your school. I was in hopes to spend the vacation with you, but that is now not possible.

My wish is you should pass the vacation under Uncle Williams advice, in the way most agreeable to yourself. Perhaps you may as well go to Boscawen, as any where. Uncle E[zekiel] will send Speeder down, if you write to him—or you may go up in the Stage Coach, & ride down on Speeder. Whatever arrangement you & Uncle William agree to, for passing the holidays, will suit me; but I think a journey into the country is probably the best. Your uncle, aunt, & cousins will be very glad to see you.

I believe I owe Mr Emerson[1] a letter which I have not time to write. He must take care of you till I come home, & unless he shall already have made you so full of knowledge as that you can hold no more, his further contributions will be desirable.

Give my affectionate love to Julia & Edward. Your loving father
Danl. Webster

P.S. Since writing this letter, I have recd y[ou]rs, with Mr Goulds report,[2] which I enclose. You must try to correct, what he finds amiss, & to add to your other attainments. Tell Mr Emerson I duly recd his letters[3] —& postpone, for a fortnight, & to personal communication, a reply thereto.

He does not well to infer assent from silence. Yrs   D. W.

ALS. NhHi. Published in Van Tyne, pp. 574–575.

1. For the problems involved in identifying Emerson, see above, Daniel Fletcher Webster to DW, February 18, 1826.

2. Not found.

3. Not found.

TO JAMES WILLIAM PAIGE

Monday Eve' [May 12, 1828]

Private

Dr. Wm.

You will see that the Tariff is engrossed, in the Senate. How I shall vote, if the final passage depends on me, nobody knows, & I hardly know myself. Today, when my name was called for the engrossment, a majority had already answered *Aye*, and my friends were exceedingly anxious that I should not appear agt. the Bill, when it could have no effect. If you see the *Telegraph* of today, you will see how marked a bird I am.[1]

In truth, I am convinced, somewhat agt. my inclination, that it is necessary to check the amount of English Importations. But no more of that for the present.

You will see that we have fixed the *time* so as to save you. That required all the address and effort that could be made. I shall take all possible pains to induce members of the House to agree to that amendment —tho', *possibly*, they may refuse.

What reconciles me, in some measure to the bill, is, that N. E. will, certainly, on the whole, be benefitted by it; and some things which are wrong & bad, we may hope to amend hereafter. If the bill, on the other hand, had failed now, I know not whether there would have been any chance hereafter of doing any thing for the manufacturers—& I *conscientiously* think, after what has passed, the interest of N. E. required that something should be done for them.

It is yet somewhat uncertain whether the Bill will become a *law*. Very likely it may be two or three days discussed in the Senate—& then it has to go to the House, where many accidents may await it. Still, the safe course is to expect the Bill to pass. I believe *it will* pass. Yrs   D. Webster

ALS. MHi.

1. In a lengthy editorial, May 12, the *United States Telegraph* had attacked Webster for his position on the tariff: he was inattentive to western interests; his only concern was for New England and woolen manufacturers.

FROM WILLIAM SULLIVAN

Monday 12th. May 1828.

Dr. Sr.

Mrs S. and I went to Mrs [Nathan] Hale's yesterday to see Julia. She was at Mrs Lee's in Brookline. In the afternoon we went there. Julia came in from the fields, accompanied by Miss Hale; in very good health —and well inclined to welcome me, on finding that I had lately seen you. She seems to me to be a little taller than when I saw her last. She is, as you must know for yourself, a softened, feminine image of her paternal origin. I expected to have seen Daniel yesterday; but did not. I saw Mr. Emerson on Saturday, who spoke of his good health and conduct. Julia was dressed in a crossbarred calico, with a ruffle round her neck—and large comb in her head—and Telemachus in her hand; I asked for her opinion of this young Hero. She replied that she had not read far enough to give one. Mr & Mrs Lee were very interrogative as to who, and what I had seen and heard, but mostly as to yourself. I endeavored, well aware of the danger of being misunderstood, and of giving impressions, not intended, to say only such things, as you would not have disapproved had you been "behind the arras." Emerson thought that Daniel was doing well, and consequently better, than at some other place which he had left. Julia's place of schooling is removed to Common Street. I understand that Misses P[eabody] are reported to sustain themselves according to their former well earned fame. Edward I have not seen. I am told that the three meet often and take a strong interest in each other's society. Little Miss Hale, who is a beauty on the maternal scale, was at Mrs. Lee's (which I find on perusal I have said before).

You probably know as much of our political state here as I do. The amalgamated 40—you have seen. It is a curious fact that, man and boy as I am for 45 yrs in Boston—and somewhat in the business walks, there are ten of the number whose persons I never saw—and some of the ten whose names I never before read. The Jackson interest, is of course, very flat here; it is probably so elsewhere in the State. The result of the next Pres. Elec. is thought to be very doubtful, and some who take more note of these things than I do, *guess*, that the Legislative meeting in Albany in Sept. will take care to give a shape to the voting in that State, if the case should so require. I should infer from the little that I see and hear that the opinion is, (unless some unlooked for changes occur,) that it is probable, we shall have a change of dynasty. Then comes this question, will the new president, attempt to live down the bad fame that has been affirmed of him—and call the first talents in the Land into his counsels; or will he be forced to submit himself to the dominion of partizans, and persevere in a course of party favoritism, & exclusion? And who can answer this?

My excursion tho' a short one as to time, was full of interest and instruction. I can now understand much better than before, the current of events—& have the means of measuring magnitudes, which distance & mist greatly misrepresent. I have come home with the impression, (no very unnatural one) tha[t] men, climate, social and political relations—property and the enjoyment of it—are all and every [one] of them, worth more in N. E. than any where else.

With great regard your truly obliged friend   Wm. Sullivan

The Ch. Jus. intended to hold a nisi pr. term here commencing tomorrow. But he has had a fag of 4 weeks at Worcester; and on Saturday Evening he told me that he should be glad to give up this design, if the bar concurred which I doubt not they gladly will. There is, however, a session of the Law term on the 15. of June. If I could have foreseen that the Judge would so incline it would have given me, what I much desired, another week in Washington. But, I am content; and consider myself as having closed my personal account with the City that is no city—but which is the place of paste board and distances; as well as of many other things not to be spoken of.   W. S.

ALS. DLC.

FROM WILLIAM ELLERY CHANNING

Boston May 14th. 1828

My dear Sir,

I wish to call your attention to a subject of general interest.

A little while ago, Mr. [Benjamin] Lundy of Baltimore, the editor of a paper called "The Genius of Universal Emancipation," visited this part of the country, to stir us up to the work of abolishing slavery at the South, and the intention is to organize societies for this purpose. I know few objects into which I should enter with more zeal, but I am aware how cautiously exertions are to be made for it in this part of the country. I know that our Southern brethren interpret every word from this region on the subject of slavery as an expression of hostility; I would ask if they cannot be brought to understand us better, and if we can do any good till we remove their misapprehensions.

It seems to me that, before moving in this matter, we ought to say to them distinctly, "We consider slavery as your calamity, not your crime, and we will share with you the burden of putting an end to it. We will consent that the public lands shall be appropriated to this object; & that the general government shall be clothed with power to apply a portion of revenue to it."

I throw out these suggestions merely to illustrate my views. We must first let the Southern States see that we are their *friends* in this affair; that we sympathize with them, and, from principles of patriotism and philanthropy, are willing to share the toil and expense of abolishing slavery, or I fear our interference will avail nothing. I am the more sensitive on this subject from my increased solicitude for the preservation of the Union. I know no public interest so important as this. I ask from the general government scarcely any other boon than that it will hold us together, and preserve pacific relations and intercourse among the States. I deprecate every thing which sows discord and exasperates sectional animosities. If it will simply keep us at peace, and will maintain in full power the national courts, for the purpose of settling quietly among citizens of different States questions which might otherwise be settled by arms, I shall be satisfied.

My fear in regard to our efforts against slavery is, that we shall make the case worse by rousing sectional pride and passion for its support, and that we shall only break the country into two great parties, which may shake the foundations of government.

I have written to you because your situation gives you advantages which perhaps no other man enjoys for ascertaining the method, if any can be devised, by which we may operate beneficially and safely in regard to slavery. Appeals will probably be made soon to the people here, and I wish that wise men would save us from the rashness of enthusiasts, and from the perils to which our very virtues expose us. With great respect, your friend   Wm E. Channing.

Copy. PHi. Published in *W & S*, 10: 98–99. On February 15, 1851, Webster forwarded a copy of Channing's letter to Gales and Seaton for publication in the *National Intelligencer*.

FROM ROBERT FIELD STOCKTON

Princeton May 14th. 1828

My Dr Sir.

It has been a source of deep regret to me, that I have not heard from you since October 1826.

I have been as you may suppose frequently assailed on the subject of *"the letter"* and with regard to Mr Adams conduct towards the Federalists.[1]

I have heretofore paid but little attention to the suggestions thrown out.

But I am of opinion that so much has been admitted by Mr. Walsh, that the sooner the *real truth* is known the better; and that the best course for both of us, wd. be for me to send the enclosed letter.[2] I have been abused as an inconsistent politician, and even *suspected* of telling what is not true—all this [I] have borne and will continue to bear, unless I have your consent to send the enclosed letter.

I am satisfied that a plan is maturing to extort all that is known about the letter—and I think the sooner I tell the story the better. I wish we had done so long ago.[3]

No one on earth knows that I have written such a letter. I beg you will return it immediately. I am most faithfully   Robert Stockton

ALS. DLC.
1. See above, pp. 334–336.
2. Stockton was probably referring to Hopkinson's publication in Walsh's *National Gazette*; see above, DW to Hopkinson, April 21, 1828. Stockton's

enclosure has not been found.
3. Stockton's version of the episode, if he made it public, has not been found.

TO NATHANIEL F. WILLIAMS

Washington May 17 [18]28
Private
Dear Sir,

I wish to obtain *a thousand dollars*, to be repaid, in Boston, on my return, say 30 days hence. Can you send me yr check on a Baltimore Bank, & let me send you, in return my acceptance for that amount, payable as above?

An early answer will oblige Your ob. sevt.   Danl. Webster

ALS. NhD.

FROM JOSEPH TINKER BUCKINGHAM

Boston. May 20, 1828
My dear Sir,

With the approbation and at the request of a number of gentlemen, who are desirous of offering to you a public testimonial of their respect, and their approbation of the independent course you have pursued in the U. S. Senate, I pray you to inform me by return of mail, if it would be agreeable to you to dine with them and such other friends as may unite with them for that purpose, immediately on your return to this place from Washington. I assure you that you will find warm hands and warmer hearts to welcome you—those of men who feel grateful for your public labors, sympathy for your domestic afflictions, and esteem for your character as a legislator, which has not been lessened by the neglect of the jealous here or the persecution of the envious and malignant in other places. It may be proper to say to you, that the feeling which dictates this request on the part of your friends is not of an exclusive or narrow character. If you should consent to their wishes, it is most probable that they would show their magnanimity of feeling by embracing in their invitations your colleague in the Senate, and some of the representatives who may have given a vote on the Tariff, different from yours.

It has been deemed most proper, and quite as agreeable to your feelings, to consult you, *confidentially*, on this subject, before making any movement in relation to it that would meet the eye of the public.[1]

Among those at whose request I have written this letter are the Messrs [Abbott] Lawrence, [Jonas Bond] Brown, Clapp, Poor, [Joseph] Coolidge, [Edward H.] Robbins, &c &c[2] and in whose names, with sentiments of deep respect for your character and services as a public man and with affectionate regard for your happiness and prosperity as a private citizen, I am Yours ever and truly   Jos. T. Buckingham

ALS. DLC.

1. For an account of the public proceedings held as a "Tribute of Respect" to Webster at Faneuil Hall, June 5, 1828, and for Webster's speech, see the *Columbian Centinel*, June 7, 11, 1828.

2. Coolidge (d. 1879; Harvard 1817) was a merchant in Boston; Robbins (1758–1829; Harvard 1775) was a Boston lawyer, former speaker of the Massachusetts House of Representatives, and lieutenant governor of the state. Clapp and Poor have not been identified.

FROM SAMUEL JAUDON

New Orleans, May 21st. 1828

Dr. Sir,

I will not attempt to describe the pleasure which the receipt a short time since of a document, franked by you afforded me. Altho' the envelope contained not a single line from you, yet I was most happy to look upon it as a token of remembrance, and as an evidence that I still retained some portion of that confidence and regard with which I had reason to think I was once honored by you. It is eight months or more since I received a letter from you—and altho' I knew the extent and weight of your engagements, and the very deep and severe affliction which has befallen you and in which I have most sincerely sympathized with you, yet I did think myself somewhat entitled to a few lines "for auld lang syne." But let that pass—the sight of your signature once more, gives me hope that if in aught I have offended, the door for reparation is still open.

My residence in New Orleans has thus far been very agreeable, and I some time since communicated to Mr. Biddle my determination to remain in charge of the Office here for some years. Marguerite has also been pleased with this place—of course, or I should have returned to my old post at the Parent Bank. The disagreeable part is now coming on, vizt. the removal of the whole family for the summer. We are not yet decided as to the course we shall take, but shall at all events leave here by the 1st. of July and get to the North either up the River or by sea as circumstances may determine.

We hear a great deal about the probability of your appointment as Minister to England. I shall be truly rejoiced if you can find it your interest to accept the mission.

I do not pretend yet to know much of the politics of Louisiana, but the friends of the Administration are sanguine of success. Nothing has occurred since my residence here, to show certainly which way the state will vote. The famous entrée on the 8th. Jany. last, if it foreboded anything, was an ill omen for the "Heroites." It excited no more attention, than a military parade of the same magnitude would do at any other time, and as the "Hero" walked along the streets, not a shout of welcome nor a move of a hat or a handkerchief answered his obsequious bows to the gazers whose curiosity, and not admiration as their conduct proved, brought to the windows and galleries. How different, I cannot help thinking, from the visit of Lafayette,—what an absence of that enthusiasm and that delirium of feeling which every where manifested itself at his presence. The late election for Mayor and Alderman too proved nothing. This was a matter that interested the City alone, and altho' many were no doubt influenced in their votes by the Presidential opinion of the candidates, yet very many wisely thought that the Presidential question was not to be influenced by this election and that the interests of the City required them not to be led away by a name. The administration candidates were not well selected—and I frankly confess, that anxious as you know I am for the success of the present Administration, I could not, and if I had a vote, I would not, have voted the administration ticket.

Marguerite desires to be very particularly remembered to you—we talk of you very often with great pleasure. She and the children as well as myself have enjoyed fine health during our residence here. I am with great regard Yours, very truly   S. Jaudon

As a further matter of politics, I may state that there is very little doubt that the administration candidate for Governor, Mr. [Pierre Auguste Charles Bourguignon] Derbigny, will be elected, and that Mr [Edward] Livingston will have permission to stay at home, malgré his intended visit to this City.

ALS. NhHi.

TO EZEKIEL WEBSTER

Philadelphia May 28 [1828]
Wednesday Morning

Dr E.

I came here last eve, & shall proceed at noon today. For a week or two I have purposed to write to you, but have had no leisure.

All I wish now particularly to suggest is, the expediency of proceeding, *as soon as possible*, to the election of a Senator. I know it would be gratifying to Mr [Samuel] B[ell] that his reelection should be promptly and handsomely done. I should be exceedingly sorry, if, among friends of the Admn. he should lose a vote. Another reason is—he may wish to go early to Concord—but probably wd. prefer his Election to be first over. Let me find a letter from you, at home. Yrs   D. Webster

ALS. NhD.

TO HENRY CLAY

Boston June 8. 1828

Private

My Dear Sir,

You will have seen some proofs of the prevailing sentiments, on public subjects, in this quarter. The best possible feeling was indicated, at the Meeting on the 5th. I do not mean in regard to myself, but on general subjects, & in respect to *others*.[1] The toast in which you were named, was recd with the most enthusiastic applause. I do not think I have ever seen in Boston a meeting comprising so much character, talent, influence & respectability. I hope it may do good.

All that we yet hear from N Hampshire is very well. Mr [Samuel] Bell, I presume, will be reelected to the Senate, this week.

One objection, My Dear Sir, which I have to writing to you, is, that your courtesy & kindness lead you always to answer me—& I feel that it is wrong, in the present state of your health, & of your engagements, to impose any new duty, tho' it be a trifling one, upon you. I will really take it as a greater proof of friendship & confidence, if, how often soever I may write, you will forbear all reply, unless when there is something which you wish to say. Yours, with constant regard,   Danl. Webster

ALS. DLC. Published in *W & S*, 16: 180.

1. On June 5, Boston citizens paid their respects to Webster with a public dinner at Faneuil Hall. See above, Joseph T. Buckingham to DW, May 20, 1828.

TO HENRY CLAY

Boston July 7th. 1828.

Private & confidential

My Dear Sir,

I am in hopes this will find you in Kentucky, in good spirits, & renewed health. If you are as well as we wish you, this way, you need be no better. A strong manifestation of kind feeling towards you, personally, has very generally appeared in all the numerous celebrations of the fourth inst., in this quarter of the Country, which have fallen under my observation. As far as I can judge, the general aspect of things is favourable. A Gentleman of the first character is now with me, from the Genessee River, recently, and who saw, on his way hither, Mr. [Francis] Granger, & many other well informed persons, who are all represented as agreeing with him that the best hopes may be entertained respecting that State.

Mr. Lewis Williams writes me a very encouraging letter from North-Carolina;[1] but you have still better means of judging of that State. After all, I remain of opinion that the battle is to be won or lost where you now are. With Kentucky on our side, we shall get gloriously through the contest. I wish some of our friends there would let us know how the face of things appears. Tell [James] Clarke to write me, but do not take that trouble yourself.

I wish now to say one word on another subject. In the multitude of things which were to be attended to at the breaking up of Congress, *a part of one thing* was omitted. The enclosed is designed to accomplish it, and put it right.[2] I would adopt another *form*, if I could think of a better. When you return to Washington, or chuse to send this there, it may be conveniently used, in the manner indicated on it.

In the mean time, have the goodness to communicate with Mr. C[larke?] and let him understand that the matter is arranged. I would not trouble you with this, if I could well avoid it, and I shall feel more at ease when I know that you have received this Letter.

Have the goodness to acknowledge it in one word.

May God bless & prosper you. Yours always truly   Danl. Webster

LS. DLC. Extract published in
W & S, 16: 180.

1. Not found.
2. Not found.

FROM ROBERT FIELD STOCKTON

Princeton July 14th. 1828

My Dr Sir

I was much gratified by the recpt. of your kind letter from Boston;[1]

which came to hand, in the course of a few days, after it appears to have been written.

If I had answered immediately as I much desired to do, I would not have thought it necessary to express any sentiment, with regard to the pleasure it afforded me—because, I am satisfied, that you must be aware of, the large portion of my affectionate regards, which you have ever possessed.

I have delayed writing to you day after day in the hope of being able to inform you accurately as to the movements of my mothers family—her health however, and other domestic matters, have prevented her coming to a decision upon that subject, until today. She will, if nothing occurs to alter her determination, leave Princeton with Julia on or about the 25th. Inst—& proceed to N. Bedford as fast as a proper regard for her health will permit. Julia will be quite happy to take charge of your Daughter whilst you are absent; and you know our Quaker friends will be over joyed to have her with them.

I feel pleased at Mr. [George] Blake's remembrance of me; and will be glad to have a letter from him—*although he is an administration man*. I will not leave Princeton, but for a few days at a time during the Summer—and therefore am not likely to see you again for some months; and until the great question which now agitates the whole country shall have been settled.

Allow me to say one word about that great matter—perhaps it is due to a proper degree of candour. You will recollect that at your suggestion I first came out as an humble supporter of Mr Adams; and as I then supposed of a wise liberal and firm administration—such an administration as would serve on all proper occasions to relieve the nation from a party persecution which had already disgraced it, and place every citizen upon the ground of virtuous conduct and fitness to serve his country. Although I never confided much in Mr. Adams, I am free to confess that I was persuaded by you, to believe that, those liberal and patriotic principles, which I knew you & your friends possessed, had been adopted by the Cabinet at Washington—and under the influence of that opinion and no other did I give my support to Mr. Adams. I fondly expected that in nominating for appointments the great question with Mr. Adams would be, "who is most fit, most faithful"—who possesses in the highest degree those talents and virtues which the office to be filled would call into action. You are aware that these hopes have been blasted and under such circumstances of indifference and contempt for the claims of a near & dear & lamented relative, which cannot be forgotten and which in my opinion ought not to be forgiven. I confess it gives me pain great pain to oppose a party to which you belong. But under these circumstances it is impossible for me to go with you—the injustice and *contempt* with which we have been treated, added to the more enlarged views which I have hinted—give rise to emotions not readily subdued—and by such a man as Saml Southard—who was not in truth worthy to be esteemed by a man like my Father—is enough to drive from the heart every feeling of civilization and humanity.

For what I have written I hope to find an excuse in our old friendship and that however we may wend our way in politics we may always retain personal good feelings towards each other.

The War is waging fiercer and fiercer in New Jersey. I send to you a document[2] which I ask you to read in your closet—candidly read—and then burn up if you please. I am most truly & affectionately

R. F. Stockton

ALS. NhD.   2. Not found.
   1. Not found.

TO JOSEPH E. SPRAGUE

Hanover July 20. 1828[1]

My dear Sir,

Your several letters have reached me here, beginning with that addressed to me at Nantucket.[2] Various things have successively occurred to put the "Address" out of my thoughts, or out of my power. I intended to have written you on the subject while at Boston, but in truth there were so many other things pressing, and I was under so urgent a necessity to get out of Town, for the sake of a little *rest*, that I omitted it. Without more of apology I wish now to say that if the paper is drawn up by another hand, I shall be very glad; if it be not and it is still wished that I should do it, I wish to suggest my opinion; according to which I would be willing to make an attempt at an address. That is that it should not be prepared and published till the first of October—or certainly not till September. The main reason for this opinion is that by the 20th of Augt. we shall be in possession of the result in Louisiana and Kentucky, of the pending elections. That result whether favorable or unfavorable will make a considerable change in our condition and prospects and the address would profitably be accomodated to the new state of things.[3]

I leave here for *home* tomorrow or tuesday. I shall be in Boston by Friday or Saturday when I hope to hear from you. Yours truly   D. W.

Copy. NhHi. Published in Van Tyne, pp. 138–139.

   1. According to the *New-Hampshire Statesman*, August 2, 1828, Daniel and Ezekiel had stopped in Hanover for a few days following a trip to northern New Hampshire. While in Hanover, Webster delivered a short address to the people of the community, a summary of which ap-

peared in the *Statesman* of the same date.

2. Not found.

3. Most likely Webster hoped to see an address to voters issued in Massachusetts, something similar to the suggestion he had made to Ezekiel. On October 11, 1828, the *Columbian Centinel* carried the "Address to the Citizens of the Commonwealth of Massachusetts," supporting the re-election of Adams. That address was perhaps drafted by Webster, revised by Sprague and others, and issued by the State Central Committee, a group of state legislators (see DW to Sprague, [August 16?, 1828], and [September 24?, 1828], below).

TO [SAMUEL BELL]

Boston July 29. 1828

Private & Confidential.
My Dear Sir

I was sorry not to see you, when I passed thro Chester; although I had nothing of particular importance to communicate, or to inquire about. As I passed only through the same parts of N. H. over which you travelled, about the same time, I can probably give you no valuable information, or suggestion, relative to the state of things in that quarter. One thing, however, occurred to me so strongly, & has occurred so often before, that I will mention it, with a view of submitting to you whether it does not require some particular attention. It is, that in the remote parts of the State, farthest from the sources of intelligence, & out of the way of much intercourse with other quarters, the Jackson party is, relatively speaking, much stronger than elsewhere. The Patriot circulates along all the borders, & is spread about with the utmost care. So I hear, too, it is in Maine. Along the line, on the Maine side, up under the mountains, & among the new settlements, no paper is seen, hardly, except the *Argus*. The effect of this, it is clear, (I mean of this almost exclusive circulation of the Patriot) was felt in the March Elections. The Towns, it is true, are small; but then if they are unanimous, or nearly so, their aggregate amount is considerable. It strikes me that efficient measures ought to be adopted, immediately, to put the good People in the remote parts of Strafford & Grafton, in possession of truth, & the enjoyment of its light. You & others round can best judge what ought to be, or what can be done; but it seems to me to be a branch of the general subject, which calls for particular attention.

You will probably have recd a communication from Hanover;[1] which I hope you will give such attention to, as you may think fit. The subject of it is deemed important, by friends, as one means of attaining the general end hoped for.

I have news from the West, of dates as late as the 19th. At that time, the very best hopes were entertained of Kentucky. Our friends were confident, that Metcalf would come in 5 or 6 thousand ahead. Ohio, too, is strong enough, tho' it is thought possible there may be one or two changes, in the Representation of the State. [John] Sloan[e] does not run. [John C.] Wright does, & expects a close race. [Philemon] Beecher also will be vigorously opposed. The rest of our friends have nothing to fear.

Indiana is not doing quite so well as we hoped. It is said Govr. [James Brown] Ray[2] has been playing double; & the people in that State are also mightily taken with the project of graduating the price of the public lands. Little fear, however, is entertained of Indiana, if Kentucky goes right. On that event much seems to depend. I trust good news will arrive from Louisiana to strengthen & encourage our friends in Kentucky. There seems no doubt that Mr [Edward] Livingston is beaten; & we hope that both [Henry H.] Gurley & [William L.] Brent are safe.

I should be glad to hear from you; & particularly to learn what you think of *Maine*. Yrs always truly   D. Webster

ALS. NhHi.   2. Ray was governor of Indiana,
    1. Not found.   1825–1831.

In the correspondence below, Webster uses his influence as a director of the Bank of the United States, and as one of its attorneys, to secure the appointment of Jeremiah Mason as president of the Portsmouth branch. For years, the Portsmouth office had been a subject of controversy. As early as 1821, a clerk had charged Edward Cutts, then president, with the responsibility for deficiencies exceeding $18,000 in the government's Pension Office there. James Shapely, Cutts' successor, had himself been lax in the renewal of notes and reportedly ended his association with the bank in 1828 under a cloud. Webster's friendship for Mason was probably not his only reason for seeking the appointment. He may have determined to preclude the employment of his friend as counsel against the bank, by Cutts, Shapely, or anyone else. In 1829, when Mason's own presidency of the branch became a subject of controversy, Biddle found it necessary to explain Webster's role in the appointment. "Mr. Webster had not the slightest agency in obtaining for him the appointment," Biddle assured Samuel D. Ingham, then secretary of the treasury. "His nomination was resolved upon without the knowledge either of Mr. Webster or Mr. Mason, and the only agency of Mr. Webster was, that, after the agent of the bank charged to make a choice had determined to recommend Mr. Mason, Mr. Webster was requested to endeavor to prevail upon him to serve; a request which the agent naturally made of Mr. Webster as a director of the bank." Reports of Committees of the House of Representatives, 22d Cong., 1st sess.,

1831–1832 (Serial 227), Document No. 460, p. 441; Fritz Redlich, The Molding of American Banking: Men and Ideas *(2 parts; New York, 1968), Part 1, p. 116; Norman Walker Smith, "A History of Commercial Banking in New Hampshire, 1792–1843" (Ph.D. dissertation, University of Wisconsin, 1967), pp. 181–183.*

TO JEREMIAH MASON

Aug 1. 1828

My Dear Sir

I have seen Mr. [Joseph] Copperthwaite[1] this morning, & had a full conversation with him respecting the state of the Bank at Portsmouth. At his request, I have agreed to write to you; & I come at once to the main matter. He thinks it important that you should take the Presidency of the Branch, if you can be persuaded to do so.[2] He says you manifested no disposition for it, but I did not learn from him that he had Suggested a probable increase of the Salary, as among the motives. It now stands, I hear at 800 Dlls. He desires me to say, confidentially, that if twice that amount would induce you to take the office, it wd. be given cheerfully.

In all probability, the amount of pay would not be a Subject of difference between you & the Bank, if you were inclined to have the office. He is to leave Boston, on Monday Morning; & I am anxious to hear from you before his departure.

I suppose you have weighed the *pros & Cons* & probably have a feeling, one way or the other, on the Subject. I do not wish to influence your judgment; but I should think it a great object with the Bank to obtain your services; & am persuaded they would pay as liberally as you should think they ought.

If you have made up your mind fully agt. it Mr. [Isaac] Waldron[3] will be appointed. In that case, the Bank will immediately crave leave to send you a large retainer, at least a proper one, & engage your professional services, with a desire that you should pay *particular* attention to its affairs, & be paid accordingly. After the receipt of this letter, I will thank you not to enter into any engagement adverse to the Bank, until there shall be time to hear from Philadelphia.

Contrive to let me have an answer on Sunday.

I write this at Beverly; having come down here to visit Mr [Israel] Thorndike's family.

I shall return to B. this Evening. Yours truly   D. Webster

Copy. NhHi. Published in *W & S*, 16: 180–181.

1. Later cashier of the parent bank at Philadelphia, Copperthwaite (usu-

ally spelled Cowperthwait) was probably an unofficial agent of Biddle's at this time, serving in much the same capacity of coordinating the bank's activities that Reuben M. Whitney later did.

2. Mason was subsequently elected president of the Portsmouth branch of the Bank of the United States.

3. Waldron (1774–1843) was a Portsmouth merchant.

TO JEREMIAH MASON

Boston Aug. 4, [1828] Monday Morning

My Dear Sir

I recd your letter last Evening,[1] & have this morning communicated its contents to Mr Copperthwaite. He is well satisfied with the letter. His instructions being to consult Gentlemen here is among the reasons why he was less explicit with you, in regard to your taking the Office, than he might otherwise have been; altho' he says what he saw & learned at Portsmouth operated very strongly to produce in his mind a wish to see you at the head of the Branch. He feels particularly gratified with the candor manifested by you, in speaking of men and things around you.

Mr Copperthwaite proceeds this morning for Philadelphia; & as soon as he arrives there will take care that you hear from him. There is probably no reason to doubt that the Board at Philadelphia will adopt the course which he shall advise. In the meantime it will be prudent to say little on the subject; & especially not to let it be understood that any augmentation of the Salary is proposed.

I write this with Mr C's knowledge and privity.

Begging to be remembered kindly to your family, I remain, as ever Yours truly   Danl. Webster

ALS. MHi.
1. Not found.

TO NICHOLAS BIDDLE

Boston Aug. 9. 1828

Private

My Dear Sir

I intended to write you earlier, in regard to the Portsmouth Office, but have omitted it, from the pressure of some other matters.

My own opinion is very clear, that the only *effectual* step is the appointment of Mr. Mason. His proposed compensation is liberal; but, then, I think he will well earn it. It appears to me that the true ground to put it on, is, to give him $1000 for discharging the duties of President, & $1000 for his professional services, in regard to the suspended debt. His eminent standing as a Lawyer, his great knowledge of every body about him, his independence, in every point of view, & the great confidence reposed in him by all, will be, all, in the highest degree useful to the Bank.

In the present state of things, his pecuniary interest will be best promoted by his engaging *agt* the Bank. And to secure his professional services, *for it*, would cost half the proposed compensation. I hardly know what can be done, but this, to inspire confidence, & give a fair opportunity to establish the rights of the Institution; tho' I think well of Mr Waldron, as a correct merchant, & an honest & respectable man. I have thought it a duty I owed to the Proprietors to speak thus decisively on the subject.

Mr. Copperthwaite, I presume, is now with you. Praying to be remembered to him, I am, with assurances of constant regard, Yours

D. Webster

ALS. NjMoHP.

FROM NICHOLAS BIDDLE

Bank of the U. States
Augt. 14. 1828

(Private)
My dear Sir,

I thank you for your favor of the 9th. inst[1] in regard to the Portsmouth Office which we have this day arranged agreeably to your recommendation. The only departure from it is that we have fixed the salary at $800 & the professional compensation at $1200. instead of making each $1000. This was done so as to preserve the symmetry of our system of compensation to the Presidents of offices of similar capital to that of Portsmouth, and not to make any invidious distinctions between them. To Mr Mason, the form is I presume indifferent.

It remains now to secure his election. You know that the Parent Board indicate their preference of a President by placing him at the head of the list, and this is usually decisive, but the election is actually with the Board of the Office, and altho' I have no reason to suppose that there will be any difficulty, yet it is always so much easier, if possible, to prevent than to overcome obstacles, that I wish you would take upon yourself to promote his election by any communication which you may deem judicious with the board of the office, whose names are subjoined.

I enclose Mr Mason's letter to you, and remain, With great regard Yrs

N Biddle, Prest.

ALS. NhHi. Printed in Reginald C.
McGrane, ed., *Correspondence of
Nicholas Biddle* . . . (Boston, 1919),

pp. 52–53.
1. See above.

TO JOSEPH E. SPRAGUE

Saturday Evening. [August 16?
1828]

My dear friend,

I hope you will not come up *tomorrow*, for though I am most sorry
to say it I have not yet succeeded to do any thing valuable. I find it exceedingly difficult to say any thing which has not been said before.[1]
Yesterday and today I have staid in my Study without being able to satisfy myself at all. Tomorrow I will write you again, not expecting to go
out of town till *Tuesday*. I have a letter this evening from Lexington
(Mr C[lay]) dated the 12th.[2] It is very good. It states in effect as follows
namely,—that General [Thomas] M[etcalf] is elected *by not less* than
1500 votes, that the Lieutenant Governor is also elected. That the late
Jackson speaker is defeated in his election. That there are ascertained
to be majorities favorable to the administration in at least two of the
districts now represented in Congress by Jackson members. That the
successor to General Metcalf in Congress is an Administration man, and
finally that in all probability there are majorities favorable to the administration in both branches of the Legislature. Yours truly always   D. W.

Copy. NhHi. Published in Van Tyne,
p. 139.
1. The purpose of the proposed
visit was probably to discuss the "ad-

dress" to the voters of Massachusetts.
See above, DW to Sprague, July 20,
1828.
2. Not found.

TO JOHN QUINCY ADAMS

Boston Sep. 13. 1828

Private & Confidential
Dr Sir

I herewith transmit copies of two letters, which passed, in Feb. 1825,
between Mr. [Henry] Warfield, of Maryland, & myself.[1] This correspondence, as far as I know, is the whole foundation of all that has been said
about the "Webster pledge."

My object now is to submit to your consideration, & that of those
around you, the expediency of publishing the letters. To that end, it
would be necessary first to obtain Mr Warfield's consent. The publication, if made, may be made, perhaps, by him, better than by others. If
Mr Clay had been at Washington, I should probably have written him,

on this subject; as I have reason to think that Mr Warfield has had some conversation with him upon it. In his absence, I am quite willing, if you so think best, that the papers should be handed to Mr. [Richard] *Rush*, & published, in such manner as his judgment may approve, Mr Warfield being first consulted. I have only to add the wish, that the mode of publication may be such as shall not make my appearance in the newspapers necessary, if any publication should be made. It strikes me that a short note from Mr Warfield to some Editor, transmiting the letters, would be the most eligible manner. But of this a better judgment can be formed by others. If thought better, on the whole, that the publication should be authorized by me, I will cause it to be done, if Mr W's consent be obtained. I do not write to him, not knowing his Address.[2] Yours always truly   Danl. Webster

ALS. MHi. Published in Van Tyne, p. 140.

1. See above, Henry R. Warfield to DW, February 3, 1825; and DW to Warfield, February 5, 1825.

2. No contemporary publication of the Webster-Warfield correspondence has been found.

FROM JONATHAN HUNT

Brattleboro' Sept. 21. 1828

Sir,

Your letter of the 15th inst. arrived during my absence,[1] at Court, & I have but a moment to return this answer, as I am now about leaving for Court again. We should be much pleased to see you & Daughter the fore part of next month at our house if convenient for you. The second Thursday of October I shall expect to be at Montpelier, or soon after that, as our Legislature will then be in session.

In relation to your proposal about our taking lodgings at Washington, which you are pleased to make, you certainly do us much honor. It is now expected that Mrs H & two children will accompany me to W. but as they are small I fear they will be an incumbrance to your comfort— if however it can be so arranged that you can be accommodated Mrs H. would be pleased with your Daughter's company. Until the receipt of your favour it was our intention to take rooms for ourselves & children; but if the arrangement could be made to accommodate you, it would afford us much satisfaction.

As Mrs. H. expects to accompany me to Montpelier, will you be kind enough to inform me by letter, at what time it will be convenient for you to make us the proposed visit. I am, Sir, very respectfully yours,

Jona: Hunt

ALS. NhHi.

1. Not found.

TO NATHANIEL SILSBEE

Boston 22 September 1828.

Dear Sir,

Enclosed you have a letter from Mr Clay, and a statement relative to the condition of affairs in New York.[1] They have been submitted to several Gentlemen in this town, and a considerable sum has been raised by subscription at a meeting this day; which, however, is not considered adequate to the emergency. It is deemed highly desirable that Gentlemen in Salem, interested in the Cause, would, on this Occasion, unite with our friends in Boston. We are, Dear Sir, Respectfully Yours,

> Danl. Webster
> Bn Gorham
> Edward Everett.

The following sums are among those subscribed

P[eter] C[hardon] Brooks	$800
John Welles	300
John Parker	400
Sam[ue]l Appleton	300
B[enjamin] Bussey[2]	200
Pat[rick Tracy] Jackson	200
N[athan] Appleton	200
A & A Lawrence	200
E. Everett	100
J. Coolidge	150
Geo. Blake	100

Messrs. [Israel] Thorndike, [David] Sears, T. H. Perkins and G[ardiner] Greene[3] were absent from the meeting but it is understood will contribute. About $4000 have been subscribed for this service; but we are satisfied that from one to two thousand dollars more are absolutely wanted. We venture to hope that you will show this to Mr [Benjamin W.] Crowninshield, to Mr [Joseph] Peabody, to Mr. D[udley] L. Pickman[4] and to other Gentlemen interested in the cause and use your efforts to promote the objects. The nature of the case admits of no delay, and a considerable part of the sum here subscribed is already forwarded.

It is unnecessary to add that this communication and the documents inclosed are in the highest degree confidential.

LS. MH.

1. An endorsement on the letter reads: "I find *no* enclosed 'letter or documents.' N. D. S."

2. Welles, Parker, Appleton, and Bussey were all bankers and merchants.

3. Greene (d. 1832) was a merchant and at the time president of the Boston branch of the Bank of the United States.

4. Peabody (1787–1842) and Pickman (1779–1846) were Salem merchants.

TO JOSEPH E. SPRAGUE

Wednesday Morning. [September 24?, 1828]

Dear Sir,

I believe you will do well to put this address into other hands at once,[1] and those other hands I am clear should be your *own*. Strike out the thing, and I will go over it with you, if you desire it and make any suggestions which occur to me. I have really been too unwell for these three weeks past to do anything. The letter which you saw yesterday must also be attended to,[2] and in my present condition I can *beg* better than I can write. Yours faithfully   D. Webster

I shall see you tomorrow if weather and health allow.

Copy. NhHi. Published in Van Tyne, pp. 140–141.

1. See above, pp. 355–356, 361.

2. Webster was probably referring to his letter of September 22, to Nathaniel Silsbee, above.

The size of Jackson's victory in the election of 1828 was a shock even to the Jacksonians. During the months preceding the election, both the National Republicans and the Jacksonians had talked of victory, but few had expected Jackson to march away with 178 of a possible 261 electoral votes, especially not Clay or Webster. In the congressional elections of 1827, and again in the summer of 1828, both men had interpreted every success of an Adams supporter as clear indication that the President would be reelected. When the voters appeared at the polls between October and November, they turned in a different verdict. Adams carried only the New England states, Maryland, and Delaware. Even in Kentucky, Clay's home state, where only recently voters had elected the Adams candidate Thomas Metcalfe governor, Jackson scored a resounding victory. When the final results were known in late November, Clay tersely remarked, "We are beaten," while Webster maintained a studied silence on the results.

TO NATHANIEL F. WILLIAMS

Boston Septr. 25. 1828

Private

Dear Sir

Your letter has remained long unanswered,[1] owing mainly to the circumstances of my absence from Town.

If more convenient for you to draw on me for the sum (500) payable in 3 or 4 mo, than to wait its adjustment as I go thro your City, you are at liberty to do so.

I believe, My Dear Sir, it is now very likely that Maryland will decide the election. We need, as you know, 131 votes. We may calculate, I trust, upon all N. E.—say 51—upon Kentucky, Ohio, Indiana, & Louisiana, 40—These make 91 votes. Eight from N. Jersey & three from Delaware will give a result of 102—Twenty nine votes will be still wanting. We have no place to look for these but N York & Maryland. We hope to have 20 Districts for us in N York—& the two Electors, also, who are chosen by the others—say 22 in all. We shall still need 7 votes. *Can you promise them to us, from Maryland?*

I should be glad to hear from you. Nothing of interest is occurring here, since the Maine Election. Give yourself no uneasiness about any part of N England. Yours truly   D. Webster

I do not at all mean to say I despair of Penna. & N. Carolina. I am looking at things, in the worst aspect.

ALS. NhD.   1. Not found.

TO [MARTIN VAN BUREN?]

Boston Sep. 27. '28

My Dear Sir

I recd your's this morning,[1] & my first inclination was that I would meet you & Mr [Henry B.] Cowles at New York, on the 4th Oct. according to your suggestion. I find, however, on reflection, that I have engagements, which would render *that day*, rather an inconvenient one, for such an appointment. Engagements are on me, for the latter end of next week, which it is not easy to shake off. I am disposed, however, to conform to your suggestion, in its general object, & varied [?] only as to *time*. At the same time, it may be worth considering, whether it be not practicable to accomplish the object by one journey, instead of two. In other words, whether it would not be as useful, in regard to the main object, & less inconvenient to ourselves, to be in N York four or five days before the sitting of the Court. Upon reflection, this rather appears to me to be, under all circumstances, the preferable course. Still, I do not feel positive about it; & if it be, in your mind, matter of doubt, the previous conference is the safer mode, & ought to be adopted. What has led to this impression, on my mind is, that we have no testimony, that I am aware of, farther off than Putnam County; that our chief labor will be, to consider, how best to use what materials we have; & that coming together, four days before the Court, each having, in the meantime, turned his attention to all known questions in the cause, there will be time enough to settle the course of the defense, & summon witnesses on any new point; if such should occur to us.[2] It would be somewhat disagreeable to me thus to extend the time of my stay in N. York, at the time of the trial; but on the whole I should prefer this, to another journey.

Nevertheless, My Dear Sir, I am disposed to follow your lead, because you have a better view of the whole ground, as well as for other reasons. Therefore I will meet you and Mr Cowles at N York, any time after hearing from you, but so as that I can be home again by the 15 or 16 October. You will probably receive this the morning of the *first*. If you answer by return of Post, I shall hear from you by the 5th.—& can meet you in N York, the 8th—9th—10th—11th or 12th, if you should so conclude.

Allowing me three days after the proper time for the arrival of your letter, you may expect my attendance, on any day you may mention, within the above mentioned period. So much for "the weightier matters of the law."

As to the rest, My D. Sir, I do not hear that the "political health of my friends," in the great State needs, at present, either prescription or nursing. If not decidedly *good*, we are assured it is very satisfactorily *convalescent*. That State, we learn, is likely to enjoy soon what is said to comprize the whole substance of mortal bliss—"*sana mens*, in corpore sano."

Adieu! I would give you the Spanish benediction, ("God preserve your *Excellency* a thousand years!") but that I have not yet heard from Herkimer, and you have not informed me what *orders you sent up*.[3] But *masters* must be sometimes *servants*; do you not find it so? Yrs truly

D. Webster

ALS. MHi.

1. Not found.

2. The purpose of the meeting between Van Buren, Cowles, and Webster was to confer on a case involv-

ing the Astor lands.

3. At the Herkimer convention in late September, New York Democrats nominated Van Buren as their candidate for governor.

TO EZEKIEL WEBSTER

Boston Sunday Eve
[September 28, 1828]

Dear E.

I learned from Mr [Ninian Clark] Betton,[1] that you expected soon to come this way. I hope it will be this week, as I shall be at home for the next ten days; & do not know how it may be, in that respect, afterw[ar]d. You told me the general run of your engagements, thro the autumn, but I have a good deal forgotten it. I am liable to be called away to N York—indeed expect I must go—but otherwise hope to be at home till late in Novr. I want much to see you, & will thank you to inform me what your plans are, & how your time is likely to be occupied.

I have a plan for our children spending a part of the winter together, which I wish to submit to you. It is, that Alice & Mary[2] & Julia & Edward come to Boston, about a month hence, all together; that at the meeting of the Legislature at Concord, Mrs W. come down & join them, & stay till you are thro' the Session, & as much longer as you can spare her; & when you come for her, let her take home with her as many of the children as she pleases. It will be, I should hope, not unpleasant to Mrs W. & might give A. & Mary an opportunity to attend to some useful things.

Pray make my most affectionate regards to your wife, & submit this matter to her serious consideration.

I had a letter from Julia yesterday, for which give her my thanks.[3] Uncle William sends to her & Edward something, by this post; & he says a letter will be found among the *things*. He & Daniel are quite well. My own health is much improved, & now pretty good.

Our most recent political news is rather cheering. Maryland, it is said, is doing exceedingly well, & may be reconed good for 9 votes. Twenty from N York will, in that case, carry us thro. Mr Story has been here, & is full of hopes. Some of our friends calculate on 26 votes in that State. The Herkimer Convention has nominated Mr V. Buren for Govr.

Pray let me hear from you. Yrs affectionately   D Webster

ALS. NhD.

1. Betton (1787–1856; Dartmouth 1814) was an attorney, having read law with both Ezekiel and Daniel Webster. After a few years in practice in Hanover, he settled in Boston, where he combined his law practice with service in the Massachusetts legislature.

2. Alice (1814–1876) and Mary (1816–1864) were Ezekiel's daughters.

3. See Julia Webster to DW, September 25, 1828, mDW 7211.

TO HENRY CLAY

Boston Oct. 1 '28

Private

My Dear Sir

I hope this will meet you at Washington, in bettered health, & good spirits. You will have recd. a short letter from me, of date ten days earlier than the present,[1] & also a letter from our friend Mr Welch.[2] I am afraid those communications would have done more good, if they could have reached their ultimate destination earlier; but altho' yours from the Springs was promptly attended to,[3] some delay, I fear, has, or may have, arisen from communicating with you, instead of writing directly to others. There were objections, however, to the latter course, which we could not well get over. If my letter & Mr Welch's were forwarded to you, they would be recd. in tolerable season. If they stopped at Washington, it will be less fortunate.

I observe, however, that the election in K[entucky] does not take place till Novr. 10.

Our friend Mr [Henry Randolph] Storrs has been here, & made us a very short visit. His hopes are good. The doubtful Districts, he says, lie in his neighborhood, & great efforts will be made in them, on both sides; & at present the expectation of himself & friends is better than it has been. We were glad to see him, & he was gratified with his visit.

I believe, My Dear Sir, Mr Adams will be reelected, if K. goes for him. What we hear from Maryland & N York is so encouraging, that no pains ought now to be spared. I think the object is fairly within reach. You will have seen that there is no fear of losing a vote in N. England. I feel some anxiety for Delaware; but the question will soon be settled there.

Is there any thing further that *I*, or *we*, can do?

God bless you   Danl. Webster

ALS. DLC.   Letter not found.
  1. Not found.   3. Not found.
  2. Welch has not been identified.

FROM KENSEY JOHNS, JR.

New Castle October 9th. 1828

Dr. Sir,

The result of our election presents Delaware on the side of the Administration by a Majority greater than last year. Our Members of the Legislature from the counties of Kent & Sussex are all elected & the electoral vote of this state is sure. Respectfully Your friend &c   K. Johns Jr

	Jackson	Administration
	Bayards Majority	Johns Jr Majority
New Castle County	325	
Kent County		294
Sussex County		450
		744
deduct Bayards majority—		325
Johns Jr. Majority in the State—		419

ALS. NhHi.

TO [JACOB MCGAW]

Boston Oct. 11. '28

My Dear friend,

I thank you for your letter of Sep. 26, detailing the incidents of your tour.[1] It has enabled me to go, pretty accurately, over your track, & I have followed you, by the means of it, repeatedly from Boston round by the West, & home to Bangor. I well understand how you should feel excited by visiting such places as Kingsbridge, White Plains, Bemis' Heights, etc. I never knew a man yet, nor a woman neither, with a sound head & a good heart, that was not more or less under the power, which those local associations exercise. It is true, that *place*, in these things, is originally accidental. Battles *might have been* fought elsewhere, as well as at Saratoga, or Bennington. Nevertheless, here they *were fought*; & nature does not allow us to pass over the scenes of such events with indifference, unless we have a good share of bluntness & stupidity, or unless the scenes themselves have become familiar by frequent visits to them. For my part, I love them all, and all such as they. An old *Drum* hangs up in the Senate Chamber of Mass., taken from the Hessians at Bennington, & I do not think I ever went into the room without turning to look at it. And that reminds me to say, that I have a pair of silver *sleeve buttons*, the material of which my father picked up on, & brought away from, that same field of Bennington. If I thought either of my boys would not value them, fifty years hence, if he should live so long, I believe I should begin to flog him, now.

The day we parted here was, in truth, very hot. I reached Falmouth, at evening, very much exhausted by heat & fatigue. The next morning we embarked for Nantucket, & had a good passage. There I staid a week, exceedingly busy, all the time, & hurrying thro' business, in order to shorten our stay. Work & heat, (a good deal too much of both) made me sick; & after I returned from the Island, it was a month before I felt quite well. Cooler weather & repose have, at length, accomplished my restoration. My health is now good, & I shall have occasion for all of it, for the next month or two, during which professional engagements are usually most pressing.

Julia & Edward are still at Boscawen. At the end of this month they will come home, & both their little cousins with them. Mrs E. Webster is to come down, & to keep all the children here, for a month or two, while her husband is engaged with the Courts, & the Legislature. My present purpose is not to be in great haste to depart for Washington, unless some urgent public duty should require it. In the present condition of my household, it is a great object to shorten my absence as far as I well can.

I rejoice that you found your little daughter, & your other connexions well; & that the journey proved so favorable to Mrs McGaw's health. Nothing is better, I think, than a tour of that sort, once in a while, to places not before visited, & to the midst of society a little different from that in our own circle. It is not only gratifying, at the moment, but furnishes many things, to think about, & talk over, for a long time. The mind requires occasionally a supply of new ideas, or else it is likely to get out of stock. New books, (or books never read before) will sometimes enable the inner man to gratify himself with a change of ideas, [(]which are his diet), & a visit to new scenes, & new circles, often does the same thing more effectually. For my part, I journey a good deal, but it is all on the beaten track from Boston to Washington. Once we made an exception, & went, as you know, to Niagara. It was a high gratification. I advise you to keep your eye on such a tour, at some time, hereafter. Why is it not a sort of duty, before we leave this world, "thus wondrous fair," to see all the wonders, which it is fairly in our power to see, &, by beholding them, to derive a new excitement to our veneration & adoration of the Deity? I confess that natural Religion—that conviction of the existence & perfection of the Deity, which the contemplation of natural objects produces,—grows daily more & more impressive on my mind.

But I must stop—or I shall write a sermon. Adieu—I have not written so tediously long a letter, in a twelve month. Give every good wish of my heart to your wife—and, as we Yankees say, "the same to yourself." Yrs always truly   Danl. Webster

ALS. NhD. Published in Van Tyne,   1. Not found.
pp. 736–738.

TO HENRY CLAY

Boston Oct 23. 1828

Private
My Dear Sir,

I am obliged to you for yours, recd two posts back.[1] One part of its object, you will have seen or heard, had been anticipated, & your friend & Neighbor will have before this recd the proper communication.

The favorable results in Maryland & Delaware seem now to put the general object fairly within our reach, with proper exertion, & common good fortune. In my judgment, nothing fair & honorable should be spared. If we hold Kentucky, I have now full faith that we shall get votes enough in New York to ensure Mr A's reelection. No doubt every useful mode of communication will occur to our friends, but I take the liberty of suggesting the expediency of letters, written or printed, from friends in Washington to friends in every part of Kentucky, laying before them the true state of things, as it is at present presented, & thus showing them the great probability that the vote of K. will decide the above. Our friends here ought to be made to feel, as the ancient combatants felt, that the issue of the contest may depend on a single arm. I know, at the same time, their zeal & steadiness; & that they will not be likely to omit reasonable exertions. Still, new hope would naturally inspire new vigor. Let me add, in a word; *if anything remains to be done, to secure the vote of K. do it.*

I have seen David Trimble's publication, which, I should think, must do good.[2] The back part of your letter is that which gives assurance of the improvement of your health. May God preserve you—for your own sake & the Country. Truly yrs   D. Webster

ALS. DLC.
1. Not found.
2. *Address of David Trimble, to the public, containing proof that he did not make statements attributed to* him, *in relation to charges against the President of the United States, and Mr. Henry Clay* (Frankfort, 1828).

FROM HENRY CLAY

Washn. 24th Oct. 1828.

(Confidential)

My dear Sir

Although some of the Congressional results in Ohio are to be regretted, my belief is unshaken that we shall get the State by a large majority. The returns in [Elisha] Whittleseys, Bartletts [Mordecai Bartley's], [Samuel F.] Vintons & MClanes [William McLean's] districts are not yet fully recd.[1] In them our majorities will be very great. [Allen] Trimble will be re-elected by many thousands, and he, you know, was the Admin. Candidate for Govr.

My intelligence from K[entucky] continues good, very good. I have heard of the safe reception there of what you have sent.[2] All has been done, and will continue to be done, that honorable men can or ought to do.

I yet think that Mr. Adams will be re-elected; but it is mortifying, and sickening to the hearts of the real lovers of free Government, that the contest should be so close; and that if Heaven grants us success it will be perhaps by less than a majority of six votes.

I thank you for the hint about Mr. B.[3] who has not yet called. Always Cordially Your friend   H. Clay

ALS. DLC. Published in Curtis, 1: 334–335.
1. McLean had declined to seek re-election, but Joseph H. Crane, the administration candidate, won over the Jackson nominee.
2. Not identified.
3. Not identified.

FROM ESTWICK EVANS

Portsmo. Octo. 28th, 1828

Dear Sir,

As the Presidential Election in New Hampshire will take place on the 3rd of next month, the people of this State, will, after that time, turn their attention to our congressional election.

It is universally understood that Mr [Ichabod] Bartlett does not wish to be again considered a candidate for Representative to Congress. He has informed many, including myself, of this fact; indeed he told me a few days since that he sent a note to this effect to the Rockingham Representatives during our last June session.

The question is now asked here, as to his successor, if I may so speak. I do not know that any one has been named excepting myself. You will readily perceive, I think, the policy of my being brought forward to take his place, by the Administration Party. No pains, you will agree, should be spared to break down those partition walls which have heretofore divided the patriotic people of this country, not, comparatively, at all, upon a difference of principle or sentiment, but upon a sense of supposed, mutual injustice, & the errors, in feeling & acting, incident to great party excitement.

The parties in this State are now, as I apprehend, about equally divided. Should Jackson be elected, there will be additions to the strength of his party here; & if Mr Adams should succeed, there will be the same sort of contest among us that now exists, & pretty much upon the same basis.

I am willing, as a matter of propriety & of public utility, to give one half of our congressional ticket to the old federal party. I consider the two old parties as now merged in the Administration & Jackson parties; & I believe it would be, not only negatively, but positively well for the country to act, in future, without any reference to former party distinctions.

I believe, sir, that I stand *well* with the Administration Party, & that they would cheerfully support me for Congress. As to the Jacksonians, a great many of them are my warm personal friends; & these would, I *presume*, vote for me in preference to any other person.

Upon these grounds I take it for granted that I should command a very large majority; my success would be the success of the Administration party, & would certainly give support to the whole ticket. The mere circumstance of my being brought forward & sustained by this party would be considered *solid* testimony in proof that republicanism is the basis of it. The Jacksonians will never doubt my integrity or my patriotism. There is not a man of them with whom I cannot most freely associate; & thousands of them would be influenced by my opinions & reasonings upon the subject of parties, on the ground of their confidence in me, & the readiness with which I can perceive from my long acquaintance with them, their suspicions & motives, & the manner in which the associating principle operates in their minds.

If the unreasonable spirit of party in this state, with reference to old distinctions, is to be done away;—if this is the object, & I believe it a very patriotic one, means must be employed to effect it. A cautious & a steady course will effect it. Let it be an open course, & one that will stand the test of enquiry. Let the congressional ticket be made up of one half *unquestionable* republicans & one half federalists, as the Jacksonians would say. When I speak of a cautious course I mean that there should not be evinced any disposition on the part of the federalists to monopolize the whole ticket directly or indirectly. This would probably not succeed & if it should, it would produce irritation & a reaction &c.

I really, sir, do not know of so politic a step, that the Administration party in this State could take, as their nominating me for Rockingham. This step of itself would do them much credit;—it would also tend to heal party differences.

This subject is not new to many of your friends in Portsmouth. Our Legislature meets about the 10th I believe, of next month, & there the conventions formed by the Representatives in each county will nominate. I am universally known as an Administration man; but am waiting to be brought forward by the A[dministration] Party, to do & to accomplish much. I am, Dear Sir, with great respect Your friend & obed servt.

E. Evans

P S I should be gratified, sir, to have you interest yourself a little upon this subject. E E

ALS. NhHi.

TO JOSEPH HOPKINSON

Boston Octr. 29. 1828

My Dear Friend

I am not willing to pass a post, without expressing to you the pleasure I feel in hearing today of your appointment to the Bench.[1] To yourself, I am aware it is of little importance; but it is a matter of consequence to the Judicial system, generally, & to your District particularly. Again I say, I rejoice.

It may be a little later than usual that I see you, this autumn. Many things make it most desirable to me to shorten the period of my absence as much as may be, & unless something urgent should arise, I incline to think it will be December before I leave home.

I pray to be remembered to Mrs. Hopkinson & Elizabeth; & to add assurance of my constant regard   Danl. Webster

Nobody will be more gratified with your appointment than Judge Story.

ALS. PHi. Published in part in Burton Alva Konkle, *Joseph Hopkinson, 1770–1842: Jurist, Scholar, Inspirer of the Arts* (Philadelphia, 1931), p. 267.

1. President Adams had appointed Hopkinson judge of the federal district court for eastern Pennsylvania.

In the correspondence below, Webster suggests to Nicholas Biddle, president of the Bank of the United States, and to Gardiner Greene, president of the Boston branch, that James W. Paige, his brother-in-law and then a partner of Nathan Appleton, be named to one of the vacancies in the directorship of the Boston branch. Distrustful of the Boston president, Webster feared that Greene might be trying to obviate his wishes; Biddle, however, quickly resolved the misunderstanding, and without opposition Paige was elected a director in 1828, to serve with Greene, Daniel P. Parker (1781–1850), a merchant and former partner of Nathan Appleton; Resin D. Shepherd, merchant; David Sears (1787–1871; Harvard 1807), a merchant, former director of the parent bank, and close friend of Webster; John Borland, merchant; George Blake, longtime personal and professional friend of Webster; Ebenezer Chadwick, merchant; Thomas Handasyd Perkins, merchant in the China trade and already one of Webster's key advisers; William Hammond, merchant; Samuel Appleton, merchant, manufacturer, and brother of Nathan; B. W. Crowninshield, former director of the parent bank, shipper, merchant, and client of Webster; and George Hallett, merchant. All in all, with Paige's nomination to the Boston board, Webster could claim as close personal or professional friends or clients seven of the twelve directors of the Boston office in 1829. But all was not well with the Boston branch: Webster's friends on the board often found Greene incommunicative and uncooperative in revealing to them the bank's activities (see below, pp. 402–404).

TO NICHOLAS BIDDLE

Boston Oct. 30. 1828

Private

My Dear Sir

As the time draws near for the appointment of Directors for the Office here, I take this mode of bringing to your notice a Gentleman, as candidate for a seat at the Board. He is Mr. J. W. Paige.[1] I must begin by saying that he is a connexion of mine, being Mrs W's half brother. Premising this, by way of due qualification of my opinion, I proceed to express that opinion frankly, which is, that he is singularly qualified to be useful to the Institution. He has been an importing merchant in this City, for 12 or 15 years; & as a man of business is exact, discreet, & diligent. The course of his business has made him extensively acquainted with the credit & standing of a large class of persons, such as are likely to have more or less to do with the Bank. He is now about changing his line of business, & in connexion with one of our most respectable merchants, Mr N[athan] Appleton, is to undertake the sale of the manufactured goods, from the larger factories in this neighborhood. This business will be very extensive, & must necessarily connect him much with the business of the southern Cities in their branches. No doubt, it would be desirable to more than one of the local Banks, that he should connect himself with such Bank—but his preference is for the Office of the U. S. B. I have therefore taken the liberty of suggesting his name to you. As a man of probity, property, intelligence, & discretion, I venture to give him a high & decisive character. As he is a friend of mine, I have thought it proper to mention his name to you, in such season as that you might have time to inquire of others. You may safely ask, of any [of] your acquaintances here, Mr Paige's character & standing as a merchant, & of his fitness, by his acquaintance with a numerous class of probable borrowers, & the nature & course of his business, for usefulness in the situation of a Director.

I write this, without knowing who goes out of the Direction this year; &, certainly, without wishing to make any vacancy, for the sake of filling it with Mr. Paige. There will, I suppose, however, be sundry vacancies of course.

I hear with pleasure that the appointment at Portsmouth is satisfactory to those concerned with the Bank. I am sure it will be most useful to the Bank itself. Yours with entire regard,   Danl. Webster

ALS. DLC.
1. Paige was elected a director of

the Boston branch of the Bank of the United States in November.

TO NICHOLAS BIDDLE

Novr. 1. 1828

Private & Confidential
My Dear Sir,

I thought it would be well to address a note to Mr [Gardiner] Greene,[1] the President of the Office, suggesting to him the propriety of nominating Mr. Paige to you, for a seat at the Board of Direction here. I have recd from him this morning a letter, of which I now enclose a copy.[2]

I wish further to state, in strict & close confidence, that I had a hint, yesterday, that Mr Greene had *already sent on* the names, whom he wished appointed. I can hardly believe that, since it would fix the character of disingenuousness upon his note to me. If such list have been sent on, I yet beg the favor of you to write Mr Greene, &, according to the expectation intimated in his letter, inquire of him whether he thinks Mr. P. a fit person to be appointed. I beg to assure you, what I am sure you will not doubt, that this appointment is not of the slightest personal interest to me, in the gross sense of that word; nevertheless, on sundry accounts, I feel some concern for it. It would seem just, I think, that the two Directors of the Parent Bank, who are on the spot here, should be consulted, as to the list.[3] *This has not been done, if any list has been already sent.* It is proper, too, perhaps, that the Gentlemen remaining at the Board, & the Cashier, a most excellent—a truly invaluable Officer— should have some voice, in such matters. How this has been, in this case I have not felt authorized to inquire; but, if a list has really been sent on, I should entertain doubts whether it had been the subject *of a very extended conversation.* You will understand me as writing this in strict personal confidence. If a list has gone on, still, it is not too late to consider the matter; & without inquiring under what circumstances it was sent, I only wish Mr. Greene to be now asked whether he recommends Mr Paige. And as introductory to this, I am quite willing you should inform Mr Greene, that I, as one of the Directors of the Parent Board, have written to the Board recommending Mr. Paige for the appointment.

In great haste, but with much true regard, Yours   Danl Webster

ALS. DLC.
1. Not found.
2. See Greene to DW, October 31, 1828, mDW 7300.

3. Webster and Nathaniel Silsbee were the two directors of the bank from Massachusetts.

FROM NICHOLAS BIDDLE

Phila. Nov. 4. 1828

(Confidential)
My dear Sir,

I received this morning your favor of the 1st inst & hasten to answer it by the return of mail,[1] in order to remove, with the least possible delay, the misapprehension in regard to the course pursued, by the gentleman whose letter to you was inclosed to me in your's. Between him & myself nothing whatever had passed in regard to the election at the date of his letter to you.

My practice is at the approach of an election to write to the President or Cashier—or both—requesting them to confer with the members of the Parent Board resident near them—and send on a list of the new Directors. I did not write last year until the 12th of November—but on receiving your first letter, in order to obtain the necessary information, I thought it better to write to Mr Greene earlier than usual, so as to allow time for an interchange of opinions. Your letter reached me on Sunday the 2d. The next morning I wrote to Mr G. as follows:

B U S. Novr. 3. 1828

Dear Sir,

Will you & Mr [Samuel] Frothingham have the goodness to confer with Mr Webster & Mr [Nathaniel] Silsbee, & give us your views as to the best mode of filling the vacancies at the approaching election. With great respect Yrs   N B

G. Greene Esq.

Prest &c.

At the same time—in order to obtain the necessary information in regard to Mr Paige, & to bring him before Mr Greene with the benefit of your nomination, I wrote a private letter to Mr Greene—stating that you had strongly recommended Mr Paige—& had named him early in order to afford an opportunity of making enquiries in regard to him—that I had "the highest respect & regard for Mr Webster—& would always have pleasure in gratifying any wish of his"—but was desirous of having the opinion of himself & the gentlemen habitually consulted on these matters, as to the nomination of Mr Paige. Thus the matter stands.

You will perceive I hope from this detail that the subject has been placed in a proper train and I have no doubt will result to your satisfaction. I have written to Mr Silsbee requesting him to confer with the gentleman named in my letter to Mr Greene, but without mentioning the name of Mr Paige, as my private letter to Mr. Greene would necessarily bring the nomination before him. I observe that Mr Greene speaks of the election of *four* new Directors—but *five* are wanted for if I do not mistake, Mr [Israel] Munson, Mr [John] Parker, Mr [John] Welles, Mr [R. S.] Rogers & Mr [Thomas H.] Perkins have all served three successive years & of course are not reeligible.[2]

I shall be happy to hear from you again on this subject—& remain meanwhile Very sincerely Yrs   N Biddle

ALS. DLC.

1. See above.

2. Biddle erred when he assumed that Perkins was ineligible for the board of directors; Perkins had not been listed among the Boston directors for at least two years and was, indeed, named to the post a few weeks later.

TO NATHANIEL F. WILLIAMS

Boston Novr 5. [1828]
Wednesday 12 o'clock

Private

Dr Sir

The accounts recd. here last evening & this morning leave us easy, as to any apprehension about N Hampshire, or the Cumberland District in Maine. You will be quite safe, I think, in considering it certain that the New England votes will be wholly undivided.

Our latest information from N York is favorable. The western part of the State, especially, is expected to be nearly unanimous for Mr. Adams. It is very probable, I think, that your City may decide the matter. Yrs truly   D. Webster

Don't make any public use of my name—as to this matter.   D W

ALS. NhD.

TO NICHOLAS BIDDLE

Boston Novr. 7. [1828]

Dr Sir

I have recd yours, this morning.[1] Mr Greene has called on me this morning, & the following arrangement is agreed on. Mr [Nathaniel] Silsbee will see it today, & no doubt approve it. It is a good list—& I assure you *much* improved by the last name. It makes a good *composition*—Greene, D[aniel] P. Parker, [Ebenezer] Chadwick, [John] Borland, [David] Sears, [George] Blake, [R. D.] Shepherd, S[amuel] Appleton, [William] Hammond, [George] Hallet, T. H. Perkins, [B. W.] Crowningshield, Paige.[2] Yours always truly   D. Webster

ALS. DLC.
1. See above, Biddle to DW, November 4, 1828.

2. All of those mentioned were named directors in November 1828.

TO [JOHN BRAZER]

1828. Boston. Novem 10.

Dear Sir.

I part with [Richard] Whately[1] not without regret, as I have not had leisure to go through with him regularly, though I have had some good snatches here & there. It is a good book. If it were not for the appearance of self conceit I would say that I have found in it twenty things which I have thought of often, & have been convinced of often, but never before seen in print. He shows sense especially in the preeminence he gives to perspicuity & energy as qualities of style. I like his hatred of adjectives & his love of Saxon words, & his idea of the true use of repetition. This last might be much further explained than it is done by him. There is something which may be called *augmentative* repetition that is capable sometimes of producing great effect. "The author of the murder stood by the side of his victim, wet, bathed with the blood he had shed," or, "The murderer stood by the side of the slain, his sandals wet with the blood—the warm, gushing blood of his victim." In this last case by the way adjectives do their office; they add definite ideas. What Mr. W says of the effect of particularization is just, especially as applied to pathetic description. The skilful & apparently natural enumeration of particulars, is certainly in its proper place one of the very best models of producing impression. All the standard works are full of this kind of composition. Perhaps the very best & most touching, is in the 12th verse of the 7 chapter of Luke. Here are comprised in that simple paragraph— A death—A funeral—The death of a young person (for his mother was living) [—]The death of a son—The death of an only son—The son of a living mother—That mother a widow. You remember much better than I do what a burst [Jean Baptiste] Massillon² has at the opening of his sermon on this text. This fine passage would have been tame enough sinking all particulars—only relating that when he came to the city he met the funeral of one who had died under very afflicting circumstances. Additional effect is given to the incident by fixing so nearly the *place* where it happened—*nigh* to the *gate* of the *city*. This minute statement of place as well as of time gives great notedness to narrative composition. Homer & DeFoe I regard as the greatest masters of this part of their art—always excepting the Scriptures. Mr. Whatelys rejection of expletives & epithets shews his just perception of strength & beauty. Yet particularization is sometimes out of place. There are cases in which comprehension or generalization is altogether preferable. Suppose one should say "The distinction of the Christian Revelation is that it is adapted not only to Englishmen but also to Frenchmen, Spaniards, Germans, Italians, Russians, Prussians etc. etc." This would be feeble. Better thus "The distinction of the Christian dispensation is that it reveals truths not to a few favored individuals, but to all the race of men— not to a single nation, but to the whole world." A book might be written upon this little question: When is effect produced by generalization— when by particularization? At least a book might be filled with apposite instances of both kinds—from our English classics—especially the Scriptures—Shakespeare & Milton. An accurate writer should avoid generalities sometimes—but not always—but *when* it would require a treatise to expound. I rejoice to see one Rhetorician who will allow nothing to words but as they are signs of ideas. The rule is a good one, to use no word which does not suggest an idea or modify some idea already suggested. And this should lead writers to adopt sparingly the use of such words as "vast," "amazing," etc. For what do they mean? Dr [Isaac] Watts,[3] (who by the way I do not deem altogether a bad poet) somewhere speaks of the flight of an angel as being with most "amazing speed." But what idea is conveyed by this mode of expression? What is "amazing speed?" It would amaze us to see an oyster moving a mile in a day. It would not amaze us to see a greyhound run a mile in a minute. On the other hand see with what unequalled skill Milton represents both the distance through which, and the speed with which, Mulciber fell from Heaven—

> "from morn
> To noon he fell—from noon to dewy eve—
> A summers day—and with the setting sun
> Dropt from the zenith, like a falling star."

What art is manifest in these few lines. The object is to express great distance & great velocity, neither of which is capable of very easy suggestion to the human mind. We are told that the angel fell a day—a long summers day[;] the day is broken into forenoon & afternoon that the time may be protracted. He does not reach the earth till sunset—& then to represent the velocity he "drops"—one of the very best words in the language to signify sudden & rapid force—& then comes a simile, "like a falling star."

Excuse my dear Sir this very hurried & presumptuous letter. You have I hope leisure to study rhetoric by investigating its principles. I have given little time, for I have had little time to give to the systematic authors—But I have observed something of the effect of speaking & writing & have endeavoured to analyze the causes of effects. "After all" says [William] Cobbett "he is a man of talents that can make a thing move.["] And after all say I he is an orator who can make one think as he thinks—& feel as he feels. And I pray you dear Sir both to think & to feel that I am With much regard Your obt. Servt   D. Webster

Copy. NhExP. Published in *PC*, 1: 463–465.

1. Whately (1787–1863), later archbishop of Dublin, had recently published his *Elementary Rhetoric*, a copy of which Brazer had probably loaned to Webster.

2. Massillon (1663–1742) was a French clergyman noted for his oratory.

3. Watts (1674–1748) was an English clergyman and religious poet.

TO JAMES HERVEY BINGHAM

Boston Novr. 18th. 1828

My dear friend,

I have recd yours of the 15th,[1] enclosing one hundred & sixty dollars, on account of your Brother Milton.[2] I owe to his diligence that I ever got any thing for my Unity land; & am therefore under obligation to him which the small sum he has recd for compensation is by no means sufficient to discharge. It is more, however, than he proposed, which was very trifling.

I really long to see you. If nothing unexpected occur to prevent, I intend to be your way early next season. I pray to be remembered to your wife; & am with unceasing regard & affection your friend, as ever,

Danl Webster

ALS. MeHi. Bingham (1781–1859; Dartmouth 1801), one of Webster's classmates and close friends, was then a lawyer and banker in Claremont, New Hampshire. A few years later he settled in Ohio, where he remained until 1849, when with Webster's influence he received an ap-

pointment as a commissioner in the land office in Washington.

1. See mDW 7320.

2. Milton Bingham (b. 1788), had negotiated the sale of the Unity lands Webster had owned since his New Hampshire days and had transmitted the money through his brother.

FROM NICHOLAS BIDDLE

Philada. Nov 28. 1828

My dear Sir

You will be glad to learn what you have no doubt anticipated, that at the election of directors of the Office at Boston, your friend Mr Paige, was chosen this day. When shall we have the pleasure of seeing you in this quarter? With great regard Very truly Yrs   N Biddle

LC. DLC.

TO NICHOLAS BIDDLE

Boston Nov 29th. 1828.

Private

My Dear Sir,

Mr [Joseph] Gales has written me from Philadelphia, desiring me to express to you my opinion of him & his establishment with a view to facilitate his pecuniary arrangements with the Bank.[1]

I can, of course, only speak in a general manner; but, so speaking, have a clear opinion that his paper is a very useful one, & think its place could not be fully supplied. Under any & all Administrations, an able & independent Press at Washington, while it is not easily established, is of very considerable public importance. The opinions which the Intelligencer steadily advocates are favourable to all the valuable Institutions of the Country, & among others to the Bank itself; & the able & candid manner in which it supports its opinions, doubtless, has given it much weight with the public.

Of course, I know nothing of the security Mr. G. has to offer; nor of the propriety or expediency of the terms proposed. And if I did, I should not do so impudent a thing as to interpose my own opinion. But that it is desirable, for the public & the *Bank*, that his establishment should continue, is a conviction which I feel strongly, & am willing to express confidentially. Yrs. ever with regard, Danl. Webster

LS. DLC.
1. Letter not found.

In the presidential campaign of 1828 Webster was singled out by the Jackson press for special attention only slightly less abusive than that accorded to Clay. But attacks upon him for his inconsistency on the tariff, for his alleged complicity in securing the President's election through the so-called "Adams pledge," for his role as administration spokesman in the Senate, were no more than the measure of his political prominence, and could be disregarded as an inevitable concomitant of leadership. Far more serious was the accusation made on October 29, 1828, in the Boston Jacksonian Republican, *to which Clay alludes below. The* Republican *asserted that Adams, in a conversation with Jefferson some years earlier, had implicated Webster along with other well-known Federalists in a plot to dissolve the Union in 1807–1808. The charge was of a piece with chronic attempts to associate Webster with the anti-national—perhaps treasonable—activities of a few members of his party. This time, however, the charges had to be taken seriously. One of the proprietors of the paper, and the author of the offending editorial, was Theodore Lyman, Jr., until his recent flirtation with the Jacksonians a close personal friend and almost daily associate of Webster. Lyman's own father, who had made a fortune in the China trade, had been of the Essex Junto; his father's lifelong friend, Harrison Gray Otis, had attended and defended the Hartford Convention; and his granduncle, Timothy Pickering, had been the spearhead of Federalist dissent since the turn of the century. If anyone of his generation was in position to know the inner history of federalism, it would be Theodore Lyman, Jr. The charge was made, moreover, at a time when Adams himself was in the midst of an acrimonious controversy with those same Massachusetts Federalists whom he had publicly accused of entertaining disunion sentiments two decades earlier.*

In Webster's reaction to the Lyman article there was an understandable bitterness, but there was also an element of political self-preservation. Less than two weeks after the accusation was made, Webster's counsel, Charles P. Curtis, then Boston city solicitor, and Richard Fletcher (Dartmouth 1806), who had read law with Webster and was now one of the rising young attorneys in the city, secured a grand jury indictment against Lyman for libel. The case was tried on December 16 and 17, 1828. It was easily shown that Adams had not in fact mentioned Webster by name, but that his involvement had been merely inferred from his later prominence in the Federal party. The merits of the case at issue, however, were quickly overshadowed as the courtroom became a sounding board for the whole state rights controversy that had raged in New England between 1800 and 1815 and was at that moment absorbing the intellectual energies of the South.

The trial ended abruptly with a deadlocked jury (rumored to have stood 10-2 for conviction), and the charges were ultimately dropped. By 1830 Webster and Lyman were back on terms of intimacy. See Josiah H. Benton, Jr., A Notable Libel Case: The Criminal Prosecution of Theodore Lyman, Jr., by Daniel Webster in the Supreme Judicial Court of Massachusetts, November Term, 1828 *(Boston, 1904); and* Documents Relating to New England Federalism, 1800–1815, *ed. Henry Adams (Boston, 1877).*

FROM HENRY CLAY

Washn. 30th Nov. 1828

My dear Sir

As I understand that you are not to be here for a month, I wish to say some things which I had intended for a personal interview.

We are beaten. It is useless to dwell on the causes. It is useless to repine at the result. What is our actual position? We are of the majority, in regard to measures; we are of the minority in respect to the person designated as C[hief] Magistrate. Our effort should be to retain the majority we have. We may lose it by imprudence. I think, in regard to the new Administration, we should alike avoid professions of support or declarations of opposition, in advance. We can only yield the former, if our principles are adopted and pursued, and if they should be[,] our honor and our probity afford a sufficient pledge that *we* shall not abandon them. To say before hand that we will support the President elect, if he adheres to our systems, is to say that we will be honest; and that I hope is a superfluous proclamation. On the other hand, if we were now to issue a manifesto of hostility, we should keep united, by a sense of common danger, the discordant confederates who have taken the field against us. They cannot remain in Corps but from external pressure. The dissentions among them this winter, the formation of the new Cabinet, and the Inaugural Speech will enable us to discover the whole ground of future operations. Above all I think that *we* ought not to prematurely agitate the question of the Succession. The nation wants repose. The agitations of the last six years entitle it to rest. If it is again to be immediately disturbed let others not us assume the responsibility.

We shall here all calmly proceed in our various spheres to discharge our duties, until the 4th. of March. The message is good. It makes no allusion to the late event. Its strongest features are the support of the Tariff and disapprobation of sentiments of disunion.

I shall return to Ashland after the 4th. of March, and there consider and decide my future course. I do not mean to look at it until then.

You have all my wishes for success in the prosecution against [Theodore] Lyman. I regretted the publication here which led to the libel, but most certainly I never supposed you to be alluded to in that publication. In the midst of all the heats of former times I believed you, as I have since found you, faithful to the Union, to the Constitution and to Liberty.

Under every vicissitude believe me Sincerely Your friend   H. Clay

ALS. DLC. Published in Curtis, 1:335–336.

FROM NICHOLAS BIDDLE

Phila. Decr. 2 1828

Private

My Dear Sir,

I received this morning your favor of the 29th ulto.[1] which did not reach me until the Com[mitt]ee to whom Mr [Joseph] Gales's application was referred had decided upon it, and their report was adopted by the Board today.

I have, indeed we all have, very favorable dispositions towards Mr Gales & would gladly assist him if it could be done with propriety. But it would be wrong for us to consider the matter in any other than simple business principles. The value of his paper & the advantage of its continuance are considerations entirely foreign to us, and the very circumstance that but for the B. U. S. any newspaper would be discontinued, or that the Bank had gone out of its way in order to sustain any newspaper either in administration or opposition would be a subject of reproach—& what alone makes reproach uncomfortable—of just reproach to the Bank. I have striven to keep the Bank straight & neutral in this conflict of parties, and I shall endeavor to persevere in that course. If then the support of the Nat[ional] Int[elligence]r offers no adequate temptation to hazard the property of the Bank, the loan is on business principles not a proper one. The responsibilities of the party now amount to a little above $50,000, for this the Bank has it is conceived just enough & no more to make the debt secure—& all the other means of the parties are already pledged for other debts. The only chance then of any accession of means is the contingency of their receiving the appointment of printers to the next Congress—a contingency which a politician may regard as surrounded by different degrees of probability—but which to a Banker seems an unsteady basis for a loan of $15000. I am very sorry that we were obliged to decline but really saw no other course, unless we were ready, in all impartiality, to furnish the means for a newspaper under the next administration. I have written thus freely because I thought it would interest you to know the fate of his application & the reasons of it. With great respect and regard Yrs   N Biddle

ALS. PHi. Published in Reginald C. McGrane, *Correspondence of Nicholas Biddle* . . . (Boston, 1919), pp. 58–59.

1. See above, DW to Biddle, November 29, 1828.

FROM JOHN HOLMES

Alfred 20 Decr. 1828

Dr Sr

Mr [William Pitt] Preble & some of his friends in Congress are getting up an excitement here *for effect* in regard to the northeastern boundary. It is attempted to induce a belief that *Mr [Christopher] Hughes* is to be promoted as minister at *the Hague* & the business is to be *taken out of the hands of the agents* & confided to him—& it is insisted that if this is to be the case—*one* of the agents (which is Preble) ought to be the minister, he understanding more of the case than Mr Hughes. So far as I understand the subject there is no intention at all of diminishing the duties of the agents & that it would be injurious to the cause to promote Mr Preble until he shall have finished his duties as Agent.

As our Legislature meet in about a fortnight I will be obliged to you to ascertain & inform me as soon as convenient how the case is, as I strongly suspect, it is all a *machinery* to get up recommendations here for Preble for minister & *for certain other purposes.* Mr Adams' obligations to Mr P. you know are *very strong.*[1] Yours truly   J Holmes

ALS. NhD.

1. Preble had only recently been appointed as one of the agents to aid Gallatin in the preparation of the northeastern boundary case, to be decided by the king of the Netherlands. Longtime champion of Maine's claims, Preble had probably heard that Adams had nominated Hughes, then chargé, as minister to the Netherlands, an appointment subsequently rejected by the Senate. In 1830, Jackson named Preble minister, a post he held until 1831, when he returned home to protest the boundary decision proposed by the arbitrator. From then until the ratification of the Webster-Ashburton Treaty in 1842, Preble continued to espouse Maine's interests; and in the negotiation of the 1842 treaty, he served as one of Maine's four commissioners.

FROM DAVID LEE CHILD

Boston Jany. 3d. 1829

Dear Sir,

I wish to ascertain in anticipation of the last of January, whether you feel willing to continue your distinguished favor to my newspaper.[1] I cannot boast of very brilliant success, but I am impressed with the belief that the Journal has not, until recently been in a form to receive all the encouragement, which the public were really disposed to give it. This I partly infer from the fact that the Weekly Journal for the country has received 500 subscribers in four months, more than 300 of whom were spontaneous. This paper occasions me no additional expense except for paper and press work. The same matter goes into it which is contained in the Daily and Triweekly. The Triweekly has between 9[00] & 1000 subscribers. The ratio of increase has been & is for the Triweekly 3 to 1 : i e, 3 who subscribe to one who discontinues. The ratio of the Weekly has thus far been more than 100 to 1. I have now issued a *Daily*, which completes a *suite* of publications as well adapted in point of form for profit & for effect as an establishment of the kind can be. My whole number of subscribers now stands at 1300, *all good men*. The *quality* is not inferior to that of any list in the United States. The capital which has been put into the concern is $18000 or near that; $10,000, I now owe. The *outlay* is considered to be over. The ratio of increase has not been diminished by the result of the election. I am not aware that I have lost more than *two* subscribers by the count by which the Republic *has lost her honor*—but mum is the word with me. I now confine my attention and give my labor to the Journal alone. I believe I have made arrangements which will ensure to the work as much success as any newspaper can expect. I have ceased to look for any other reputation or support than that which I may obtain as editor. All my views are directed to my duties in that capacity. I trust I need not say that an ardent & constant desire to fulfil all my engagements & obligations to some kind friends & especially to you, has had & will continue to have a due influence over my actions. Gen Dearborn is perfectly willing to endorse for me again & I shall have a third person in the room of Mr. Blake, to whom I feel not the less obliged altho he wishes to be relieved from responsibility on my account. I consider the whole property in the Journal to be of the value of $20,000.

I have wished for some time to make this exposition to you & I called to do it personally the Evening before your departure.[2] I remain Very Respecty. Yr. Most obt. Svt.   D L Child

ALS. NhD.

1. For a discussion of Webster's association with the *Massachusetts Journal*, see above, pp. 69–70.

2. Like Blake, Webster also declined: his endorsement of the letter reads, "Ansd—declining." Yet, his former association with the *Journal* remained a base for attack from his political enemies. See, for example, the pamphlet, *Extracts from the Writings and Speeches of Daniel Webster, and from a Paper Sustained by his* Endorsements, called the *Massachusetts Journal* (n.p.; n.d.), probably published sometime during the 1836 presidential campaign; DW to Caleb Cushing, December 6, 1835, mDW 12759; Cushing to DW, December 2, 1835, mDW 12750; and the *National Intelligencer*, December 2, 1835.

Much of Webster's correspondence in 1829 reveals a despondency, a pessimistic attitude, seldom exhibited by him. He was deeply concerned over the welfare of his children. Since the death of Grace in January 1828 he had left them in New England with friends and relatives. Lonesome without them, he hoped to take them to Washington during the congressional and court sessions, but that prospect apparently revolved around Ezekiel's success in the New Hampshire congressional contest. Ezekiel's defeat in March, followed by his sudden death in early April, doomed those hopes to have his and Ezekiel's family in Washington with him. He despaired, moreover, of the political situation. Jackson's election, the hordes of officeseekers in the familiar surroundings of Washington, the Jacksonian plurality in the Senate, and the uncertainty of his own role on the new political scene led him to question the wisdom of his returning to Washington. To his close friends, he confided that he might retire.

Just when Webster changed his mind is not certain, but the decision must have been influenced by his marriage in December to Caroline Le Roy (1797–1882) of New York, daughter of Herman Le Roy, a prominent merchant. Throughout much of the summer, he had been traveling about New England and New York, visiting friends, looking after the settlement of Ezekiel's estate, and seeking a companion. In fact, in late May, he had visited Stephen Van Rensselaer, to renew an acquaintance with the Patroon's daughter and to explore the possibility of marriage (see pp. 413–414, below). Whether he met Caroline prior to or after that visit has not been established; but his courtship of Caroline apparently proceeded rapidly, and on December 12, 1829, they were married in a private ceremony in New York.

TO EZEKIEL WEBSTER

Washgtn. Jan 17. '29

Dr. E.

The enclosed will give you a *brief* of all that is to be said of the state of things here.

I came here on the 12th. after a severe cold journey. But three judges are yet here. We expect a fourth tonight, and I must go into Court on Monday. Not much is doing in the Senate. Mr. [Charles A.] Wickliffe's motion about the mode of choosing Officers of the House, which was intended mainly to affect the choice of *printer* was today laid on the Table, by a majority of 7 or 8 votes.[1]

You did right to go on the Ticket. I showed Mr. [Samuel] Bell your letter.[2] He says your fears that Republicans will strike off your name are groundless—& that you will get as many votes as any of the rest. I believe you will all be chosen. Let me know from time to time, how the prospect is. Mr. [Jacob B.] Moore's remark in a late Journal is true—it is the most important election in N. H. since the adoption of the Constitution.[3] I hope our friends will not lose it for want of attention.

Let me hear from you.   D. W.

—Gen J. will be here abt. 15. Feb.

—Nobody knows what he will do; when he does come.

—Many letters are sent to him; he answers none of them.

—His friends here pretend to be very knowing; but, be assured, not one of them has any confidential communication from him.

—Great efforts are making to put him up to a general sweep, as to all offices; springing from great doubts whether he is disposed to go it.

—Nobody is authorized to say, whether he intends to retire, after one term of service.

—Who will form his Cabinet, is as well known at Boston as at Washington.

—The present apparent calm is a suspension of action—a sort of syncope arising from ignorance of the views of the President elect.

My opinion is

—That when he comes, he will bring a breeze with him.

—Which way it will blow, I cannot tell.

—He will either *go with the party*, as they say in N. Y., or *go the whole hog*, as it is elsewhere phrased, making all the places he can for friends & supporters, & shaking a rod of terror at his opposers;

Or else, he will continue to keep his own counsels, make friends & advisers of whom he pleases, & *be President upon his own strength.*

The first, would show boldness, where there is no danger; & decision, where the opposite virtue of moderation would be more useful.

The latter would show real nerve, & if he have talents to maintain himself in that course, true greatness.

My *fear*, is stronger than my *hope*. Mr Adams is in good health, & complains not at all of the measure meted out to him.

Mr Clay's health is much improved, & his spirits excellent. He goes to

K[entucky]—in March—& I conjecture will be pressed into the next H.R.

His chance of being at the head of affairs is now better, in my judgment, than ever before.

—Keep N. E. firm & steady, & she *can* make him Prest. if she chooses.

—Sundry important nominations are proposed; probably to know Genl. J's pleasure.

The above contains all that is known here, at this time.

ALS. NhD. Published in *PC*, 1: 466–468.

1. On January 15, Wickliffe had proposed that "all elections by the House of Representatives shall be by viva voce, by a call of the names of the members alphabetically from the roll." *Journal of the House of Representatives*, 20th Cong., 2d sess., 1828–29, p. 165.

2. Ezekiel discussed his congressional candidacy in a letter to DW, January 9, 1826, mDW 7636.

3. Moore had written: "We regard the next State election as the most important which will have occurred since the adoption of our constitution. It is to decide the question, whether there is virtue enough left in the people firmly to resist the approach of that military spirit which has overcome and scathed with moral desolation so many states of the Union. It is to decide whether the people of New-Hampshire dare still to think and act for themselves—to choose able and faithful men to office —to maintain by their suffrage those republican principles of equality and justice which have characterized our State and National Governments: or whether the FREE MEN of New-Hampshire have become so lost to honor, so recreant to duty, as to yield without a struggle the fruits of their double conquest to the infuriated zealots of the military aristocracy." *New-Hampshire Journal*, January 12, 1829.

FROM JOSEPH HOPKINSON

Philad. Jany 18. 1829

My dear Sir

I sent you, a few days since, some remarks on the Charge of your Ch. Justice on the late libel case;[1] in which I fear I have not succeeded in a clear expression of my objections. Indeed altho I thought I saw distinctly the errors of the charge, I found it difficult to draw a line round them to be obvious to every reader. The colours so run into each other that a separation of them is, in some instances, scarcely possible. I have no doubt you will discover what I mean, and, if it be obscure, you may make it luminous by some change of expression. I wish you to understand that I place the whole thing at your disposal. If you should think we have not made out a good case against the charge, and that it cannot be made so by any modification, you will frankly say so, and there is an end of it; but if it can be made to answer any good purpose, why let us have it.

I see you soon got into the debate on the subject of having no national debt. I will at some day have a little talk with you. I know it is a very popular opinion; & an event to be bragged of, when almost every other Government in the world, perhaps every one, is groaning and sweating under an intolerable debt, in some cases without a hope or prospect of ever discharging it. There is nevertheless, I think much to be said in favour of the *policy* and *convenience* of a moderate, manageable debt; the interest of which can be paid by the ordinary revenue, without any additional taxation; and the principal be always in the power of the government. I leave these matters, however, to those whose right and business it is, to settle them. The people of Europe will hardly be able to imagine that we have any government at all here, if we have no debt, they are so inseparable, time immemorial, in their minds. When our debt shall be paid they will suppose we mean to break up, and will see no further use for a Government; as they are accustomed to see their own entirely occupied with creating debts and providing means to pay them.[2]

Will any thing be done in Congress of general importance; or will the whole system stand still until the new sun appears to give it new movements, gravitations and attractions? Truly Yrs   Jos Hopkinson

ALS. MHi.

1. Hopkinson's "remarks" on the charge to the jury in the Theodore Lyman, Jr., libel case have not been found.

2. Hopkinson was probably referring to some newspaper comment upon Webster's remarks in the Senate on January 14, when, during the debate on the distribution of the revenue, Webster said: "he had no doubt that there were individuals who were interested in keeping up the stock, and in delaying the redemption of the debt; they were those who had loaned money to the country, and who found in the Government a regular and solvent debtor; they were those wealthy citizens, who were disposed to loan money to the Government, and such as must have connection with all Governments." *Register of Debates in Congress*, 20th Cong., 2d sess., 1828–29, p. 40.

TO JOSEPH HOPKINSON

Washington Jan. 23. 1829

Private

My Dear Sir

I am your debtor for two letters.[1] Your remarks on a certain subject I have not yet found time to peruse. If, after reading them, I entertain any *doubt* of their doing good, I shall retain them for further consideration. It will be just that I should take care that your zeal for your friend shall do no harm, to you, or to the public. Since I came here, the answering of my correspondents, whose letters lay piled up in a mass truly formidable, with affairs in Court & other things, have left me no leisure.

You have been *misinformed*, in what you have heard as to the Committee having reported.[2] All I can say at present, is, that since my arrival here I have made that subject matter of particular attention. Mr. [John M.] Berrien, Chairman of the Comm[itt]ee, has been *sick a week*. He hopes to be in the Senate on Monday, & by the end of next week I shall probably have something, good or evil, to communicate.

The truth is, there will be an attempt to postpone all the nominations, which are of consequence, till after the 3rd. March. This, at least, will be aimed at, as a general measure; tho' it is intimated that there may be *exceptions*; & that y*ours* may be *one*.

It is far from certain that that course will be adopted, by a Majority, even as a general measure; & if it should be, I am of opinion it will not affect your case. I have little doubt you will be confirmed.

I know not whether I can, now, give you more particulars, with propriety; & even what I have already said you must consider as entirely confidential.

As far as I can yet learn, the state of things here is this—

—Nobody knows Gen. J's purposes. Many letters are sent to him—*none answered.*

—No one knows, by communication from him, whether he will *turn out*, or *keep in*, official incumbents—Nor what he would wish done, in relation to pending nominations.

—Nobody knows whether he intends to be President a *second Term.* There is a *pause*, in the action of parties. One waits to see the other move; & the other waits to receive a hint from headquarters—or, perhaps, to suite [suit?] and reconsider the opinions & purposes of its own members. Yrs. always truly   D. Webster

I find the Judge [Story] delighted with his little visit at Philadelphia. You may show this to Mr. [Robert] W[alsh]. Say to him that I feel fully his personal regard & kindness.

ALS. PHi.
1. Only one of the letters, Hopkinson to DW, January 18, 1829, above, has been found.

2. The allusion here is probably to the progress of Hopkinson's confirmation as district judge of Pennsylvania by the Senate.

TO JOSEPH HOPKINSON

Jan. 23 [1829]

Dr Sir

I have not seen what I am reported to have said on the sub ect of the National Debt. Be assured I uttered no *nonsense* on that occasion. It is quite impossible you & I should differ on the subject. I thought a manifest effort was made to raise a new score of merit for Gen J. on the ground that he would not suffer the sinking fund to be diverted from its object. One Gentleman said broadly that the new Admin[istration] would have to encounter a most formidable effort to perpetuate the National Debt &c.; & another said there was a *"party"* in this Country constantly aiming at that object. What I said was in answer to these things.[1] Adieu! D. W.

P.S. I have found opportunity this Evening to read your remarks. They are excellent & *unanswerable*. I will write you further.

ALS. PHi.
1. See above, Hopkinson to DW, January 18, 1829.

When Webster returned to Washington in December 1828, he entrusted his children to the care of Achsah Pollard Webster, Ezekiel's wife. With Alice Bridge and Mary Ann—daughters by Ezekiel's first marriage, Achsah stayed at the Webster house in Boston while Ezekiel remained in Concord to attend to his duties in the New Hampshire legislature and before the court.

TO MARY ANN WEBSTER

Washington Jan. 24. 1829

My dear Mary Ann,

I believe my next letter is due to you. It is a good while since I wrote, but the reason is, I have been & am very busy. Today I have a letter from Mr Paige,[1] who says your mother is gone to Salem, which I was glad to learn, as her friends there will be very glad to see her. I suppose Alice sits at the head of the table, in her absence.

The Senate does not sit today; but the Court does; & I am obliged to be very much in the latter place, at present. I perceive by letters from Boston that it rained there, very much, on Sunday, the 11th. inst. Now it *snowed* here, on that same day, more violently than I ever knew it to do before; six or eight inches falling, in the course of the day.

My last letter, except Uncle's, was from Julia;[2] & my next will be *to* her. I shall write again soon; & when you do not hear from me, you must conclude that I am well, & have nothing to say.

Excuse this *broken* sheet—I did not notice the imperfection, till I had nearly finished my letter. Your affectionate uncle   Danl. Webster

ALS. NhD.
1. Not found.

2. See Julia Webster to DW, [January] 27, 1828 [1829], mDW 7706.

FROM EZEKIEL WEBSTER

Boston Jany 25. 1829

Dear Brother,

Our Court after a sitting of two days adjourned on Thursday Morning. I left Concord Saturday morning and arrived here last evening. I found all our folks well. From their own account they got along very well and are quite happy. I shall stay only a few days. I received your letter of the 17. the day I left home.[1] I am glad to hear that Mr. Clay's health is improving & that he is [in] good spirits. I have always been of the opinion that the failure of Mr Adams would be favorable to Mr Clay.

[Isaac] Hill starts for Washington tomorrow & he says that he shall not return till April. His friends say that he will be appointed Post Master General.[2] He is evidently preparing to leave Concord, as the people there believe. He took all the mail contracts in the name of Horatio Hill.[3] On the first of January his paper appeared, as printed by one of his journeymen. He seems to be making arrangements in some of his other concerns. I am inclined to think he intends to go into the Post Office—if he can. The Jackson men in N. England are pressing his claims, it is said, for the office. He promises by means of the Post Office to bring over New England, but if he fails in this he will print the administration paper at Washington. He may however, be disappointed in all his hopes. Could the Senate agree to his nomination as P. M. G.? I am not able to give you much information about New Hampshire. I think the result of the election very doubtful. The people cannot be excited to such exertions—as they made in Nov. last, at least the administration folks cannot. Our adversaries will be busy enough. They are full of confidence & hope and they calculate that Jackson's election will carry the doubtful & hesitating & many of those who wish for office to their side. This will happen in many instances, but in what numbers nobody can say. Letters from Gov. [John] Bell and our other friends from W. would do much to stir up a good spirit, and impress us with the importance of the approaching election. From present appearance no extraordinary exertions will be made, and without great efforts—the State government & all will be lost.

Write me as often as you can find leisure. Yours truly

Ezekiel Webster

ALS. NhD.

1. See above.

2. Although not named to the position of postmaster general, Hill received a recess appointment as the second comptroller of the Treasury in 1829; his nomination was subsequently rejected.

3. Horatio Hill was the youngest brother of Isaac Hill.

TO JOSEPH HOPKINSON

Washington Jan. 30. 1829

Private

My Dear Sir

What you suggest, in yours of the 27th is very satisfactory.[1] I like N.

York, for the purpose mentioned, as well as Philadelphia. Indeed I pray you do nothing, in such a case from mere regard to me. Consult only your own source of what the cause of sound principles requires.

I have no views to give you, at present. The spirit here is not so good as I could wish. Yet I do not give up the hope of sundry good things being done. The rumour of Genl. J's death has subsided. My own private opinion, however, still is, that he is very ill, & I have doubts whether he will ever reach this place. Remember this prediction—or this *doubt*,—but of course let not the world be the wiser for it. Yrs   D. Webster

ALS. PHi.

1. Hopkinson, in his letter to DW of January 27, 1829, mDW 7702, had discussed the use of certain words and phrases in his "Remarks" on the charge to the jury in the Lyman libel case.

FROM JOSEPH HOPKINSON

My dear Sir   Philad. Jany. 30. 1829

I have given my remarks on the "Charge" to Mr. [Robert] Walsh,[1] leaving it exactly as you had it, except that I have added a page upon the admission of the evidence to show that the persons named by the defendant were his particular friends; and concluding with your remarks, a little amplified, upon the local air and character of the whole proceeding. When I sent the paper to you it was but just finished, and I feared I had not sufficiently explained my views and objections. Upon a reperusal I am better satisfied with it, and think my criticisms, be they right or wrong, are clearly stated and cannot be misunderstood, at least, by professional readers. The subject is one of general concern and a fair subject for examination, if fairly treated; and so I think it is. Had any thing escaped from my pen which might be deemed harsh or disrespectful to the Judge, it would have struck you or our friend and you, I trust, would have pointed it out. We may look, I presume, for a counter attack, but I think we have no indefensible point. But we shall see. Will any of the Boston papers republish the review? That is a matter you may manage through some of your friends. I think we shall have it out here on Monday.

I observe that an attempt to go into Executive business, on Tuesday, failed by a party vote, but I know not what inference should be drawn from this circumstance.

Remember me to my good and valued friends on the bench, C. Justice—Judges W[ashington]—and S[tory]. Did you receive a newspaper from me for them—a few days since, containing an opinion &c. Yrs

J Hopkinson

ALS. MHi.   1. Not found.

FROM EZEKIEL WEBSTER

Boston Jany 31. 1829

My dear Brother

I intend to go to Boscawen Monday morning. I have had a very pleasant week. The children are all well and very happy. It is very good coasting on the Common & Edward is delighted.

Mr [Nathan] Hale tells me that the correspondence between Mr Adams & "other folks" is now in his press & will be out in a few days. From his account of it—I apprehend, the business will not end with the present publication. I trust Mr Adams' answer will not be satisfactory to any body. There was never a publication, I so much regretted as Mr. A's *"Explanation"* in the Intelligencer.[1] You will see the account of Col [Timothy] Pickering's death, before this reaches you. Judge [Clifton] Clagget also died very recently.[2]

I can give you nothing from New Hampshire, in addition to what I said in my last. There is a good deal of anxiety here to know what the Senate will do with the nominations now before you. Yours truly

E. Webster

ALS. NhD. Published in Van Tyne, p. 141.

1. The "Letter of Massachusetts Federalists to John Quincy Adams," November 26, 1828; Adams' reply, December 30, 1828; and Adams' statement in the *National Intelligencer*, October 21, 1828, are all conveniently printed in *Documents Relating to New-England Federalism, 1800–1815*, ed. Henry Adams (Boston, 1877).

2. Pickering had died on January 29; Clagett, on January 25.

TO EZEKIEL WEBSTER

Feb. 5. '29

My Dear E.

I thank you for your letter from Boston,[1] & wish I had any thing good to tell you from here. But I have not. Those events in N. Jersey & Louisiana have quite depressed us.[2] We are beaten, where we had decisive majorities, by private disagreements, & individual partialities. The next Senate will contain a majority favorable to Gen Jackson, at least who have favored his election, even tho' a Delaware or a N. H. member should be removed to the Cabinet. Neither of these, however, is likely. There are greater & stronger claimants. The City is already full of hungry friends, & will *overflow*, before the 3. of March. Mr. [Isaac] Hill & his cavalcade have not yet arrived, but we understand they are on the road; viz Col [John?] McNeil[, Jr.], Col [John Pine?] Decatur, &c, &c.[3] Mr [Nathaniel] Green[e], of the Boston Statesman, has been here a month, & a Delegation from the other branch of the Jackson family in Boston arrived last night. It consists of Genl. [John P.] Boyd, Col [Henry]

Orne, & Dr. [William] Ingalls.[4] Most of these persons are doomed to taste of disappointment.

It is not possible Hill can get the P. Office. He may, very probably, get some little office, such as an auditorship—& will be kept here, as a supporter, & as charged with the conversion of N. E. But I incline to think he will lose his importance, as soon as he leaves home.

Gen Jackson will be here, in a day or two. I am of opinion his health is very feeble, & that there is not much chance of his lasting long.

We have *done* nothing in the Senate. It is difficult to fortell results—with some, especially the *Federalists* who joined Genl. Jackson's cause, there is as much bitterness as you ever saw in the Concord Patriot.

It is eno. to disgust one with all public employment.

I have spoken to two or three of the N. Hamp. Gent[lemen]. They will do what they can. The outside of yr affairs looks promising enough, but I suppose it is, as you say, very doubtful how the Election will go. It is of great importance, & I hope no proper pains will be spared.

I shall write you again soon—& I hope oftener than hitherto. Yrs

D. Webster

ALS. NhD. Published in Van Tyne, pp. 143–144.

1. See above, EW to DW, January 31, 1829.

2. The legislatures of both states had recently elected Jacksonians as United States senators: Mahlon Dickerson had been elected from New Jersey to succeed Ephraim Bateman, resigned; Edward Livingston had defeated Dominique Bouligny in the Louisiana election. *Niles' Weekly Register*, 11 (February 7, 1829): 385–386.

3. McNeil (1784–1854), a native of Hillsborough and veteran of the War of 1812, was appointed a supervisor of the port of Boston in 1830. Decatur was Hill's nominee for customs collector in Portsmouth. In 1830, the Senate rejected his nomination.

4. Orne (1786–1861; Dartmouth 1812) was a Boston lawyer, sometime editor of the *Boston Yankee*, and a contributor of political pieces supporting Jacksonians to the *Boston Statesman* and *Boston Bulletin*; Ingalls (1769–1851; Harvard 1790) was an eminent physician in Boston.

FROM JOSEPH HOPKINSON

Phila Feby. 5. 1829

My dear Sir

A gentleman of the bar, a friend of mine, but an active friend also of Genl. J— has just called on me on the subject of my nomination. He had written to two or three of his friends in the Senate strongly urging the confirmation. One of them writes him that he has clearly ascertained that if my name could be brought by itself before the Senate, it will unquestionably be affirmed. Now may not this be done—may not a Committee report separately on the nomination—or be discharged from mine

& that be referred to another. I mention this matter to you, leaving it to you to manage it as you shall think expedient. Yrs truly

Jos. Hopkinson

ALS. MHi.

TO RICHARD SMITH

feb. 9. 1829.

Dr Sir

Please transfer my Washington Corporation Stock, say 5000, to Ch[arles] J. Catlett Esq,[1] or order, on his paying you therefor, for my account, 4.500.[2]   D. Webster

ALS. MB.

1. Catlett was a merchant in the dry goods business in the District of Columbia and a justice of the peace in Alexandria.

2. The Washington Corporation stock had probably been transferred to Webster in 1827 as payment of his legal fees in the lottery case, *Clark* v. *City of Washington*, 12 Wheaton 40 (1827). See DW to Thomas Swann, December 21, [1827], mDW 6506.

TO JOSEPH HOPKINSON

Senate Chamber
friday 2 o'clock
[February 13, 1829]

Private & Confidential
Dr Sir

It is understood that the Senate decided *some things*, yesterday—tho not all.[1] The Jud[iciary] Com[mitt]ee met today—& have also agreed on *some* things—& not on others.

I think it now nearly certain, I hope quite, that *your* nomination *will be confirmed.*

I owe you for three or four letters, a debt I shall pay as I have the requisite leisure. Yrs faithfully   D. Webster

ALS. PHi.

1. On February 12, the Senate rejected Adams' nomination of John J. Crittenden to fill the vacancy on the Supreme Court occasioned by the death of Robert Trimble. *Journal of the Executive Proceedings of the Senate,* 1789–1828 (3 vols.; Washington, 1828), 3: 644.

FROM EZEKIEL WEBSTER

Feby 15th. 1829

Dear Daniel,

I do not write to you oftener for two reasons, one I have nothing to say, the other that you have no leisure to read letters that say nothing. I can give you nothing new in regard to affairs in N Hampshire. The truth is that the people made such an effort last Fall, were so disappointed in the result and so disgusted with the conduct of Mr Adams, that they have not any heart to make any exertions. They always supported his cause from a cold sense of duty, & not upon any liking of Mr Adams. We soon satisfy ourselves that we have discharged our duty to the *cause* of any man, when we do not entertain for *him* our personal kind feeling; nor cannot, unless we disembowel ourselves, like a trussed turkey—of all that is human nature within us. During the last contest— this cause alone had no little effect in producing all its disasters. If there had been at the head of affairs a man of popular character like Mr Clay, or any man, whom we were not compelled by our natures—instincts and fixed fate to hate, the result would have been different. People cannot have strong affection for the cause—& strong dislike for the man. The measures of his Administration were just & wise and every honest man could support them, but many honest men, would not, for the reason I have mentioned.

At what time do you expect to be home?

We are anxious here to see the first movements of Gen. Jackson, as they will indicate the course of his policy.

I hear from Boston often, & you I suppose every day. Yours truly

E Webster

ALS. NhD. Published in *PC*, 1 : 469.

TO DANIEL FLETCHER WEBSTER

Senate Chamber
Tuesday 17. Feby. [1829]

My Dear Son,

I have recd a letter from you today, before I have found time to answer your last.[1] *That* gave me singular pleasure, as it contained a very gratifying report from Mr [Frederick P.] Leverett.[2] I have nothing more at heart, My Dear Son, than your success and welfare, & the cultivation of your talents & virtues. You will be, in the common course of things, coming into active life, when, if I live so long, I shall be already an old man, & shall have little left in life but my children, & their hopes & happiness. In contemplation of these things, I look with the most affectionate anxiety upon your progress, considering the present as a most critical & important period in your life.

Such reports, as that last recd, give me good spirits; & I doubt not, My Dear Son, that the consciousness that your good conduct & respectable progress in your class, & among your fellows, give me pleasure, will stimulate your affectionate heart, with other motives, to earnest & assiduous endeavors to excel. I pray Heaven to bless you, & prosper you.

At present my time is exceedingly occupied, between the Senate & the Court—& I suppose it will continue so to be, till the 3rd of March. It is very cold here; much the severest winter I ever experienced at Washington. Yours mo. affectionately, D. Webster

ALS. NhHi. Published in *PC*, 1: 448–449, under date of February 17, 1828.

1. See DFW to DW, February 5, 12, 1829, mDW 7743, 7754.

2. Leverett (1803–1836; Harvard 1821) was headmaster of the Boston Latin School.

TO ACHSAH POLLARD WEBSTER

Senate Chamber Feb. 19, 1829

My Dear Sister,

I must begin with apology; or, let me rather say, with confession. For tho' I am willing to confess great & censurable omissions, I have little to urge by way of *apology*, & nothing which amounts to *justification*. Let me pray you, therefore, in the exercise of your clemency, to adopt the rule which Hamlet prescribes for passing judgment on the Players. Do not treat me according to my deserts, (for if so, "who would escape whipping") but according to your own bounty & dignity. The less I deserve forgiveness, the more will forgiveness exalt your forbearance & mercy.

The children, under your good superintendence, have written me, continually, day by day, very good letters. Mr. Paige, also, has been kind, as he always is. Your own letters have completed my circle of domestic correspondence, & I must say that it has been very punctual & highly gratifying.[1] And now, what can I tell you, worth hearing?

Gen Jackson has been here about ten days. Of course the City is full of speculation, & *speculators*. "A great multitude," too many to be fed without a miracle, are already in the City, hungry for office. Especially I learn that the *Typographical* Corps is assembled in great force. From N. H. our friend [Isaac] Hill, from Boston Mr [Nathaniel] Greene, from Con[necticu]t Mr Norton,[2] from N York Mr [Mordecai M.] Noah, from Kentucky Mr [Amos] Kendall, & from every where else somebody else. So many friends, ready to advise, & whose advice is so *disinterested*, make somewhat of a numerous *Council* about the President elect; & if report be true, it is a Council which only "makes that darker, which was dark enough before." For these reasons, or these with others, nothing is settled yet, about the New Cabinet. I suppose Mr. Van Buren will be Secy. [of] State;[3] but beyond that I do not think any thing is yet determined.

For ten or twelve days, our Senate has been acting with closed doors, on certain nominations to office by Mr. Adams. What we have done is not yet known; tho' one day it will be known probably.[4]

The general spirit prevailing here, with the friends of the New President, is that of a pretty decided *party* character. It is not quite so fierce as our N. E. Jackson men are actuated by; still I think it likely to grow more & more bitter, unless, *which is highly probable*, the party itself should divide.

We have all read the dispute between Mr Adams & the Boston Gentlemen. Thus far, I believe the universal feeling is, that Mr. Adams has the worst side of it. I hear, however, that he is about to reply, in another pamphlet!![5]

The late Mayor arrived here yesterday. Today, I went with him to the H. of R. The first person [ms. cut] Mr Randolph—[ms. cut] winter. He does not seem in a speaking humour.

The fashionable world is, & has been, full & gay. Crowds have come & are coming to see the Inauguration &c. I have been to three parties— to wit, Mrs Adams last, Mrs Clay's last, & Mrs [Peter Buell] Porter's last. Mrs Porter, wife of the Sec of War, is a fine woman, whom we visited at Niagara, when there 4 yrs ago. With these manifestations of regard for the setting sun & stars, I have satisfied my desire of seeing the social circles. If there should be a ball on the 22, I shall attend, as usual, to commemorate the great & good man, born on that day.

Judge Story is well, & in his usual spirits. The Court is deeply engaged, & as soon as I get rid of these secret sessions of the Senate, I have enough to do in it.

We are looking to N. Hamp. I shall not engage lodgings for you & your husband next winter, till I see the *returns*. [ms. cut]

AL (signature removed). NhD. Published in *PC*, 1: 470–471.

1. Apparently none of Achsah Pollard Webster's letters to DW about this time has survived.

2. Not identified.

3. Following the interim appointment of James A. Hamilton, Van Buren assumed the duties of secretary of state on March 28, 1829.

4. One of the appointments under consideration was that of Joseph Hopkinson; and, according to Webster's hint, in a party split on March 14, the Senate voted to remove the injunction of secrecy on certain of Adams' nominations. *Journal of the Executive Proceedings of the Senate, 1829–1837* (Washington, 1887), 4: 23–24.

5. See above, Ezekiel Webster to DW, January 31, 1829.

TO JOSEPH HOPKINSON

Senate Chamber
Febry. 23. 1829.
4 oclock

My Dear Sir,

You are a *Judge, dum diu bene se gesserit.* Yrs thankfully

D. Webster

ALS. PHi. Published in Burton Alva Konkle, *Joseph Hopkinson, 1770–* *1842: Jurist, Scholar, Inspirer of the Arts* (Philadelphia, 1931), p. 267.

TO [HENRY WILLIS KINSMAN?]

Feb. 23. '29

Dr Sir

There is a note, indorsed by Mr [Nathan] Hale, which will be due, I think, 1/4 March for $1000—& which must be paid. I enclose a draft for $900—& shall write you again soon.

The new Cabinet pleases *nobody*. Yrs   D. W.

ALS. MBevHi.

TO EZEKIEL WEBSTER

feb. 23. [1829]

Private

Dr E.

I wrote you last Eve' abt. Capt [George?] Stones business[1]—I will see it attended to, the earliest moment I can leave the Senate.

A prodigious excitement has been produced by the new Cabinet List. It has set all Washington in a *buz*—friends rage, & *foes laugh*. Nobody will say he was privy to it—nobody justifies it. The clamor, (for that is not too strong a name) became so loud, that we hear today of a change, that is, that Mr [John] McLean is to be Secretary of War, instead of *Major [John H.] Eaton.*[2] This will in some matter alleviate the discontents; but still I think they are deep, & likely to be permanent. This very first step of Genl Jackson presents him his first difficulty; & every other step will repeat it. His friends have no common principle—they are held together by no common tie—& my private opinion is, tho' I do not wish to be quoted for that, at present, is, that Genl J. has not character enough to conduct his measures by his own strength. Somebody must & will lead him. Who it will be, I cannot say—but I have an opinion.

I will write you again soon. I think I see unsettled times before us. Let me know what prospects your election wears. Take all the care of it you well can. Yrs   D. W.

ALS. NhD. Published in Van Tyne, pp. 141–142.

1. Stone (1760–1834), a veteran of the Revolutionary War and at the time a farmer at Boscawen, was probably making a claim for services rendered during the Revolution. In his letter to Ezekiel, February 21, 1829, mDW 7776, Webster reports that he has been by Secretary of War Porter's office on several occasions on behalf of his "old friend & client Capt Stone."

2. McLean remained in the cabinet as postmaster general, and Eaton, contrary to rumors, was named to the War Department post.

Washington Feb. 26 1829

Dr E

The cabinet arrangements have been announced; & they are as I wrote you. It is, on the whole, a very *weak* Cabinet; & if it gets along, it must be rather by its weakness, than its strength. If, with *this* Cabinet, Gen J. takes a high handed course, he will not & cannot sustain himself. Hundreds of partizans are, & thousands will be, exceedingly disappointed, by the disposition of Office; & clamor & discontent will arise. In Va. especially the Cabinet is *unpopular*—greatly so. Now, under these circumstances, I rather expect Genl J. will take a *moderate* course— perhaps a *vacillating* one. The elements of dissension will be in the Cabinet itself. Mr Calhoun, (who tho not nominally in the Cabinet, is likely to be *near* the President) & Mr Van Buren & Mr McLean will all be looking out for the *succession*. I think it possible the state of things may be much as it was under the last 4 yrs of Mr Madison.

We shall have time to *see* & to *know* something before I leave here. The great point, at present, is the N. Hamp. election. Depend on it, this is the turning point. If Govr [John] Bell should now succeed, there will be little difficulty hereafter.

Pray let your friends be wakened up; & do your best.

I shall stay here till about the 20 March. By that time, I shall hear from N. Hamp:. If it should look likely that you are to be here, I shall leave my *Books* here, so that if I do not come back, you can take care of them. Otherwise, I shall box them up, & send them home, to be brought back, if I come back. On this point, I have much to say when I see you. Yrs as ever   D. Webster

ALS. NhD. Published in Van Tyne, pp. 144–145.

Boston Feby 1829

Dear Sir

I enclose with this a copy of a letter which I have addressed to Mr Biddle the President of the United States Bank, together with copies of a correspondence I have had with the Bank here—presenting altogether as it appears to me a most extraordinary transaction.[1]

With all the light I can get upon the subject I can find no other ground on which the idea originated that we deposited the money in other banks—but that we paid the large drafts on us for the monthly payments, (in reference to which the Bank had made an arrangement with the Columbian Bank, who gave for a long time 30 days credit without interest for the benefit of the circulation) in our *checks* on the U. S.

Bank instead of sending to that Bank for the *bills*, as is customary— and arose wholly from the entire confidence placed in our signatures. The truth is the President is an old woman & wholly unfit for the place— and the whole business is managed by the Cashier, who assumes airs as I should think very unbecoming his situation—this whole difficulty has arisen from his perverseness.[2] I cannot imagine on what ground he has set himself so against this account. There never has been the slightest personal difference or difficulty. I can imagine nothing more probable than that I never called on him to ask his good offices, which I believe he is very fond of having done. But I have no doubt the poor old Presid[en]t actually thought that the Bank was in danger from this acct.— when supported by my brother [Samuel] & Jas. Paige.

It is of no importance to us whether we do our business at this Bank or others—although doing so much in Southern drafts, it is worth more to them. It is unquestionably to them the most valuable account in Boston. But the management of this Bank has been on the most proven & contracted principle in my opinion whereas their true policy should be the most liberal—so as to secure all the first rate business, instead of second & third rate as at present. A thorough change is wanted. I should think Mr. [David] Sears was the man for President.

It strikes me that it is a very useless and absurd bye-law that no director can examine any account of the Bank without leave of the board. This makes the Cashier the unchecked arbiter of the value of every account—and is wholly useless in any point of view. What possible objection can there be to having the ledger open to any director—it is done I believe at every other Bank and I take this restriction to be copied from the musty rules of the Bank of England.

The report itself from what I can learn is a most extraordinary one and has already occasioned the resignation of Mr Sears and Mr [Daniel P.] Parker and I suppose my brother will follow. We have removed our account, to the New England Bank so that I do not see that Mr Paige will have much inducement to remain under the present administration. After you have looked over the papers I should be glad of your opinion— and whether I have taken any too strong ground in reference to the representation of overdrawing. It is true this is not stated in the body of the report—but in a statement of the account accompanying it—and which *was to be considered a part of it*. It purports to be taken from the books—but the words "over-drawn" are the gratuitious additions of the committee.—and insisted on being put in—or kept in—by Mr. [Resin D.] Shepherd & others after they had ascertained that there was no such thing. I suppose it is not very probable that any thing will be done at Phila. untill Mr Silsbee & yourself reach there on your return. I should like to have you communicate to him the accompanying papers—& this letter if you think proper—although you will perceive it is of a confidential character.

AL copy. MHi.

1. Not found. On the disagreement between Appleton and certain directors of the Boston branch and the president and cashier, see Nicholas Biddle to Gardiner Greene, February 21, March 10, 1829; and Biddle to

Nathan Appleton, August 28, 1829, Biddle Letterbooks, DLC.

2. Appleton was referring to Gardiner Greene and Samuel Frothingham, president and cashier, respectively, of the Boston branch of the Bank of the United States.

TO ACHSAH POLLARD WEBSTER

Washington Sunday Morning
Mar. 2. [1829]

Dear Sister

I had letters yesterday from Mr P[aige] & from Alice,[1] which ought to have been recd two days earlier. This, I suppose, is to be placed to the acct. of your great snow storm.

With less snow, we have very cold weather here. There has not been a warm day since I came here, although I have often seen the peach trees in blossom in February. The ground is still covered with snow, the river hard frozen, & the weather steadily cold. It will make bad travelling for those who leave here the 4th.

Tuesday is the last day of the session of Congress. A special session of the Senate is called, to meet on Wednesday the 4th. I suppose it will not last beyond two or three days. Gen Jackson will then nominate his new Cabinet, & make such *changes* in Office, as he sees fit. On this latter subject, very little is known about his intentions. Probably he will make some removals, but I think not a great many immediately. But we shall soon see.

The Court will probably continue its session a fortnight longer—& then I shall set my face northward. I hope your patience will hold out. Consider how cold it must be up at Boscawen—& how *busy* your husband is *now*—& how soon he will come to Boston, after the tenth, either for congratulation, or condolence. He will need a week, in either case, & that will bring March so far along, that I trust you will be able to content yourself till I come.

My health is good, but I find, to confess the truth, that I am growing indolent. I would be glad to have more decisive *volitions*. I do nothing, in Congress or the Court, but what is clearly necessary; & in such cases, even, my efforts "come haltingly off." In short I believe the truth is, that

I am growing old—& age, you know—or rather you have heard—requires *repose.*

Adieu! Yrs with much affectionate regard   Danl Webster

ALS. NhD. Published in *PC*, 1: 472.   1. Not found.

TO EZEKIEL WEBSTER

Washington March 2. '29

Dear E.

Nothing of importance has occurred since I wrote you last. The Cabinet list stands as it did. There is much dissatisfaction, especially among the Virginia Gentlemen. Yet they must submit. The general idea now is, that Genl. J. will make no great number of *changes.* The Cabinet is not strong enough to carry on a mere *party* Administration. This the Genl. will know soon, if he does not know now.

I shall stay here till 20th inst—send me word of your earliest Election returns. Yrs   D. W.

ALS. NhD. Published in Van Tyne, p. 145.

TO ACHSAH POLLARD WEBSTER

Washington March 4. 1829
first year of the Administration
of Andrew Jackson—
& the first day

My Dear Sister

I thank you for yours, recd today;[1] & thank you both for the letter itself, & for your *pardon,* which it contains, & of which I stood in so much need. Your benignity is memorable, & praiseworthy. To be serious, however, My Dear Sister, let me say, once for all, that I have a very affectionate regard for you; that I am very glad you are my sister, & the wife of the best of all brothers; & that if, like him, I am not the most punctual of all correspondents, I am like him, also, in sincerity & constancy of esteem. If you find, in your connexion with my own little broken circle, but one half as much pleasure as you bestow, you will have no reason to regret it. Your presence with my children thro' the winter has relieved me from a pressing weight of anxiety.

Today, we have had the Inauguration. A monstrous crowd of people is in the City. I never saw any thing like it before. Persons have come 500 miles to see Genl Jackson; & they really seem to think that the Country is rescued from some dreadful danger.

The Inaugural Speech you will see. I cannot make much of it, except that it is *Anti Tariff*—at least, in some degree. What it says about *reform in Office* may be either a prelude to a general change in Office, or a mere *sop* to soothe the hunger, without satisfying it, of the thousand expectants for office who throng the City, & clamor all over the Country. I expect some changes, but not a great many at present.

The show lasted only half an hour. The Senate assembled at 11. The Judges & foreign Ministers came in. The President Elect was introduced, & all seated by ½ past 11. The Senate was full of Ladies. A pause ensued till 12. Then the President, followed by the Senate &c. went thro' the great Rotunda, on to the Portico, over the Eastern front door, & those went with him who could, but the crowd broke in, as we were passing the Rotunda, and all became confusion. On the Portico, in the open air, (the day is very warm & pleasant) he read his Inaugural, & took the oath. A great shout followed from the multitude, & in fifteen minutes, "silence settled, deep & still." Every body was dispersed.

As I walked home, I called in at a Book Store, and saw a vol which I now send you. It may serve to regulate matters of etiquette at Boscawen.

I hope to write Edward tonight. If not, I shall not fail to do so tomorrow. Yrs very sincerely & truly   D. Webster

ALS. NhD. Published in *PC*, 1: 473–474.
    1. Not found.

TO EZEKIEL WEBSTER

Washington Mar. 15. 29
Sunday Eve'

Dear E.

The Senate will probably adjourn tomorrow, & I hope the Court will rise, or at least will dismiss me by Wednesday or Thursday. I shall be immediately off. My books are in trunks—I shall hear from N. H. tomorrow, & dispose of them according to circumstances. If no change takes place in my own condition, of which I have not the slightest expectation, & if you are not elected, *I shall not return.* This *inter nos*— but my mind is settled. Under present circumstances, public & domestic, it is disagreeable being here; & to me, there is no novelty to make compensation. It will be better for me & my children, that I should be with them. If I do not come, in a public, I shall not in a Professional character—I can leave the Court now as well as ever; & can earn my bread as well at home as here.

Your company, & that of your wife, would make a great difference. I have not much expectation that you will be returned. Our fortune is, as connected with recent & current political events, that if there be opposite chances, the unfavorable one turns up. You had a snow of five feet, which, of itself, might turn the election, against the well-disposed and indifferent, & in favor of the mischievous & the active. I shall not be disappointed, if I hear bad news.

I make my point to be home the first day of April, when I trust I shall meet you. We will then settle what is best to do with the children. I shall want Julia & Edward to stay a little while with me. Edward, I think, should then go to Boscawen. I hardly know what I shall think best to do with Julia. Yrs as ever   D. Webster

We have had one important cause here. It is from N. York respecting what is called the Sailors Snug harbour. I have made a greater exertion in [it] than in any other since D. C. vs Woodward—& than it is probable I shall ever make in another.[1]

ALS. NhD. Published in *PC*, 1: 474–475.

    1. *John Inglis* v. *Trustees of the Sailor's Snug Harbour in the City of*

New York, 3 Peters 99 (1830). The case came before the Court in its January 1829 term.

FROM ELIZABETH LANGDON-ELWYN

Phila. April 9th. 29.

My dear Mr Webster,

It gave me great pleasure to hear of your safe arrival at Boston & that you found all well there—but your letter gratified me in many ways. We heard of you at Princeton & N. York through our kind friend Mr [George] Blake—from others, who had no direct information, however, of your movements, we were told *much more*. You were certainly to do so & so— no doubt, you would do this—& that—to all which I assented with the best grace possible, not liking to appear ignorant of what they knew so well. Yet, if there is any one thing I dislike more than another it is the hearing from officious, inquisitive tho' well meaning friends, about those I know much better & care much more for—than they do. However correct they may be, they are apt to be rudely positive, & this makes me angry—but I am, at least sufficiently a woman of the world—to know how to acquiesce very amiably on such occasions. On one subject which is spoken of, I am satisfied. Be not alarm'd—it is of a public nature —& I have a right to speak as well as the rest—& smile, or be vex'd, as you may at a woman's presumption, I will say, that, I hope it is not true, as is asserted, that you mean—to desert in despondency, the post of honour which you now hold. The time is far distant, I trust, when you can justly consider that best to be found only in a "private station." Your country has strong claims upon you. Come once more, at least. I wish to add a great deal <more>, but dare not—if I incur much censure for my temerity it will grieve me, but no argument can alter my opinion. Events have prov'd that I was right last year altho' I differ'd in sentiment from your best friends on an important point (politically speaking always,) & some now acknowledge it—this has given me courage—& must be my apology.

We have still cool & rainy weather, & since you left us—affairs under my roof have not borne a cheerful aspect. My older daughter has been afflicted by the return of severe headaches, which no remedies appear'd to diminish until yesterday. Sunshine, & change of air will restore her— & for us all a change of scene would be useful.

I shall be *impatient* for an assurance from you that I have not offended past forgiveness.

Forget, too, if you please all, but that I am sincerely & respectf[ull]y Yr friend   E. L-E.

No one knows of my writing or I should have some remembrances to send—you may be assur'd of all the best wishes of this house.

ALS. NhHi. Elizabeth Langdon-Elwyn (d. 1860) was the only child of John Langdon, former congressman, senator, and governor of New Hampshire. She had married Thomas Elwyn, a native of England; they had settled in Philadelphia where her husband had practiced law. One of their sons, John Langdon, had read law with Jeremiah Mason and Webster following his graduation from Harvard in 1819.

TO ACHSAH POLLARD WEBSTER

Boston April 15. 1829

My Dear Sister,

We had a very good journey here, & arrived last Evening at abt. 8 oclock. Mr Paige is here. He reached home from N York on Sunday Eve'. No news met him, till he came into the House here. Julia has come home this morning. She seems well, except her usual cough. I think I shall consult Dr. [John C.] Warren, as to that. My losses have been such that I feel alarmed for every thing that remains.

Mary will put up your articles, & Edward's clothes; & perhaps we may send them by the Coach which carries this. I hear that Mrs Ticknor & Mrs Hale are well as usual.

Your house alone, My Dear Sister, is not solitary & melancholy. It is the same here. Yours truly & affectionately   Danl Webster

ALS. NhD. Published in PC, 1: 475.

TO CYRUS PERKINS

Boston, April 17, 1829.

My dear Friend,

You will have heard of the sudden death of my brother. The event necessarily called me to Boscawen, from which place I returned a day or two ago. It has quite overwhelmed us all. Mrs. Webster and the oldest daughter were here, when it happened. The messenger brought us the news at three o'clock, on Saturday morning, the 11th instant. The death took place the previous afternoon at four o'clock. You will probably have seen some account of it. It seems to me I never heard of a death so instantaneous. He fell in an instant, without any effort to save himself, and without any struggle or sign of consciousness, after he reached the floor. On receiving the tidings, Mrs. Webster and her daughter, and myself and two sons, set off immediately, and arrived at Boscawen that evening at nine o'clock. The funeral was attended the next day. Mrs. Webster's constitution is feeble, and I knew not how she would get through the dreadful scene; yet she did get through. I left her far better than was to have been expected; and a letter received to-day says she continues so.[1] It was not possible for me to stay long from home, on so sudden a call; but I must return in two or three days to Boscawen, to pay proper attention to the circumstances of the family. My brother has left two daughters, one fourteen and one twelve years old; and a wife, a fine woman, to whom he had been married about four years. He has left a competency to those dependent on him; but it will require care and oversight to preserve it, and make the most of it.

This event, my dear Sir, has affected me very much. Coming so soon after another awful stroke, it seems to fall with double weight. He has been my reliance, through life, and I have derived much of its happiness from his fraternal affection. I am left the sole survivor of my family. Yet I have objects of affection in my children, and I do not intend to repine; though I confess I cannot well describe the effect of this event on my feelings.

I ought to acknowledge the receipt of two letters from you, yet unanswered. It is probable, that but for this melancholy occurrence, I should have been in New York the first of May. Now, it is hardly likely I shall be there before the sitting of the court, on the 25th.

I pray you give our love to Mrs. Perkins. We know she sympathizes with us, in all our afflictions. Remember me also to Mr. [Benjamin] Clarke's family,[2] whom I had not the pleasure of seeing as I came home. Yours always truly,   Danl Webster

Text from PC, 1: 475–476. Original not found.

1. Not found.

2. Clark (1774–1840; Dartmouth 1800) was then a lawyer in New York City.

TO JEREMIAH MASON

Boston, April 19, 1829.

My Dear Sir,

I thank you for your kind letter.[1] You do not and cannot overrate the strength of the shock which my brother's death has caused me. I have felt but one such in life; and this follows that so soon that it requires more fortitude than I possess to bear it with firmness, such perhaps as I ought. I am aware that the case admits of no remedy, nor any present relief; and endeavor to console myself with reflecting, that I have had much happiness in lost connections; and that they must expect to lose beloved objects in this world, who have beloved objects to lose. My life, I know, has been fortunate and happy beyond the common lot, and it would be now ungrateful, as well as unavailing, to repine at calamities of which, as they are human, I must expect to partake. But I confess the world, at present, has for me an aspect any thing but cheerful. With a multitude of acquaintance, I have few friends; my nearest intimacies are broken, and a sad void is made in the objects of affection. Of what remains dear and valuable, I need not say that a most precious part is the affectionate friendship of yourself and family. I want to see you very much indeed, but know not whether I shall be able soon to visit Portsmouth. You will be glad to know that my own health is good. I have never, for ten years, got through a winter without being more reduced in health and strength. My children also are well. Edward is at Boscawen, where he will probably stay through the summer, or as long as the family may be kept together there. Daniel hopes to go to college in August. Julia proposes to pass the summer, or part of it, with Mrs. Lee, and must afterwards be disposed of as best she may.

This occurrence is calculated to have effect on the future course of my own life, and to add to the inducements, already felt, to retire from a situation in which I am making daily sacrifices and doing little good to myself or others. Pray give my love to your family. Yours affectionately and entirely   Danl Webster

Text from *PC*, 1: 477. Original not found.

1. See Jeremiah Mason to DW, April 16, 1829, mDW 7926.

FROM JACOB MCGAW

Bangor May 1—1829

Dear Sir,

There are seasons that sooner or later present themselves to us, which are too sacred to admit the presence of even dear friends. But those seasons are hallowed by the knowledge that the same friends share our griefs or our joys with us. My own experience leads to the conclusion that others possess these feelings in common with me.

How to approach the subject with which my heart is full and yours is overflowing I do not know.

Bereavement of friends who were dear to you, is not a new case, though the arrows of affliction have not fallen thick upon you that I know of. If however your wounds had been quite numerous; few, very few of them could have been so severe as the one recently received.

A State has lost one of her most highly valued citizens, and the Bar of N. H. one of its brightest ornaments. But some other citizen may supply his place to the State, and some other lawyer adorn the Bar, of which he was the pride. Would to God, it were possible that another brother possessing equal excellence and equal love with him whom you have lost could be granted you. I know that it is unavailing to utter such a wish; but it is my privilege to mourn in such cases.

The friends of my youth are pretty fast dropping off, and leaving me with but few (and that number constantly diminishing) who are really dear to me; and though my heart clings close to those friends who remain, yet, on the whole, my desire of living becomes weaker and weaker every year.

Amid the vicissitudes and trials of life there is consolation in the assurance that, though no chastening, for the present seemeth to be Joyous but grievous: nevertheless, afterward it yieldeth the peaceable fruits of righteousness unto them which are exercised thereby.

That every dispensation of divine Providence may bring you to the enjoyment of more of the smiles of the blessed Saviour is the earnest prayer of Your friend   Jacob McGaw.

ALS. NhHi. Published in *PC*, 1: 478.

TO RICHARD PETERS, JR.

Boston May 7. 1829

Dr Sir

I thank you for your kind letter of the 30th April.[1] In the death of my Brother I have, indeed, sustained a loss, which admits neither of description, nor compensation. At no very advanced age, I find myself the last of a large family of Brothers & Sisters; & with the last survivor I have, this life enjoyed a degree of affectionate friendship, more than commonly intense, I believe, even for the relation which existed between us. His death was like tearing away one half of all that remained of myself. He has left two children, both daughters, aged fourteen & twelve; & a wife, not their mother, much younger than himself.

I have not brought my mind to consider how far this occurence may influence the question to which you refer. I do not, at present, intimate any intention of leaving my present situation in the Senate. Things look bad enough, in my opinion, for the Country; but whether there is any chance of improvement of prospects, I cannot judge. You thought, last winter, that I spoke strongly of the infatuation of the times, & the extravagance of personal devotion. I think you will see it all verified.

I will endeavor to look up the briefs you ask for, tomorrow, & send them to you.

A Gentleman from Halifax, Mr Archbold [Samuel George William Archibald], Solicitor Genl of that Province,[2] has brought letters from our friend Judge [Brenton] Halliburton,[3] & is a sensible & agreeable man. His wife & son, & perhaps daughter, are with him. Not expecting to go farther South, he has no letters from Philadelphia, tho' he now intends visiting your City. I have given him your address, & asked him to call on you; saying I would write you this.

With my best regards to your family, I am, Dr Sir, Yours always truly
Danl Webster

ALS. PHi.
    1. Not found.
    2. Archibald (1777–1846) had been appointed solicitor-general of Nova Scotia in 1825.

3. Sir Brenton Halliburton (1775–1860) had been appointed to the provincial bench of Nova Scotia in 1807 and was made chief justice in 1833.

TO BOSWELL STEVENS

Boston May 7. 1829

My Dr Sir

I feel some interest in regard to the *successor* to my Brother as a Professional Gentleman to reside in Boscawen. As to individuals, I have no preferences to gratify, & no objections to interpose. My only wish is that a man of respectability & character, & one who is acceptable to the good people of the Place, may occupy the vacant situation, if any one shall occupy it. My present purpose is merely to say one word respecting a very small consideration, connected with this matter. Mr. [John] Greenough & Mr. W[orcester] W[ebster] are competitors in trade, in the Village.[1] The locality of the Atty's Office seems, or may seem, to them, an object of some utility to them; or of comparative advantage.

Now I only wish to say that who ever goes there, with my approbation, must be prepared to hold an entirely independent course, in such matters as these. He should build or buy suitable accomodations for himself, & neither do nor appear to do any thing, in that respect or any other, that should make him a party to little village competitions. I read this letter to W. W. & wish you would show it to Mr Greenough, to whom I have expressed already similar sentiments. A man who has not power to hold an even balance, in such matters, cannot be a useful addition to the Society of the village. Yrs always truly   D. Webster

ALS. NhD.

1. Greenough (1780–1862) was a prominent merchant of Boscawen, having moved there in 1814 and purchased the house and business formerly owned by Timothy Dix. On several occasions, he served as state legislator. Webster (b. 1794) kept a store on the Boscawen Plain.

TO STEPHEN VAN RENSSELAER

Boston May 15. 1829

Private and Confidential

My Dear Sir,

Before you have read much of this letter, I fear you will think it a very foolish one. I am so far of that opinion myself, that I should not send it, if I had not the fullest confidence, both in your kindness, and your discretion. Relying on these, I persuade myself that no seriously evil consequences will result, in any event, from what I am about to say.

My object is no other than to express a wish to be permitted to visit you, and to cultivate an acquaintance in your family. For yourself, My Dear Sir, I hope you will allow me to say, I have a deep & fervent regard. My acquaintance, political or general, has not brought to my knowledge any Gentleman, for whom I entertain that feeling, in greater strength. Of Mrs Van Rensselaer I know less, but think not less highly. There is another member of your Family, with whom my acquaintance has not been great; yet it has been sufficient to assure me of her uncommon good sense, refined manner, and amiable temper; and I have the best reasons for not entertaining a doubt of her domestic habits & dispositions, or of the solidity & excellence of her religious & moral principles. I think it right to say, frankly, that from the time I first saw her, I have admired her character & manners; and can add, with entire truth, that since I have brought myself to think on the subject of a change in my own condition, she has been the leading object of my reflections. I am well aware that she cannot know much of me. My only hope, at present, is, that the little she does know may render her not unwilling to know more.[1]

It was my purpose to speak to you on this subject before parting in New York. But circumstances did not favor that intention. I have since thought of going to Albany, but have esteemed it, on the whole, more ingenuous, since I should have regard to a particular object in such visit, not to make it before disclosing to you & Mrs. Van Rensselaer all my motives.

What I now propose is only to ask, whether there be any objection to my visiting your house, & cherishing an acquaintance in your family;

leaving every thing else, in the freest manner, to such a course as inclination and events may afterwards give to it? Not unconscious that difficulties may appear to lie between me & my object, I hope, still, that I may be pardoned, if my feelings prompt me not to withdraw my attention from that object, until it shall be intimated, from the proper source, that those difficulties, or some of them, are deemed insurmountable. Such an intimation, whenever made, would be received as it ought to be. It would cause disappointed feeling; but it would, in no respect, lessen my high regard for You & Yours.

This is a case, My Dear Sir, for the utmost frankness; & I am quite sure that *all* those, to whom I have not hesitated thus freely to expose my feelings, will treat me with that frankness; and if nothing is found, in this letter, which can be *approved*, I trust, nevertheless, that it can all be *pardoned*, on account of the true & sincere esteem, in which it has originated.

Two persons, your friends & mine, know of the writing of this letter, & no one else. Nor will knowledge of it be further communicated.

From the 25th. of this month to the first of June, I expect to be in New York; which I mention only for the reason that you may know where I am, if you should wish to write me, within that time. Thro' June, professional engagements will oblige me to be at home. I hope for leisure for the residue of the summer.

Praying you to accept, & to communicate, my best wishes & regards, I am, Dear Sir, most truly Yours,   Danl Webster

ALS. NhD.

1. An endorsement on the letter, not in Webster's hand, reads: "The lady is Catherine Van Rensselaer, who married G. W. Wilkins."

FROM JAMES BARBOUR

London May 17th. 29.

Dear Sir

Lord and Lady Holland, who have been kind to me by marked attentions, made some inquiries of me about land claims in the East.[1] As it was a subject with which I was far from being acquainted, I took the liberty of referring to you as one, whom we esteemed worthy of all confidence, and to whom I would submit their papers. They, accordingly, sent me the accompanying packet.[2] In fulfilment of my promise I beg to transmit them to you, hoping that you will be able to give them some beneficial advice—and altho no compensation was alluded to, I take it for granted, they will cheerfully pay whatever you may think yourself entitled to. I shall be happy to be the organ of communication—should I remain here. The uncertainty as to my position has been exceedingly mortifying. My Friends have advised me to stand my ground. Having so recently received the unanimous ratification of my nomination from the Senate; and in this age of *Severe reform* having subjected my Country to some expense by an outfit and salary, I did not feel myself at liberty to withdraw. The sinister rumors from home coupled with the singular appearance here of the essays of Senex—and commendations in favor of the Author, whose name stood conspicuous on the title page[3]—and the unqualified declaration that the Author was to be substituted for me at this Court,[4] and withal seeing the relentless spirit of the new administration against its adversaries, I had every reason to believe that I should be forthwith recalled. The result was of no sort of consequence, except that my position was humiliating—being placed in the predicament of a public functionary from whom the confidence of his Country was withdrawn. For altho at home, the circumstances being known, are without effect on me—yet abroad the world look only to the superficial fact that the Minister has been involuntarily forced to retire, and is hence in disgrace with the powers that be. Thus situated I have deemed it due to myself to abstain from presenting myself to the Government here except on occasions belonging to the routine of office, and such as are indispensable. I have frankly disclosed my predicament to my own Government, and have asked them to come at once to some definitive resolution in regard to this mission: and that if I am to be recalled the sooner it is done the better. As a friend I have felt anxious to submit the propriety of my course to you as I have done to many others with whom I have been politically associated. The truth is that a residence here, however, desirable on many accounts does not suit any but the wealthy. The expenses are in the ratio of about 4 to 1 compared to Washington and to maintain a style even respectable—and to reciprocate the Courtesies one receives, requires at least double the amount of the appointment. Nothing is more painful than to be wanting in a reciprocity of hospitality—except insolvency—and yet you are compelled to elect between these alternatives, unless you are blessed with a large share of that which commands the good things of this world.

The Country is certainly a most interesting one—its rural husbandry is above all praise and is incredible but to the eye of the beholder. The intercommunication by roads, by rail roads, and by canals is I presume unsurpassed by any country on the globe. If labor saving machinery has multiplied the capacity of the Country for manufacturing production these channels of intercourse have been equally operative in increasing the power of the nation, in their diffusion thro' the empire and the world. And I apprehend that here the same power applied to conveyance availing wholly of these facilities would effect 4 to 1 what could be effected on the Continent. And it is a problem difficult to solve what are the relative advantages of a People thus circumstanced with a corresponding number of People deprived of their advantages. They have certainly been to this nation one of the most fruitful springs of those effects which for scale and duration have astonished the world. But I rather think they have been abused. Like a prosperous individual who has had a long career of success they have supposed in this Country that its powers were without limit. Levying as they did a tribute on all nations they became reckless of expense—and confident they were adequate to any emergency they did not hesitate to draw largely even on futurity—that fateful bane of nations—till they have increased the burden almost beyond endurance. The advance of other nations, less embarrassed in manufactures, has thrown immense masses of their products on the hands of the manufacturers—they have acted on their operatives either by diminishing their wages or shutting up their factories. And the latter in turn have risen against calamities too severe to be borne. To their importunate cries for bread—they have been advised to a philosophic quiet —and their forcible attempts to obtain it have been repelled by the bayonet. Trade stagnates—labor is unemployed—bread is scarce—and their revenue must be most sensibly affected—and as I believe far beyond the admissions of the Chancellor of the Exchequer. The Government has been greatly relieved by the settlement of the Catholic question. It enables them to look abroad with more confidence and to speak in a higher, and what is highly important, in a more imposing tone to foreign nations. This Country in common with all Europe is looking intensely on the East. Russia has indeed declared that she seeks not territorial aggrandizement—but she claims pecuniary indemnities for the war which all the world knows Turkey can never pay—like the man who cannot pay his debts without the sale of his patrimony. So Turkey must relinquish her fairest provinces *now*. The next war Constantinople itself must go. Meanwhile G. Britain is looking on with the keenest Jealousy— but she stands in a very embarrassing predicament. Her Greek Treaty meets her at every turn. Prussia wishes to keep that question open so as to keep G. Britain and France from co[a]lescing with Turkey to arrest her uplifted arm. She contends therefore for enlarged limits. France unites with her in these views because of the principal part she has enacted on the scene—while England wishes to close it by confining the boundaries to the Morea and the Cyclades. Prussia has declared herself the firm friend of Russia and that she will strike at any power that interferes—which intimidates Austria and compels her to keep the peace—between Russia and Prussia she might find another trigram. I have endeavored to give you a rapid sketch of the political board and the position and character of the pieces. I think it is conjectured only to be said that Turkey must fall without aid—and so thinking I believe G. Britain will at every hazard interpose. By entreaty first—but by force if necessary. The first gun she fires involves all Europe.

From the King down I have had the most positive and reiterated assurances of a wish to cultivate the most friendly relations with us. The Duke of Wellington declaring that he had nothing so much at heart. Amid the learned and benevolent societies, who contribute to form and control public opinion I have been received always with respect—sometimes with enthusiasm. I have on those occasions, unhesitatingly, assured them of a kindred spirit in my own Country—and have adverted to show strong ties which recommend and secure our friendship. Whenever I have done so I have been made perfectly sensible that these People are most sincere in their good feelings towards us—as professed.

The Government indeed (without complaining of it) have adverted to the tariff as a measure of an unfriendly character to them. This I have repelled—and they stood rebuked when I pointed to their own example —which we had not even approached—altho it was particularly onerous to the principal productions of our Country. I feel quite sure that we have the fairest prospect of a long and undisturbed tranquility. As to the points between us, their settlement will depend rather on their own merit, than on the character for ability of the Minister. I have written a long letter which I beg you to place to the real motive[—]a sincere friendship for you.   James Barbour

I have a painful weakness in my eyes which will account in part for this scrawl.

ALS. ViU.
1. Henry Richard Vassall Fox (1773–1840) and Elizabeth Vassall Fox (1770–1845), Lord and Lady Holland, had probably inquired about their interests in the Holland Patent, a grant of 20,000 acres of land to the first Lord Holland in 1769. David Maldwyn Ellis, *Landlords and Farmers in the Hudson-Mohawk Region, 1790–1850* (Ithaca, 1946), p. 49.

2. Not found.
3. Littleton Waller Tazewell, *A Review of the Negociations between the United States of America and Great Britain, Respecting the Commerce of the Two Countries* (1829). On the essays, see James Barbour to Martin Van Buren, May 13, 1829, Van Buren Papers, DLC.
4. Louis McLane, rather than Tazewell, succeeded Barbour.

FROM JOHN WHITTEMORE

Dixville June 22, 1829

Sir

The inhabitants of this town are now reduced to two. My Children are all gone but my youngest daughter and if there is no better prospect we must quit before winter. The roads are so bad there is but little travel. Last year the bridges were all carryed off and two large Slides came down in the notch. We did sevinty days work on the road before teams could pass, Mr Parsons[1] and others worked about twenty more, the prospect was so bad that my sons were determined not to winter here again, Mr [Jeremiah] Gerrish[2] told me the last time I saw him that you and he had agreed not to sell any single lots nor do any thing on the road, now Sir if this is right I ought not to complain but I must hear some other reason for its being just before I can believe it. We have done at least five hundred days work on the road and the proprietors have done nothing. I am no begger. All I ask is justice amongst men. Your much lamented brother told me that Daniel would be willing to lay out a hundred or two dollars on the road if that would satisfy me but that you considered such sum only as an entering wedge for a larger sum but I am not Lawyer enough to see the propriety of such argument. Beside two hundred dollars well layed out with what the people would do provided that sum was promised to be paid those that should do the work. When done under the superintendance of some good men that put an Interest in the road would make it tolerable good so that the reverse of curses would rest on the proprietors heads, you can guess pretty near what men say when they get their horses off the notch and have them lay in the gulf two or three days, which has several times been the case, I think it would be for your Interest to sell the land by lots to setlers and I should like good neighbours very much—now sir if you will assist in repairing the road you will let me know how and when. General Town from Charlton[3] has been here if you see him he can tell you my situation and that of the road. I am your long neglected and very Humble Servant

John Whittemore

ALS. NhHi. Published in *PC*, 1: 479–480. Whittemore (1776–1846), a native of Salisbury, had moved to Dixville in 1812 as the agent of Webster to look after Webster's and Gerrish's land interests in the township. For a discussion of Webster's acquisition of the land, see *Correspondence*, 1: 123–124.

1. Not identified.
2. Gerrish (1764–1836) was a gunsmith in Boscawen and Webster's partner in the Dixville landholdings.
3. Not identified.

TO NATHAN HALE

Thursday Morning [July 2, 1829]

Dr Sir

I congratulate you sincerely on the happy occurrence in your family. How is Mrs H. today?

In the course of the day, I hope to see you, & to have a little conversation on another subject.

In the mean time, I have a draft to pay, which requires 300 more than I shall have till Monday? Have you such a sum as that, which is *sleeping* for want of use? I will give a check payable on Monday. Yrs.

D. Webster

ALS. MHi.

TO EDWARD CUTTS, JR.

Boston July 6. '29

Dr Sir

I am obliged to you for your letter of the 17th of June.[1] In regard to the subject, about which it was written, I feel no other disposition to put an end to the claim than what arises from a wish to avoid the trouble. I am quite sure I never did any thing unjust, or improper, in the purchase of the land; time has removed most of the circumstances from my mind—& I suppose I could not well be called on, now, to retain them.

What I have offered, I have offered simply for peace, & out of respect to Mr [Peyton R.] F[reeman]'s[2] opinion.

If 300 Dlls will satisfy the party, I will pay it. In September I hope to be in Portsm. & will hand you the money—if not then, you may draw on me for it. The parties may consider this as final, on my part. I cannot, in duty to myself, go any farther. You can inform me whether the offer be accepted.

After this week, I expect to be out of Town till Aug 1.—shd. like, therefore, to hear from you this week, as I wish this matter off my mind.

I pray you to remember me, with much regard, to Madam [Jacob] Sheafe;[3] & to give my respects also to Mrs Cutts. Yours always truly

D. Webster

ALS. CSmH. Cutts (1782–1844; Harvard 1797) was a lawyer in Portsmouth.

1. Not found.

2. Freeman (1775–1868; Dartmouth 1796) was also a Portsmouth lawyer, having previously served as deputy secretary of state for New Hampshire and as clerk of the United States district court. For additional information on the dispute, see Freeman to DW, November 16, 1829, below.

3. Mrs. Sheafe's husband, a Portsmouth merchant, had died on January 25, 1829.

FROM WILLIAM WIRT

Baltimore—July 8. 1829.

My dear Sir

Mrs. W. instructs me to return you her cordial thanks for your attention to her gratification in the letter of *excerpts*—and you must permit me to disburthen myself of the pressure of my own feelings so far as to assure you that I shall *resent* through life (to use an expression of Boyle's) your unwearied and affecting kindness to me through the whole of my visit to your land of poetic beauty and Arcadian hospitality—that is to say, provided the Arcadians were the people which the poets describe and not those whom the divers [?] historians represent them to have been. All figure and levity apart, my visit to Boston comes back to me, at times, more like a delightful dream than a reality, so far did it surpass all the other comparatively "dull realities of civil life" that I have encountered in the course of my mortal pilgrimage. I have either been supremely fortunate and caught you, all, in your *mollia* or rather *mollissima tempora*, or the Southerners who have, heretofore, visited you are ungrateful dogs not to have chaunted your character in louder strains. I can tell you, however, that I find here, among the gentlemen of this place, a full response to my strongest notes of admiration. I have not met with a *gentleman* who has visited your country who is not in perfect unison with me. Mr. [Robert?] Oliver[1] says that your whole population is the best in the world—that there is nothing in Europe or America to compare with it—and I know nothing that can compare with it, but the unmixed native stock of Virginia. With a few slight peculiarities, the people of Virginia are identical with those of your people whom I have seen. I make the remark not as Mr. [Benjamin] Gorham seemed to suppose in the way of compliment—for there is no compliment on either side—but as a striking philosophical fact—and I wish to Heaven it were more perfectly known to those most deeply interested to know it. The political elements of disunion are at work among us, and it will require all the attraction of cohesion which mutual knowledge & love of each other's characters can generate to hold us together—and most happy should I be if I could devise any mode by which I could successfully contribute to such a result. Can you tell me how? "Gentle shepherd tell me—how."

I am glad to hear that our friend [George] Blake is well—and can well imagine the pleasure of your ride. I wd. have given *an ingot of gold* to have been with you, tho' I might have spoiled your subject. But I have been even with you both—for I have talked you over, too, again & again —and my listeners seemed well disposed to give me *my time*—those listeners have generally been "wife, children and friends"—and enter keenly into all the sensibilities which my reception in Boston must I think have awakened in a heart even of stone, which mine, however, chances not to be. By the way of secret and in your ear, I am unaffectedly surprized that such a speech as I made in our cause,[2] should have been thought worthy of so much news-paper notice. I was not conscious and cannot see to this moment that it was at all beyond an every day speaking in the Supreme court—and yet one who did not know me would suppose from these eulogies that the people of Boston had caught *a hippopotamus at the least*. Be it so—it is a silly bird, they say, that bewrays its own nest. But you & I know a thing or two more upon this subject. Mean time how happy & secure you must feel with the house of your fame on its' everlasting rock—like the rocks that form the *substratum* of your blissful country. I wish I had been as wise all my life as you have been—gone always for substance and not for show. My show, through the earlier years of my life, was the eclipse of my substance—and the shadows of that eclipse will haunt me thro' life. Even Gibraltar port has been always in its' sunlight—defying the thunders of the clouds & the ocean—and there may it ever stand in its' proud pre-eminence. It is fit that it should be so—and none but a *sacrilege* would wish to disturb the order of nature.

If you should meet with our friend Mr Justice Story assure him of my constant and grateful remembrance of his kindness. Would to Heaven that I had such an Oracle of the law in my neighborhood in the form of a Judge of the Supreme court. How does he continue to carry such a load of law with such buoyancy of spirits. I do not observe that his richly [laden] argosy sinks the thousandth part of an inch the deeper, with all her load, but makes her way as gaily & sportingly as if she were a mere gondola for pleasure. Such is the effect of a happy construction—and there is no builder, at best, like nature.

May I beg you, too, to present me, as occasion may offer, respectfully and gratefully to Chief Justice [Isaac] Parker and the members of the court of whose indulgence & kindness I shall cherish through life a religious sense. And to every enquiring friend, if it be not too troublesome, give the assurance that their kindness has not been sown on barren ground but that I have left Massachusetts under a sense of obligation for the delicate & polite hospitalities, I recd.—which neither time nor chance can diminish. With best regards to Mr. Pa[i]ge & your kin— Yrs truly   Wm. Wirt

P.S. Mrs. W. finding that I was writing to you wants that I shall thank you in her name, *with stronger emphasis*, for your fraternal kindness to me as well as for the *excerpts* you have sent her. So please to record her thanks with centuple accent. The young ladies, too, desire me to tender their thanks for your kind remembrance of them and to offer you their cordial greetings and salutations. I will write to my friend Blake as soon as I have disposed of some questions of law from Florida—meantime I pray you to offer him my kindest regards.

ALS. MHi. Published in Van Tyne, pp. 617–619.

1. Oliver (1757–1834) was a prominent merchant in Baltimore.

2. In June Wirt had traveled to Boston to appear against Webster in *Farnam* v. *Brooks*, 9 Pickering 212 (1830). Webster represented Brooks.

TO JOHN AGG

Boston Aug. 10. '29

My Dear Sir

It has given us all very great pleasure to hear from you and Mrs. Agg. We are here going on very dully. Julia is spending the summer at Brookline, with Mrs [Eliza Buckminster] Lee, Edward is in the Country; & Mr P[aige,] Master Danl. & myself constitute the family. D. will soon leave us for College, & Mr. P. & myself shall then have the whole house to ourselves. My health is rather better, I think, than usual; but, partly on pretence of bettering it, & partly because I am willing to get away from home for a while, I believe I shall go to the South shore, & stay there, with some occasional visits to town, for the month to come. I have been to Vermont, passed over the Mountains with the intent of visiting Lake George, but gave up that purpose, in consequence of not being joined by my expected company, & after spending a day at Albany, I returned to Brattleboro, from which place Mr and Mrs [Jonathan] Hunt accompanied me to Boston, & have spent a few days with us. They leave us today, much to our regret.

Mr Paige is gone to Lowell. I have not had occasion to lay Mrs Agg's reproaches before him. He works very hard, & complains bitterly of hard times. In that he is not singular.

Nobody here says any thing of politics. There is a very general feeling of dissatisfaction, & a silent reference to Mr Clay, as the man who, if any, is likely to be supported, as the means of bringing about a change. But nobody moves, at present.

I am sorry your prospects with the Journal are so very bad. The paper might have been useful, but things have been so conducted, that those who would willingly have befriended the establishment do not think of it with any pleasure. At least that is my case.

As yet, I have made no arrangements for the winter. It is hardly probable, however, my children will accompany me to Washington. They are of an age, when it seems necessary to [keep] them diligently at school.

I pray you to remember me, most kindly, to Mrs Agg. We wish you were here with us, to pass this hot month on our sea side. Yrs always truly   D. Webster

ALS. NhD.

TO NATHAN HALE

[August 10?, 1829]

My Dear Sir,

I have arranged with Mr [Frederick P.] Leverett that D. shall go & stay with him, one fortnight, & then be examined. In the mean time, inquiry is to be made for the best place to send him after Commencement.

Poor Julia seems unprovided for, for the next ten days, on acct. of Mrs Lee's expected visit to Dover. I understand your two eldest daughters are absent, and it has occurred to me that Mrs H. might be willing to have Julia to help her & Susan take care of the baby.

I am going away, tomorrow, to *Marshfield*—near our old shooting place at Scituate. I mean to stay there a week—to read in foul weather, & shoot in fair. I should like it much, if you could name a day in which you would join me. There is good boat shooting, of brown backs & yellow legs—& very comfortable *beds*—& agreeable people. I can so describe the place to you, as to bring you to the very house, without inquiry or doubt.

Suppose you leave here on *friday* at one oclock—a good trotting horse will bring you there before dark—(or even at 2 oclock)—I will have a boat, & guns ready—*Saturday* we will shoot—Sunday, go to meeting—come up to Hingham or Quincy Sunday Eve'—& home *Monday.*

I shall be at home all day, today, & quite alone. If you wish to confer on any of these matters, perhaps you will find time to call. Yrs
D. Webster

ALS. MHi.

TO JEREMIAH MASON

Boston Aug. 10. 1829

My Dear Sir

My stay in Vermont was protracted, so as to run into this month. I will meet you at Nahant, with pleasure, or at Hampton, at the House near the Beach, if we can fix on any time. This week & next you will be at Court—& I believe I shall go down to the south shore. The week following is Commencement. Commencement day, & the day after, I will give to visiting you, wherever you may choose—keeping out of places

where we shall be obliged to see others. The Hotel at Lynn, is a very good place—with spare rooms enough. It is far better than Nahant. Yrs
                                        D. Webster

ALS. NhD. Published in Van Tyne, p. 619.

TO ELIZABETH LANGDON-ELWYN
                                        Boston, September 8, 1829.
My Dear Mrs. Langdon Elwyn,

I have been long your debtor for two kind letters, received by me early in the season.[1] I know not how to account for, much less excuse, so long a delay. But the summer has been running away, and occurrences happening which occupied my attention from week to week. My brother's death was an unexpected stroke, and has devolved on me, in addition to the pain arising from the loss of so good a brother, many new cares and duties. I have lived to be the last of a pretty large circle of brothers and sisters. It not only fills me with wonder, but with melancholy, to look round about the places of my early acquaintance. Every body is gone. While my brother lived, there was yet something to hold to; but now, the last attraction is gone. There was a large, valuable, and most pleasant farm which belonged to us, and which he had taken excellent care of for years, but it causes me great pain now to visit it. A new generation has sprung up around it, and I see nothing interesting to me but the tombs of my parents, and my brothers and sisters.

I have been from home but once, except to New Hampshire. Julia and I went to Brattleboro' in July, and intended to visit Lake George. I proceeded to Albany where I was to be joined by Mr. [Jonathan] Hunt's family, of Brattleboro', and Julia, but Mrs. Hunt was taken sick, so that part of the journey failed, and I returned to Brattleboro' and thence home. I got home just in season to see your neighbor and my friend— in the stage-coach, passing out of town on her return home. If all Boston talk be true, it is possible we may have the pleasure of seeing her again in this quarter. Some people's hearts, it seems, are not so cold as their occupations.

We have had sundry and divers good citizens of the South among us in the course of August; among others your neighbor, Mr. [Nicholas] Biddle, was here just long enough to let us look at him. He is always most welcome, as he is always most agreeable; but, if instead of cashiers and other officials, he would bring fellow travellers of another kind with him, it would enhance our pleasure. Our Yankees have a great opinion of him. They think he takes good care of their money; although they do not see in him any of the marks of one of the children of Israel. He will have told you, that he had occasion to visit our town of Portsmouth. Mr. [Jeremiah] Mason was recently here, and expressed high satisfaction at the result of Mr. Biddle's visit, and much respect for him.

Of news in our circle, I dare say your daughters know more than I do. All that has come to my knowledge, is, that Mr. Charles Adams and Miss [Abigail] Brooks are married, and saw their friends last evening; and that Mr. [Benjamin] Gorham is engaged to Mrs. Coles.[2] The latter fact I learn from Mr. Gorham himself, and the former I infer from having received a legal portion of wedding cake.

I send you a copy of Mr. [Charles] Sprague's poem, which I did not hear, and have not read; but I subscribed for six copies, being told it was a poetical poem. I have seen no such production among us, lately, though I have met with several prose ones. Judge Story edified us with a good discourse, on his inauguration as professor.[3]

What shall I say of your friend Mr. Blake? He has been very gay and gallant through the season of company, and is in fine health and spirits. I know not if he intends becoming a relative of yours, but I believe that when he goes out for a drive, if no special order be given, the coachman sets off, as of course, for Mrs. [Caroline Langdon] Eustis's.

I hear with much regret of the illness of Mrs. R.,[4] understanding she is in Portsmouth. I hope she will find an atmosphere somewhat less damp than that of New York, favorable to her. We saw little of Charles [Langdon-Elwyn][5] while he was here, everybody was engaged. I sought him diligently, to have his company at dinner with Mr. Biddle, but he had gone to carouse with the Phi Beta Kappa.

I pray you make my best respects to Emily and Matilda.[6] For all I have heard of them lately, I am mainly indebted to Mr. [Jules von] Wallenstein, whom also I salute. Say to —— I have still in my eye the parting but reproachful shake of her finger through the coach window. She cannot say, I did it, "never shake," &c. Yours always, very truly,

Daniel Webster

Text from *PC*, 1: 480–482. Original not found.

1. See above, Elizabeth Langdon-Elwyn to DW, April 9, 1829; and see April 16, mDW 7924.

2. Not identified.

3. Story had recently accepted the appointment as the first Dane Professor of Law at Harvard.

4. Not identified.

5. (d. 1848; Harvard 1826), son of Elizabeth.

6. Daughters of Elizabeth.

TO SOLOMON VAN RENSSELAER

Boston Sep. 11. 1829

My Dear Sir

I regret exceedingly, that before your letter came to hand,[1] I had made an appointment to go to N. Hampshire sooner after the 20th instant, on business which it is not practicable to postpone. So long an interval had occurred since I saw you, that I had been led to think you had concluded that it would be best to leave a meeting to accident. I hope, very sincerely, it may yet so happen, that I may see the Genl. [Stephen Van Rensselaer?] before I go South. The last week in October, and the two first weeks in Novr. I expect to pass in New York. It would gratify me, if circumstances should call him to the City about that time. The opinions which I expressed to you, especially such as relate to the state of things in this part of the Country, have been much confirmed by events which have since occurred. It will not be possible to repress, for many months longer, some public demonstration of the general sentiment. I am, Dr Sir, with very sincere regard Yours,   Danl. Webster

ALS. NjMoHP.
  1. Not found.

TO NATHANIEL F. WILLIAMS

Boston Oct. 7. 1829

Dear Sir

I return your draft accepted. We look anxiously for the result of your late elections, and that of Delaware.[1] In this part of the Country, we stand as we have done, except, probably, with still fewer approvers of the present rule.

I hope to see you abt. the first of Decr. Yrs always truly

Danl. Webster

ALS. NN.
  1. In the Maryland general elec-
tions, the National Republicans won; in Delaware, the Jacksonians.

FROM JOSIAH STODDARD JOHNSTON

Phil. Oct. 19th. 1829

My dear Sir

After walking up and down Broadway for a month, looking at the same people & the same objects, listening to the same rattling & grating sounds & witnessing the confusion worse confounded, we sought a relief in the sameness and tameness of this City of peace & brotherly love. We heard nothing but noise & saw nothing but confusion, very good things no doubt while we can take a part in the busy scene & forget ourselves in the eagerness of pursuit & very agreeable while the novelty lasts. But here we have more quiet & repose—an entire freedom from political strife as well as the dissipations of society. A month of tranquility here will give us a rest for the gay & animated scenes of the Capitol. All is still at Washington—they have determined to hush up the affair—& shroud themselves in profound mystery. This gave rise to various surmises & auguries. But the veil has not been rent & we are suffering under the dread of an explosion in the War or Navy departments. Whether [John H.] E[aton] will be sent to Russia or [John] B[ranch] to N. Carolina—Whether he will hold them together by force—or blow them all up no one knows. I have letters from Mr. Clay of the 5 & 8. He is well. He had just returned from the Green River—where he was well recd. & well entertained. The demonstrations were very enthusiastic. He has but one more engagement at Mercer. The Legislature are decidedly in his favor & they will act as may be most advisable, during the present Session. They will either pass Resolutions approbatory of his conduct or nominate him—& this begets a very important question—when & where this nomination ought to be made—In the West—in the North or in the middle this winter or the next—or whether it is not better to wait until we see the indications at Washington. Mr. Clay is aware of the exception that may be taken to the premature agitation of this question—as well as of the motives that ought to induce them to wait for the development of opinions.

The result in Maryland (& perhaps Jersey) is not the effect of any change of opinion, but of the stimulus of success, continuing to animate one party while the other is dispirited by defeat. But I do not argue unfavorably of the final result. They will be rallied again & I have no doubt the issue of this will diffuse new spirit among them. It is said some members of the Senate are dissatisfied. But have they the independence to resist? no not one. The people disapprove but the party holds together.

Mr. R.[1] remained a short time at N. York & returned to Baltimore. The Govr. having appeared some time above the horizon at N. York & Philadelphia, passed off in a very erratic Course towards the West & was last seen in the quarter of Richmond.

Mr. [Robert] Walsh is about to pay you a visit. He may account to you for the vote of Penna. The vote of [Joseph] Ritner has astonished the political world. His name was never heard here during the Election & I did not know he was a Candidate until I heard he was near being elected.[2] I do not know how to account for the defection but I am told there is a little anti-Wolf & anti-Masonry mixed. The majority in Lancaster may make [James] Buchannon quake. It is the precursor of breaking down the nominations. Little Delaware is erect. We shall have [John Jones] Milligan in the Senate.[3] Entre nous—McLane & [William C.] Rives went off on bad terms.[4] Something had occurred, I know not what. There was no intercourse. What a delightful time they will have of it!!

Majr. [Henry] Lee[5] more wisely chose to go alone—yours with great regard   J. S. Johnston

I had forgotten to say any thing about my wife—& now I think of it what can I say!—except that she is in status quo—she praises the people of Boston—the fashion of New York—& the quietness of Phila. & if I can judge from what is going on with Mrs. Pratt & Miss Cora,[6] she intends to assist to make Washington fashionable this winter.

She sends her regards to you & her congratulations on the marriage of Miss [Maria] Parker[7]—& her remembrance to all her friends.

ALS. NhD.

1. Not identified.

2. In the Pennsylvania gubernatorial race, Joseph Ritner, the Anti-Masonic candidate, polled a surprising 24,959 votes, compared to Wolf's 46,888.

3. Instead of Milligan, Arnold Naudain was elected to the Senate from Delaware.

4. The disagreement, if such there was, may have been over Rives' appointment as minister to France. As John A. Munroe, in *Louis McLane: Federalist and Jacksonian* (New Brunswick, 1973), p. 257, points out, there is no evidence that McLane, who had been appointed minister to Great Britain and was to make the trip abroad with Rives, was consulted on the appointment. Furthermore, there apparently was some misunderstanding about when and where they would board the *Constellation* for departure to Europe (p. 267).

5. Lee was appointed consul-general at Algiers.

6. Not identified.

7. In his diary, Charles Francis Adams reported a "rumor of an engagement between Mr. Webster and a young lady" of Boston, identified in one of his letters as "Miss Parker" (*Diary of Charles Francis Adams*, vol. 2. *July 1825–September 1829*, ed. Aïda DiPace Donald and David Donald, Cambridge, Mass., 1964, p. 360). In mid-August Maria Parker married Simon Adams of Lowell (*Columbian Centinel*, August 19, 1829).

FROM JOHN LOWELL, JR.

Richmond. November 2, 1829.

Sir,

I have been in this place rather less than three weeks, and during that time I have daily attended the debates both in the committees & in convention.[1] I have also associated with members of both parties, and have found your letters of introduction of much advantage.

I now sit down to give you my impressions concerning the state of affairs here; since you were pleased to request me to do so.

The right of suffrage, contrary to the expectation of many, has become a secondary object. A majority seems disposed to extend that right somewhat according to the plan recommended in the report of the legislative committee, which plan would still restrict it very much, according to our Northern notions.

The great question is the appointment of representation in the house and senate; and on this question the house is geographically divided. The Western party claims the basis of white population for both houses; and the tide-water party that of population white population & taxation equally combined. The country below the Blue Ridge pays at present three fourths of the taxes; but its' white population only exceeds that of the Western district by about 19,000. If the white basis prevail, the power of the trans-Alleghany country will remain the same; that of the tide-water district will be diminished at least one fourth; and the populous counties of the valley, as well as some counties just below the Blue Ridge, will gain all that the others lose.

The gentlemen of the West appeal to the natural rights of man & of majorities; those from the tide water district predict danger to their slave property from taxation, & other legislation. But all guarantees are refused, & the contest, as among the members of the convention, turns wholly on the possession of political power. Accordingly several large slave counties join the West; & slave-holders who live in them do not fear the experiment. The East is said to have lost heretofore by obstinacy and petulance. It will certainly gain nothing now by the opposite virtues. The East certainly possesses men of the most talent & education in the house; and men who besides have a perfect knowledge of the whole theory of government and of the nature of man, as exhibited from the time of the creation to that of George Mason's constitution in 1776. Although the Western members have not this general information; some of them exhibit a practical sense somewhat resembling that of our country legislators in Massachusetts.

Mr. Munroe made a speech to day; in which he recommended a compromise by placing the house on the basis of white population, and the senate on that of the combined ratio. Mr. Madison is understood to be in favor of this plan, & perhaps also General [Robert B.] Taylor.[2] They are probably the only men who are in favor of it; unless some Eastern men should adopt it for fear of being forced to accept worse terms. Still, so equally are the parties divided, that a general impression prevails that this measure will be carried; as the moderate men will alternately throw themselves into either scale.

Judge Marshall goes with the East.

Mr. Munroe comes from a district in the Western interest, Messrs. Madison and Taylor from the East; and they are I believe the only men whose votes have not coincided precisely with their geographical position.

If, after the white basis is adopted for the house, General Taylor should still act with the West; it is thought possible that there may be a tie, 48 to 48, on the question of amending the senatorial basis of the present constitution. This result would be equivalent to a victory in the opinion of the Western members; who profess that they will not accept the compromise, but demand the whole. It seems that the East and West are also divided on the subject of internal improvements, & from what I can learn, I should suppose that the doctrine of a liberal construction of the U. S. constitution was gaining ground rapidly in the West. Manufactures are said to be springing up in that country. The allurement of extensive patronage can no longer be offered to the aspirants for political distinction, by the leading men of ancient Virginia: and these unrestrained differences of opinion & local jealousies forbode, in the opinion of intelligent men of both parties, less internal tranquillity than has heretofore existed in the commonwealth.

The West must certainly triumph at last, if it do not immediately; and in the mean time Virginia will scarcely be at leisure to regulate the concerns of the nation, as well as her own internal affairs.

Some gentlemen express a belief that, if the presidential election could be deferred till six years from the present day, Virginia would give her vote to Mr. Clay. Others again, affirm that nine out of ten of the whole population are for a narrow construction of the constitution.

I believe both parties to be much too confident.

The internal parties of Virginia will probably be more marked, if the election of governor be given to the people: but the present opinion is that the choice will still be reserved to the legislature.

This convention certainly contains many able men, but what I have here seen and heard confirms me in the opinion that Virginia does not owe her predominance in the national councils either to the talent or to the information of her sons, but to the undeviating consistency of her own course, & to the perseverance with which she supports those [who] represent her sentiments. Still, if I mistake not, the floodgates [of] democracy are about to be opened upon the native soil of [Jefferson.] The tide may rise gradually, but I do not believe it can be excluded. It may enrich the economic wealth, but it will not admit the existence of so solid a political fabric, as has heretofore overshadowed the land.

In the remarks that I have made concerning the politics of Virginia, I have principally confined myself to the opinions which are entertained by some of those gentlemen whom I have met in this place.

I expect to leave Richmond next week, and remain very respectfully, Your obedient servant,   John Lowell, Jr.

ALS. NhHi.

1. The Virginia Constitutional Convention, which Lowell was observing and reporting on, had assembled in Richmond on October 5, 1829, and continued to sit until January 15,

1830.

2. Taylor, a graduate of William and Mary, a lawyer and commander of the American forces at Norfolk during the War of 1812, represented Norfolk in the Constitutional Convention. Because he differed with his constituents on the question of representation, he resigned his seat. *Niles' Register*, 37 (November 14, 1829): 188–189.

FROM PEYTON R. FREEMAN

Portsmouth Novr. 16. 1829

Sir,

Since the last letter of Mr [Edward] Cutts to you[1] on the Rindge claim, hearing nothing from you for some time, I suppose you consider the matter of attempting an amicable compromise through him as at an end. I was somewhat surprised at the smallness of the sum which Mr Cutts informed me he had named to you—which I did not know of at the time & never should have acceded to on any other consideration than the sort of reference made by us to his award or mediation. I was much more surprised that you did not promptly accede to that proposal of Mr Cutts, made by him as an expedient to mediate an adjustment so as to avoid the unpleasant occasion of deciding on the merits of a claim so apparently involving your professional reputation, when the sum named for aught shown by you as yet, is but about one third of what I think you ought in justice to pay.

Did you or not in the summer of 1815 obtain a deed from Saml. Pearse[2] as Executor of Isaac Rindge[3] purporting for the consideration of $100 to convey to you 2 hundred acre lots in New Chester?[4]

Did you at or about the same time execute two deeds of said lots, each purporting for the consideration of $200 (400 Drs. in both) to convey one of said lots to your brother Ezekiel Webster?

Were you then or had you previously been engaged & acting as Attorney or counsel for John P. Rindge[5] in a contest between him and Saml. Pearse respecting the settlement of his Admn. account of Is. Rindges estate? & were or were there not other persons, minors interested with your client in the subject matter of that controversy? So far, (unless there is forgery in the case) is easily answered now, for the facts are matter of record & they still remain uncontradicted & unexplained by you.[6] Did you then absolutely know, if the decision of that contest should be in your clients favor, that Pearse was solvent & able to answer to the estate for the full value of those lots & that he certainly would justly account therefor? If not, you certainly stood in a situation too favourable for making a good bargain at the expense of the interests you were intrusted with & had undertaken to protect: And unless your client and all persons interested with him in the matter, with full information of their rights & the circumstances affecting them (at least as far as you might know them), & being in a *capacity* to *protect* their rights, had consented to the contract, you *could not with a safe conscience make any bargain whatever for yourself with your clients adversary* which MIGHT AFFECT THOSE INTERESTS. Thus far the case presents a transaction which the law views with a jealous eye, which it will scrutinize with rigor, & of which any concealment on your part or neglect voluntarily & seasonably to disclose to the parties interested all the circumstances affecting their rights without waiting for their detection by other means must operate to your disadvantage in the mind of an enlightened casuist. How? When? & to whom have you ever made such disclosure? Supposing the land was sold in a year or two after the deeds given for only $600. (& I cannot find that it ever passed to a bona fide purchaser *for less*)—that sum with simple interest would now be over $1000. What should prevent your being justly held for that amount?

Was or was not Jno. P Rindge at the time said deed to you was executed indebted to you, or had you a claim on him, for fees & services relating to his claims on the estate or to the settlement of the administration acct.? And to what amount was your claim? Was or was not the deed obtained by you from Pearse under colour or for the purpose of an indemnity for said claim in case Rindge should abandon his appeal from the allowance of the admn. account & you should be unable to obtain payt. of him other wise? Did you or did you not afterward receive satisfaction for your claim against Rindge *of him*? If this *was not, What was* the actual consideration received or agreed on by Pearse for giving you the deed? Did you pay any & what sum or in any wise pay or allow any thing valuable to Pearse pending the appeal in consideration of said deed, & to what amount? And did you take care that the amount of such payment or allowance should be credited in s[ai]d Administration acct. or immediately or seasonably made known to Rindge or any person contesting that acct. that Pearse might be charged with it? Or that the estate should be benefitted by such allowance or payt.? And how & in what manner *was* or *might* the estate have been benefitted by the consideration of that sale?

These inquiries with many others we have a right to make, & if you see fit to resist the claim on you [we] request you to answer. If you can contrive or imagine any probable explanation which I think ought to satisfy me of the injustice of that claim I will abandon it at once. But as the case stands unexplained by you it does appear to me that you are altogether in the wrong—and I will add, that I hope you will consider your reputation too valuable to be put in competition with the possible gain by you of so paltry a sum as six or eight hundred dollars in a transaction like this, & will delay no further to make a just compensation.[7] Your humble Servt.   Peyton R. Freeman

ALS. NhHi.

1. Not found.

2. Not identified.

3. Rindge (c. 1736–1806), a native of Portsmouth, had apparently remained a Loyalist throughout the Revolution.

4. In 1837, New Chester changed its name to Hill in honor of Governor Isaac Hill.

5. John P. was most likely a son of

Isaac Rindge.

6. The case referred to was *Rindge* v. *Pearse*, filed in the Rockingham Superior Court of Judicature in November 1813, but not finally disposed of until February 1819.

7. As early as February 27, Freeman had written Webster, urging him to send the sum Freeman had previously suggested (see mDW 7799).

TO EDWARD CUTTS, JR.

Boston Novr. 18. 1829

Dear Sir

I have recd another long letter from Mr Freeman, on the subject of the claim set up by him agt me, in the name or on the behalf of the Rindge heirs.[1] I certainly regard this as being in the last degree unfounded, &, in short, vexatious. Mr Freeman's letter seems written, *in terrorem*, & does not incline me to make any further sacrifices, in order to appease him. I believe I wrote you, last June, that I would buy peace, at the cost of 300 Dlls.[2] That offer will not be encreased; it may stand, a reasonable time to be answered; & if not accepted it must then be considered as withdrawn. As I wrote you before, I made this offer out of respect to Mr Freeman's opinions, for whom I have always entertained friendly regard, & always wish to. I know, that in the case itself, there was nothing either in fact or intention, in the slightest degree improper.

I leave home for W[ashington] the day after Thanksgiving—say, the 27th inst. Yrs with great regard   D. Webster

ALS. MB.

1. See above.

2. See above, DW to Cutts, July 6, 1829.

TO [JACOB MCGAW]

Boston Novr. 18 1829

My Dear Sir

I have a thousand thanks to give to you & Mrs McGaw for your kind invitation to leave Julia with you, for the winter.[1] I assure you, there are no persons living, to whom I would more cheerfully give such a pledge of confidence. I know you would both love her, for her own sake, & for her father's & mother's also. But Julia is at present so exceedingly well situated, & so attached to her present condition, that it seems it would be wrong to change it. She has passed the summer at Brookline, with Mrs Lee (Eliza Buckminster) & had her instruction from Miss Searle,[2] a young Lady of our acquaintance, of the best character & qualifications, who lives at Brookline with her mother & sisters. Julia has become quite attached to her, &, now that Mrs Lee has come into town for the winter, Miss Searle has taken her altogether to herself. In addition to being in an excellent family, & having good means of instruction, she is near town, so that her uncle Paige, & other friends, can see her frequently in my absence. Under these circumstances, with hearty & repeated thanks for your friendship & kindness, I have concluded to leave her where she is.

And now, My Dear Sir, I must tell you & Mrs McGaw, *in confidence*, a little news; nothing less than my expectation of being again married. The affair is not of long standing; but it looks so much like terminating in a marriage, that I may venture to mention it to you, to go no further, till you shall hear of it from other quarters. The Lady is Miss Caroline LeRoy, of New York, aged 31 yrs, or thereabouts. She is the daughter of a highly respectable Gentleman, now some years retired from mercantile business. Mrs McGaw will want to know all about her—what I can say is, that she is amiable, discreet, prudent, with enough of personal comeliness to satisfy me, & of the most excellent character & principles. With this account of the Lady, your wife must rest content till she has the means of personal acquaintance, which I sincerely hope may happen soon. Tell her, she will be sure to like her. Whether this same Lady will go to Washington, the first of next month, or whether she will be so cruel as to oblige me to go without her, & to return for her to New York, about Christmas, are secrets worth knowing, but which are not known to me. I shall endeavor to set forth strongly the inconvenience of a winter journey from W. to New York & back.

I hope to get away on the 27th inst.—& intend taking Julia to New York, to make a little visit to Mrs [Cyrus] Perkins, & for the purpose of giving her an opportunity of seeing the aforesaid Lady.

With grateful & affectionate remembrance to you all, I am, My good old friend, very truly Yours   Danl. Webster

ALS. NhD. Published in Van Tyne, pp. 577–578.
1. See McGaw to DW, September
27, 1829, mDW 8094.
2. Not identified.

TO LETITIA BRECKENRIDGE PORTER

Boston Nov. 19. 29

My Dear Mrs Porter,

I ought to have answered your letter a month ago,[1] but I have been to New York, & came home only a few days since. It gives me great pleasure to learn that your harbor is *permanently* built & secured. It is the accomplishment of a great object, &, in time, much benefit must of course be derived from it. The *sub agent* of the War Department certainly deserves well of his Employers! I shall preach of the advantages of Black Rock, and its neighborhood, to all the young men I see, with a shilling in their pockets, because I really think those advantages to be great, & that Capital might be invested there, with as much promise of profits as any where else. The *times* have *pinched* New England, like a vise. We hope we are getting over the hardest of the *screwing*, & if this should turn out to be so, our emigrants to the West would be more likely to be able to possess the means of business & credit, wherever they might fix themselves.

Every body, here, is frightened, at the idea of any investment, *beyond his own power of oversight.* So many establishments have failed, & brought with their failure, such severe losses, that our Capitalists, who mean to spend their days where they are, are extremely inclined to keep every thing very close. Black Rock must be built up by young & active men, of some Capital, who will go with it, take care of it, & hope to encrease it. I cannot but think, if the times should grow a little more favorable, such adventurers may be found.

I go to W. in ten days. The society will be so much changed, it must look like another place; & I fancy it may be a place of queer things. If I see any thing which I think would make you laugh, I will give you an account of it. I met with Mr [James] Barbour in New York. He is well, in fine spirits, delighted with England, & yet willing to get home; but sufficiently angry, with all, at the manner of his return.

He talked better than I ever heard him. I did not see his family.

Pray remember me to Genl. P[orter]. If he has anything to say about the politics of N York, I wish he wd. write me at Washington. I will not betray him, since he is a "Jackson Agent." Yours with very true regard
D. Webster

ALS. NBuHi. Mrs. Porter was the wife   under Adams.
of Peter Buell Porter, secretary of war   1. Not found.

TO NATHAN HALE

Friday Morning [November 20, 1829]

D Sir

This is instead of one, not used, after being indorsed by you, some time ago, but burnt.

You will be glad—so shall I—when the occasion for troubling you with these matters & things shall cease—Yr. 300 Dlls is at your command, when needed. Yrs[1]   D Webster

ALS. MHi.
1. Hale endorsed the letter: "Nov 20, 1829. $100 in 3 m. ans NH."

TO EDWARD CUTTS, JR.

Boston Nov. 29 '29

Dear Sir

Enclosed you have my check for $300. It would puzzle me to write a discharge, & I shall be content with whatever you send.

Perhaps it may be to following effect—"recd &c of DW in full of a claim set up by us agt. him to account for price or value of lands conveyed to him by S[amuel] P[earse] &c; for which he says that he is not liable to acct"—or any other form—except only, that I cannot service any discharge, which would imply an admission, on my part, of any rightful claim.

I shall go so[uth] in two or three days. Yrs always with regard

D Webster

ALS. NhHi.

TO DANIEL FLETCHER WEBSTER

New York Decr. 14. 1829

My Dear Son,

You have been informed that an important change in my domestic condition, was expected to take place. It happened on Saturday.

The Lady who is now to bear the relation of mother to you, & Julia & Edward, I am sure will be found worthy of all your affection & regard; & I am equally certain that she will experience from all of you the utmost kindness & attachment. She insists on taking Julia with us to Washington; thinking it will be better for her, & that she will also be good company.

We shall leave New York in about a week. I recd your first letter,[1] which gave me pleasure, & hope to have another from you, before I leave N. York. You will not fail to write me once a week, according to arrangement. The enclosed note[2] you will of course answer. If you dispatch your answer at once, without waiting for the keep sake, it will arrive here before our departure. Let it come enclosed to me. The "keep sake" is an elegant gold watch. You must send for it to Mr. Paige, by a careful hand. Mr. Paige will not be home under ten days from this time.

I hope, My Dear Son, that I shall continue to hear good accounts of you—& am always, with much affection, Yr father   D. Webster

ALS. NhD. Published in *PC*, 1: 482.   2. Not found.
    1. Not found.

FROM JAMES BARBOUR

Barboursville Decr. 22nd. '29
Dear Sir

The exceedingly great pressure of my domestic affairs has deprived me of the opportunity of replying to your esteemed favor—received some days past.[1] I was quite satisfied, when I saw you among the guests at the dinner given to Mr [James] Brown,[2] that a new and adequate motive had been presented to you, to induce you to change the purpose you entertained when I consulted you on the propriety of my refusal. I still feel satisfied that I acted correctly—apart from the real necessity there was of my hastening home.

When in Philadelphia I spent the only evening I was there, with Mr [John] Sergeant. I found he entertained the same opinion you hold as to Mr Clay—as the only man around whom the Friends of a better state of things could rally, with the least prospect of success. Mr [Samuel L.] Southard writes me to the same effect—for he was absent from Trenton when I passed—so that I did not see him as I wished. Since my return home I have received a letter from Mr Clay, in which there is much more of hope, than despondency. As I suggested to you, I visited the Convention. My reception there was on the whole highly gratifying—but the full blooded Jacksonians stood aloof—and obviously eyed me with jealousy—and I might add with hatred. The more moderate and reasonable indulged their good feelings—and gave me a most hearty and friendly welcome. I regretted to learn that as yet few or none of his Jacksons Party, had disavowed him. I could discover, however, as I thought some repressed indignation waiting for a favorable occasion to blaze out. [Thomas] Ritchie is more and more zealous in his favor—and he continues to brandish the uplifted rod of his denunciation over the heads of his disciples. I found Van Buren there. His visit was said to be an unprofitable one. His reception, except with his Good Friend Ritchie and his Partizans, any thing but flattering. As far as I could learn—he—Calhoun & Clay stand on pretty equal ground—the union of the two former *at this time* I believe would be sovereign in carrying Virginia as the prejudices against Clay are continually kept alive by the Enquirer—and it is impossible to bring back the People to a just way of thinking as it regards him—they reading almost, exclusively, the Enquirer. What new Parties may grow up under the excitement prevailing from the proceedings of the Convention, it is impossible to say. Could I have sacrificed my conscience to popularity I had a plain path before me—that of advocating universal suffrage—but my best judgement led me to the conclusion that the freehold franchise was our last hope—and hence I unhesitatingly avowed my sentiments in its favor and was immediately placed among the Aristocrats. Turning my back on Politics I have given up the whole of my time to my own affairs—the more necessary as they are somewhat deranged by my long absence in the public service. The field is a large and interesting one, and I am, as yet at least, more happy than in any former period of my life. Tho never suffering myself to be depressed, unreasonably, yet there were times and seasons of vexation. Now I scarcely look even at the papers—and at peace with myself, and no one to say why or what doest thou, I am undisturbed with the folly or the crimes of Mankind.

Still I feel I owe much to my Country for its numerous proofs of confidence and kindness—and still more to Posterity and to the last hope of the World. If I could believe I could render any service to either, by committing myself again to the troublous scene, I would do so with whatever sacrifice it might be attended—but as long as the disastrous mania continues, which has so long, and so degradingly, prevailed I see but little hope from human efforts. If therefore you have any propitious omens do let me hear of them. I write as if the mail were a safe conveyance; and the sacredness of private correspondence respected—in this I may be mistaken.

I assure [you] of my high respect and cordial friendship

James Barbour

ALS. NhD.
1. Not found.
2. Merchants and businessmen of Philadelphia had held a public dinner for Brown upon his retirement as minister to France.

Calendar, 1825–1829

(Items in italic are included in this volume.)

1825

Jan 1	To David Lewis. ALS. PPL. mDWs. Expresses willingness to assist him in the case of the *James Lawrence.*	
[*Jan 1*]	*Lines on the death of Charles Webster.*	3
Jan 1	From Grace Fletcher Webster. ALS. NhHi. mDW 4603. Van Tyne, p. 554. Remarks on the activities of the family and the death of Charles.	
Jan 4	Petition of Rufus Lincoln for a pension. ADS. DNA, RG 233. mDW 41196.	
Jan 4	From Nahum Mitchell (enclosure: petition of Rufus Lincoln). ALS. DNA, RG 233. mDW 41200. Reports on the Lincoln petition for a pension.	
Jan 4	From Josiah Quincy. ALS. DLC. mDW 4606. Recommends a direct grant from Congress for the islands in Boston harbor.	
Jan 4	Resolution requesting the Committee on the Judiciary to inquire into the expediency of compensating messengers of electors. AD. DNA, RG 233. mDW 41024.	
[*Jan 5?*]	*To George Ticknor.*	4
[Jan 5]	From Josiah Quincy. ALS. DLC. mDW 4614. Again discusses grant for Boston harbor.	
Jan 6	Resolution requesting the Committee on the Judiciary to inquire into the expediency of changing the times of the district court of Louisiana. AD. DNA, RG 233. mDW 41026.	
Jan 7	To Edward Cutts, Jr. ALS. MB. mDW 4618. Reports that the original papers in the case of the *Calliope* have not yet been found.	
Jan 7	From Grace Fletcher Webster. ALS. NhHi. mDW 4622. Van Tyne, pp. 554–555. Relates her despondency over Webster's long absence from Boston.	
Jan 7	Resolution requesting the Committee on the Judiciary to consider the matter of establishing "national penitentiaries." AD. DNA, RG 233. mDW 41028.	
Jan 8	*From Grace Fletcher Webster.*	5
Jan 9	To Leverett Saltonstall. ALS. DLC. mDWs. Reports that "under present circumstances" he cannot "oblige" him in the case of the *Argonaut, Peele* v. *the Merchants Insurance Co.*, an unreported Supreme Court case (1827).	
[Jan 10]	To George Ticknor (for Mrs. Ticknor). ALS. DLC.	

	mDW 4693. *W & S*, 16:94. Sends copy of his "Lines on the Death of Charles Webster."	
Jan 10	*From Grace Fletcher Webster.*	5
Jan 10	Resolution requesting the Committee on the Judiciary to determine what, if any, legislation is necessary for the "impartial administration" of justice in the territories. AD. DNA, RG 233. mDW 41030.	
Jan 11	*To John C. Calhoun.*	6
Jan 11	*From Lucius Horatio Stockton.*	8
Jan 11	From Robert Field Stockton. ALS. DLC. mDW 4638. Discusses the probability of George Blake's appearing in the case, *The Marianna Flora*, 11 Wheaton 1 (1826), for him.	
Jan 11	Petition of the Boston Marine Society for a floating light in Boston harbor. ADS. DNA, RG 233. mDW 41127.	
Jan 12	*From Grace Fletcher Webster.*	9
Jan 13–March 18	From William Tudor. ALS. NhD. mDW 4645. Discusses a libel case against him and comments on United States relations with Peru.	
Jan 14	From S[amuel] D. Ingham. ALS. DNA, RG 233. mDW 41070. States that he has been unable to find the report on the Wernwag petition.	
Jan 14	*From Grace Fletcher Webster.*	10
Jan 15	From Cyrus Perkins. ALS. DLC. mDW 4682. Sends his condolences on the death of Charles.	
Jan 15	*From Grace Fletcher Webster.*	11
Jan 16	*To Ezekiel Webster.*	12
[Jan 16]	To George Ticknor. Printed. Curtis, 1: 227–228. Discusses his lonesomeness since the Ticknors have left Washington, his shock at [Robert Goodloe] Harper's death.	
Jan 17	*To Mrs. George Ticknor.*	12
Jan 17	From Grace Fletcher Webster. ALS. NhHi. mDW 4696. Discusses the health of the family.	
Jan 17	Memorial of merchants of Boston, Mass., against duty on sales at auction. Printed DS. DNA, RG 233. mDW 41269.	
Jan 17	Petition of Samuel G. Perkins of Boston regarding certain claims on the Dutch Government. ADS. DNA, RG 233. mDW 41287.	
Jan 17	Resolution asking that claims on the Netherlands by U.S. citizens be reported if not injurious to the public interest. AD. DNA, RG 233. mDW 41032.	
Jan 18	From Edmond J. Lee. ALS. DNA, RG 233. mDW 41081. Asks DW to support giving federal courts diversity jurisdiction in matters involving citizens of the District of Columbia and those of other states.	

Jan 18	*To Ezekiel Webster.*	*13*
Jan 18	From Grace Fletcher Webster. ALS. NhHi. mDW 4703. Van Tyne, pp. 556–557. Discusses family affairs.	
Jan 18	From George Ticknor. Printed. Curtis, 1: 228. Reports the reaction in Baltimore to the death of Harper.	
Jan 19	From Alexander Macomb. LC. DNA, RG 77. mDWs. Sends letter from Calhoun to McLane recommending appropriation for erection of sea walls in Boston harbor.	
Jan 19	From George Ticknor. Printed. Curtis, 1: 231–232. Comments on DW's speech and Harper's death.	
Jan 20	To John Q[uincy] Adams (enclosure: James A. Holden to DW, Nov 8, 1824). ALS. DNA, RG 59. mDWs. Sends James A. Holden's application for appointment as commercial agent at Aux Cayes.	
Jan 20	From H. H. Huggeford (enclosed in James Barnes to DW, Feb 2, 1825). ALS. DNA, RG 94. mDWs. Recommends James Barnes for appointment as cadet to West Point.	
Jan 20	*To George Ticknor.*	*14*
Jan 20	From Grace Fletcher Webster. ALS. NhHi. mDW 4706. Van Tyne, p. 557. Reports on family affairs in Boston, ordination which she attended at church.	
Jan 21	To [Judah Hays]. ALS. IGK. mDW 4710. Details reasons for not presenting Hays' memorial before Congress immediately on receipt of it.	
Jan 21	From Daniel Brent. LC. DNA, RG 59. mDW 55665. Reports that he has been unable to find the papers on the *Calliope* in the state department.	
Jan 22	From Cadwallader D. Colden. AL. NhD. mDW 4712. Requests to borrow Webster's set of Blackstone's *Commentaries*.	
Jan 22	*From Grace Fletcher Webster.*	*15*
Jan 24	Petition of Benjamin Connor of Ohio for compensation of damages suffered during the Revolutionary War. ADS. DNA, RG 233. mDW 41162.	
Jan 25	From Henry Alexander Scammell Dearborn. ALS. NhHi. mDW 4720. Thanks DW for documents and discusses the President's recommendation for the suppression of piracy.	
Jan 25	From Judah Hays. ALS. DLC. mDW 4725. Responds to Webster's letter of Jan 21 concerning his memorial.	
Jan 25	*To Jeremiah Mason.*	*16*
[Jan 25]	*To George Ticknor.*	*16*

Jan 25   From Joseph Head and Thomas W. Philips. LS.
NhHi. mDW 4728. Reports a vote of thanks to
DW by the board of directors of the West Boston
Bridge Corporation for the services Webster
rendered the company as agent in Washington
the previous winter.

Jan 25   From Grace Fletcher Webster. ALS. NhHi. mDW
4730. Reports on family and friends.

Jan 26   To John Haven. LS. NhHi. mDW 4734. Urges
Haven to pay Sheafe the Spanish claim awarded
him in the case of the *Industry.*

Jan 26   To [John Collins Warren]. ALS. MHi. mDWs.
George Washington Warren, *History of Bunker
Hill Monument Association* . . . (Boston, 1877),
p. 125. Webster requests that he be able to
postpone his decision regarding Bunker Hill
oration until he reaches home.

Jan 26   From Grace Fletcher Webster. ALS. NhHi. mDW
4736. Van Tyne, pp. 557–558. Thanks DW for
letter and reports news from Ezekiel.

Jan 26   To Henry C. Carey & Isaac Lea. ALS. DLC. mDW
[1825–1838] 38294. Sends payment.

Jan 27   From Daniel Brent. ALS. DNA, RG 76. mDW
55616. Discusses the location of the *Calliope*
papers; encloses letter from James Monroe to
John Quincy Adams, March 15, 1816, mDW
55616.

Jan 28   *From Grace Fletcher Webster.*   *17*

Jan 28   Judiciary Committee report on an unidentified
petition of the inhabitants of the Western
District of Pennsylvania. AD. DNA, RG 233.
mDW 41051. Report that the petition ought not
to be granted.

Jan 28   Bill (H.R. No. 302) to change the time of holding
the district court for the Eastern District of
Louisiana. AD. DNA, RG 233. mDW 40922.
Approved on March 3, 1825.

Jan 28   Resolution requesting the Committee on the
Judiciary to consider changing the time of
holding the courts in the Western District of
Virginia. AD. DNA, RG 233. mDW 41034.

Jan 29   From James Trecothick Austin. ALS. DLC. mDW
4746. Asks DW to give attention to Long Island
in Boston harbor.

Jan 29   *To Joseph Hopkinson.*   *17*

Jan 29   From Grace Fletcher Webster. ALS. NhHi. mDW
4750. Van Tyne, p. 558. Discusses family affairs
in Boston.

Jan 31   From James Greenleaf. ALS. DNA, RG 233. mDW
41069. Discusses the question of compelling
testimony in courts of the United States.

Jan 31	To James William Paige. ALS. MHi. mDW 4753. Reports that he has spoken to Livermore on the Kelley (?) appointment.
Jan 31	From Porter, Bradley & Co. (enclosed in James Barnes to DW, Feb 2, 1825). ALS. DNA, RG 94. mDWs. Recommends James Barnes for appointment as cadet to West Point.
Jan 31	From Grace Fletcher Webster. ALS. NhHi. mDW 4755. Van Tyne, p. 558. Remarks on opposition to DW in Congress; reports occurrences on the Boston scene.
[Jan]	To S[amuel] L[ewis] Southard. ALS. DNA, RG 45. mDWs. Reports the receipt of Russell's warrant; has forwarded it to him and his friends.
Jan [?]–Feb 22	From [?]. AL. NhHi. mDW 4764. Expresses sympathy with the Websters over the death of Charles.
[Jan]	From Julia Stockton. ALS. NhHi. mDW 4768. Expresses her high regard for Mrs. Webster.
[Jan]	To Mrs. George Ticknor. ALS. NhD. mDW 4762. Reports that because of rheumatism he will not be able to dine with the Ticknors.
Feb 2	From James Barnes (enclosures: Henry H. Huggeford to DW, Jan 20, 1825; Porter, Bradley & Co. to DW, Jan 31, 1825). ALS. DNA, RG 94. mDWs. Asks DW's assistance in securing appointment to West Point.
Feb 2	From Samuel Jaudon (enclosed in DW to JQA, [Feb 5, 1825]). ALS. DNA, RG 59. mDW 55515. Recommends Benjamin Carman for appointment as consul to Montevideo.
Feb 3	From John Pitman. ALS. NhHi. mDW 4770. Requests DW's aid in securing an increase in salary for district judges, and particularly for him in Rhode Island.
Feb 3	*From Henry R. Warfield.* 18
Feb 3	From Grace Fletcher Webster. ALS. NhHi. mDW 4780. Van Tyne, p. 559. Reports on family life in Boston.
Feb 4	To Joshua Haven. ALS. NjMoHP. mDW 4784. Reports the receipt of Haven's letter and his satisfaction with it.
Feb 4	To James Monroe. ALS. NhD. mDWs. Recommends Richard D. Harris for navy agent at Boston.
Feb 4	To Samuel Lewis Southard. ALS. NhD. mDW 4786. Sends Southard endorsements of Ezra Davis for navy agent at Boston, but reminds him that he favors another.
Feb 4	To George Ticknor. Printed. Curtis, 1: 234.

Feb 18   To [John Quincy Adams]. ALS. MHi. mDW 4832. Introduces a Mr. Scott, applicant for sergeant at arms to the House of Representatives and a relative of Judge Washington.

Feb 19   From Daniel Putnam. ALS. MB. mDWs. Discusses Webster's review of the *Battle of Bunker Hill,* in the *North American Review,* and urges him to correct certain aspects of General Putnam's role in his next speech at Bunker Hill.

Feb 19   From John Randolph (with copies of related correspondence and memoranda). Copy. DLC. mDW 4844. Van Tyne, pp. 111–112. Asks DW to clarify a comment he made the previous summer about Randolph; sends note by Thomas H. Benton.

Feb 19   From George Ticknor. ALS. NhD. mDWs. Sends account of the affairs of Harvard College for Judge Story; reports that Mrs. Ticknor saw Mrs. Webster yesterday.

Feb 19   Resolution requesting the Committee on the Judiciary to inquire into the expediency of a law to adjust claims growing out of the War of 1812. AD. DNA, RG 233. mDW 41036.

Feb 22   To John Quincy Adams. ALS. MHi. mDW 4860. Introduces William Tileston, manufacturer of Boston.

Feb 23   To [?]. ALS. NhHi. mDW 4862. *W & S,* 16: 100–101. Thanks him for letter on Massachusetts politics and reports rumors of cabinet appointments.

Feb 24   From [Buckner Thruston]. AD. DNA, RG 233. mDW 41296. Discusses the Van Ness petition questioning Thruston's judicial character.

Feb 25   To Thomas Hart Benton (enclosure: memo to Benton on DW's disagreement with John Randolph, Feb 25, 1825). ALS draft and copy. NhHi. mDW 4868. Van Tyne, pp. 111–112. Sends Randolph's original communication and reports that no copies have been preserved.

[Feb 25]   From Thomas Hart Benton. Printed. Van Tyne, p. 112. Reports that arrangement with Randolph is "entirely satisfactory."

Feb 25   To John Randolph. Copy. DLC. mDW 4844. *W & S,* 16: 102–104. States that he remembers

saying nothing in 1824 "which can possibly be
considered as affecting Mr. R's veracity."

Feb 25   To Buckner Thruston. Copy. DNA, RG 233. mDW
41299. Requests Thruston's appearance at
committee hearing on February 26.

Feb 25   To John P. Van Ness. Copy. DNA, RG 233. mDW
41297. Requests his presence at the hearing of
Buckner Thruston.

Feb 26   *To [John Quincy Adams]*.   *34*

Feb 26   To James Miller. ALS. NWM. mDW 4880. Reports
that he received Miller's medals and will deliver
them on his return to New England.

[Feb 26]   To [James Monroe]. AD. DNA, RG 107. mDW
57160. On behalf of James Miller, expresses
gratitude for medal granted him in recognition
of Miller's service during the War of 1812.

Feb 26   *To Ezekiel Webster*.   *35*

Feb 27   *To Ezekiel Webster*.   *35*

Feb 28   To [Edward Everett]. ALS. MHi. mDW 4889. Asks
Everett for letters of introduction for [Joel
Roberts] Poinsett, who contemplates a trip to
the Mediterranean.

Feb 28   From Grace Fletcher Webster. ALS. NhHi. mDW
4890. Van Tyne, p. 563 (excerpt). Reports on
the family and friends in Boston.

Feb   [Articles of Assoc. of the N. E. Society for the
Improvement of Wool]. Printed DS. ScU. mDWs.

March 1   *From Grace Fletcher Webster*.   *36*

March 3   From John C. Calhoun (to DW, et al.). Copy. DNA,
RG 77. mDWs. Reports that no officer in the
Engineer Corps will be available during the
current year to carry out the surveys requested
by the Massachusetts legislature.

March 5   From Grace Fletcher Webster. ALS. NhHi. mDW
4898. Van Tyne, p. 564. Reports on visits from
friends, on the family, and on rumors of the
DW–Randolph dispute.

March 6   To [John Collins] Warren. ALS. MHi. mDWs.
George Washington Warren, *History of the
Bunker Hill Monument Association . . .* (Boston,
1877), pp. 126–127. Discusses a
misunderstanding over whether a speech is to be
made at the laying of the cornerstone of the
Bunker Hill monument in June.

March 8   *To Ezekiel Webster*.   *37*

[March 8]   From Grace Fletcher Webster. ALS. NhHi. mDW
4904. Reports on problems of securing
domestic help and on the affairs of the family.

March 9   From Daniel Fletcher Webster. ALS. NhHi. mDW
4908. Van Tyne, p. 565. Thanks DW for recent
letter; relates affairs of the family.

March 10	*From Grace Fletcher Webster.*	*38*
March 15	To Ezekiel Webster. ALS. NhD. mDW 4916. Speculates on the reason he has not received a report on New Hampshire's election from Ezekiel.	
March 20	From Thomas Appleton (enclosure: Spiridione Balbi to DW, Feb 15, 1825, LS and translation). ALS. DLC. mDW 4919. Introduces Balbi.	
[March 23]	To Alexander Bliss. ALS. DLC. mDW 4940. Instructs Bliss on note collection; reports his plans to leave for home the next day.	
March 29	To Henry Clay. ALS. DNA, RG 59. mDWs. Introduces John C. Jones, a merchant of Boston.	
March 29	*From Joseph Vance.*	*39*
March 29	Deed to land: Transfer from Timothy Williams, Lewis Tappan to Daniel Webster, March 29, 1825. AD. MWalB. mDW 39620.	
[March ?]	From Horatio Greenough (to the Committee of the Bunker Hill Monument Association). AL. MHi. mDWs. *Letters of Horatio Greenough, American Sculptor,* ed. Nathalie Wright (Madison, 1972), pp. 3–5. Submits model of obelisk for Bunker Hill monument.	
[March ?]	To [Edward Everett]. ALS (incomplete). MHi. mDW 3475. States that if Everett needs any documents for the *Annual Register,* he will furnish them, if he is notified before he leaves for home (may be later than 1825).	
[April 1]	To Edward Everett. ALS. MHi. mDW 4946. Introduces Samuel Adams of Greenland, N.H., who wishes to present plan for Bunker Hill monument.	
April 4	To [Bushrod Washington?] ALS. NhD. mDW 4948. Introduces Benjamin A. Gould, instructor in Boston Latin School.	
April 4	To Thomas Jefferson. ALS. NNPM. mDW 4950. Introduces Benjamin A. Gould.	
April 7	*To Henry Clay.*	*40*
[c. April 10]	To Jules von Wallenstein. ALS fragment. Judge Samuel J. Feigus, Uniontown, Pa. mDWs. Reports on summer plans; mentions Clay's letter [address] of March 26 to Kentucky constituents.	
[April 12]	To Ezekiel Webster. ALS. NhD. mDW 4955. Reports that [Jonathan] Hartwell is willing to buy Ezekiel's house.	
[April 18]	*Deed to Land: Transfer from Lewis Tappan to Daniel Webster.*	*40*
April [24?]	To Ezekiel Webster. ALS. NhD. mDW 4960. States his willingness to sell certain books to Ezekiel.	
April 25	Report of committee on plans for monument at Bunker Hill. ADS by DW et al. MHi. mDWs.	

	George Washington Warren, *History of the Bunker Hill Monument Association* . . . (Boston, 1877), pp. 158–159. Recommend that award for obelisk design of memorial be granted to Horatio Greenough.	
[c. April 25]	To the Secretary of the Suffolk Bar Association. DS. MBBA. mDWs. States that John Everett began reading law in his office on December 20, 1822.	
April 26	To John Quincy Adams. ALS. MHi. mDW 4962. Introduces a Mr. Wigglesworth and a Mr. Watts of Boston.	
April 27	*From John Evelyn Denison.*	42
May 2	*To [John Evelyn Denison].*	44
May 2	*To Joseph Hopkinson.*	45
May 3	[Certificate of honorary membership, Rockingham Agricultural Society]. Printed form with MS insertions. MWalB. mDW 4973.	
[May] 4	From John Evelyn Denison. Printed. Curtis, 1: 246. Thanks Webster for letter; reports meeting with Rufus King; and expresses continuing and strong friendship.	
May 7	*To Jonathan Goodhue.*	48
May 7	To Jeremiah Mason. Copy. NhHi. mDW 4979. Urges Mason to visit him in Boston soon.	
May 9	From Israel Thorndike. ALS. NhD. mDW 4980. Requests DW to represent him in a case.	
[May 12]	To Edward Everett. ALS. MHi. mDW 4981. States that even though he has another engagement in the evening he can meet with Everett if he is "wanted."	
May 21	To Jeremiah Mason. ALS. MHi. mDW 4983. Van Tyne, pp. 114–115. Discusses New Hampshire electoral possibilities and strategy.	
[May 22]	*To Jeremiah Smith.*	49
May 23	To DeWitt Clinton. Copy. NhHi. mDW 4989. Introduces Jeremiah Smith.	
May 23	To William Duer. Copy. NhHi. mDW 4991. Introduces Jeremiah Smith.	
May 23	*To James Kent.*	49
May 23	*To Jeremiah Mason.*	50
[May 27]	To James William Paige. ALS. NhHi. mDW 4993. Van Tyne, p. 612. Reports the arrival of Daniel at Sandwich where he is trout fishing.	
May 31	From Benjamin Jarvis. ALS. DLC. mDW 4995. Asks DW to use his influence in getting his son appointed consul to Greece.	
June [2?]	To Ezekiel Webster. ALS. NhD. mDW 5029. States that George Sullivan has some business in Concord and will want to consult with him on Sunday.	

June 4	*To Henry Cabot.*	51
[June 5?]	To Ezekiel Webster. ALS. NhD. mDW 5031. Has suggested to Sullivan that he will probably be unable to make satisfactory settlement; unless Ezekiel believes otherwise, Sullivan will not go to Concord.	
[June 5–10?]	To [Edward Everett]. ALS. MHi. mDW 5026. Discusses the selection of their lodgings in Washington.	
June 6	*To John Evelyn Denison.*	53
June 7	To R. Elwell. ALS. NhD. mDW 5011. States that he will be happy to represent Bell and Shaw in an insurance cause provided a $50 retainer fee is paid.	
June 9	To Edward Everett. AL. MHi. mDW 5014. Invites Everett to visit him on Tuesday evening.	
June 13	From Robert Walsh, Jr. ALS. DLC. mDW 5016. Regrets that he will not be able to accept honorary membership in the Bunker Hill Monument Association in person on June 17.	
[June 15?]	*To George Ticknor.*	54
[c. June 17?]	To Alexander Hill Everett. ALS. MHi. mDW 5201. Thanks Everett for work on Europe and invites him to dinner with the Ticknors and Lafayette.	
June 20	*To Ezekiel Webster.*	55
June 21	Opinion respecting powers and duties of Boston Overseers of the Poor (by William Prescott, Charles Jackson, and Daniel Webster). Printed. Josiah Quincy, *A Municipal History of the Town and City of Boston . . .* (Boston, 1852), pp. 172-175.	
June 23	To Rufus King. ALS. NhHi. mDW 5022. Introduces the Reverend John G. Palfrey.	
[June 25]	*To George Ticknor.*	55
[July 3]	*To James William Paige.*	56
July 8	To Samuel Frothingham. ALS. PHC. mDW 10982. Reports that he has drawn on his account for $400 and suggests that if there are problems with the draft he should see James W. Paige.	
July 8	*To James William Paige.*	56
July 9	From Daniel Brent. LC. DNA, RG 59. mDW 55667. Sends copies of *Calliope* papers he had requested from London.	
July 15	*To Mrs. George Blake.*	57
July 16	To James William Paige. ALS. NhHi. mDW 5039. Reports on his visit and reaction to Niagara Falls.	
July 17	To Mrs. George Blake. ALS. DLC. mDW 5043. Revises certain descriptive comments of the falls contained in his letter of July 15.	
July 17	*From John Evelyn Denison.*	63

July 18   From John L. Sullivan. ALS. NhD. mDW 5051. Reports success in purchasing *"a certain double barrel'd fowling piece"* for Webster.

July 24   From the Marquis de Lafayette. ALS. NhHi. mDW 5054. Van Tyne, p. 614 (under 1828). Introduces Count de Vidua of the Piedmont.

July 25   From Nathaniel Coffin. ALS. MHi. mDW 5056. Comments on hearing Webster at Bunker Hill; reminisces of college days (mailed letter with postscript a year later; postscript dated June 20, 1826).

[July 26]   To [Mrs. George Ticknor?]. AL fragment. NhD. mDW 5060. Reports several occurrences while returning from Niagara Falls.

July 30   *To Jonathan Goodhue.*   65

July   *From "Acacius."*   66

[Aug 2]   To Edward Everett. ALS. MHi. mDW 5066. Thanks Everett for his two notes, and suggests that they "forbear, *for the present*, to make any publication on the subject."

Aug 7   To John Fabyan Parrott. ALS. NhHi. mDW 5068. Reports that he has not yet presented Parrott's "paper" in Washington but will do so at the earliest opportune time.

Aug 12   *From James Madison.*   69

Aug 17   *From Caleb Cushing.*   70

Aug 19   From Jules von Wallenstein. ALS. DLC. mDW 5074. Reports on friends and politicians in Washington, Baltimore, New York, and Newport, R.I.

Aug 22   *From Robert Walsh, Jr.*   70

Aug 25   *To Edward Everett.*   71

[Aug]   To [Edward Everett]. ALS. MHi. mDW 5086. Thanks Everett for copy of his Concord speech and sends him a copy of his Bunker Hill oration.

Aug [?]   To George Ticknor. ALS. NhD. mDW 5088. Reports that another visit will have to be postponed temporarily since the Websters and the Blakes are going to Sandwich.

Sept 3   To William Allen. ALS. NhD. mDW 5091. Introduces Count de Vidua of Piedmont and Mr. Niederstetter, chargé d'affaires of the king of the Netherlands.

Sept 4   From Edward Everett. LC. MHi. mDW 5094. Requests documents on French spoliations claims previous to 1800, to be used in article he is writing for Jared Sparks.

[Sept 4?]   To Edward Everett. ALS. MHi. mDW 5199. States that documents he has on the French spoliation question are in his trunk of Spanish papers in the bank.

Sept 4	From Jules von Wallenstein. ALS. NhD. mDW 5095. Sends news of politicians and friends in Washington.
Sept 14	To Joseph Hopkinson. ALS. PHi. mDW 5098. Congratulates Hopkinson on his labor in defense of Captain Charles Stewart.
Sept 16	To Ezekiel Webster. ALS. NhD. mDW 5101. Urges Ezekiel and his family to visit them in Boston.
[c. Sept 17]	From Jules von Wallenstein. ALS. NhHi. mDW 5114. Reports on Washington friends.
Sept 21	From Edward Everett. LC. MHi. mDW 5105. Asks Webster for a legal opinion involving land he hopes to purchase in Cambridge.
[Sept 22?]	To [Edward Everett]. ALS. MHi. mDW 5197. Advises on his proposed land purchase.
Sept 24	To James Kent. ALS. DLC. mDW 5107. Introduces William Smith, son of Jeremiah Smith.
Sept 26	Deed transfer from Daniel Ladd to DW. ADS. MWalB. mDW 39835-272. For land in Plymouth, N.H.
Sept 28	To Henry Clay. ALS. DLC. mDW 5110. *W & S*, 16: 116. Hopkins and Hargreaves, *Papers of Henry Clay*, 4: 698–699. States that he is sending under separate cover his views on trade with England; comments on voters' approval of Clay in New York and New England.
Sept 28	To Henry Clay. LS. DNA, RG 59. mDWs. Hopkins and Hargreaves, *Papers of Henry Clay*, 4: 695–698. Discusses the U.S.-England trade question.
Oct 6	To Henry Willis Kinsman. ALS. MH. mDW 5118. Urges Kinsman to pressure Upton to pay notes due.
Oct 11	To Henry Willis Kinsman. ALS. NhD. mDW 5121. Again urges Kinsman to see that Upton pays immediately.
Oct 13	To Charles Brickett Haddock. Printed. *PC*, I: 396–397. Agrees to lend him $500; congratulates him on two orations.
Oct 17	To James Barbour. ALS. DNA, RG 74. mDWs. Asks Barbour to forward a letter, by a friend of Webster, to Lieutenant Leonard.
Oct 17	From Henry Clay. ALS. DNA, RG 76. mDW 55621. Reports that the Sheafe papers relating to the *Calliope* are now in the State Department.
Oct 23	To Joseph Hopkinson. ALS. PHi. mDW 5124. Expresses his gratification with Hopkinson's recent visit; mentions his involvement in Circuit Court cases; asks Hopkinson to urge Walsh to publish excerpts from Ticknor's recent pamphlet on Harvard University.

[Oct 25]	Deed of land to David Reed. DS. NhHi. mDW 39628. Transfer of land near Federal Street, Boston.
Oct 27	To Ezekiel Webster. ALS. NhD. mDW 5128. Urges Ezekiel to bring his wife on the forthcoming visit to Boston.
[Nov 7]	To Edward Everett. ALS. MHi. mDW 5133. Asks Everett to look over several items he received and to burn or otherwise dispose of them.
Nov 7	From Edward Everett. LC. MHi. mDW 5135. States that he does not care to be concerned in publishing the Evans' [?] letter.
Nov 15	From Nathaniel Chamberlain. ALS. DLC. mDW 5136. Introduces Yahola-Micco, a chief of the Creeks, and other Creek Indians visiting Washington.
Nov 17	To Joseph Hopkinson. ALS. PHi. mDW 5139. Reports that he and his family are preparing to leave for Washington.
Nov 17	From J[?] Richardson. ALS. DNA, RG 233. mDW 42094. Comments on petitions being sent to Webster.
Nov 17	To John Collins Warren. Printed. *PC*, 1: 397. Expresses a desire to assist Warren in raising money for a college gymnasium; sound body necessary for a sound intellect.
Nov 18	To Henry Clay. LS. DNA, RG 59. mDW 55517. Recommends Benjamin Gardner for appointment as consul at Palermo.
Nov 18	Receipt from Gilbert Stuart. Printed. Lawrence Park, comp., *Gilbert Stuart: An Illustrated Descriptive List of his Works* (4 vols.; New York, 1926), 2: 796–797. For $100 on painting of DW.
[Nov 19]	To Joseph Story. ALS. MHi. mDW 5142. *W & S*, 16: 116–117. Asks Story for a draft of a bankruptcy law and for his views on court reorganization.
[Nov 24]	To James William Paige. ALS. NhHi. mDW 5144. Van Tyne, p. 115. Reports their arrival in New York and the news of several important business failures.
Nov 28 [1825–1827?]	From Aaron Burr. AL. MHi. mDW 7326. George F. Hoar, "Daniel Webster," *Scribner's Magazine*, 26 (1899): 218. Sends Webster the "three Bills of Exceptions in the cases whose titles were furnished yesterday."
Nov 29	From Nathaniel Searle. ALS. DNA, RG 59. mDWs. Recommends Richard W. Greene for district attorney in Rhode Island.
Nov 30	From Richard W. Greene. ALS. DNA, RG 59.

	mDWs. Solicits appointment as district attorney in Rhode Island.
Dec 2	To Henry Willis Kinsman. ALS. NhD. mDW 5149. Asks Kinsman to send him the course of study used in Webster's law office.
Dec 6	To Henry Clay. ALS. DNA, RG 59. mDW 55520. Recommends Richard W. Greene for district attorney in Rhode Island.
Dec 6	From Charles Pelham Curtis. ALS. DLC. mDW 5151. Asks DW to assist him in a case against W. Samuel Williams.
Dec 6	From Richard W. Greene. ALS. DNA, RG 59. mDWs. Encloses letter of Nov 29, 1825, from Nathaniel Searle, endorsing his candidacy for district attorney in Rhode Island.
Dec 7	To John W. Taylor. ALS. NHi. mDW 5153. Asks Speaker of the House Taylor to examine and comment on his resolutions to amend the rules of that body.
[c. Dec 9]	To James Barbour. LS. DNA, RG 107. mDW 57164. As member of the select committee on the organization of the Executive Department, DW requests information regarding the War Department.
Dec 9	From W. Cranch (with enclosures). ALS. DNA, RG 233. mDW 41377. Encloses sketch of a bill involving the taking of evidence in the courts of the United States.
Dec 10	From Samuel Mifflin. ALS. DLC. mDW 5156. Discusses appealing the case, *Comegys* v. *Vasse*, 1 Peters 193 (1828), to the Supreme Court and claims before the Spanish claims commission.
Dec 11	To Alexander Bliss. ALS. DLC. mDW 5159. Instructs Bliss on the payment of a note he had accepted from Samuel Jaudon.
Dec 11	*To Jeremiah Mason.* 72
Dec 12	To Henry Clay. ALS. DNA, RG 59. mDWs. Again recommends Richard W. Greene for district attorney in Rhode Island.
Dec 12	To James William Paige. ALS (and signed by other members of the Webster family). MH. mDW 5165. Thanks Paige for his recent letter; comments on the failure of W. Samuel Williams.
Dec 12	Resolution to amend the rules of the House. AD. DNA, RG 233. mDW 41526.
Dec 13	Petition of Daniel Jackson and others. ADS. DNA, RG 233. mDW 42166.
Dec 15	From Winslow Lewis. ALS. DNA, RG 233. mDW 42096. Discusses salary increases for keepers of lighthouses.

Dec 19 Resolution on the inexpediency of constructing canal across Florida. AD. DNA, RG 233. mDW 41545.

Dec 21 To James Barbour. ALS. DNA, RG 107. mDW 57155. Discusses the law relating to the power of the Secretary of the Treasury over fines and forfeitures.

Dec 21 *To Alexander Bliss.* 73

Dec 22 *To Alexander Bliss.* 74

Dec 22 Bill for altering the time of holding the sessions of the Supreme Court. AD. DNA, RG 233. mDW 41307.

Dec 22 Bill to amend the judicial system of the United States. AD and printed document. DNA, RG 233. mDW 41312.

Dec 22 Report from the Committee on the Judiciary on the petition of Daniel Clark. AD. DNA, RG 233. mDW 41963.

Dec 22 Note for $1,000. ADS. MWalB. mDW 39630.

[c. Dec 22] Hartwell deed. ADS. MWalB. mDW 39835–278, 39640.

Dec 23 From Richard Rush (enclosure: R. R. to John Welles et al., copy). AL. DLC. mDW 5172. Encloses opinion on the Welles memorial.

Dec 23 To E. B. Williston. ALS. VtNN. mDWs. Informs Williston of the copyright owners of two of his recent speeches.

Dec 28 *To Joseph Hopkinson.* 74

Dec 28 From the Marquis de Lafayette. ALS. NhHi. mDW 5179. *PC*, 1: 398–400. Comments on European and American political developments; praises DW's Bunker Hill speech.

Dec 30 From Daniel Brent. LC. DNA, RG 59. mDWs. Sends letter of Harvey Strong, late consul of the United States at Glasgow.

Dec 30 *From William King.* 75

Dec 31 From Clement Cornell Biddle. ALS. DLC. mDW 5188. Forwards a copy of the English bankruptcy law for DW's consideration.

Dec 31 To Joseph Story. Printed. *PC*, 1: 400–401. Discusses the bankruptcy and judiciary reorganization questions.

[Dec ?] From George Ticknor. Printed. Curtis, 1: 259. Inquires about appointment as visitor to West Point.

[1825–1827] To Alexander Bliss. ALS. DLC. mDW 38271. Reports that he has had a severe attack of rheumatism; instructs Bliss on the payment of certain notes.

[1825–1827] [Order sheet for copies of the Presidential Message]. DS. DLC. mDW 5208.

[1825–1829]	To John Quincy Adams. AL. MHi. mDW 5193. Declines dinner invitation.
[1825–1829]	To John Quincy Adams. AL. MHi. mDW 5195. Declines dinner invitation.
[1825–1839]	From Lewis Burr Sturges. ALS fragment. NhD. mDW 38879. Asks Webster's assistance in securing a government pension.
[c. 1825–1852]	Names of persons to send documents to. AD (MS book). NhD. mDW 12109.

1826

[c. Jan 2]	To [James Barbour?]. ANS. DNA, RG 94. mDWs. Endorses Amory's recommendation of Wm. M. Wallach for appointment to West Point.	
Jan 3	Resolution, that it is expedient to establish a uniform system of bankruptcy, from Committee on the Judiciary. AD. DNA, RG 233. mDW 41968.	
Jan 3	Resolution to inquire into expediency of repealing the act regulating duties on imports and tonnage. AD. DNA, RG 233. mDW 41547.	
Jan 4	From Benjamin Tappan. ALS. PHi. mDW 5211. Requests Webster's assistance in securing an appointment to West Point for Grenville S. Winthrop, his brother-in-law.	
[Jan 4]	To [Edward Everett]. ALS. MHi. mDW 5209. Accepts invitation for the evening.	
[c. Jan 4]	To [James Barbour]. ANS. PHi. mDW 5213. Recommends Grenville S. Winthrop for appointment to West Point.	
Jan 5	Committee on the Judiciary, bill better to provide for taking evidence in the courts of the United States in certain cases. AD, printed document with MS insertions. DNA, RG 233. mDW 41361.	
Jan 6	Resolution on reprinting old House of Representatives journals. AD. DNA, RG 233. mDW 41555.	
Jan 8	*To Joseph Hopkinson.*	75
Jan 8	To George Ticknor. Printed. Curtis, 1: 257–259. Apologizes for not writing sooner; discusses the Panama mission; reports on friends and social life in Washington.	
Jan 11	To Joseph Gales and W. W. Seaton. ALS. NhD. mDW 5218. Sends "Communication" for publication in the *National Intelligencer.*	
Jan 13	*From Timothy Fuller.*	76
Jan 13	From Henry Wheaton. ALS. DLC. mDW 5225. Reports that he has sent Webster a copy of the British bankruptcy act.	

Jan 13   From Alden Bradford. ALS. DNA, RG 233. mDW 42115. Endorses John Simson's petition for a pension.

Jan 13   Report on the petition of Thomas Cooper, from Committee on the Judiciary. AD. DNA, RG 233. mDW 41966.

Jan 14   From John Temple Winthrop. ALS. DLC. mDW 5227. Asks Webster to support the appointment of Grenville S. Winthrop as cadet to West Point.

Jan 15   To [?]. ALS. Richard Upton, Concord, N.H. mDW 5231. Does not at present recommend the employment of counsel in the Ruggles case.

Jan 16   From Joseph H. Dorr. ALS. DNA, RG 233. mDW 42157. Sends affidavit in support of the Mowry petition (under date of Jan 23).

Jan 16   Petition of lighthouse keepers asking additional compensation for their services. ADS. DNA, RG 233. mDW 42090.

Jan 17   From W. Cranch. ALS. DNA, RG 233. mDW 41371. Suggests several amendments to the "bill better to provide for taking evidence in the Courts of the United States in certain cases."

Jan 17   Bank note to Samuel Jaudon for $2,968. ADS. DLC. mDW 39631.

Jan 18   Resolution directing the Committee on the Judiciary to inquire "whether any cases have occurred in which Attorneys of the United States have received compensation from defendants in causes under their care." AD. DNA, RG 233. mDW 41679.

Jan 19   To Samuel D. Ingham. AL draft. DNA, RG 233. mDW 41825. Requests Ingham to forward to the Judiciary Committee any information he may have on the Ingersoll charges.

Jan 19   Resolution on attesting judicial records, from Committee on the Judiciary. AD. DNA, RG 233. mDW 41631.

Jan 21   From Isaac Parker. ALS. DLC. mDW 5232. Asks Webster to suggest a possible office for his son, Charles, in Washington and to recommend him for it.

Jan 23   Petition of Jabez Mowry and Samuel Crackbon asking compensation for items confiscated during War of 1812. ADS. DNA, RG 233. mDW 42132.

Jan 23   Committee on Military Pensions, petition of John Simson. ADS. DNA, RG 233. mDW 42115.

Jan 24   From James Barbour. Printed. *Senate Documents*, 21st Cong., 1st sess., Doc. No. 109 (Serial 193), pp. 7–9. Enumerates the services and duties of

the Department of War and suggests that
perhaps some of its duties might be transferred
to a new department.

[*Jan 24*]   *To Charles Jared Ingersoll.*   79

Jan 26   From Richard Rush. Printed. *Senate Documents,*
21st Cong., 1st sess., Doc. No. 109 (Serial 193),
pp. 6–7. Answers DW's communication of Jan
23, on behalf of the select committee on
reorganizing the Executive Department; states
that Treasury Department probably needs
enlarging.

[Jan 26]   To Samuel Lewis Southard. LS. DNA, RG 45.
mDWs. Asks, on behalf of the select committee
on the reorganization of the Executive
Department, if there are any needed changes in
the Navy Department.

Jan 27   From James Hervey Bingham. ALS. NhHi. mDW
5270. Reports the death of his father and asks
for instructions regarding the sale of Webster's
Unity lands for which Bingham's father had a
contract from Webster.

Jan 27   From Charles Jared Ingersoll. ALS. DNA, RG 233.
mDW 41665. Reports that he will send a
communication to the Judiciary Committee in
a few days.

Jan 28   From Charles Jared Ingersoll. ALS. DNA, RG 233.
mDW 41669. Responds to the charges against
him.

Jan 29   To Ezekiel Webster. ALS. NhD. mDW 5274. *PC,*
1: 401–402. Discusses congressional action on
the judiciary bill, the Panama mission, and the
bankruptcy question; comments on political
views in that body.

Jan 29   *John Davis to George Bancroft.*   80

Jan 31   To Ezekiel Webster (with enclosure: Pension
Office to DW, Jan 1826, extract in DW's hand).
ALS. NhD. mDW 5278. Sends extract of letter
from Pension Office respecting Truel, a
Revolutionary War veteran who reportedly
deserted.

Jan 31   From Richard Rush. AL. DNA, RG 233. mDW
41799. Encloses paper by John Sergeant
touching the Ingersoll investigation.

Jan 31   Report on the relief of Thomas Stevenson and
John Francisca. AD. DNA, RG 233. mDW
41971.

[*c. Jan. 31*]   *From Henry Clay.*   82

[c. Feb 1]   To Henry Clay. LS. DNA, RG 59. mDW 55506.
Asks for information regarding needed reforms
in the organization of the state department.

Feb 2   From Samuel L. Southard. Printed. *Senate*

	Documents, 21st Cong., 1st sess., Doc. No. 109 (Serial 193), p. 12. States that no alteration is required in the organization of the Navy Department.	
Feb 3	From Charles Jared Ingersoll. ALS. MH. mDW 5282. Requests Webster to get a case Ingersoll is to argue before the Supreme Court postponed for a few days.	
Feb 3	From John Fabyan Parrott. ALS. DLC. mDW 5284. Asks Webster's assistance in securing for him the appointment as postmaster of Portsmouth.	
Feb 3	Resolution on the Panama mission. AD. DNA, RG 233. mDW 41567. Requests President Adams to submit as much information as possible on the proposed congress to the House of Representatives.	
Feb 4	*To Jared Sparks.*	83
Feb 4	*From Nicholas Biddle.*	83
Feb 4	From Jeremiah Mason. ALS. MH. mDW 5291. Curtis, 1: 264–265. Comments at length on Webster's judiciary and bankruptcy bills.	
Feb 6	Petition of Walley and Foster on the subject of drawbacks. ADS. DNA, RG 233. mDW 42124.	
Feb 6	Resolution instructing the Judiciary Committee to consider the expediency of a law providing that in states where there are two or more circuit or district courts the process instituted in one court may be executed in any other part of the state. Copy. DNA, RG 233. mDW 41570.	
Feb 7	To Nicholas Biddle. ALS. PU. mDW 5295. Sends list (not found) of cases before the Supreme Court in which the bank is a party.	
Feb 7	Resolution instructing the Judiciary Committee to consider proposing a law to allow liens on executions. Copy. DNA, RG 233. mDW 41576.	
Feb 8	Resolution requesting the Judiciary Committee to consider recommending law for changing the time of courts in Louisiana. Copy. DNA, RG 233. mDW 41578.	
Feb 10	From Nicholas Biddle. ALS. DLC. mDW 5297. Informs Webster of the Supreme Court cases the board of the Bank of the United States wishes him to "take charge of."	
Feb 12	*From Isaac Parker.*	84
Feb 13	Report from the Committee on the Judiciary on process of execution in the U.S. courts. AD. DNA, RG 233. mDW 41633.	
Feb 13	Bill to amend the laws concerning executions for districts of Kentucky, Louisiana, and Ohio. AD. DNA, RG 233. mDW 41388.	

Feb 14	*From Lewis Tappan.*	*85*
Feb 15	To Samuel Lewis Southard (from B. W. Crowninshield, DW, et al.). ADS. DNA, RG 45. mDWs. Discusses the impact of the war between Brazil and the provinces of La Plata on American commerce in the area.	
Feb 16	*From Nicholas Biddle.*	*86*
Feb 16	From [Henry Clay]. Draft with revisions in Clay's hand. DLC. mDW 5308. *Senate Documents*, 21st Cong., 1st sess., Doc. No. 109 (Serial 193), pp. 3–5. Hopkins and Hargreaves, *Papers of Henry Clay*, 5: 109–112. Replies to Webster's inquiries (DW was chairman of the House select committee on the reorganization of the Executive Department) concerning organizational changes and funding required by the state department.	
Feb 17	To John Quincy Adams. LS. DLC. mDW 5315. With William Brent, Edward Livington, H. R. Storrs, and H. W. Dwight, Webster recommends Raphael Semmes as collector for Georgetown.	
Feb 18	*To Alexander Bliss.*	*88*
[Feb 18]	From [Henry C. Carey and Isaac Lea]. AL. DNA, RG 233. mDW 41403. Propose to Webster (chairman of the Judiciary Committee) that their company be appointed to furnish a reporter to the Supreme Court and publish the reports of cases.	
Feb 18	*From Daniel Fletcher Webster.*	*89*
Feb 20	From [Anon]. AL. NhHi. mDW 5323. Gives opinion on the proposed bankruptcy law.	
Feb 20	From Lyman Law. ALS. DLC. mDW 5327. Asks Webster to look into two cases a neighbor of his has before the Supreme Court.	
Feb 20	Resolutions of the Bar *re* death of Honorable Thomas Todd (addressed to the *National Intelligencer*). AD, signed by William Wirt, Chairman. Samuel J. Feigus, Uniontown, Pa. mDWs.	
Feb 22	From Nicholas Biddle. LC. DLC. mDWs. Sends Webster a newspaper which discusses "how the matter of signing Bank notes is managed in England."	
Feb 23	*From John Evelyn Denison.*	*89*
Feb 23	Summons for witnesses in the Ingersoll investigation. DS. DNA, RG 233. mDW 41820.	
Feb 24	Report from the Committee on the Judiciary on the Orleans Navigation Company. AD. DNA, RG 233. mDW 41908.	
Feb 26	To Alexander Bliss. ALS. DLC. mDW 5330. Discusses the case, *State Bank* v. *Welles*, 3 Pickering 15, 394 (1827).	

Feb 26 To Henry Willis Kinsman. ALS. Dr. Gurdon S.
Pulford, Palo Alto, Calif. mDW 5333. Assures
Kinsman of his "respect & friendship."

Feb 28 To John Quincy Adams. Printed. Van Tyne, pp.
116–117. Recommends the appointment of a
Mr. Seawall [?] to some post.

March 1 To [James Barbour?]. ALS. NhD. mDW 5335.
Recommends the appointment of George Ticknor
to the commission for the next examination of
cadets at West Point.

March 1 *To Nicholas Biddle.*   *93*

March 1 To Nicholas Biddle. ALS. PU. mDW 5340. Printed.
W & S, 16: 121–122. Reports on several cases
before the Supreme Court involving the bank.

March 1 From John Sergeant. ALS. DLC. mDW 5343.
Inquires about a Bank of the United States case
before the Supreme Court; retains Webster in
three other cases.

March 1 To George Ticknor. Printed. Curtis, 1: 259–260.
Tells Ticknor that he has called at War
Department about Ticknor's appointment as
visitor to West Point; discusses social life and
politics of Washington.

March 1 Report by the Committee on the Judiciary of a bill
to establish a southern judicial district in
Florida. AD. DNA, RG 233. mDW 42235.

March 2 Resolution under which Webster was appointed to
a select committee on the Ohio and Michigan
boundary. Copy. DNA, RG 233. mDW 41580.

March 3 To [Joseph Anderson]. ALS copy. DNA, RG 233.
mDW 41773. On behalf of the Committee on the
Judiciary, asks Anderson when he first had
interview with Ingersoll on the subject of the
sales of Waln's property.

March 3 To Nicholas Biddle. ALS. PU. mDW 5345. Reports
on the Supreme Court decision in the case,
Finley v. *the Bank of the United States*, 11
Wheaton 304 (1826).

March 3 *To Alexander Bliss.*   *94*

March 3 To C[harles] King (from DW and Thomas Addis
Emmet). ALS copy. PHi. mDW 5351. Give
opinion on a claim involving the Treasury
Department.

[March 3] From Grace Fletcher Webster. ALS. NhHi. mDW
5354. Discusses social and family life in Boston.

March 8 Bank note to Webster for $1,000. ADS. DLC.
mDW 39632.

March 12 To Samuel Lewis Southard. ALS. DNA, RG 45.
mDWs. On behalf of a friend of Mr. Tudor, asks
that a letter be forwarded by the Navy
Department.

March 12	From the Marquis de Lafayette. ALS. NhHi. mDW 5357. *PC*, 1: 403–404. Expresses opinions on South American independence, the political situation in Russia, and the virtues of democracy.	
March 13	To [Nicholas Biddle]. ALS. PU. mDW 5361. *W & S*, 16: 122–123. Reports on the progress of cases involving the bank before the Supreme Court.	
March 13	Resolution instructing the Judiciary Committee to inquire into the expediency of selling the real estate of the United States acquired in the satisfaction of debts. Copy. DNA, RG 233. mDW 41582.	
March 14	*From Jared Sparks.*	95
March 15	To Nicholas Biddle. ALS. PU. mDW 5365. *W & S*, 16: 123. Reports success in the Ohio causes, *Williams* v. *The Bank of the United States*, 11 Wheaton 414 (1826), and *Mills* v. *The Bank of the United States*, 11 Wheaton 431 (1826), before the Supreme Court.	
March 16	Bank draft for $4,451.25. ADS. DLC. mDW 39634.	
March 17	From Joseph Anderson. ALS. DNA, RG 233. mDW 41787. Reports that he had interview with C. J. Ingersoll on the Waln debt in February 1820.	
March 18	To Alexander Bliss. ALS. DLC. mDW 5367. Discusses his personal finances and a bank case.	
March 18	From Richard Rush. ALS. DLC. mDW 5369. Reports that the decision on the Charles King claim will not be altered by the Treasury Department.	
March 19	To Alexander Bliss. ALS. DLC. mDW 5373. Inquires when several of his notes will fall due.	
March 20	*To Jared Sparks.*	95
March 20	To [the Directors of the Charles River Bridge Co.]. AL draft. NhHi. mDW 5375. Van Tyne, pp. 117–118. Comments on the bridge controversy.	
March 21	*To Nicholas Biddle.*	96
March 22	From Charles Jared Ingersoll. ALS. DNA, RG 233. mDW 41841. Sends additional depositions to the Judiciary Committee.	
March 22	From Richard Peters, Jr. ALS. DNA, RG 233. mDW 41717. Reports his knowledge of the "character and conduct" of John S. Wolf of Philadelphia.	
March 22	From Nathaniel R. Poles. ALS. DNA, RG 233. mDW 41883. Supports the testimony of John S. Wolf before the Judiciary Committee (on the investigation of Ingersoll).	
March 24	*From Bushrod Washington.*	97
March 27	*To [Jeremiah Mason].*	98
March 27	*From James Madison.*	100

March 28 Bill to provide for reports of decisions of the Supreme Court. Copy. DNA, RG 233. mDW 41400.

March 30 To John Tappan. ALS. NhD. mDW 5394. Reports the decision of the Supreme Court in *United States* v. *Tappan*, 11 Wheaton 419 (1826).

March 31 From Robert Barnard. ALS. DNA, RG 233. mDW 41904. Asks the Judiciary Committee to support his petition for a patent for improvements in the tanning of leather.

March [?] To Alexander Bliss. ALS. DLC. mDW 5397. Asks Bliss to attend to a draft of Samuel Jaudon which Webster had accepted.

March [?] Report by the Committee on the Judiciary on its investigation into the charges against Charles J. Ingersoll. AD. DNA, RG 233. mDW 41667.

April 2 To Emeline Colby Webster. ALS. DLC. mDW 39185. DW forwards letter for Emeline, his "cousin."

April 3 *From John Marshall.* *100*

April 7 *To Alexander Bliss.* *100*

April 9 To [Joseph E. Worcester]. ALS. MHi. mDW 5422. Thanks Worcester for the information and suggestions, particularly regarding census procedures.

April 12 *From Frederick De Peyster, et al.* *101*

April 12 *From Henry Wheaton.* *102*

[April 16?] To Joseph Story. Printed. *PC*, 1: 382–383 (under date of April 8, 1825). Mentions the Randolph-Clay duel and discusses the progress of legislation in Congress.

April 19 From William Thornton (to the chairman of the Committee on the Judiciary). ALS. DNA, RG 233. mDW 41957. Asks for reforms in the Patent Office and on patent legislation.

April 20 From John Mason. ALS. DNA, RG 233. mDW 41916. States that he is sending a memorial on the Orleans Navigation Company, which he hopes will be submitted to the Judiciary Committee.

April 20 From John Mason. LS. DNA, RG 233. mDW 41918. Discusses the Orleans Navigation Company and his appearance as a witness before the Judiciary Committee in February.

April 26 From William Thornton (to the chairman of the Committee on the Judiciary). ALS. DNA, RG 233. mDW 41960. Requests increase in salary and the right of franking letters.

April 28 To James Barbour. ALS. John W. King, Concord, N.H. mDW 4964. Asks that Lt. [John] Child[e]

	might be given a furlough to assist in the survey of some public work in Massachusetts.	
April 28	To [Alexander Bliss]. ALS. DLC. mDW 5416. Instructs Bliss on the payment of notes.	
[April 28]	To [Stephen] Pleasonton. ANS. DNA, RG 206. mDW 57180. Requests Pleasonton to forward to the Judiciary Committee the papers relating to the case, *United States* v. *Sill and Noyes*.	
April 28	From Stephen Pleasonton. LC. DNA, RG 206. mDWs. Sends the correspondence relating to *United States* v. *Sill and Noyes*.	
April 29	*To Mrs. George Blake.*	103
May 2	*To Jeremiah Mason.*	105
May 2	*From John Sergeant.*	106
May 2	From J. W. Simonton. ALS. DNA, RG 233. mDW 42241. According to Webster's suggestion, Simonton has prepared and encloses a communication showing the necessity of a district court at Key West.	
May 3	*To [John Evelyn Denison].*	107
May 3	From Nathaniel Williams. ALS. DNA, RG 45. mDWs. Introduces William Alfred Patterson.	
May 4	From Henry Alexander Scammell Dearborn. ALS. CtY. mDW 5435. Praises Webster's Panama speech and expresses the hope that the bankruptcy bill will pass.	
May 5	Report from the Committee on the Judiciary on an amendment to the House bill to amend the judicial system of the United States (in DW's hand). AD. DNA, RG 233. mDW 41657.	
May 7	*From Susan Decatur.*	110
May 7	*From Jeremiah Mason.*	111
May 8	*To Alexander Bliss.*	112
May 8	*To Joseph Story.*	113
May 8	Bill from the Committee on the Judiciary for altering the times of holding the courts in the District of Columbia. AD. DNA, RG 233. mDW 41424.	
May 9	To Edward Cutts, Jr. ALS. MB. mDW 5447. *W & S*, 16: 132. Reports on the state of the *Calliope* case.	
May 10	To Alexander Bliss. ALS. DLC. mDW 5450. Instructs Bliss on the payment of several notes.	
May 10	Resolution for printing Livingston's penal code (in DW's hand). AD. DNA, RG 233. mDW 41594.	
May 11	From Susan Decatur. ALS. DLC. mDW 8812. Asks Webster to confer with her on her claim for Stephen Decatur.	
May 12	Report by the Committee on the Judiciary "to whom was referred the Message from the	

Senate, on the subject of the disagreeing votes
of the two Houses on the amendments proposed
by the Senate to the Bill to amend the
Judicial System of the United States." Printed.
House Reports, 19th Cong., 1st sess., 1825–26,
Doc. No. 207 (Serial 142).

May 13
To Alexander Bliss. ALS. DLC. mDW 5453.
Encloses letter for Judge Story, "not knowing
whether he is in Boston or Salem."

May 14
From Nathaniel Potter. ALS. DLC. mDW 5455.
Asks Webster for an opinion on whether a
recent act of the Maryland legislature violates
the charter of the University of Maryland.

May 15
To [Jeremy Robinson]. DS by DW, et al. DLC.
mDW 5456a. Signers testify to Robinson's
character and support him in his bid for some
public office.

May 16
From Theodore Dwight. ALS. NHi. mDW 5457.
States that the proposed collection of duties on
canal boats at Buffalo will be a very unpopular
measure.

May 17
Report by the Committee on the Judiciary on
process in courts (in DW's hand). AD. DNA,
RG 233. mDW 41659.

May 18
Resolution for printing journals of the House (in
DW's hand). AD. DNA, RG 233. mDW 41596.

May 20
To Samuel Lewis Southard. Copy. DNA, RG 59.
mDWs. Recommends William Coolidge for a
clerkship in the Navy Department.

May 20
From William Gaston. ALS. CtY. mDW 5461.
Discusses a slander case he is to argue and
asks Webster to give character witnesses in
behalf of his clients.

[May 20]
To Gulian Crommelin Verplanck. ALS. NHi. mDW
5459. Asks Verplanck to return Judge Joseph
Story's letter to Webster on the proposed
alteration in the revenue law.

May 20   *From John Marshall.*   *114*
[May 21]
To Alexander Bliss. ALS. DLC. mDW 5466.
Expresses shock over the news of Mrs. Blake's
death.

May 22
To [Samuel Frothingham]. ALS. PHC. mDW 5469.
Sends $500 for deposit in his account.

May 22   *From Gulian Crommelin Verplanck.*   *115*
May 22
Report of the Select Commitee of the House of
Representatives, on the subject of reorganizing
the Executive Departments. Printed. *Senate
Documents*, 21st Cong., 1st sess., Doc. No. 109
(Serial 193).

May 29   *From William Plumer, Sr.*   *115*
May 31   *To William Gaston.*   *116*

May 31	To Jeremiah Mason. Printed. *W & S*, 16: 133–134. Reports their arrival home, comments on Mrs. Blake's death, and discusses New Hampshire politics.	
May ?	To William Ellery Channing. LS by Isaac Parker, William Prescott, DW, et al. RHi. mDW 5481. Express hope that Channing will publish some of his sermons.	
June 8	*To Henry Clay.*	*118*
June 9	Purchase of property from Lewis Tappan for $8,790. Printed document with MS insertions. MWalB. mDW 39635.	
June 11	To Jeremiah Mason. ALS. MBG. mDW 5488. Arranges to have dinner with Mason.	
June 12	From Jules von Wallenstein. ALS. NhHi. mDW 5490. Reports on news of friends in New York and Philadelphia.	
June 14	*From Henry Clay.*	*119*
July 7	*From Francis Johnson.*	*120*
July 8	To Albert H. Tracy. ALS. NN. mDW 5499. Introduces George Blake, district attorney for Massachusetts.	
July 11	*From John Evelyn Denison.*	*123*
July 11	*From Joseph Story.*	*126*
July 18	To Elisha Whittlesley. ALS. OClWHi. mDW 5510. Introduces William [?] Prescott, one of Webster's colleagues of the Boston bar.	
July 19	*From Timothy Pickering.*	*127*
July 22	From George Washington Adams (with enclosure: JQA to John Sergeant, July 20, 1826, copy). ALS. DLC. mDW 5517. Sends Adams' letter and also the volume containing the "Dissertation on the Canon and Feudal Law."	
July 22	From Timothy Pickering. ALS. NhHi. mDW 5519. Discusses the question of who (Adams or Lee) moved the resolutions for independence in 1776.	
July 24	To Sylvanus Thayer. ALS. NWM. mDW 5525. Introduces Colonel McDougall of the British Service.	
July 26	From the Marquis de Lafayette. Printed. *PC*, 1: 407–408. Remarks on the Monroe Doctrine and Greek independence.	
July 27	To [Aaron] Ward. ALS. MB. mDW 5528. Will try to let Ward know of Adams' proposed departure from the Boston area as soon as he can ascertain it.	
Aug 3	From Josiah Quincy. ALS. NhHi. mDW 5596. *PC*, 1: 408–410. Congratulates Webster on his Adams-Jefferson eulogy, but asks if he meant to portray John Harris as opposing independence.	

Aug 4 From Edwin R. Wallace. ALS. NhHi. mDW 5600.
Thanks Webster for his assistance in planning
his course for the study of law.

[Aug 5] To Edward Everett. ALS. MHi. mDW 5605. Invites
Everett to dine with him and Charles R.
Vaughan, British minister to the United States.

Aug 7 To [Timothy Pickering]. ALS. MHi. mDW 5607.
W & S, 16: 137. Thanks Pickering for lending
his correspondence with John Adams; reflects
on the motion for independence.

Aug 9 From Edward Everett. LC. MHi. mDW 5610. Sends
an enclosure on the Turks and suggests that
they are not "such unconscionable people as I
tho't them."

Aug 10 To Horace Hall. LS. CSmH. mDW 5611.
Recommends Nathan Hale's map of New
England and requests Hall to promote it.

Aug 10 To Mills Olcott. LS. NhD. mDW 5613.
Recommends Hale's map of New England and
requests Olcott to promote it.

Aug 10 To Peleg Sprague. LS. Duxbury Rural and
Historical Society, Duxbury, Mass. mDWs.
Recommends Hale's map of New England.

Aug 10 To Benjamin Vaughan. LS. PPAmP. mDW 5616.
Recommends Hale's map of New England and
requests Vaughan to promote it.

Aug 12 To Ezekiel Webster. ALS. NhD. mDW 5627.
Instructs Ezekiel to sell the Tarleton lands for
whatever he can.

Aug 12 *From John Forsyth.*   *128*

Aug 14 To Henry Clay. ALS. DNA, RG 59. mDW 55435.
Asks Clay to forward a packet of materials from
a Mr. Grulé to Joel R. Poinsett.

Aug 14 To Ezekiel Webster. ALS. NhD. mDW 5624.
Encloses a letter from and one to William
Haddock, involving debt settlement.

Aug 24 To Ezekiel Webster. ALS. NhD. mDW 5627.
Discusses his own travel plans and expresses
satisfaction with the dates of Ezekiel's proposed
visit.

Aug 30 From Joseph Hopkinson. ALS. DLC. mDW 5629.
Curtis, 1: 279. Thanks Webster for his
"Commemoration Discourse" on Adams and
Jefferson.

Aug 30 *From Richard Rush.*   *128*

[Aug] "Dear Lady, I a little fear." Copy. John R.
Morison, Peterborough, N.H. mDW 39346. Bela
Chapin, comp., *The Poets of New Hampshire*
(Claremont, N.H., 1883), pp. 778–779. Poem.

[Sept 1] To John W. Taylor. ALS. NHi. mDW 5636. Urges

Taylor to join him in dinner with General
H. A. S. Dearborn.

Sept 1   From Henry Alexander Scammell Dearborn. ALS.
NHi. mDW 5638. Thanks Webster for the
information on Taylor; glad that he will dine
with them tomorrow.

Sept 1   From Tobias Watkins. ALS. NhD. mDW 5641.
Thanks Webster for the copy of his
Adams-Jefferson discourse.

Sept 2   From William Plumer, Sr. ALS. NhD. mDW 5643.
Thanks Webster for the copy of his
Adams-Jefferson discourse.

Sept 3   From Jeremiah Mason. Printed. Curtis, 1: 280.
Expresses regret that he was unable to be at
Cambridge for Story's oration; praises Webster's
discourse.

Sept 4   From Daniel Fletcher Webster. ALS. NhHi. mDW
5646. Describes his trip to Boscawen to visit
Ezekiel.

Sept 5   To the Marquis de Lafayette. ALS. NIC. mDW
5650. Introduces a Mr. Buckingham of Boston,
who is to depart for Europe.

Sept 6   From Samuel Burr. ALS. MHi. mDWs. Sends
authority for Webster to receive the money
appropriated for the Bunker Hill monument.

Sept 6   From Jared Sparks. Printed. H. B. Adams, *The
Life and Writings of Jared Sparks* (2 vols.;
Boston, 1893), 1: 271. Asks Webster to review
Cardozo's tract on political economy.

Sept 8   From James Kent. ALS. DLC. mDW 5651.
Recommends William Johnson for district judge
of New York.

Sept 9   From James Kent. AL (signature removed). DLC.
mDW 5654. Retracts his recommendation of
Johnson, since the latter would be unwilling to
accept the office.

Sept 11   To Simón Bolívar. LS. Archivo del Libertador,
Caracas, Venezuela. mDWs. *Correspondencia de
Extranjeros Notables con el Libertador*, ed.
Daniel F. O'Leary, (2 vols.; Madrid, 1920), 2:
181–184. Expresses gratitude with Bolívar's
acceptance of membership in the Bunker Hill
Monument Association.

Sept 20   To Richard Rush. ALS. NjP. mDW 5656. Thanks
Rush for his comments on the Adams-Jefferson
discourse.

Sept 20   To the Committee of the Suffolk Bar Association.
LS (with insertions by DW). MBBA. mDWs.
States that Edward Vernon Child has read law
in his office since October 1823.

Sept 22	From Edward Everett. LC. MHi. mDW 5662. Discusses Burr's letter of Sept 6 and other affairs of the Bunker Hill Monument Association.	
Sept 22	*To Charles Folsom.*	*129*
Sept 22	To Ezekiel Webster. ALS. NhD. mDW 39189. Discusses Sawyer deed and his unwillingness to part with certain of his books.	
[Sept 23]	To [Edward Everett]. ALS. MHi. mDW 5663. Comments on letter to Bolívar and discusses dinner plans.	
Sept 24	From James Hervey Bingham. ALS. NhHi. mDW 5665. Reports that he is now cashier of the Claremont bank; discusses sale of some of Webster's land.	
Sept 30	*From Noah Webster.*	*130*
Oct 6	To Levi Lincoln. ALS. MHi. mDW 5672. Webster states that he is unable to accept invitation because of a jury trial.	
Oct 12	*To Jared Sparks.*	*132*
Oct 12	*To John C. Wright.*	*133*
Oct 13	*To Henry Clay.*	*135*
Oct 14	To Ebenezer T. Andrews. ALS. NhD. mDWs. Wants to give his note for amount due on Upton's; if cash is necessary for payment, it can be so paid, since "I expect to be in funds from Missouri."	
Oct 14	To Charles Brickett Haddock. Printed. *PC*, 1: 410–412. Discusses the settlement of New Hampshire and the "moral character" of the early settlers.	
Oct 14	*To William Buell Sprague.*	*136*
Oct 14	*To Noah Webster.*	*137*
Oct 14	Purchase of property from Stephen Hartwell for $1,500. Printed document with MS insertions. MWalB. mDW 39640.	
Oct 15	To Emeline Colby Webster. ALS. DMaM. mDW 5684. Forwards letter of Dr. Lindsly.	
Oct 23	From Eliza Buckminster. ALS. NhHi. mDW 5686. Requests that Webster use his influence to secure the appointment of Thomas Hickling as consul general to the Azores.	
Oct 23	From John Farrar (enclosed with DW to Henry Clay, Oct 24, 1826). ALS. DNA, RG 59. mDW 55526. Recommends Thomas Hickling as consul general to the Azores.	
Oct 24	To Henry Clay (with enclosure: John Farrar to DW, Oct 23, 1826). ALS. DNA, RG 59. mDW 55523. Recommends Thomas Hickling as consul general to the Azores.	
Oct 25	Bank note for $1,500. DS. NjMoHP. mDWs.	

	Asks that Webster recommend her son for appointment to West Point.	
Dec 6	To Henry Alexander Scammell Dearborn. ALS. MeHi. mDW 5729. Attests to the character of Captain Joseph Flanders, who is seeking an appointment as inspector.	
Dec 6	*To Grace Fletcher Webster.*	*142*
Dec 8	From Caleb Stark. ALS. DLC. mDW 5740. Asks Webster to support his claim for revolutionary services, now before Congress.	
Dec 8	*To Grace Fletcher Webster.*	*143*
Dec 9	To Mrs. [?] Meredith. ALS. PHi. mDW 5742. States that he has conferred with Secretary of the Navy Southard about the appointment of her son as midshipman.	
Dec 10	From Isaac Parker. ALS. DLC. mDW 5746. Asks Webster to examine again his claims against the United States.	
[Dec 11]	To [Edward Everett]. ALS. MHi. mDW 5750. Asks Everett and his wife to join him in dinner at Mr. Vaughan's.	
Dec 12	To James Lloyd. ALS. MH. mDW 5752. Discusses the British colonial question.	
Dec 12	To [Henry G.] Rice. ALS. MHi. mDW 5756. Reports on the status of Rice's petition in the House of Representatives.	
Dec 13	To Joseph Hopkinson. ALS. PHi. mDW 5758. Asks Hopkinson to "look at the enclosed, and 'do the needful.' "	
Dec 13	To Emeline Colby Webster. ALS. DMaM. mDW 5760. Asks her to visit him and Dr. Sewall in Washington.	
Dec 13	From Jacob Harvey (with enclosure: Charles March to DW, Dec 13, 1826). ALS. DNA, RG 59. mDW 55529. Recommends the appointment of Reuben Harvey as consul at Cork.	
Dec 13	From Charles March (enclosed with Jacob Harvey to DW, Dec 13, 1826). ALS. DNA, RG 59. mDW 55533. Recommends the appointment of Reuben Harvey as consul at Cork.	
Dec 14	*To Nathan Hale.*	*143*
Dec 14	From Moses W. Brigham (enclosed with DW to Samuel L. Southard, Dec 20, [1826]). ALS. DNA, RG 45. mDWs. Asks Webster to request the Navy Department to furnish him with a statement regarding the discharge of Philander A. Paul Jones.	
Dec 15	To Caleb Stark. ALS. NN. mDW 5766. States that he will pay the "necessary attention" to Stark's claim.	
Dec 16	To Alexander Bliss. ALS. DLC. mDW 5767. States	

that he has received Bliss' notes in the Bank
case.

Dec 16   To Henry Alexander Scammell Dearborn. ALS.
NhD. mDW 5769. Since Dearborn's letter
arguing for the repeal of the last section of
the appraisement act of 1823 is at home,
Webster asks him to restate his views on the
subject.

Dec 16   From Clarkson Crolius, et al. LS. DLC. mDW 5771.
Ask that Webster support their petition for
compensation for services rendered during the
War of 1812.

Dec 18   From Bradford Sumner (enclosed with DW to
Henry Clay, c. March 5, 1827). ALS. DNA, RG
59. mDW 55546. Recommends E. Kingman for
some political office.

Dec 20   From DeWitt Clinton. AL (signature removed).
DLC. mDW 5775. Reports that the comptroller
of New York will be forwarding the retaining
fee for the case of New York against the Astor
claim, in which Van Buren will also serve as
counsel.

Dec 20   To Joseph Hopkinson. ALS. PHi. mDW 5773.
Discusses the appointment of the New York
judge and the opposition to Wheaton.

Dec 20   To Samuel Lewis Southard (enclosure: Moses W.
Brigham to DW, Dec 14, 1826). ALS. DNA, RG
45. mDWs. Forwards letter of Moses W.
Brigham and suggests that, if Brigham's request
is not burdensome, the Navy Department
comply with his request for information
regarding the discharge of Philander A. Paul
Jones.

Dec 22   From Nicholas Biddle. LC. DLC. mDWs. Inquires
about the bill on the signing of bank notes.

Dec 23   From Isaac P. Davis. ALS. DNA, RG 233. mDW
42109. Encloses petition on the hemp question;
discusses drawbacks and its importance to
merchants and manufacturers.

Dec 25   From Isaac Winslow. ALS. NhHi. mDW 5780.
Reports the age of his nephew, for whom
Winslow sought an appointment to the Naval
Academy.

Dec 26   From J[ohn] McLean. LC. DNA, RG 28. mDW
57047. Discusses expenses for post office
supplies, probably in response to a query by
Webster.

Dec 28   To John Quincy Adams. AL. MHi. mDW 5781.
Declines dinner invitation for Jan 2, because
of a previous engagement.

Dec 28   To John Quincy Adams. AL. MHi. mDW 5781. Accepts invitation to dinner for Jan 5.

Dec 28   *To [Nicholas Biddle].*   *144*

Dec 28   To Nathan Hale. ALS. MHi. mDW 5786. Corrects the weather figures he sent Hale earlier in the day.

Dec 28   Fom William Learned Marcy. ALS. MHi. mDW 5788. Encloses $500 retaining fee for an Astor land case.

Dec 29   To John Quincy Adams. ALS. MHi. mDW 5790. Introduces a Mr. Knapp, who was seeking appointment to some office.

[Dec 31]   To Edward Everett. ALS. MHi. mDW 5791. *PC*, 1: 413. Conveys Vaughan's invitation to dinner; comments on the cold weather.

[1826]   To John Sergeant. ALS. PHi. mDWs. Asks for notes in the case, *Hinde v. Longworth*, 11 Wheaton 199 (1826); comments on activities in the Senate.

[1826–1844]   To [Samuel Ayer] Bradley. ALS. NhD. mDW 38277. Invites Bradley to join him and W. W. Seaton for dinner.

[?]   To Emeline Colby Webster. ALS. DMaM. mDW 5796. Suggests several works on Spain covering the years 1800–1824.

1827

Jan 1   To Ezekiel Webster. ALS. NhD. mDW 5799. Sends letter for Kent; comments on the weather and Calhoun's appeal against Elijah Mix.

Jan 2   Bill to establish uniform system of bankruptcy throughout the United States. Printed document with MS insertions. DNA, RG 233. mDW 41427.

Jan 2   *From Nicholas Biddle.*   *145*

Jan 2   Petition to the Committee on Commerce for a drawback on Russian hemp. ADS. DNA, RG 233. mDW 42104.

Jan 2   Resolution to inquire into expediency of repealing the last section of the act of March 1, 1823, regulating the collection of duties on imports and tonnage. AD. DNA, RG 233. mDW 41598.

Jan 3   To Samuel Frothingham. ALS. PHC. mDW 5800. Deposits $500 check from the treasurer of the state of New York.

Jan 4   From Samuel Fessenden. ALS. NhHi. mDW 5801. Discusses Preble's claim for prize money in the destruction of the frigate *Philadelphia*, then before Congress.

Jan 4   *From John Temple Winthrop.*   *145*

Jan 5
From Grace Fletcher Webster. ALS. NhHi. mDW
5805. Discusses the health of the family and the
weather in Boston.

Jan 6 *To Nicholas Biddle.* *146*

Jan 8
From William Tudor. ALS. NhHi. mDW 5809.
Asks Webster to exhort the Bunker Hill
Monument Association to make a Bolivian
dignitary, Marshal LaMar, an honorary
member of the society.

Jan 8
Petition of Isaac P. Davis regarding his contract
with navy commissioners. ADS. DNA, RG 233.
mDW 42191.

Jan 9
From Henry Warner. ALS. DLC. mDW 5815.
Discusses the question of the United States'
sending aid to the Greeks.

Jan 10
To [Joseph E.] Sprague. Printed. PC, 1: 414.
Discusses the importance of re-electing Mills
to the Senate from Massachusetts.

Jan 11
To James Barbour. ALS. DNA, RG 49. mDWs.
Recommends John E. Brackett of New York for
appointment as a cadet.

Jan 11
From John P. Sheldon. ALS. DNA, RG 217. mDW
57194 (incorrectly dated 1826). Details abuses
practiced by U.S. officers in Michigan Territory.

Jan 11
Bill to amend the judicial system of the United
States. Printed document with MS insertions.
DNA, RG 233. mDW 41520.

Jan 12
To Mrs. John Agg. ALS. NhD. mDW 38176. States
that he is suffering under the "general
complaints"; hopes to see her and her mother
in a few days.

[Jan 14?]
From G[abriel] H. Thompson (enclosed in DW to
Samuel Lewis Southard, March 19, 1827). ADS.
DNA, RG 45. mDWs. Asks Webster to aid him
in securing government assistance in the
development of instruments "to establish a
perfect System of Navigation and Surveying."

Jan 15
Petition of Nehemiah Parsons to the Committee
on Commerce for a new registry for his ship
Isis. ADS. DNA, RG 233. mDW 42039.

Jan 16
From E. Appleton. ALS. DNA, RG 59. mDW 55540.
Recommends John Larkin Payson for a
consulship at Messina.

Jan 16
To David Daggett. LS. CtY. mDW 5819. Requests
the use of Daggett's notes in arguing the case of
M'Gill v. *the Bank of the United States,* 12
Wheaton 511 (1827), before the Supreme Court.

Jan 16 *To Emeline Colby Webster.* *146*

Jan 16
From Grace Fletcher Webster. ALS. NhHi. mDW
5823. Harvey, *Reminiscences,* pp. 324–325.
Discusses the activities of the family in Boston.

Jan 17	From Ezekiel Webster. Printed. *PC*, 1: 415–417. Recounts his meeting with John Bell and the attempts of the Adams Republicans to exclude Federalists from their meetings.	
Jan 17	From Grace Fletcher Webster. ALS. NhHi. mDW 5827. Van Tyne, p. 566. Discusses the weather, the family, and newspaper reports of Webster's activities.	
Jan 18	*From Grace Fletcher Webster.*	*147*
Jan 20	From Thomas B. Wales (with enclosure: Thomas B. Wales to John Quincy Adams, Jan 19, 1827). ALS. DNA, RG 59. mDW 55537. Recommends John L. Payson for a consulship at Messina.	
Jan 21	From George Cheyne Shattuck. ALS. NhHi. mDW 5833. Thanks Webster for the support he has given for the awarding of Revolutionary War pensions in Congress.	
Jan 21	*From Grace Fletcher Webster.*	*148*
Jan 22	From Aaron Burr. Copy. NhHi. mDW 5840. Discusses the Eden case; asks Webster to inform him of the "position of our causes on the [Court] Calendar."	
Jan 23	From Thomas P. Cope. ALS, with AN by DW. NhD. mDW 5842. Asks Webster's opinion on increasing Biddle's salary; Webster endorses letter that he concurs.	
Jan 25	To Aaron Burr. LS. NhD. mDW 5848. Discusses their cases before the Supreme Court.	
Jan 25	To Henry Clay (with enclosures: E. Appleton to DW, Jan 16, 1827; Appleton, et al. to Henry Clay, Jan 16, 1827). ALS. DNA, RG 59. mDW 55535. Sends recommendations of John Larkin Payson for consulship at Messina.	
Jan 25	To Thomas P. Cope. LC. DLC. mDW 5851. Webster concurs in the proposal to raise Nicholas Biddle's salary.	
[Jan 26]	To Henry Clay. ALS. DNA, RG 59. mDWs. Encloses additional papers supporting the candidacy of J. L. Payson for the consulship at Messina.	
Jan 26	*From Samuel Torrey.*	*150*
Jan 27	*From Ezekiel Webster.*	*151*
Jan 27	Report from the Committee on Ways and Means on William Otis' petition. AD. DNA, RG 233. mDW 42036.	
Jan 29	*From Grace Fletcher Webster.*	*154*
Jan 29	From Noah Webster. Printed. E. E. F. Skeel, comp., *Notes on the Life of Noah Webster* (2 vols.; New York, 1912): 2: 301. Inquires about the progress of a new copyright law before the Judiciary Committee.	

Jan 30	From John McLean. LC. DNA, RG 28. mDW 57044. Discusses the passage of the mail between Washington and Boston.
Jan 31	From John Davis, et al. ALS. DLC. mDW 5868. Send memorial drawn up by members of the Massachusetts Historical Society, asking the consideration of Congress in their quest to acquire copies of materials relating to the American colonies in British public offices.
Jan ?	From Simón Bolívar. AL draft. Archivo del Libertador, Caracas, Venezuela. mDWs. Reports the receipt of the news of his being named honorary member of the Bunker Hill Monument Association; expresses his gratitude.
[Jan–March]	To John Quincy Adams. ALS. DLC. mDW 5192. Recommends appointment of Ogden as one of the commissioners under the St. Petersburg arbitration.
Feb 1	To Richard Rush. AL (signature removed). DNA, RG 217. mDW 57192. Encloses letter from John P. Sheldon of Detroit respecting abuses practiced by U.S. officers in Michigan Territory.
Feb 1	From John McLean. LC. DNA, RG 28. mDW 57048. Reports the instructions he has given the Boston postmaster regarding the delivery of newspapers.
Feb 2	To John Quincy Adams. AL. MHi. mDW 5870a. Accepts invitation to dine with Adams on Feb 9.
Feb 2	From Grace Fletcher Webster. ALS. NhHi. mDW 5872. Expresses concern that Webster is having trouble with rheumatism; reports on the family.
Feb 4	To [Nicholas Biddle]. ALS. PU. mDW 5875. Discusses the bill on the punishment of crimes which he plans to report.
Feb 4	To Samuel Jaudon. ALS. ViU. mDW 5876. Reports on the Dandridge and other Bank cases before the Supreme Court.
Feb 5	*From Grace Fletcher Webster.* 155
Feb 5	Report of Committee on Claims on George Johnston's petition. AD. DNA, RG 233. mDW 41611.
Feb 6	Report of the Committee on the Judiciary on a bill for the punishment of crimes. AD. DNA, RG 233. mDW 41973.
Feb 6	Resolution for the appointment of a joint committee on the order of business in the Senate and the House. AD. DNA, RG 233. mDW 41600.
Feb 8	To John Quincy Adams. ALS. MHi. mDW 5883. States that he is enclosing letters recommending

the appointment of a Mr. Sewall to some post,
whom Webster also favors.

Feb 8   From Grace Fletcher Webster. ALS. NhHi. mDW
5885. Discusses friends in Boston and party she
attended the previous evening at S. G. Perkins'.

Feb 10   From Isaac Parker. ALS. DLC. mDW 5888. Asks
Webster to assist in getting John Lee appointed
Collector of Customs.

Feb 10   From Grace Fletcher Webster. ALS. NhHi. mDW
5891. Van Tyne, pp. 567–568 (excerpt).
Discusses family and friends in Boston.

Feb 11   To James Trecothick Austin. ALS. NhD. mDW
5894. Reports on the position of the case of
Franklin Insurance Company v. *Lord* on the
United States Supreme Court docket.

Feb 12   Petition from Hartford, Connecticut, against
Sunday mails. ADS. DNA, RG 233. mDW 42119.

Feb 12   Resolution for additional regulation of appeals
from the Circuit Court in the District of
Columbia. AD. DNA, RG 233. mDW 41602.

Feb 12   Report of the Committee on the Library on the
memorial from the Massachusetts Historical
Society. AD. DNA, RG 233. mDW 41978.

Feb 14   From Nicholas Biddle. LC. DLC. mDWs. Discusses
the forthcoming decision in the Dandridge case.

Feb 15   From Grace Fletcher Webster. ALS. NhHi. mDW
5900. Van Tyne, p. 568 (excerpt). Comments on
Webster's failure to write, family affairs; states
her belief that Mills will not be chosen senator
by the Massachusetts legislature.

Feb 16   From Grace Fletcher Webster. ALS. NhHi. mDW
5904. Van Tyne, p. 568 (excerpt). Reports that
Governor Lincoln declines the Senate seat;
discusses family affairs.

Feb 17   To R. S. Coxe (from DW and John Crafts Wright).
ALS. DLC. mDW 5907. Reply to Coxe's query on
the construction of the act relating to
compensation to witnesses imprisoned, passed
at the last session of Congress.

Feb 17   From Grace Fletcher Webster. ALS. NhHi. mDW
5908. Reports on her social life in Boston.

Feb 19   From Grace Fletcher Webster. ALS. NhHi. mDW
5911. Reports the receipt of a letter from Jules
von Wallenstein and discusses the family.

Feb 19   Memorial of Citizens of Boston and vicinity to
Congress against the contemplated increase of
duty on certain woolen goods imported. Printed.
State Papers, 19th Cong., 2d sess., 1826–27,
Doc. No. 115 (Serial 152).

Feb 20	To [Nicholas Biddle]. ALS. PU. mDW 5914. *W & S*, 16: 140–141. Reports on the progress of cases before the Supreme Court in which the bank is involved.	
Feb 20	To Henry Clay. ALS. DNA, RG 59. mDWs. Recommends [Fromentin] Winder, son of General William H. Winder, for appointment as clerk in the State Department, if he is deserving.	
Feb 20	From Nathaniel Goddard (to DW and Francis Baylies). Printed. *State Papers*, 19th Cong., 2d sess., 1826–27, Doc. No. 115 (Serial 152), p. 4. Transmits petition of citizens of Boston and vicinity against the pending woolens bills.	
Feb 21	*To Jacob McGaw.*	*158*
Feb 21	From William Hubbell and Daniel Gano. ALS. NhHi. mDW 5922. Express gratitude to Webster for his efforts in Congress in behalf of pensions for Revolutionary War veterans.	
Feb 23	*To [William Coleman].*	*160*
Feb 23	From Nicholas Biddle. LC. DLC. mDWs. Discusses one aspect of the McGill case and its possible relationship to the Dandridge cause.	
Feb 24	To John Quincy Adams. ALS. MHi. mDW 5925. Recommends the appointment of William Fowle of Alexandria for the office of surveyor.	
Feb 24	To Nicholas Biddle. ALS. PU. mDW 5928. Discusses cases before the Court in which the bank is a party and his role as attorney for the bank.	
Feb 24	To Nicholas Biddle. ALS. PU. mDW 5934. States that the Court has not yet handed down its decision in the Dandridge case.	
Feb 24	From Nicholas Biddle. Copy. DLC. mDW 5938. Introduces Thomas Dunlap, an attorney from Philadelphia.	
Feb 24	To Samuel Jaudon. ALS. NHi. mDW 5936. Discusses the "Vasse's case," *Comegys* v. *Vasse*, 1 Peters 193 (1828).	
Feb 24	*From Grace Fletcher Webster.*	*163*
Feb 24	Committee on the Judiciary, Report on the Orleans Navigation Company. Printed. *House Reports*, 19th Cong., 2d sess. 1826–27, Doc. no. 89. (Serial 160).	
Feb 25	*To Nicholas Biddle.*	*165*
Feb 25	*From Philip Reed.*	*166*
Feb 26	*To Nicholas Biddle.*	*166*
Feb 26	*To Samuel Jaudon.*	*167*
Feb 26	From Nicholas Biddle. ALS. DLC. mDW 5955. Discusses the employment of counsel for a case originating in Cincinnati.	
Feb 27	From Elizabeth Langdon-Elwyn. ALS. NhHi. mDW	

	5957. Introduces a Mr. Markoe of Philadelphia, who hopes to obtain an appointment to West Point.	
Feb 27	From Elizabeth Langdon-Elwyn. ALS. NhHi. mDW 5959. Explains reasons for her recommending Mr. Markoe.	
Feb 27	From Jacob Gillett. ALS. NhHi. mDW 5963. Asks Webster's assistance in obtaining an appointment in the customs office of New York.	
Feb 27	From Grace Fletcher Webster. ALS. NhHi. mDW 5967. Comments on Richard Stockton's being killed in a duel, and on the family.	
Feb 28	From Daniel Brent. LC. DNA, RG 59. mDW 55670. Discusses the petition of Reuben Shapley, presented before Congress on Dec 27, 1821.	
[March 1]	Resolution to suspend Joint Rule 17 so far as relates to William Morrison and the surveyor of public lands in Mississippi and Louisiana. AD. DNA, RG 233. mDW 41608.	
March 2	From Nicholas Biddle. LC. DLC. mDWs. Discusses several court actions in which the bank is involved.	
March 2	To Alexander Macomb. ALS. CU. mDW 5970. Assures Macomb that Emerson's evaluation and recommendation of a Mr. Smith is reliable.	
[March 3]	*To John Quincy Adams.*	*168*
March 3	Resolution for the clerk to purchase stationery for the next Congress. AD. DNA, RG 233. mDW 41604.	
[c. March 5]	To Henry Clay (enclosure: Bradford Sumner to DW, Dec 18, 1826). ALS. DNA, RG 59. mDW 55544. Attests to the respectability of Sumner, who recommends E. Kingman for office.	
March 5	*From Grace Fletcher Webster.*	*168*
March 6	To Alexander Bliss. ALS. DLC. mDW 4902. Instructs Bliss on payments he is sending; remarks that he began argument in Ruggles case that day.	
March 6	To Jacob Gillett. ALS. DLC. mDW 38387. Acknowledges Gillett's letter of Feb 27 and states that he will "cheerfully" assist him in obtaining an appointment in the customs office of New York if he can.	
March 8	*From Grace Fletcher Webster.*	*169*
March 9	From Grace Fletcher Webster. ALS. NhHi. mDW 5978. Reports the arrival of Bliss in Boston.	
March 10	*To Nicholas Biddle.*	*170*
March 10	To Samuel Frothingham. ALS. NhExP. mDW 5981. Sends draft for $3,500 to be deposited in his account.	
[March 10?]	From Austin Eli Wing (enclosure: Queries by	

[William Woodbridge]). ALS. MiD–B. mDW
6058. Discusses the affairs of the Bank of
Michigan.

[March 10?]   Queries by [William Woodbridge] in *Bank of
Michigan* v. *A. E. Wing* (enclosed with A. E.
Wing to DW, [March 10?], 1827). AD. MiD-B.
mDWs.

March 12   To Alexander Bliss. ALS. DLC. mDW 4914.
Reports that the Supreme Court has handed
down a favorable decision in the Ruggles case.

March 12   To Alexander Bliss. ALS. DLC. mDW 5982. Asks
Bliss to send an enclosed item to a Mr. Wright.

March 12   *From Charles Richard Vaughan.*   170

March 14   To Alexander Bliss. ALS. DLC. mDW 5989.
Discusses decision handed down by the Supreme
Court in *Ogden* v. *Saunders*, 12 Wheaton 213
(1827).

March 14   To William Fowle. ALS. MdHi. mDW 5993.
Reports that he has examined the papers
involving some company in a court case;
concludes that the decision rendered by the
judge is correct.

March 14   To Austin Ely Wing (with enclosure: case for
opinion in *Bank of Michigan* v. *A. E. Wing*,
with DW's opinion). ALS. MiD–B. mDW 5997.
Discusses the case and suggests that the
Michigan territorial legislature perhaps lacked
the power to incorporate the bank.

March 17   To James Lloyd. ALS. MH. mDW 6004.
Acknowledges receipt of letter in behalf of a
Mr. Knox, probably a candidate for appointment
to the Naval Academy.

March 17   To Samuel Lewis Southard. ALS. Ia-HA. mDW
6006. Sends him Lloyd's recommendation of
Knox and asks Southard to "consider
recommendations as favorably" as he can.

March 17   *To Emeline Colby Webster.*   171

March 17   Prospectus of the Wilmington *Delaware Journal.*
Printed DS, signed by Edward Everett, DW,
et al. MHi. mDWs. Propose the establishment
of newspaper to support the Adams
administration.

March 19   To Nicholas Biddle. ALS. PU. mDW 6011. *W & S*,
16: 144–145. Discusses cases before the
Supreme Court involving the bank.

March 19   To Richard Rush. AL (signature removed). DNA,
RG 217. mDW 57226. Discusses Wallack's claim
for indemnity for loss of property on the
Niagara frontier.

March 19   To Samuel Lewis Southard (with enclosure:
petition from G. H. Thompson, [Jan 14?, 1827]).

	ALS. DNA, RG 45. mDWs. Disposes of Thompson's petition by sending it to Southard.	
March 19	To Emeline Colby Webster. ALS. DMaM. mDW 6015. Forwards Dr. Sewall's letter to her.	
March 22	From Nicholas Biddle. Printed. *House Reports*, 22d Cong., 1st sess., Doc. No. 460 (Serial 227), p. 496. Asks if the Bank of the United States can, in accordance with the provisions of its charter, hold and improve the real estate that has come into its hands in satisfaction of debts.	
March 22	From Nicholas Biddle (to DW and Horace Binney). Printed. *House Reports*, 22d Cong., 1st sess., Doc. No. 460 (Serial 227), p. 50. In an effort to foil counterfeits, Biddle asks Webster and Binney if the bank will be violating its charter by establishing uniformity in the notes of the branches of the bank and by allowing the presidents and cashiers of those branches to sign notes for $20 and less.	
March 23	*To John Quincy Adams.*	*172*
March 23	To Nicholas Biddle. Printed. *House Reports*, 22d Cong., 1st sess., Doc. No. 460 (Serial 227), p. 496. Transmits opinion regarding the power of the bank to hold and improve land.	
March 23	[Opinion regarding power of United States Bank to hold and improve land]. ADS. PU. mDW 6019. *House Reports*, 22d Cong., 1st sess., Doc. No. 460 (Serial 227), pp. 496–497.	
March 23	To Nicholas Biddle (from DW, Horace Binney, and Wm. Wirt). Printed. *House Reports*, 22d Cong., 1st sess., Doc. No. 460 (Serial 227), p. 51. Give opinion regarding the signing of checks.	
March 24	*To Peter Force.*	*173*
March 24	*To Charles Miner.*	*173*
March 24	*To Nathaniel F. Williams.*	*174*
March 24	To John Agg. ALS. NhD. mDW 7888. Comments on an editorial in the New York *Evening Post*; states that he encloses several paragraphs which Agg might publish.	
March 25	*To Henry Clay.*	*175*
March 26	*To John Quincy Adams.*	*178*
March 26	*To Mrs. George Ticknor.*	*178*
March 27	*To John Quincy Adams.*	*179*
March 27	To James William Paige. ALS. DLC. mDW 6051. Reports his arrival in New York and his anxiety to reach Boston.	
March 29	*From John Test.*	*181*
March 31	To George Blake, et al. Printed. *Niles' Register*, 32 (April 7, 1827): 103 (incorrectly dated in *W & S*, 13: 23–24). Declines invitation to a	

April 16   To Joseph Story. ALS. MHi. mDW 6105. *W & S,*
                16: 160. Asks Story for a legal opinion on river
                navigation.

April 18   From Jared Sparks. Printed. Herbert B. Adams,
                Life and Writings of Jared Sparks (2 vols.;
                Boston, 1893), 2: 138–139. Reports on the
                agreement reached with Henry Clay regarding
                the publication of the Revolutionary
                correspondence.

April 19   To Joseph Gales and W. W. Seaton. ALS. NN.
                mDW 6107. Sends items placed in his hands by
                Israel Thorndike.

April 20   *From Henry Clay.*   *193*

April 25   From Richard Rush. AL (signature removed).
                DLC. mDW 6112. Reports that the Castine
                appointment was made before Webster's letter
                of April 16 reached him.

April 27   *To Joseph E. Sprague.*   *195*
April 30   *To John C. Wright.*   *195*

May 6   From Thomas Swann. ALS. DLC. mDW 6123.
                Reports on action in carrying out the Court's
                mandate in the lottery prize case, *Clark* v. *City
                of Washington*, 12 Wheaton 40 (1827).

May 7   *To Henry Clay.*   *197*
May 8   *From Nicholas Biddle.*   *200*

May 10   To Nicholas Biddle. ALS. DLC. mDW 6132.
                Thanks Biddle for the copy of the eulogy.

May 14   *From Henry Clay.*   *200*

May 14   From Samuel A. Talcott. ALS. DLC. mDW 6138.
                Requests Webster's "personal attendance" in the
                case of New York against Astor, coming up in
                the Court.

May 15   To Jacob Cutter. ALS. NhD. mDW 6142. States
                that he would "be glad to dispose of the old
                house, on almost any terms."

[c. May 15]   To [Samuel Lewis Southard]. ANS, with
                testimonial. MHi. mDW 6144. Endorses a
                testimonial for Andrew Ellison, Jr.

May 18   *To Henry Clay.*   *202*

May 18   From John D. and Hannah W. Sweat. ALS. NhD.
                mDW 6280. Report on their hardships and ask
                Webster's financial assistance.

May 20   From the Marquis de Lafayette. Printed.
                Portsmouth Journal, October 6, 1827.
                Reminisces on his recent visit to America;
                mentions Rufus King's visit to La Grange.

May 22   *To Levi Lincoln.*   *204*

May 22   To Samuel Lewis Southard. ALS. CtHi. mDW
                6158. Comments on and endorses the excellent
                recommendations of Charles Peirce.

May 23   *To Joseph E. Sprague.*   *206*

June 22	*To Henry Clay.*	223
June 22	From Mary Pyne March. ALS. NhHi. mDW 6257. Again recommends her brother for chaplain at West Point.	
June 22	*To Ezekiel Webster.*	224
June 25	From William Sturgis, et al. LS. DLC. mDW 6261. Invite Webster to dinner in celebration of the anniversary of American independence.	
June 27	From Henry Wheaton. ALS. DLC. mDW 6263. Discusses and thanks Webster for several loans of money.	
June 29	From Nicholas Biddle. LC. DLC. mDWs. *Correspondence of Nicholas Biddle*, ed. Reginald C. McGrane (Boston, 1919), pp. 41–42. Discusses the selection of a bank director.	
June 30	*To John Quincy Adams.*	225
[*June* ?]	*To Joseph Gales.*	227
[June]	To Ezekiel Webster (enclosure: John D. and Hannah W. Sweat to [DW], May 18, 1827). ALS. NhD. mDW 6278. Sends $10 to John D. and Hannah W. Sweat.	
July 1	From Nicholas Biddle. LC. DLC. mDWs. Sends report on the bank, since Webster was unable to attend the semiannual meeting of the directors.	
July 8	*From John Quincy Adams.*	228
July 11	To Samuel Jaudon. ALS. NHi. mDW 6294. Declares that he does not wish to state his preference of the two candidates for office, probably in one of the branches of the Bank of the United States.	
July 12	*To Ezekiel Webster.*	229
July 15	*To [John W. Taylor].*	229
[*July* 17]	*To Joseph Story.*	231
July 20	To Ezekiel Webster. ALS. NhD. mDW 6306. *PC*, 1: 421–422. Discusses the party proceedings at Concord, N.H.; expresses pleasure with Ezekiel's decision to go to Harrisburg.	
July 24	*To Henry Clay.*	232
July 25	*To Samuel Jaudon.*	233
July 26	From James Brown. AL (signature removed). NhD. mDW 6316. Introduces a Mr. Rumpft, "Minister of the Free Towns of Germany."	
July 28	*To John Evelyn Denison.*	233
July 28	*To the Marquis de Lafayette.*	236
Aug 11	From James Savage (enclosed with DW to S. L. Southard, Aug 13, 1827). ALS. DNA, RG 45. mDWs. Introduces Lieutenant Henry Bruce, his nephew, and solicits Webster's assistance in securing an appointment for him to a sea post in the navy.	

	appointment of O. W. B. Peabody as United States attorney for New Hampshire.	
Oct 8	To Francis Hopkinson (with abstract of reply, Oct 13, 1827). ALS. NhD. mDWs. Reports that he cannot assist Mrs. Grant in collecting a debt from Hutchinson, since Hutchinson has "not a cent."	
Oct 8	From Elijah Paine. ALS. NhHi. mDW 6381. Reports his acceptance of various drafts for money by DW and Henry Wheaton.	
Oct 9	To Ezekiel Webster. ALS. NhD. mDW 6385. Van Tyne, pp. 120–121. Discusses New Hampshire politics.	
Oct 13	From Francis Hopkinson (abstract). ANS. NhD. mDWs. Informs Webster that "Mrs. Grant had determined to prosecute Hutchinson for the Bigamy."	
Oct 13	From Edward Wyer. ALS. DLC. mDW 6388. States that he is enclosing correspondence with a Russian count (enclosures not found); comments on men and events in Washington.	

Oct 24	To Caleb Cushing. ALS. DLC. mDW 6402. Discusses the dropping of Nazro's claim for damages if the suit against Nazro should be discontinued.	
Oct 24	From John Temple Winthrop and David Lee Child (enclosed in DW to Samuel Lewis Southard, Oct 25, 1827). ALS. DNA, RG 45. mDWs. Recommend that John Jay Jerome of Boston be given a contract with the government to supply groceries to the naval yard at Charlestown.	
Oct 25	To [John Agg]. ALS. NhD. mDW 6406. Reports that he expects a contentious session of Congress.	

Oct 25	To Samuel Lewis Southard (with enclosure: John Temple Winthrop and David Lee Child to DW, Oct 24, 1827). ALS. DNA, RG 45. mDWs. Endorses Winthrop's and Child's recommendation.	
[Oct 27]	To Thomas Handasyd Perkins. ALS. MHi. mDW 6412. Because of illness, will not be able to get together with him and Edward Everett in the evening.	

Oct 30	From John Agg. Copy. DLC. mDW 6418. Reports on the Washington scene, political news from	

Dec 3	From Elijah Hunt Mills. ALS. NhHi. mDW 6460. *PC*, 1: 423–424. Sends enclosure for Mr. Barrell; discusses his health; asks to be informed of events in Washington.	
Dec 4	To James William Paige. Dictated letter. NhHi. mDW 6463. Van Tyne, pp. 570–571. Reports that Grace has improved slightly and he is convalescing.	
Dec 4	From James Wadsworth (enclosure: James Wadsworth to DW, Dec 5, 1827). LS. MHi. mDW 6533. Asks that his letter on the Indian question be laid before the President and secretary of war.	
Dec 5	*To James William Paige.*	257
Dec 5	From James Wadsworth (enclosed in James Wadsworth to DW, Dec 4, 1827). LS. MHi. mDW 6535. Submits recommendations which he believes will "raise the Indian to the dignity of a civilized man."	
Dec 7	To Samuel Frothingham. ALS. PHC. mDW 6469. Sends draft for deposit to his account.	
Dec 7	*To John Collins Warren.*	258
Dec 8	To Samuel Frothingham. ALS. PHC. mDW 6477. Sends instructions on payments and deposits.	
Dec 8	*To John Collins Warren.*	259
Dec 9	To Mrs. [Tristam?] Burges. ALS. CtY. mDW 6481. Reports on his and Grace's health.	
Dec 9	*To Nathaniel Silsbee.*	260
Dec 9	To George Ticknor. Printed. Curtis, 1: 306. Discusses Grace's condition.	
Dec 9	*To John Collins Warren.*	260
[Dec 10]	*From Joshua Phillips.*	261
Dec 10	From George Ticknor. Printed. Curtis, 1: 306–307. Reports on his distribution of Webster's letters to Boston friends; comments on Grace's illness.	
Dec 11	To Mrs. George Ticknor. Printed. Curtis, 1: 307–308. Thanks Mrs. Ticknor for her letter to Grace; reports on Grace's condition.	
Dec 13	To Mrs. Nathan Hale. ALS. MNS. mDW 6489. Thanks Mrs. Hale for her expression of concern; reports on Grace's condition.	
Dec 14	From Mrs. [Frederick?] Tudor. AL. NhHi. mDW 39089. Inquires of DW's and Mrs. Webster's health; sends DW a sprig of fern to relieve him of the pain of his rheumatism.	
Dec 15	*From Henry Willis Kinsman.*	262
Dec 15	From Thomas Washington. ALS. DLC. mDW 6494. Reports that the fee in *McLemore v. Powell*, 12 Wheaton 554 (1827), has been collected.	
Dec 16	Memorial of a committee on behalf of the	

surviving officers of the Revolutionary Army.
ADS. DNA, RG 46. mDW 42296.

Dec 17 To Samuel Lewis Southard. ALS. MB. mDW
6497. Recommends Colonel Wallach's son for
some appointment.

Dec 17 To Ezekiel Webster. ALS. NhD. mDW 6499. *PC*,
1: 426. Reports his arrival in Washington on
Dec 16; comments on Grace's condition.

Dec 18 To Joseph Story. Printed. *PC*, 1: 426–427.
Discusses Grace's health, his living
accommodations in Washington.

Dec 18 Account of DW's Senate compensation. AD. DLC.
mDW 39650. Runs to 1835, July 4.

Dec 19 *To Elijah Hunt Mills.* 262

Dec 21 To Thomas Swann. ALS. PHi. mDW 6506.
Discusses his fees in the lottery case, *Clark* v.
City of Washington, 12 Wheaton 40 (1827).

Dec 21 From Bushrod Washington. AL (signature
removed). NhHi. mDW 6509. Discusses the
claim of a Mrs. Blodgett, of Philadelphia,
against the United States.

[Dec 22?] To Mrs. John Agg. ALS. NhD. mDW 6515.
Thanks her for letters and presents for the
children; mentions Grace's condition.

Dec 22 *To David Daggett.* 264

Dec 24 From James Lloyd. ALS. DLC. mDW 6522.
Introduces Gustavus Colhoun and solicits
Webster's attention to Colhoun's efforts to
get appointment as midshipman.

Dec 25 *To James William Paige.* 264

[Dec 26] To Jeremiah Mason. Printed. *PC*, 1: 430–431.
Reports on his and Grace's illnesses.

[Dec 28?] *To James William Paige.* 265

[Dec 28] From Grace Fletcher Webster. ALS. MHi. mDW
6512. Harvey, *Reminiscences*, pp. 326–327.
Expresses relief on hearing that DW is in
Washington and comments on her health.

[Dec 29] From Grace Fletcher Webster. ALS. MHi. mDW
6519. Harvey, *Reminiscences*, pp. 327–328.
Reports that she is feeling some better.

Dec 31 To John Quincy Adams (with enclosures: James
Wadsworth to DW, Dec 4, 1827, LS; Dec 5,
1827, LS). ALS. MHi. mDW 6532. Sends Adams
Wadsworth's letters; states that he is leaving
for New York to visit Grace.

[Dec 31?] To Mrs. John Agg. ALS. NhD. mDW 6544. Sends
along Grace's last letter to him to give Mrs. Agg
knowledge of the "present state of her health."

Dec 31 To Henry Willis Kinsman. ALS. NhD. mDW 6541.
Reports his intention to leave for New York on
the morning of Jan 1.

[1827]   To William Wirt. ALS. MdHi. mDW 6546. Asks
          Wirt to answer letter on Cherokee matter.

[1827?]   To [Nathan Hale]. ALS. MHi. mDW 38436. Invites
          the Hales to join the Lees in dinner at the
          Websters'.

[1827–1829] To Samuel Lewis Southard. ALS. CtHi. mDW
             6548. Sends some item from the attorney
             general of New York.

[1827–1829] To Ezekiel Webster. ALS. NhD. mDW 6549. Hopes
             to see Ezekiel on Friday morning.

[1827–1831] To [John Agg]. ALS. NhD. mDW 38168. Has
             taken a "sudden & violent cold" and may not be
             able to visit in the evening.

[1827–1831] To John Agg. ALS. NhD. mDW 38171. States
             that he will dine with Agg on Sunday should
             the weather prove good.

[1827–1832] To John Agg. ALS. NhD. mDW 38162. Asks Agg
             if he has any reliable news from the West;
             plans visit to see his brother's family.

[1827–1841] To Mr. and Mrs. John Agg. AL. DLC. mDW
             38174. Invites them to dinner.

1828

Jan 1   To Henry Clay. Printed. *W & S*, 16: 166–167.
          Remarks on his vote on a bill, "the whole
          business" of which he believes "originated with
          General J[ackson]."

Jan 3   From A. W. Putnam. ALS. DLC. mDW 6551.
          Forwards items relating to a land claim in
          Arkansas Territory.

Jan 4   *To Nathaniel Silsbee.*   267

Jan 4   From William A. Kent. ALS. DLC. mDW 6557.
          Asks Webster to inquire if Mrs. Israel Evans is
          entitled to receive any bounty lands.

Jan 4   *From Nathaniel Silsbee.*   268

Jan 6   To [John Agg]. ALS. NhD. mDW 6562. Reports
          his arrival in New York; discusses Grace's and
          the family's health, friends.

[Jan 6] *To James William Paige.*   269

Jan 6   *To John Collins Warren.*   270

[Jan 7?] To James William Paige. ALS. MHi. mDW 6577.
          Reports that Grace "had a good night, & is
          much better today than yesterday."

Jan 8   To Sarah Goodridge. ALS. NhD. mDW 6579.
          Responds to her letter of Dec 27 (not found)
          and reports their satisfaction with the
          miniature.

Jan 8   *To Nathaniel Silsbee.*   272

Jan 8	*To Ezekiel Webster.*	272
[Jan 8?]	To James William Paige. ALS. MHi. mDW 6581. Reports on Grace's condition.	
Jan 8	From Charles Brickett Haddock. ALS. NhD. mDW 6588. Asks Webster's advice regarding accepting a position with the Female High School in Boston.	
Jan 9	*From Jeremiah Mason.*	273
Jan 10	*To Joseph Story.*	276
[Jan 11]	To Joseph Story. ALS. DLC. mDW 6605. States that Grace "passed another very good night."	
Jan 12	To William Carroll. AL (signature removed). DNA, RG 267. mDWs. Asks Carroll to inform the Supreme Court that his two cases from Louisiana will not be argued, if they are called for the following week.	
[*Jan 12*]	*To Joseph Story.*	277
[Jan 13?]	To James William Paige. ALS. MHi. mDW 6613. Reports on Grace's condition.	
[*Jan 14*]	*To [Joseph Story].*	278
Jan 15	*To Jeremiah Mason.*	279
Jan 15	To Joseph Story. ALS. DLC. mDW 6619. Reports on the state of Grace's health.	
Jan 16	To Joseph Story. ALS. DLC. mDW 6620a. Reports on Grace's health.	
[Jan 17]	To Joseph Story. ALS. DLC. mDW 6621. Discusses Grace's weakening condition and his own frustrations at not knowing "what to do."	
Jan 17	*To Ezekiel Webster.*	280
[Jan 18]	To Joseph Story. ALS. DLC. mDW 6627. Reports that Grace continues to lose strength.	
Jan 19	*To Joseph Story.*	280
Jan 19	From Eliza Buckminster Lee. ALS. NhHi. mDW 6633. Thanks Webster for his letter and expresses her deep concern over Grace's illness.	
[*Jan 20*]	*To Joseph Story.*	281
Jan 20	From John Agg. ALS. NhHi. mDW 6641. Expresses his concern over Grace's illness and his fear that she will not recover.	
Jan 20	From Eliza Buckminster Lee. ALS. NhHi. mDW 6646. Expresses her willingness to visit Mrs. Webster should she ask to see her.	
Jan 20	*From Nathan Hale.*	282
Jan 20	Bill to amend the judicial system of the United States. AD. DNA, RG 46. mDW 42215.	
[Jan 21]	To Ezekiel Webster. ALS. NhD. mDW 6660. States that Mrs. Webster is near death.	
Jan 21	To Joseph Story. ALS. DLC. mDW 6654. Reports that he believes Mrs. Webster can "hardly live half an hour."	

	Court; DW was appearing as counsel for the defendants.	
Feb 3	From Samuel Hubbard. ALS. NhHi. mDW 6704. Expresses his sympathy with the Websters, but finds consolation in the belief that Mrs. Webster —and his wife who had recently died—"lived & died in the faith & hope of the Gospel of our Glorious Redeemer."	
Feb 5	*To Joseph Story.*	291
[Feb 5]	From Julia Webster. ALS. NhHi. mDW 6710. States that the Webster children will miss DW very much while he is at Washington.	
Feb 7	*To James William Paige.*	291
Feb 8	From Edward Webster. ALS. NhHi. mDW 6716. States that he likes school very much.	
Feb 9	To Joseph Story. ALS. DLC. mDW 6718. Reports that after a week's journey he has reached New York; will proceed on to Washington as his health and the roads permit.	
Feb 9	From David Ellis. ALS. NhHi. mDW 6721. Sends petition requesting payment of claim which he holds on the Boston Customs Office.	
Feb 9	*From Julia Webster.*	292
Feb 10	To Henry Willis Kinsman. ALS. NNC. mDW 6726. Sends bank note for renewal; comments on the bad condition of the roads and his slow progress to Washington.	
Feb 10	From Heman Lincoln. ALS. NhHi. mDW 6728. Expresses his sympathy for DW.	
Feb 10	From Delia Tudor. ALS. NhHi. mDW 6732. Asks Webster to counsel and represent her in a case in which she seeks financial support from her estranged husband.	
Feb 10	From Edward Webster. ALS. NhHi. mDW 6735. Reports on his activities in Boston.	
Feb 10	From Julia Webster. ALS. NhHi. mDW 7750. Reports on a visit from Achsah Pollard Webster.	
Feb 11	*From Patrick Tracy Jackson.*	293
Feb 11	From Elijah Hunt Mills. AL (signature removed). NhD. mDW 6742. Expresses his sympathy with DW and discusses the management of the Boston Post Office and his desire to be appointed postmaster there.	
Feb 11	Petition of Jonathan Chapman of Boston for debentures on rum shipped to Palermo in 1818. ADS. DNA, RG 46. mDW 42683.	
Feb 12	From Daniel Webster. ALS. DLC. mDW 6748. DW's nephew asks for a loan of from $200 to $500.	
Feb 13	From Julia Webster. ALS. NhHi. mDW 6750. Reports on the family's activities in Boston.	

	mDW 42692. Encloses documents in support of his claim.	
Feb 27	To Thomas Kemper Davis. ALS. MWalB. mDW 6793. Sends him a copy of his speech on judicial process.	
[Feb 27]	*To James William Paige.*	303
Feb 28	Memorial of Enoch M. Miley for payment of pension, referred to the Committee on Pensions. ADS. DNA, RG 46. mDW 42292.	
Feb 29	From Elijah Hunt Mills. ALS. NhHi. mDW 6799. Apologizes for seeking the office of treasurer; states that he did so because of newspaper report of the treasurer's death and speculation regarding his successor; still seeks federal employment.	
Feb 29	To Mrs. John Agg. ALS. NhD. mDW 6803. Sends her a lock of Grace's hair.	
March 1	*From Thomas Handasyd Perkins.*	304
March 1	*From Ezekiel Webster.*	307
March 2	*From Eliza Buckminster Lee.*	307
March 2	From Daniel Fletcher Webster. ALS. NhHi. mDW 6816. Sends his school report and states that "for some reason or other, I have not done so well, this month, as I could wish."	
March 3	From Julia Webster. ALS. NhHi. mDW 6818. Reports on her activities in Boston.	
March 4	From Edward Webster. ALS. NhHi. mDW 6822. Reports on his activities.	
March 6	From Eliza Buckminster Lee. ALS. NhHi. mDW 6824. Encloses a letter from [Nathan?] Parker and urges DW to write Julia more frequently.	
March 6	Memorial of manufacturers of salt of Barnstable, Mass., asking that duty on imported salt be repealed. ADS. DNA, RG 46. mDW 42322.	
March 7	*From Henry Alexander Scammell Dearborn.*	308
March 7	From Julia Webster. ALS. NhHi. mDW 6831. Thanks Webster for a long letter; reports on her and her cousin's activities.	
March 7	*From Thurlow Weed.*	309
March 8	To James Barbour. ALS. DNA, RG 94. mDWs. Recommends the appointment of T. Browne Dix, brother of John A., as cadet to West Point.	
March 8	To [Samuel Frothingham]. ALS. PHC. mDW 6836. Sends deposit for his bank account.	
March 8	From Thomas W. Ludlow. ALS. NhHi. mDW 6837. Discusses the court cases, *Konig* v. *Bayard*, 1 Peters 250 (1828), and *Schimmelpennich* v. *Bayard*, 1 Peters 264 (1828).	
March 10	*To Mrs. Edward Everett.*	309

March 11   From Edward Webster. ALS. NhHi. mDW 6943. Reports on his studies at school.

March 12   To John Quincy Adams. AL. MHi. mDW 6845. Accepts invitation to dinner.

March 12   *From Gerry Fairbanks.*   310

March 12   From Charles Brickett Haddock. ALS. NhHi. mDW 6851. States the loss he feels by the death of "that dear aunt," Grace Fletcher Webster; mentions the election in New Hampshire.

March 13   *To James William Paige.*   312

March 13   *From the Marquis de Lafayette.*   313

March 14   From Jonathan Chapman. ALS. DNA, RG 46. mDW 42688. Discusses his request for debenture on rum.

March 15   To Mrs. Edward Everett. ALS. MHi. mDW 6861. Thanks her for letter (not found) and expresses his pleasure in knowing that she has named the Everett daughter after Grace.

March 15   *To Eliza Buckminster Lee.*   313

March 15   To Nathaniel F. Williams. AL. NhD. mDW 6864. Asks that a draft be sent to Washington where he will pay it; reports that political prospects "look better."

March 15   From Samuel A. Talcott. ALS. DNA, RG 45. mDWs. Requests Webster to recommend the appointment of Peter L. Gansevoort as a midshipman.

March 17   From Gustavus Colhoun. ALS. DNA, RG 45. mDWs. Asks Webster to assist him in securing warrant appointing his son to the navy.

March 17   From Thomas W. Ludlow. ALS. NhHi. mDW 6866. Acknowledges Webster's report on the decision in the Bayard cases, *Konig* v. *Bayard*, 1 Peters 250 (1828), and *Schimmelpennich* v. *Bayard*, 1 Peters 264 (1828).

March 17   *From Ezekiel Webster.*   314

[March 17]   *From Ezekiel Webster.*   316

March 17   From Julia Webster. ALS. NhHi. mDW 6874. Gives a statement of her daily activities.

March 18   *To Ezekiel Webster.*   316

March 18   From Aaron Burr. ALS. MeB. mDW 6883. Thanks Webster for his letter (not found) advising him of the "favorable termination of the Eden suits."

March 18   From Daniel Fletcher Webster. ALS. NhHi. mDW 6885. Thanks his father for his advice concerning studies.

March 20 [19]   *To Ezekiel Webster.*   317

March 20   *To Jeremiah Mason.*   318

March 21   *To Charles Brickett Haddock.*   319

March 22	To Jared Sparks. ALS. MH. mDW 6892. Encloses a letter to George Canning and offers to assist him more if Sparks should want it.	
March 22	To Samuel Smith. ALS. DNA, RG 46. mDW 42693. Returns Jonathan Chapman's petition and vouches for the truth of its statements.	
March 22	*To Joseph E. Sprague.*	320
March 22	To William Wirt (with enclosure: memorandum of agreement, with ANS by DW, March 1828). ALS. ICHi. mDW 6896. Returns papers to Wirt, with his opinion in behalf of Governor Ninian Edwards.	
March 23	To Mrs. George Ticknor. Printed. Curtis, 1: 322. Thanks her for the interest she takes in the children; reports that his health is good.	
March 23	*To Ezekiel Webster.*	321
[March 23]	From William Wirt. ALS. DLC. mDW 6904. Thanks Webster for his prompt reply to the request for an opinion in behalf of Governor Ninian Edwards of Illinois.	
March 25	From Robert Blair Campbell (enclosure: Campbell to John Randolph, March 25, 1828). ALS. NhHi. mDW 6907. Van Tyne, pp. 137–138. Sends his answer to Randolph's request for his recollection of Webster's comments on Randolph's letter to his constituents in 1824 relating to the committee investigating Crawford.	
March 25	From Peyton R. Freeman (with endorsement by DW). ALS and ANS. DLC. mDW 6910. Seeks appointment as cashier of the proposed branch of the Bank of the United States at Portland; Webster attests to Freeman's "integrity."	
March 25	From Julia Webster. ALS. NhHi. mDW 6912. Details her activities in Boston.	
March 27	*From Jeremiah Mason.*	322
March 27	From Daniel Fletcher Webster. ALS. NhHi. mDW 6915. Reports on his studies and activities in Boston.	
March 29	From Nicholas Biddle. ALS draft. DLC. mDW 7890. Introduces Matthew L. Bevan to Webster.	
March 29	*From Ezekiel Webster.*	323
March 31	*From Ezekiel Webster.*	324
April 1	*From Estwick Evans.*	325
April 2	To Nathaniel F. Williams. AL. NhD. mDW 6930. Refers cryptically to an item he is forwarding Williams.	
April 2	From Julia Webster. ALS. NhHi. mDW 6932. Reports on her activities in Boston.	
April 3	From Paul Farnum. LS. NhHi. mDW 6936. Urges	

	permanent appointment in the Post Office Department.	
May 28	*To Ezekiel Webster.*	352
May 29	From David Sears, et al. LS. NhD. mDW 7099. To show their respect for Webster, invite him to dine with them at the Exchange Coffee House in Boston on June 5.	
May [?]	To Mrs. George Ticknor. Printed. Curtis, 1: 324. Thanks her for letter; states that he, Ticknor, and Prescott are preparing to go to the President's for dinner.	
[May–June]	To Samuel Lewis Southard. ALS. NjP. mDW 7101. Introduces G. Evans, who wants to see Southard on business.	
June 4	From Nathaniel Williams (enclosed with DW to H. Clay, June 8, 1828). ALS. DNA, RG 59. mDW 55551. Recommends John Stricker for appointment as secretary of the legation in Paris.	
June 8	To Henry Clay (with enclosure: Nathaniel Williams to DW, June 4, 1828). ALS. DNA, RG 59. mDW 55554. Endorses Williams' recommendation of John Stricker for secretary of the legation in Paris.	
June 8	*To Henry Clay.*	352
June 8	From Aaron Burr. ALS. NjMoHP. mDW 7107. Discusses an aspect of Story's opinion in the Comegys case and its impact on the Eden suits in the New York courts.	
June 12	To [John Agg]. ALS. NhD. mDW 7110. Thanks him for the *National Journal*; reports on his children.	
June 13	From Henry Clay. Printed. Curtis, 1: 329. Expresses his gratification with Webster's reception in Boston.	
June 16	To John Quincy Adams. LS. CtHi. mDW 7112. Recommends a Mr. Larkin for appointment as navy agent in Portsmouth.	
June 19	To [Ezekiel Webster]. ALS. NhD. mDW 7114. *PC*, 1: 458–459. Discusses his summer plans and his hopes to visit Boscawen.	
June 26	To John Quincy Adams. ALS. MHi. mDW 7118. States that George Long, applicant for the position of navy agent at Portsmouth, should not be given serious consideration, because his "character is not absolutely above suspicion" and he would not be satisfactory to the community.	
June 26	From Peter Lorillard. ALS. NhHi. mDW 7120. Asks Webster to represent him in a case.	

June 27	From Thomas W. Ludlow. ALS. NhHi. mDW 7126. Discusses the Bayard cases with Webster.
July 4	From Richard S. Coxe. ALS. DLC. mDW 38308. Acknowledges receipt of $150, payable on the fee in David Canter's case.
July 6	To William Baylies (from DW and William Sullivan). ALS by Sullivan, signed also by DW. MHi. mDW 7130. Ask Baylies to appear as a referee in case before the Supreme Judicial Court of Massachusetts at Nantucket in August.
July 7	*To Henry Clay.* 353
July 7	From Nicholas Biddle. LC. DLC. mDWs. Sends Webster a statement of the affairs of the bank, since he was unable to attend the last semiannual meeting of the directors.
July 9	To Mrs. John Agg. ALS. DCHi. mDW 7137. *Records of the Columbia Historical Society*, 28 (1926): 238. Forwards Julia's letter (not found) and invites her and John Agg to Boston for a visit.
July 9	To R. W. Greene. ALS. MWA. mDW 7139. Apologizes for having been absent on the previous Saturday when Greene called; details his plans for Greene and proposes meeting him in late July in Boston.
July 10	To [William Buell] Sprague. ALS. NhHi. mDW 7141. Sends a "small pamphlet" and reaffirms his high regard and esteem.
July 10	From William Baylies (to DW and William Sullivan). ALS draft. MTaHi. mDWs. Consents to serve as a referee in the case mentioned in Sullivan and Webster's letter of July 6.
July 14	*From Robert Field Stockton.* 353
July 14	From Jules von Wallenstein. ALS. DLC. mDW 7143. Asks Webster to assist him in his present financial troubles.
July 16	From Thomas Rich. ALS. NhHi. mDW 7147. Van Tyne, p. 614. Thanks Webster for his gift of $20 and asks him to convey his appreciation to an anonymous donor of $50.
July 20	*To Joseph E. Sprague.* 355
July 26	To John Thomas. ALS. MHi. mDW 7150. Reports that the Webster children are in New Hampshire; will perhaps visit in his vicinity in early August.
July 28	To Ezekiel Webster. ALS. NhD. mDW 7152. Reports that he has forwarded Ezekiel's two letters, and that members of Ezekiel's family have arrived in Boston.
July 29	*To [Samuel Bell].* 356
Aug 1	*To Jeremiah Mason.* 358

Sept 22	Check for $1,000. DS. DLC. mDW 39661.	
Sept 22	Check for $30. DS. DLC. mDW 39662.	
Sept 23	Check for $1,155. DS. NhD. mDW 39663.	
[Sept 24?]	*To Joseph E. Sprague.*	364
Sept 25	*To Nathaniel F. Williams.*	364
Sept 25	Statement regarding persons who have recommended Thomas Hardy. ADS. NhD. mDW 7214. Attests to the character of those who wrote recommendations.	
Sept 25	From Julia Webster. ALS. NhHi. mDW 7211. Reports on her studies at the Boscawen Academy.	
Sept 26	Check for $250. DS. DLC. mDW 39664.	
Sept 27	To R. W. Greene. ALS. MWA. mDW 7217. Arranges a time for meeting with Greene.	
Sept 27	*To [Martin Van Buren?].*	365
Sept 27	Deed to land on High Street, Boston, transferred from DW to Isaac P. Davis. Printed DS with MS insertions. NhD. mDW 39665.	
[Sept 28]	*To Ezekiel Webster.*	366
Sept 29	To John Quincy Adams. ALS. MHi. mDW 7227. Encloses letters recommending Caswell of Ohio for district judge, whom Webster also endorses.	
Sept 29	Check for $287.50. DS. DLC. mDW 39669.	
Sept 29	Check for $10.50 to Mr. Hardy. DS. DLC. mDW 39668.	
Sept 29	Check for $32.33. DS. DLC. mDW 39670.	
[Sept]	To John Collins Warren. ALS. MHi. mDW 7231. States that he will "gladly" take care of some unidentified matter.	
Oct 1	To John Agg. ALS. NhD. mDW 7233. Discusses their lack of communication recently; reports on his and the children's activities.	
Oct 1	*To Henry Clay.*	367
Oct 1	To Jeremiah Mason. ALS. NhHi. mDW 7239. W & S, 16: 182–183. Discusses a court case with him.	
Oct 1	From John E. Frost. ALS. NhHi. mDW 7242. Hopes that Webster has received his letter containing a draft for the balance due Sheafe.	
Oct 1	From Edward Webster. ALS. NhHi. mDW 7246. Reports on his speaking at school.	
Oct 2	From Julia Webster. ALS. NhHi. mDW 7248. Tells Webster of a composition she has written.	
Oct 4	To [the Secretary of the Suffolk Bar Association]. ANS. MHi. mDWs. States that Charles Francis Adams has read law in his office since Aug 15, 1827.	
Oct 7	To Jeremiah Mason. ALS. NhD. mDW 7251. W & S, 16: 183. Asks Mason to appear for the defendant in the case, *Carrington* v. *The*	

	Merchants Insurance Company, in the forthcoming circuit court in Boston.	
Oct 7	From William Buell Sprague. ALS. DLC. mDW 7255. Asks Webster for autographs from letters to send to an English friend.	
Oct 9	*From Kensey Johns, Jr.*	368
Oct 11	*To [Jacob McGaw].*	368
Oct 13	From Timothy Farrar. ALS. DNA, RG 46. mDW 42802. Discusses the petition of Onesimus Newhall.	
Oct 13	Petition of Onesimus Newhall for Revolutionary pension. DS. DNA, RG 46. mDW 42794.	
Oct 14	To [Jonathan Hunt]. AL. NPV. mDW 7266. Reports that he had written to Washington recommending Caswell for judge in Ohio before the receipt of Hunt's letter of Sept 21; comments on the election in the various states.	
Oct 15	From Samuel A. Talcott. ALS. NhHi. mDW 7268. Reports that the Astor causes will not be tried this fall.	
Oct 21	To O. Ellsworth Williams. ALS. CtHT. mDW 7270. Discusses the execution against Stephen Hartwell; Webster authorizes Williams to draw on him for amount of debt and costs.	
Oct 22	From William Buell Sprague. ALS. DLC. mDW 7272. Thanks Webster for his friendly letter and the autographs.	
Oct 23	*To Henry Clay.*	370
Oct 23	From David Hayden, Jr. ALS. NhHi. mDW 7277. Clarifies certain items in documents previously sent to Webster regarding their claim to be presented before Congress.	
Oct 24	*From Henry Clay.*	371
Oct 28	*From Estwick Evans.*	372
Oct 29	To David Hayden, Jr. AL draft. NhHi. mDW 7286. W & S, 16: 183. Recommends that claim should probably first be presented in the House of Representatives, perhaps by Edward Everett.	
Oct 29	*To Joseph Hopkinson.*	373
Oct 30	*To Nicholas Biddle.*	374
Oct 31	From Gardiner Greene (enclosed with DW to Nicholas Biddle, Nov 1, 1828). Copy. DLC. mDW 7300. States that he believes James W. Paige is fully qualified for the board of directors of the Boston branch of the Bank of the United States; will add his name to the list.	
Nov 1	*To Nicholas Biddle.*	375
Nov 1	From Mrs. R. McIntyre (with abstract of reply). ALS. NhHi. mDW 7301. Asks if Webster wants a room in her boarding house in Washington; Webster declines her offer.	

Nov 3   To Mrs. Nathan Hale. ALS. MHi. mDW 7303.
             Sends her some small gift.
Nov 4   *From Nicholas Biddle.*   *376*
Nov 5   *To Nathaniel F. Williams.*   *378*
Nov 5   From Richard Fletcher. ALS. NhHi. mDW 7309.
             Requests that he be allowed to return the
             retaining fee sent him by C. P. Curtis and that
             he be allowed to appear as counsel in Webster's
             behalf in the suit against Theodore Lyman, Jr.,
             without cost—"I shall be very happy to perform
             any professional duty in return for the benefits
             of your early instruction."
Nov 5   From Joseph Hopkinson. ALS. MHi. mDW 7311.
             Comments on his appointment as a district
             judge and on the presidential election.
Nov 7   *To Nicholas Biddle.*   *378*
Nov 10   *To [John Brazer].*   *378*
Nov 15   From James Hervey Bingham. ALS. NhHi. mDW
             7320. Forwards $160 from "Brother Milton."
Nov 18   *To James Hervey Bingham.*   *380*
Nov 24   From Thomas Handasyd Perkins (enclosed with
             DW to H. Clay, Nov 26, 1828). ALS. DNA, RG
             59. mDW 55557. Asks Webster to forward a
             memorial to Henry Clay recommending William
             Henry Low of Salem for the consular post at
             Canton.
Nov 25   From Henry Wheaton. ALS. DLC. mDW 7323.
             Discusses the move by Peters to begin
             publishing the decisions of the Supreme Court.
Nov 26   To Henry Clay (with enclosure: T. H. Perkins to
             DW, Nov 24, 1828). ALS. DNA, RG 59. mDW
             55556. Forwards and endorses the petition from
             Perkins, Nov 24.
Nov 28   *From Nicholas Biddle.*   *381*
Nov 29   *To Nicholas Biddle.*   *381*
Nov 30   *From Henry Clay.*   *383*
Dec 1   To Emeline Colby Webster Lindsly. ALS. DMaM.
             mDW 7334. Expresses his best wishes to her
             on her marriage to Dr. Harvey Lindsly.
Dec 2   To Warren Dutton. ALS. NhD. mDW 7337.
             Thanks him for a present.
Dec 2   *From Nicholas Biddle.*   *384*
Dec 4   To Mrs. John Agg. ALS. NhD. mDW 7342.
             Encloses letter from Julia; reports on the
             children.
Dec 11   From Thomas L. Winthrop, et al. (with enclosure:
             memorial on Sunday mails service). Facsimile.
             NhHi. mDW 7345. Protest the transportation
             and delivery of mail on Sunday.
Dec 15   To Mrs. Cyrus Perkins. Copy. NhHi. mDW 7348.
             Van Tyne, p. 615. Will not be able to stay with

	the Perkins family as he makes his trip to Washington; will be traveling with George Blake.	
Dec 20	*From John Holmes.*	385
Dec 27	Memorial of sundry Boston merchants asking that the collector of customs be required to settle accounts under old tariff laws. ADS. DNA, RG 46. mDW 42269.	
Dec 28	To Samuel Lewis Southard. LS. NjP. mDW 7351. Recommends Joseph Snelling for appointment as a lieutenant in the Marine Corps.	
[Dec 30?]	To Nathaniel F. Williams. ALS. NhD. mDW 7353. Reports that he will most likely be at Barnum's on the forthcoming Tuesday.	
[Dec]	Petition of Josiah Jordan for Revolutionary pension. ADS. DNA, RG 46. mDW 42788.	
[1828]	[Autobiographical notes]. Copy. NhHi. mDW 7355. *W & S*, 13: 549–551.	
[1828?]	Memorandum: "Dates of the deaths of my mother, brothers, and sisters." AD. NhHi. mDW 39343.	
[1828?]	To Sarah Goodridge. ALS. MHi. mDW 38403. Arranges to see her.	
[1828?]	To Sarah Goodridge. ALS. MHi. mDW 38404. Arranges to see her.	
[1828–1829]	To John Agg. ALS. NhD. mDW 38161. Apologizes for not answering Agg's letter promptly, but he has been troubled with poor eyesight since August.	
[1828–1829]	To Mrs. John Agg. ALS. NhD. mDW 38181. Sends James W. Paige's regards; states that Paige will be writing her soon.	
[1828–1841]	To John Agg. ALS. NhD. mDW 38164. Requests that Agg stop by to see him for a few minutes.	

1829

Jan 1	From Henry Willis Kinsman. LC, Kinsman Letterbook. NhD. mDW 7388. Reports on Webster's bank accounts and a fire in Kinsman's office.	
Jan 2	From Henry Willis Kinsman. LC, Kinsman Letterbook. NhD. mDW 7388. Sends a copy of Capt. Bunker's testimony and a statement of the case *Coffin* v. *Phoenix Insurance Company*.	
Jan 3	*From David Lee Child.*	386
Jan 5	From Henry Willis Kinsman. LC, Kinsman Letterbook. NhD. mDW 7389. Reports on Webster's finances, the speeches of the retiring and newly inaugurated mayors of Boston.	
Jan 6	From Julia Webster. ALS. NhHi. mDW 7631.	

	Informs Webster of her New Year's Day activities.
Jan 7	To Henry Willis Kinsman. ALS. NNC. mDW 7633. Thanks him for several letters; suggests that since the fire described in Kinsman's letter of Jan 1 is the third that has hit their offices, Kinsman might be on the lookout for better offices in the spring.
Jan 7	From Henry Willis Kinsman. LC, Kinsman Letterbook. NhD. mDW 7389. Reports on the acceptance of several of Webster's notes at various banks.
Jan 7	From Robert Treat Paine. ALS. DNA, RG 45. mDWs. Seeks appointment as astronomer to an exploring expedition about to be undertaken.
Jan 8	From Mary Ann Webster. ALS. NhD. mDW 6591. Discusses the activities of the Webster children (erroneously dated 1828 by writer).
Jan 9	From Ezekiel Webster. ALS. NhD. mDW 7636. PC, 1: 466. Comments on the meeting of the New Hampshire legislature and on the congressional nomination in the state; much against his wishes, he will again be a candidate for Congress.
Jan 10	From Edward Webster. ALS. NhHi. mDW 7640. Reports on the activities of the family.
Jan 13	From William C. Aylwin. ALS. CSmH. mDW 7642. Encloses several letters (not found) recommending John A. Bates for purser in the navy.
Jan 14	To John Quincy Adams. AL. MHi. mDW 7645. Accepts invitation to dinner.
Jan 14	From Daniel Fletcher Webster. ALS. NhHi. mDW 7647. Informs Webster of his diligent studying.
Jan 16	From Henry Willis Kinsman. LC, Kinsman Letterbook. NhD. mDW 7391. Details his efforts to renew Webster's note endorsed by Isaac P. Davis.
Jan 16	From William Taggard. ALS. NhHi. mDW 7649. Encloses a check for the balance due on the draft Webster gave him.
Jan 17	*To Ezekiel Webster.*
Jan 17	From Knowles Taylor. ALS. NhHi. mDW 7658. Proposes a course of action in the Senate on the question of Sunday mails.
Jan 17	From Julia Webster. ALS. NhHi. mDW 7660. Tells Webster of the social activities of friends and members of the family.
Jan 18	To [?]. AL incomplete. MWalB. mDW 7662. Mentions that he will support the nomination

387

of a Mr. Hooper before the Senate; comments
on the municipal politics of Boston.

Jan 18 *From Joseph Hopkinson.* 389

Jan 19 To [Samuel Lewis Southard]. ALS. DNA, RG 45.
mDWs. Recommends Robert Treat Paine for
appointment as astronomer to an exploring
expedition.

Jan 22 From Henry Willis Kinsman. LC, Kinsman
Letterbook. NhD. mDW 7391. Gives statement
of the status of several of Webster's bank notes.

Jan 23 *To Joseph Hopkinson.* 390

Jan 23 *To Joseph Hopkinson.* 391

Jan 23 From Henry Willis Kinsman. LC, Kinsman
Letterbook. mDW 7391. Reports that he has
renewed the note for $900 endorsed by Nathan
Hale; gives account of other notes about to fall
due.

Jan 24 To Joseph Hopkinson. ALS. PHi. mDW 7678.
Thanks Hopkinson for his comments on one
of Webster's proposed publications, probably
relating to the libel case against Theodore
Lyman, Jr.

[Jan 24] To Joseph Hopkinson. AL. PHi. mDW 7681.
Further discusses the proposed essay involving
the Lyman libel case.

Jan 24 *To Mary Ann Webster.* 392

Jan 24 From Lemuel Shaw, et al. ALS. DLC. mDW 7689.
Forwards a memorial on the subject of the
protective tariff.

Jan 25 To Josiah Quincy. Printed. Van Tyne, pp.
615–616. Praises Quincy's address, delivered on
the occasion of his retirement as mayor of
Boston in 1828.

Jan 25 From Daniel Fletcher Webster. ALS. NhHi. mDW
7691. Discusses his school work.

Jan 25 From Edward Webster. ALS. NhHi. mDW 7693.
Reports that he has a new sled.

Jan 25 *From Ezekiel Webster.* 392

Jan 26 To John Quincy Adams. AL. MHi. mDW 7700.
Declines invitation.

Jan 26 From Nicholas Biddle. LC. DLC. mDWs. Inquires
about disagreements among the directors of
the Boston branch of the Bank of the United
States.

Jan 26 From Nicholas Biddle. LC. DLC. mDWs. Discusses
the selection of a director for the branch bank
at Savannah, Georgia.

Jan 26 From Henry Willis Kinsman. Abstract, Kinsman
Letterbook, NhD. mDW 7392. Encloses letter
to Mrs. Eleanor Talbot.

Feb 16   From Henry Willis Kinsman. LC, Kinsman
        Letterbook. NhD. mDW 7396. Acknowledges
        receipt of letter and bank notes.

Feb 17   To Peter Buell Porter (from DW and Benjamin
        Gorham). ALS by DW, signed also by Gorham.
        NBuHi. mDW 7761. Want to see Porter on the
        subject of appointment of cadets to West Point.

Feb 17   *To Daniel Fletcher Webster.*   *398*

Feb 17   From Nicholas Biddle. LC. DLC. mDWs. Reports
        that he is enclosing an extract of a letter from
        J. Cumming, president of the branch bank at
        Savannah.

Feb 17   From Henry Willis Kinsman. LC, Kinsman
        Letterbook. NhD. mDW 7397. Reports that he
        has been unable to get any information
        regarding a C. D. Atkinson; suggests that the
        name may be an assumed one.

Feb 17   From Julia Webster. ALS. NhHi. mDW 7766.
        Reports on the activities of the family and
        children in Boston.

[c. Feb 18]   From Henry Willis Kinsman. LC, Kinsman
        Letterbook. NhD. mDW 7397. Acknowledges the
        receipt of bank notes to be renewed.

Feb 19   *To Achsah Pollard Webster.*   *399*

Feb 19   From Samuel Upton. ALS. NhHi. mDW 7773.
        Asks Webster to write a letter supporting him
        in his campaign for Congress; queries Webster
        about Jackson's probable course.

[c. Feb 20]   From Henry Willis Kinsman. LC, Kinsman
        Letterbook. NhD. mDW 7397. Sends a copy of
        a book divided into halves to avoid paying
        excess postage above that of the senator's
        franking privilege.

Feb 21   To Ezekiel Webster. ALS. COMC. mDW 7776. In
        accordance with Ezekiel's wishes, Webster
        promises to confer with Peter B. Porter,
        Secretary of War, about Captain Stone's claim.

Feb 23   *To Joseph Hopkinson.*   *400*

Feb 23   *To [Henry Willis Kinsman?].*   *401*

Feb 23   *To Ezekiel Webster.*   *401*

Feb 23   To Mary Ann Webster. ALS. NhD. mDW 7784.
        PC, 1: 471. Wishes her a speedy recovery from
        her illness.

Feb 23   From R. W. Greene. ALS. NhHi. mDW 7786.
        Introduces a Colonel Mallett, the son-in-law of
        Governor James Fenner of Rhode Island.

Feb 23   From Henry Willis Kinsman. LC, Kinsman
        Letterbook. NhD. mDW 7397. Reports that he
        has just received a notice that a Webster note
        for $1,000 is due at the American Bank.

Feb 23   From Daniel Fletcher Webster. ALS. NhHi. mDW
7788. Reports on the activities of the family.

Feb 26   *To Ezekiel Webster.*   402

Feb 26   From William Taggard. ALS. NhHi. mDW 7794.
Asks Webster for legal advice.

Feb 26   From Daniel Fletcher Webster. ALS. NhHi. mDW
7797. Discusses his progress in Latin and
Greek; reports on the family and the weather.

Feb 27   From Peyton R. Freeman. ALS. NhHi. mDW 7799.
Asks Webster to send promptly "the small sum
which I mentioned to you," or "otherwise I
can hold myself no longer bound by the
proposal."

Feb 27   From Henry Willis Kinsman. LC, Kinsman
Letterbook. NhD. mDW 7398. Reports on the
action he has taken regarding several of
Webster's bank notes; informs him of those
falling due in early March.

Feb 27   From Edward Webster. ALS. NhHi. mDW 7802.
Reports on the health and activities of the
family.

Feb 28   From Henry Willis Kinsman. LC, Kinsman
Letterbook. NhD. mDW 7398. Asknowledges
receipt of a bank draft for $900.

Feb 28   Motion by Webster for communications from the
President relative to instructions to the
ministers to Panama, etc. AD. DNA, RG 46.
mDW 42226.

Feb   *From Nathan Appleton.*   402

[Feb ?]   To Mrs. John Agg. ALS. NhD. mDW 38189.
Declines invitation; comments on the Birth
Night ball.

March 1   From Eliza Buckminster Lee. ALS. NhHi. mDW
7846. Offers Webster the "assurance of my
constant and affectionate regard."

March 2   To Joseph Hopkinson. ALS. PHi. mDW 7848.
Requests Hopkinson to examine the papers in
the district court of Pennsylvania relating to
the claim against Judge Isaac Parker by the
Treasury Department and to report to him on
them.

March 2   *To Achsah Pollard Webster.*   404

March 2   *To Ezekiel Webster.*   405

March 3   From Henry Willis Kinsman. LC, Kinsman
Letterbook. NhD. mDW 7399. Sends letter from
T. G. Coffin to Curtis, dealing with the case,
Coffin v. *Phoenix Insurance Company*;
discusses case.

March 3   From Henry Willis Kinsman. LC, Kinsman
Letterbook. NhD. mDW 7400. Reports the

	payments of Webster's note endorsed by Nathan Hale; has also paid on the Willis note.
March 3	From Isaac Parker. ALS. DLC. mDW 7858. Reports that he is satisfied with the "proposed arrangement" with the Treasury Department if it will not jeopardize his claim.
March 3	From Julia Webster. ALS. NhHi. mDW 7860. Reports on activities in Boston.
March 4	*To Achsah Pollard Webster.* *405*
March 4	From Joseph Hopkinson. ALS. MHi. mDW 7868. Reports that a case factually related to Isaac Parker's original claim was argued before the recent term of the district court over which Hopkinson presided.
March 5	From Joseph Hopkinson. ALS. MHi. mDW 7870. Sends a statement of the fees and charges due Parker.
March 7	To Lemuel Shaw. ALS. MBS. mDW 7872. Reports that he will return to Boston as quickly as possible after March 18 to argue the Charles River Bridge case.
March 7	From Henry Willis Kinsman. LC, Kinsman Letterbook. NhD. mDW 7400. Reports on Webster's notes endorsed by Nathan Hale, Isaac P. Davis, and George Blake.
March 8	To Henry Willis Kinsman. ALS. NNC. mDW 7875. Sends notes to be looked after; reports on his expected departure for Boston on March 18.
March 9	Bank draft for $700 to DW. ADS. DLC. mDW 39671.
March 10	Motion by Mr. Chambers to direct the secretary of the Senate to subscribe for copies of congressional documents proposed to be published by Gales and Seaton. AD. DNA, RG 46. mDW 43100.
March 11	From Henry Willis Kinsman. LC, Kinsman Letterbook. NhD. mDW 7401. Reports on the disposition of certain notes; has had some difficulty with one.
March 13ʻ	From Henry Willis Kinsman. LC. Kinsman Letterbook. NhD. mDW 7401. Reports the receipt of certain notes and the intervention of James W. Paige, with regard to the one giving some difficulty.
March 15	*To Ezekiel Webster.* *406*
March 16	To Achsah Pollard Webster. ALS. NhD. mDW 7881. Reports that he hopes to leave Washington on March 19.
March 17	From Henry Willis Kinsman. LC, Kinsman Letterbook. NhD. mDW 7402. States that he

has taken care of the notes Webster has
forwarded; comments on New Hampshire
elections; and reports that James W. Paige's
case, *Adams* v. *Paige*, 7 Pickering 542 (1829),
before the Massachusetts Supreme Court was
decided against him.

March 20   From Elizabeth Langdon-Elwyn. ALS. NhHi.
mDW 7883. Expresses the hope that Webster
will spend the day with her family in
Philadelphia as he makes his way from
Washington to Boston.

March 21   From Henry Willis Kinsman. Abstract, Kinsman
Letterbook. NhD. mDW 7402. Informs Webster
of a note due (addressed to New York).

March 21   From Henry Willis Kinsman. Abstract, Kinsman
Letterbook. NhD. mDW 7402. Informs Webster
of a note due (addressed to Philadelphia).

March 22   To Achsah Pollard Webster. ALS. NhD. mDW
7886. Reports that he is leaving Washington
but expects that he will have to stop in
Baltimore because of the snow and cold
weather.

March 27   From Henry Willis Kinsman. LC, Kinsman
Letterbook. NhD. mDW 7402. Sends list of bank
notes about to fall due.

[March 30]   To Henry Willis Kinsman. ALS. NhD. mDW 7892.
Reports that he has just arrived in New York,
having been detained at Philadelphia and
Princeton, because of his error regarding the
departure of steam boats.

[March 30]   To Achsah Pollard Webster. ALS. NhHi. mDW
7894. Reports on his arrival in New York and
on his visit with Mrs. Stockton at Princeton.

[March]   To William Bainbridge. ALS. NHi. mDW 7897.
Asks where Bainbridge's friend, Colonel Miller
lives, since he has occasion to see him.

April 4   To the Secretary of the Suffolk Bar Association.
DS. MBBA. mDWs. Certifies that George
Edward Winthrop read law in his office from
November 1827 to November 1828.

April 9   *From Elizabeth Langdon-Elwyn.*   407

April 11   From Timothy Farrar, et al. ALS by Farrar,
signed also by others. DLC. mDW 7904. State
that they are enclosing a copy of the resolutions
of the Concord bar and court on the death of
Ezekiel Webster.

April 13   From Greene Carrier Bronson. ALS. DLC. mDW
7906. Reports that five of the Astor suits in
which Webster is to appear as counsel for the
people of New York will come before the circuit
court in late May.

April 13   From Julia Stockton. ALS. NhHi. mDW 7908.
         Asks Webster to hand an enclosed letter to
         Mary Mason, who is in Boston; thanks him for
         letter and lozenges.

April 13–18   From [?]. AL. NhHi. mDW 7910. Expresses her
         condolences on the death of Ezekiel Webster.

April 15   To Lemuel Shaw. ALS. MBS. mDW 7914. States
         that because of recent events he will not be able
         to prepare his address to the bar.

April 15   To Boswell Stevens. ALS. NhD. mDW 7619. Asks
         Stevens, who is taking care of Ezekiel's court
         papers and whom Mrs. Webster wishes to settle
         the estate, the whereabouts of a certain parcel
         of Ezekiel's papers.

April 16   To Achsah Pollard Webster. ALS. NhD. mDW
         7922. Reports that James W. Paige is sending
         some sherry; urges her to take care of her
         health.

April 16   From Elizabeth Langdon-Elwyn. ALS. NhHi.
         mDW 7924. Expresses her sympathy on the
         death of Ezekiel.

April 16   From Jeremiah Mason. ALS. NhHi. mDW 7926.
         Van Tyne, p. 616. Expresses his sympathy on
         the death of Ezekiel; "his loss is, in my
         estimation, nothing less than a public
         calamity."

April 18   From Lemuel Shaw. ALS. MBS. mDW 7929. Tries
         to arrange a time for mutual discussion of the
         Charles River Bridge case.

April 21   Transfer of land in Salisbury, N.H., from Israel
         W. Kelly to DW. ADS. MWalB. mDW 39673.

April 26   Bank draft for $500, payable to Henry W.
[1828–?]   Kinsman. AD. DLC. mDW 40649.

April 29   From Greene Carrier Bronson. ALS. DLC. mDW
         7931. Reports that the trial of the Astor suits
         will begin on Monday, June 1.

[April]   From P. AL. NhHi. mDW 7936. Expresses
         sympathy on the death of Ezekiel.

May 6   From Caleb Cushing. ALS. NhD. mDW 7944.
         Reports a favorable jury verdict in a case in
         which Webster had presented an "able &
         conclusive argument."

May 8   From Israel W. Putnam. ALS. DLC. mDW 7953.
         Expresses his condolences on the death of

	Ezekiel Webster; reports on the construction of the church at Portsmouth and requests Webster to redeem his pledge of $75.	
May 11	To R. S. Smith. ALS. WaU. mDW 7957. Requests the renewal of a note for $1,000, signed by Thomas Swann.	
May 11	From Arthur Livermore. ALS. DLC. mDW 7960. Thanks Webster for letter of April 15 (not found), probably regarding the death of Ezekiel.	
May 15	*To Stephen Van Rensselaer.*	413
May 16	To Achsah Pollard Webster. ALS. NhD. mDW 7966. Van Tyne, p. 576. Reports on the Webster activities in Boston, his forthcoming departure for New York; remarks that there have been numerous "disasters among the Commercial Gentlemen."	
May 17	*From James Barbour.*	414
May 18	To Joseph Hopkinson. ALS. PHi. mDW 7979. Asks Hopkinson for his views on the question of judgments creating liens in federal courts.	
May 19	To William Cabell Rives. ALS. DLC. mDW 7983. Congratulates Rives on his appointment as minister to France and introduces David Sears and his wife.	
May 30	To Samuel Frothingham. ALS. NhD. mDW 7985. Asks Frothingham to discount a note and credit his account; reports that he delivered the cash Frothingham sent to New York.	
May 30	From Tench Ringgold. ALS. DLC. mDW 7987. States that he will try to collect the amount of Joseph Gales' debt to Ladd & Co.	
May 30	From Richard Wallach. ALS. DLC. mDW 7989. Reports on the efforts to collect the amount Joseph Gales owes to Ladd & Co.	
May [?]	To William Cabell Rives. ALS. DLC. mDW 7990. Introduces Caleb Cushing.	
May	Receipt to Greene C. Bronson for $100. ADS. NN. mDW 39675. For expenses in attending the New York circuit court as counsel for the state in the Astor cases.	
June 12	To Fletcher & Aylwin (from DW and Lemuel Shaw). Copy. MBS. mDW 7993. Notify the defendants that they will not oppose evidence taken by a certain date.	
June 22	*From John Whittemore.*	417
[July 2]	*To Nathan Hale.*	418
July 2	From Peter Chardon Brooks. ALS. DLC. mDW 8001. Encloses certain papers for Webster and thanks him for the "kindness and patience, so	

	uniformly shown, towards an anxious, and . . . troublesome, client," in *Farnam* v. *Brooks*, 9 Pickering 212 (1830).	
July 6	*To Edward Cutts, Jr.*	*419*
July 6	From Nicholas Biddle. LC. DLC. mDWs. Reports on the affairs of the bank, since Webster has again missed the semiannual meeting of the directors.	
July 8	*From William Wirt.*	*419*
[July 13]	To Edward Everett. ALS. MHi. mDW 8010. Wants to have a "little conversation" with Everett before he sets off "on a journey of a week."	
[July 16]	To Henry Willis Kinsman. ALS. NhD. mDW 8013. Requests Kinsman to forward important letters received in Boston to Brattleboro.	
July 24	From Ichabod Bartlett. ALS. CtY. mDW 8015. Asks Webster to write a letter of introduction for James H. Haven to William C. Rives; since a certain "newspaper correspondence," Bartlett reports that he and Rives "have preserved a very sullen silence toward each other."	
July 25	From Henry Willis Kinsman. LC, Kinsman Letterbook. NhD. mDW 7409. Forwards letters to Brattleboro; reports on what he has done with several of Webster's notes.	
July 25	Promissory note for $300 to James W. Burdett. ADS. DLC. mDW 39677.	
July 27	Promissory note for $900 to Nathan Hale. ADS. DLC. mDW 39679.	
July 29	To Henry Willis Kinsman. ALS. NNC. mDW 8017. Returns note for deposit to his bank account; reports that he is "setting my face eastward, & hope to be punctual to the appointed time—Aug. 1."	
July	From William Eayrs. ALS. DNA, RG 76. mDWs. Discusses the collection of an unpaid award under Spanish claims, the commission of which was concluded in 1824.	
Aug 3	From Daniel Dewey Barnard. ALS. CtY. mDW 8019. Expresses his disappointment at not finding Webster in Boston, but hopes to renew his acquaintance with DW at a later date in Boston.	
Aug 6	From William Eayrs. ALS. DNA, RG 76. mDWs. Again confronts Webster on the question of an uncollected Spanish claim.	
Aug 9	From John Marshall. ALS. George C. Whipple, Jr., Carmel, N.Y. mDW 8020. Introduces a Mr. Williams of Virginia.	
Aug 10	*To John Agg.*	*422*

in action against the former treasurer of
Phillips Exeter Academy (or the executor of his
sureties), whose account was in arrears.

Sept 12   From Elizabeth Langdon-Elwyn. ALS. NhHi. mDW
           8074. Queries Webster about his summer
           activities; discusses friends, acquaintances,
           and events in Philadelphia.

Sept 14   To Jeremiah Smith. ALS. NhExP. mDW 8080.
           Agrees to take on the Phillips Exeter case and
           hopes to confer with Smith shortly.

Sept 14   Bank draft for $52 payable to Mr. Hughes. DS.
           NhHi. mDW 39684.

Sept 16   Bank draft for $260 payable to S[amuel]
           F[rothingham]. DS. DLC. mDW 39685.

Sept 17   Bank draft for $139. DS. DLC. mDW 39686.

Sept 17   Bank draft for $150. DS. DLC. mDW 39687.

Sept 19   To Jeremiah Smith. ALS. NhExP. mDW 8082.
           Agrees on a time to confer with Smith; states
           that he will write a letter introducing William
           Smith, who is going west.

Sept 24   To Daniel Caswell, Jr. Copy. NhHi. mDW 8083.
           Introduces William Smith, son of Jeremiah.

Sept 24   To Henry Clay. ALS. NhD. mDW 8085. Van Tyne,
           p. 146. Introduces William Smith.

Sept 24   To William Henry Harrison. Copy. NhHi. mDW
           8088. Introduces William Smith.

Sept 24   To John McLean. Copy. NhHi. mDW 8090.
           Introduces William Smith.

Sept 24   To John Marshall. Copy. NhHi. mDW 8092.
           Introduces William Smith.

Sept 27   From Jacob McGaw. ALS. DLC. mDW 8094.
           Asks that Webster allow Julia to spend the
           winter with them, to go to school and to be the
           companion of their only daughter.

Sept 28   Bank draft for $400. DS. DLC. mDW 39688.
           Payable to Henry W. Kinsman.

Oct 3   Promissory note for $500 to James B. Mills & Co.
           ADS. DLC. mDW 39689.

Oct 6   To the Secretary of the Suffolk Bar Association.
           DS. MBBA. mDWs. Certifies that Edward B.
           Emerson has read law in his office since
           November 1824.

Oct 6   From Charles Chauncey. ALS. DLC. mDW 8098.
           Reports the transfer of $300 to Webster's
           credit and the purchase of ten bank shares for
           him.

Oct 6   From Rufus Choate. ALS. MHi. mDW 8100.
           Informs Webster that William Hook of Salem
           wishes to retain him as counsel in a case
           against B. Merrill.

Oct 7   *To Nathaniel F. Williams.*   426

notes and memorandum of judgments in the
Sherburne and Blunt case.

Dec 15   To Nathan Hale. ALS. MHi. mDW 8162.
Discusses notes; reports that he expects to leave
for Washington soon, but will write Mrs. Hale
"about 'great events' " before he does.

Dec 15   To Henry Willis Kinsman. ALS. NhD. mDW 8164.
Discusses the Hale note, which neither he nor
Hale recalls.

Dec 15   Petition of inhabitants of Cohasset and Scituate
asking for a survey of the Cohasset harbor.
ADS. DNA, RG 46. mDW 42642.

Dec 16   From Charles Pelham Curtis. ALS. DLC. mDW
8167. Congratulates Webster on his marriage;
encloses petition from a widow requesting
payment of a claim on the government.

Dec 17   Bill for the relief of Jonathan Chapman. Printed
document with MS insertions. DNA, RG 46.
mDW 42470.

Dec 18   From Thomas March. ALS. NhHi. mDW 8170.
Asks Webster's intervention in the settlement of
accounts between his brother Charles and
himself; encloses papers relating to the matter
and asks Webster if he wrote Charles approving
of his conduct.

Dec 20   From Daniel Fletcher Webster. ALS. NhHi. mDW
8174. Congratulates his father on his marriage
and hopes to "have the pleasure of seeing my
mother soon"; reports on his reading.

Dec 21   To [?]. ALS. PHi. mDW 8177. Sends deposit to
his bank account.

Dec 21   To Nathan Hale. ALS. MHi. mDW 8179. Reports
the payment of two drafts; discusses other
notes. Van Tyne, pp. 718–719, publishes from
a newspaper clipping a letter, reportedly by
Webster, which seems to be a mixture of
excerpts from this letter; DW's to Hale,
December 15; and DW's to Kinsman, also
December 15.

Dec 22   *From James Barbour.*   437

Dec 23   From James C. Doane. ALS. DNA, RG 46. mDW
42647. Forwards petition of residents of
Cohasset and Scituate asking for a survey of
the Cohasset harbor.

Dec 24   To Henry & John White. ALS. MdHi. mDW 8189.
Ships boxes to Baltimore through Robert White.

Dec 28   From Daniel Dewey Barnard. ALS. DLC. mDW
8191. Congratulates Webster on his marriage.

Dec 30   From Henry White. ALS draft. MdHi. mDW 8193.
Reports that Webster's three boxes have not yet

	arrived, but they will be shipped on to Washington when they do.
[Dec 31]	To John Collins Warren. ALS with circular. MHi. mDW 8194. Sends him the circular from Andrew Anderson, November 1829.
[1829]	To Richard Peters. ALS. PHi. mDW 8201. Proposes that Peters meet with him and Story for dinner.
[1829]	To Achsah Pollard Webster. ALS. NhD. mDW 8203. Reports on the health of the family; hopes to make a trip to Boscawen before the end of the week.
[1829?]	To John Agg. ALS. NhD. mDW 38169. Asks to see copies of newspapers in Agg's room.
[1829?]	To [John Gorham Palfrey?]. ALS. NhExP. mDW 38781. Encloses a short poem, which, Webster writes, "your mornings discourse reminded me of."
[1829?]	To [John Gorham Palfrey]. ALS. MH. mDW 8200. Invites the Palfreys to dinner.

Index

The following abbreviations are used: JQA, John Quincy Adams; BUS, Bank of the United States; DW, Daniel Webster; EW, Ezekiel Webster; GFW, Grace Fletcher Webster. As in Volume 1, the entry for Webster is confined to personal details, avocations, feelings, opinions, and writings and speeches. The reader is referred to specific entries within the main body of the Index for information on Webster's political activities.

Page-entry numbers between 439 and 524 refer to material in the Calendar. Numbers set in bold-face indicate pages where individuals are identified. Individuals identified in the *Dictionary of American Biography* are denoted by an asterisk immediately following the name; those identified in the *Biographical Directory of the American Congress* are denoted by a dagger.

E 337.8 .W24 1974 ser.1 v.2
Webster, Daniel, 1782-1852.
The papers of Daniel
Webster